The National Churches of England, Ireland, and Scotland
1801–1846

The National Churches of England, Ireland, and Scotland 1801–1846

STEWART J. BROWN

OXFORD
UNIVERSITY PRESS

Great Clarendon Street, Oxford OX2 6DP
Oxford University Press is a department of the University of Oxford.
It furthers the University's objective of excellence in research, scholarship,
and education by publishing worldwide in

Oxford New York

Athens Auckland Bangkok Bogotá Buenos Aires Cape Town
Chennai Dar es Salaam Delhi Florence Hong Kong Istanbul Karachi
Kolkata Kuala Lumpur Madrid Melbourne Mexico City Mumbai
Nairobi Paris São Paulo Shanghai Singapore Taipei Tokyo Toronto Warsaw

and associated companies in Berlin Ibadan

Oxford is a registered trade mark of Oxford University Press
in the UK and certain other countries

Published in the United States
by Oxford University Press Inc., New York

First published 2001

British Library Cataloguing in Publication Data
Data available

Library of Congress Cataloging in Publication Data
Data applied for

ISBN 0-19-924235-6

1 3 5 7 9 10 8 6 4 2

Typeset in Bembo
by Jayvee, Trivandrum, India
Printed in Great Britain
on acid-free paper by
T.J. International Ltd.,
Padstow, Cornwall

To my Parents

Preface

On 1 January 1801, the Parliaments of Great Britain and Ireland were united, and a new State, the United Kingdom, came into being. There were, however, no joyous celebrations to mark the event. The mood was one of sombre resignation in Britain, and of a profound sense of loss in Ireland. The making of the union had been a matter of political expediency. It was imposed on Ireland by the British Government of William Pitt in the aftermath of the Irish rising of 1798–9, a rising that had brought with it sectarian civil war and French military intervention, and that had been brutally suppressed with widespread atrocities inflicted on the civilian population. There had been some 30,000 deaths. For the Government, the Act of Union was meant to end the instability in Ireland, an instability that encouraged rebellion and provided opportunities to Britain's enemies. To gain a majority of votes for Union in the Irish Parliament, Pitt's Government had resorted to widespread bribery of its members. To win the acquiescence of Ireland's Catholic majority, politicians had promoted the belief that Union would be followed by Catholic Emancipation, freeing Catholics from most of the remaining civil disabilities that had been imposed on them by the exclusively Protestant Irish Parliament in the late seventeenth and early eighteenth centuries. However, once the Union was enacted, the prospects of Catholic Emancipation were quickly dashed, thwarted by the opposition of George III, who represented the view of probably the large majority of the British people that the United Kingdom must be a Protestant State. Pitt resigned over the failure of Emancipation, but then soon returned to office. Most of the Irish people remained disaffected.

The United Kingdom that was created in 1801 faced other difficulties. The State was in the midst of a prolonged struggle with Revolutionary France, an ideological as well as a military struggle, against an enemy determined to spread its political revolution by force to the whole of Europe. There was, meanwhile, another kind of revolution beginning at home. In parts of Great Britain—London, the Midlands, South Wales, and the central Lowlands of Scotland—there was a rapid growth of manufacturing, associated with new technologies and new forms of factory organization. These new forms of production threatened traditional handicraft skills and patterns of work. The concentration of population in manufacturing towns and villages placed unprecedented strains on traditional systems of poor relief, education, and public order. In the countryside, the spread of enclosures was bringing revolutionary changes in agricultural organization, ending centuries-old agricultural practices and disrupting rural communities.

These changes in manufacturing and agriculture brought with them unprecedented suffering for large sections of the labouring orders, and this in turn meant widespread disaffection among labouring men and women. The ideas associated with the French Revolution—the end of privilege, the equality of all citizens before the law, government representative of the popular will—were spreading, accompanied by demands for fundamental political reforms. Itinerant Methodist, Baptist, and Independent preachers, moreover, were carrying a new-style gospel message to the populations of the growing towns and villages, a gospel that emphasized the equality of all souls before God, and that divided communities between the saved and the reprobate. With the spread of this village preaching, a growing number of the population were becoming Dissenters from the established order in Church and State. Many of those drawn into Dissent were also embracing millenarian views, with expectations of the imminent Second Coming of Christ and a world turned upside down.

The pressing task for the political leaders after 1801 was to consolidate the new State, to make the United Kingdom a union of peoples as well as of Parliaments, to achieve a moral unity, to overcome sectarian divisions, to insulate the common people against the revolutionary ideas, and to roll back the expansion of Dissent. There was a need to combine the diverse peoples of the United Kingdom into a single State, to provide them with a common education and shared set of moral and spiritual values, to inspire them with a sense of common purpose. In 1801, the constitutional responsibility for providing such a moral and spiritual instruction to the population of each historic kingdom belonged to the established Church—the Church that had been established by law as the religious expression of the kingdom and the guardian of the people's faith. After 1801 it was increasingly to the established Churches of England, Scotland, and Ireland that political leaders looked for the work of defining the spiritual culture for the new State. By clause V of the Act of Union of 1801, the established Churches of England and of Ireland were joined, forming the United Church of England and Ireland. The provisions of this Church union were, according to the act, to 'remain in full force for ever'. During the first quarter of the nineteenth century the State devoted unprecedented resources and effort to strengthening the established Churches, giving particular care to promoting the work of the Churches at the grassroots, parish level. Leaders in Church and State worked closely together to improve residency among the parish clergy, to promote more regular pastoral visiting and more frequent religious services in the parishes, to build and repair churches, and to increase the number and quality of local schools in connection with the established Churches. The hope was that the revived established Churches would become truly national, asserting their influence and authority over the whole population of these islands, including the Catholic majority in Ireland—organizing the British and Irish peoples into close-knit parish communities in which the inhabitants would live in unity and harmony under the spire of the parish church. State and Church, throne and altar, would work together to mould the peoples of the three kingdoms into a single Protestant nation-state—homogenous, benevolent, paternalistic, communal, traditional. This project of nation-building was already well advanced for England and Scotland by 1801; now the work would be brought forward to completion, transforming the peoples of England, Scotland, and Ireland into Protestant Britons. A coherent set of values and beliefs would be mediated from above, from a Protestant monarch, a Protestant Parliament, and Protestant national Churches.

This book explores the role of the national Churches of England, Ireland, and Scotland in this project of creating a unified Protestant nation-state between the Act of Union in 1801 and the fall of the Peel Government in 1846. It is a study in the relations of Church, State, and national identity in an era that witnessed the spread of ideas of democratic nationalism throughout the North Atlantic world. The approach is a narrative one, and the author takes the view that the struggles over established religion in the three kingdoms during this period form a single story. The period was one of considerable *sturm und drang* in the religious life of these islands—with the supporters of the national Churches struggling to achieve national unity and social harmony under Christian influence, and opponents fighting in the political arena for what they viewed as religious liberty, the rights of individual conscience, and the independence of the Churches from State control. The struggle found expression in the New Reformation, Catholic Emancipation, and anti-tithe struggles in Ireland, in the Radical and Voluntary onslaught on the established Churches in Britain, and in the conflicts over State-supported church extension and national education. The struggle led to tensions within the national Churches themselves, contributing to the prophetical visions of the Irvingites, the Oxford Movement in England, the Disruption of the Church of Scotland, and the Maynooth controversy. In the background was the rapid growth of industrialization and urbanization in Britain, troubling the religious conscience of the nation with scenes of social deprivation, social dislocation, profound social inequality, and social injustice. There was also the growth of a Catholic Irish nationalism, with the threat of renewed sectarian warfare in Ireland. It was a time of momentous change in the religious and social life of Britain and Ireland. When the Union of 1801 was enacted, the United Kingdom was a predominantly rural, semi-confessional State, with the established Churches still claiming the adherence of the large majority of the inhabitants of these islands and viewed as vital to the constitution. When the Peel Government fell in 1846, the 'railway age' was well advanced, and the established Churches could claim the adherence of only a minority of the inhabitants of the United Kingdom. The State could not form a system of national education under the control of the established Church, the constitutional role of the established Churches was becoming a formal one, and the project of structuring the societies in the three kingdoms around the parochial establishment had largely ended. The prospect of creating a unified, largely homogenous Protestant nation faded during these years, and the United Kingdom emerged by mid-century as a more pluralist, multi-denominational society.

Readers will note that the fourth major nation within the United Kingdom, Wales, does not figure prominently in this account. This is not because the author does not recognize the importance of the Welsh experience in shaping the United Kingdom or does not see the central role of religion in defining a national identity in

Wales. Rather, it is because Wales did not exist as a separate kingdom with its own religious establishment in the post-Reformation era. Further, the conflicts over the place of the established Church in Wales did not become particularly acute, nor did the Welsh Churches become extensively politicized, until near the end of the period covered by this book. The book also does not explore the efforts begun during this period to expand the influence of the established Churches to the Empire, especially to the colonies of European settlement.

The book began its life as a series of Chalmers Lectures presented at the Universities of Glasgow and Aberdeen, and I wish to express my gratitude to the Trustees of the Chalmers Lectureship for their encouragement. The University of Edinburgh has assisted with sabbaticals and travel support. I have received valuable support and assistance from a number of research libraries in Britain and Ireland. Special mention must go to the staff at New College Library at the University of Edinburgh; they have been unfailing in their professionalism and commitment. Numerous people have been generous with their assistance and advice as I prepared the book. Mr Owen Dudley Edwards provided invaluable guidance on the argument of the second chapter and both he and Professor A. C. Cheyne read and commented sagely on much of the text. Mr Donald J. Withrington has been generous with his extensive knowledge of nineteenth-century religious and educational history, and has been a continual source of encouragement and inspiration. I have gained insights over the years from the students in my seminar on 'Religion, Liberalism and Nationalism in Britain and Ireland, 1780–1850'. Others who have helped with information and guidance include Dr Peter Nockles, Professor Jonathan Clark, Professor Anthony Waterman, Professor W. R. Ward, Professor David Bebbington, Professor Emmet Larkin, Dr Henry Sefton, Professor David Miller, Dr Callum Brown, Dr John Wolffe, Dr David M. Thompson, Dr John Walsh, Professor Duncan Forrester, Dr Jane Dawson, Dr Andrew Ross, Professor Hugh McLeod, Dr Clyde Binfield, Dr Mark Smith, Dr Deryck Lovegrove, and Mr Liam Upton. My wife, Teri, offered her steady support and sound advice throughout the process of preparing the book.

Contents

1

'Guardians of the Faith': The Established Churches of the United Kingdom, 1801–1828

The Established Churches of the Three Kingdoms in 1801

In 1801, the United Kingdom of Great Britain and Ireland was a semi-confessional Protestant State, in which subjects were expected to conform to the worship and discipline of the established Church of the historic kingdom in which they resided. The established Churches were fundamental to the constitution of the State; they represented the State in its religious aspect, they gave a religious sanction to the social and political order, they celebrated the faith that bound generation to generation, past, present and future, they taught the people the essentials of the faith and their religious duties, they gave out the sacraments and provided religious discipline. They were the religious authority in the land. 'Westminster Abbey', observed the early nineteenth-century Tory politician and diarist J. W. Croker, 'is part of the British constitution.'[1] The national Church establishments had emerged during the sixteenth-century Reformation, when the English, Irish, and Scottish monarchical States officially ceased to support the Roman Church and instead recognized particular forms of Protestant worship, ecclesiastical polity, and doctrine. The sixteenth-century States had not created the national Churches; rather they had acted to enforce a uniformity in doctrine, liturgy, and discipline within the existing Churches; the word 'established', the historian and theologian J. N. Figgis argued, referred 'not to the origin of the Church, but to its control'.[2]

[1] Cited in H. W. Carless-Davis, *The Age of Grey and Peel* (Oxford, 1929), 151.

[2] J. N. Figgis, *Churches in the Modern State*, 2nd edn. (London, 1914), 9–12; W. L Sachs, *The Transformation of Anglicanism* (Cambridge, 1993), 9–12; O. Brose, *Church and Parliament: The Reshaping of the Church of England 1828–1860* (Oxford, 1959), 11.

The Reformation settlements in all three kingdoms were consolidated gradually, and were secured in their more or less permanent form in England only after 1660 and in Scotland and Ireland after 1690. In England and Scotland, the final Reformation settlements represented, on the whole, forms of liturgy, doctrine, and polity that were acceptable to the large majority of the respective populations. In Ireland, by contrast, the Tudor monarchy imposed a version of the English Protestant settlement on the Irish Church, and this took hold among only a small portion of the population, mainly recent English settlers. The Churches by law established came to be described as such in the late seventeenth century, after the State began granting official toleration to religious groups that refused to conform to the national Church. Only with the introduction of religious toleration did it make sense to refer to an established Church as distinct from Dissenting Churches.

In 1801, there were, properly speaking, two established Churches in the United Kingdom—the Episcopal United Church of England and Ireland and the Presbyterian Church of Scotland. The United Church of England and Ireland was a recent innovation, created by clause V of the Act of Union of 1801, which had combined the respective establishments of England and Ireland 'into one Protestant Episcopal Church' whose 'doctrine, discipline and government' were to 'remain in full force for ever'. However, this ecclesiastical union was more a project for the future than a present reality. The conditions and circumstances of the two Churches were so different that for purposes of parliamentary legislation, and in the eyes of most observers, they were separate institutions.[3] It was more accurate to speak of three established Churches, corresponding to the three historic kingdoms.

The largest of the three was the Church of England. It was episcopal in its organization, with two archbishops and twenty-four bishops, including four bishops in Wales. The King-in-Parliament was its supreme temporal governor; its bishops, the lords spiritual, sat in the House of Lords. It was also a parochial Church, ministering to the people through parish churches, each surrounded by defined territorial districts. In theory, the Church possessed independent governing bodies, the Convocations, or provincial assemblies of the

[3] See e.g. A. Knox, 'On the Situation and Prospects of the Established Church' (4 June 1816), in the *Remains of Alexander Knox*, 2nd edn., 4 vols. (London, 1836), i. 53.

clergy of the archdioceses of Canterbury and of York. However, the Convocations had been gradually deprived of their powers following the Reformation, losing their right to revise canon law under Henry VIII and their right to fix clerical taxation under Charles II. There had been no sitting Convocations between 1664 and the Revolution of 1688, or between 1689 and 1700. In 1700, William III made an experiment of allowing them again to sit. In 1717, however, following a series of rancorous annual sessions, the Crown suspended the Convocations as debating bodies. Now Parliament, as the lay synod of the Church of England, assumed increasing authority over the governance of the Church.[4]

The dioceses of the Church of England varied greatly in size, from Rochester, with fewer than 100 parishes, to Norwich and Lincoln, with 1,100 and 1,250 parishes respectively.[5] The diocesan bishops were responsible for maintaining ecclesiastical discipline through diocesan or consistory courts, for examining and ordaining new clerics, for confirming children, and for conducting regular, usually triennial, visitations of the parishes in the diocese. They were assisted in their administrative and judicial functions by one or more archdeacons, who exercised authority under the bishop over specified territorial districts within the diocese, and who presided over archidiaconal courts, which provided another level of ecclesiastical discipline within the dioceses. Central to the religious life of each diocese was its cathedral, the 'mother-church' of the diocese. While monasteries and convents had been suppressed at the Reformation, the Church of England had preserved its cathedral establishments for the provision of worship on a grand scale and the advancement of theological learning. By the later eighteenth century, cathedrals were also becoming centres for musical performances, often for charitable purposes, with reconstructed organs and massed choirs.[6] There were only twenty-two proper cathedral buildings in 1801, in varying physical condition, and twenty-six cathedral chapters, one chapter for each diocese, with additional chapters at Westminster Abbey and (Royal) St George's chapel, Windsor (both of which had no diocesan responsibilities). Each cathedral had its dean and chapter. Most chapters included about twelve prebendaries, who were

[4] N. Sykes, *Church and State in England in the XVIIIth Century* (Cambridge, 1934), 298–310.

[5] P. Virgin, *The Church in an Age of Negligence* (Cambridge, 1989), 158.

[6] F. C. Mather, 'Georgian Churchmanship Reconsidered: Some Variations in Anglican Public Worship 1714–1830', *Journal of Ecclesiastical History*, 36 (1985), 262–3.

expected to be resident 90 days a year (though they could receive a licence for non-residence if they held a university position, royal chaplaincy, or similar position). Prebendaries were expected to preach occasionally and defend through their scholarship the orthodox Trinitarian faith. They were also to provide links between the Church and the wider world of learning; John Hoadley, for example, prebendary of Winchester cathedral from 1737 to 1760, made his contributions as a 'poet and dramatist'.[7] Each cathedral also supported a number of minor canons, with responsibility for daily services and music in the cathedral, and for pastoral care in the cathedral city.[8] In the twenty-eight chapters, there were approximately 520 prebendaries and 260 minor canons or officers, or a total of about 780 chapter livings.[9]

It was, however, in the approximately 10,500 parochial benefices that the Church performed its main task of providing public worship, religious instruction, and pastoral care to the people of England and Wales. The entire country had been divided into territorial parishes between the eleventh and twelfth centuries, with the parish system becoming fixed during the high Middle Ages.[10] Nearly every parish had its church, often a venerable medieval structure, which in most parishes served as the main public building, the place for communal meetings as well as worship. Each parish, moreover, had an incumbent, an ordained priest charged to provide religious instruction and ordinances to the parish population. The parish incumbents were supported from the tithes (a notional tenth of the value of the production of all land, though with much land exempt), from the produce of the glebe, from rentals on Church property, from endowments, and in some parishes from rents charged for seats in the church. Each parochial benefice had its own distinctive form of income and was in effect an independent ecclesiastical corporation,

[7] W. R. Ward (ed.), *Parson and Parish in Eighteenth-Century Hampshire: Replies to Bishops' Visitations* (Winchester, 1995), pp. xx–xxi.

[8] J. Gregory, 'Canterbury and the Ancien Régime: The Dean and Chapter, 1660–1828', in P. Collinson, N. Ramsay, and M. Sparks (eds.), *A History of Canterbury Cathedral* (Oxford, 1995), 226–7; P. Barrett, *Barchester: English Cathedral Life in the Nineteenth Century* (London, 1993), pp. xi–xv.

[9] Virgin, *Church in an Age of Negligence*, 60–1.

[10] For the development of the parish system in England and Wales, see the excellent survey by D. M. Palliser, 'Introduction: The Parish in Perspective', in S. J. Wright (ed.), *Parish, Church and People: Local Studies in Lay Religion 1350–1750* (London, 1988), 5–28.

with the parish incumbent possessing the living as a form of freehold property. Indeed, it might be said that the Church of England was not one establishment, but an amalgam of some 10,500 separate parochial establishments, each with its own distinctive endowment. Clerical incomes had risen steadily from the late eighteenth century, along with the general increase in agricultural incomes associated with the spread of enclosures, improved crop rotations and the drainage of land. In 1815 the average clerical income was £387 a year. The incomes of individual parish livings, however, varied considerably, with 16 per cent of English benefices valued at under £100 a year, and 4 per cent valued at between £1,000 and £2,000 a year.[11] Those on the bottom rungs of the clerical ladder were little better off than unskilled labourers; those on the higher rungs were at a level with the well-off gentry. This was especially true of clerics who possessed, as they had a legal right to do, a plurality of livings.

The doctrinal standards of the established Church were expressed by the Thirty-Nine Articles, first issued by Convocation in 1563 and reaching their final form in 1571. The Articles were not a confessional statement, but rather a collection of short summaries of doctrine, open to interpretation and comprehending different shades of Trinitarian belief and both Calvinist and Arminian interpretations of justification by faith. The Church of England, in short, was not a confessional Church on the pattern of Reformed Churches on the Continent, but was rather a distinctively English national Church.[12] There was a sense that Anglicanism represented a middle way between the extremes of Roman Catholicism and Puritanism, between Rome and Geneva, manifesting 'ideals of balance, proportion and harmony'. This was expressed in the special services on 30 January to mark the execution of Charles I by Cromwellian Puritans, and on 5 November, to mark the Church's preservation from Catholic 'tyranny'.[13] More important than the Thirty-Nine Articles for most Anglicans was the Book of Common Prayer,

[11] Virgin, *Church in an Age of Negligence*, 50, 136; J. Walsh and S. Taylor, 'The Church and Anglicanism in the "Long" Eighteenth Century', in J. Walsh, C. Haydon, and S. Taylor (eds.), *The Church of England, c.1689–c.1833: From Toleration to Tractarianism* (Cambridge, 1993), 6–7.

[12] G. Rowell, '"Church Principles" and "Protestant Kempism": Some Theological Forerunners of the Tractarians', in P. Vaiss (ed.), *From Oxford to the People: Reconsidering Newman and the Oxford Movement* (Leominster, 1996), 20.

[13] Walsh and Taylor, 'The Church and Anglicanism in the "Long" Eighteenth Century', 56–7.

rooted in pre-Reformation service books and informing worship with its sombre cadences and 'melodic Cranmerian prose'. Anglicanism was largely a religion of this book. The Prayer Book, the historian Anthony Waterman has observed, 'was something that every church-going English man, woman and child—that is to say, the vast majority of the population—heard continually from earliest infancy to the last hours of their lives. Common people with no education at all knew large portions of it by heart simply by hearing it so often.'[14] The sacraments were essential to the religious life. The eucharist in most parishes was celebrated infrequently—an average of once a quarter in most parishes, and monthly in larger villages and towns—but this may have meant it was held in greater awe.[15]

Within early nineteenth-century Anglicanism, there were two main, but contrasting views of the relationship of Church and State. The first reflected the Lockeian social contract language of early eighteenth-century Whiggism, with its rejection of divine-right monarchy and its pragmatic view of the origin and nature of government. It received its fullest expression in William Warburton's *The Alliance between Church and State*, published in 1736.[16] For Warburton, Church and State were two sovereign and independent societies that had entered into a compact with one another, agreeing to co-operate for the good of the commonwealth. In this compact, the Church received from the State 'Security from all exterior Violence' and endowments for the support of its clergy.[17] In return, the Church undertook to provide religious and moral instruction to the population, helping to educate a loyal and law-abiding populace. In the alliance, the State was the predominant partner, and the

[14] F. Knight, *The Nineteenth-Century Church and English Society* (Cambridge, 1995), 43; A. M. C. Waterman, 'The Nexus between Theology and Political Doctrine in Church and Dissent', in K. Haakonssen (ed.), *Enlightenment and Religion: Rational Dissent in Eighteenth-Century Britain* (Cambridge, 1996), 198.

[15] Sykes, *Church and State in England in the XVIIIth Century*, 250–1; Gregory, 'Canterbury and the Ancien Régime', 230; Mather, 'Georgian Churchmanship Reconsidered', 269–72.

[16] W. Warburton, *The Alliance between Church and State, or, the Necessity and Equity of an Established Religion and a Test-Law Demonstrated* (London, 1736); for discussions of Warburton's theory in its context, see Sykes, *Church and State in England in the XVIIIth Century*, 316–26; R. W. Greaves, 'The Working of the Alliance: A Comment on Warburton', in G. V. Bennett and J. D. Walsh (eds.), *Essays in Modern English Church History: In Memory of Norman Sykes* (London, 1966), 163–80; J. N. Figgis, 'William Warburton, Bishop of Gloucester, 1698–1779', in W. E. Collins (ed.), *Typical English Churchmen: From Parker to Maurice* (London, 1902), 215–53.

[17] Warburton, *The Alliance between Church and State*, 63–73.

Church had voluntarily relinquished a portion of its sovereignty in return for civil protection.[18] The State, Warburton acknowledged, had no competence to recognize religious truth. He did not, however, view this as a problem—for the fundamental purpose of the Church–State alliance, as an alliance, was not so much to inculcate religious truth as to promote civil order and social harmony.[19]

More prominent among late eighteenth- and early nineteenth-century Anglicans, however, was the view that Church and State were essentially one, that they represented different aspects of the nation's soul.[20] For probably most orthodox Anglicans, Warburton's theory of a voluntary compact between Church and State was perverse.[21] Rather, they viewed the monarchical state as imbued with a divine nature; Church and State were alike ordained by God for the right ordering of the commonwealth. This view received its classic expression from the sixteenth-century Anglican apologist Richard Hooker: 'Seing there is not any man of the *Church of England*, but the same man is also a member of the *Commonwealth*; nor any man a member of the Commonwealth which is not also of the *Church of England* . . . no person appertayning to the one can be denied to be also of the other.'[22] In this view, Christian subjects owed the same loyalty and obedience to their monarch and magistrates that they owed to their bishops and clergy. Had not the Old Testament shown that rulers must nurture true religion, with disaster befalling a people whose rulers ignored this sacred task? Did not the Prayer Book employ language consecrating the State and celebrating a sacred kingship?[23] Proponents of the divine unity of Church and State

[18] Ibid. 114. [19] Ibid. 150–4.

[20] For recent discussions of orthodox Anglican political theory in the 'long' eighteenth century, see especially J. C. D. Clark, *English Society 1688–1832* (Cambridge, 1985), 216–35; P. B. Nockles, *The Oxford Movement in Context: Anglicanism High Churchmanship 1760–1857* (Cambridge, 1994), 44–67; F. C. Mather, *High Church Prophet: Bishop Samuel Horsley (1733–1806) and the Caroline Tradition in the Later Georgian Church* (Oxford, 1992), 226–30; H. T. Dickinson, *Liberty and Property: Political Ideology in Eighteenth-Century Britain* (London, 1977), 13–27, 53–6, 167–8, 290–318; J. J. Sack, *From Jacobite to Conservative* (Cambridge, 1993), 188–216; R. Hole, *Pulpits, Politics and Public Order in England 1760–1832* (Cambridge, 1989), 11–22.

[21] S. Taylor, 'William Warburton and the Alliance of Church and State', *Journal of Ecclesiastical History*, 43 (1992), 271–86.

[22] R. Hooker, *Of the Laws of Ecclesiastical Polity* (1593–1662), bk. viii, ch. 1.2, Folger edn., eds. G. Edelen, W. Speed Hill, P. G. Stanwood, 3 vols. (Cambridge, Mass., 1977, 1981), iii. 312.

[23] G. F. A. Best, 'The Protestant Constitution and its Supporters, 1800–1829', *Transactions of the Royal Historical Society*, 5th series, 8 (1958), 105; Waterman, 'The Nexus between Theology and Political Doctrine', 193–209.

rejected both the Lockeian theory of the social contract, with its implied right of a people to resist their rulers, and its ecclesiastical cousin, the Warburton theory of the utilitarian alliance of Church and State. Social order did not originate in any collective human decision taken in remote history, but was ordained by a paternalistic God who had given his children government as a gracious act; the origins of society were to be found in Scripture and not in abstract theories of natural law. Governments and established Churches were alike instituted by God to curb sinful human nature. The response of subjects to the 'powers that be' should be passive obedience and non-resistance. To do otherwise was rebellion against God and would breed only confusion, as it had in the 1640s and 1650s, when both the civil and religious order had together collapsed through human pride and presumption, until God in his grace restored Church and State together in 1660. This insistence on the identity of Church and State became especially prevalent after 1760, in response to the republican ideas spread by the American and French Revolutions. Despite the apparent imperfections of this union, Bishop Samuel Horsley observed in an unpublished essay in 1790, 'the Christian must regard the intimate and inseparable Union of Religion and Civil Government as the grand Disideratum with respect to human Happiness'.[24] In a speech in the House of Commons in 1792 against a motion to repeal the penal laws directed against Unitarians, the moral philosopher and politician Edmund Burke declaimed against the Warburtonian view of Church and State as two separate societies joined in voluntary compact:

> An alliance between church and state in a Christian commonwealth is, in my opinion, an idle and fanciful speculation. An alliance is between two things that are in their nature distinct and independent, such as between two sovereign states. But in a Christian commonwealth the church and the state are one and the same thing, being different integral parts of the same whole.[25]

The connection of Church and State in England was expressed in the coronation ceremony and in the constitutional requirement that the monarch conform to the established Church. It was represented

[24] S. Horsley, 'Thoughts on Civil Government', ed. A. Robinson, in S. Taylor (ed.), *From Cranmer to Davidson: A Church of England Miscellany* (Woodbridge, 1999), 211.

[25] E. Burke, *Speeches of the Right Honourable Edmund Burke in the House of Commons*, 4 vols. (London, 1816), iv. 56–7 (11 May 1792).

by the presence of the bishops in the House of Lords. The system of ecclesiastical courts, including the diocesan and archidiaconal courts, and the appeal courts administered by the archdiocese of Canterbury, exercised authority over such civil matters as wills and marital disputes, as well as over moral offences by both clergy and laity. The Church kept State festivals—the discovery of the Gunpowder plot, the execution of King Charles the Martyr, the Restoration of 1660—and the general Fasts proclaimed by the Crown in times of national emergency. The connection of Church and State was further expressed by the Test and Corporation Acts, which restricted entry into most offices of trust in England to communicants of the established Church. The Corporation Act of 1661 required members of municipal corporations to affirm that they had received communion within the Church of England in the year preceding their election. The Test Act of 1673 required all holders of Crown office to take communion according to the usages of the Church of England and make a declaration against the Roman Catholic doctrine of transubstantiation.

The connection of Church and State was further expressed by the role of the parish in local government. The parish was the fundamental unit of both ecclesiastical and civil government. The parish vestry, consisting of the parish incumbent and the parishioners who owned or occupied property rated for poor relief, had responsibility for levying the church rate for the maintenance of the parish church and provision of communion elements, for levying rates for poor relief and repair of bridges, and for other matters of local administration. In many parishes, the vestry also administered a variety of charitable endowments, including alms-houses, hospitals, and schools. Such endowments often evinced a concern for both the spiritual and physical welfare of the recipients. A charity in a Hampshire parish, for example, paid 20*s.* to the parish incumbent for preaching a sermon on 'death, resurection and judment' [*sic*] each Michaelmas Day, and 30*s.* to those 'poor people' who turned up for the event.[26] The most important parish officers were the churchwardens, appointed jointly by the vestry and incumbent, who had responsibility for overseeing the repair of the church, supervising the collection and

[26] W. R. Ward (ed.), *Parson and Parish in Eighteenth-Century Surrey: Replies to Bishops' Visitations* (Guildford, 1994), pp. xvi–xx; Ward, *Parson and Parish in Eighteenth-Century Hampshire*, pp. xxviii–xxxi.

expenditure of the church rate, enforcing canon law, and maintaining parish discipline, including regular church attendance and the suppression of brawling, immorality, and profanity. In disciplinary matters, churchwardens had the power to summon persons to appear before the archdeacon's or bishop's court, though by the beginning of the nineteenth century the penances that could be assigned were almost exclusively ecclesiastical and the impact was limited. By 1750 the ecclesiastical courts had largely ceased attempting to enforce church attendance; in the diocese of Chester, the last attempt to discipline persons for non-attendance at the parish church was in 1778. A Parliamentary Commission reported in 1832 that almost no cases of sexual immorality or brawling had appeared before the ecclesiastical courts for many years.[27]

Parish incumbents generally co-operated closely with local landed gentlemen, who in turn exercised considerable authority in the parishes, both informally as landlords and employers and formally as justices of the peace. This squire–parson alliance prevailed in most rural parishes. During the eighteenth century, moreover, parish ministers were increasingly appointed as justices of the peace, serving on the magistrates' bench and imposing civil sentences, including the death penalty, for civil crimes. As the ecclesiastical courts ceased attempting to enforce discipline among the general population, the growing number of clerical magistrates after 1760 marked a revival of the role of the clergy in maintaining social order. Clerics were appointed as magistrates in part because they were educated men with a close knowledge of local society.[28] It would hardly have been healthy for local communities, wrote a historian of Oxfordshire, 'if there had been no magistrate with that particular knowledge of and feeling for the poor which is acquired by the faithful discharge of pastoral duties'.[29] The total number of clerical magistrates increased by 18 per cent between 1761 and 1831; by 1831 perhaps a quarter of all magistrates in England were clergymen, and

[27] R. B. Walker, 'Religious Changes in Cheshire, 1750–1850', *Journal of Ecclesiastical History*, 17 (1966), 80; *Parliamentary Papers*, 'Reports . . . by the Commissioners appointed to Inquire into the . . . Ecclesiastical Courts in England and Wales', (199) xxiv.1 (1831–2), 44–64; Knight, *Nineteenth-Century Church and English Society*, 182–7.

[28] D. Hempton, *Religion and Political Culture in Britain* (Cambridge, 1996), 8–9; Virgin, *Church in an Age of Negligence*, 121; D. McClatchey, *Oxfordshire Clergy 1777–1869* (Oxford, 1960), 178–201.

[29] J. C. Blomfield on William Jocelyn Palmer, rector of Mixbury, 1807–52, and JP; cited in McClatchey, *Oxfordshire Clergy*, 181.

in five English counties it was over 40 per cent. One clergyman in every six was an active magistrate.[30] Clergymen also served as surveyors of the highways, turnpike trustees, land tax commissioners, and other functionaries. They recommended recipients for parish poor relief. Such roles reflected an increasing interdependence between the clergy and propertied classes.[31] 'In many respects', the historians John Walsh and Stephen Taylor have recently observed, 'the close relationship of gentry and clergy made the alliance of church and state more of a *social* reality at the end of the eighteenth century than at any time since the middle ages.'[32] But this could also mean an identification of the clergy with the interests of the gentry. During this period the clergy wore secular clothing outside church; parsonages were becoming larger and more elaborately furnished, and the better-off clergy increasingly emulated the manners, morals, and pastimes of the gentry. These were, the Victorian novelist Anthony Trollope would later recall, 'halcyon days' for much of the clergy, when they were no longer expected to leave 'the dining-room when the pudding came in'. Rather 'the parson in his parsonage was as good a gentleman as any squire in his mansion or nobleman in his castle'.[33] If clergymen served on the magistrates' bench with the landlords, many also drank, rode, and hunted with the landlords, and grew distant from the majority of their parishioners. This was a serious weakness in a spiritual body that by scriptural precept was to be no respecter of persons.

There were, in truth, widespread problems with the Church of England as a national institution for nurturing the faith of the people. The fixing of the parish system in the Middle Ages had made it difficult for the Church to adapt to the growth and shifts of population in the late eighteenth and early nineteenth centuries. There were ample parish churches and relatively small parish populations in the rural south-east of England. However, London and the new

[30] E. Evans, 'Some Reasons for the Growth of English Rural Anticlericalism, *c.*1750–*c.*1830', *Past and Present*, 66 (Feb. 1975), 101; Virgin, *Church in an Age of Negligence*, 8, 118–19; A. D. Gilbert, *Religion and Society in Industrial England* (London, 1978), 80–1.

[31] G. F. A. Best, *Temporal Pillars: Queen Anne's Bounty, the Ecclesiastical Commissioners and the Church of England* (Cambridge, 1964), 61–74; Walsh and Taylor, 'The Church and Anglicanism in the "Long" Eighteenth Century', 28; G. Kitson Clark, *Churchmen and the Condition of England 1832–1885* (London, 1973), 35–6; A. Warne, *Church and Society in Eighteenth-Century Devon* (Newton Abbot, 1969), 148–65.

[32] Walsh and Taylor, 'The Church and Anglicanism in the "Long" Eighteenth Century', 28.

[33] A. Trollope, *Clergymen of the Church of England* (London, 1866), 59.

population centres, especially in the manufacturing and mining districts of the north and west, had too few parish churches, resulting in parish populations of 10,000 or more, far too large to be served by a single pastor. There were serious legal difficulties involved in subdividing parishes, which were civil as well as ecclesiastical units, or in building new chapels within existing parishes, as the new chapels might infringe on the rights and incomes of the parish churches. These difficulties restricted new church building. The result was that many people were outside the pastoral care of the established Church. The extreme inequalities in the value of parish livings meant that ambitious clerics were continually on the move, always seeking to advance up the preferment ladder to better-paid livings and frequently neglecting their existing parish responsibilities in their climb. At the same time the losers in the competition for preferment could grow frustrated and bitter. There were also numerous parishes in which the tithes and property were inadequate to support an incumbent in decent comfort. In 1809, despite a century of efforts by the State to increase the value of small livings through Queen Anne's Bounty, some 3,300 benefices were valued at less than £150 a year, regarded as a minimum income for a married professional man with a family, while 860 parish livings were worth less than £50 a year, well below that line.[34] A frequent metaphor used to describe the distribution of clerical incomes in the eighteenth and early nineteenth centuries was that of the lottery, in which many drew blanks and a favoured few found prizes.

Probably the Church's most obvious weakness was the widespread pluralism and non-residence among its clergy. According to returns made to Parliament in 1831, some 33 per cent of the beneficed clergy in England and Wales held more than one living, and 6 per cent held three or more. Only 44 per cent of the parishes of England and Wales had an incumbent who actually resided within the parish boundaries. Many technically non-resident incumbents, to be sure, resided near their parishes and provided regular Sunday services and pastoral care. In some cases, especially in rural districts, pluralism was probably a sensible tactical move. It enabled the Church to make the most efficient use of its resources by combining two or three very small and neighbouring parishes under a single incumbent, who would then have an adequate income while he was able to provide for the pastoral

[34] Best, *Temporal Pillars*, 204.

needs of the parishes. In many other cases, however, pluralism was a means by which clerics increased their incomes by taking the revenues of parish livings or cathedral offices for which they performed no duties. Such pluralism all too frequently led to neglect of the pastoral needs of parishioners. It could mean an abuse of a sacred trust, a placing of self-interest above the needs of the Church.

When an incumbent could not serve the parish, he was required to employ at his own expense a curate to supply his place. Incumbents, however, frequently paid the curates starvation wages; in 1810 most curates received stipends of only £20 to £30 a year, but some were as low as £10 a year. These were the 'serfs' of the Church, the clerical underclass. Undervalued and poorly supervised, many grew despondent and neglected their pastoral duties. Most would remain humble curates throughout their working lives, until incapacitated by old age or illness, and 'cast upon the world to starve'.[35] They would share the fate of George Eliot's Amos Barton, curate of Shepperton, in *Scenes of Clerical Life*—despised by parishioners for their lowly status and shabby appearance, beaten down by poverty, lacking social graces and opportunities for study, and liable to be dismissed without notice at the whim of the incumbent. Some curates, on the other hand, imbibed the ethos of their superiors and became pluralists themselves, multiplying the number of their curacies, or combining their curacy with a parish living or a schoolmaster's post.[36] In 1812, moreover, there were an estimated 1,000 parishes that were served by neither a resident incumbent nor a curate.[37] The Church also suffered from abuses of the system of patronage. Virtually every living in the Church had a legal patron, who possessed the right to present an ordained clergyman to that benefice. Patronage was a property right, and advowsons, or the right of presentation, could be bought and sold in the open market, generally fetching between five and seven times the annual value of the living. There was a lively market in advowsons in the early nineteenth century. Over 50 per cent of patrons were lay persons—for example, the King, nobles, squires, colleges, merchants, or lawyers—while some clergymen owned advowsons in a personal capacity.[38] It was not

[35] Virgin, *Church in an Age of Negligence*, 191–227; A. Tindal Hart, *The Curate's Lot: The Story of the Unbeneficed English Clergy* (London, 1970), 107–9.

[36] W. R. Ward (ed.), *Parson and Parish in Eighteenth-Century Hampshire*, p. xx.

[37] Gilbert, *Religion and Society in Industrial England*, 7.

[38] M. J. D. Roberts, 'Private Patronage and the Church of England, 1800–1900', *Journal of*

always clear who owned a particular patronage. 'The advowson', complained the incumbent of Mickleham in Surrey to his bishop in 1788, 'has been for sometime hawked about, and is supposed to be sold to Mr Talbot, solicitor at law and steward to Lord Donegal.'[39] All too often patrons made presentations to serve their personal or family interest. In 1783, for example, the enterprising John Leroo purchased the advowson of the parish of Long Melford in Suffolk for £2,600, presented himself as vicar in 1789, then proceeded to claim all possible tithe and financial benefit from the benefice, raising its annual income from £460 to £1,200. Soon after Leroo's death, the advowson sold for £12,400.[40] Such financial dealings represented a form of trade in souls, filling parish livings with incumbents more concerned with maximizing their income than serving their parishioners. Moreover, clerics seeking, or having received, patronage were expected to defer to the wishes of their patrons, thus sacrificing to a degree their independence as spiritual guides and pastors.

These problems were serious. However, they must be set alongside the positive contributions of the established clergy. While it is difficult to measure clerical diligence, many parish clergy were clearly dedicated pastors and men of blameless lives, who regularly catechized the young, visited their parishioners, encouraged family devotion, distributed charity, and supported local schools. Theirs was a pastoral commitment rooted in the missionary zeal of the Reformation, and promoted by such eighteenth-century archbishops as William Wake and Thomas Secker.[41] Mark Smith's recent study of religion in Oldham and Saddleworth suggests that the standard of eighteenth- and early nineteenth-century pastoral work was often high.[42] For the large majority of the population in late eighteenth- and early nineteenth-century England who adhered to the established Church, the parish church provided the rites of

Ecclesiastical History, 32 (1981), 199–204; W. A. Evershed, 'Party and Patronage in the Church of England 1800–1945' (Univ. of Oxford D.Phil., 1985), 33–5; Virgin, *Church in an Age of Negligence*, 171–81.

[39] W. R. Ward (ed.), *Parson and Parish in Eighteenth-Century Surrey*, p. xiv.

[40] Ibid. 182.

[41] J. Gregory, 'The Eighteenth-Century Reformation: The Pastoral Task of Anglican Clergy after 1689', in Walsh, Haydon, and Taylor (eds.), *The Church of England, c.1689–c.1833*, 67–85, and J. Gregory (ed.), *The Speculum of Archbishop Thomas Secker*, Church of England Record Society, 2 (Woodbridge, 1995), pp. xxi–xxx.

[42] M. Smith, *Religion in Industrial Society: Oldham and Saddleworth 1740–1865* (Oxford, 1994), 32–62.

passage—baptism, confirmation, marriage, and burial—that marked off the stages in their lives. Medieval church buildings and parish churchyards provided a continuity between the generations. Weekly worship was conducted with due decency. Parish clergy, often assisted by their wives and daughters, distributed charity, gave out moral guidance, provided consolation in bereavement, and communicated a sense of transcendence to their communities. The people of rural England, observed the poet Robert Southey, in 1820,

> are familiar from their childhood with the sound of the church bell, in all its varied imports of joy and sorrow: the sight of the font and the altar brings with it to them hallowed and tender recollections, and their family graves are in the green and quiet church-yard, where they themselves know that they shall one day find room as well as rest.[43]

The teachings of the parish clergy often dwelt on the practical duties of the Christian life, on the virtues of charity, benevolence, forbearance, and submission to the will of God. Their sermons offered hope to those who knew painful illness, loss of children, and pervasive poverty. Recalling his youth as the son of the archdeacon of Totnes, James Anthony Froude in the 1820s described religion in the rural parish church as

> orthodox without being theological. Doctrinal problems were little thought of. Religion, as taught in the Church of England, meant moral obedience to the will of God. . . . The creeds were reverentially repeated; but the essential thing was practice. People went to church on Sunday to learn to be good, to hear the commandments repeated to them for the thousandth time, and to see them written in gilt letters over the communion table.[44]

The Church of Ireland, like its sister establishment in England, was Protestant and episcopal, with a parochial organization. Its worship was based on the Book of Common Prayer, and it acknowledged the King-in-Parliament as its supreme temporal governor. Even before its union with the Church of England in 1801, its Irish apologists frequently referred to it as the Church of England in Ireland. Yet there was a fundamental difference between the two establishments. While the Church of England ministered to the large majority of the people of England and Wales, the Church of Ireland was the Church

[43] [R. Southey], 'New Churches', *Quarterly Review*, 23 (July 1820), 558.

[44] J. A. Froude, 'The Oxford Counter-Reformation', in J. A. Froude, *Short Studies on Great Subjects*, 4 vols. (London, 1890), iv. 239.

of only a small minority, perhaps 10 per cent, of the Irish people. Most of its adherents, moreover, were concentrated in Ulster and Leinster; in the south and west, they comprised only about 3–5 per cent of the population.[45] There was a great gulf between what was expected of it as an establishment and what it was possible for it to do.[46] For it was deeply resented as an alien force by Ireland's overwhelming Catholic majority, as well as by Ireland's Presbyterian population. *Sasanach* (Englishman) was the Irish-language term to denote an adherent of the established Church.[47] 'It is not the religion of the people of Ireland,' observed the champion of the establishment principle, Edmund Burke, in 1794, 'No Church, in no Country, is so circumstanced.'[48] For their own part, however, adherents of the Irish Church viewed themselves as a 'favourite People', a beleaguered minority, guardians of God's truth in a hostile land.[49]

The Church of Ireland was administered by four archbishops and eighteen bishops, all Crown appointments. The archbishop of Armagh was the primate, with the archbishop of Dublin second in authority. Before the Act of Union of 1801, all Irish bishops had held seats in the Irish House of Lords, and most spent considerable time in Dublin, performing their parliamentary duties. By the terms of the Act of Union, however, only four Irish bishops sat in the House of Lords at Westminster, according to a prescribed order of rotation, and this gradually had a positive effect in ensuring more regular residence in their dioceses. The eighteenth-century bishops were largely English or Anglo-Irish; of 123 bishops serving the Irish Church in the eighteenth century, sixty-seven came from mainland Britain and another fifty-six were Anglo-Irish. They were frequently concerned with pursuing patronage and seeking translations to better-endowed bishoprics. The Convocation of the Irish Church, like that of the English Church, had been suspended early in the

[45] D. G. Boyce, *Nineteenth-Century Ireland: The Search for Stability* (Dublin, 1990), 11–12.

[46] D. Bowen, *The Protestant Crusade in Ireland 1800–1870* (Dublin, 1978), 47. Overemphasis on its claims as an establishment has, Sean Connolly has noted, resulted in much injustice in the treatment of the Church of Ireland as a Church. S. J. Connolly, *Religion, Law, and Power: The Making of Protestant Ireland 1660–1760* (Oxford, 1992), 171–2.

[47] L. Swords, *A Hidden Church: The Diocese of Achonry 1689–1818* (Blackrock, Co. Dublin, 1997), 137.

[48] E. Burke to Earl Fitzwilliam, 21 Oct. 1794, cited in I. McBride, *Scripture Politics: Ulster Presbyterians and Irish Radicalism in the Late Eighteenth Century* (Oxford, 1998), 19.

[49] R. Eccleshall, 'Anglican Political Thought in the Century after the Revolution of 1688', in D. G. Boyce, R. Eccleshall, and V. Geoghegan (eds.), *Political Thought in Ireland since the Seventeenth Century* (London, 1993), 40, 43, 44.

eighteenth century, leaving the bishops with considerable authority over the local affairs of the Church, but depriving the Irish Church of a strong sense of corporate identity and missionary purpose.[50] There were a total of thirty-two dioceses in Ireland, so that some of the twenty-two bishops exercised authority over more than one diocese. The dioceses varied considerably in size, from Tuam with an area of some 1,135,600 acres, to Waterford with an area of 31,300 acres; and in population, from Dublin with a population of 501,977 in 1830, to Kilfenora with a population of only 36,405.[51] Most of the dioceses had a cathedral. Few of the medieval cathedral structures had survived, and some cathedrals were very modest structures that also served as parish churches. There were, however, also some impressive buildings, including St Patrick's Cathedral, Armagh, with its majestic nave (restored in 1765), St Mary's Cathedral, Limerick, with its great limestone altar, and the two Dublin cathedrals of St Patrick's and Christ Church. In general Irish cathedrals were far less well endowed than those of England. While thirty of the dioceses had a dean and chapter, Irish prebendaries were not resident to the same degree as in England—many never visited their dioceses—and they did not play a national role as preachers and apologists for the faith. There were about 180 prebendaries and another 140 cathedral officers, or a total of about 320 holders of chapter livings—the majority of whom also held parish livings.[52]

Ireland was divided by law into some 2,400 legal parishes. However, many of these civil parishes had been united for ecclesiastical purposes, making a total of about 1,200 parish livings. The parish clergy were supported by tithes and other forms of Church property, and as in England, each parish formed a miniature ecclesiastical corporation, with the living held as a form of freehold property. While the clergy of the established Church were by law responsible for providing worship, religious instruction, pastoral care, and ecclesiastical discipline to the entire population of Ireland, in practice they restricted themselves to their own adherents. They were not a missionary Church. Some clergy recognized a responsibility before God to bring the whole of Ireland's people within their fold, but

[50] J. Falvey, 'The Church of Ireland Episcopate in the Eighteenth Century: An Overview', *Eighteenth-Century Ireland*, 8 (1993), 103–14.

[51] [T. H. Lister], 'State of the Irish Church', *Edinburgh Review*, 61 (July 1835), 498.

[52] Ibid. 492–4; D. A. Chart, 'The Broadening of the Church', in W. A. Phillips (ed.), *History of the Church of Ireland*, 3 vols. (Oxford, 1933), iii. 275–8.

were unclear about how to do so without fomenting strife with their Roman Catholic or Presbyterian neighbours. Many others, however, seemed happy enough to collect their incomes, minister to the Protestant minority, fraternize with the gentry, and not bother themselves about the Catholic poor in their parishes. There were no doubt many like the Revd Phineas Lucre in the Irish Protestant William Carleton's novel, *Valentine McLutchy* (1845): 'Without piety to God, or charity to man, he possessed, however, fervent attachment to his church. . . . If he neglected the widow and the orphan whom he could serve, he did not neglect the great and honorable, who could serve himself.'[53]

The Church of Ireland had adopted the Anglican Book of Common Prayer early in the reign of Elizabeth I, and the Anglican Thirty-Nine Articles in 1634–5. Thus, like the Church of England, it was not a confessional Church on the pattern of Continental Protestantism. For its defenders it was a branch of the ancient Church, with its bishops representing an episcopal succession going back to St Patrick, and from St Patrick to the Apostles. Its claim to be the established Church rested, not upon the numbers of its adherents or the support of the State, but rather on its perception of itself as the sole branch of the holy catholic and apostolic Church within Ireland. It was the guardian of the true faith in a largely heathen land. The eighteenth-century Church of Ireland venerated the teachings of the Caroline divines, with their emphasis on the evil of schism and the importance of proper order and decorum.[54] Most parish churches celebrated the sacrament of Holy Communion about four times a year, generally at the major festivals of the Christian year. With between a third and half of the adult Church of Ireland adherents regularly taking the sacrament, it formed an important event in the life of the Church.[55]

The relations of Church and State were close. The Irish establishment commemorated the festivals that helped to consecrate the Irish kingdom, especially that of St Patrick, the apostle of the Irish, and

[53] W. Carleton, *Valentine McClutchy, the Irish Agent* (1845), in *The Works of William Carleton*, 2 vols. (New York, 1881), ii. 213.

[54] P. Nockles, 'Continuity and Change in Anglican High Churchmanship in Britain, 1792–1850' (University of Oxford D.Phil., 1982), 344–9; F. R. Bolton, *The Caroline Tradition of the Church of Ireland* (London, 1958).

[55] W. A. Phillips (ed.), *History of the Church of Ireland*, iii. 285; Connolly, *Religion, Law and Power*, 186–7.

the birthday of William III, the nation's 'deliverer'.[56] All magistrates had to conform to the established Church and some 10 per cent of the Irish justices of the peace were clerics. Local government was largely administered by general parish vestries, made up of the incumbent and ratepaying inhabitants of the parish, who were responsible for levying small local taxes for church repairs, road maintenance, and other minor public works, and for employing constables to maintain public order. Participation in the general vestries was not restricted to members of the established Church, and Catholics and Presbyterians frequently attended. However, the vestry officers—including two churchwardens and the parish clerk—were required by law to conform to the established Church.[57]

In the eighteenth century, the principle of the Church–State connection in Ireland was expressed most visibly in the penal laws that were directed mainly against Ireland's Roman Catholic majority.[58] Imposed by a triumphant and exclusively Protestant Irish Parliament following the Jacobite war of 1689–91, the penal laws were aimed at keeping the Jacobites and their French and Spanish allies at bay, sustaining the confiscations of Catholic land, reducing the defeated Catholic majority to a condition of subservience, and persuading the Catholic élite to conform to the established Church. The penal laws severely curtailed the activities of the Roman Catholic Church in Ireland and deprived Catholics of the right to own and bequeath landed property, bear arms, and educate their children in Catholic schools. By an act of 1697, all bishops and religious orders were expelled from the country. Catholic pilgrimages to Irish holy places were outlawed. In 1704, the Irish Parliament required all Catholics to take an oath of allegiance and abjuration, renouncing the Stewart pretender, Roman 'errors', and authority of the Papacy, in order to vote in parliamentary elections, sit in Parliament, or hold Crown office. Priests were required to register with a magistrate, and provide securities for good behaviour. In 1704, the Irish Parliament also passed a Test Act, requiring all persons holding Crown office to

[56] J. R. Hill, 'National Festivals, the State and "Protestant Ascendancy" in Ireland, 1790–1829', *Irish Historical Studies*, 24 (1984), 30–9.

[57] McBride, *Scripture Politics*, 22; D. H. Akenson, *The Church of Ireland: Ecclesiastical Reform and Revolution, 1800–1885* (New Haven, 1971), 52–4.

[58] For recent reassessments of the penal laws and their impact, see Connolly, *Religion, Law, and Power*, 263–313; T. Bartlett, *The Fall and Rise of the Irish Nation* (Dublin, 1992), 17–29.

receive the sacrament of communion within the established Church. The sacramental test was imposed on both Catholics and Protestant Dissenters, effectively excluding them from political participation.[59]

If enforced, the penal legislation would have effectively destroyed the Roman Catholic Church in Ireland. The enforcement, however, was sporadic. The penal acts were strictly enforced in the area of landownership, and here they had a major impact, reducing the amount of Catholic-owned land in Ireland from 14 per cent in 1703 to 5 per cent in 1776.[60] But the provisions against the Catholic clergy and Catholic education were only erratically enforced, especially after 1730, as the Protestant minority felt more secure and the difficult work of harrying Catholic priests and teachers seemed less pressing, especially to a Protestant élite that had no real interest in converting the Catholic peasantry. In the later 1770s, influenced by Enlightenment ideas of toleration and the need of the imperial State for the military service of Irish Catholics, the Irish Parliament began repealing or modifying the penal acts, until by the mid-1790s much of the penal legislation had been withdrawn.[61] Catholics continued to be denied the right to sit in Parliament and hold most Crown offices by the required oath of abjuration, but they could now own land and vote in parliamentary elections. The Government of William Pitt proposed to emancipate Catholics from their remaining civil disabilities and grant them full rights of citizenship as part of the Union of Britain and Ireland in 1801. But Catholic Emancipation was thwarted by the opposition of George III, who would not compromise on the terms of his coronation oath and who had the support of conservative opinion in England for his conscientious stand. From the mid-1780s, moreover, there was a growing feeling among Irish Protestants that Catholic relief measures might be going too far. They began to employ the term 'Protestant ascendancy' to describe the proper social and political order in Ireland, and to insist that further encroachments on this ascendancy would threaten not only Protestantism and property in Ireland, but also the connection of Ireland and England. Conservative Protestant attitudes in Ireland continued to harden after 1801.[62]

[59] W. A. Phillips (ed.), *History of the Church of Ireland*, iii. 185–7, 195–7.

[60] Bartlett, *The Fall and Rise of the Irish Nation*, 22–3. [61] Ibid. 82–172.

[62] J. Hill, 'The Meaning and Significance of "Protestant Ascendancy", 1781–1840', in *Ireland after the Union*, Proceedings of the Second Joint Meeting of the Royal Irish Academy and the British Academy (Oxford, 1989), 1–22; J. Kelly, 'The Genesis of "Protestant

While probably most Irish Protestants were rallying to the defence of the 'Protestant ascendancy', liberals in England and Ireland continued to direct attention to the injustices of Irish society and to call for further reform. They focused particular criticism on the Irish establishment. In an age of reason, it seemed less and less defensible to maintain an established Church for a small minority of the population. There was also the glaring problem of the tithe, the notional 10 per cent of all agricultural produce, which was levied on tenants regardless of their religious affiliation to support the established Church. An act of 1735 had exempted land under pasture from the payment of tithe, and this had had the effect of throwing the burden of tithe from the large landowners on to the mainly Catholic small tenant farmers, with even the potatoes necessary to sustain the Irish poor subject to tithe in Munster and much of Leinster. In the west of Ireland parish of Coolaney and Collooney, the tithe book for 1813 revealed that the estate of Templehouse, seat of the Percival family, and the estate of Nymphsfield, seat of the O'Hara's, were both totally exempt from tithe, while Catholic smallholders were obliged to bear the tithe burden.[63] All this meant that the poorest peasantry in western Europe was forced to pay heavily to maintain an established Church attended by a small minority, including owners of large estates who were largely exempt from tithe. There was, not surprisingly, sporadic peasant resistance to the tithe; in some districts, secret, oath-bound agrarian bands, Whiteboys, Rightboys, and Defenders, threatened clerics with violence for insisting on their tithe rights. But tithe was not the only problem plaguing the Church of Ireland. A minority establishment, in which many parishes had few if any Protestants, in which bishops often provided little leadership, and that lacked a sense of corporate identity and mission, was hardly calculated to inspire the best efforts from its clergy. A survey of the Irish Church, commissioned by the archbishop of Armagh in 1807, revealed widespread pluralism and non-residence. Of 1,133 beneficed clergy reported in the survey, 274 held more than one benefice and 561 were habitually non-resident, many of them living in England. The unions of parishes, moreover, had created situations in which parish churches were too distant for many parishioners to

Ascendancy"', in G. O'Brien (ed.), *Parliament, Politics and People: Essays in Eighteenth-Century Irish History* (Dublin, 1989), 93–127.

[63] Swords, *A Hidden Church: The Diocese of Achonry*, 148.

attend. A further survey in 1808 revealed that of 775 reporting parishes, only 582 had churches in good repair, and only 199 had glebe houses (residence houses) in decent condition.[64]

These problems were serious, and posed real threats to the maintenance of both the Irish establishment and the Protestant ascendancy. For many, however, the legislative Union of 1801 and the creation of the United Church of England and Ireland promised a new beginning.[65] By uniting the Irish establishment to that of England, the act of Union promised to preserve the Irish Church from its growing number of opponents. From being the Church of a small minority in Ireland, the Irish establishment had become a branch of the majority Church in the United Kingdom. The United Church, moreover, would contribute to the consolidation of the Union by promoting a common Anglican faith. The established Church in Ireland, argued the Protestant convert William Phelan in 1823, educated its members in loyalty to the 'English' State:

> In feelings, principles and associations—in all those subtle elements which constitute the social being, her children are Englishmen. . . . The church has been no illiberal preceptress. She gladly admits the lights of science, literature, well-ordered freedom, sober philanthropy, and she points to England as the fountain of them all. She has taught her followers to blend England with all their dearest, their holiest, their most enobling recollections—to trace thither the pedigree of their blessings—to make it their heart and spirit, the country of their earthly affections, and the guide to that better country, whose foundation is in the Heavens.[66]

In 1801, it remained to be seen whether the Irish establishment could extend its influence beyond its small minority of adherents, educate a larger portion of the Irish people in loyalty to the 'English' State, transform the Protestant ascendancy into a Protestant majority, and make the Union live in the hearts of the Irish people.

The third of the established Churches in the United Kingdom, the Church of Scotland, was an anomaly. Where the establishments in England and Ireland were Episcopalian in structure, the Church of Scotland was Presbyterian, with government through a hierarchy of

[64] E. Brynn, 'Some Repercussions of the Act of Union on the Church of Ireland, 1801–1820', *Church History*, 40 (1971), 292–5; Akenson, *The Church of Ireland*, 128–9.

[65] E. Brynn, *The Church of Ireland in the Age of Catholic Emancipation* (New York, 1982), 29–30; Akenson, *The Church of Ireland*, 72–3.

[66] [W. Phelan], *The Case of the Church of Ireland Stated, in a Letter Respectfully Addressed to His Excellency the Marquis Wellesley . . . by Declan* (Dublin, 1823), 49.

representative Church courts. Where the doctrine of the English and Irish Establishments was loosely expressed in the comprehensive Thirty-Nine Articles, the doctrine of the Church of Scotland was closely defined by the Westminster Confession of Faith, a systematic exposition of seventeenth-century Reformed, or Calvinist, theology. Where worship in the established Churches of England and Ireland was informed by the Book of Common Prayer, the Scottish establishment had no prayer-book and its services emphasized the sermon and extempore prayer. Where the Churches of England and Ireland had preserved their cathedrals, the Reformed Church of Scotland had broken with its medieval past, abolishing its cathedral establishments and demolishing many cathedral structures. Where the established Churches of England and Ireland recognized the King-in-Parliament as the supreme governor of the Church, and were represented in Parliament by bishops in the House of Lords, the Church of Scotland expressly rejected the notion of the royal supremacy, had no direct ecclesiastical representation in Parliament, and insisted that Church and State were two distinct kingdoms. The Scottish establishment was also small in comparison with its sister establishments. In 1815, out of a total population of nearly 20 million inhabitants of the United Kingdom, about 18 million were at least notionally under the care of the Episcopalian United Church of England and Ireland, while fewer than 2 million were under the Presbyterian Church of Scotland.

The Scottish establishment was an anomaly that the monarchical state had been reluctantly forced to accept. When the Reformation had come to Scotland in 1560, Scotland had been an independent country. The Scottish Reformation had been a popular movement, pursued *against* the opposition of the Crown, and Scotland's Reformers had looked for their model not to Canterbury and the Henrician Reformation, but rather to Calvin's Geneva. By the later 1570s the Scottish Reformed Church had embraced Presbyterianism, again despite the opposition of the Crown. Church and State in Scotland had thus remained separate, eyeing one another with distrust. In 1603, Scotland's Stewart king, James VI, came to the throne of England as James I, and England and Scotland were united under a single Crown. Efforts by James and his son Charles I to use their new power to move the Scottish Church towards convergence with the Episcopal Churches of England and Ireland led to an armed rising in Scotland, under the banner of the National

Covenant, which in turn plunged the three kingdoms into revolution by the early 1640s. Following the Restoration of the monarchy in 1660, Charles II restored episcopacy and revived the effort to move the Scottish Church towards convergence with the sister establishments. The result was military resistance by the Presbyterian Covenanters and brutal repression by the State, with Covenanters killed on sight on the hills and moors during the 1680s. Following the Glorious Revolution of 1688–9, William III reluctantly acquiesced in the decision of the Scottish Convention to establish Presbyterianism and to require all ministers to subscribe to the Westminster Confession of Faith. It was for William a matter of political expediency. The majority of the Scottish people seemed committed to Presbyterianism and he therefore resisted the claim by high Anglicans that he must, for truth's sake, require an Episcopalian establishment in Scotland. William's religious conscience, the Whig historian T. B. Macaulay would later insist, 'was perfectly neutral. For it was his deliberate opinion that no form of ecclesiastical polity was of divine institution.'[67] The restored Presbyterian establishment shrewdly made no attempt to revive the Covenants. When, five years after William's death, England and Scotland entered into the legislative Union of 1707, securities were added to ensure that the new-formed British Parliament would not interfere with the Scottish Presbyterian establishment.

The Presbyterian Church of Scotland was governed not by a hierarchy of bishops, but by a hierarchy of Church courts, from the kirk-session at the parish level rising to the district presbytery, the provincial synod, and finally the national General Assembly. One of the salient features of Scottish Presbyterianism was the parity of ministers, with no single minister superior to, or exercising authority over, a fellow minister. At the foundation of the Presbyterian system was the parish, with its kirk-session of minister and elders. There were approximately 970 parishes in Scotland, each with a parish church and minister. The minister was ordained when appointed to his first parish. He was assisted by a number of elders, usually between seven and twelve—but often as few as one or two—who were also ordained, but who were commonly regarded as laymen. The minister and ruling elders met together regularly as a parish court, or kirk-session, with responsibility for supervising the moral

[67] T. B. Macaulay, *History of England*, 5 vols. (New York, 1862), iii. 206–7.

and spiritual discipline of the parishioners, as well as parish education and poor relief. In rural parishes, the kirk-session shared authority in parish government with the parish court of heritors, or principal landowners. In burgh (town) parishes, the kirk-session shared responsibility with the magistrates and burgh council.

Above the kirk-session was the presbytery, exercising a territorial jurisdiction over several contiguous parishes, usually between eight and eighteen, within a convenient travelling distance of one another. There were sixty-nine presbyteries in the early nineteenth-century Church. Presbytery courts included the minister and one ruling elder from each of the parishes within the presbytery's boundaries and they usually convened once a month. Presbyteries were responsible for hearing appeals from kirk-sessions, for examining and licensing candidates for the ministry, for ordaining new ministers, and for supervising the work of ministers within their boundaries. They had the power to depose ministers for heretical teaching, neglect of pastoral responsibilities, or immoral conduct. Further, they could recommend motions ('overtures') for Church legislation to the General Assembly, or supreme court of the Church. Above the presbytery was the synod, made up of all the members of several presbyteries, and meeting once or twice a year for sessions of two to three days, usually in early May and in October. There were sixteen synods in the Church. Synods heard appeals from the presbytery decisions and reviewed acts of presbyteries. They could also recommend Church legislation to the consideration of the General Assembly. The General Assembly, or supreme ecclesiastical court in the Church of Scotland, met once a year for a week-long session, usually in late May, in Edinburgh. The Assembly consisted of three to five representatives from each presbytery, and a ruling elder from each royal burgh and university, making a total of some 360 members, with about 200 ministers and 160 ruling elders. It met in the presence of a Lord High Commissioner, who represented the monarch, and it was presided over by a Moderator, who was elected by the Assembly for a term of one year. The General Assembly was the court of final appeal for decisions of the lower Church courts. It also had the power to approve overtures for new acts of Church law, though once approved an overture had to be sent back to the presbyteries for their final approval before it could become law. At the close of its annual session the General Assembly appointed a Commission, which met three times during the year to handle any ongoing Assembly business. All church courts, with the exception of kirk-sessions, were conducted in public, 'open to spectators from every class of the people'.[68]

The doctrinal standards of the Church of Scotland were defined by the Westminster Confession of Faith, a systematic exposition of Reformed doctrine drafted by the Westminster Assembly of Divines in 1645–6 and adopted by the Church of Scotland in 1647. The Westminster Confession left little room for diversity of interpretation. It proclaimed a transcendent God who had ordained all things by his divine decrees, including the salvation of the elect saints and the damnation of the reprobate. It insisted in uncompromising language on the depravity of human nature and on salvation by grace alone. All candidates for the ministry of the Church were required to subscribe to the Confession and teach its doctrines. Worship in the Church was defined by the Westminster Directory of Public Worship, which provided for a simple service, emphasizing the sermon and the singing of psalms. The Church recognized two sacraments, baptism and communion. In most parishes, communion was celebrated twice a year, in sacramental occasions of three or four days' duration, which included prayer services, examination of communicants in doctrine and morals, extensive preaching, and thanksgiving services. In these communal festivals, or 'holy fairs', the parish minister would be assisted by neighbouring ministers. People would attend in large numbers from neighbouring parishes, combining piety with socializing, hearing sermons, drinking ale, exchanging news, and finding marriage partners.[69]

The ministers of the Scottish establishment were supported from the teind, or tithe, a notional 10 per cent of all agricultural produce, with half paid by the tenant and half by the landowner. Ministers were required to reside in the parish, conduct one service each Sunday, visit their parishioners regularly, and catechize the young.[70] The minister and elders had responsibility for education, poor relief, and moral discipline in the parish. At the Reformation, the Church

[68] H. Moncreiff Wellwood, *Account of the Life and Writings of John Erskine* (Edinburgh, 1818), 414.

[69] For the distinctive sacramental occasions in Scottish Presbyterianism, see L. E. Schmidt, *Holy Fairs: Scottish Communions and American Revivals in the Early Modern Period* (Princeton, 1989), 11–51, 69–168; G. B. Burnet, *The Holy Communion in the Reformed Church of Scotland 1560–1960* (Edinburgh, 1960), 126–254.

[70] For the pastoral visiting and catechizing of the eighteenth-century clergy, see especially Moncreiff Wellwood, *John Erskine*, 71–6.

of Scotland had committed itself to the goal of universal literacy, to ensure that every person could read the Bible, and to provide a ladder of educational opportunity to enable every male child to develop his capacities for service to the commonwealth. This was to be achieved in part by providing a primary school in every parish. By the Act for Settling of Schools in 1696, the heritors, or principal landowners, in each parish were responsible for providing a school and schoolmaster. Schoolmasters were elected by the heritors, examined and approved by the kirk-session, and required to subscribe to the Westminster Confession of Faith. In 1816, Scotland had 942 parish schools, or nearly one in every parish.[71] Although in many districts the parish schools were proving inadequate for Scotland's growing population, the general literacy rate in the country was one of the highest in Europe.

The kirk-session exercised responsibility over moral discipline in the parish.[72] In the Scottish establishment, discipline was corporate in its character. The elders were responsible for discovering moral and religious infractions, including extramarital sex, drunkenness, lying, quarrelling, profanity, and unfair business practices. Offenders would be summoned to appear before the kirk-session, examined, and if found guilty, admonished and assigned a penance, which usually involved paying a fine to the poor relief fund or having to stand or sit, sometimes dressed in sackcloth, before the congregation for a specified number of Sundays. Kirk-sessions had the power to call witnesses and examine them on oath.[73] By 1801, it should be noted, most kirk-session discipline involved cases of extramarital sex, with elders pressing unmarried pregnant women to reveal the names of fathers, who could then be forced to contribute to the children's support.[74] According to the Scottish poor law, moreover, the kirk-session was responsible for the distribution of parish poor relief, with the funds derived primarily from voluntary church-door collections

[71] R. D. Anderson, *Education and the Scottish People 1750–1918* (Oxford, 1995), 3–23; S. Mechie, *The Church and Scottish Social Development 1780–1870* (Oxford, 1960), 138–9.

[72] For accounts of kirk-session discipline in the early modern Church of Scotland, see I. M. Clark, *A History of Church Discipline in Scotland* (Aberdeen, 1929), 85–186; G. D. Henderson, *The Scottish Ruling Elder* (Aberdeen, 1935), 100–45; A. Edgar, 'The Discipline of the Church of Scotland', in R. H. Story (ed.), *The Church of Scotland*, 5 vols. (Edinburgh, n.d.), v. 427–556; R. Mitchison and L. Leneman, *Sexuality and Social Control: Scotland 1660–1780* (Oxford, 1989).

[73] Moncreiff Wellwood, *John Erskine*, 409.

[74] L. Leneman and R. Mitchison, 'Acquiescence in and Defiance of Church Discipline in Early Modern Scotland', *Records of the Scottish Church History Society*, 25 (1995), 20–1.

for the poor. Only if these funds proved insufficient were the kirk-session and heritors empowered to levy an assessment, or poor rate, on parish property. Even in assessed parishes, the kirk-session distributed poor relief. By law, no relief was to be given to the able-bodied poor, though kirk-sessions frequently ignored this rule, especially during periods of poor harvests and high unemployment.[75]

In Scottish Presbyterianism, Church and State comprised two separate and distinct societies, 'twa kingdoms'—one under the sole headship of Christ and one under the worldly monarch—which had entered into a compact for mutual benefit. In the alliance, the State employed its power of the sword to protect the endowments of the Church, while the Church employed its spiritual power to elevate the population through religious and moral instruction.[76] This was a version of contract theory, and implied a Christian right to resist an 'ungodly' monarch. The Presbyterian political theory received one of its most eloquent expressions in 1596, when at Falkland Palace the clergyman Andrew Melville had plucked James VI's sleeve, called him 'God's sillie vassal', and instructed him that the Church was the kingdom of Christ, 'whose subject King James the Sixth is, and of whose kingdom not a king, nor a lord, nor a head, but a member'.[77] The eighteenth-century Church of Scotland did not repudiate the struggle of the seventeenth-century Covenanters against the Stewart monarchs, nor did it share the Anglican view of Charles I as a martyr-king. The Scottish Church continued to insist on its independence from the State in spiritual matters. 'That establishment is the most perfect', wrote the Church of Scotland minister Alexander Ranken in 1799, 'in which [Church and State] interfere the least with each others' functions and immediate objects, and in which, at the same time, they can most readily co-operate in promoting successfully the present order, and the future happiness of man.'[78] Church of Scotland ministers could not be elected to the House of Commons or vote in parliamentary elections, and the Church had no official representation at the coronation ceremony or

[75] R. Mitchison, 'The Making of the Old Scottish Poor Law', *Past and Present*, 63 (1974), 72–3, 89, 90–1.

[76] G. Hill, *View of the Constitution of the Church of Scotland* (1803), 3rd edn. (Edinburgh, 1835), 6–13; J. Inglis, *The Importance of Ecclesiastical Establishments; a Sermon, preached . . . before the Society . . . for the Benefit of the Sons of the Clergy of the Church of Scotland* (Edinburgh, 1821), 11–15.

[77] J. H. S. Burleigh, *A Church History of Scotland* (Oxford, 1960), 204–5.

[78] A. Ranken, *The Importance of Religious Establishments* (Glasgow, 1799), 3.

representatives in the House of Lords.[79] There was, moreover, no movement in late eighteenth-century Scotland, similar to that in England, for the appointment of clerical magistrates. (A few were appointed, mainly in the Highlands, but only when there was a shortage of landed gentlemen able to serve.[80]) Scotland had no Test Act, requiring candidates for civil office to take communion within the established Church. From the 1560s the Scottish Parliament had imposed civil disabilities on Roman Catholics, including laws against priests and Catholic landownership. The British Parliament had also imposed penal restrictions upon Scottish Episcopalians in 1719, in the aftermath of the Jacobite rising of 1715, with additional restrictions added after the Jacobite rising of 1745–6. The penal restrictions on Episcopalians tended to be ignored as the Jacobite threat waned, and were finally repealed in 1792, while most of the penal restrictions on Catholics were repealed in 1793.

The Union of 1707 had not been without difficulties for the Presbyterian Church of Scotland, which now became part of a predominantly Anglican State. The greatest of these difficulties was the issue of patronage, or the right of laymen to own advowsons and present ministers to vacant church livings. Despite guarantees in the Union treaty that Parliament would not interfere in Scotland's religious settlement, Parliament had in 1712 restored lay patronage in the Church of Scotland. Patronage, however, had long been opposed by strict Presbyterians, who believed it gave patrons—most patronage was in the hands of the Crown or members of the gentry and aristocracy—a privileged status within God's Church. It was an offence against the principle, sacred for most Scots, that Christ's Church was to be no respecter of persons and that all were equal (and equally depraved) in the eyes of God. The Stewart monarchs had consistently sought to enforce patronage. But in 1690, when the Presbyterians had regained control of the Scottish establishment, they had immediately moved to abolish lay patronage and to place the right of presenting ministers in the hands of the kirk-sessions and heritors in the parishes. Parliament's decision to reimpose patronage in 1712 had been made without consulting with the Scottish Church, and many Presbyterians viewed it as a return to the old Stewart policy of moving Scotland's Church towards conformity

[79] J. Cunningham, *The Church History of Scotland*, 2 vols. (Edinburgh, 1859), ii. 549.

[80] A. E. Whetstone, *Scottish County Government in the Eighteenth and Nineteenth Centuries* (Edinburgh, 1981), 39.

with that of England. The Scottish Church courts strenuously resisted the Patronage Act, viewing it as an unwarranted intrusion by the State into Church affairs. Initially most lay patrons had declined to exercise their right of presentation. Then, from about 1730, they increasingly exercised their right, treating it as a means of increasing their local influence by placing 'their' men in local churches, men who would emphasize in their sermons the importance of civil order and deference to the powers that be, and who might also be congenial companions for dinner and cards at the laird's house. The result was considerable disorder in the Scottish Church, with parishioners resisting patronage settlements with violence, and presbyteries often refusing to ordain patron's candidates. Ordinations often had to be conducted in the presence of armed troops, brought in to suppress popular resistance. There were clashes between parishioners and troops, and even loss of life. Individuals and whole congregations seceded from the established Church rather than submit to patronage.[81] But repeated Church petitions to Parliament to remove the hated law proved unavailing, and gradually the protests died down. By the early nineteenth century, the majority in the Scottish Church had grown to live with patronage, while continuing to regard it as a sore grievance.[82]

The Church of Scotland did not suffer to the same extent as its sister establishments from the abuses of pluralism and non-residence. There was only one type of pluralism permitted within the Church in 1801—the uniting of a parish living with a university chair—and this was needed because of the poor endowments of most chairs. Non-residence was comparatively rare. Church law required residence from all parish clergy, and presbyteries were strict in enforcing this law.[83] The Scottish Church did, however, suffer from serious financial problems, many of them stemming from the lay impropriations of monastic lands and parish teinds at the Reformation. In 1750 over half the teinds in Scotland were in the possession of the landed classes and clerical stipends were often meagre. No fewer

[81] For the patronage controversy in the eighteenth-century Church of Scotland, see R. Sher and A. Murdoch, 'Patronage and Party in the Church of Scotland, 1750–1800', in N. McDougall (ed.), *Church, Politics and Society: Scotland 1408–1929* (Edinburgh, 1983), 197–220.

[82] Moncreiff Wellwood, *John Erskine*, 473.

[83] R. Burns, *Plurality of Offices in the Church of Scotland Examined* (Glasgow, 1824), 82–124; G. Cook, *Substance of a Speech delivered in the General Assembly, 22 May 1816, containing an Inquiry into the Law and Constitution of the Church of Scotland respecting Residence and Pluralities* (Edinburgh, 1816).

than 273 parish livings, over 28 per cent of the total, provided less than £50 a year.[84] There was a lack of adequate church accommodation. The parish system had been fixed in the later Middle Ages, and there was an insufficient number of parish churches in the rapidly growing industrial towns and cities of the central Lowland belt. In the industrializing city of Glasgow, parishes had as many as 12,000 inhabitants in 1815, far beyond the capacity of a single pastor. High pew rents in the urban churches effectively excluded the poor from attendance. In the Highlands and Islands, moreover, there was a severe shortage of parish churches and ministers. There parishes were often of vast territorial extent, with sea, mountains, lochs, and moors making travel extremely difficult and with many communities far removed from any church or school provision. But the greatest problem was that of patronage, which was contributing to the appointment of a growing number of parish clergy whose allegiance was more to the patron-class, the gentry and aristocracy, than to the mass of their parishioners.

The three established Churches, then, were diverse institutions. While the English and Irish establishments were similar in doctrine, worship, and polity, they differed profoundly in their relationship to their populations—the English establishment claiming the adherence of perhaps 90 per cent of the population of England and Wales in 1801, while the Irish establishment ministered to perhaps 10 per cent of the Irish population. While the English and Scottish establishments were similar in their relationship to their respective nations, both ministering to some 90 per cent of their populations, they differed radically in doctrine, worship, and polity—and it seemed difficult to believe that the same State could maintain two such contradictory ecclesiastical systems. Many Anglicans refused even to recognize the Scottish establishment as a Church.[85] And yet, despite their differences, the three establishments shared much in common, guarding the nation's Protestant faith, disseminating religious teachings, and preserving a Christian social order. All three represented the principle that the United Kingdom was a Christian State, which would ultimately stand or fall according to its success in disseminating Christian teachings to its diverse peoples.

For all three, the fundamental unit was the parish. It was at the

[84] J. Cunningham, *Church History of Scotland*, ii. 482–3.

[85] e.g., C. Daubeny, *On the Nature, Progress and Consequences of Schism* (London, 1818), 237–62.

parish level that the established Churches most touched the lives of the peoples of the three kingdoms. In thousands of parishes the parish church was the main public building, rich in historical associations, surrounded by the churchyard and the graves of the ancestors. In thousands of parishes a parish clergyman gave religious instruction and provided the rites of passage—baptism, confirmation (in England, Wales, and Ireland), marriage, and burial—that marked the stages of life. He visited the parishioners, especially the sick and infirm, he supervised the collection and distribution of parish charities. In the parish church were kept the records of births, marriages, and deaths. Many parishes maintained schools for the education of children, and most provided relief for the parish poor. It was, to be sure, a paternalistic social ideal. Religious authority came from above; the parish clergy were closely allied with the dominant landed classes, through patronage obligations, education, and shared governmental duties, while the lower social orders were to accept the teachings and discipline given to them. There was an element of social control. Yet in their religious and moral teachings parish clergy also militated against much brutal abuse of power, blatant pursuit of self-interest, and open injustice, while helping maintain standards of decency in local society.[86] 'Intermixed with the concerns of his parishioners', maintained the Anglican *British Review* in August 1817, 'he is often the guardian of their temporal as well as their spiritual interests: he is the depository of the charities of the wealthier class, and the savings of the poorer: and by the influence and authority thus placed within his reach, he is often enabled to render charity and moral reform subservient to one another.'[87] The parish churches represented order and harmony among living inhabitants and continuity between the present and the past generations. 'Happy are they who grow up in the institutions of their country', enthused the *Quarterly Review* in October 1813, 'and share like brethren in the feelings of the great body of their countrymen! The village spire is that point amid the landscape to which their eye reverts oftenest. . . . They love the music of the Sabbath bells, and walk in cheerfulness along the church path which their fathers trod before them.'[88]

[86] For assessments of the communal ethics of the old parish ideal, see Kitson Clark, *Churchmen and the Condition of England*, 5–16; Gilbert, *Religion and Society in Industrial England*, 74–6; Knight, *The Nineteenth-Century Church and English Society*, 61–2.

[87] 'Basis of National Welfare', *British Review*, 10 (August 1817), 188.

[88] 'History of Dissenters', *Quarterly Review*, 10 (October 1813), 139.

At the same time, however, in all too many parishes, the established Churches were not approaching this ideal. In the United Church of England and Ireland, widespread pluralism and non-residence too often led to the neglect of pastoral duties. Too many clerics pursued personal advancement at the expense of their pastoral responsibilities, seeking the favour of those who counted in society and could serve their interests, while neglecting those who did not count and could not serve them. There were too many clerical entrepreneurs, such as John Leroo, chasing the prizes of a clerical career. In Ireland, there was not only pluralism and non-residence, but also a lack of missionary purpose: the established clergy who were resident confined their ministry to the small Protestant minority, while viewing the overwhelming majority of Catholics almost with indifference. They were the national Church of the Protestants only. They were prepared to collect the tithe from an impoverished Catholic peasantry but otherwise view them as inhabitants of another country. In Scotland, where there was very little pluralism and non-residence, patronage was creating a distance between many parish ministers and the majority of their parishioners. Many Scottish ministers were becoming too deferential to the patron-class, emulating their manners and morals, and growing distant from the large majority of their parishioners. Behind the ideal of the confessional State and often gorgeous descriptions of parish communities, there was another reality.

The Challenge of Dissent

Between about 1790 and 1815 the situation for the established Churches was fundamentally changed. Amid the upheavals of the Revolutionary and Napoleonic Wars, and the beginnings of large-scale industrialization and urbanization, a large and increasing portion of the population of the United Kingdom ceased to participate in the religious establishments. They ceased to view the parish church as the centre of their world and the parish incumbent as their pastor. They stepped out of the traditional communal culture of the parish, with its rites of passage, its festivals, fast days, and processions, and all its historic and familiar associations. They declined to 'walk in cheerfulness along the church path which their fathers trod before them'. These twenty-five years brought an unprecedented growth in Dissent, and a consequent waning of the influence and authority of the established Churches. Supporters of the establishments grew apprehensive. As the eighteenth century drew to a close, they made grim comparisons between the growth of Dissent under the shadow of the American and French Revolutions, and the emergence of the Puritan sects in the 1640s and 1650s, when the monarchy, House of Lords, and established Churches had been overthrown and the world turned upside down.[89] 'Let the state of religion in the days of Cromwell be considered,' demanded the *British Review* in September 1811, 'let the numberless divisions and heresies which arose among the professors of christianity be remembered—let the wild and mischievous fanaticisms which then prevailed be called to mind.'[90]

In England, Protestant Dissent had its origins in late sixteenth- and early seventeenth-century Puritanism, and especially in the Puritan sects that had mushroomed amid the revolutionary strife of the 1640s and 1650s. These Puritan sectaries, filled with prophetic fervour for a godly commonwealth, had executed Charles I in 1649 and overthrown the established Church. They had sought to achieve the godly society in England and make their nation a beacon to the world. Yet deeply divided among themselves, they had failed to achieve the new Jerusalem. Their dreams of the godly commonwealth faded and in 1660 the monarchy and established Church were restored. The monarchical State then moved to suppress the Puritan sectaries. The religious settlement of 1660–2 led to the ejection of some 2,000 Puritan clergy—about 20 per cent of the total number of clerics in the Church—from church livings. Many of the Puritan sects of the commonwealth years—Seekers, True Seekers, Levellers, Diggers, Ranters—were swept away or driven deep underground. But other groups persevered. Their activities were severely curtailed by the Clarendon Code of the 1660s, which debarred Dissenters from holding municipal office, meeting for communal worship, or receiving pastoral care from those who had ministered to them before the Restoration. They were deprived of the right to hold Crown Office by the Test Act of 1673. In some districts, magistrates and local gentry hounded Dissenters without mercy. Some fell away, joined the established Church. But others endured the trials,

[89] N. U. Murray, 'The Influence of the French Revolution on the Church of England and its Rivals' (University of Oxford D.Phil., 1975), 166–80.

[90] 'State of the Church', *British Review*, 2 (September 1811), 108–9.

worshipped when necessary in secret conventicles, remembered their prophetic dreams, suffered imprisonment and in some cases death through ill-treatment in prison.[91] James II's Declaration of Indulgence of 1687 and the Glorious Revolution of 1688 brought an end to the worst of the persecution. With the Toleration Act of 1689, Parliament granted Protestant Dissenters in England and Wales a limited freedom of worship—provided that they took oaths of allegiance to the sovereign and registered their places of worship with a bishop or magistrate, and that their ministers subscribed to the doctrinal portions of the Thirty-Nine Articles.

With the easing of persecution, Dissenting groups were allowed to become more open in their worship, to erect chapels and schools, and to form connections. There were four main bodies of Protestant Dissenters in the eighteenth century—Presbyterians, Independents, Baptists, and Quakers. The first three were broadly Calvinist in theology, while the Quakers embraced George Fox's doctrine of the 'inner light' leading to a direct personal engagement with God. Early eighteenth-century Protestant Dissenters were not actively conversionist. Their concern was more to preserve the religious tradition they had inherited, honour the memory of those parents and grandparents who had endured persecution, and obey God according to their consciences. They tended to keep to themselves, marry within the communion, and nourish a sense of themselves as a chosen people, a remnant saved and preserved by Providence. As the years passed, they grew more distant from the enthusiasm of the seventeenth century, embraced regular patterns of worship and moved towards a more intellectual faith, emphasizing freedom of conscience and the capacity of the rational individual to find religious truth in Scripture. Their ministers achieved high intellectual standards; their academies for the higher education of ministers and laity, such as Philip Doddridge's academy at Northampton, offered a broad and demanding curriculum. By the 1730s many Dissenting congregations, especially among the Presbyterians, were moving from the Calvinism of their fathers to a rational faith, with an emphasis on the ethical teachings of Jesus, that could lead to Arianism and Unitarianism.

After 1715, Protestant Dissenters gained important concessions from Whig-dominated Parliaments. The Act for Quieting and

[91] M. R. Watts, *The Dissenters*, 2 vols. (Oxford, 1978, 1995), i. 220–62.

Establishing Corporations of 1719 ensured that if a Dissenter's right to hold municipal office were not challenged within six months of his being appointed to office, he could not thereafter be removed for his nonconformity. After 1726 Parliament passed an Indemnity Act nearly every year, which circumvented the Corporation Act by allowing Dissenters to take the qualifying sacrament in the Church of England after they had taken office.[92] The spirit of concession, however, reached a limit during the 1730s, when a Dissenting campaign failed to secure the repeal of the Test and Corporation Acts. None the less, Dissenters were becoming increasingly confident and secure. While Baptists and Quakers tended to remain in insular communities, Presbyterians and Independents held office in the municipalities, and established themselves in professional and commercial occupations; by the 1770s the occupational structures of urban Dissenters were virtually the same as those of members of the established Church. One prominent Dissenter described the Test Act in 1790 as '*a cobweb*, which any fly may break through'.[93] In the late 1760s a group of Dissenting leaders, mainly Arian or Unitarian in doctrinal allegiance, and including Joseph Priestley and Richard Price, revived the campaign for full civil rights for Dissenters. In doing so, these 'rational Dissenters' challenged the connection of Church and State—denouncing Church establishments as a corruption of the liberating message of Christianity. The movement culminated in a campaign between 1787 and 1790 for the repeal of the Test and Corporation Acts, which included meetings across the country, the formation of committees of correspondence, and petitions to Parliament. The campaign, however, was defeated amid the fears aroused in England by the French Revolution, and the leaders of rational Dissent, now associated with the radical political opposition, were silenced by Church and King mobs in the early 1790s.[94]

If the eighteenth-century growth of rational Dissent posed a serious challenge to the Church–State connection in England, another, far more serious challenge came from the rapid expansion of the

[92] K. R. M. Short, 'The English Indemnity Acts 1726–1867', *Church History*, 42 (1973), 366–76.

[93] Watts, *The Dissenters*, i. 285–6; J. E. Bradley, *Religion, Revolution, and English Radicalism* (Cambridge, 1990), 50, 61–9; P. Langford, *Public Life and the Propertied Englishman 1689–1798* (Oxford, 1991), 72–7.

[94] U. Henriques, *Religious Toleration in England 1787–1833* (London, 1961), 31–66; J. C. D. Clark, *English Society*, 315–46; Watts, *The Dissenters*, i. 471–88; Murray, 'The Influence of the French Revolution on the Church of England', 125–63.

more emotive Evangelical Dissent. In the 1720s and 1730s a new movement of warm, conversionist, and biblicist Christianity made its appearance in England and Wales. This movement, as W. R. Ward has argued, originated among displaced Protestants in Central Europe in the aftermath of the Thirty Years War, was brought to England by religious refugees from the Continent, and was spread by such organizations as the Society for Promoting Christian Knowledge and by the preaching of people such as John Wesley, George Whitefield, and Howell Harris.[95] The new Evangelicalism emphasized a heartfelt, Bible-centred gospel message, aimed at eliciting a personal decision for Christ. Wesley, Whitefield, and their followers, dubbed Methodists by their opponents, sought for a time to keep this intense conversionist zeal within the structures of the established Church. They became itinerant preachers, travelling on circuits around the country, holding meetings, braving drunken mobs, and organizing their converts into class meetings and extra-parochial societies. Their rejection of the parish system, however, antagonized bishops and parish clergy, who viewed their itinerant preaching and societies as a threat to proper ecclesiastical order. By the 1780s Wesley's followers were being forced out of the established Church, and local magistrates were requiring Methodists to register their society meeting-houses as Dissenting places of worship under the terms of the Toleration Act.[96] The break of the Methodists from the established Church was clarified in 1791, as the circuit system of preaching was developed and expanded to cover the whole of the United Kingdom.

The social and political unrest of the 1790s brought an explosive growth of this Evangelical Dissent. The beginning of the French Revolution aroused new aspirations and millenarian expectations, and these increased as the Revolutionary armies advanced beyond the French borders, overran the Papal States and seized the Pope. A new world was being born. The 1790s were also a time of social dislocations and misery, associated with the beginnings of industrialization, rapid urbanization, and the pressures of war. This social unrest contributed to the heady mixture of prophetic enthusiasm. The numbers of Methodists expanded rapidly, while older Dissenting denominations, especially Independents and Baptists, also embraced

[95] W. R. Ward, *The Protestant Evangelical Awakening* (Cambridge, 1992), 296–316.
[96] Gilbert, *Religion and Society in Industrial England*, 78–9.

the new Evangelicalism. Voluntary societies were formed to support the itinerant preachers, and numerous itinerants, many without ordination in any Church, some scarcely literate, travelled between villages, preaching in simple, homespun language in the fields, in cottages, or in barns, making converts and gathering them into congregations.[97] The meetings were often loud and unruly, with direct, energetic preaching, intense pressure for conversion, lengthy, spontaneous prayers, and screams and convulsions among the excited crowds. The movement was characterized by a buoyant optimism. Formal liturgies were thrown aside. The itinerants were often unpaid, being fed and housed by their followers. Women, such as the Methodists Sarah Crosby, Elizabeth Ritchie, and Ann ('Praying Nanny') Cutler, proved powerful itinerant preachers.[98] New congregations of labouring people formed Sunday schools to provide basic literacy to children and adults, and frequently provided food, clothing, and fuel to their poorest members. The movement had particular success in rural areas, especially in the north and west, where the parochial structures of the established Church were weak.[99] The growth was impressive. Between 1781 and 1787, 878 places had been registered as Dissenting meeting-houses. This increased to 1,812 registrations between 1788 and 1794, and 3,378 registrations between 1795 and 1801.[100] After 1805, itinerant preachers from the United States, including Lorenzo 'Crazy' Dow, with his long, patriarchal beard and wild eyes, began bringing to England the revivalist influences of the Second Awakening on the Western frontier. These influences included camp meetings—large outdoor gatherings which continued for several days. The first English camp meeting was held in May 1807 at Mow Cop in Staffordshire.[101]

Along with this rapid growth of Dissent after 1790 came millenarian enthusiasms and new prophecies. For many, the events surrounding the French Revolution, including the apparent fall of the Papacy,

[97] D. W. Lovegrove, *Established Church, Sectarian People: Itinerancy and the Transformation of English Dissent, 1780–1830* (Cambridge, 1988), 14–65.

[98] D. M. Valenze, *Prophetic Sons and Daughters: Female Preaching and Popular Religion in Industrial England* (Princeton, 1985), 28–73; D. C. Dews, 'Ann Carr and the Female Revivalists of Leeds', in G. Malmgreen (ed.), *Religion in the Lives of English Women, 1760–1930* (London, 1986), 68–87.

[99] Watts, *The Dissenters*, ii. 325–7; Lovegrove, *Established Church, Sectarian People*, 130, 151.

[100] Murray, 'The Influence of the French Revolution on the Church of England', 201.

[101] R. Carwardine, *Trans-Atlantic Revivalism: Popular Evangelicalism in Britain and America 1790–1865* (Westport, Conn., 1978), 60–1, 102–7; Watts, *The Dissenters*, ii. 139–40.

were signs and wonders that presaged the beginning of the millennium. Even the Rational Dissenters, Richard Price and Joseph Priestley, came to view the revolutionary upheavals of the early 1790s in this light.[102] Price proclaimed in a sermon in 1793 that the events unfolding around them were 'leading to the final happy state of the world'; Priestley, writing to a friend in December 1798, confessed that he anticipated 'the personal appearance of Jesus'.[103] The Church of the New Jerusalem, based on the teachings of the Swedish mystic Emanuel Swedenborg, was established in London by five ex-Wesleyan preachers in 1787 and expanded rapidly during the 1790s. Richard Brothers, a retired naval lieutenant, gathered a number of followers in the mid-1790s with his prophetic writings and his claim that he was the nephew of Jesus Christ, destined to lead the 'invisible' or spiritual Hebrews in Europe back to the Holy Land and thus inaugurate the millennium. There was a revival of the Muggletonians, a seventeenth-century sect, who proclaimed that the age of the Spirit had begun and the New Jerusalem was imminent. Others were drawn to the prophetic teachings of Joanna Southcott, a dairymaid and domestic servant, who in 1792 proclaimed herself the 'woman clothed with the sun' (Revelation 12), and claimed to be called by the Spirit to seal believers in preparation for the approaching Last Judgement. By 1804, over 8,000 had come forward to be sealed, and by 1807, some 14,000, and by 1814 some 20,000. Many of her followers continued to believe in her even after she failed in her promise to give birth to the messianic Shiloh and died in 1814. The mood of expectation was reflected in William Blake, whose poetry and etchings were saturated with a strange divinity. It was a time of new visions of society. In 1793, the former Dissenting minister William Godwin published his *Enquiry Concerning Political Justice,* with its gospel of anarchism, rooted in veneration for private judgement and the seventeenth-century Commonwealthman's distrust of monarchy and established religion.[104] The year before, Mary Wollstonecraft (Godwin's future wife) had published *A Vindication of the Rights of Woman,*

[102] J. Fruchtman, Jr., 'The Apocalyptic Politics and Richard Price and Joseph Priestley: A Study in Late Eighteenth-Century English Republican Millenialism', *Transactions of the American Philosophical Society*, 73: 4 (1983).

[103] Ibid. 41, 30.

[104] J. F. C. Harrison, *The Second Coming: Popular Millenarianism 1780–1850* (London, 1979), 57–134; E. P. Thompson, *Witness against the Beast: William Blake and the Moral Law* (Cambridge, 1993), 52–105; M. Butler, *Romantics, Rebels and Reactionaries* (Oxford, 1981), 41–52.

with its call for equal rights of citizenship for men and women, and its bold declaration of the right of women to experience sexual pleasure. Robert Owen had developed his socialist ideas largely through his experiences in managing his father-in-law's cotton mill in Scotland, and his first major work, *A New View of Society*, written in 1812–13 appealed to experience and reason in its calls for radical social reform. By 1817, however, Owen was proclaiming a 'new religion' of socialism, with a millenarian promise of social perfection in the present generation.[105]

By 1815, the established Church was losing its dominance over religious life in England and Wales. The village preaching and cottage religion of the New Dissent was challenging the old paternalist authority in thousands of rural parishes. Increasing numbers were making a conscious decision to step out of the traditional communal life of the parish and enter a separatist meeting-house. After 1790, moreover, the New Dissent was increasingly making its presence felt in the industrializing towns and cities, with Sunday schools playing an important role in recruitment, especially in the textile towns with their high levels of child labour.[106] Many urban labourers were drawn to the millenarian prophecies or new social visions. Efforts by supporters of the established Church to restrict the activities of the itinerants and Sunday schools through parliamentary legislation proved abortive. Proposals for legislative action were made in 1799–1800, but no bills were brought forward.[107] When in 1811 Lord Sidmouth attempted to introduce legislation to tighten the licensing of itinerant preachers, the Dissenters, led by Congregationalists, Baptists, and Calvinistic Methodists, hastily organized a national movement of protest. The Government then withdrew its support and Sidmouth's bill was defeated without a division.[108] Parliament followed this climb-down with yet further concessions to Dissent. In 1812 it abolished two seventeenth-century acts against Dissenters, the Conventicle Act and Five Mile Act. The following year

[105] W. H. Oliver, 'Owen in 1817: The Millennialist Moment', in S. Pollard and J. Salt (eds.), *Robert Owen: Prophet of the Poor* (London, 1971), 166–87; J. F. C. Harrison, *Quest for the New Moral World: Robert Owen and the Owenites in Britain and America* (New York, 1969), 92–3.

[106] W. R. Ward, *Religion and Society in England 1790–1850* (London, 1972), 12–16; T. W. Laqueur, *Religion and Respectability: Sunday Schools and Working Class Culture 1780–1850* (New Haven, 1976), 63–76.

[107] W. R. Ward, *Religion and Society in England*, 52.

[108] Ibid. 55–60; Watts, *The Dissenters*, ii. 369–72; Lovegrove, *Established Church, Sectarian People*, 135–7; Hole, *Pulpits, Politics and Public Order in England*, 195–8.

Parliament granted legal toleration to Unitarians.[109] By 1811, there was evidence that the number of active members of Dissenting congregations was equal to or greater than the numbers of active adherents of the established Church.[110]

Scotland experienced a similar emergence and perseverance of Dissent in the late seventeenth and eighteenth centuries, followed by an explosive expansion of Evangelical Dissent from the 1790s. Dissent in Scotland had its origins in the introduction of non-Presbyterian sects from England following the seventeenth-century Cromwellian conquest and in the refusal of devout Presbyterians to conform to the Episcopalian establishment imposed by Charles II after the Restoration of 1660. The Covenanters, as we have seen, suffered heavily during their years as Dissenters between 1660 and 1688. With the Revolution of 1688–9 and the restoration of Presbyterianism in the established Church, it was the turn of devout Episcopalians to be forced out of the establishment and find themselves treated as Dissenters. Some sixty Episcopalian clergy were 'rabbled' out of their livings by Presbyterian mobs in 1689; others were gradually removed from their livings through legal action. Episcopalian congregations emerged and survived, largely under the protection of aristocratic families. They also remained loyal to the Stewart dynasty, looking over the water for the tall ships that would bring the Stewarts back from their exile in France. In 1712, the predominantly Anglican British Parliament passed a Toleration Act for Scottish Episcopalians, despite angry protests from the Presbyterian establishment. Scottish Episcopalians, however, continued to give their allegiance to the exiled Stewart monarchs. They paid a heavy price for their support for the Jacobite risings in 1715 and 1745. Penal acts were imposed in 1719, 1746, and 1748 upon Scottish Episcopalians who did not 'qualify' by renouncing allegiance to the Stewarts and adopting the English Prayer Book. In suppressing the Jacobite rising in 1745–6, Hanoverian forces burned Episcopal meeting-houses and scattered congregations. Only with the waning of the Jacobite threat after 1760 did the persecution gradually ease. In 1792 the penal laws were finally rescinded. The Scottish Episcopal Church emerged from the penal times as a

[109] R. W. Davis, *Dissent in Politics 1780–1830: The Political Life of William Smith, MP* (London, 1971), 190–207.

[110] E. Halévy, *England in 1815* (London, 1949), 428.

remnant, with six bishops, about fifty priests, and perhaps 11,000 adherents among the Jacobite non-jurors, and another twenty-three priests and 4,000 adherents among the qualified congregations—representing about 1 per cent of the population.[111] In the early nineteenth century, the Episcopal Church began to revive, gaining influential converts among the landed and urban professional classes. Its struggle and endurance appealed in an era that saw the Romantic rehabilitation of the Jacobite cause in the novels of Sir Walter Scott, a convert to the Episcopal Church.

Other Dissenting bodies also emerged. There were Cameronians—severe Presbyterian Covenanters who took their name from Richard Cameron, killed in 1680 while resisting rule by the 'uncovenanted' Charles II. Alienated by the refusal of the British Crown to adopt the Covenants, the Cameronians withdrew from the established Church in 1690 and worshipped as Dissenters. There were Glassites—a gentle, charitable sect of followers of John Glas (1695–1773) who was deposed from the ministry of the Church of Scotland in 1730 after he embraced the view that the Church must be entirely independent of the State. From 1733 these small groups of Dissenters were joined by larger bodies of Presbyterian seceders from the national Church. Many devout Presbyterians were by now growing disenchanted with the established Church, objecting to what they perceived as its laxity towards the Calvinist standards of the Westminster Confession and deference to the wealthier classes at a time of spreading economic improvement. They deplored the established Church's failure to resist more forcibly Parliament's reimposition of lay patronage in 1712, or to denounce the worldly luxuries of the rich. In 1733, following a dispute over patronage in the General Assembly, a small party of four ministers in the neighbourhood of Stirling, led by the brothers Ralph and Ebenezer Erskine, withdrew from the Church of Scotland and formed themselves into the Associate Presbytery, commonly known as the Secession Church. They gained a growing number of adherents, mainly tough-minded Lowland farmers and artisans who hated patronage and relished a strict Calvinist discipline. The Secession Church split in 1747 over a disagreement on whether or not it was proper for Christians, on becoming magistrates or town councillors, to take an oath of loyalty to the State.[112]

[111] R. Strong, *Alexander Forbes of Brechin: The First Tractarian Bishop* (Oxford, 1995), 12–13.

[112] J. McKerrow, *History of the Secession Church*, 2nd edn. (Edinburgh, 1854), 208–38.

Despite the split, both branches of the Secession Churches continued to expand, establishing seminaries for the training of ministers and creating additional presbyteries. The year 1761 saw the formation of the Relief Church under the leadership of Thomas Gillespie, who had been deposed from the ministry of the Church of Scotland in 1752 for his outspoken opposition to patronage. The Relief Church attracted Presbyterians who objected to patronage, but were uncomfortable with the uncompromising Calvinism of the older Secession Churches. Embracing a more liberal interpretation of Calvinist doctrine—Gillespie said he would share communion with all who recognized Christ—the Relief Church expanded steadily, mainly in the rural Lowlands.[113] By 1801 there were over 300 Secession or Relief congregations, with perhaps 150,000 adherents, representing nearly 10 per cent of Scotland's population.[114]

Amid the social and political unrest of the 1790s, the new Evangelicalism reached Scotland and transformed Scottish Dissent. The leading figures in this movement were the brothers James and Robert Haldane, the one a former captain of an East India Company ship, the other a wealthy landowner. Converted to evangelical Christianity in the mid-1790s through the influence of David Bogue, a Scottish Congregational minister who had settled in England, the Haldanes embraced a home mission directed to the growing numbers in Scotland who were outside organized Christianity, especially in the towns and more remote rural districts. In 1798, they created the Society for Propagating the Gospel at Home, which supported itinerant preachers who travelled on circuits through the country and established new churches on a congregational pattern. By 1800 there were fourteen Congregational churches in Scotland; by 1807 this had increased to eighty-five. Much of the money that supported this rapid expansion came from the sale of Robert Haldane's estate.[115] In 1808, the Haldanes embraced Baptist teachings and entered the small denomination of Scottish Baptist Churches, together with many of their followers.

[113] G. Struthers, *The History of the Rise, Progress and Principles of the Relief Church* (Glasgow, 1843), 60–165, 186–9; C. Brown, *The Social History of Religion in Scotland since 1730* (London, 1987), 36–7, 121–2.

[114] Sher and Murdoch, 'Patronage and Party in the Church of Scotland', 201; Ranken, *Importance of Religious Establishments*, 115–26.

[115] A. Haldane, *The Lives of Robert Haldane of Airthey and of his Brother, James Alexander Haldane*, 4th edn. (Edinburgh, 1855), 1–356; H. Escott, *A History of Scottish Congregationalism* (Glasgow, 1960), 45–85.

They joined a Baptist denomination which had already embraced the new Evangelical ethos, and Baptist itinerants were soon enjoying considerable success in the Highlands and Islands.[116]

The ethos of Evangelical Dissent also permeated the older Presbyterian Secession Churches. In the later 1790s some members of the Secession Churches began experiencing 'new light' regarding the teachings of the Westminster Confession on Church and State. They came to reject the principle of an established Church and covenanted nation, and to embrace instead the belief that church membership should be purely voluntary, based on the individual's decision for Christ. Between 1799 and 1804 the majority in both branches of the Secession Church embraced these New Light teachings, breaking with their more traditionalist brethren and forming new denominations.[117] The New Light movement marked a major shift in the prevailing attitude among Presbyterian Dissenters, from one of hope that the established Church would eventually be purified and the Covenants restored, to a rejection of any connection of Church and State. For New Light Dissenters, religion grew more individualistic. They ceased looking back to the seventeenth-century Covenants, and were drawn to democratic and reformist ideas. According to one recent estimate, nearly 30 per cent of the Scottish population were Dissenters by the 1820s, with higher percentages in the industrializing towns and cities.[118] Most of them had rejected belief in the connection of Church and State. They stepped out of the traditional communal culture of the parish, with its kirk-session discipline, parish poor relief, parish education, and communion seasons.

In Ireland, as we have seen, the overwhelming majority of the population was outside the established Church. This was largely because of the failure of the Reformation to take root in Ireland. Historians have suggested various reasons for this failure—the divisions during the crucial early decades of the Reformation over how best to evangelize among the masses, the alienation of the old English settler class, who had felt neglected by the Tudor State and therefore declined to assist the Tudors' religious policies, the paucity of

[116] D. E. Meek, 'Evangelical Missionaries in the Early Nineteenth-Century Highlands', *Scottish Studies*, 28 (1987), 1–34.

[117] McKerrow, *History of the Secession Church*, 430–75.

[118] C. Brown, *The Social History of Religion in Scotland*, 31.

resources available to the Irish Protestant establishment as a result of appropriations of Church property by the gentry and aristocracy.[119] Whatever the reasons, by the early seventeenth century the effort to secure the conformity of the Catholics to Protestantism had stalled and the established Church had developed an exclusionist mentality, restricting its ministry to the English settler class.[120] A second opportunity to extend the influence of the established Church came following the defeat of the Jacobite forces in Ireland in 1691. The Protestant State had at last gained firm political control over the whole of Ireland, making the goal of achieving full religious conformity a realistic one. However, while the victorious Irish Parliament imposed penal laws on the defeated Catholics, it did not encourage the established Church to evangelize among them. Most Protestant landowners had no interest in such a mission. Would not a strengthened, missionary established Church try to reclaim the former Church property now resting comfortably in the landowners' possession?[121] And would not a mass movement of Catholics into the established Church be accompanied by calls for the return of properties confiscated from them in the past?[122] Landlords were thus prepared to leave the Catholics alone, and the Church followed their lead. Not surprisingly, there were only about 5,800 converts to the established Church during the eighteenth century, and the overwhelming majority in Ireland remained outside the established order in Church and State.[123]

The Catholics of Ireland were a defeated people at the beginning of the eighteenth century, many of them living in appalling poverty. They endured sporadic but often severe persecution in the early

[119] B. Bradshaw, 'Sword, Word and Strategy in the Reformation in Ireland', *Historical Journal*, 21 (1978), 475–502; N. Canny, 'Why the Reformation Failed in Ireland: *Une Question Mal Posée'*, *Journal of Ecclesiastical History*, 30 (1979), 423–50; N. Canny, 'The Formation of the Irish Mind: Religion, Politics and Gaelic Irish Literature', *Past and Present*, 95 (May 1982), 91–116; K. Bottigheimer, 'The Failure of the Reformation in Ireland: *Une Question Bien Posée'*, *Journal of Ecclesiastical History*, 36 (1985), 196–207; S. G. Ellis, 'Economic Problems of the Church: Why the Reformation Failed in Ireland', *Journal of Ecclesiastical History*, 41 (1990), 239–65.

[120] Bradshaw, 'Sword, Word and Strategy in the Reformation in Ireland', 502.

[121] T. Bartlett, *The Fall and Rise of the Irish Nation: The Catholic Question 1690–1830* (Dublin, 1992), 25–9; [S. O'Sullivan], 'Modern Reformation in Ireland', *Blackwood's Magazine*, 26 (July 1829), 85–6.

[122] J. Brady and P. J. Corish, 'The Church under the Penal Code', in P. J. Corish (ed.), *A History of Irish Catholicism* (Dublin, 1971), iv. 5–6.

[123] T. P. Power and K. Whelan (eds.), *Endurance and Emergence: Catholics in Ireland in the Eighteenth Century* (Dublin, 1990), 101–27.

years of the penal code. Yet by the 1730s the worst of the persecution was behind them and the Catholic community began to recover. In the towns, a Catholic commercial middle class emerged and began to prosper by developing trading networks in Ireland and the Continent. Some Catholic families, moreover, found ways around the penal laws to hold on to or purchase landed estates.[124] The best-known example of this were the Catholic O'Connells of Kerry, who both held on to their lands and prospered through the smuggling trade with the Continent. The Catholic Church emerged from the era of severe persecution reasonably intact. A report on Irish Catholics to the Irish House of Lords in 1731 indicated that there were approximately 1,700 Catholic clergy, 900 churches, and a Catholic population of about 1.8 million. The rural churches, or 'mass-houses', were often rudimentary turf structures, and services frequently had to be held in the open air, but in the towns Catholics were beginning to erect substantial stone churches. Through the custom of 'stations', or holding confessions in private dwellings if there was no appropriate church structure nearby, the priests were able to extend their influence to more remote villages and hamlets. Although Catholic education had been proscribed by law, the Catholic Church none the less supported a network of some 550 schools. 'The Church organisation', observed the historian Patrick Corish, '[had] weathered the storm.'[125]

Catholic Ireland did not come out for the Jacobites at the risings of 1715 and 1745, and with the waning of the Jacobite threat after 1746, the enforcement of the penal legislation was further eased. The manpower needs of the British army during the Seven Years' War brought a relaxation of prohibitions on the recruitment of Irish Catholics, while the influence of the Enlightenment reduced religious intolerance among educated Protestants. The derogatory term 'popery' was increasingly replaced in polite conversation by the more enlightened 'Roman Catholicism'.[126] With the gradual rescinding of the penal laws between 1778 and 1793, the condition of Catholics in Ireland began to resemble that of Protestant Dissenters in England: they were granted limited toleration but excluded from full participation in the political life of the State. The

[124] Power and Whelan, *Endurance and Emergence*, 57–100.

[125] P. J. Corish, *The Catholic Community in the Seventeenth and Eighteen Centuries* (Dublin, 1981), 82–115.

[126] Hill, 'National Festivals, the State and "Protestant Ascendancy"', 34.

Catholic leadership grew more confident, sending loyal addresses to the Crown, organizing petitions to Parliament, and pressing through constitutional means for their full emancipation from all remaining civil disabilities. The Catholic population was also growing at a faster rate than the Protestant population—through high fertility combined with an improved diet resulting from increased potato cultivation. In 1731, Catholics probably represented less than two-thirds of Ireland's total population of under 3 million. By the end of the century, however, they represented some 80 per cent of Ireland's population of nearly 5 million.

The largest body of Protestant Dissenters in Ireland, the Presbyterians, were concentrated in Ulster. They had come from Scotland in the early seventeenth century as part of the State-sponsored plantation of the province. These Scottish settlers had resisted assimilation to the established Church and preserved a distinctive identity through their communal forms of piety, their links to Scottish Presbyterianism, and their sense of themselves as a covenanted people.[127] During the civil unrest of the 1640s and 1650s Presbyterian clergymen had taken possession of many parish livings in the established Church in Ireland. With the Restoration of 1660 they were ejected from those livings and subjected to civil disabilities as Dissenters. The Protestant State, however, did not rigorously persecute Presbyterians, recognizing them to be Protestants whose loyalty should be cultivated. During the later 1660s the State allowed the Presbyterian clergy in Ulster to form presbytery courts, and in 1672 the government of Charles II began secretly making a modest annual grant, or *regium donum*, to the Irish Presbyterian clergy. Following the Jacobite war of 1689–91, the Irish Presbyterians supported William III, who in turn allowed them to organize themselves into a Synod of Ulster and doubled their *regium donum*, which now became a public grant. Yet toleration for Presbyterians was limited. The Synod of Ulster had no legal status and Presbyterians were vulnerable to harassment by local magistrates and established clergy, among them the irascible William Tisdall, vicar of Belfast, who despised Presbyterians no less than Catholics as enemies of the State. 'By the Fundamental Principles of both Presbyterian and

[127] M. J. Westerkamp, *Triumph of the Laity: Scots-Irish Piety and the Great Awakening 1625–1760* (Oxford, 1988), 15–42; D. W. Miller, *Queen's Rebels: Ulster Loyalism in Historical Perspective* (Dublin, 1978), 13–16; E. W. McFarland, *Ireland and Scotland in the Age of Revolution* (Edinburgh, 1994), 6–9; McBride, *Scripture Politics*, 26–34.

Popish Policy', he insisted in 1713, 'there is no Allegiance due to any Christian Prince who does not profess . . . what either call the true Religion.'[128] The Test Act of 1704 excluded Presbyterians, together with Roman Catholics, from most Crown offices.[129]

Forced from active involvement in Irish political life, Presbyterians remained a separate people, marrying within their communion, and providing their own poor relief and schools. Their ministers were usually educated in Scotland, mainly at Glasgow University.[130] They were not conversionist. Through much of the eighteenth century they were occupied with internal doctrinal disputes, which contributed to a series of secessions from the Synod of Ulster. The numbers of Presbyterians remained relatively stable through the eighteenth century, with any natural increase in their numbers offset by high levels of emigration to the North American colonies. There were an estimated 515,000 Presbyterians in Ireland in the 1780s, including some 432,000 in the Synod of Ulster and 83,000 in the secession communions.[131] During the 1770s and 1780s many Ulster Presbyterians expressed sympathy for the colonists in the American war, and were active in the Volunteer movement in Ireland, which forced the British State in 1782 to grant increased autonomy to the Irish Parliament. In the 1790s some Ulster Presbyterians were drawn into republican politics, taking a lead in the United Irishmen movement, which sought to unite Protestants and Catholics in a movement to create an independent Irish republic with no established Church and full religious toleration. The 1790s also witnessed a prophetic and apocalyptic movement in Ulster Presbyterianism, especially in the countryside, with widespread expectations of the return of Christ and the coming of the millennium.[132] In 1798, filled with republican fervour and millenarian hopes, and expecting substantial military aid from Revolutionary France, the United Irishmen led an armed rising, which gained wide Presbyterian and Catholic support. As the rising

[128] W. Tisdall, *A Seasonable Enquiry into that Most Dangerous Political Principle of the Kirk in Power* (Dublin, 1713), 7.

[129] P. Brooke, *Ulster Presbyterianism: The Historical Perspective 1610–1970*, 2nd edn. (Belfast, 1994), 46–67; Connolly, *Religion, Law and Power*, 161–2.

[130] J. M. Barkley, 'The Presbyterian Minister in Eighteenth Century Ireland', in J. L. M. Haire *et al.*, *Challenge and Conflict: Essays in Irish Presbyterian History and Doctrine* (Antrim, 1981), 46–60.

[131] McBride, *Scripture Politics*, 27–8, 115.

[132] Ibid. 195–201; Hempton, *Religion and Political Culture in Britain and Ireland*, 98–100.

spread, many established clergymen fled the country with indecent haste. But poorly led and ill-organized, the rising degenerated into sectarian civil war, especially in the south-east of Ireland, and it was crushed with extreme brutality, leaving an estimated 30,000 dead. The rising of 1798 illustrated the real dangers of an Ireland with an overwhelming Catholic and Dissenting population now being infused with the new religious enthusiasm and democratic fervour.

The unrest of the 1780s and 1790s also introduced a new aspect to Irish religious life—the expansion of Evangelical Dissent. The foundations for this had been laid by the activities of Moravian and Methodist itinerant preachers in the 1740s, and the Methodist mission began gaining ground in the 1780s. Membership of Methodist societies in Ireland rose from 3,124 in 1770 to 19,292 in 1800 and 29,357 by 1815.[133] Following the rising of 1798, the Irish Methodist conference began making more sustained efforts to convert the Catholic population, sending out three full-time Irish-speaking missionaries in 1799. By 1816, the conference was supporting twenty-one missionaries among the Catholic population.[134] This mission to the Catholics was a new development in Ireland, and one which, if successful, could seriously threaten the position of the Irish establishment. Meanwhile, visits by the American Methodist preacher Lorenzo Dow in 1800 and 1806 introduced the revivalist piety of the American Second Awakening into Ireland. After the 1798 rising, moreover, Ulster Presbyterians increasingly withdrew from their former association with republican politics and, under the influence of such young Evangelicals as Henry Cooke, began embracing the new-style emotional, conversionist, biblicist Evangelicalism.[135]

The twenty-five years of struggle against Revolutionary and Napoleonic France had witnessed one of the most important changes in the history of Britain, the explosive expansion of the New Dissent, with itinerant village preaching, evangelical fervour, and millenarian enthusiasms. This had been combined with a new

[133] D. Hempton and M. Hill, *Evangelical Protestantism in Ulster Society 1740–1890* (London, 1992), 10–13.

[134] D. N. Hempton, 'The Methodist Crusade in Ireland, 1795–1845', *Irish Historical Studies*, 22 (1980), 35–7; I. M. Hehir [now Whelan], 'Evangelical Religion and the Polarization of Protestant–Catholic Relations in Ireland, 1780–1840' (University of Wisconsin Ph.D., 1994), 225–41.

[135] R. F. Holmes, *Henry Cooke* (Belfast, 1981), 8–9; Hempton and Hill, *Evangelical Protestantism*, 37–40, 43–4.

assertiveness among the growing Roman Catholic majority in Ireland. Before 1790, probably 90 per cent of the population of Britain had been at least nominal adherents of the established Church of England or Church of Scotland. By 1815, perhaps a third of the population of Britain were Dissenters, while the numbers of active members of Dissenting bodies began to approach those of active adherents of the established Churches. Tens of thousands had stepped out of the old parish system, with its historic associations, rites of passage, and communal culture, and had made their way into a Dissenting sect, often embracing millenarian visions of a new world order, a rule of the saints. For a State which based much of its public order on the parish system, this mass secession was deeply alarming. In Ireland, with perhaps a third of the population of the United Kingdom, nearly 90 per cent of the population were outside the established Church. In 1798, sections of this overwhelming majority, both Catholics and Presbyterians, had risen against the State, and there had been nightmarish scenes of mass bloodshed. The religious strife reminded contemporaries of the seventeenth century, though with the religious enthusiasm of that era now fed by the new democratic forces that had brought revolution to America and France. The growing numbers of Dissenters and Catholics seemed to threaten not only the religious unity of the three kingdoms, but also social and political cohesion. Many of them were dissatisfied and disaffected, without loyalty to the established order of Church and State. 'The increase of these Meeting Houses', wrote Bishop Cleaver of Chester in 1799, 'is chiefly owing to the facility which they afford of privately discussing Political Topics and of forming Political Combinations.' Their members, he added, are 'better known by their Democratical principles, than by a Religious zeal'.[136] 'How long will it be', asked the conservative *Quarterly Review* of the New Dissent of England and Wales in 1810, 'before these people begin to count hands with the Establishment?' 'The sectarian spirit', it continued, 'which is thus formed and fostered, is nourished at the expense of national spirit, and their growth is like an incysted tumour in the body politic. Their hopes and feelings are concentrated in the interests of the connection; not in those of the country.'[137]

[136] Cited in G. M. Ditchfield, 'Ecclesiastical Legislation during the Ministry of the Younger Pitt, 1782–1801', in J. P. Parry and S. Taylor (eds.), *Parliament and the Church, 1529–1960* (Edinburgh, 2000), 76.

[137] 'On the Evangelical Sects', *Quarterly Review*, 4 (1810), 509, 510.

Church Parties and Controversies

The challenges confronting the established Churches from the later eighteenth century—especially the expansion of the New Dissent—were profound, and the Churches were far from united over how to respond. Among the difficulties for established religion at this time, many would have included party-spirit within the Churches. Parties are inevitable in the Church, given the imperfect nature of its human material. People disagree over the interpretations of the body of religious teachings that have been given them, and they seek out like-minded men and women to help them convince the Church as a whole that theirs is the orthodox position. By the early nineteenth century each of the three established Churches contained two main parties—loose, informal, but recognizable groupings of clergymen and laity, which disagreed in fundamental ways over the nature of the Church and its proper response to Evangelical Dissent. The nature and role of ecclesiastical parties in this period is problematical, not least because their numbers and influence have frequently been exaggerated by historians, resulting in a distorted picture of polarized Churches. The party divisions should not be exaggerated. Most Church adherents of the time would have denied that they had any party affiliation, and would have viewed party-spirit in Christ's Church as an evil, a rending of Christ's seamless robe. None the less, contemporaries recognized the presence of parties, and if pressed, many would have admitted to having a party orientation.[138] Within the United Church of England and Ireland the two main groupings were the High Church party, dominated in the early years of the nineteenth century by a group of influential London-based clerics and lay members, the 'Hackney Phalanx', and the Evangelical party, also dominated at this time by an influential London-based clerical and lay group, the 'Clapham Sect'. The Presbyterian Church of Scotland also included two loose but identifiable parties—the Moderates and the Evangelicals.

The High Church party in the late eighteenth- and early nineteenth-century Church of England placed emphasis on the visible Church—its sacraments, traditions, doctrines, and ceremonies.[139]

[138] For a discussion of party-spirit in the Church, see R. Whately's Bampton Lectures, *The Use and Abuse of Party-Feeling in Matters of Religion considered in Eight Sermons preached before the University of Oxford* (Oxford, 1822), 16–67.

[139] For the High Church party, see especially P. Nockles, 'Church Parties in the

Rooted in the Anglicanism of Archbishop Laud and the seventeenth-century Caroline divines, they viewed the Church of England as a branch of the holy catholic and apostolic Church. Its tradition provided the sole guide to religious truth for the nation; its doctrine was derived from Scripture, the Fathers, and the Councils; its sacraments communicated divine grace, its ceremonies elevated and sanctified the nation.[140] Schism from the Church of England was a rejection of Christ's Church, a form of rebellion born of human pride. 'Communion with the Church', argued the High Church divine, Charles Daubeny, in his *Guide to the Church*, 'is conformity to the Divine plan for our salvation; separation from it is setting up a plan of our own.'[141] High Anglicans rejected Calvinism, which they believed encouraged spiritual pride among the 'elect' and which they held responsible for the Puritan rebellion and the death of the martyr-king Charles I.[142] Amid the unrest of the early 1790s, High Churchmen tended to associate Dissenters with the Puritan regicides of the 1640s.[143] While denouncing Dissenters as schismatics, they denied that the Church of England was in schism from Rome. Rather, they insisted that the English Church, in its corporate character as a branch of the one Church, had separated at the Reformation from the corrupted Latin branch in order to preserve its apostolic purity.[144] In political theory, they emphasized the Pauline doctrine that God had ordained the powers that be and that the subject was under a divine command to obey the worldly powers.[145] Government existed because of sinful human nature; authority from above was required to control human sin and pride. The social hierarchy was also divinely ordained: God had ordered

pre-Tractarian Church of England 1750–1833: the "Orthodox"—Some Problems of Definition and Identity', in J. Walsh, C. Haydon, and S. Taylor (eds.), *The Church of England c.1689–c.1833: From Toleration to Tractarianism* (Cambridge, 1993), 334–59.

[140] Mather, *High Church Prophet*, 207–8; Y. Brilioth, *The Anglican Revival: Studies in the Oxford Movement* (London, 1925), 23–4.

[141] C. Daubeny, *A Guide to the Church* (1798), 3rd edn., 2 vols. (London and Bath, 1830), i. 139; Daubeny, *On the Nature, Progress and Consequences of Schism*, 149–50.

[142] G. Best, 'The Evangelicals and the Established Church in the Early Nineteenth Century', *Journal of Theological Studies*, NS 10 (1959), 74.

[143] Sack, *From Jacobite to Conservative*, 192–202.

[144] H. Marsh, *An Appendix to the 'Comparative View of the Churches of England and Rome'* (Cambridge, 1816), 18–19; Daubeny, *On the Nature, Progress and Consequences of Schism*, 17–23; Nockles, *Oxford Movement in Context*, 164–70.

[145] e.g., Sermon xliv, *Sermons by Samuel Horsley*, 2 vols. (London, 1824), ii. 426–51; Mather, *High Church Prophet*, 302–3.

the commonwealth according to a law of subordination, with some individuals born subject to others.[146]

The High Church party had particular strength in London and in provincial towns such as Manchester, Bath, Wigan, Liverpool, and Newcastle—towns which had preserved a traditional corporate identity.[147] In the 1790s leading High Church figures included Samuel Horsley, bishop of Rochester, William Stevens, a successful hosier, and Jonathan Boucher, a former American Loyalist and now vicar of Epsom. Such men were active in the management of the older Church missionary societies—the Society for Promoting Christian Knowledge and the Society for the Propagation of the Gospel. From about 1810 a group of largely London-based High Anglicans, based in the parish of Hackney, began acting together to revive the social authority of the established Church.[148] Dubbed the Hackney Phalanx, they represented a web of friendships and family connections, with powerful influence at the highest levels of the Church. The central figure in the group was the wealthy and well-connected merchant Joshua Watson, who retired from business in 1814 at the age of 43 to devote himself to religious and philanthropic work. Watson's brother, John James Watson, was vicar of Hackney, and the independently wealthy Henry Handley Norris served as Watson's curate.[149] The Phalanx had influence with Lord Liverpool, the Tory prime minister from 1812 to 1827, and with Charles Manners-Sutton, archbishop of Canterbury from 1805 to 1828. During Liverpool's administration, they influenced the appointments to bishoprics, archdeaconries, and prebendaries; so much so that the Phalanx leader H. H. Norris became known as the 'bishop maker'.[150]

[146] A. M. C. Waterman, '"The Grand Scheme of Subordination": The Intellectual Foundations of Tory Doctrine', *Australian Journal of Politics and History*, 40, Special Issue (1994), 121–33; J. C. D. Clark, *English Society 1688–1832*, 222–3; Hole, *Pulpits, Politics and Public Order in England*, 142.

[147] Mather, *High Church Prophet*, 16–17.

[148] Discussions of the Hackney Phalanx include E. Churton, *Memoir of Joshua Watson*, 2 vols. (London, 1861), i. 54–102; A. B. Webster, *Joshua Watson: The Story of a Layman, 1771–1855* (London, 1954), 18–32; C. Dewey, *The Passing of Barchester: A Real Life Version of Trollope* (London, 1991), 125–41; E. A. Varley, *The Last of the Prince Bishops: William Van Mildert and the High Church Movement of the Early Nineteenth Century* (Cambridge, 1992), 63–5; Nockles, *Oxford Movement in Context*, esp. 270–4; K. Hylson-Smith, *High Churchmanship in the Church of England* (Edinburgh, 1993), 101–20.

[149] For an attempt at identifying the membership of the Hackney Phalanx, see Dewey, *The Passing of Barchester*, 149–68.

[150] Nockles, *Oxford Movement in Context*, 271–2.

There was a High Church party in Ireland which largely mirrored that of England, though more defensive in its character. Grounded in the writings of Jeremy Taylor, William King, and other seventeenth-century Irish divines, Irish High Church divines viewed their Church as the one true branch of the catholic Church in Ireland—a guardian of the true faith, confronted by hostile forces on both sides.[151] 'Those who consider the State of the Church of Ireland', noted William Tisdall, vicar of Belfast in 1715, 'must observe, that She is plac'd like an *Isthmus*, betwixt two Raging Seas, of *Popery* and *Presbytery*: That these *troubled Waters*, however they may seem to swell and foam at each other, do both beat with Violence against her.'[152] Irish High Churchmen of the early nineteenth century portrayed their Church as representing a middle way between the corruptions of Roman Catholicism and of Presbyterianism.[153] Leading early nineteenth-century Irish High Churchmen included the two friends Alexander Knox, a lay theologian who had for a time been personal private secretary to Lord Castlereagh, and John Jebb, later bishop of Limerick.[154] Both Knox and Jebb had close connections with the Hackney Phalanx, while the appointment of Richard Mant to an Irish bishopric in 1820 created yet another link between the Phalanx and the Irish Church.[155]

The Evangelical party within the Church of England consisted of those who had come under the influence of the larger eighteenth-century transatlantic religious awakening, but had not joined the ranks of Evangelical Dissent. Rooted in the conversionist zeal of the Reformation and the godly commonwealth ideal of late sixteenth- and seventeenth-century Puritanism, Evangelicals embraced the hope of achieving a Christian society of converted individuals. Emerging as an identifiable movement in the Church from the 1740s, Evangelicals had begun forming local clerical societies for

[151] Eccleshall, 'Anglican Political Thought in the Century after the Revolution of 1688'; Nockles, 'Continuity and Change in Anglican High Churchmanship in Britain', 344–9; P. Nockles, 'Church or Protestant Sect? The Church of Ireland, High Churchmanship and the Oxford Movement, 1822–1869', *Historical Journal*, 41 (1998), 457–93.

[152] [W. Tisdall], *The Case of the Sacramental Test, Stated and Argued* (Dublin, 1715), 2.

[153] Gunstone, 'Alexander Knox', 472; Brilioth, *The Anglican Revival*, 53–5; W. Magee, *A charge delivered at his Primary Visitation, in St Patrick's Cathedral, Dublin, on Thursday, the 27th of October, 1822* (London, 1822).

[154] Brilioth, *The Anglican Revival*, 45–55; J. T. A. Gunstone, 'Alexander Knox, 1757–1831', *Church Quarterly Review*, 157 (1956), 463–75.

[155] W. B. Mant, *Memoirs of the Right Reverend Richard Mant, Lord Bishop of Down and Connor and of Dromore* (Dublin, 1857), 64–113; Dewey, *The Passing of Barchester*, 159–60.

Bible study and prayer, such as that set up by Samuel Walker in Truro in about 1740, or London's Eclectic Society, established in 1783.[156] By the end of the 1790s, according to one recent estimate, there were about 300 to 500 Evangelical clergymen within the Church of England; although they were but a small faction of the total number of clergy, contemporaries viewed them as the Church's most 'aggressive and formidable' party.[157] In doctrine, they emphasized Christ's atonement for the sins of humankind, the gospel of personal salvation through the transforming power of the Cross, the inspiration of the Bible, and a disciplined life of service to God within the world.[158] While Anglican Evangelicals respected the Church 'as the highest conceivable human authority', they did not share to the same degree the High Church reverence for the visible Church. 'The ordinances of the Church', insisted the Evangelical rector of Clapham, John Venn, in 1805, 'are not placed on the same footing as divine commandments.'[159] Christ did not restrict his grace to any particular Church, and true Christians could be found within the Dissenting communions as well as within the establishment. According to the historian Geoffrey Best, the Church Evangelicals believed that 'any church could be, and established churches usually were, good, but Christ in the hearts of men was better'.[160]

During the 1790s a circle of wealthy Evangelicals, based in the then fashionable London suburb of Clapham, began exercising influence within the established Church. Dubbed the Clapham Sect, the Evangelical circle was united by ties of marriage and friendship, and included successful merchants, barristers, and politicians. Most formidable was William Wilberforce, heir to a commercial fortune, MP for Yorkshire, and close friend of the Tory prime minister, William Pitt. With their connections and organizational skills, the Clapham circle embraced a number of causes, including the abolition of the slave trade, the spread of Protestant missions in the expanding British empire, the reformation of morals at home, the multiplication of Sunday schools and day schools for the labouring orders, and the

[156] G. R. Balleine, *A History of the Evangelical Party in the Church of England* (London, 1933), 50–143; K. Hylson-Smith, *Evangelicals in the Church of England 1734–1984* (Edinburgh, 1988), 34.

[157] Murray, 'The Influence of the French Revolution on the Church of England', 5.

[158] D. Bebbington, *Evangelicalism in Modern Britain* (London, 1989), 2–17.

[159] J. Venn in the *Christian Observer*, 4 (May 1805), 145, cited in M. Hennell, *John Venn and the Clapham Sect* (London, 1958), 127.

[160] Best, 'The Evangelicals and the Established Church', 65.

improvement of social conditions. In 1797 Wilberforce published his influential manifesto, *A Practical View of the Prevailing Religious System of Professed Christians in the Higher and Middle Classes of this Country, contrasted with Real Christianity*, in which he called on the upper social orders to advance beyond the nominal Christianity that characterized too much established religion of the country, and to take up the 'serious' Christianity that alone could save the nation from 'moral degeneracy'. In the House of Commons, Wilberforce led a group of nearly thirty MPs, the 'Saints', who voted together on issues which they viewed as affecting the moral and religious well-being of the nation, and who gained respect as an independent and often highly effective political force. Among their parliamentary achievements were the abolition of the slave trade in 1807 and the opening of India to missionary activity in 1813.[161]

A second major centre of Evangelical activity developed at Cambridge, in the circle surrounding Charles Simeon, minister of Trinity church from 1783 until his death in 1836. Simeon exercised a profound influence over students through his preaching at Trinity, his evening lectures, and his 'conversation parties'. Perhaps his most important contribution was to direct Evangelical attention to the importance of the parish. Evangelical ministers, he maintained, should be pastors as well as preachers, regularly visiting the homes of every inhabitant of the parish, including Dissenters and Roman Catholics, and encouraging household piety and communal responsibility. They should minister to all, and seek to regain all those alienated from the established Church. Simeon had a strong sense of the Church as a corporate body. Although he respected individual Dissenters, he condemned schism and believed that Evangelicals should work to restore the Christian unity of the nation under the established Church.[162] He developed patronage networks, working

[161] E. M. Howse, *Saints in Politics: The Clapham Sect and the Growth of Freedom* (London, 1953); I. Bradley, 'The Politics of Godliness: Evangelicals in Parliament, 1784–1832' (Oxford Univ. D.Phil., 1974); L. Stephen, 'The Clapham Sect', in *Essays in Ecclesiastical Biography*, 2 vols. (London, 1849), i. 287–383; M. Hennell, *John Venn and the Clapham Sect* (London, 1958), 169–214; F. K. Brown, *Fathers of the Victorians* (Cambridge, 1961); B. Hilton, *The Age of Atonement: The Influence of Evangelicalism on Social and Economic Thought 1795–1865* (Oxford, 1988), 3–35.

[162] C. Smyth, *Simeon and Church Order: A Study of the Origins of the Evangelical Revival in Cambridge in the Eighteenth Century* (Cambridge, 1940), 289–98, 311; M. Webster, 'Simeon's Doctrine of the Church', in A. Pollard and M. Hennell (eds.), *Charles Simeon (1759–1836): Essays written in Commemoration of his Bi-Centenary* (London, 1959), 123–35.

to place Evangelical students in parish livings. In 1817, he set up the Simeon Trust, using a large legacy left him by his elder brother to establish a fund for purchasing the patronage of parish livings, so that Evangelicals could be presented to the livings. In 1815, the Church of England gained its first Evangelical bishop when Henry Ryder was made bishop of Gloucester.[163]

In Ireland, an Evangelical movement had emerged in the established Church during the 1780s. At the centre of this movement was Bethesda chapel, a proprietary Church of Ireland chapel built in the mid-1780s in a fashionable district of Dublin. Under the chaplaincy of Benjamin Mathias, a formidable preacher who was presented to the chapel in 1805, the Bethesda congregation became in many respects an Irish equivalent to the Clapham Sect, providing central leadership to the Church of Ireland Evangelical movement. From the late eighteenth century a number of graduates of Trinity College were drawn to Evangelical teachings, largely through their attendance at Bethesda chapel, and these graduates, once ordained, carried their Evangelical piety with them to parishes throughout the country.[164] In some districts, Evangelicals formed clerical societies for regular Bible study and theological discussion—such as the Ossory Clerical Society, formed in 1800 under the leadership of Peter Roe, the Evangelical rector of Odagh.[165] In 1816, Evangelicalism gained its first member of the Irish bench when Power le Poer Trench, bishop of Elphin, was converted to Evangelicalism. Three years later, Trench became archbishop of Tuam.[166]

Of the many Evangelical initiatives of the first two decades of the nineteenth century, probably the greatest was the British and Foreign Bible Society, an interdenominational voluntary association formed in 1804 in London largely through the efforts of the Clapham Evangelicals. The object of the Society was both simple

[163] G. B. Davies, *The First Evangelical Bishop: Some Aspects of the Life of Henry Ryder* (London, 1958), 4–7.

[164] J. Liechty, 'Irish Evangelicalism, Trinity College Dublin, and the Mission of the Church of Ireland at the End of the Eighteenth Century' (St Patrick's College, Maynooth, Ph.D. 1987), 121–82; Hehir, 'Evangelical Religion and the Polarization of Protestant–Catholic Relations in Ireland', 48–57; A. R. Acheson, *'A True and Lively Faith': Evangelical Revival in the Church of Ireland* (Belfast, 1992), 8–11.

[165] S. Madden, *Memoir of the Life of the Late Rev Peter Roe, Rector of Odagh and Minister of St. Mary's, Kilkenny* (Dublin, 1842), 69–95. For the clerical societies, see also D. Massy, *Footprints of a Faithful Shepherd: A Memoir of the Rev Godfrey Massy, Vicar of Bruff* (London, 1855), 60–70.

[166] Bowen, *Protestant Crusade in Ireland*, 71–2.

and grandiose—to provide each inhabitant of the world with a Bible printed in his or her native language. This, many believed, would bring the conversion of the world and usher in the millennium. The work of translating and printing the Bibles was financed by voluntary subscriptions and supervised by a London committee of management. For the first five years support for the Society was largely restricted to London. Beginning about 1809, however, national interest was aroused and branches began appearing in towns and counties throughout Britain and Ireland. By 1816, 541 branch societies had been formed. During its first five years, between 1804 and 1809, the Society had distributed some 150,000 Bibles; during the second five years, however, with the rapid growth of the auxiliary societies, it distributed 800,000 Bibles.[167] The Bible Society movement was brought to Ireland in 1806 with the formation of the Hibernian Bible Society, which distributed both English- and Irish-language Bibles to the Catholic population. The local Bible Society branches in England and Ireland not only spread Evangelical influence through society, but also united Evangelicals from both the established and Dissenting Churches.

The Bible Society movement placed little emphasis on the visible Church; its language suggested that the spread of the Bible alone would be sufficient for world conversion, and its members treated the divisions between Church and Dissent as of little account. For these reasons, most High Church Anglicans bitterly opposed the movement. The established Church, they insisted, already had an agency for distributing Bibles, the Society for Promoting Christian Knowledge, formed in 1698. Loyal subjects should support this Society, which distributed not only Bibles, but also copies of the Book of Common Prayer, catechisms, psalters, and devotional works intended to provide guidance in interpreting Scripture.[168] High Anglicans criticized the Bible Society for blurring the differences between Church and Dissent, and for forming popular associations outside the established order in Church and State, which were too reminiscent of political reform societies. 'It is a *political*, not a religious association,' insisted Thomas Sykes in 1812. 'Jack [John

[167] R. H. Martin, *Evangelicals United: Ecumenical Stirrings in Victorian Britain, 1795–1830* (Metuchen, NJ, 1983), 92.

[168] H. H. Norris, *A Practical Exposition of the Tendency and Proceedings of the British and Foreign Bible Society*, 2nd edn. (London, 1814), 62; Hole, *Pulpits, Politics and Public Order in England*, 190; Sack, *From Jacobite to Conservative*, 212–13.

Owen, Secretary of the Bible Society] was a Jacobin once, and Jack is a Jacobin still. He has only changed colour, as the complexion of times and places require.'[169] By distributing Bibles without notes or guidance, the Bible Society was luring the untutored lower social orders into false interpretations and religious enthusiasm, feeding the popular millenarian movements and the Dissenting bodies. 'If we neglect to provide the poor of the establishment with the Book of Common Prayer, as well as the Bible', argued Herbert Marsh in 1812, 'we certainly neglect the means of preventing their seduction from the Established Church.'[170] H. H. Norris argued that the branches of the Bible Society were competing with the structures of the established Church, 'parcelling out the country into new departments, and erecting a lay eldership in each, to supersede the ministrations of the regular Clergy'. 'They are, at most, but tolerators of Episcopacy', observed the Irish High Churchman William Phelan in 1817, 'and they think lightly of the pastoral office.'[171] The Bible Society controversy reached its greatest intensity between about 1810 and 1820, with High Anglicans seeking to thwart the formation of additional branches and Evangelicals denouncing their opponents as enemies of the Bible.

The early nineteenth-century Church of Scotland was also divided into two main parties—the Moderates and the Evangelicals—which confronted one another within the system of Church courts. The Moderates were the dominant party, and had maintained an ascendancy in the Scottish Church since the 1760s. Reflecting the ethos of the Scottish Enlightenment, Moderates, under the leadership of the versatile William Robertson, celebrated historian, minister of an Edinburgh church, and Principal of Edinburgh University, had worked to move the Church away from the doctrinaire Calvinism of the seventeenth century towards a more tolerant, world-affirming faith. Moderates called on the Church to promote a culture of improvement, and the clergy to be active in all aspects of the intellectual life of the nation. They sought to end the distrust that had plagued relations of Church and State in the past and to achieve a more co-operative alliance. While they did not directly challenge

[169] T. Sykes to H. H. Norris, 22 December 1812, Bod. MS Eng. Lett. c. 789, fos. 38–9.

[170] H. Marsh, *An Enquiry into the Consequences of Neglecting to give the Prayer Book with the Bible* (Cambridge, 1812), 11.

[171] Norris, *A Practical Exposition of the Tendency and Proceedings of the British and Foreign Bible Society*, 43; W. Phelan, *The Bible, not the Bible Society* (Dublin, 1817), 95.

the Calvinism of the Westminster Confession of Faith, they did play down predestination and the atonement, while emphasizing practical morality and human reason. Their ecclesiastical policy was based on a consistent support for lay patronage in the Church. The established Church, they insisted, was obligated to enforce patronage so long as it remained the law of the land. More than that, they believed that patrons, mainly educated landed gentlemen or Crown officials, presented a superior quality of clergymen to Scottish church livings—men of refinement, good manners, and intellectual accomplishments, who would exercise a civilizing influence on their parishioners. On the whole, Moderates looked on the growth of Dissent as an inevitable result of a liberal and tolerant society, in which the established Church no longer had the power to enforce attendance at its services. During a celebrated General Assembly debate over schism in 1766, Robertson had referred to Scotland's increasingly diverse religious landscape as a 'bed of flowers' in which 'the great part of the beauty arises from the variety in shape, size and colour'.[172] During the political unrest of the 1790s the Moderate party had aligned itself with the Tory party of William Pitt and Henry Dundas, denouncing popular reform movements and religious enthusiasm while insisting upon non-resistance to the powers that be.[173] As a consequence, admitted the Moderate James Lapslie in 1791, the Moderate clergy had become stigmatized in the popular mind 'as the servile flatterers of men in power, who have no regard to the spiritual interests of their flock'.[174] None the less, they continued to benefit from Crown patronage and they retained control of the General Assembly of the Church.[175]

The Evangelical movement in the Church of Scotland, like that in the English and Irish establishments, was part of the larger eighteenth-century Evangelical awakening. The Evangelical party, or as

[172] *Scots Magazine*, 28 (June–July 1766), 337–41.

[173] E. Vincent, 'The Responses of Scottish Churchmen to the French Revolution, 1789–1802', *Scottish Historical Review*, 73 (1994), 191–215; C. Kidd, 'The Kirk, the French Revolution, and the Burden of Scottish Whiggery', in N. Aston (ed.), *Religious Change in Europe 1650–1914* (Oxford, 1997), 213–34.

[174] J. Lapslie, *A Foederal Union amongst the Different Sects of Christians, and particularly of this Kingdom, Proposed and Recommended. A discourse, delivered before the Synod of Glasgow and Air, at Glasgow, April 1791* (Glasgow, 1795), 33.

[175] R. B. Sher, *Church and University in the Scottish Enlightenment: The Moderate Literati of Edinburgh* (Princeton, 1985); I. D. L. Clark, 'From Protest to Reaction: The Moderate Regime in the Church of Scotland, 1752–1805', in N. T. Phillipson and R. Mitchison (eds.), *Scotland in the Age of Improvement* (Edinburgh, 1970), 200–24.

it was usually called in the eighteenth century, the Popular party, emerged during the 1750s, largely in opposition to patronage. For the Popular party, patronage was an evil, subordinating the spiritual needs of parish communities to the will of individual patrons. Patronage, they believed, often resulted in the appointment of worldly men to parish livings, ministers who preached manners and morality rather than the familiar old message of salvation by grace alone. They deeply regretted the loss of those dedicated Presbyterians who seceded from the established Church in protest against patronage. By the 1790s, however, having failed to secure the abolition of patronage, the Popular party increasingly directed its attention to other matters, and especially to the increasing numbers of people who were growing up outside any Church affiliation. A new generation of Evangelicals was now coming of age, men and women who were strongly influenced by both the thought of the Scottish Enlightenment and the Evangelical movement in England. Led by John Erskine, Stevenson Macgill, and Sir Henry Moncreiff Wellwood (the only titled clergyman in the Scottish Church), Scottish Evangelicals participated in the broader culture of improvement, joining literary and philanthropic societies and founding in 1810 the *Edinburgh Christian Instructor*, a monthly review of religious, political, and scientific literature. They embraced the anti-slavery and missionary commitments of the English Evangelicals. From 1810 Church of Scotland Evangelicals began establishing branches of the British and Foreign Bible Society while they shared the commitment of Simeon and other Anglican Evangelicals to an activist parish ministry.[176]

The party divisions within the establishments of the three kingdoms should not be exaggerated. At the same time, they were real and party-spirit was intensifying. The revival of party in the late eighteenth and early nineteenth centuries reflected a growing awareness that the established Churches were in danger and that they needed reform. Party divisions reflected genuine commitment to Church revival on the part of clergy and laity. For the High Church parties of England and Ireland, reform and renewal would be achieved by holding firmly to Church principles and preserving the

[176] J. McIntosh, *Church and Theology in Enlightenment Scotland: The Popular Party, 1740–1800* (Edinburgh, 1998); J. Macinnes, *The Evangelical Movement in the Highlands of Scotland, 1688–1800* (Aberdeen, 1951); S. J. Brown, *Thomas Chalmers and the Godly Commonwealth in Scotland* (Oxford, 1982), 43–9.

sacraments and traditions of the visible Church. For English and Irish Evangelicals, Church renewal would come through individuals embracing a personal faith, and working to convert others through preaching and the dissemination of Bibles. Moderates in Scotland saw the hope for the establishment to rest in a learned clergy, linked to the landed and professional élite, contributing to social improvement through scholarship and moral example. Scottish Evangelicals sought to revive a popular Church, rooted in a traditional communal culture and disseminating a biblical faith. But all parties were agreed that Church reform was an imperative.

Parliamentary Initiatives—Church Reform and Church Extension

The nineteenth-century movement for the reform of the established Churches began, significantly, not within the Churches themselves but in Parliament and in the Tory Government of William Pitt and his successors, which were for their part responding to growing popular impatience with the abuses in the establishments. In the late eighteenth century individuals had begun raising private legal actions against Church of England clerics who violated long-neglected acts of Henry VIII prohibiting non-residence, pluralism, and commercial farming. The actions were treated seriously in the civil courts, and this prompted parliamentary action to provide protection for members of the clergy indulging only moderately in these practices. In 1803, Sir William Scott, a High Church Tory, MP for Oxford University, and brother of the Lord Chancellor, Lord Eldon, introduced a bill to permit clergymen to be non-resident under specified conditions and to engage in certain types of farming. At the same time Scott's bill gave bishops enlarged powers to restrict more blatant forms of non-residence. The bill passed easily through both houses. In 1805, Parliament began requiring bishops to submit annual returns of the extent of non-residence in their dioceses, to show that they were using their new powers to achieve real improvements in clerical residence. Scott, meanwhile, tried to follow up his 1803 act with legislation to improve the incomes and conditions of the long-suffering curates. Parliamentary intervention, he believed, was needed to ensure that these clerical 'serfs' received an adequate income, and his bill would have forced non-resident incumbents to provide their curates with a specified percentage of the value of the parish living the curate served. Scott's curacy bill, however, encountered strong opposition in a Parliament keenly sensitive to the rights of property. For Scott's opponents, the Church was a corporation, or rather an amalgam of thousands of separate parochial corporations, in which each incumbent held his living as a form of personal property. While it was generally acknowledged that non-resident incumbents should employ curates, most MPs also felt that incumbents should be free to negotiate the best terms they could with their curates without outside interference. If Parliament could force incumbents to pay curates a specified portion of the parish income—or, in short, a minimum wage—could it not also force manufacturers and shopkeepers to do likewise with their employees? Some attacked Scott's bill as a Jacobinical measure, which aimed at securing equality of clerical incomes through State action. High Anglicans feared Scott's bill would open the way for further parliamentary interference in Church government. Scott failed to get his curacy bill passed in 1803 and 1804, and then dropped the measure.[177]

The cause of the working curates was now taken up by the Tory Attorney-General, Spencer Perceval, an energetic barrister and devout Evangelical. The curates, he believed, were a largely impoverished and exploited body of men whose treatment by unscrupulous incumbents disgraced the Church. Legislation was required to force incumbents to pay their curates a fair share of the income of the living. If incumbents were unhappy with this, they should reside in their parishes and do the duty themselves. The purpose of Church property, he insisted, was not to provide incomes for the clergy, but to provide religious instruction and pastoral care for parishioners. Perceval brought forward curacy bills in the Commons in 1805, 1806, and 1808, experiencing defeat on all three occasions.[178] None the less, the debates over his bills forced Parliament to begin considering seriously the nature and purpose of an established Church. Was an established Church an amalgam of independent parish corporations, in which the incumbents held their livings as freehold

[177] W. R. Ward, *Victorian Oxford* (London, 1965), 22–3; W. L. Mathieson, *English Church Reform 1815–1840* (London, 1923), 24; S. Walpole, *Life of Spencer Perceval*, 2 vols. (London, 1874), i. 281–4.

[178] D. Gray, *Spencer Perceval: The Evangelical Prime Minister 1762–1812* (Manchester, 1963), 22–3; Walpole, *Life of Spencer Perceval*, i. 284–6.

property, or was it a national institution, its property held in trust for the religious and moral instruction of the people? Were incumbents to enjoy freedom from outside interference regarding their livings, or did Parliament have authority to redistribute Church property in order to provide the nation with an improved parish ministry?

In 1809, following the death of the duke of Portland, Perceval became prime minister. Rather than immediately revive his curates bill, he shifted instead to a different tactic for improving the parish ministry. He acknowledged that a major cause of non-residency and pluralism was the large number of poorly endowed parish livings in the Church of England—many of which could not decently support a resident incumbent. The number of poor livings had long been recognized as a problem. Since 1704, Queen Anne's Bounty, a fund established by Anne out of certain ecclesiastical revenues which had been confiscated by Henry VIII at the Reformation, had been used to augment the endowments of poorer parish livings. The fund, however, was a relatively modest one, and progress towards augmenting the large number of poor livings was proving agonizingly slow. In May 1809, to speed up this process, Perceval's Government called for a grant of £100,000 from the public revenues to be used to increase the endowments of the poorer parish livings. Speaking for the grant in the Commons on 7 June 1809, Perceval argued that if the Church relied solely on Queen Anne's Bounty it would require another forty years to raise all its poor livings to £50 per annum. However, if Parliament would approve an annual grant of £100,000 for the next four years, it would raise all livings to the £50 minimum by the end of that period. He further announced that he would request the Crown to ask for returns on poor livings in the establishments in Ireland and Scotland, with the aim of providing similar grants for those establishments. His ultimate aim was to raise all parish livings throughout the three kingdoms to a minimum of £150 per annum, ensuring that each could support a resident clergyman and eliminating any reason for non-residence.[179] Perceval was warmly supported by Wilberforce and the Saints, while in the Upper House, Lords Liverpool and Harrowby spoke on behalf of the grant, which was approved without a division in both Houses. Parliament went on to approve a total of eleven annual grants of £100,000, or

[179] *Cobbett's Parl. Debates*, 14 (1809), 920–1; Gray, *Spencer Perceval*, 24–5.

a total of £1,100,000, to improve small livings in the Church of England between 1809 and 1821.[180]

Parliament made similar moves to improve the parish ministry in the Church of Ireland. Since the late 1770s the Irish Parliament had provided modest grants to assist the building and repair of glebe houses and improve the endowment of benefices in the Irish establishment. These grants had been made to the Board of First Fruits, a body established in 1711 when Queen Anne agreed to remit the First Fruits, a tax on clerical incomes which yielded only modest amounts, to the Church of Ireland for the purpose of improving small livings. In 1808, the United Kingdom Parliament greatly augmented these grants to the Irish Board of First Fruits, while at the same time it increased the powers of the Board, enabling it now to use its revenues for building and repairing churches, as well as building glebe houses and improving small livings. The aim was to increase clerical residence and ensure regular worship. These parliamentary grants to the Board of First Fruits averaged £10,000 a year in 1808 and 1809, and then rose to £60,000 a year between 1810 and 1816, declining to £30,000 a year between 1817 and 1821. Between 1801 and 1822, the Board of First Fruits distributed nearly £1,000,000. While much of this money was wasted on unnecessary repairs or diverted to personal uses by unscrupulous clerics, the grants did promote substantial new building. The number of glebe houses in the Irish establishment increased from 418 in 1807 to 765 in 1819, weakening the force of one often-cited reason for non-residence. During the same period more than 200 new parish churches were constructed.[181] In 1808 Parliament passed an act on clerical residence in the Church of Ireland, which strengthened the powers of bishops in enforcing residence in their dioceses. These included the power to sequester the parish income of a non-resident incumbent, and to employ one-fifth of that income to pay the salary of a curate. Further, after three years of persistent non-residence, the bishop was empowered to declare the living vacant, and have a new incumbent appointed. These measures contributed to a steady improvement in residence, from about 46 per cent of the incumbents resident in 1806 to over 65 per cent resident in 1819. Along with the

[180] Virgin, *The Church in an Age of Negligence*, 17; Mathieson, *English Church Reform*, 18.

[181] Akenson, *The Church of Ireland*, 113–22; Brynn, *The Church of Ireland*, 127–35; Brynn, 'Some Repercussions of the Act of Union on the Church of Ireland, 1801–1820', 295.

improvement in residency and decline in pluralism, there was an increase in the number of clergymen in the Irish establishment, from 1,253 in 1806 to 1,977 by 1826.[182] Efforts were also made to encourage the formation of parish schools. With the help of additional subsidies from the Government, the number of parish schools in the Irish establishment increased from 361 and about 11,000 pupils in 1788 to 549 and some 23,000 pupils in 1810. After 1800, moreover, Parliament began making annual grants to the Association for Discountenancing Vice and Promoting the Practice of the Christian Religion, which maintained schools in connection with the established Church. These annual grants started at a modest level of £300, but then rose dramatically, up to some £9,000 a year by 1823; by 1819, the Association was educating about 8,000 pupils in its schools.[183]

Nor did Parliament neglect the Scottish establishment. Although non-residence was not permitted within the Church of Scotland, that Church did have many poor livings. In 1750, some 350 livings, over a third of the total, were worth less than £50 a year, and the total income of all the clergy was under £50,000. Efforts of the clergy to obtain an increase in their stipends had been repeatedly blocked after 1750 by the landed interest. The principal landowners, or heritors, had appropriated the tithes, or teinds, of the medieval Church at the Reformation, and were responsible for paying the stipends of the clergy out of those teinds, while retaining the rest for their own personal use. Thus the heritors, who retained about half the teind in Scotland after the payment of clerical stipends, had a vested interest in keeping the stipends of the parish clergy low. Then in 1810 the Perceval Government successfully sponsored an act increasing the minimum stipend of a Scottish parish minister to £150 a year. Because in about a fifth of the parishes the teinds were not large enough to provide the new minimum stipend, Parliament also provided an annual grant of £10,000 from the public revenues to the Scottish Church to help poorer parishes pay the increased amount.[184]

In May 1812, Perceval was assassinated in the lobby of the House of Commons by a mentally unbalanced Baltic merchant. The

[182] Akenson, *The Church of Ireland*, 127.

[183] D. H. Akenson, *The Irish Education Experiment: The National System of Education in the Nineteenth Century* (London, 1970), 81–2; Akenson, *The Church of Ireland*, 139–41; H. R. Clayton, 'Societies formed to Educate the Poor in Ireland in the late 18th and early 19th Centuries' (Trinity College, Dublin, M.Litt., 1981), 104–21.

[184] J. Cunningham, *Church History of Scotland*, ii. 608–10; M. Fry, *The Dundas Despotism* (Edinburgh, 1992), 297–8.

Church reform movement he had initiated, however, was by now bringing significant material improvements to the established Churches in the three kingdoms. Perceval's Government had committed itself to a comprehensive programme of Church reform, including improved conditions for curates, the reduction of non-residence, and the achievement of a minimum of £150 a year for all parish livings in the three establishments.[185] In this work, Perceval had been supported by a group of devout lay Anglicans, including Lords Harrowby and Liverpool and Nicholas Vansittart. Significantly, although Perceval received some support from Wilberforce and the Saints in Parliament, he was not closely allied with any Church party, nor did he receive much practical help from the bishops. The lead in the movement for reforming the national Churches was taken not by the Churches but by Parliament—setting a pattern that would continue into the 1830s.

After Perceval's murder, the Tory Government, now under the leadership of Lord Liverpool, carried on the commitment to Church revival. In June 1812, a few weeks after the assassination, Perceval's curates bill, which had been allowed to lapse in 1808, was revived by his friend, Lord Harrowby (the brother of the future Evangelical bishop of Gloucester). In an emotional speech in the House of Lords, Harrowby announced that Perceval had intended to revive the bill as part of a larger 'system of measures for strengthening the establishment of the Church of England'. In now introducing the bill, Harrowby was acting 'only as the executor of a much-lamented friend'.[186] The alarming growth of Dissent in recent years, he argued, could be countered only by a comprehensive programme of reform of the established Church. While much had been done to strengthen the Church in recent years, its situation remained grave: there was still far too much non-residence, far too many small livings, far too many exploited curates, far too much pastoral neglect. Still more dangerous was the insufficiency of church accommodation in the establishment, especially in the rapidly growing towns and cities. 'In the most populous parishes', Harrowby

[185] For a sketch of the Government's Church reform programme, see the speech of Lord Harrowby in the House of Lords on 18 June 1810; *Hansard's Parl. Deb.* xvii (1810), cols. 753–68.

[186] Lord Harrowby, *Substance of the Speech of the Earl of Harrowby, on Moving for the Recommitment of a Bill for the Better Support and Maintenance of Stipendiary Curates, on Thursday, the 18th of June, 1812* (London, 1812), 1.

insisted, 'places of worship, according to the Church of England, are notoriously deficient. The people have no option but the entire neglect of all divine worship, or the attendance upon a worship which makes them dissenters from the establishment.'[187] The parliamentary Church reform movement connected with Perceval's name, Harrowby concluded, must continue. Parliament agreed, despite the fact that the majority of bishops in the House of Lords opposed the measure as an infringement on the rights of incumbents. The stipendiary curates bill now passed through both Houses and became law.

Having acted to improve clerical incomes, residency, and the lot of the curates, Parliament now turned to church extension—or the effort to increase the number of churches, especially in the towns and cities. The lack of sufficient church accommodation for Britain's rapidly growing population was widely recognized as a serious problem. Indeed, Perceval had been preparing a church extension measure before he was assassinated in 1812.[188] The final phase of the struggle with Napoleonic France absorbed the nation's attention in the years after Perceval's death, but late in 1814 the church extension issue was revived. This time the initiative came not from Parliament, but from the High Church Hackney Phalanx, which had been calling for additional churches since the early years of the century. In 1814 Phalanx leaders began pressing the church extension cause with Tory politicians, and especially Lord Liverpool. In 1815, the High Church clergyman Richard Yates published a vigorous pamphlet, *The Church in Danger*, in the form of a letter addressed to Liverpool. Yates called attention to the increase in population during the past century, which had rendered church accommodation scandalously inadequate, especially in the growing towns and cities. There were now over-crowded urban parishes with 30,000–40,000 inhabitants, far too large for a single parish clergyman to provide pastoral care. In the central districts of London, out of a total population of 1,162,300, there was accommodation in established churches for only 216,000, leaving 946,000 unable to attend public worship in their national Church.[189] When new churches were built, they had

[187] Lord Harrowby, *Substance of the Speech*, 33–4.

[188] *Hansard's Parl. Deb.*, xvii (18 June 1810), cols. 765–6; M. H. Port, *Six Hundred New Churches: A Study of the Church Building Commission* (London, 1961), 6–7.

[189] R. Yates, *The Church in Danger . . . in a Letter to the Right Hon. Earl of Liverpool* (London, 1815), 31, 50–1.

to charge high pew rents in order to repay the building loans, thus effectively excluding the poor. A large urban underclass was emerging, with no religious or moral instruction; these were the abandoned masses drawn to the millenarian visions of Brothers and Southcott. Was it any wonder that both Church and State were in danger? 'Shut out, in fact, from the Pale of our Church', Yates observed,

> these numbers are necessarily driven to join the ranks of injurious opposition, either in Dissent, and Sectarian Enthusiasm;—or in the infinitely more dangerous opposition of Infidelity, Atheism, and ignorant depravity. Such a Mine of Heathenism, and consequent profligacy and danger, under the very meridian (as it is supposed) of church illumination, and accumulated around the very centre and heart of British Prosperity, Liberty, and Civilization, cannot be contemplated without terror.[190]

Late in 1815, the High Church layman John Bowdler drafted a memorial to the prime minister that was signed by 120 prominent laymen, calling on Parliament to provide additional churches, as this task was beyond the capacity of either private subscriptions or the resources of the Church. 'Parliament alone can do it', the memorialists insisted, 'and we conceive it to be one of its chief duties to provide places of worship for the members of the established religion.'[191] In 1816 the Government announced that it would bring forward a church extension measure in the following year.

The post-war financial crisis precluded any Government measure in 1817. In May 1817 the Phalanx, aided by the Clapham Evangelicals and the prime minister, formed the Incorporated Church-Building Society, intended to promote close co-operation between Church and Parliament, the Evangelical and High Church parties, for the cause of church extension. Formally launched at a public meeting in February 1818, the new society had the backing of the Church hierarchy and included all the bishops as vice-presidents. In March 1818 Nicholas Vansittart, Chancellor of the Exchequer and a Church Evangelical, introduced the Government's church extension proposals in the House of Commons.[192] These included a grant of £1,000,000 from the public revenues, the encouragement of private subscriptions, and the creation of a Church-Building

[190] Ibid. 51–2.
[191] A. B. Webster, *Joshua Watson*, 62; Port, *Six Hundred New Churches*, 9.
[192] *Hansard's Parl. Deb.*, xxxvii (1818), cols. 1116–27.

Commission to oversee the church-building campaign. Provision was also to be made for the subdivision of parishes. The new churches and their ministers were to be supported from modest seat rents, though a 'large proportion' (eventually defined as a fifth) of the seats were to be free. Each new church was to offer three services each Sunday. Vansittart maintained that the new churches would contribute to public order and the security of property by elevating the moral condition of the lower social orders. The new churches would also strengthen the religious and moral unity of the nation. Many thousands, he insisted, worshipped at Dissenting meeting-houses only because there was no room for them in the parish church. 'To give to all such an opportunity of returning', he continued, 'must be the most anxious wish of every true friend of the church.'[193] In moving the second reading of the bill in the House of Lords two months later, Liverpool described the bill as 'the most important measure [he had] ever submitted to their lordships' consideration'.[194] He insisted that at least 100 new churches could be built from the £1,000,000 grant. More than this, he predicted that the parliamentary grant would greatly stimulate private subscriptions, raising the total number of new churches that would result from the parliamentary grant to 200 or more. These hundreds of new churches together would form a fitting national monument to Britain's victory over Napoleonic France, a rededication of the nation to God. The Church of England would at last begin rolling back the gains made by Dissent during the past three decades.[195]

The measure passed easily through Parliament, and late in 1818 the new Church-Building Commission, which included both archbishops, six bishops, six archdeacons, and a number of High Church and Evangelical leaders, began its work. It was permitted to make grants for new churches only in parishes with populations of more than 4,000, in which there was no room in the existing parish church for more than 1,000 persons, or in which more than 1,000 persons lived more than 4 miles from the parish church. Applications for the new churches were to come from the localities, and were to have the support of the majority of property-holders or ratepayers in the district. There were strict requirements on the type of church to be constructed, with the Commission insisting on the most economical

[193] *Hansard's Parl. Deb.*, xxxvii (1818), col. 1125.
[194] Ibid., xxxvii (1818), col. 709.
[195] Ibid. cols. 709–21.

forms of construction, though efforts to impose a few basic designs were thwarted by local insistence on diversity in the new churches. Despite higher than expected building costs and other difficulties, there was progress. In its first report to Parliament, in February 1821, the Commission reported that eighty-five new churches had either been built or were under construction, and all but £80,000 of the original £1,000,000 grant had been committed. Another twenty-five applications for new churches had been approved but building was postponed for lack of funds. In 1824 the State received an unexpected repayment of £2,000,000 from Austria on a war-time loan that had been written off, and the Liverpool Government successfully requested a further parliamentary grant of £500,000 from the windfall to the Church-Building Commission. In distributing this second State grant, the Commission gave smaller amounts to individual projects, thus requiring that more money be raised through private donations. By 1831 the Treasury had provided a total of £1,440,000 in church extension grants, building 188 new churches and chapels—known as 'Waterloo churches'—with seating for 260,000, over half of it free.[196] Even more important, the Commission's work stimulated extensive voluntary church-building in the Anglican establishment during the 1820s, with local church-building societies raising over £6,000,000 in private contributions and building hundreds of new churches, mainly in the urban districts.[197] There were, to be sure, problems. Proposals for erecting new churches very often led to disputes between parishioners and incumbents, with the latter frequently viewing a potential new church in the parish as a rival for pew rents or an expression of discontent with their ministry.[198] The new churches were often too large and expensive—the new church at St Pancras in London cost over £76,000—and many failed to attract reasonable congregations.[199] Further, their architectural mixtures of classical Grecian and modern styles, including porticoes modelled after Greek temples topped with high steeples, attracted few admirers. One notable critic was the celebrated architect Augustus Pugin. 'A more meagre,

[196] R. A. Soloway, *Prelates and People: Ecclesiastical Social Thought in England 1783–1852* (London, 1969), 298.

[197] W. R. Ward, *Religion and Society in England*, 110.

[198] See e.g. Thomas C. Adams to H. H. Norris [February 1825], Bodl. MS Eng. Lett. c. 789, fos. 146–7.

[199] W. R. Ward, *Religion and Society in England*, 110–11; B. F. L. Clarke, *Church Builders of the Nineteenth Century* (London, 1938), 20–6.

miserable display of architectural skill', he wrote in 1836, 'never was made, nor more improprieties and absurdities committed, than in the mass of paltry churches erected under the auspices of the commissioners.'[200] None the less, for all their aesthetic failings, the Waterloo churches were increasing church accommodation and signalling the nation's revived commitment to the established Church.

In requesting the first English church-building grant in 1818, the Government had also announced its intention to bring forward a similar measure for the Scottish establishment. The General Assembly of the Church of Scotland had responded immediately, appointing a Church Accommodation Committee in May 1818. After some years of deliberation, the Church Committee and the politicians agreed to concentrate the Scottish church-building efforts on the remote Highlands and Islands. The Reformation had had only localized impact in the Highlands, and much of the largely Gaelic-speaking population there had remained either Catholic or pagan. Beginning in the early eighteenth century, the established Church had pursued a mission to the Highlands and Islands, sending out missionaries and catechists—assisted after 1724 by a Royal Bounty of £1,000 a year. The Society in Scotland for Promoting Christian Knowledge (SSPCK) had also been active in supporting missionaries and schools in the region. These efforts had proved successful at thwarting the efforts of Catholic missionaries and in bringing Protestantism to the region, often through heroic individual efforts. For example, the Gaelic-speaking John MacDonald, the 'Apostle of the North', itinerated widely through the Highlands during his long Church of Scotland ministry from 1807 to 1849, and was said to have preached over 10,000 sermons during the last thirty-six years of his life, with crowds of thousands attending his open-air services. Gaelic Schools Societies were established in Edinburgh (1811), Glasgow (1812), and Inverness (1818) to raise funds to support Gaelic, Scripture-based schools in the Highlands. Still, the difficulties were immense, and more churches and schools were desperately needed.[201]

[200] A. W. Pugin, *Contrasts: or, A Parallel between the Noble Edifices of the Middle Ages and Corresponding Buildings of the Present Day* [1st edn. 1836], 2nd edn. (London, 1841), 49.

[201] J. Macinnes, *The Evangelical Movement in the Highlands of Scotland*, 197–261; D. Ansdell, *The People of the Great Faith: The Highland Church, 1690–1900* (Stornoway, 1998), 6–55; A. Macinnes, 'Evangelical Protestantism in the Nineteenth-Century Highlands', in G. Walker and T. Gallagher (eds.), *Sermons and Battle Hymns: Protestant Popular Culture in Modern Scotland* (Edinburgh, 1990), 43–68.

In 1823 Parliament provided a grant of £50,000 for building additional churches and manses in the Highlands and Islands. The act also provided an additional sum for endowing the ministers' stipends. The celebrated engineer Thomas Telford provided the design for inexpensive church buildings, and by the end of the 1820s forty-three new churches had been erected, and endowments provided for forty-two ministers—representing a total State investment of about £180,000.[202] The investment encouraged additional efforts on the part of the Church. In 1824, the General Assembly created a Highlands and Islands Committee to co-ordinate its mission in the region. Two years later the General Assembly was supporting thirty-nine missionaries and twenty-three catechists in the Highlands, and planting new parish schools.[203] In the early 1830s the SSPCK was supporting ten missionaries, thirty-three catechists, and 261 teachers (including 105 women) in the region.[204] These efforts proved highly successful in bringing the Reformation to the Highlands and Islands and transforming what had been a stronghold of Catholicism and Jacobitism into a region dominated by evangelical Presbyterianism.

The parliamentary Church reform movement between about 1808 and 1828 marked a major reversal of fortune for the established Churches of the three kingdoms. After having provided no grants of public money to the establishments for over a century, Parliament had suddenly adopted a policy of combining moderate reforms with generous financial infusions. In the two decades after 1808 Parliament provided £2,600,000 in new grants of public money to the Church of England, nearly £1,000,000 in grants to the Church of Ireland, and over £350,000 in grants to the Church of Scotland. Much of this money was provided at a time when the State was engaged in a life-and-death military struggle with Napoleonic France. Never before had the established Churches of the three kingdoms received direct financial aid from the State on such a scale as in these years. By the early 1820s there was a new confidence and sense of purpose in the established Churches. After some twenty-five years of relative decline, the establishments seemed poised to

[202] I. F. Maciver, 'Unfinished Business? The Highland Churches Scheme and the Government of Scotland, 1818–1835', *Records of the Scottish Church History Society*, 25 (1995), 376–99; A. Maclean, *Telford's Highland Churches* (Inverness, 1989).

[203] J. Sinclair, *Analysis of the Statistical Account of Scotland* (London, 1826), part ii, 55–6; D. Chambers, 'The Church of Scotland's Highlands and Islands Education Scheme, 1824–1843', *Journal of Educational Administration and History*, 7 (1975), 8–17.

[204] A. Macinnes, 'Evangelical Protestantism', 44.

revive their influence and authority. Church leaders felt a new confidence in Parliament. This was evident in the church-building campaign, in which both the Hackney Phalanx and the Clapham Sect had co-operated closely with Liverpool's Government in obtaining parliamentary grants and organizing local church-building efforts. The conflict between the ecclesiastical parties in the Churches seemed to be easing by the 1820s, as the parties—High Church and Evangelical in the United Church, Moderate and Evangelical in the Church of Scotland—found a shared goal in reviving the parish ministry and expanding the number of parish churches. A new era seemed to be dawning. Parliament, the established Churches, and the propertied orders were embracing a common purpose, the revival of social harmony and stability in the three kingdoms through a restored parish system.

The Church Response—Diocesan Reform and Renewed Confidence

By the early 1820s the new confidence and sense of purpose within the Church of England was finding expression at the diocesan level, in what the historian Arthur Burns has described as a 'diocesan revival'.[205] This movement was stimulated by a greater commitment on the part of government to appoint men of proven ability and energy to the episcopal bench. Lord Liverpool insisted that merit and not political partisanship be the primary consideration in episcopal appointments. Liverpool also expected those recommended for bishoprics to set an example by giving up their pluralities and sinecures. Bishops appointed after 1815 were mainly High Church, but included Evangelicals as well.[206] Among the new bishops were the Evangelical Henry Ryder, consecrated bishop of Gloucester in 1815 and translated to Lichfield and Coventry in 1824, William Van Mildert, consecrated bishop of Llandaff in 1819 and translated to Durham in 1826, Charles James Blomfield, consecrated bishop of Chester in 1824 and translated to London in 1828, Robert Gray,

[205] A. Burns, *The Diocesan Revival in the Church of England, c.1800–1870* (Oxford, 1999), 1–22; R. A. Burns, 'A Hanoverian Legacy? Diocesan Reform in the Church of England, c. 1800–1833', in Walsh, Haydon, and Taylor (eds.), *The Church of England*, 265–82.

[206] W. Gibson, 'The Tories and Church Patronage: 1812–30', *Journal of Ecclesiastical History*, 41 (1990), 266–74; Gibson, *Church, State and Society, 1760–1850*, 53–8; Best, *Temporal Pillars*, 261; E. R. Norman, *Church and Society in England 1770–1970* (Oxford, 1976), 72.

consecrated bishop of Exeter in 1827, John Kaye, scholar and Church reformer, consecrated bishop of Bristol in 1820 and translated to Lincoln in 1827, the Evangelical Charles Sumner, consecrated bishop of Llandaff in 1826 and translated to Winchester in 1827, and his brother, John Bird Sumner, consecrated bishop of Chester in 1828. These were men who before elevation to the episcopal bench had achieved prominence for their scholarship or pastoral work, and who were committed to improving the discipline and professionalism of the clergy in their dioceses. The powers of the bishops, meanwhile, had been considerably increased by the Church reform legislation, including the residence act of 1803 and the stipendiary curates act of 1813.[207] The new group of bishops was prepared to exercise those powers. On becoming bishop of Chester, for example, Blomfield immediately raised the requirements for ordination, acted to end clerical fox-hunting, and improved the incomes of curates, in order to 'provide for the proper pay of the *workmen*'.[208]

Beginning about 1820, bishops began treating the triennial visitations of their dioceses more seriously. Frequently neglected in the eighteenth century, the visitations now became a regular part of diocesan life and a means to monitor progress in Church reform. Bishops insisted on more thorough returns from the clergy on the condition of their parishes. They also devoted more care to preparing their charges to the clergy—viewing the charges as opportunities to defend the establishment, to encourage the clergy in their pastoral work, and to report on progress in reducing clerical nonresidency and increasing the numbers of churches and schools. During the 1820s the charges were increasingly published. The visitations and charges contributed to the development of dioceses as self-conscious communities, bound together by a shared commitment to expanding the pastoral outreach of the Church.[209] In the effort to improve clerical discipline, bishops made greater use of the office of archdeacon, appointing a number of able, activist archdeacons, including the High Churchmen J. J. Watson, Charles Daubeny, and George Cambridge, who revived regular archidiaconal visitations of the parishes, strengthened archidiaconal courts for the disciplining of clergy and laity, and published charges to the

[207] Knight, *The Nineteenth-Century Church and English Society*, 153.

[208] C. J. Blomfield to H. H. Norris, 2 September 1824, Bodl. MS Eng. Lett. c. 789, fos. 127–9; A. Blomfield, *Memoir of Charles James Blomfield* (London, 1864), 77.

[209] A. Burns, *The Diocesan Revival*, 23–32.

clergy.[210] Bishops and archdeacons demanded greater exertion from the parish clergy, insisting, for example, on two services each Sunday instead of the customary single service. Between 1825 and 1831, for example, Henry Ryder increased the number of churches in his diocese offering two Sunday services from 263 to 354—out of a total of some 600 churches. In many dioceses there was also a general shift from quarterly to monthly communions in rural as well as town parishes.[211] Another significant innovation was the revival of the office of rural dean. Rural deans, or heads of small groups of parish priests, nominally ten, had filled an important administrative role in the medieval Church, but the office had fallen into disuse in all but a few dioceses by the eighteenth century. Bishops then began reviving the office after 1800, and by 1830 rural deans were operating in most of the dioceses of the Church of England. Rural deans visited parish churches and monitored their state of repair, scrutinized the conduct of parish clergy and churchwardens, and mediated disputes between clergymen. They could also speak for the parish clergy, articulating their needs and concerns to the bishops.[212]

Another manifestation of diocesan revival was the formation of diocesan societies for the promotion of philanthropic and missionary causes. Thomas Burgess, bishop of the Welsh diocese of St David's, had pioneered this development with the creation in 1804 of the diocesan Church Union Society, for distributing Bibles and tracts, and forming parish libraries and schools.[213] Burgess established a similar society in the diocese of Salisbury following his translation there in 1827. From 1825, responding to the stimulus provided by the parliamentary grants, bishops promoted the formation of diocesan church-building societies, which built hundreds of new churches during the next two decades. The later 1810s also saw the formation of the first diocesan committees for promoting the building of schools. These worked in conjunction with the National Society for the Education of the Poor, which had been formed in 1811 to raise funds for the founding of schools in connection with the established Church.[214]

210 A. Burns, *The Diocesan Revival*, 41–9.

211 Knight, *The Nineteenth-Century Church and English Society*, 76–8, 80; Davies, *The First Evangelical Bishop*, 14.

212 A. Burns, *The Diocesan Revival*, 75–81; Knight, *The Nineteenth-Century Church and English Society*, 177–81.

213 J. S. Harford, *Life of Thomas Burgess* (London, 1840), 227–34.

214 A. Burns, *The Diocesan Revival*, 115–16.

The diocesan reform movement spread from England to Ireland. The Governments of Perceval and Liverpool sought to ensure that Crown presentations to the Irish bench went to men of proven ability, and by the early 1820s there was a new group of resident, mainly High Church Irish bishops, dedicated to strengthening clerical discipline and diocesan administration. They included the High Church scholar Richard Mant, consecrated bishop of Killaloe and Kilfenoragh in 1820, and translated to Down and Connor in 1823, the Oxford scholar Richard Lawrence, consecrated bishop of Cashel in 1822, the High Church theologians John Jebb, consecrated bishop of Limerick in 1822, and William Magee, consecrated archbishop of Dublin in 1822, and the able, generous, cultivated, and well-connected Lord John George Beresford, an Irish bishop since 1805, who was elevated to the archbishopric of Armagh and primacy of the Church of Ireland in 1822.[215] As the Union of 1801 had reduced the representation of the Irish bishops in the House of Lords to four, most Irish bishops now resided more regularly in their dioceses, and gave increased attention to supervising the clergy and visiting parishes. Under Beresford's primacy, Irish bishops used the powers given them by the parliamentary acts of 1808 and 1824 to reduce non-residency, pluralism, and pastoral neglect. After 1800, Irish bishops also revived the office of rural dean; by 1820, rural deans were active in sixteen of the twenty-two Irish dioceses, with an average of six rural deans in each of these sixteen dioceses. Residency continued to improve, from 65.2 per cent of the clergy habitually resident in their parishes in 1819 to 74.8 per cent resident by 1832.[216]

With their increasing residency, Irish bishops and clergymen became more active on boards of local charities and hospitals, and began to show greater concern for all the inhabitants of their dioceses and parishes, Catholics as well as Protestants. Amid the distress of 1816–17, Church of Ireland parsons were conspicuous in local relief efforts. During the famine of 1821–2, Power le Poer Trench, archbishop of Tuam, was said to have purchased at his own expense 40 tons of meal for distribution to the poor of his diocese and to have given £700 to the general charity funds of the town of Tuam.[217]

[215] Akenson, *Church of Ireland*, 131–2; Brynn, *The Church of Ireland*, 77–81; J. Jebb to C. A. Ogilvie, 31 October 1822, Bodl. MS Eng. Lett. d. 123, fos. 49–50.

[216] Akenson, *The Church of Ireland*, 128–9, 131–2.

[217] Swords, *A Hidden Church: The Diocese of Achonry*, 154; J. W. Murray, *Sketches of the Lives and Times of Eminent Irish Churchmen from the Reformation Downwards* (Dublin, 1874), 155.

According to John Jebb, bishop of Limerick, the efforts of the resident-established clergy during the famine saved thousands of lives. 'As collectors and distributors of bounty', Jebb insisted of the Irish clergy, 'as purveyors of food, as parcellers of employment, as overseers of labour, on roads, in bogs, in public works; by their exertions in these and similar departments, the Irish peasantry (under Providence) were saved from famine and its attendant pestilence, and I would hope, were formed to permanent habits of industry, morality, and grateful feeling.'[218] For Jebb, the established clergy had a vital role to play in providing material relief and moral guidance to their parish populations, however small the attendance might be at their Sunday services. 'Throughout the South', he asserted in his episcopal Charge of 1823, 'the clergy have the melancholy pre-eminence of being, I had almost said, the single class to whom the people look up for relief in their distresses, for counsel in their difficulties, and, in too many districts, for common honesty, and civility, in the ordinary transactions of life.' 'Thus situated', he added, 'their influence is, of necessity, very considerable; and, in most parishes, the poorer inhabitants feel, that the rector is to them the most important individual in the neighbourhood.'[219] In those areas of Ireland where the landlords were habitually absentee, the resident parish clergymen increasingly stood in for the landowners, engaging 'in a thousand offices of charity in a country where such ministrations are specially wanted'.[220]

In the Presbyterian Church of Scotland, where there were no dioceses, a corresponding Church reform movement was pursued within the ecclesiastical courts. It began in 1813 with a campaign by the Evangelicals to eliminate the one form of plurality permitted in the Scottish establishment—the union of a parish living with a university chair. The Moderate party had long defended such unions, arguing that they encouraged the parish clergy to provide leadership in the intellectual life of the nation. The Evangelicals, however, insisted that the duties of the parish ministry, if performed with proper diligence, required a minister's full-time efforts. The established clergy, the Evangelicals argued, could not afford to neglect

[218] J. Jebb, *A Speech delivered in the House of Peers, Thursday, June 10, 1824, on Occasion of the Third Reading of the Irish Tithe Composition Amendment Bill* (London, 1824), 78.

[219] J. Jebb, Bishop of Limerick, *A Charge, delivered to the Clergy of the Diocese of Limerick . . . on Thursday, the 19th of June 1823* (Dublin, 1823), 37–8.

[220] 'The Church in Ireland', *Quarterly Review*, 31 (March 1825), 522; R. B. McDowell, *Public Opinion and Government Policy in Ireland 1801–1846* (London, 1952), 22.

their parish duties, especially in the industrializing Lowland towns and cities, where the Church was losing its hold over the people. In 1817, the Evangelical campaign achieved a partial victory when the General Assembly passed a new pluralities act, stipulating that no one holding a university position could also be admitted to a parish living outside the boundaries of the university town, and instructing presbyteries to be strict in disciplining ministers found to be neglecting their parish duties.[221]

The leading figure in the Evangelical campaign against pluralism was the Church of Scotland minister Thomas Chalmers, who in the early 1820s emerged as Britain's foremost proponent of the parish ideal. Having begun his ministry in a small rural parish in Fife, Chalmers was translated to a large Glasgow parish church in 1815. From his arrival, he was deeply disturbed by the conditions in the industrializing city of Glasgow, very different from the close-knit parish communities he had known in Fife. He had never encountered such poverty as he found in his Glasgow parish—families crowded into cold, barren rooms in rat-infested buildings, pervasive drunkenness, children in rags dying of disease and chronic malnutrition. In Glasgow, the traditional parish system with its communal associations had largely broken down. The city churches had little connection with their parish populations, but attracted their mainly middle- and upper-class congregations from throughout the city, while seat rents in the churches effectively excluded the poor. There was no system of parish schools. The care of the poor was largely the responsibility of voluntary societies or of the civic authorities. The costs of poor relief, moreover, were soaring, while conditions for the urban poor seemed to be deteriorating. Chalmers became convinced that the fundamental problem in Glasgow and other large towns was the breakdown of communal spirit, and that the only way to restore this spirit was to adapt the parish system to the new urban environment. In 1819, he convinced the Glasgow town council and magistrates to permit him to conduct an 'experiment' in urban ministry in a new parish, St John's, that was being created in a working-class district of the city.[222] In return for the co-operation of the civic

[221] S. J. Brown, *Thomas Chalmers and the Godly Commonwealth*, 84–8.

[222] For the St John's experiment, ibid. 116–44; A. Cage and E. O. A. Checkland, 'Thomas Chalmers and Urban Poverty: The St. John's Parish Experiment in Glasgow, 1819–1837', *Philosophical Journal* (Glasgow), 13 (1976), 37–56; Mechie, *The Church and Scottish Social Development*, 47–63.

authorities in his experiment, Chalmers promised to eliminate the need for any legal poor relief in the parish, removing all St John's paupers from the civic relief rolls. He would do so by transforming the large city parish into a stable and largely self-sufficient community. Chalmers based his parish plan on two fundamental principles—'territoriality', or the territorial subdivision of his crowded urban parish into more manageable 'proportions', and 'aggression', or regular house-to-house visiting by a parish agency of lay church officers. He first subdivided his parish of St John's, with its population of over 10,000, into twenty-five proportions, each representing a neighbourhood of about 400 inhabitants. He then organized a parish agency of elders and deacons, assigning an elder and deacon to each proportion. They were to engage in 'aggressive' visiting, designed to carry religious and moral influences to every household. The elders were to focus their efforts on the moral and spiritual development of the parishioners, elevating the moral condition of the community. Deacons were to be responsible for the material condition of the parishioners, and especially for the care of the poor. They were to work for the elimination of legal poor relief first by encouraging paupers to recover their independence through labour, thrift, and temperance. For poor persons unable to work, the deacons would appeal for support to the person's extended family and neighbours, and only as a last resort draw from the parish church's modest church-door collection for the poor. The aim was to replace institutional poor-relief with individual self-help and communal benevolence.

Chalmers also introduced other programmes for the elevation of his parishioners. He revived the parish school system, establishing four day schools to provide inexpensive education to children of the parish, with fees waived for the very poor. He organized a parish Sunday school society, with a voluntary Sunday school teacher assigned to establish a school in each proportion of the parish. He began a Sunday evening service, which the labouring poor were encouraged to attend in their working clothes. Finally, he collected contributions and erected a chapel-of-ease to provide additional church accommodation for the parishioners. It was, however, his poor-relief programmes that most attracted outside attention. By 1823, the St John's deacons had managed to remove all St John's paupers from the civic relief rolls, saving Glasgow's ratepayers some £300 a year. For the propertied classes, anxious about the soaring costs of poor relief in industrializing Britain, Chalmers's St John's experiment seemed to offer a humane means to reduce or even eliminate legal poor relief. Further, Chalmers claimed that his parish programmes were based upon a scientific understanding of human nature and political economy. In particular, he invoked the arguments of the English clergyman and political economist T. R. Malthus, who maintained that poverty was the inevitable result of population growth pushing beyond the food supply and creating a large 'redundant' population, which was condemned to a marginal subsistence and early death. The only way to alleviate poverty, Malthus argued, was for people in sufficient numbers to adopt 'moral restraint', voluntarily restricting sexual activity in order to limit population growth. Chalmers insisted that his parish programmes would do just that. They would revive a traditional communal responsibility, by which couples would delay marriage until able to support a family, thus reducing their child-bearing years. He maintained that in Scottish rural districts in the previous century the parish system had proved effective in preserving communal responsibility, limiting population growth, and ensuring the decent care of the poor. It was only with the breakdown of the parish system that both population and poor-relief costs had begun their upward spiral. Chalmers's parish ideas won the warm support of his mentor. 'I consider you as my ablest and best ally,' Malthus wrote to Chalmers in July 1822.[223]

Between 1819 and 1826, Chalmers published a three-volume work, *The Christian and Civic Economy of Large Towns*, in which he described his experiment in the urban ministry and developed his arguments in support of established Churches.[224] Only through the principles of 'aggression' and 'territoriality', he maintained, could Christian communities be restored in the new industrial towns and cities. As people had no natural taste or inclination for religion and morality, religious and moral influences had to be brought to them through regular, 'aggressive', house-to-house visiting. Only established churches possessed the legal authority to conduct such aggressive visiting. The parish programmes he had developed in Glasgow,

[223] T. R. Malthus to T. Chalmers, 21 July 1822, Thomas Chalmers Papers, New College Library, Edinburgh CHA 4.21.51.

[224] T. Chalmers, *The Christian and Civic Economy of Large Towns* (1819–26), repr. as *The Christian and Economic Polity of a Nation* in *The Collected Works of Thomas Chalmers*, 25 vols. (Glasgow, 1835–42), vols. xiv–xvi.

he further argued, were applicable not only to the Presbyterian establishment in Scotland, but also to the English and Irish establishments. The Episcopal Churches could readily appoint parish visitors similar to the St John's elders and deacons. Through a proper parochial system, he insisted, legal poor relief could be eliminated and social harmony restored throughout all three kingdoms. He found encouragement from the Clapham Evangelicals in England. Wilberforce recommended Chalmers's social writings to Lord Liverpool in 1820, and Chalmers's St John's experiment and parish programmes attracted broad interest in the English establishment.[225] Here was a further argument for building more established Churches in the industrializing towns and cities—an argument that claimed to be based on the latest teachings of political economy and to be 'scientifically' verified through social experimentation.

Chalmers's *Christian and Civic Economy* also marked a major contribution to the movement within the established Church to Christianize the discipline of political economy. From the early years of the nineteenth century a number of Church of England clergymen, among them Thomas Malthus, John Bird Sumner, Edward Copleston, and Richard Whately, had been endeavouring to show that the teachings of the political economists—including the self-regulating market, the emphasis on rational individualism, the limited wage-fund, the inevitability of inequality and poverty, and the competition for limited resources—were consistent with a providential world order emphasizing individual responsibility and free moral choice. The project reached the height of its influence in the 1820s, as the economy was recovering from the post-war depression and the established Churches were embracing a new sense of mission.[226] It was perhaps no accident that Chalmers's St John's experiment coincided with the first phase of State-supported church-building. His parish ideal profoundly influenced some of those bishops active in the early diocesan reform movement. John Bird Sumner, bishop of Chester and Christian political economist, embraced many of Chalmers's ideas. In his first episcopal *Charge* to

[225] W. Wilberforce to Lord Liverpool, 16 September 1820, BL Add. MSS 38191, fos. 274–9; Carless-Davis, *The Age of Grey and Peel*, 152–4; Hilton, *The Age of Atonement*, 55–60; Best, *Temporal Pillars*, 155n.

[226] A. M. C. Waterman, *Revolution, Economics and Religion: Christian Political Economy 1798–1833* (Cambridge, 1991); Hilton, *The Age of Atonement*, 36–70; Norman, *Church and Society in England*, 41–7.

his clergy at Chester in 1829, he recommended the creation of district-visiting societies of lay parochial visitors who would conduct regular house-to-house visiting on Chalmers's principle of 'aggression'.[227] By 1828, Charles James Blomfield, the new bishop of London, was arguing that charity tended to corrupt the morals of the poor and that Christian philanthropy should be directed towards building new churches. These churches would in turn shape Christian communities that would eliminate the need for much institutional poor relief. He also began cautiously recommending that the London clergy introduce lay visitors on Chalmers's model.[228]

While some followed Chalmers in looking to political economy for arguments in support of the parochial establishments, others were invoking a romantic vision of the past, celebrating the role of the established Churches in shaping national identity. There was, to be sure, a romantic element in Chalmers's parish ideal, reflected in his descriptions of a traditional communal morality that he claimed had permeated rural Scotland a century before. His descriptions of simple, virtuous peasants and close-knit parish communities united under the influence of well-loved ministers and schoolmasters were more myth than reality, but they appealed to a public being influenced by the historical novels of Chalmers's fellow countryman, Sir Walter Scott. In 1822 the English poet William Wordsworth published his *Ecclesiastical Sketches*, a series of 102 sonnets providing meditations on the history of Christianity in England, and more particularly on the Church of England as an expression of the highest religious aspirations of the nation.[229] A revolutionary idealist in his youth, Wordsworth had by about 1820 found his way to the conservative High Church piety of his brother, Christopher Wordsworth, a prominent figure in the Hackney Phalanx. His sonnets celebrated the English Church in history, its first missionaries, its Saxon monasteries, its Reformation martyrs, its persecutions and its triumphs, its sacraments and its pastoral care, its cathedrals and ruined abbeys. The *Sketches* were an expression of a romantic

[227] J. B. Sumner, *Charge addressed to the Clergy of the Diocese of Chester at the Primary Visitation in August and September 1829*, 23–4, 32–9; N. Scotland, *John Bird Sumner, Evangelical Archbishop* (Leominster 1995), 54, 105; Soloway, *Prelates and People*, 321; Best, *Temporal Pillars*, 163.

[228] Soloway, *Prelates and People*, 150–1, 322–3.

[229] S. Gilley, 'John Keble and the Victorian Churching of Romanticism', in J. R. Watson (ed.), *An Infinite Complexity: Essays in Romanticism* (Edinburgh, 1983), 229–30; S. Gill, *William Wordsworth: A Life* (Oxford, 1989), 342–4.

English patriotism, presenting the Church as an elevating and ennobling presence, uniting the nation in reverence for ideals that transcended selfish interests. The sonnet 'Pastoral Care', for example, celebrated the ideal of the resident parish incumbent, 'the learned pastor' set amid a rural parish, providing 'a genial hearth, a hospitable board, and a refined rusticity' and 'meek and patient as a sheathèd sword'. Yet in the pulpit, 'arrayed in Christ's authority', meekness falls away as he 'lifts his awful hand'

> For re-subjecting to divine command
> The stubborn spirit of rebellious man.

Four of the sonnets commemorated the church-building movement. In the first of these, 'New Churches', the church-building movement becomes the highest purpose of the State, transcending even the glory of its victory over Napoleonic France. The new churches are channels for irrigating the land with spiritual influence, bringing life to what must otherwise be desert.

> But liberty, and triumphs on the main,
> And laurelled armies—not to be withstood,
> What serve they, if, on transitory good
> Intent, and sedulous of abject gain.
> The state (ah surely not preserved in vain!)
> Forbear to shape due channels which the flood
> Of sacred truth may enter—till it brood
> O'er the wide realm, as o'er the Egyptian plain
> The all-sustaining Nile. No more—the time
> Is conscious of her want; through England's bounds
> In rival haste, the wished for temples rise!
> I hear their Sabbath bells' harmonious chime
> Float on the breeze—the heavenliest of all sounds
> That hill or vale prolongs or multiplies!

While Wordsworth was composing his *Ecclesiastical Sketches*, his friend, the romantic poet Robert Southey, a former republican idealist who had embraced a High Church piety about 1810, was writing his own apology for the Anglican establishment, *The Book of the Church*, which he described 'as a running commentary' upon Wordsworth's series of sonnets.[230] Published in two volumes in early 1824, *The Book of the Church* provided a history of the Church of

[230] R. Southey to G. C. Bedford, 15 April 1821, cited in C. C. Southey, *The Life and Correspondence of Robert Southey*, 6 vols. (London, 1850), v. 65.

England from its beginnings in Roman England up through the Glorious Revolution of 1688, when the Protestant constitution of Church and State was at last consolidated. For Southey, the established Church was the expression of the highest ideals of the English people, the conscience of the nation, the guardian of English liberties and civilization against heathenism, superstition, and tyranny.[231] His book sought to awaken the educated classes to the value of their establishment. 'Manifold as are the blessings', Southey proclaimed in opening his book, 'for which Englishmen are beholden to the institutions of their country, there is no part of those institutions from which they derive more important advantages than from its Church Establishment, none by which the temporal condition of all ranks has been so materially improved.'[232] 'We owe to it', he continued, 'our moral and intellectual character as a nation; much of our private happiness, much of our public strength.'[233] Three years later, in 1827, Anglicanism was further celebrated with the publication of *The Christian Year* by the romantic conservative Oxford scholar and curate of Hursley, John Keble. Written in the tradition of the great seventeenth-century Anglican poets Henry Vaughan and George Herbert, Keble's work was an extended meditation on the Book of Common Prayer, a series of poems commemorating the days of the Christian calendar, each opening with the Scripture passage recommended for that day in the Prayer Book. A High Churchman, Keble portrayed a natural world permeated by Christian imagery, a world in decay awaiting its redeemer—with the Anglican Prayer Book providing a key to understanding the mysteries of creation.[234] He contributed to a reconciliation of the High Church and Evangelical movements, bringing to High Churchism, 'the emotions of Evangelicalism, while he avoided angry collisions with Evangelical opinions'.[235] In *The Christian Year*, John Henry Newman later recalled, 'Keble struck an original note and woke up in the hearts

[231] S. Gilley, 'Nationality and Liberty, Protestant and Catholic: Robert Southey's Book of the Church', in S. Mews (ed.), *Religion and National Identity, Studies in Church History*, 18 (Oxford, 1982), 418–22; D. Pym, 'The Idea of Church and State in the Thought of Three Principal Lake Poets: Coleridge, Southey and Wordsworth', *Durham University Journal*, 83 (1991), 19–26.

[232] R. Southey, *The Book of the Church*, 2 vols. (London, 1824), i. 1.

[233] Southey, *Book of the Church*, ii. 528.

[234] G. Rowell, *The Vision Glorious: Themes and Personalities of the Catholic Revival in Anglicanism* (Oxford, 1983), 26–31; Nockles, *Oxford Movement in Context*, 197.

[235] J. A. Froude, *Short Studies on Great Subjects*, iv. 265.

of thousands a new music, the music of a school, long unknown in England.'[236]

In 1825 the romantic poet and theologian Samuel Taylor Coleridge began writing one of the most cogent apologies for the established Church to emerge from the revival years.[237] Like Wordsworth and Southey, Coleridge had been a republican idealist in his youth in the 1790s, but by the 1820s had embraced a conservative High Anglicanism. His *On the Constitution of the Church and State*, published in 1829, explored the idea behind the established Church. For Coleridge, the realm consisted of three estates—the first estate, or landowners, the second estate, or merchants and manufacturers, and the third estate, or National Church. The first estate, with its fixed landed property, represented permanency and stability. The second estate, with its entrepreneurial spirit and productive capacities, represented progress and personal freedom. But most important of all was the third estate, the National Church, which provided the ultimate cultural grounding for the first two estates, resolving the tensions between permanency and progress, ensuring harmony and peace in society. The National Church was an independent corporate body, which represented the idea of cultivation, of 'the harmonious developement of those qualities and faculties that characterise our *humanity*'.[238] Its purpose was 'to form and train up the people of the country to obedient, free, useful, organizable subjects, citizens, and patriots, living to the benefit of the state, and prepared to die for its defence'.[239] It was a permanent social body, dedicated to the cultivation of mind and the transmission of knowledge.

For Coleridge, perhaps the most important feature of the National Church was its parochial system, by which it divided the entire country into small territorial districts, placing in each district a learned person, whose sole responsibility was the moral, intellectual, and spiritual cultivation of the inhabitants of that parish. The parish clergy not only provided religious and moral instruction, but also served as moral examples to the community. The National

[236] J. H. Newman, *Apologia Pro Vita Sua*, Modern Library Edition (New York, 1950), 47.

[237] 'It was', observed Stephen Prickett, 'a defence of the old order . . . rather than a reconstruction of a new'; *Romanticism and Religion: The Tradition of Coleridge and Wordsworth in the Victorian Church* (Cambridge, 1976), 255; P. Allen, 'S. T. Coleridge's *Church and State* and the Idea of an Intellectual Establishment', *Journal of the History of Ideas*, 46 (1985), 89–106.

[238] S. T. Coleridge, *On the Constitution of the Church and State* (1829), ed. J. Colmer (London, 1976), 42–3.

[239] Ibid. 54.

Church was not supported by taxes levied on the other two estates; it had its own fixed property, the tithes or teinds, and was thus an independent spiritual force.[240] Unfortunately much of the fixed property of the National Church had been 'wrongfully' alienated at the Reformation, and this had undermined the Church's spiritual independence and weakened its ability to fulfil its task of cultivating parish communities.[241] The State therefore now had an obligation to redress that historic wrong by directing new public money to Church reform and church extension, and to restoring the parish system.

The new intellectual vitality of established Christianity found expression at Oxford University in the 1820s.[242] In the early 1820s Oriel College, which had previously led the development of competitive examinations in the University, became home to a brilliant circle of scholars, including Edward Copleston, Richard Whately, Edward Hawkins, Renn Dickson Hampden, and Joseph Blanco White. Also included were Thomas Arnold and John Keble, who had resigned their Oriel fellowships for parish livings in the early 1820s but retained connections with the college. Dubbed the Noetics, or free-thinkers, because of their passionate love for debate, the Oriel circle brought a new intellectual militancy to the University as a whole, including an unwillingness to be bound by old dogmas and an insistence upon subjecting time-honoured assumptions to rigorous scrutiny. To this they added a commitment to reviving the influence of the established Church. Their intellectual defence of the established Church was given an added urgency by perceived threats to the faith emanating from the biblical and historical scholarship emerging from the German universities.[243] The original Oriel circle was joined in the mid-1820s by a promising set of younger fellows, among them John Henry Newman, Richard Hurrell Froude, Edward Bouverie Pusey, and Robert Isaac Wilberforce. These younger Oriel men shared with the older Noetics a loyalty to the establishment and love for controversy, but added a warmer, more emotional piety and a strong commitment to

[240] J. Morrow, 'The National Church in Coleridge's *Church and State*: A Response to Allen', *Journal of the History of Ideas*, 47 (1986), 646–52.

[241] Coleridge, *On the Constitution of the Church and State*, 52–3.

[242] For the renaissance at Oxford, see the brilliant brief sketch by David Newsome in *The Parting of Friends: A Study of the Wilberforces and Henry Manning* (London, 1966), 62–70.

[243] H. J. Rose, *The State of the Protestant Religion in Germany* (London, 1826); J. W. Burgon, *Lives of Twelve Good Men* (London, 1891), 71.

the pastoral ministry of the Church; most of them reportedly knew Keble's *The Christian Year* by heart.[244] The influence of Oriel spread to other Oxford colleges, aided by a growing sense of corporate identity within the University as a whole in the 1820s. The new idealism included a commitment to making the established Church a force for the moral and spiritual elevation of the nation. Keble had set an example of pastoral commitment when in 1823 he had resigned his Oriel fellowship for the curacy in the rural parish of Southrop near Fairford.[245] In 1828, Newman was appointed vicar of St Mary the Virgin in Oxford, where he inspired students with his high sense of the pastoral priesthood. Nor was this new zeal for the parish priesthood confined to Oxford. Trinity College, Cambridge, home to Julius Hare and Connop Thirlwall, formed another centre for disseminating a practical Anglican divinity. In 1826, Hugh James Rose delivered a series of lectures on 'The Commission and Consequent Duties of the Clergy' at Cambridge University—presenting a high view of the sacred responsibilities of the parish priest, including the priest's responsibility before God for the eternal fate of each of his parishioners. 'If, indeed,' Rose observed, 'it will be a hard task at that awful day [of judgement] for every man to give an account of his own soul, what a task is theirs of whom God will require an account of the souls of other men!'[246] Here was both a revival of the ancient catholic doctrine of the priesthood and an awesome vision to inspire the younger priests filling the new churches being erected across the land.

There were also new ventures for the education of the Anglican clergy. In 1816, George Law, bishop of Chester, founded the College of St Bees in Cumberland as a seminary for men who could not afford to attend Oxford or Cambridge. Six years later Thomas Burgess, bishop of St David's, founded St David's College, Lampeter, for the same purpose, receiving a gift of £1,000 from George IV.[247] The founding in 1828 of the non-denominational University of London, with no teaching in theology—what Hugh James Rose

[244] D. Newsome, *Godliness and Good Learning: Four Studies on a Victorian Idea* (London, 1961), 16.

[245] For Keble's ideal of community, see J. H. L. Rowlands, *Church, State and Society: The Attitudes of John Keble, Richard Hurrell Froude and John Henry Newman, 1827–1845* (Worthing, 1989), 27–43.

[246] H. J. Rose, *The Commission and Consequent Duties of the Clergy*, 4th edn. (London, 1847), 149.

[247] Harford, *Life of Thomas Burgess*, 293–4, 318–22, 328–37, 355.

dubbed as 'Godless Gower Street' in the *British Critic*—antagonized High Anglicans, and the Hackney Phalanx took the lead in establishing a new Anglican college in the capital. In June 1828, supporters held a public meeting in London, with ten Anglican bishops, the prime ministers, and other leaders of Church and State on the platform, to appeal for funds, and King's College, London, was founded later that year and opened in 1831. In 1829 the High Church party began planning a similar Anglican college in the north, which led to the opening of Durham University in 1833.[248]

In Scotland, Thomas Chalmers was instilling a new spirit at quiet St Andrews University, where he had gone to teach moral philosophy after leaving the Glasgow parish ministry in 1823. At his crowded lectures on moral philosophy and political economy he aroused student enthusiasm for the programmes in parish ministry that he had developed in Glasgow. Further, he encouraged his students to establish local Sunday schools for children and Bible classes for adults, and conduct house-to-house visiting among the labouring orders in St Andrews. 'Such a change', wrote one of Chalmers's St Andrews students to his father on 15 December 1824, 'I did not certainly expect to see in my day. On the whole, our college seems at present to present an aspect something similar to that of the University of Oxford in the days of Hervey and Wesley.'[249] Chalmers also pressed for extensive university reforms in Scotland, including the abolition of all remaining pluralities, improved university patronage, and better administration of university funds. In 1825, he described the university chair as a fulcrum for elevating the nation: '"Give me, said Archimedes, a place where to stand, and I will move the world". Now, such a place is a college pulpit. That is a spot on which I desire to stand, and move the moral and spiritual world through the youth of our land.'[250] Chalmers's calls for university reform contributed in 1826 to the Government's decision to appoint a Royal Commission of Inquiry into the Scottish Universities. In 1828, he was appointed to the Chair of Divinity at the University of Edinburgh, arguably the most influential position in the Scottish establishment. His aim was to prepare zealous pastors, with a firm understanding of political economy and social ethics, who would

[248] A. B. Webster, *Joshua Watson*, 44–6; Varley, *Last of the Prince Bishops*, 149–79.

[249] W. Orme, *Memoirs of John Urquhart* (Philadelphia, 1855), 69–70.

[250] *Report of the Debate of the General Assembly of the Church of Scotland on the Overtures anent the Union of Offices* (Edinburgh, 1825), 17.

carry to all the parishes of Scotland the programmes in house-to-house visiting, education, and poor-relief reform that he had pioneered in Glasgow. As in Oxford, students at Edinburgh embraced the ideal of the resident parish incumbent, the clerical scholar who would bring cultivation, communal values, and Christian knowledge to his parishioners.[251]

'In no other age and no other country can any parallel to these things be found,' enthused Robert Southey of the Church revival movement in the *Quarterly Review* in 1820. 'In no other age and no other country have there ever been seen such desires on the part of government, and such exertions on the part of the higher ranks for bettering the condition of the people.'[252] By the mid-1820s, the revived confidence and sense of purpose in the established Churches was making its influence felt in society, especially among the middle and upper social orders. Writing to a friend in 1824, Southey observed that those among his acquaintances who had been 'unbelievers some thirty years ago' were now, for the most part, 'settled in conformity with the belief of the national Church' and that there was 'less [infidelity] in the higher classes than at any time since the Restoration'.[253] The Church reform movement initiated in Parliament in the early years of the century and associated in particular with the assassinated Evangelical prime minister, Spencer Perceval, had brought substantial improvements in clerical residence in the English and Irish establishments, and improved conditions for the poorer clergy in all three established Churches. The church-building campaign stimulated by the parliamentary grants of 1818 and 1824 was adding scores of new churches in England and the Scottish Highlands. Through the diocesan reform movements in the English and Irish Churches, and the parochial reform movement in the Scottish establishment, leaders within the Churches had taken up the cause of reform and were working for continued improvements in clerical residency, discipline, and pastoral care. The writings in defence of the establishments by Chalmers and the Christian political economists, by Wordsworth, Southey, Coleridge, and the romantics, appealed to social science, national identity, and romantic feeling, and developed sophisticated arguments in support of the

[251] For the influence of this ideal at Oxford, see Newsome, *The Parting of Friends*, 70.
[252] [R. Southey], 'New Churches', *Quarterly Review*, 23 (July 1820), 580.
[253] Southey, *The Life and Correspondence of Robert Southey*, v. 185–6.

parish system. The established Church ideal was gaining a new intellectual respectability. More and more young men were attracted into the ministry. In the Church of England the number of ordinands rose from an average of 277 a year between 1800 and 1809, to an average of 387 a year between 1809 and 1819 and an average of 531 a year between 1820 and 1829.[254] In his evidence before the Royal Commission on the Scottish Universities in August 1827, Chalmers pointed to a similar increase in the numbers seeking ordination in the Church of Scotland, to the point where there were five times more students of divinity in the Scottish universities than there were vacancies in the Church.[255] Party divisions grew muted by the 1820s, as High Anglicans, Scottish Moderates, and English, Irish, and Scottish Evangelicals alike found common ground in their shared commitment to improving the parish ministry and strengthening parish communities. The parish was at the centre of the reform movement. The aim was to organize the whole of the three kingdoms, from Portsmouth to Wick, from Galway to Norwich, into living parish communities, each with its resident clergyman and its parish church disseminating a common set of religious and moral teachings.

Probably the most striking characteristic of the Church reform and Church extension movement between about 1808 and 1828 was the close co-operation between Church and State. The State had taken the lead in the reform movement and had invested unprecedented amounts of public money in strengthening the established Churches. 'Certainly, in the years immediately prior to 1828', the historian Peter Nockles has recently observed of the Church of England, '. . . the union of church and state appeared to be working more in the church's interests . . . than at any time since the reign of Charles II.'[256] There was a concerted effort by both Parliament and Church authorities in all three kingdoms to roll back the gains made by Dissent in the decades of the revolutionary and Napoleonic wars. The liberal Tory Governments of Perceval and Liverpool had been most forward in this movement, and underlying their effort there can be discerned a view that the parochial structures of the established Churches could contribute to the process of nation-building

[254] Virgin, *The Church in an Age of Negligence*, 136, 165.

[255] *Parliamentary Papers*, Reports from Commissioners, Universities (Scotland): 3. St. Andrews, 1837 (94), xxxvii. 65–75.

[256] Nockles, *Oxford Movement in Context*, 64.

in the three kingdoms. The Union of 1801 had brought Britain and Ireland together in a unitary parliamentary monarchy. But the act of Union had not created a nation. Here, then, was a task for the religious establishments. They would educate the diverse peoples of England, Wales, Ireland, and Scotland in shared Protestant religious and moral values, including loyalty to the powers that be. They would help to form national character, to define a common language of discourse, to inculcate civic virtues, to inspire people with national causes, and ensure that national ideals would be transmitted from generation to generation. Their church bells would ring out national triumphs; from their pulpits, the nation would speak in its religious aspect; in their reviving parish schools, a new generation would be imbued with a Christian national identity. As both Chalmers and Coleridge had recognized, the establishments would form citizens of the United Kingdom as well as Christians. The parochial establishments would mould the diverse peoples of the three historic kingdoms into a single nation-state, discouraging Dissent and dampening the millenarian enthusiasms of the revolutionary era, restoring public order, and building upon the triumph over Revolutionary and Napoleonic France to achieve at last the ideal of the Protestant nation. And if the Church reform movement was achieving success in Britain, including the dissemination of established Christianity in formerly Catholic and pagan districts of the remote Scottish Highlands, in Ireland the early 1820s brought signs of an even greater triumph—nothing less than the conversion of the Irish Catholic population to the Protestantism of the established Church.

2

'Second Reformation': The Struggle for the Religion of Ireland, 1822–1833

The Scripture Education Movement

On 24 October 1822, William Magee, the recently appointed archbishop of Dublin, presented his first charge to the clergy of his archdiocese. Speaking in Dublin's St Patrick's Cathedral, he called attention to the attacks being directed against the established clergy through the 'malevolence' of anti-tithe agitators and radical reformers. The clergy, he insisted, were 'beset with difficulties and perils' and 'more than usual hostility prevails against our Zion'. On the whole, he continued, the established clergy were men of blameless lives, undeserving of the attacks falling heavily upon them. Recent years had brought dramatic improvements in clerical discipline, residency, and pastoral commitment; indeed, 'at no time within the memory of any now living, has the Established Clergy, as a Body, been less deserving of reproach than at present'. In one sense, however, the established clergy did have to bear some responsibility for 'that irreligion, which now too fatally prevails among our people'. For despite their improved discipline and commitment, most established clergymen were, Magee believed, too conciliatory, too anxious to maintain peaceful relations with Roman Catholics and Dissenters; they were not sufficiently zealous in their divine commission as ministers of the one catholic and apostolic Church in Ireland. 'Fearful of incurring the charge of bigotry', the clergy did not contend vigorously 'for the *apostolic origin and succession of the Christian ministry*; the only ground on which the just rights of the Church can be maintained'. The time had now come for the established clergy to put aside compromise and accommodation, and embrace a mission to reclaim the Irish masses who were largely sunk in religious error. The established clergy must recover a sense of responsibility for the religious and moral instruction of the whole

Irish people; they must become militant, and work to bring the entire Irish population into conformity with the United Church of England and Ireland. In fulfilling their commission, the established clergy must boldly denounce the errors of both the Roman Catholics on the one side and the Presbyterian Dissenters on the other:

> We, my Revd Brethren, are placed in a station, in which we are hemmed in by two opposite descriptions of professing Christians: the one, possessing a Church, without what *we* can properly call a Religion; and the other possessing a religion, without what *we* can properly call a Church: the one so blindly enslaved to a supposed infallible Ecclesiastical authority, as not to seek in the Word of God a reason for the faith they profess; the other, so confident in the infallibility of their individual judgement as to the reasons of their faith, that they deem it their duty to resist all authority in matters of religion.[1]

It was not enough for the Church of Ireland to be content to be the guardian of the truth, to hold the *via media* between the two extremes; the time had come for it to evangelize among both groups. The most effective means for this work, moreover, was a committed parish ministry. The clergy must reside in their parishes, developing close connections with the people, working to create a sense of community, and above all seeking to draw all inhabitants of Ireland within its fold: 'The true relation of the Clergy to the people (it cannot be too often repeated) is a *pastoral* one.' Only through an effective pastoral ministry would the Church of Ireland become in truth the national Church of the Irish people.

Magee's first Charge was reported widely in the Irish press. Here was one of the new breed of bishops, an accomplished theologian and a High Churchman with close connections to the Hackney Phalanx, a man representing the spirit of the reform movement in the established Churches of the three kingdoms, issuing a call to action to the clergy of the United Church in Ireland. A native of Enniskillen, in Ulster, Magee had been born to an impoverished linen merchant and his Presbyterian wife in 1766. Entering Trinity College, Dublin, in 1781, he had an outstanding academic career, becoming a fellow of the College in 1788 and publishing an effective treatise on the doctrine of atonement in 1801. Committed from

[1] W. Magee, *A Charge delivered at his Primary Visitation, in St Patrick's Cathedral, Dublin, on Thursday, the 27th of October, 1822* (London, 1822), 5, 12–13, 25–6.

childhood to the 'British constitution and the established Church' as two great symbols of 'order and stability', and advanced for his talent rather than his connections, Magee was consecrated bishop of Raphoe in 1819 and then translated to Dublin in 1822.[2] At one level, Magee's first Charge in Dublin was defensive in tone, reflecting the concerns of a beleaguered established Church under threat from anti-tithe agitators and a more confident Catholic Church.[3] But this champion of the established order in Church and State did not seek only for the preservation of the existing tithes, properties, and privileges of the established Church—or for peaceful coexistence with the Catholic majority and the Presbyterians. Rather, he called for a bold denunciation of the religious 'errors' of Catholics and Presbyterians, and a concerted effort through the parochial system and pastoral ministry to bring most of the Irish population into conformity with the established Church. He did not see himself as formulating new policy in his Charge of 1822. He was expressing the aims of the Church reform movement that had begun in the early years of the nineteenth century, with improvements in clerical residency and discipline, and with grants of public money for repairing churches and building glebe-houses. He summoned the clergy of his archdiocese to build upon the achievements of the reform movement and expand their authority over the religious and moral life of the whole nation.[4] For Magee, the established Church in Ireland now had the potential to succeed where the sixteenth-century Irish Reformation had failed; there was a real opportunity to unite the Irish people within the true Protestant faith. And many were prepared to take up his call for a new militancy on the part of the established Church. 'My friend and tutor the Archbishop of Dublin has just delivered a most admirable Charge', John Jebb informed his friend Charles Ogilvie of Balliol College, Oxford, on 31 October 1822, 'from which, and from his practical following up of the principles advanced in it, I cannot but augur the happiest results.'[5]

[2] For Magee, see A. H. Kenney, 'Memoir of William Magee', in *Works of William Magee*, 2 vols. (London, 1842), pp. i, ix–lxxx; Liechty, 'Irish Evangelicalism, Trinity College Dublin, and the Mission of the Church of Ireland', 250–312; [J. Wills], 'William Magee, Archbishop of Dublin', *Dublin University Magazine*, 26 (Oct. 1845), 480–93; 28 (Dec. 1846), 750–67.

[3] J. Hill, *From Patriots to Unionists: Dublin Civic Politics and Irish Protestant Patriotism, 1660–1840* (Oxford, 1997), 330–5.

[4] Bowen, *The Protestant Crusade in Ireland*, 92–3.

[5] J. Jebb to C. A. Ogilvie, 31 October 1822, Bodl MS Eng. Lett. d. 123, fos. 49–50.

Others, however, were less happy with Magee's Charge, which was viewed by Irish commentators as a declaration of 'religious war'.[6] Magee's remarks seemed particularly provocative, coming as they did at a time of heightened religious and political strife. Agricultural distress in the south and west was fuelling a violent popular campaign against the payment of tithe, and the conflict had already resulted in loss of life. The growing political movement for Catholic Emancipation in both Britain and Ireland was contributing to violent confrontations between Orangemen and Catholics in the north of Ireland. Magee's Charge caused offence to both Presbyterians and Catholics, but the most vigorous response came from Irish Catholics and liberal Protestant advocates of Catholic Emancipation.[7] 'The Catholics have a Church, without a Religion,' thundered the liberal *Dublin Evening Post*, 'We do not remember any thing so thoroughly offensive to the people of Ireland . . . Such a charge, coming from such a man, must strike home, wound deeply and rankle long.'[8] Catholic leaders publicly condemned Magee's Charge; insults were exchanged between Protestants and Catholics on the streets of Dublin and relations between the communities grew increasingly strained.[9] When on 6 November a severed calf's head was thrown upon the altar of a Catholic chapel in Ardee, Patrick Curtis, the Catholic archbishop of Armagh and primate of Ireland, asserted publicly that Magee's Charge had incited the outrage.[10] As the symbol of the new militancy of the established Church, Magee became a hated figure among the Catholics of Ireland—so much so that he soon feared to leave his residence without being armed.[11] Daniel O'Connell would even claim in a public speech that the fact that Magee 'walked unharmed' was proof against the imputation that the Irish people were prone to assassinate their enemies.[12]

[6] Hill, *From Patriots to Unionists*, 334.

[7] W. D. Killen, *The Ecclesiastical History of Ireland*, 2 vols. (London, 1875), ii. 420–1; R. S. Brooke, *Recollections of the Irish Church* (London, 1877), 19.

[8] *Dublin Evening Post*, 29 October 1822.

[9] W. J. Fitzpatrick, *Life, Times and Correspondence of the Rt. Rev. Dr. Doyle, Bishop of Kildare and Leighlin*, 2 vols. (Boston, 1869), i. 214–30; J. MacHale, *Letters of John MacHale, Archbishop of Tuam* (Dublin, 1893), 121–37.

[10] *Dublin Evening Post*, 12, 16, 21 November 1822.

[11] W. Magee to J. Jebb, 29 May 1824, Trinity College, Dublin, Jebb Papers, MS 6396–7/196.

[12] [J. Wills], 'William Magee, Archbishop of Dublin', *Dublin University Magazine*, 28 (Dec. 1846), 760.

Perhaps the most effective response to Magee came from James Doyle, who only three years previously had been appointed Catholic bishop of Kildare and Leighlin. Doyle had served as an interpreter with the British army during the Peninsular campaign, and had personal connections with the Marquess Wellesley, the lord-lieutenant of Ireland. Having witnessed as a boy the atrocities that had followed the rising of 1798, he had developed an abhorrence of sectarian violence and intolerance. An intelligent man who was committed to achieving practical benefits for Irish Catholics within the Union, Doyle represented a new, more confident mood in Irish Catholicism.[13] In a letter to the *Dublin Evening Post*, Doyle challenged Magee's claim that the established Church was the true catholic and apostolic Church in Ireland, with an exclusive commission to preach the word, administer the sacraments, and provide pastoral care to the Irish people. For Doyle, the established Church in Ireland was merely a national Church, exercising at best a local ministry, with no warrant to claim the title of catholic or universal. Further, Doyle denied that the established clergy in Ireland could demonstrate an authority based on apostolic succession. To Magee, he threw out the challenge:

> As an Archbishop of the Established Church, I would beg leave to ask you, my Lord, who are you, and where did you come from? What Earth produced you? Turn over the records of your Church, tell us the names of the Bishops who preceded you; show us how they were connected with the Apostles, or with those who received the Faith from them. Produce your claim to that title of 'Apostolic', which you so ostentatiously put forth.[14]

After 1822, Doyle emerged as the principal spokesperson for Irish Catholicism, and the leading opponent of the movement proclaimed by Magee for expanding the authority of the established Church among Irish Catholics.

The controversy surrounding Magee's Charge was an early episode in a period of intense religious struggle in Ireland during the 1820s, which would have profound consequences not only for the

[13] Doyle has been well served by biographers. See W. J. Fitzpatrick, *The Life, Times, and Correspondence of the Right Rev. Dr Doyle, Bishop of Kildare and Leighlin*, 2 vols. [1st edn., Dublin, 1861] (Boston, 1869); T. McGrath, *Religious Renewal and Reform in the Pastoral Ministry of Bishop James Doyle of Kildare and Leighlin, 1786–1834* (Dublin, 1999), and T. McGrath, *Politics, Interdenominational Relations and Education in the Public Ministry of Bishop James Doyle of Kildare and Leighlin, 1786–1834* (Dublin, 1999).

[14] *Dublin Evening Post*, 7 November 1822.

established Church in Ireland but also for the established Churches in Britain. The next five years witnessed a vigorous effort on the part of many supporters of the established Church to build on the achievements of the early nineteenth-century reform movement and to achieve a 'New Reformation' or a 'Second Reformation' in Ireland—that is, to succeed where the sixteenth-century Reformation had failed, and to gain at last the conformity of the large majority of the Irish people to Protestantism, and more particularly to the United Church of England and Ireland. It was a movement that united the Irish Evangelical and High Church parties in a common cause, and which captured the attention and aroused the enthusiasm of religious and political leaders in Britain. The New Reformation movement of the 1820s involved the combined efforts of voluntary Bible and educational societies, of parish clergymen and bishops, and of prominent members of the Irish landed classes. For a brief period in the 1820s, it seemed that the established Church might well achieve the ascendancy over the religious, moral, and intellectual life of Ireland that had eluded it at the sixteenth-century Reformation. The parliamentary and diocesan reforms of the first two decades of the nineteenth century would now bear fruit. The established Church would break the hold of the Catholic Church over Ireland and assert its authority over the religious and moral instruction of the Irish people. This in turn would be a triumph for the establishment principle in all three kingdoms, and a major step towards the goal of integrating the three kingdoms into a single nation-state with a shared set of religious and moral values. At the same time, the New Reformation movement aroused vehement opposition from Irish Catholics, who had no intention of relinquishing their Faith and conforming to what they regarded as an alien Church. The New Reformation intensified the political pressure in Ireland for Catholic Emancipation and contributed to the popular support for the Catholic Association organized in May 1823, some six months after the delivery of Magee's Charge, by the Catholic barristers Daniel O'Connell and Richard Lalor Sheil.

While many would later view Magee's Charge of 1822 as marking the beginning of the New Reformation movement, Evangelicals in the Church of Ireland had been treating Catholic Ireland as a mission field from at least the beginning of the nineteenth century, with the rising of 1798 stimulating Protestant missionary efforts.[15] The early Evangelical missions in Ireland had been conducted largely through extra-parochial voluntary societies, and had involved co-operation between British and Irish Evangelicals. Believing that Irish Catholics were deprived of access to the Scriptures by a combination of illiteracy and the opposition of the Catholic priests to the free circulation of the Bible, Evangelicals had concentrated their efforts on distributing Bibles and supporting Scripture-based educational ventures. One of the earliest of the Evangelical societies in connection with the established Church of Ireland was the Association for Discountenancing Vice and Promoting the Knowledge and Practice of the Christian Religion, which had been founded in 1792 in Dublin for the purpose of spreading Protestant influence in Irish society. The Association printed and distributed religious tracts and supported schools. From 1800, it began receiving parliamentary grants to assist its educational work; these grants rose from a modest £300 a year in 1800 to £9,000 a year by 1823. It was educating some 8,000 pupils in 1819.[16] The Evangelical British and Foreign Bible Society became active in distributing Bibles in Ireland from its formation in 1804. Initially the Society had agreed to distribute only English-language Bibles, in the belief that the Irish language was dying out. By the end of 1809, however, on the advice of preachers and teachers active in the Irish-speaking south and west, the Society agreed to begin printing and distributing the New Testament in Irish, and in 1823 it decided to print and distribute the entire Bible in Irish. In 1808, Evangelicals in Dublin founded the interdenominational Hibernian Bible Society, in association with the British and Foreign Bible Society, as a means to facilitate the distribution of Bibles in Ireland. Drawing upon considerable financial support from England, the Hibernian Bible Society established auxiliaries in most Irish counties and many market towns. These branches assumed responsibility for distributing the Bibles among poor, mainly Catholic families in the surrounding districts, while their regular meetings served to strengthen Evangelical fervour in the localities,

[15] K. Whelan, *The Tree of Liberty: Radicalism, Catholicism and the Construction of Irish Identity 1760–1830* (Cork, 1996), 141–2.

[16] H. R. Clayton, 'Societies Formed to Educate the Poor in Ireland in the Late 18th and Early 19th Centuries' (Trinity College, Dublin M.Litt., 1981), 104–48; I. Hehir, 'Evangelical Religion and the Polarization of Protestant-Catholic Relations in Ireland, 1780–1840' (Univ. of Wisconsin, Madison, Ph.D., 1994), 155–8; Akenson, *The Church of Ireland*, 139–41.

especially among the Protestant laity. By 1829, the Hibernian Bible Society claimed to have distributed 209,000 Bibles in Ireland.[17] The Bible Society became the central institution in Irish Evangelicalism, representing the view that Catholicism's hold on the Irish peasantry resulted from their ignorance of the Scriptures. Other forms of Protestant religious literature were provided by the Irish branch of the Religious Tract and Book Society (1816), which was reported to have distributed over a million tracts in Ireland between 1819 and 1833.[18]

The achievements of the Bible Society encouraged further Evangelical educational efforts aimed at teaching the labouring poor to read the Bible for themselves. The Hibernian Sunday School Society was formed in 1809 in Dublin, to encourage and co-ordinate the formation of local Sunday schools, and to provide grants, Bibles, and tracts to these local schools. The schools were taught by voluntary workers and offered basic instruction in reading as well as knowledge of the Scriptures. The Sunday School Society had considerable success, in large part through the zeal of its secretary, James Digges La Touche, a prominent member of the Bethesda Chapel circle, the Dublin version of the Clapham Sect. The number of schools increased dramatically after 1816, and by 1825 the Society claimed to be assisting more than 1,700 Sunday schools with some 150,000 pupils.[19] Another Evangelical educational society was the London Hibernian Society, an interdenominational venture formed in 1806 by English and Irish Congregationalists initially to support itinerant preaching, the formation of schools, and the distribution of Bibles and tracts. 'Britons,' the Society announced in its opening prospectus, with reference to the recent act of union, 'Ireland is now your sister!'[20] 'The hope', the Society further observed in 1806, '. . . that the Irish will ever be a tranquil and loyal people . . . must be built on the anticipated reduction of popery.'[21] By 1814, the London Hibernian Society had decided to cease supporting preaching and to concentrate on education, supporting schools in which the Bible was required reading, and providing instruction in both the

[17] Hempton and Hill, *Evangelical Protestantism in Ulster Society*, 52–5.

[18] Ibid. 52; R. F. Foster, *Modern Ireland 1600–1972* (London, 1988), 302–3.

[19] Hempton and Hill, *Evangelical Protestantism in Ulster Society*, 59–60; Hehir, 'Evangelical Religion', 277–81; Clayton, 'Societies Formed to Educate the Poor in Ireland', 68–99; Akenson, *The Church of Ireland*, 135–6.

[20] Clayton, 'Societies Formed to Educate the Poor in Ireland', 173.

[21] Cited in Whelan, *The Tree of Liberty*, 141.

English and Irish languages. The Society was based in London, where it gained high-level supporters among Church of England Evangelicals—William Wilberforce was a vice-president in the 1820s and the duke of Gloucester, nephew and son-in-law of George III, served as patron. (The latter, known as Silly Billy for his vacuous expression and, some suspected, no less vacuous mind, was valued more for his connections than his leadership.[22]) By the early 1820s, moreover, the Society had become dominated by clergy and lay members of the established Church, while the Dissenting presence had grown very small. In 1818, the London Hibernian Society claimed to be educating some 32,000 pupils in nearly 400 schools; five years later, it claimed to have over 61,000 pupils.[23] The Irish Society for Promoting the Education of the Native Irish through the Medium of their own Language, founded in 1818, was far more concerned than the London Hibernian Society with recruiting Irish-speaking teachers and supporting schools in which Irish was the primary language for instruction. By 1825, the Irish Society was maintaining seven Irish-speaking teachers, who moved among some 140 separate schools, teaching adults as well as children, mainly in Connaught and Munster.[24]

The above societies were generally open about their aim to proselytize among the Irish. On the other hand, the Society for Promoting the Education of the Poor in Ireland, or as it was commonly known, the Kildare Place Society, had been formed in 1811 with the professed goal of promoting the development of a national system of non-denominational schools, in which Protestant and Catholic children would be educated together and, it was hoped, develop mutual understanding and empathy. The Kildare Place Society employed the educational programmes being developed by the English Quaker, Joseph Lancaster, including the use of the monitor system, the establishment of model teacher training schools for both men and women, the use of a national set of textbooks, and the development of an effective system of school inspection. The Bible, without note or comment, was to be used in all its schools. In its

[22] F. K. Brown, *Fathers of the Victorians*, 311–14.

[23] Clayton, 'Societies Formed to Educate the Poor in Ireland', 173–95; Hehir, 'Evangelical Religion', 241–75; Akenson, *The Irish Educational Experiment*, 83; Hempton and Hill, *Evangelical Protestantism in Ulster Society*, 55–6.

[24] Hehir, 'Evangelical Religion', 284–7; Clayton, 'Societies Formed to Educate the Poor in Ireland', 222–31; Hempton and Hill, *Evangelical Protestantism in Ulster Society*, 56–7.

early years, it enjoyed broad support from members of the Church of Ireland, the Presbyterian Churches and the Roman Catholic Church. Daniel O'Connell had a place on the board of managers, and representatives of the Catholic gentry served as patrons of local schools. After 1816, Parliament began making modest grants to help support the Society's educational work. By 1819, however, the management of the Society had come under the domination of Church of Ireland Evangelicals, who placed increasing emphasis on the centrality of the Bible in its schools, with decidedly Protestant teaching. The Society also began providing subsidies to avowedly Protestant schools and proselytizing agencies, including grants to 340 schools of the London Hibernian Society and to fifty-seven schools of the Association for Discountenancing Vice.[25] The Kildare Place Society, moreover, turned a blind eye to the proselytizing zeal of certain schoolmasters. This new direction in the Society no doubt reflected the growing confidence and sense of mission in the established Church. In 1820, O'Connell resigned from the board of management in protest against these alleged proselytizing activities, and became a vehement opponent of the Society and especially of the grants of public money it received each year. By 1824, Bishop Doyle had also became a strong opponent of the Society, and helped to convince the Catholic hierarchy to withdraw all support; in 1824, the Catholic bishops petitioned Parliament to end its grants to the Kildare Place Society. Some MPs grew concerned over the charges of proselytism, though the House of Commons as a whole continued to increase its grant to the Society—from £6,000 in 1816 to £10,000 in 1821 and £22,000 in 1824. By 1825, the Kildare Place Society maintained nearly 1,400 schools with over 102,000 pupils, and had become a driving force in what was becoming known as the Scripture education movement.[26]

The growth of the Evangelical Scripture education movement in Ireland after 1806 raised expectations of a great transformation in Irish religious life. In a country where the legacy of the eighteenth-century penal laws and the poverty of the Catholic Church meant

[25] *Hansard's Parl. Deb.*, 3 ser. vi (1831), col. 1266; McGrath, *Politics, Interdenominational Relations and Education in the Public Ministry of Bishop James Doyle*, 191.

[26] *Hansard's Parl. Deb*, NS x (1824), 837–47, 1399–1413, 1476–84; Akenson, *The Irish Educational Experiment*, 85–90; Hehir, 'Evangelical Religion', 331–9; Fitzpatrick, *Life, Times and Correspondence of Dr. Doyle*, i. 235–6; McGrath, *Politics, Interdenominational Relations and Education*, 157–206.

there were still inadequate educational opportunities for the Catholic poor, many Irish Catholic parents were prepared to brave the censures of their priests and send their children to a school supported by Kildare Place Society, London Hibernian Society, Irish Society, Sunday School Society, or one of the other Evangelical Scripture education societies. In 1825, the first report of the Irish Education Commission estimated that nearly 390,000 pupils in Ireland were attending one of the Scripture education schools, as compared to only about 20,000 children in such schools in 1812.[27] According to statistics supplied by the Kildare Place Society, the total number of Scripture education schools in Ireland had increased from 239 in 1812 to some 4,150 by 1824.[28] The annual April meetings of the Bible, missionary, and Scripture educational societies, held in the Rotunda of Dublin, brought together hundreds of delegates by the early 1820s. The April meetings served as important events in the life of the Protestant community in Ireland, helping to build confidence and strengthen the sense of common purpose.[29] Supporters of the Scripture education societies believed that as the younger generation of Irish Catholics learned to read the Bible for themselves, they would reject the authority of the Catholic priests and be drawn inexorably to the Protestant faith. 'The progress of knowledge in Ireland', enthused one advocate, 'through the circulation of the Holy Scriptures and education, is becoming daily more apparent. And perhaps in nothing does it appear more, than in the growing independence of the people in spiritual matters, and the declining influence of the priests.'[30]

The Evangelical Scripture education movement received support from a number of prominent Irish Protestant landowning families.[31] Members of these families had frequently come under the influence of 'heartfelt' Evangelical religion, and they sought to communicate the gospel, especially to Catholic tenants on their estates. Religious motivations were probably combined with feelings of guilt over the wretched poverty of much of the Irish peasantry and a genuine belief that Scripture education would help to alleviate such poverty by

[27] *Practical Observations upon the Views and Tendencies of the First Report of the Commissioners of Irish Education Inquiry* (London, 1826), 35.

[28] Speech of J. L. Foster, 29 March 1824, *Hansard's Parl. Deb.*, NS x (1824), col. 1478.

[29] Brooke, *Recollections of the Irish Church*, 35.

[30] R. Steven, *Remarks on the Present State of Ireland* (London, 1822), 16.

[31] I am indebted here to the discussion of the Evangelical gentry in Hehir, 'Evangelical Religion', 390–418.

encouraging greater thrift, temperance, hard work, delayed marriage, and smaller families, while at the same time teaching the duties of humility, deference, respect for property, and non-resistance to the powers that be. Many of these families were of the lesser gentry, but they also included such prominent aristocratic names as Farnham, Roden, Powerscourt, Lorton, Mandeville, Mountcashel, and Gosford. The families were frequently connected by ties of marriage and friendship, and formed Evangelical networks of considerable power and influence. Evangelical landowners served as patrons of local branches of the Bible Society or Scripture education societies—providing funds, chairing meetings, and enhancing the social status of Evangelical activity. County Wicklow was especially strong in this Evangelical paternalism. Among the Wicklow Evangelical gentry was Thomas Parnell, 'Tract Parnell'—described as 'a big solemn man whose pockets bulged with tracts'. 'When he arrived [for a visit]', it was said, 'the household knew they were in for a discourse, at least an hour long after evening prayers.'[32] Such people used their authority to promote Scripture education on their estates. On taking control of the Kingscourt estate near Cavan in 1823, Lord Farnham began establishing schools in connection with the Evangelical Irish Society. By 1826, he was maintaining at his own expense seven schools with some 700 pupils on his estate. A large new established church was completed in the town of Cavan in 1825, and County Cavan became a main base for the Irish Society's Scripture education activities, with fifty-one Irish Society schools in the county in 1825. One of the 'greatest blessings resulting from the system of Scriptural education', the earl of Roden later maintained, was that 'it brought the landlords of Ireland and their tenants together'.[33] Lord Ennismore was said to have dismissed twenty-three labourers and servants in June 1824, when they refused to send their children to the Kildare Place School on his estate in county Cork. Similar allegations were made against Lords Carbery, Lorton, Roden, and Rathdrum.[34] Women of the gentry classes were frequently the most active in Evangelical causes, organizing Sunday

[32] T. C. F. Stunt, *From Awakening to Secession: Radical Evangelicals in Switzerland and Britain 1815–35* (Edinburgh, 2000), 161–2.

[33] Speech on 28 February 1832, *Hansard's Parl. Deb.*, 3rd ser. x (1832), col. 856.

[34] Ibid. 410–11, 418; *Practical Observations upon the Views and Tendencies of the First Report of the Commissioners of Irish Education Inquiry*, 78n.; N. D. Emerson, 'Church Life in the Nineteenth Century', in Phillips (ed.), *History of the Church of Ireland*, iii. 342.

schools, distributing Bibles and tracts, and visiting the homes of the poor to provide charity and Christian advice. The liberal *Dublin Evening Post* complained in 1826 of what it termed the new-style 'Bible gentry' and their 'ostentatious' support for the Bible Society and Scripture education societies: 'it is the *fashion* in the high places to patronise these Societies and their itenerant [*sic*] orators'.[35] The larger landowners, however, were not always active in Scripture education. In the city of Cork and the surrounding county, for example, the larger gentry and aristocracy remained aloof and the leadership in the Scripture education movement was provided by dedicated Evangelical clergy of the established church, with support from the minor gentry, shopkeepers, and merchants, and their wives and daughters.[36]

The High Church party within the established Church of Ireland had initially looked upon the work of the Bible Society and Scripture education societies with dismay, even hostility. In 1817, William Phelan had published an influential attack on the Bible Society in Ireland, criticizing it for encouraging co-operation between Church and Dissent and for placing too much reliance on individual Bible reading, to the neglect of the teachings, liturgy, and sacraments of the established Church.[37] Critics such as Phelan gave expression to fears that had been growing for some time among the predominantly High Church Irish bishops, who had hitherto given the Bible Society cautious support, but who were growing uncomfortable with the theological discussions occurring at Bible Society meetings and with the blurring of distinctions between Church and Dissent. In 1821 William Stuart, archbishop of Armagh and primate of the Church of Ireland, withdrew his name as one of the presidents of the Hibernian Bible Society, and his lead was followed by all the bishops except Power le Poer Trench, the Evangelical archbishop of Tuam.[38] Yet for all their concerns about the Bible Society, the High Church

[35] 'State of Ireland', *Dublin Evening Post*, 17 October 1826.

[36] I. d'Alton, *Protestant Society and Politics in Cork 1812–1844* (Cork, 1980), 71–2.

[37] W. Phelan, *The Bible, not the Bible Society, being an Attempt to Point Out that Mode of Disseminating the Scriptures, which would most Effectually Conduce to the Security of the Established Church, and the Peace of the United Kingdom* (Dublin, 1817). See also the comparisons of the Bible Society and the seventeenth-century Puritan zealots made by the High Church dean of Achonry, A. H. Kenney, in his *Principles and Practices of Pretended Reformers in Church and State* (London, 1819), 422–38.

[38] Hempton and Hill, *Evangelical Protestantism in Ulster Society*, 66; J. D. Sirr, *A Memoir of the Hon. and Most Revd. Power le Poer Trench, Last Archbishop of Tuam* (Dublin, 1845), 459–64; Nockles, 'Continuity and Change in Anglican High Churchmanship', 349–50.

bishops and clergy could hardly oppose Scripture education or the aim of converting the Irish Catholic population. When the new High Church archbishop of Dublin delivered his famous Charge in 1822, he was in one sense appealing for an end to party divisions by calling upon the whole established Church, the High Church and Evangelical parties, to unite in a crusade to gain the conformity of the Irish people. He sought to combine the parliamentary and diocesan Church reform movements, which had been proceeding under mainly High Church leadership, and the Scriptural education movement, proceeding under Evangelical leadership. He aimed, in short, to bring the spirit of the Evangelical crusade within the structures of the established Church.[39] The dramatic improvements made since 1808 in clerical residence, in provision of parish churches, in pastoral zeal, and in diocesan administration would be combined with the fervour of the Evangelical Bible and Scripture education societies. To the substantial parliamentary grants to the established Church made since 1808 would now be added the large sums of money that the Evangelical societies were able to collect from supporters in Britain as well as Ireland. After 1822 there were signs of a new spirit of co-operation between the Evangelical and High Church parties in the shared goal of extending the influence of the established Church.[40] It was the beginning of what one historian has described as a distinctive High Church Evangelicalism in the nineteenth-century Church of Ireland.[41]

This was, significantly, also a time of considerable instability in Ireland and growing threats to the Church of Ireland. In the south and west of Ireland the followers of 'Captain Rock', a symbol of agrarian vengeance, pursued a campaign of terror and intimidation directed against landlords, soldiers, and tithe collectors. This period also witnessed the spread of the prophecies of Pastorini. In 1790, the English Catholic Charles Walmesley published in Dublin, under the pseudonym Signor Pastorini, a commentary on the Apocalypse of St John the Apostle, in which he prophesied that God's wrath would descend on the heretics some fifty years after 1771. From

[39] Hehir, 'Evangelical Religion', 384.

[40] T. C. F. Stunt, 'Evangelical Cross-Currents in the Church of Ireland, 1820–1833', in W. J. Sheils and D. Wood (eds.), *The Churches, Ireland and the Irish*, Studies in Church History, 25 (Oxford, 1989), 219.

[41] D. Bowen, 'Alexander R. C. Dallas: The Warrior Saint', in P. T. Phillips (ed.), *The View from the Pulpit* (Toronto, 1978), 27.

about 1817, roadside peddlers began hawking cheap popular versions of Pastorini's prophecy in the form of small tracts, penny handbills, or broadside ballads. While the versions varied, most predicted that the year 1825 would bring the extirpation of Protestantism in Ireland. The distribution of Bibles by the various Bible and Scripture education societies apparently fed this popular preoccupation with Pastorini's prophecies, and it was said that Irish peasants would concentrate their reading on the Book of Revelation. Pastorini's prophecies aroused alarm among Protestants, who feared the prophecies would incite acts of violence, even massacres of Protestants.[42] 'Is it surprising', asked an Irish correspondent of the home secretary, Sir Robert Peel, in March 1823, 'that the Protestants are alarmed?' 'Will any rational man believe', he added, 'with such encouragement and such hopes of an early completion held out by these sanguinary prophecies, that the Ribbonman's oath to wade knee-deep in Protestant blood . . . is the oath only of a few shoeblacks, tailors and coal-porters?'[43]

In the House of Commons, Radicals and some Whigs portrayed the anti-tithe disturbances in Ireland as an understandable reaction by impoverished peasants to the extreme wealth of the Irish establishment. In March 1823, the Radical MP Joseph Hume proposed an extensive reform of the Church of Ireland, including the gradual reduction of the Irish hierarchy to one archbishop and four bishops, and the rationalization of clerical incomes. The money saved, Hume insisted, should be regarded as the property of the nation, to be applied by Parliament to any religious purpose it chose.[44] Hume's proposals were regarded as too extreme, but there was a general sense that something had to be done to ease the burden of Irish tithe. Early in 1823, the Tory Government brought forward a bill to commute Irish tithe from the notional 10 per cent of agricultural produce into a money payment based on the average value of the tithe over a course of seven years. The Irish tithe composition act of 1823, however, was made voluntary rather than compulsive, with the result that relatively few parish vestries took advantage of its provisions.[45]

[42] J. S. Donnelly, Jr., 'Pastorini and Captain Rock: Millenarianism and Sectarianism in the Rockite Movement of 1821–4', in S. Clark and J. S. Donnelly, Jr. (eds.), *Irish Peasants: Violence and Political Unrest* (Dublin, 1988), 102–39.

[43] C. S. Parker, *Sir Robert Peel*, 3 vols. (London, 1891), i. 340.

[44] Akenson, *The Church of Ireland*, 106–7.

[45] Ibid. 109; B. Jenkins, *Era of Emancipation: British Government of Ireland 1812–1830* (Kingston and Montreal, 1988), 200–4.

Popular hostility to tithe continued to simmer. Some Irish clergymen, meanwhile, were feeling abandoned by what they viewed as Parliament's continual criticism and harassment of the Irish establishment, and the readiness of English 'friends' of the Irish Church publicly to condemn its shortcomings.[46] 'How fortunate', quipped Magee to Jebb in March 1824, 'that the *English* branch of the Church is pure and free from blame, [and] that all enquiry is confined to this side of the Channel.'[47] 'The language now adopted with respect to the Church . . . (and not entirely by Opposition members)', complained the Church of Ireland clergyman Robert Burrowes of Parliament in May 1824, 'opens the minds of the immediately rising generation to the question, whether the Established Church is of benefit to Ireland.'[48] Adding to Irish Protestant anxiety was the issue of Catholic Emancipation, which continued to gather support in Parliament. In 1821 the House of Commons passed an Emancipation bill, which was then rejected by the Lords. But support for the Protestant constitution was wavering among British politicians. Emancipation had been defined as an 'open question' in the Liverpool Government from 1812, which meant it was effectively sidelined, but by the early 1820s pro-Emancipation ministers were becoming the majority in the Cabinet. For most Irish Protestants, this foreshadowed disaster for the Irish Church. Emancipation, they feared, by empowering the Irish Catholic majority, would quickly lead to the overthrow of the established Church in Ireland. There was certainly evidence to support such a fear. In June 1823, Bishop Doyle published a lengthy treatise, confidently addressed to the lord-lieutenant, Lord Wellesley, in which he combined a vigorous appeal for Catholic Emancipation with condemnation of tithes and a call for the abolition of the established Church.[49] 'This church, my lord', insisted Doyle,

> deserted by the legislature, has since not ceased to tremble for her existence. She fears that England is not greatly interested in her, and that her natural protectors are now weak or indifferent, or too far removed. She knows that her wealth and possessions are immense, calculated to awaken the jealousy

[46] J. Jebb to R. Jebb, 15 April 1824, Trinity College, Dublin, Jebb Papers, MS 6396–7/187.

[47] W. Magee to J. Jebb, 31 March 1824, Trinity College, Dublin, Jebb Papers, MS 6396–7/184.

[48] R. Burrowes to J. Jebb, 5 May 1824, Trinity College, Dublin, Jebb Papers, MS 6396/7/190.

[49] McGrath, *Politics, Interdenominational Relations and Education*, 16–19.

of her friends, and excite the envy of her enemies. She fears the legislature would examine her tithe, and inquire whether she holds [it] by any other than their free gift; and knowing, that she does not answer the ends for which any Christian Church has ever been erected, she apprehends that they might new-model her constitution, or lay claim to some portion of her spoils.[50]

Rockite outrages, Pastorini's prophecies, parliamentary criticism, growing support for Catholic Emancipation—all this served to strengthen the sense within the Irish establishment that decisive action was urgently needed. But amid these threats there was also good reason for confidence. With the unprecedented State investment in the established Church since 1808 and with the expanding Scripture education movement, the Church seemed poised for a breakthrough in its mission to the Irish people. If the Church could begin to make converts through Scripture education and pastoral commitment, if it could once break the hold of the Catholic Church over peasant communities, it might well find that vast numbers of Irish Catholics were prepared to conform—because they would recognize the established Church was the true Church in Ireland, because they would see Protestantism as a more rational, less superstitious faith, and because they would wish to participate fully in the political, moral, and religious life of the nation-state that was being consolidated in the aftermath of the Union of 1801. If Parliament was not as supportive by 1823–4 as it had been in previous years, the proper response for the Church was now to take the lead, to respond to Magee's Charge of October 1822, and to show the politicians what it could accomplish by its own spiritual and moral power. It must become a popular missionary Church. There was, meanwhile, an example of just such a process of large-scale conversions to the established Church occurring nearby, across the narrow North Channel in the largely Gaelic-speaking Highlands and Islands of Scotland. There the erection of new churches and schools in connection with the established Church was achieving impressive results in spreading an Evangelical Presbyterianism and a loyalty to the British State among communities whose grandfathers had risen for the Jacobite cause in 1745 and fought as Catholics or Episcopalians at Culloden.[51] Surely the Church of Ireland, if it had faith, could lead a

[50] J.K.L. [James Doyle], *A Vindication of the Religious and Civil Principles of the Irish Catholics*, 3rd edn. (Dublin, 1823), 9.

[51] See e.g. J. Glassford, *Letter to the Right Honourable the Earl of Roden, on the Present State of Popular Education in Ireland* (Ireland, 1829), 9–12.

similar movement among the Irish Gaels and secure at last the established Protestant Faith in Ireland.

The Bible War

The Catholic Church in Ireland seemed, in many respects, to be ill prepared to resist a sustained proselytizing campaign by the established Church. The hold of the bishops and priests over the Irish Catholic population was less than secure. As the historian of the nineteenth-century Catholic Church in Ireland, Emmet Larkin, has observed, there was a serious shortage of priests for the rapidly growing Catholic population. In 1800 there were only about 1,850 priests and twenty-six bishops for a Catholic population of nearly 4,000,000; by 1820, the Catholic population had probably reached 5,000,000, while the number of priests had scarcely increased. Clerical discipline was lax, with sexual misconduct and alcoholism all too frequent. Clerical morale was weakened by considerable inequalities in clerical incomes, and many priests were hard-pressed financially. At the same time, parish priests could seem unnecessarily wealthy to impoverished Catholic tenant farmers, who had to pay tithes for the support of the established clergy as well as fees for the maintenance of their own priests, and there were widespread complaints about clerical avarice and mercenary priests.[52] While Catholic organizations, most notably the Christian Brothers, struggled to provide schools for Catholic children, they did not have access to the resources of the established Church and Scripture education societies, with their parliamentary grants and massive voluntary contributions from Britain. The overwhelming majority of Catholic schools were small fee-paying schools that received no State support of any kind; many of these were so-called 'hedge schools', meeting in barns or turf buildings, starved of books and materials. In 1826, of more than 400,000 children being educated in Catholic schools in Ireland, fewer than 31,000 benefited from State grants—and this at a time when the State was providing large subsidies to the Scripture education societies.[53]

[52] E. Larkin, 'The Devotional Revolution in Ireland, 1850–75', *American Historical Review*, 77 (June 1972), 625–52; D. Bowen, *Souperism: Myth or Reality? A Study of Catholics and Protestants during the Great Famine* (Dublin, 1970), 51–4; S. J. Connolly, *Priests and People in Pre-Famine Ireland 1780–1845* (Dublin, 1982), 58–73.

[53] P. J. Dowling, *The Hedge Schools of Ireland* (Dublin, 1968), 33, 42; Jenkins, *Era of Emancipation*, 214.

One who recognized the urgency of the educational crisis confronting the Catholics in Ireland was James Doyle, bishop of Kildare and Leighlin. The State, he observed in a pamphlet on the Scripture education movement published in the autumn of 1824, refused to entrust Catholics with public funds for the education of their children: 'It is said to the Catholics: you and your clergy are only tolerated by the state; and therefore the government cannot be expected to confide in you the regulation of public instruction.' This was, Doyle argued, deeply insulting as well as unjust to people who contributed by their taxes to the public funds. Even worse was the insistence of the State on funding and encouraging the Scripture education societies, and thus 'interposing [their] authority between us and our children'.[54] 'Behold,' he wrote of the Scripture education societies,

> . . . the force with which these societies press on an impoverished and broken-hearted people. Funds to the amount of, or exceeding £200,000 a year, are at their disposal; the influence of the landlord, an influence paramount to every other, the zeal of the inspector, the power of the press, and of the tongue—calumnies incessantly repeated, the hallowed name of the word of God, the thirst of the people for education, their excessive poverty, all these form a moral phalanx more formidable than that of Macedon, and if God and the unbroken spirit of the people did not assist us, we could not resist it.

'We have', he added, 'borne many things, but we have never borne a persecution more bitter than that which now assails us.'[55] Doyle's pamphlet, published and promoted by the respected Catholic Dublin bookseller Richard Coyne, went through four editions and helped greatly to arouse Catholic opinion against the Scripture education movement.[56]

This growing Catholic opposition to the Scripture education societies proved an important factor in convincing Catholic bishops and priests to give open support to the Catholic Association, a political organization formed in May 1823 by the Irish Catholic barristers Daniel O'Connell and Richard Lalor Sheil. The main purpose of the Catholic Association was to mobilize Catholic opinion in support of Catholic Emancipation. Early in 1824, however, the Catholic Association broadened its activities, establishing the

[54] J.K.L. [James Doyle], *Letters on the State of Education in Ireland; and on Bible Societies* (Dublin, 1824), 13–14.
[55] Ibid. 22–3.
[56] Fitzpatrick, *Life, Times and Correspondence of Dr. Doyle*, i. 363–6.

famous 'Catholic rent', a financial exaction to be collected in every parish, with subscriptions of a penny a week encouraged from the poor and larger contributions expected from the better-off. The bulk of the Catholic rent, about two-thirds of the total, was to be used to provide legal counsel for Catholic victims of political persecution and to subsidize pro-Emancipation newspapers. Significantly, the remaining third would be directed primarily to supporting Catholic popular education, building Catholic churches and residence houses for parish priests, and improving the incomes of the priests. In short, the Catholic Association would endeavour, through voluntary contributions, to provide the Catholic Church and community with the same kinds of subsidies that the parliamentary State was providing to the established Church and Scripture education societies.[57] In this it is difficult not to discern the influence of James Doyle, the first Catholic bishop to join the Association. O'Connell also took up the cause of Catholic burials, which emerged as an issue in the tense months following Archbishop Magee's Charge. The churchyards belonged to the established Church, which had the legal power to insist that only the Anglican service was read at burials, though a convention existed by which the Anglican incumbents turned a blind eye when Catholic priests recited the *De profoundis* at the burial of a Catholic. In September 1823, however, the sexton of Dublin's St Kevin's church had kept both eyes ruthlessly open, disrupting a Catholic burial service in the churchyard and causing considerable pain to the family. Largely through Archbishop Magee's efforts in the House of Lords, Parliament passed an Irish Burials Acts in 1824, which required Catholic priests to have the permission of the established clergyman before carrying out a burial in the parish churchyard; the established clergyman was also empowered to determine the time of the burial. O'Connell exploited the burials controversy to great effect, highlighting the anguish caused to Catholic families and demonstrating the readiness of the Association to demand basic human rights for Catholics.[58] The Association's open opposition to the revived established Church convinced many Catholic bishops and priests to give it their active

[57] F. O'Ferrall, *Catholic Emancipation: Daniel O'Connell and the Birth of Irish Democracy 1820–30* (Dublin, 1985), 52–3; O. MacDonagh, *The Life of Daniel O'Connell 1775–1847*, 2nd edn. (London, 1991), 209–11.

[58] McGrath, *Politics, Interdenominational Relations and Education*, 119–21; O'Ferrall, *Catholic Emancipation*, 49; MacDonagh, *Life of Daniel O'Connell*, 209.

support. Before 1823 the Catholic clergy in Ireland, haunted by memories of the French Revolution and the bloodbath of 1798 and under pressure from Rome to avoid political activities that would involve resistance to the British State, had remained aloof from the political agitation for Catholic Emancipation. By the spring of 1824, however, substantial numbers of Catholic priests were assisting the Catholic Association in enrolling members, collecting the rent and drafting petitions.[59]

In the late summer of 1824, O'Connell and Sheil found an opportunity to demonstrate the readiness of the Catholic Association to confront the Scripture education movement. On 9 September, the two men were in Cork to attend a dinner being held in honour of Sheil when they 'discovered by accident' that there was to be a meeting of the Ladies Auxiliary of the Munster Hibernian Bible Society in the county court-house, at which two British organizers sent out from the London headquarters of the Hibernian Bible Society—the young Englishman Baptist Noel and the Scotsman 'Captain' James E. Gordon—were to speak. Gathering a crowd of supporters, O'Connell and Sheil entered the court-house and broke into the meeting, issuing a challenge that Noel and Gordon were happy to accept. Over the course of the next two days the Catholic champions engaged Noel and Gordon in spirited debate over the aims and objectives of the Scripture education movement. O'Connell was in his element. On the second day, he entertained the crowd in a speech of over three hours, warning them that the Bible societies were encouraging the spread of religious fanaticism and would turn their children into Protestant sectarians, even 'Muggletonians'. He suggested that Noel and other English supporters of the Hibernian Bible Society should concentrate on alleviating the widespread irreligion and ignorance in England, rather than play at 'converting' Irish Catholics, who were already Christians, and possessors of the pure catholic and apostolic Faith. Ireland, he insisted, was not a mission field. He reminded Gordon, the Scot, of how the Scottish Covenanters had resisted the attempt to impose an alien Anglican Church on his countrymen in the seventeenth century: if the Scottish people should be allowed to preserve their Presbyterian faith, so too the Irish majority should be left in peace in their

[59] O'Ferrall, *Catholic Emancipation*, 61–3; O. MacDonagh, 'The Politicisation of the Irish Catholic Bishops, 1800–1850', *Historical Journal*, 18 (1975), 37–42.

Catholicism. The crowd grew excited and began shouting down Protestant speakers, until the meeting broke up in confusion.[60] It was a significant moment. For the first time, Catholic leaders had stood up to debate openly with proponents of the Scripture education movement. O'Connell and Sheil had demonstrated that lay Catholics could present an intelligent defence of their faith and were neither sunk in ignorance nor held in blind subjection to the priests. They had affronted the dignity of the Protestant ascendancy and challenged the assumptions of Protestant superiority. For the Catholic crowd, the event evidently instilled a new sense of pride in their religious and cultural heritage.

News of the disruption of the Bible Society meeting in Cork encouraged Catholics in the south and west of Ireland to take similar action against the Evangelical societies in the following weeks. On 21 September 1824, a Catholic crowd disrupted a meeting of the Church Missionary Society in Cork. Constables were called in to clear the hall of the intruders, but the meeting had to be discontinued. On the same day, a meeting of the Hibernian Bible Society was interrupted in Clonmel. Catholic crowds disrupted Bible society meetings at Waterford on 28 September and at Kilkenny on 14 October.[61] A crowd led by local priests violently broke up the meeting of the Galway branch of the Hibernian Bible Society in the county court-house on 19 October, despite the presence of Power le Poer Trench, the Evangelical archbishop of Tuam, who chaired the meeting.[62] Soon, in an effort to avoid violent clashes, local Catholic and Protestant leaders began agreeing to hold formal debates, or 'biblical discussions', with admission by ticket only. Such debates ranged widely over the place of the Bible in the Christian faith, the nature of the Church's authority, and the weight to be attached to private judgement. The debates were well attended, and champions emerged on both sides, including Richard Pope and Robert Daly for the established Church, and Eneas McDonnell and Tom Maguire for the Catholic Church. On 18–19 November 1824 Protestants

[60] *Constitution or Cork Morning Post*, 10, 13, 15, 17, 27 September 1824; D. O'Connell to his wife, 11 September 1824, in M. R. O'Connell (ed.), *The Correspondence of Daniel O'Connell* (Dublin, 1974), iii. 77–8; J. Wolffe, *The Protestant Crusade in Great Britain 1829–1860* (Oxford, 1992), 35.

[61] Bowen, *The Protestant Crusade in Ireland*, 98–9; *Dublin Evening Post*, 28 September, 5 October 1824; *Constitution or Cork Morning Post*, 18 October 1824.

[62] Sirr, *Memoir of Power le Poer Trench*, 466–82; *Constitution or Cork Morning Post*, 25, 27 October 1824.

carried the struggle to the door of the person they regarded as the leading figure behind the new Catholic religious militancy, organizing a debate at Carlow, the episcopal seat of James Doyle, bishop of Kildare and Leighlin. Doyle declined to be drawn into the debate, but three Catholic champions agreed to engage three Protestant champions. In the event, the meeting ended in disorder and the Protestant speakers had to escape through a back door to avoid confronting a large and excited Catholic crowd.[63]

The disruptions of the Bible Society meetings and the subsequent biblical discussions aroused considerable interest in Ireland and Britain. The confrontations, dubbed the 'Bible war' by the press, revealed the growing militancy on the part of both the established Church and the Catholic Association. The confrontations highlighted how widely the networks of Bible societies, 'Bible gentry', and Scripture schools had spread throughout Ireland. The Bible war also brought public attention to the Catholic Association, which now put itself forward as the defender of Catholics against the aggression of the established Church. At the meeting of the Catholic Association on 10 November 1824, speakers subjected the Scripture education movement to scathing criticism. Significantly, the beginning of the Bible war in the autumn of 1824 coincided with a major expansion of popular support for the Catholic Association, including the development of a national system for collecting the Catholic rent.[64] O'Connell now insisted that as much as half the rent should be sent to the parishes to support Catholic education and assist the priests in their struggle with the 'biblicals'.[65] The Catholic clergy in turn increasingly took a leading part in recruiting subscribers and collecting rent for the Catholic Association. 'The Catholic clergy', Thomas Wyse, a Catholic landowner and prominent figure in the Catholic Association, later observed, with reference to the Bible war,

> had been roused to a spirit of combination by the necessities of self-defence. Their repugnance to public exhibition was overcome; they stept

[63] Mrs H. Madden, *Memoir of Robert Daly, Lord Bishop of Cashel* (London, 1875), 105–7; Fitzpatrick, *Life of Dr Doyle*, i. 374–6; McGrath, *Politics, Interdenominational Relations and Education*, 126–7; Evidence of John S. Rochfort before the Commission on the State of Ireland, *Parliamentary Papers*, 8 (1825), 430–46.

[64] Wolffe, *The Protestant Crusade in Great Britain*, 34–5; O'Ferrall, *Catholic Emancipation*, 56–85.

[65] Bartlett, *The Fall and Rise of the Irish Nation*, 332.

out beyond the modesty of their habitual functions into the activity of public life; they began to feel the usual excitements of such scenes, to acknowledge the *guardia certaminis* of such a warfare: the church became gradually militant.[66]

Supporters of the established Church, on the other hand, portrayed the Bible war as the final effort on the part of Catholic priests and Catholic agitators to halt the inevitable spread of God's word to a benighted Catholic peasantry. The disruptions of the Bible society meetings were, they believed, desperate acts by individuals sensing the waning of their former power and influence, a power and influence that had depended on keeping the Irish people in ignorance. The effort would surely fail. Education and the free discussion of scriptural truths were preparing the ground for the final triumph of the Reformation to Ireland. 'When we advert . . . to the scenes which preceded the Reformation', noted the Evangelical *Christian Observer* of London in November 1824, 'we find them so far at least analogous to those now passing in Ireland.' The confrontations of the Bible war, it added, 'called the attention of the mass of the laity to the points in dispute, and thus secured that attention which is always useful to the cause of truth, and fatal to that of error'.[67] William Magee, archbishop of Dublin, was another who believed that the Bible war presaged the victory of Protestantism and the established Church in Ireland. In April 1825, Magee gave evidence before a parliamentary committee investigating the 'state of Ireland'. He argued that there was now a real prospect that the established Church would gain the adherence of the majority of the Irish people, if the Church would provide decisive leadership only to the Scripture education movement. 'In truth', he explained, 'with respect to Ireland, the Reformation may, strictly speaking, be truly said only now to have begun.' He maintained that the numbers of Protestants in Ireland had never been as low as was usually claimed in statistical accounts. Many people counted as Catholics, he insisted, were in truth Protestants who had drifted into Catholic chapels because of insufficient church accommodation in the establishment or pastoral neglect from the established clergy. They were now, at best, uncertain Catholics and were usually irregular in their attendance at

[66] T. Wyse, *Historical Sketch of the Late Catholic Association of Ireland*, 2 vols. (London, 1829), i. 231–2.

[67] *Christian Observer* (November 1824), 727.

Catholic chapel. Some, he claimed, even attended Catholic chapels out of a mistaken belief that the Catholic Church was the established Church in Ireland. However, now that the Protestant clergy were becoming more zealous in their pastoral duties and were beginning to visit regularly the homes of their parishioners, they had discovered large numbers of such latent Protestants, yearning to be brought back into the Church of Ireland. The Bible war, moreover, was clarifying the real weakness of their faith for many Catholics, nominal Catholics at best, who were also ready to come over to the established Church. What was now needed, he maintained, was more commitment on the part of both the State and the upper social orders to strengthening and extending the parochial establishment. While much had been accomplished in recent years in improving clerical residency and building and repairing churches, far more needed to be done to make the established Church the truly national institution which the Irish people required. Far from being over-endowed, the Church of Ireland was actually starved of the resources it needed for the great national mission that lay before it. There were, Magee asserted, over 90,000 Protestants residing in Dublin, but only twenty-five established churches in the city, which made it impossible for most Protestants to worship according to the established faith, and this contributed to the drift into Catholicism or Dissent. Ireland needed more parish churches, with low seat rents, to enable the poor to attend regularly. It needed bold, zealous parish clergymen, prepared to risk confrontation. It needed, moreover, support from the upper classes, with wealthy Protestants giving preference to adherents of the established Church in employing servants and labourers and in granting leases to tenant farmers. Above all, Magee insisted, Parliament must resist the agitation for Catholic Emancipation. Any further political concessions to the Catholics would be viewed as a victory for the Catholic Association and would signal to Irish Catholics that their religion was a matter of indifference to the State. It must be made clear to the Irish people that conformity to the Church by law established was a requirement for full political rights, and that Catholics and Protestant Dissenters could look only for toleration. 'The constitution of this realm', he observed, 'knows of one allegiance, ecclesiastical, as well as civil.'[68] For Magee, the victory of

[68] W. Magee, *The Evidence of his Grace, the Archbishop of Dublin, before the Select Committee of the House of Lords on the State of Ireland* (Dublin, 1825), 4–33, 112.

the established Church in Ireland would be achieved at the parish level, through the zeal and commitment of a resident clergy.

In the diocese of Limerick, meanwhile, one clergyman of the established Church was beginning to achieve visible results through just such an active parish ministry. The Evangelical Richard Murray had commenced his duties as the newly appointed vicar of Askeaton, about 15 miles west of Limerick, in October 1824, amid the first excitement of the Bible war. He immediately began regular house-to-house visiting among all his parishioners, Protestant and Catholic, established a parish school emphasizing Scripture education, conducted Bible classes for adults in his home, and distributed Bibles and religious tracts. His wife also began a Sunday school in their home. He made no effort to coexist peacefully with the local Catholic priests, but on the contrary became their open adversary. He insisted upon all his legal rights as a parish clergyman of the Established Church—including reading the Anglican burial service at every funeral in the Askeaton churchyard, despite the pain this caused to bereaved Catholics. Gradually his zealous and uncompromising parish ministry began having results. By the end of 1825 forty Catholics in his parish had conformed to the established Church; by April 1827, between 160 and 170 Catholics had conformed. Murray secured the confidence of his bishop, the High Church John Jebb, which reflected the growing spirit of co-operation between the Evangelical and High Church movements. Murray also encouraged neighbouring parish clergymen to adopt his aggressive methods, in part through his leadership at meetings of the Limerick clerical association.[69] The achievements at Askeaton indicated what could be achieved through a revived parish ministry.

In 1825, as the established Church grew in confidence, the campaign for Catholic Emancipation was suffering serious setbacks. In March 1825, Parliament passed the Unlawful Societies Act, which suppressed the Catholic Association as a threat to public order and parliamentary authority in Ireland. In February 1825, Sir Francis Burdett had introduced another Catholic Emancipation bill in the Commons. The bill, which had been prepared with the assistance of Daniel O'Connell, included two controversial provisions, which O'Connell described as 'wings' to assist its flight through

[69] C. Forster, *The Life of John Jebb*, 2 vols. (London, 1836), ii. 433–45; Massy, *Footprints of a Faithful Shepherd: A Memoir of the Rev. Godfrey Massy*, 112–55; H. Hamilton to J. Jebb, 8 December 1825, Trinity College, Dublin, Jebb Papers, MS 6396–7/240.

Parliament. These were the State payment of the Roman Catholic clergy (which would have given the State a considerable degree of control over the activities of the Catholic Church in Ireland) and the disenfranchisement of the 40-shilling freeholders in parliamentary elections. The wings were unpopular in Ireland, where many Catholics viewed them as a betrayal of the Emancipation movement. In the event, though the bill was passed by the Commons, it was decisively defeated in the House of Lords in May 1825 by a vote of 178 to 130. The prime minister, Lord Liverpool, spoke with passion against any further concessions to the Catholics. During the debates on Burdett's bill, British public opinion was mobilized against Emancipation, and over 400 anti-Emancipation petitions were sent to the House of Commons, many of them organized by the established clergy in Britain. The defeat of the bill was greeted with public rejoicing in England, including the ringing of church bells.[70] O'Connell managed to hold on to the leadership of the Emancipation movement in Ireland, but his reputation had been dented. In July 1825, he formed the New Catholic Association, which carefully avoided all activities proscribed by the Unlawful Societies Act. As a result its activities were largely defensive during the last half of 1825 and first half of 1826.[71]

With the king and the House of Lords promising to block the passage of any Emancipation measure indefinitely, the established Church seemed to have time in which to expand its influence and authority among the Irish people through the Scripture education movement, the biblical discussions, and the improving discipline and zeal of its parish clergy. The Catholic hierarchy was growing alarmed at the militant mood in the established Church and sought to end the Bible war. In January 1826 the Irish Catholic bishops issued a pastoral address in which they asked for co-operation between Protestants and Catholics in educational matters and denied any intention to subvert the established Church.[72] In Britain attitudes towards the Irish establishment were growing more respectful. 'I remark a curious change as to the Irish branch of the church,' wrote John Jebb from London to his intimate friend Alexander Knox, on 30 May 1826, 'it is certainly less calumniated now, than it was, by the

[70] O'Ferrall, *Catholic Emancipation,* 86–102; G. I. T. Machin, *The Catholic Question in English Politics 1820–1830* (Oxford, 1964), 47–64;

[71] MacDonagh, *Life of Daniel O'Connell,* 221–2.

[72] A. Macaulay, *William Crolly: Archbishop of Armagh, 1835–49* (Dublin, 1994), 67.

liberals, and by laymen in general.'[73] Some in Britain called for more resolute waging of the Bible war. In his sermon before the London Hibernian Society in April 1826, the passionate Church of Scotland preacher Edward Irving insisted that the gradualism of Scripture education had gone far enough; it was now time for the revived established Church in Ireland to begin preaching boldly and directly to Irish Catholics.[74] They should call for the conformity of Irish Catholics without fear of violent confrontations. Should the Church begin boldly preaching the Reformation', Irving acknowledged, 'the liberals will cry out, "COMMOTION. CIVIL WAR! BLOODSHED!" And I answer, "COME WHAT WILL, SOULS MUST BE SAVED!" . . . No; though Satan bring all hell into the field, still the Gospel must be preached! Though the earth gape, and the mountains be removed, still the gospel must be preached!'[75] For Irving, there was no time to lose. Souls were being lost now. It was time to act decisively.

The New Reformation

The belief that the reviving established Church would have time gradually to gain the conformity of the Catholic population in Ireland was dealt a blow at the general election of June–July 1826. In the United Kingdom as a whole the general election was a modest victory for opponents of Catholic Emancipation, who achieved a net gain of thirteen anti-Catholic MPs.[76] But in Ireland there was a disturbing development: in June, the New Catholic Association gained an unexpected victory when it effectively organized the Catholic 40-shilling freeholders in county Waterford, securing the defeat of the powerful anti-Emancipation Beresford interest. The Catholic Association victory in Waterford, which was largely unexpected, encouraged last minute challenges to anti-Catholic candidates in most of the other counties, resulting in several further victories. For the first time, Irish tenants were mobilized in large numbers to vote against anti-Catholic Protestant landlords, in a move that threatened to embitter relations between landowners and tenants. There would almost certainly have been further Catholic Association victories in the general election had there been more

[73] C. Forster (ed.), *Thirty Years' Correspondence between John Jebb, Bishop of Limerick, and Alexander Knox*, 2 vols. (London, 1834), ii. 544.

[74] 'Sermon report', *The Pulpit*, 160 (11 May 1826), 225–39.

[75] Ibid. 235.

[76] Machin, *The Catholic Question in English Politics*, 86–7.

time to organize the Catholic tenant voters in all the counties. O'Connell now ordered the collection of a New Catholic Rent, to help tenants who might be victimized by their landlords for their behaviour in the election.[77] 'A darker cloud than ever seems to me to impend over Ireland', Sir Robert Peel, the home secretary, observed to Sir George Hill, MP for Londonderry, on 16 July 1826, 'that is, if one of the remaining bonds of society, the friendly connection between landlord and tenant, is dissolved.'[78] It was no longer clear that the established Church would have an indefinite period of time in which to win over the Catholic population. There was need for a new departure.

The revolt of the 40-shilling freeholders in the election of 1826 convinced at least one prominent landowner that it was time for the Irish Protestant landed classes to give more active support to the efforts of the established Church to bring the 'Reformation' to Ireland. This was John Maxwell, fifth baron Farnham, a leading opponent of Catholic Emancipation, later portrayed by the novelist William Carleton as 'an amiable, benevolent, but somewhat credulous nobleman'.[79] Farnham had acquired a reputation for brutality stemming from an incident in which, as a magistrate, he had personally flogged a boy for a petty infraction.[80] On assuming control over his 29,000-acre estate in Cavan in 1823, however, he sought to make it a model of Christian moral management. As has been seen, he supported Scripture education schools, and his patronage helped to make Cavan a centre for the educational activities of the Evangelical Irish Society. In 1826, he appointed a 'moral agent', William Krause, a Waterloo veteran and now a part-time student at Trinity College, Dublin, who was to promote sabbatarianism and supervise the moral and religious life of the tenants and their families.[81] The election of the summer of 1826 in county Cavan had been bitterly fought. Although the Farnham interest had secured victory, some 800 40-shilling freeholders had for the first time defied their landlords and voted for the pro-Emancipation candidates. The election included

[77] O'Ferrall, *Catholic Emancipation*, 120–45; MacDonagh, *Life of Daniel O'Connell*, 223–31.

[78] Parker, *Sir Robert Peel*, i. 413.

[79] E. Carleton, *Valentine McClutchy, the Irish Agent* (1845), in *The Works of William Carleton*, 2 vols. (New York, 1881), ii. 214.

[80] W. R. Brock, *Lord Liverpool and Liberal Toryism 1820 to 1827*, 2nd edn. (London, 1967), 272.

[81] C. S. Stanford, *Memoir of the Late Rev. W. H. Krause* (Dublin, 1854), 36–8; Hempton and Hill, *Evangelical Protestantism in Ulster Society*, 86–7; Hehir, 'Evangelical Religion', 415–22.

violent clashes and at least two deaths, and it was followed by widespread victimization of tenants who had voted against their landlords. There was already high unemployment in the Cavan district owing to the collapse of the local linen industry, while the harvest in the autumn of 1826 was particularly bad.[82]

In September 1826, amid these social and political tensions, Farnham was approached by three Catholic schoolteachers who told him that they had been converted to Protestantism by teaching children to read the Bible. Fearing violence from local Catholics once their conversions became known, the teachers asked for Farnham's protection to enable them to conform to the established Church. Farnham received them on to his estate and also let it be known that he would offer his protection and assistance to all Catholics wishing to conform. On 8 October, seventeen Catholics conformed in the large new parish church in Cavan.[83] As the news spread, others ready to conform made their way to Farnham's estate, where it was rumoured they received food, clothing, and lodging. By 4 November, forty-seven Catholics had conformed in Cavan. Farnham was convinced that this marked the long-expected breakthrough in the Reformation movement. 'I can with truth assure you', he wrote to Sir Robert Peel on 4 November, 'that the Roman Catholic religion has already received a severe blow.' Farnham attributed the surge of conversions to the spread of Scripture education, the biblical discussions, and above all to the alienation experienced by many Catholics over the 'recent conduct [of] the R.C. Clergy in mixing Politics and Religion' and over the Catholic clergy's 'continual cravings after money in the shape of their own dues, Cathc rent, new rent, etc.' If the government would remain firm in its support of the Protestant constitution and established Church, he continued to Peel, 'we might hope that the light of reason would break in on the deluded people, and an explosive inroad be made upon the Roman Catholic Church in this country'.[84]

The numbers of converts continued to increase. By early December 1826 over 250 Catholics were reported to have conformed to the established Church in Cavan.[85] The Protestant *Dublin*

[82] D. Gallogly, *The Diocese of Kilmore 1800–1950* (Cavan, 1999), 24–31.

[83] Speech of Lord Farnham, Cavan Reform Meeting, *Dublin Evening Post*, 3 February 1827.

[84] Lord Farnham to Sir R. Peel, 4 November 1826, BL, Peel Papers, Add. MSS 40389, fos. 254–7.

[85] *Dublin Evening Mail*, 11 December 1826.

Evening Mail reported on 4 December that the entire Catholic populations of many parishes in the county of Cavan were now preparing to conform. 'So rapidly is the spirit of desertion spreading in this County', it asserted, 'that all we apprehend is a lack of shepherds to collect the straying flock and guide them to the fold.' 'Never, since the days of England's Reformation', it continued, 'has such a scene been presented to the Empire.'[86] Leading Evangelicals, including such champions of the Bible war as Richard Pope and Captain James E. Gordon, hurried to Cavan to assist in the work of gathering in the converts, preaching to crowds of 2,000 and more in the Cavan court-house.[87] Popular ballads celebrated the Protestant victories. Among these were 'Satan's Conclave or the Late Conversion from Popery in Cavan Church', which portrayed a conclave in hell called by Satan to find the cause for the sudden fall in the number of Catholics arriving in hell:

> Then Satan cast his glaring eyeballs round
> And spoke while hell re-echoed with the sound,
> What means this scant supply, what means this dearth
> Of Papists now, o' what's occurred on earth?[88]

Protestant newspapers hailed the events at Cavan as the beginning of the 'Reformation' in Ireland. Here, it seemed, was the fruit of years of effort to improve the discipline of the parish clergy and spread the benefits of Scripture education to the Catholic population. The events at Cavan, enthused the *Dublin Evening Mail* on 11 December, were a demonstration of 'what has long been the impression on all serious and reflecting minds, that the great mass of our population wanted but a fit occasion to shake off the intolerable burden of Popery with which they have been so long pressed to earth'.[89]

The reports from Cavan were taken seriously by the Irish Catholic hierarchy. In mid-December a deputation of five Catholic bishops led by the primate, Patrick Curtis, archbishop of Armagh, arrived in Cavan to investigate the reported conversions and encourage the Catholic community to resist the proselytizing movement. Brushing aside a challenge to engage with Protestant debaters in yet another biblical discussion, the Catholic bishops preached to the

[86] Ibid. 4 December 1826.
[87] *Dublin Evening Post*, 19 December 1826; Stanford, *Memoir of W. H. Krause*, 223–4.
[88] Gallogly, *The Diocese of Kilmore*, 37–8.
[89] *Dublin Evening Mail*, 11 December 1826.

Catholic faithful and interviewed local people. They claimed to uncover evidence of widespread bribery, by which beggars, unwed mothers, and unemployed schoolteachers were lured into conforming to the established Church with gifts of food and clothing, promises of pensions, or offers of employment. Other converts were simply people of weak or susceptible minds, who were caught up in the frenzied atmosphere of religious enthusiasm. The bishops asked the magistrates to take sworn depositions from those who claimed to have been offered bribes, which might then be publicized in order to expose the activities of the proselytizers at Cavan. Not surprisingly the magistrates declined to become involved, especially as the bishops did not intend to pursue action in the civil courts. None the less Catholic leaders publicly proclaimed that the Cavan conversions were the fruits of bribery or fanaticism, and that the converts were 'vile' people of weak minds or characters.[90] As one of the deputation, the stalwart John MacHale, bishop of Killala, described the scenes he encountered at Cavan: 'the highways were covered with carts, conveying to the strong citadel of the Reformation, a precious cargo of vagrants'. Children, he insisted, were being abducted by the missionaries, while 'fanatical females' fell into trances and prophesied.[91] A Catholic ballad described the converts as

> Worthless vagrants from the highway ditches,
> Naught but the very refuse of the nation,
> With prostitutes and beggars without breeches.
> And Protestants in Catholic disguise.

Those making their way to Cavan to conform were dismissed by other Catholics as 'turn-coat rogues' who 'sold their souls for soup and hairy bacon'.[92]

For Farnham and many others, on the other hand, the 'highways covered with carts' on their way to Cavan signalled the beginning of the expected mass movement into the reinvigorated Irish established Church. To the claims by Catholic leaders that the converts came from the 'vile rabble', Protestant champions responded that, if true, their condition was due to their Catholic faith. 'Who made them *vile*?',

[90] *Dublin Evening Post*, 19, 23, 30 December 1826; Gallogly, *The Diocese of Kilmore*, 43–6; Macaulay, *William Crolly: Archbishop of Armagh*, 97–8; Hempton and Hill, *Evangelicalism in Ulster Society*, 89–90.

[91] MacHale, *Letters of John MacHale, Archbishop of Tuam*, 228–9.

[92] Gallogly, *The Diocese of Kilmore*, 39.

asked the Dublin author Caesar Otway, 'who kept them *vile*? and, who left them *vile*?' Further, added Otway, 'vile rabble as they are, are not their souls precious in the sight of God? worth a world's ransom in the sight of Jesus, who came to the poor, who preached to the poor, who died for the poor?'[93] On 26 January 1827 Farnham and his supporters held a public meeting in Cavan to publicize the Reformation achievements and announce the formation of a new Reformation Society to promote and co-ordinate the movement on a national level. In his speech at the meeting, Farnham trumpeted the Reformation breakthrough. By now there were over 450 converts in Cavan, and other conversions were being reported elsewhere in the country. He vehemently denied the allegations that bribery or threats were being used to gain converts, or that the converts came from the lowest social ranks. On the contrary, he insisted that the converts came from all social orders and that most were of respectable moral character. The real causes of the Reformation breakthrough were not bribes or fanaticism, but the spread of Scripture education and the growing dissatisfaction among Catholics with their priests. Many Catholics, he asserted, had resented the conduct of the priests in the recent general election, when they had pressured the Catholic 40-shilling freeholders into voting against their landlords' interests, thus disrupting the ties of paternalism and deference which should exist in rural society and leaving the tenants 'alienated from their landlords'. Now a great opportunity had come. An experiment had been made at Cavan, which had shown that Catholics were prepared to conform in large numbers if they were given encouragement by the natural leaders of society, the landowners and the established clergy, The established Church in Ireland, backed by 'the united efforts of the British Empire', was at last in a position to bring the Reformation to Ireland. At the same time, Farnham warned, were the New Reformation movement to fail, it would open the way for the enactment of Catholic Emancipation, which in turn would lead to the disestablishment of the Protestant Church. Without the bonds of common religious and moral values, it would not be long before Ireland and Britain would separate and the United Kingdom be dissolved. 'If something be not effected in this way', Farnham averred, '*and we are obliged to abandon our Church Establishment, which now stands in such manifest jeopardy, it*

93 C. Otway, *Letter to J.K.L., on the Subject of his Reply to Lord Farnham* (Dublin, 1827), 10.

requires not much foresight, and still less of the spirit of prophecy, to foretell, that many years will not elapse until a separation takes place between the two countries.'[94] After this appeal, the meeting supported enthusiastically the establishment of the Reformation Society. 'In every point of view', declared the *Dublin Evening Mail* on 29 January, 'this is the most important meeting that has ever been held in Ireland. . . . Cavan this day presents a grand spectacle to the world'.[95] 'In Ireland', Farnham's moral agent, W. H. Krause, informed his sister in Glasgow on 19 February 1827, 'there is a shaking of the dry bones, and a stir throughout the country, such as never was known in this land.' 'Bold champions of truth,' he continued, 'holy men of God, are everywhere crying to the deluded Roman Catholics—"Come out of her, my people;" and blessed be God, the cry has been effectual in many parts. . . . Pray for poor Ireland.'[96]

The Reformation movement was now spreading beyond Cavan. The Catholic priest in Portarlington, for example, informed Doyle in February 1827 that 'the mania of religious phrenzy has lately manifested itself amongst us, and never were bibles in such requisition in our town as they are at present'.[97] In Dublin, regular bulletins of the numbers of converts were published in the newspapers and placarded on walls.[98] It was, the *Dublin Evening Mail* proclaimed in late March, a moment 'big with futurity': 'these are "signs and wonders" which must be taken as unerring harbingers—prophetic admonitions of events that must be'.[99] By April 1827, 1,340 conversions had been reported at different places around Ireland.[100] In Dublin, a talented group of clerical authors embraced the New Reformation movement. Led by the Revd Caesar Otway, Church of Ireland curate of Lucan, the group included Harcourt Lees, the Protestant converts Mortimer and Samuel O'Sullivan, Tresham Dames Gregg, and Peter Roe. Although mocked by the wits of Dublin's Comet Club for his fanatical Protestantism, the lean Caesar Otway (so lean, it was said, that he could take refuge from a rainstorm by climbing up a gun barrel), was also a gifted travel writer, whose *Sketches of Ireland*,

94 *Dublin Evening Post*, 3 February 1827.
95 *Dublin Evening Mail*, 29 January 1827.
96 Stanford, *Memoir of W. H. Krause*, 168.
97 McGrath, *Politics, Interdenominational Relations and Education*, 136.
98 W. J. O'Neill Daunt, *Eighty-five Years of Irish History 1800–1885*, 2 vols. (London, 1886), i. 93.
99 *Dublin Evening Mail*, 26 March 1827.
100 Sirr, *Memoir of Power le Poer Trench*, 539.

Tour of Connaught, and *Erris and Tyrawley* provided admirable depictions of the folk-life and geography of Ireland. In 1827, Otway founded a new periodical, *The Christian Examiner*, to promote the Reformation movement. He recruited a young Protestant convert from the Clogher valley in South Tyrone, newly arrived in Dublin, William Carleton, to write stories of Irish peasant life based on his own experiences; the aim was to use a form of cultural anthropology to reveal the 'superstitions' and 'ignorance' of the Irish Catholic poor, and thus their need for Protestantism and civilization. Carleton's first contribution, 'A Pilgrimage to Patrick's Purgatory' (an autobiographical account of his pilgrimage to Lough Derg, an episode which, he claimed, had undermined his Catholic faith), began appearing in serial form in April 1828. His descriptions of Irish Catholic rural religion and life were honest, uncompromising, and genuine, with the stamp of genius, and they captured the attention of the reading public. Carleton's writings also transcended Otway's purposes. Indeed, his stories from this period, published in his two volumes of *Traits and Stories of the Irish Peasantry* (in 1830 and 1833 respectively), remain the best portrayals of early nineteenth-century Irish rural life.[101]

In England, considerable interest was excited by this movement that seemed destined to achieve at last the conformity of the Irish people to the established Church. *The Times* published reports of the conversions from the Irish press.[102] The Whig clergyman Thomas Arnold, at first sceptical about the reports of mass conversions in Ireland, was convinced after reading Farnham's speech of 26 January. 'I am inclined to hope and believe', he wrote to the Revd F. C. Blackstone of Basingstoke on 2 March 1827, 'that the conversions are real, and caused by good motives.' 'If so,' he added, 'they afford certainly a most cheering prospect of future good for Ireland.'[103] C. J. Blomfield, the High Church bishop of Chester, also became convinced in March that the Reformation had begun in Ireland and that the movement 'should be encouraged and promoted, and . . . put into such a train, as may be likely, with the blessing of God, to carry

[101] D. J. O'Donoghue, *The Life of William Carleton*, 2 vols. (London, 1896), ii. 1–14; B. Kiely, *Poor Scholar: A Study of William Carleton* (1948; new edn., Dublin, 1997), 79–94; W. Carleton, *Traits and Stories of the Irish Peasantry*, 2 vols. (Gerrard's Cross, 1990).

[102] *The Times*, 26 December 1826; 21 March, 10 April, 7, 23 May, 8 June 1827.

[103] T. Arnold to F. C. Blackstone, 11 January, 2 March 1827, Bodl. MS Eng. Lett. d. 348, fos. 30–3.

on the work to completion'. He was especially 'anxious that the sound and orthodox churchmen should take the lead'.[104] On 16 March, the Irish Protestant earl of Roden, a relation of Farnham, referred in the House of Lords 'to that glorious Reformation which is now working its way through every part of the country' and which was rendering any further concessions to Catholics unnecessary.[105] In early April 1827, John Jebb assured the English Tory Evangelical politician Sir Robert Inglis that across Ireland large numbers of Catholics were preparing to conform.[106] Writing in the conservative Edinburgh *Blackwood's Magazine* of May 1827, the Evangelical Church of Ireland clergyman Robert Daly reminded British readers of the benefits to be expected from the triumph of the Reformation movement in Ireland. 'If its people were Protestants', Daly asserted of Ireland,

> it would be free from its present divisions and distractions; the Catholic question, which is now used as an instrument for filling it with almost every kind of evil and for placing . . . the peace between it and Britain in peril, would be unknown. If its people were Protestants, they would be free from spiritual tyranny; they would be accessible to instruction and civilisation; the subject would not be arrayed against the ruler, and the tenant against the landlord; neighbour would not be seeking the ruin of neighbour; society would be placed under these bonds, feelings and regulations without which it can never know prosperity.[107]

Here, then, was the most effective means to secure permanently both the Union and the Protestant constitution, preserve the landed interest, and bring order and prosperity to Ireland. Here was the way to set the Catholic question permanently to rest.

In the spring of 1827, supporters of the Irish Reformation carried the movement to Britain. On 21 May, they held a large public meeting in London, packing the spacious Freemasons Hall with a fashionably dressed audience, for the purpose of founding the British Society for Promoting the Religious Principles of the Reformation. Speakers at the meeting included leaders of the Irish Reformation—the earl of Roden, Lord Farnham, James E. Gordon, Baptist Noel—along with such leaders in the English Church as Henry Ryder, the

[104] C. J. Blomfield to J. Jebb, 27 March 1827, Trinity College, Dublin, Jebb Papers, MS 6396–7/278.

[105] House of Lords, 16 March 1827, *Hansard's Parl. Deb.*, NS xvi (1826–7), cols. 1232–3.

[106] J. Jebb to Sir R. Inglis, 7 April 1827, cited in Wolffe, *The Protestant Crusade in Great Britain*, 38–9.

[107] Cited in Hehir, 'Evangelical Religion', 427.

Evangelical bishop of Lichfield and Coventry, and J. W. Cunningham, the Evangelical vicar of Harrow. The bishop of Salisbury was a member of the organizing committee.[108] The aims of the new British Reformation Society were defined as first, to assist 'the resident gentry and clergy of Ireland, and other societies' in distributing Bibles and spreading scriptural education, and second, to encourage scriptural education among the Irish in Britain, especially the estimated 130,000 Irish-born Catholics residing in London. Lord Roden assured the enthusiastic audience that the conversions being reported in Ireland were genuine, and that already 'Popery had had a greater shake than it had received from the first day of its admission' into Ireland. Within four years the British Reformation Society had established thirty-nine branch societies throughout England and Scotland. Dominated by Evangelicals in the established Church, the Reformation Society also had connections with the Albury circle, a group of Evangelicals associated with the wealthy banker Henry Drummond, and including the Scottish clergyman Edward Irving, who were attracted to prophecy and who believed in the imminent approach of the Second Coming, the end of the world, and the Last Judgement.[109] For these enthusiasts, the end of the Catholic Church in Ireland was one of the 'signs and wonders' to be looked for in the unsettled last days before Christ's return. For other Church Evangelicals, the Reformation Society promised to unite Irish, English, and Scottish Evangelicals in the campaign to win Ireland for Protestantism, consolidate the union, and preserve the Protestant constitution.

Supporters of the Reformation movement devoted themselves to organization. In the final months of 1827 and early months of 1828, Irish Protestants held 'Reformation meetings' and formed auxiliaries of the Reformation Society in Carlow, Kilkenny, Waterford, Fermoy, Drogheda, Downpatrick, Belfast, and other towns.[110] On 14 December 1827 a great Reformation meeting was held in the Rotunda of Dublin, presided over by Archbishop Magee, to inaugurate the Dublin Metropolitan Reformation Society.[111] The local Reformation societies distributed bibles, tracts, and prayer-books,

[108] *Dublin Evening Mail*, 25 May 1827.

[109] *The Times*, 22, 23 May 1827; Wolffe, *The Protestant Crusade in Great Britain*, 36–52.

[110] *Dublin Evening Mail*, 19, 22, 24 October, 2, 12 November 1827; 11, 28 January, 8 February, 28 March, 11, 14 April 1828.

[111] *Dublin Evening Mail*, 17 December 1827.

supported bible readers who visited the homes of the Irish Catholic poor, and appointed supervisors to co-ordinate the local missions. Reformation societies were forbidden to use bribes or any other inducements to conform, and special efforts were made to involve the parish clergy of the established Church.[112] The aim was to organize the established Church into a great popular mission. In January 1828 the High Church *British Critic* of London published a review of the first year of the 'Irish Reformation'.[113] Between September 1826 and September 1827, it claimed, nearly 2,400 Catholics had conformed to the established Church in Ireland.[114] While the centre of the Reformation was in Cavan, there were also significant clusters of converts in Sligo, Galway, and Limerick. Branches of the Reformation Society were multiplying, uniting landowners and established clergy for local mission work. The *British Critic* acknowledged that the Reformation movement was encountering strong resistance from the Catholic Church in Ireland, and that some converts had subsequently returned to Catholicism. The struggle was becoming a desperate one. However, it insisted, now that the established Church had entered into a direct confrontation with the Catholic Church in Ireland, it could not withdraw. Further, as the established Churches of England and Ireland were united, the struggle for the Reformation in Ireland was one that must also affect the established Church in England. With a clear reference to the pressure for Catholic Emancipation, the *British Critic* maintained that the established United Church was in 'the deadly gripe of an antagonist, who will never relinquish the struggle, until he shall have been wholly overcome. Either England must subdue the Papacy by reforming Ireland, or the Papacy will overthrow the Church and Constitution of England'.[115]

The Reformation movement in Ireland, however, was not proving as vigorous on the ground as speakers at the Reformation Society meetings or authors in the Protestant press were portraying it. The popular movement announced with such enthusiasm at Cavan in 1826–7 was not bringing the expected wave of conversions in the localities. The 2,400 conversions in the first year of the Reformation movement were hardly a great number when set

[112] Gallogly, *The Diocese of Kilmore*, 47.
[113] 'The Irish Reformation', *British Critic* (January 1828), 1–58.
[114] Ibid. 53. [115] Ibid. 55.

against an Irish Catholic population of over 5 million. Further, according to the O'Connellite *Dublin Evening Post*, the Cavan conversions had 'come to a full stop' by the end of July 1827.[116] As 1827 drew to a close, Protestant newspapers ceased to publish numbers of new converts, and conversions apparently became rare. 'There has been', the London Dissenting *Eclectic Review* observed of the Irish Reformation movement in January 1828, 'a long pause in the announcement of its progress, and we fear, it is a "pause prophetic of its end".'[117] The Second Reformation did not end in 1828, but it lost momentum as it failed to fulfil the expectations raised in the winter and spring of 1826–7. The missionary societies remained active, and in 1828 Church Evangelicals formed an Established Church Home Mission in an attempt to revive the campaign. But it was without success: and the prospect that the movement would rapidly achieve the conformity of the majority of the Irish people to the established Church faded during 1828. 'The labourers in this vineyard', Thomas Wyse observed in 1829 of the Reformation movement, 'began valiantly, but threw aside their spades before noon. . . . The bubble burst; the joint-stock company dispersed; the defaulters escaped: saintship fell to a grievous discount: a few sufferers railed and wept . . . and the rest of the nation . . . shook their heads and laughed openly at the imposture.'[118] 'They had existence for a short period,' observed one Irish witness of the Reformation societies before a parliamentary committee in 1832, 'and they have not left a vestige behind them of their boasted labours.'[119] After so much public investment in the established Church and the Scripture education societies, the lack of success of the much-heralded Reformation movement was ignominious.

The growth of the Reformation movement had been circumscribed in part by organized resistance of the Catholic community. The Catholic hierarchy had reacted quickly to the activities on Farnham's estates in Cavan, and the deputation of bishops, including the primate, which had travelled to Cavan in December 1826 had done much to strengthen Catholic resistance to the Reformation

[116] *Dublin Evening Post*, 31 July 1827.

[117] *Eclectic Review*, 29 (January 1828), 30.

[118] Wyse, *Historical Sketch of the Late Catholic Association*, i. 230.

[119] Evidence of John Dunn, Esq., 21 February 1832, Second Report of the Select Committee of the House of Commons on Tithes in Ireland, *Parliamentary Papers*, xxi (508), 1831–32, ques. 2794, p. 265.

missionaries. The allegations that bribes were being offered to secure converts to Protestantism proved an effective, if not always fair, way to demean those conforming to the established Church. Converts were dismissed by a correspondent in the O'Connellite *Dublin Evening Post* of 31 July 1827 as 'starving and half naked wretches [who] were bribed with a dinner, a pair of trowsers, or a petticoat, to foreswear themselves'. 'These conversions', O'Connell assured his wife in March 1827, 'are exceedingly foolish things. They are buying wretches in every direction who are a disgrace to them and no loss to the church they desert.'[120] Despite the denials by Lord Farnham and other Protestant gentry that there had been any use of bribes, the charge stuck and proved destructive to the reputations and social relations of converts, while at the same time placing an increasingly impenetrable barrier between Reformation missionaries and Catholic communities. Facing rejection by their families and communities, many converts returned to the Catholic Church. In late September 1827, the Irish Catholic primate Patrick Curtis reported to Rome that, in the presence of a crowd of 5,000, a large number of converts had renounced their defection with tears of repentance.[121]

In *The Bible Saints of Cavan*, Matt Dolan, a Ballymachugh tinker, ridiculed one of these 'converts', who had taken the alleged bribes on offer, only to return to the Faith once the harvest was in.

> He was fed like a game-clock in Farnham
> And slept on a feather bed,
> But he only took a loan of that religion,
> Until the new 'praties' [potatoes] came in.[122]

William Carleton would later borrow this image of converts taking a temporary 'loan' of the Protestant religion in his novel *Valentine McClutchy, the Irish Agent*, written in 1844. Carleton had by now put his own New Reformation enthusiasms behind him and his novel darkly parodied the movement. As the Reformation reached the fictional parish of Castle Cumber, one local wag circulated the rumour that the Reformation Society was offering five guineas to each Catholic who would conform to the established Church. Almost

[120] *Dublin Evening Post*, 31 July 1827; D. O'Connell to his wife, 22 March 1827, in O'Connell (ed.), *Correspondence of Daniel O'Connell*, iii. 302.

[121] Macaulay, *William Crolly, Archbishop of Armagh*, 98.

[122] Cited in Gallogly, *The Diocese of Kilmore*, 50.

immediately a crowd gathered in front of the residence-house of the parish incumbent, the Revd Phineas Lucre, anxious to claim the money. These ranged from the profligate, prepared to sell their conversions for the best price, to the jokers, who were ready to take the money and go through the recantation ceremony, only to return to the Catholic Church in six months' time, to the genuinely starving—spectral, ragged figures who gave the proceedings a macabre aspect. The last to speak with the Revd Lucre was Raymond-na-hattha, who proposed to 'borrow' Lucre's religion (and money) but only till 'the new praties comes in'. Then he promised he would 'bring it back safe'. Once Lucre made it clear that there would be no payments for converts, the crowd quickly evaporated.[123]

Also contributing to the solidarity of the Catholic community in Ireland were movements towards a richer communal devotional life. The year 1825 had been a holy year, with a jubilee indulgence for those making the pilgrimage to Rome. In the year 1826, the new pope, Leo XII, had extended to Catholics throughout the world the jubilee indulgence, conditional upon prescribed penitential exercises. The devout in many parishes followed the exercises, which strengthened their devotional life and religious identity.[124] The Catholic leadership also provided a robust intellectual defence of the faith. In February 1827, a group of Dublin Catholics, encouraged by Bishop Doyle, established the Catholic Book Society, to provide for the publication and distribution of inexpensive editions of Catholic works.[125] Between 19 and 25 April 1827, Tom Maguire, a Leitrim priest who had gained a reputation as a speaker during the Bible war, engaged Richard Pope, the leading Protestant champion, in a prolonged public debate before large crowds in Dublin. While both sides claimed victory, Maguire had presented a lucid and reasoned defence of key Catholic doctrines which had greatly impressed both his opponent and the Protestant members of the audience.[126] According to Daniel O'Connell, who co-chaired the debate, 'this simple, unpretending priest from the bogs of Leitrim has given a

[123] Carleton, *Valentine McClutchy; the Irish Agent*, chs. 11–12.

[124] Ibid. 98; Fitzpatrick, *Life, Times and Correspondence of Dr. Doyle*, i. 465–7.

[125] Fitzpatrick, *Life, Times and Correspondence of Dr. Doyle*, ii. 14–5.

[126] *Authenticated Report of the Discussion which took place between the Rev Richard T. P. Pope and the Rev Thomas Maguire* (Dublin, 1827); *Dublin Evening Mail*, 20, 23, 25, 27, 30 April, 16 July 1827, *Dublin Evening Post*, 19, 21, 24, 26 April, 4 August 1827; Bowen, *The Protestant Crusade in Ireland*, 107–8; Fitzpatrick, *Life, Times and Correspondence of Dr. Doyle*, ii. 33–4.

death-blow to the doctrines of the Established Church'.[127] After this and the many other public debates of the Bible war, the claims of Reformation missionaries that Irish Catholics were benighted children needing education and civilization lost credibility. At the popular level, the millenarian dreams of such Protestant enthusiasts as Lord Farnham were met by similar hopes among the Catholic peasantry, with Irish poets speaking of an approaching 'deliverance' from Protestantism—the 'sons of Luther' and 'Calvin's hated breed'.[128] Probably most important, Catholic communal identity had always been far stronger than New Reformation leaders such as William Magee had understood. Recent work by the historian Emmet Larkin has demonstrated the continued importance for early nineteenth-century Catholic communities of 'stations', or the custom of holding communion and confessions in private homes where church accommodation was inadequate. The numerous 'hedge schools', moreover, reflected the willingness of hard-pressed Catholic farming and labouring families to pay for their children to receive Catholic schooling. 'There never was a more unfounded calumny', insisted William Carleton in about 1829, 'than that which would impute to the Irish peasantry an indifference to education.'[129] Far from achieving the conformity of Catholic Ireland, the Reformation movement strengthened this existing Catholic devotional and communal solidarity, helping in the process to forge a new Irish Catholic national identity. It is significant that the Catholic bishops followed Doyle's lead in joining the Catholic Association, until by 1829 every member of Ireland's Catholic hierarchy had joined.[130]

'Can any man who has gained permission to take off his strait-waistcoat, and been out of Bedlam three weeks', asked Sydney Smith in the *Edinburgh Review* of March 1827, 'believe that the Catholic question will be set to rest by the conversion of the Irish Catholics to the Protestant religion?' Rather than press on with the New Reformation campaign, Smith argued, it was time to recognize that the majority of the Irish people would remain Catholic, and that

[127] Cited in Gallogly, *The Diocese of Kilmore*, 42.

[128] G. O'Tuathaigh, 'Gaelic Ireland, Popular Politics and Daniel O'Connell', *Journal of the Galway Archaeological and Historical Society*, 34 (1974–5), 29–33.

[129] E. Larkin, 'The Rise and Fall of Stations in Ireland, 1750–1850', unpublished paper (1997); Dowling, *Hedge Schools of Ireland*; Carleton, *Traits and Stories of the Irish Peasantry*, i. 271.

[130] MacDonagh, 'The Politicization of the Irish Catholic Bishops', 42–3.

only by granting Emancipation would it be possible for the Irish Catholics to become loyal subjects of the United Kingdom.[131] In 1827, James Doyle, bishop of Kildare and Leighlin, issued a lengthy pamphlet in response to William Magee's trumpeting of the New Reformation in his episcopal Charge of 1827. Doyle insisted that the New Reformation was weakening and would fail. For all its considerable wealth and status, the learning of its clergy and the backing of the State, the established Church would not break the hold of the Catholic Faith over the majority of the Irish people. The idea of a confessional State, with its claims for the union of Church and State, was not viable in Ireland, and could not be made so in an increasingly liberal and tolerant age. 'The civil liberty and true religion of a country', he insisted, 'are greatly impaired by any union of the church and the state.'[132] The time had come to adopt an alternative plan for the organization of the country. Doyle expressed his support for a liberal parliamentary State, with untrammelled debate in the legislature, with an independent judiciary, a free press, and freedom of religion. 'In such a country', he maintained,

> no union of Church and State is necessary, no combination of artificial power is required, no juggling of ascendancy—no corporate monopoly—no unhallowed commixture of what is human with what is divine. The liberties and happiness of all the people should be the basis of such a state. . . . In such a state, the Catholic Church, and every other church or sect might hold its assemblies, preach the Gospel, and minister its rules in peace; they might exclude from their respective assemblies, and place abroad among the heathens and publicans, if you will, all those who dissented from their doctrine, or disbelieved their creed. But the prince and the legislature, whilst it yielded them protection, should see that they troubled not the public peace, and in place of arming them with earthly power, to inflict vengeance on dissent, or to oppress with temporal penalties, the brother who might disobey, it should teach them all that the kingdom consigned to their care was not of this world, and that the loyal and industrious heretic was as acceptable to the state as the most orthodox of any, even the most exalted communion.[133]

Doyle's portrayal of a liberal, tolerant, and essentially secular parliamentary State, to emerge out of the struggles of the Bible war and

[131] [S. Smith], 'The Catholic Question', *Edinburgh Review*, 45 (March 1827), 423–45, 436.

[132] [J. Doyle], *A Reply by J.K.L. to the late Charge of the Most Rev Doctor Magee, Protestant Archbishop of Dublin* (Dublin, 1827), 97.

[133] Ibid. 91–2.

New Reformation campaign in Ireland, was published simultaneously in Dublin and London.[134] For Doyle, the New Reformation was weakening rather than strengthening the establishment; it was the gasp of an established Church 'flushed in her decline'.[135]

Catholic Emancipation

'It is really a pity', James MacHale, Catholic priest in Hollymount, observed in the *Dublin Evening Post* on 31 May 1827, 'that it was at the eleventh hour—unfortunately for the Parson, later than the eleventh hour, that the Reformation began here. Unfortunately, when Liverpool and Eldon, and the other rewarders of bigoted and proselytising Parsons are out of office.' 'Had they but known the strange shifting of events', MacHale added with reference to the Reformation leaders, 'they would not have thus striven to purchase public ridicule.'[136] Another reason for the faltering of the Reformation movement in Ireland, as MacHale noted, was that it coincided with a ministerial crisis at Westminster, a crisis which brought to an end the long-standing Liverpool Government, with its firm commitment to strengthening and extending the established Churches in the three kingdoms. On 17 February 1827, Lord Liverpool, a staunch opponent of Emancipation, suffered an apoplectic stroke that ended his political career. After some hesitation, on 10 April the king called George Canning, now the dominant figure in the Government and a pro-Catholic, to become prime minister. This was followed by the resignation of leading anti-Emancipation ministers, including Sir Robert Peel, the duke of Wellington, and Lord Eldon. As a result, Canning's Cabinet had a decided pro-Catholic majority. During the spring and early summer of 1827, Canning consolidated his pro-Catholic Government's position, appointing some moderate Whig ministers. Then, on 8 August 1827, Canning unexpectedly died. On 9 January 1828, after some months of political instability, the king called the anti-Emancipation duke of Wellington to form a Government. Peel returned to his former office as home secretary. Significantly the leading anti-Catholic, Lord Eldon, was not invited back into office, in part a reflection of

[134] Fitzpatrick, *Life, Times and Correspondence of Dr. Doyle*, ii. 19–28.

[135] McGrath, *Politics, Interdenominational Relations and Education*, 144.

[136] *Dublin Evening Post*, 31 May 1827.

his age (he was 76 at the time) but also an indication that Wellington and Peel now recognized that concessions would have to be made to pro-Catholic opinion, concessions to which Eldon could not be expected to agree. The Reformation movement was failing to make significant progress in converting Irish Catholics to the established Church and politicians such as Peel had disassociated themselves from the New Reformation campaign.[137] By the end of 1827 it was becoming clear that the Union of Britain and Ireland could not be consolidated on the basis of the Protestant confessional State.

The first blow to the constitution of Church and State came in the spring of 1828 with the Repeal of the Test and Corporation Acts in England and Wales. These acts, it will be recalled, had been passed in the later seventeenth century as a means of excluding Dissenters from holding many civil offices. The Corporation Act of 1661 required all borough officers to take oaths of supremacy and allegiance, and to have received the sacrament according to the rites of the Church of England during the twelve months prior to being elected to office. The Test Act of 1673 imposed similar requirements on those holding most Crown offices, including military officers. The annual Indemnity Acts passed after 1727 had allowed Dissenters whose consciences would permit occasional conformity to the Church of England to take the qualifying sacrament after election to office. By the early nineteenth century, moreover, the Test and Corporation Acts were being largely ignored. In 1827, for example, out of 260 members of the City of London corporation, only ninety had taken the sacramental test.[138] None the less, the existence of these acts represented the principle that Church and State were inextricably united and that only members of the established Church could be entrusted with civil office. For High Anglicans, the Test and Corporation Acts were integral to the Protestant constitution; for Dissenters, they were a badge of inferiority.

In March 1827, following Lord Liverpool's stroke and removal from office, the four main Dissenting organizations in England and Wales—the General Body of Dissenting Ministers of London and Westminster, the Dissenting Deputies of the Three Denominations (Presbyterians, Independents, and Baptists), the Protestant Society

[137] Peel had expressed his rejection of the proselytizing aims of the Scripture education movement in his speeches on the renewal of the grant to the Kildare Place Society, 19 March 1827; *Hansard's Parl. Deb.*, NS xvi, cols. 1262–3, 1265–6.

[138] Watts, *The Dissenters*, ii. 418.

for the Protection of Religious Liberty, and the Unitarian Association—met to revive the campaign for the repeal of the Test and Corporation Acts. They formed a United Committee and entered into discussions with parliamentary leaders. On the whole, Dissenting leaders sought to keep their campaign for repeal of the Test and Corporation Acts separate from the movement for Catholic Emancipation. English and Welsh Dissenters were deeply divided over Catholic Emancipation. The older Dissenting denominations, and especially middle-class Dissenters in the larger cities, tended to support Emancipation. The New Evangelical Dissent, however, with its base among the poorly educated lower social orders in the villages, remained more fearful of Rome and less tolerant.[139]

Lord John Russell, a younger son of the sixth duke of Bedford, was commissioned to introduce the repeal motion in the House of Commons. On 26 February 1828 Russell introduced a motion in the Commons for the House to go into committee to examine the Test and Corporation Acts. The Government, led by Huskisson, Palmerston, and Peel, opposed the motion on the grounds that it was inexpedient and unnecessary, but the Government was defeated by a vote of 237 to 193. Two days later, on 28 February, the Commons passed without a vote a resolution in favour of repealing the Test and Corporation Acts. The resolution was in many respects unexpected. There had been little real agitation on the part of Dissenters outside Parliament. At the same time, with no sign of strong feeling in the country against repeal, the Government decided to drop its opposition to Russell's repeal motion. As Peel explained to his former tutor, Charles Lloyd, now bishop of Oxford, it was difficult for the Government to insist that the Test and Corporation Acts were needed to preserve the established Church in England, when neither Scotland nor Ireland maintained sacramental tests to uphold their established Churches. He had also become convinced that the Government would be soundly defeated in the Commons if it opposed repeal.[140] In March, Peel held consultations with the archbishop of Canterbury and other bishops of the Church of England in an effort to gain their acquiescence to a compromise motion, one

[139] R. W. Davis, 'The Strategy of "Dissent" in the Repeal Campaign of 1820–28', *Journal of Modern History*, 38 (1966), 374–87; Watts, *The Dissenters*, ii. 419–22.

[140] Sir R. Peel to the bishop of Oxford, 20 March 1828, in R. Peel, *Memoirs of the Right Honourable Sir Robert Peel* (London, 1856), i. 77–80; N. Gash, *Mr Secretary Peel: The Life of Sir Robert Peel to 1830* (London, 1961), 460–4.

which would replace the sacramental test with a declaration.[141] There was some difficulty in deciding on the wording of the declaration, but on the whole the bishops went along with the Government's advice. The repeal bill passed easily through the Commons. In the House of Lords, the venerable Lord Eldon vehemently opposed the bill, which he denounced as a short-term measure that would have far-reaching consequences for the Protestant constitution. 'The principle of expediency', he asserted in the debate on the second reading of the bill,

> was a low ground of legislation. That Church . . . was not an establishment erected for mere purposes of convenience, but was essentially and inseparably connected with part of the State. . . . The Constitution required that the Church of England should be supported: and the best way of affording that support to her was to admit only her own members to offices of trust and emolument.

'Their lordships', he warned, 'should take care that they did not put those asunder whom the Constitution had joined together.'[142] In late April 1828, however, the House of Lords agreed to the repeal of the Test and Corporation Acts, replacing them with the requirement that all candidates for office declare 'on the true faith of a Christian, not to weaken the established church'. No bishop opposed repeal in the Lords.[143]

Supporters of repeal had endeavoured to keep it separate from the question of Catholic Emancipation.[144] Yet it grew clear to both its supporters and opponents that repeal would open the way for Catholic Emancipation. O'Connell had certainly recognized this, and had thrown the Catholic Association behind the cause of repeal: some 100,000 Irish Catholics had petitioned for the repeal of the Test and Corporation Acts in England.[145] Parliament passed the Repeal Act with so little resistance largely because the majority in both the Commons and Lords had come to accept the inevitability

[141] E. Hughes, 'The Bishops and Reform, 1831–3: Some Fresh Correspondence', *English Historical Review*, 56 (1941), 459.

[142] H. Twiss, *The Public and Private Life of Lord Chancellor Eldon*, 2 vols. (London, 1846), ii. 203.

[143] J. C. D. Clark, *English Society 1688–1832*, 394–7; Peel, *Memoirs of Sir Robert Peel*, i. 68–100; Varley, *William Van Mildert*, 129–34; Watts, *The Dissenters*, ii. 417–24; Halévy, *A History of the English People in the Nineteenth Century*, ii. 263–6; Gash, *Mr Secretary Peel*, 464–5; R.W. Davis, *Dissent in Politics 1780–1830: The Political Life of William Smith*, 244–8.

[144] R.W. Davis, 'The Strategy of "Dissent" in the Repeal Campaign', 391–3.

[145] O'Ferrall, *Catholic Emancipation*, 181–2.

of Emancipation. The Protestant constitution was becoming indefensible. The passing of repeal, an ecstatic Lord Holland wrote to his fellow Whig [and namesake] Henry Fox, on 10 April 1828, 'is the greatest victory over the *principle* of persecution & exclusion yet obtained. . . . [I]t explodes the real Tory doctrine *that Church & State are indivisible*.'[146] For Lord John Russell, writing to the Irish Catholic poet Thomas Moore on 31 March, it was 'a gratifying thing to force the enemy to give up his first line, that none but Churchmen are worthy to serve the State, and I trust we shall soon make him give up the second, that none but Protestants are'.[147]

The decisive moment for Catholic Emancipation came soon after the passage of the Repeal Act, with the Catholic Association's famous victory in the by-election for county Clare. In May 1828 there was a Cabinet reshuffle following the resignations of Huskisson and the other Canningites from the Wellington Government. Vesey Fitzgerald, a popular Protestant landlord and liberal pro-Catholic, was appointed president of the Board of Trade. This required him to stand again for re-election in his county Clare seat. Normally there would have been no question of opposing Fitzgerald's election. However, in January 1828, the Catholic Association had pledged to increase the pressure for Emancipation by opposing the election of any supporter of Wellington's Government. Initially, no candidate could be found to stand against Fitzgerald. Then in late June 1828, in a risky but ultimately effective tactical move, O'Connell agreed that he would personally oppose Fitzgerald. Although as a Catholic he could not take the oath of abjuration required to assume a seat in Parliament, there was no legal obstacle to his standing as a candidate. The Catholic Association provided O'Connell with funds and organizational support. Probably the decisive factor, however, was the influence exercised by Catholic priests. Bishop Doyle, the leading figure in the defeat of the Reformation movement, issued a public letter in support of O'Connell's candidacy. Father Tom Maguire, the veteran Catholic champion during the Bible war, travelled about the county speaking in support of O'Connell. An estimated 150 priests were active in the election, pressing the 40-shilling freeholders hard to vote for O'Connell against the instructions of their landlords. Among these priests was the gaunt Father John Murphy of

[146] Cited in J. C. D. Clark, *English Society 1688–1832*, 396–7.

[147] Cited in Halévy, *History of the English People*, ii. 266.

Corofin, who marched his parishioners in order to the polling place and whose very glare was regarded by O'Connell's opponents as a form of intimidation. The only surprise in the election result was that Fitzgerald did as well as he did, polling 982 votes to O'Connell's 2,057. O'Connell was declared elected.[148] Fitzgerald was devastated. 'All the great interests broke down', he complained to Peel on 5 July 1828, 'and the desertion has been universal. Such a scene as we have had! Such a tremendous prospect as it opens to us!' 'The conduct of the priests', he added, 'has passed all that you could picture to yourself.'[149]

The Clare election revealed starkly the new political situation in Ireland, the legacy in part of the Bible war and New Reformation struggle. The Catholic priests were now politically active and firmly aligned with the Catholic Association in the Emancipation movement. That even a popular, pro-Catholic landlord such as Fitzgerald could be unseated demonstrated the vulnerability of all established political interests in Ireland. 'Probably at the next general election', the lord-lieutenant and Waterloo veteran Lord Anglesey had observed to the Whig Lord Holland on 1 July 1828, 'the returns will be chiefly Catholic. And what then?'[150] During the late summer and autumn Ireland seemed to be heading towards civil war. In counties Tipperary, Limerick, and Clare, large bodies of Catholic men assembled and marched in orderly, semi-military processions through towns and villages, with green flags or banners, harps, fifes and drums, green sashes, and cockades. Although the marchers were mainly peaceful and unarmed, the processions, estimated to include as many as 10,000 men, created widespread alarm among Protestants. For their part, Irish Protestants organized a network of Brunswick Clubs in the aftermath of the Clare election, with the aim of 'preserving the Integrity of the Protestant Constitution'. Many of the Evangelical gentry, including Lord Farnham, now shifted their attentions from the mainly religious Reformation Societies to the political Brunswick Clubs. In the North, the Orange lodges were also active in organizing Protestant resistance to Catholic demonstrations.

[148] O'Ferrall, *Catholic Emancipation*, 188–99; MacDonagh, *Life of Daniel O'Connell*, 248–56.

[149] W. V. Fitzgerald to Sir R. Peel, 5 July 1828, in Peel, *Memoirs of Sir Robert Peel*, i. 114.

[150] Marquess of Anglesey, *One-Leg: The Life and Letters of Henry William Paget, First Marquess of Anglesey* (London, 1961), 200.

In September, John Lawless, a Catholic lawyer from Belfast and a leading figure in the Catholic Association, began a propaganda tour in the north, accompanied by a large crowd of Catholic supporters. On 23 September a pitched battle between Lawless's procession and local Orangemen was only narrowly averted by Government forces in county Monaghan. It now seemed only a matter of time before serious violence erupted in the north. There were, moreover, concerns about how Catholics in the army would behave if they were ordered to suppress Catholic demonstrations. With their power over the Catholic marches and demonstrations, O'Connell and the Catholic Association had emerged as the real guarantors of public order in Ireland.[151] In Britain tensions were also mounting. British opponents of Emancipation were also forming Brunswick Clubs and these were co-operating with existing anti-Catholic Orange lodges and Pitt Clubs to arouse Protestant opinion. On 24 October 1828 the Kent Brunswick Club organized a meeting on Penendon Heath, near Maidstone, which attracted an estimated 60,000 people. At this meeting anti-Catholic champions debated publicly with pro-Catholics, in an English version of the Irish Bible war.[152]

By August 1828, both Wellington and Peel, hitherto leading opponents of Emancipation, had become convinced of its necessity. Not only was Ireland moving towards civil war, but the Government feared the next dissolution of Parliament would bring repeats of the Clare election result across the south and west of Ireland. On 1 August Wellington informed the king with brutal realism that while 'rebellion was pending in Ireland . . . the government was faced with a House of Commons it dared not dissolve which contained a majority who believed the only solution was Catholic emancipation'.[153] Concerned to calm the popular excitement in Britain and Ireland, Wellington's Cabinet secretly prepared an Emancipation measure during the last months of 1828 and early weeks of 1829. The challenge for the Government was to persuade the king to give up his conscientious opposition to emancipation, and to devise a bill that would provide securities for the United Church of England and Ireland and gain sufficient support in the House of Lords. In November, Wellington consulted with some bishops of the Church

[151] W. Hinde, *Catholic Emancipation: A Shake to Men's Minds* (Oxford, 1992), 99–115; Gash, *Mr Secretary Peel*, 535–6; O'Ferrall, *Catholic Emancipation*, 200–15.

[152] Machin, *The Catholic Question in English Politics*, 131–42.

[153] Cited in Varley, *William Van Mildert*, 136.

of England, and on 26 December he met at Lambeth with the archbishop of Canterbury and the bishops of London and Durham. The Anglican hierarchy, he found, was adamantly opposed to any Emancipation measure.[154] The king also remained recalcitrant. Undaunted, the Cabinet set to work on drafting the Emancipation bill in late January 1829. Wellington felt the best security for a lasting settlement in Ireland would be to combine Emancipation with a degree of State control over the Catholic clergy, and the Cabinet discussed plans for the licensing and payment of the Roman Catholic clergy, or in short, the creation of a Catholic establishment in Ireland. In the event, the Cabinet decided against licensing and payment of priests.[155] Rather, ministers agreed on two main securities for the maintenance of the political order in Ireland. First, the Irish 40-shilling freehold voters, who had proved so susceptible to the influence of the Catholic priests during the Waterford and Clare elections, were to be disenfranchised. Secondly, the Catholic Association was to be suppressed. By the end of January the ministerial plan for Emancipation was substantially complete, the king was, with considerable difficulty, brought to acknowledge the necessity of the plan, and on 5 February, the king's speech opening the new session of Parliament announced the Government's intention to introduce Emancipation.

Most people in Britain were shocked by the news that the Tory Government had decided to reverse its opposition to Emancipation. In response, opponents of Emancipation, with their networks of Brunswick societies, Reformation societies, Pitt Clubs, and Orange lodges, launched a campaign of public meetings across Britain and Ireland, which brought a flood of anti-Catholic petitions to Parliament: some 720 anti-Catholic petitions were received by the end of February, as opposed to only 220 petitions supporting Emancipation. The numbers of signatures added to the weight of the anti-Catholic petitions, with one from Glasgow bearing nearly 37,000 signatures, one from Kent with 81,400 signatures, and one from Ireland with 168,000 signatures.[156] For the anti-Catholics, the Protestant Constitution and established Churches had been betrayed

[154] Ibid. 136; Hinde, *Catholic Emancipation*, 129; Machin, *The Catholic Question in English Politics*, 159; C. J. Lewis, 'The Disintegration of the Tory-Anglican Alliance in the Struggle for Catholic Emancipation', *Church History*, 29 (1960), 34.

[155] Machin, *The Catholic Question in English Politics*, 160; Gash, *Mr Secretary Peel*, 554–5.

[156] Machin, *The Catholic Question in English Politics*, 148.

by a Tory Government pledged to their support. The world was turned upside down. 'The friends of the constitution', John Jebb, bishop of Limerick, complained to Peel on 11 February, 'have been discountenanced, almost as enemies; its enemies encouraged, altogether as friends.'[157]

Peel, who had been elected MP for Oxford University in 1826 as an anti-Catholic, now felt honour-bound to resign his seat and present himself again to the constituency. At Oxford, opposition to Peel was mobilized by the celebrated author of *The Christian Year*, John Keble, and a group of younger fellows, including Richard Hurrell Froude and John Henry Newman of Oriel College. For Newman, the contest was one between religious principle and political expediency: the established Church and Protestant constitution must not be weakened, not even for the 'pacification of Ireland', and Oxford University must not be put 'under the feet' of Wellington (who was chancellor of the University as well as prime minister). In the last days of February, Peel was defeated amid uproarious scenes by the Tory Evangelical and anti-Catholic, Sir Robert Inglis, in what Newman described to his mother as a 'glorious Victory', which 'proved the independence of the Church and of Oxford'.[158] The Government immediately found another parliamentary seat for Peel, the pocket borough of Westbury, which was vacated by the resignation of Sir Manasseh Lopes, a notorious borough owner. The effects of the Oxford contest proved lasting. It had highlighted the unpopularity of Emancipation, and suggested that the Government could get the bill through Parliament only by manipulating corrupt aspects of the old political system.[159] And it had called into question the connection of Church and State in England. Indeed, the organizers of Peel's defeat—Keble, Newman, Froude, encouraged by the Irish High Churchman John Jebb—would increasingly use their Oxford forum to call upon the Church to assert its 'spiritual independence' from a State prepared, in their view, to sacrifice religious principle to political expediency.[160]

On 5 March 1829 Peel introduced the Government's Emancipation

[157] J. Jebb to Sir R. Peel, 11 February 1829, BL, Add. Ms 40398, fo. 233.

[158] I. Ker, *John Henry Newman: A Biography* (Oxford, 1988), 33–4; S. Gilley, *Newman and his Age* (London, 1990), 72–4; Ward, *Victorian Oxford*, 71–5.

[159] M. Brock, *The Great Reform Act* (London, 1973), 56–7.

[160] Nockles, *The Oxford Movement in Context*, 69; P. Brendon, *Hurrell Froude and the Oxford Movement* (London, 1974), 94.

bill in what was widely acknowledged as the best speech of his career.[161] There would be no peace, he maintained, until the Catholic question had been addressed. During the preceding half century the Catholics of Ireland had been granted most civil and political rights in the State. Parliament could not now call a halt to that process and continue to deprive Irish Catholics of full political rights without the risk of civil war. The Catholic majority in Ireland had sufficient political power to disrupt the processes of constitutional government, and they were profoundly alienated by their disabilities. In the interest of consolidating the Union, Parliament must now grant Emancipation. Peel acknowledged that many continued to place hope in the Reformation movement in Ireland and believe that the Irish Catholics could be converted to Protestantism, if only the State would resist concessions. 'I would ask of those', Peel stated, 'most strenuous for arguing [against Emancipation] mainly upon religious grounds, what progress have we made in Ireland in the propagation and establishment of religious truth, under the system of penal and disqualifying laws? Where are our conversions?' For Peel, the weakness of the Reformation movement resulted largely from the 'penalties and disabilities' imposed on the Irish Catholics; these had created a sense of grievance, closing Catholic communities off against the Protestant missionaries. Now that the Reformation movement was failing, nothing would be lost in removing those 'penalties and disabilities'. It was also possible that New Reformation missionaries would find Catholics in Ireland less resistant after they had been granted Emancipation:

> Be the cause what it may, the fact is certain, that the reformation in Ireland has hitherto made no advance. We lose nothing, we endanger nothing in this respect by the change of system; but on the other hand, let us cherish the hope that increased intercourse between Protestant and Roman Catholic will inspire feelings of mutual charity and good will; that the agents of Protestant benevolence will be regarded with less of suspicion and distrust—that truth, moral and religious will have a freer scope for exertion—that the Protestant faith, by confiding in its own intrinsic purity, in the progress of knowledge, and the love and affection of the people, may find an energy and expansive force, which it has not found, in Ireland at least, in the monopoly of civil privileges.[162]

[161] Gash, *Mr Secretary Peel*, 570–6; C. Greville, *The Greville Memoirs*, ed. H. Reeve, 3 vols. (London, 1874), i. 183–4.

[162] *Hansard's Parl. Deb.*, NS XX (1829), cols. 753–4.

Despite determined opposition from anti-Catholic ultras, the Emancipation bill proceeded smoothly through the Commons, with a majority of 188 at the first reading on 10 March and a majority of 180 at the second reading on 17 March. The bill then moved rapidly through the House of Lords, receiving its first reading on 31 March and passing its third reading with a majority of 104 on 10 April. Despite a final appeal against Emancipation from the majority of bishops of the Church of Ireland, on 13 April the king reluctantly assented to the bill.[163]

The Emancipation Act marked a fundamental transformation of the Protestant constitution of the United Kingdom. Catholics were now allowed to hold most civil and military offices. Irish Catholics were permitted to sit in Parliament. British Catholics were allowed to sit in Parliament and, provided they met the necessary property qualifications, to vote in parliamentary elections. There were, to be sure, safeguards for the established religion. Catholics were still excluded from a small number of offices, among them the offices of lord high chancellor of England and lord-lieutenant of Ireland. Before taking their seats in parliament, Catholics were required to take an oath abjuring 'any Intention to subvert the present Church Establishment as settled by Law within this Realm' and pledging to do nothing 'to disturb or weaken the Protestant Religion or Protestant Government, in the United Kingdom'. In Ireland, moreover, Emancipation was accompanied by the disenfranchisement of the 40-shilling freeholders and the enactment of a £10 property qualification, reducing the Irish electorate from about 100,000 to some 16,000. For all these safeguards, Emancipation represented a fundamental departure from the idea of the Protestant commonwealth. No longer could it be assumed that the Union of the three kingdoms would be consolidated on the basis of a shared Protestant faith as mediated through the established Churches. The State acknowledged that the large majority of the Irish people would remain outside the established Church.

For O'Connell, writing to Edward Dwyer, former secretary of the disbanded Catholic Association, on 14 April 1829—what O'Connell termed 'the first day of freedom'—the winning of Emancipation was a revolution. 'It is', he averred, 'one of the greatest

[163] O'Ferrall, *Catholic Emancipation*, 256; W. Magee to J. Jebb, 5 March 1829, Trinity College, Dublin, Jebb Papers, MS 6396–7/333.

triumphs recorded in history—a bloodless revolution more extensive in its operation than any other political change that could take place.' Out of respect for their Protestant opponents, O'Connell would not allow illuminations and celebrations to mark the victory. Bishop Doyle, also regarded as one of the architects of victory, similarly refused to sound any note of triumphalism, but rather felt relief that civil war had been avoided. Yet many Irish Catholics viewed Emancipation with an almost millenarian sense of expectation. It was a moment of liberation, achieved 'without either a crime or a tear'. Surely this victory would be followed by others—the abolition of tithe, state-funding of Catholic education, the end of the Protestant establishment, even the repeal of the Union and the restoration of an Irish parliament in Dublin.[164] O'Connell and the Catholic Association had a right to be jubilant in the spring of 1829. They had won the Bible war and halted the Scripture education and Reformation movements. They had forced Parliament to recognize that it could not consolidate the United Kingdom on the basis of the Protestant establishment, but that it must provide equal political rights to the different Christian denominations. Further, they had achieved Emancipation against the desires of probably the large majority of the British population. Significantly, several months after the Emancipation victory, O'Connell offered his services to the Jewish community in Britain, to act as parliamentary spokesman for the cause of Jewish Emancipation.[165]

The passing of Emancipation was a heavy blow to the established Church in Ireland, especially coming so soon after the New Reformation hopes. The Church of Ireland as a whole had strenuously opposed Emancipation, and many in that Church believed that they had been betrayed not only by politicians but also by leaders in the Church of England. The High Church John Jebb blamed Emancipation in large part on the English Evangelicals. 'The political, ecclesiastical, and, I must add, moral rottenness of Evangelicalism', he confided to his brother on 10 April 1829, 'is lamentably illustrated in the Bps of Winchester, Chester, and Lichfield; in Dean Pearson, and Mr Daniel Wilson, etc.'[166] He refused to have any further contact with those fellow Irish bishops who had 'voted

[164] MacDonagh, *O'Connell*, 268–9; Fitzpatrick, *Life, Times and Correspondence of Dr. Doyle*, ii. 125–7.

[165] MacDonagh, *O'Connell*, 269.

[166] J. Jebb to R. Jebb, 10 April 1829, Trinity College, Dublin, Jebb Papers, MS 6396–7/339.

in Parliament for the destruction of our Church'.[167] Archbishop Magee's health failed in the months following Emancipation, and rumours spread that he had lost his sanity. He died in August 1831.[168] In September 1829 a meeting of Protestants was held in Cork, chaired by the earl of Mountcashel: this meeting called now for a 'Third Reformation' to save the established Church in Ireland. The failure of the Second Reformation movement and the passing of Emancipation, argued Mountcashel and his supporters, indicated that renewed efforts were required to reform abuses in the Irish Church, including the reduction of clerical pluralism and non-residence and the improvement of small livings. Others, however, opposed attempting to reform the Church of Ireland separately from the Church of England, fearing that if Parliament were to treat the two establishments as distinct institutions, it might also decide that the Church of Ireland could be disestablished without adversely affecting the Church of England. There were rumours in the autumn of 1829 that Wellington's Government would introduce a sweeping Church reform programme for the entire United Church of England and Ireland.[169]

In truth, Wellington's Government had been gravely weakened by the passing of Emancipation and was in no position to undertake extensive Church reform. Not only the ultra-Tories, but many moderate Tories as well, had been alienated by the 'betrayal' of the Protestant constitution by the Tory ministers, especially Peel and Wellington. There was also anger over the Government's decision to push Emancipation through Parliament despite the lack of any popular mandate in Britain. Some ultras, led by the marquess of Blandford, now professed support for the cause of parliamentary reform, arguing that a more representative Parliament would never have passed Emancipation. There had been few calls for parliamentary reform during the 1820s, but now that Emancipation had ended the idea of an unalterable Protestant constitution, popular attention fastened on the evils of corrupt boroughs and ministerial manipulation. In December 1829, Thomas Attwood and several supporters founded the Birmingham Political Union to press for parliamentary

[167] J. Jebb to H. H. Norris, April 1831, Bodl. Eng. Lett. c. 790, fo. 38.

[168] Kenney, 'Memoir of William Magee', pp. lxix–lxxx.

[169] Halévy, *History of the English People in the Nineteenth Century*, ii. 279–80; *Christian Guardian* (November 1829), 405–11; H. Newland, *An Apology for the Established Church in Ireland* (Dublin, 1829), 8–21.

reform; the opening meeting in late January 1830 attracted an estimated 12,000–15,000 people. George IV died at the end of June 1830, and the general election that followed in July and August found the Tory party still deeply divided. The result was a number of Whig successes, especially in the counties and 'open' boroughs. Upheavals on the Continent during the summer of 1830—the revolution in Paris in July and the rising in Belgium in August 1830—further contributed to a sense that the old order was falling away. Beginning in September 1830, agrarian unrest spread through much of southern England, with bands of hard-pressed tenant farmers and agricultural labourers destroying threshing machines, burning ricks and barns, and threatening landlords and tithe-collectors. In November 1830 Wellington's Government was brought down by a combination of ultra-Tories, Whigs, Radicals, and independents, and a Whig Government was formed under Earl Grey, committed to fundamental reforms in Church and State. In March 1831 Lord John Russell introduced a Government bill for parliamentary reform.

The Tithe War and the Reduction of the Irish Establishment

During the debates over Catholic Emancipation, some political and religious leaders had argued that Emancipation would help revive the Reformation movement in Ireland. They insisted that the disabilities imposed upon Catholics had served to alienate them from Protestant influences, raising a wall of resentment against the influence of Scripture education and Protestant missionaries. Remove the penalties and disabilities, free the established Church from reliance upon political privilege, and the wall of resentment would come down. The established Church would then bring its Scriptural teaching and preaching to an Irish people prepared to receive them.[170] Peel, as we have seen, advanced this argument in his speech introducing the Emancipation bill in the Commons. The idea also received a memorable expression from the Scottish Evangelical Thomas Chalmers at an Edinburgh public meeting on 14 March 1829, convened to show support for Emancipation. In advocating

[170] e.g. J. B. Sumner, Bishop of Chester, *A Letter to the Clergy of the Diocese of Chester, occasioned by the Act of the Legislature granting Relief to his Majesty's Roman Catholic Subjects* (London, 1829), 23; Peel's speech introducing the Emancipation bill, *Hansard's Parl. Deb.*, NS xx, cols. 753–4; T. Arnold, *The Christian Duty of Granting the Claims of the Roman Catholics* (Oxford, 1829), 54–66.

Emancipation, Chalmers insisted, he was not 'Pro-Catholic'. Rather, he argued that the policy of imposing civil disabilities on people for their religious beliefs had failed: 'this notable expedient for keeping down the Popery of Ireland has only compressed it into a firmness, and closed it into a phalanx, which, till opened up by emancipation, we shall find to be impenetrable'. But with Emancipation, the flagging Reformation movement would be revived, and Protestantism would triumph. 'Give the Catholics of Ireland', he exclaimed,

> their emancipation; give them a seat in the Parliament of their country; give them a free and equal participation in the politics of the realm; give them a place at the right ear of majesty, and a voice in his counsels; and give me the circulation of the Bible, and with this mighty engine I will overthrow the tyranny of Anti-christ, and establish the fair and original form of Christianity on its ruins.

The delivery of this passage, according to one newspaper report, 'elicited a burst of applause so deafening and enthusiastic, that the effect was altogether sublime'.[171] Many of those liberal Evangelicals who cheered Chalmers with such enthusiasm, however, were soon disappointed. For the passing of Emancipation was not followed by a revived Protestant mission in Ireland. Nor did a grateful Irish Catholic population now welcome Protestant Bible and educational societies, missionaries, or zealous parish clergy.

On the contrary, there was a continued hostility to the established Church, reflected in the Irish tithe war that began in late 1830. There had been a long history of resistance to the payment of tithe to the established Church, including violent resistance organized by secret agrarian societies, Whiteboys, Rockites, Carders, Threshers, Ribbonmen, among others. With the achievement of Emancipation, attention was again focused on the tithe, and the injustice of forcing Ireland's impoverished and overwhelmingly Catholic peasantry to support a minority Protestant establishment. There was widespread feeling among Catholic tenant farmers that as O'Connell had brought them Emancipation, so he would now bring an end to the tithe and even the disestablishment of the Church of Ireland. Economic pressures also contributed to the revived anti-tithe agitation. The 1820s had seen grain and cattle prices fall by as much as 25 per cent. This was followed by a poor harvest in 1829, which

[171] W. Hanna, *Memoirs of Dr Chalmers*, 4 vols. (Edinburgh, 1849–52), iii. 235–6, 239.

placed many tenant farmers in desperate circumstances and led to widespread appeals to the clergy for a voluntary reduction of their tithe demands.[172] In the aftermath of Emancipation, however, many established clergy, feeling threatened, embittered, and betrayed, were in no mood to be magnanimous over tithe.

The final phase of the Irish anti-tithe agitation, known as the 'tithe war', is generally regarded as beginning in the autumn of 1830 in the parish of Graiguenamanagh, on the borders of the counties of Kilkenny and Carlow. This parish had a population of 4,779 Catholics and only 63 Protestants. A conflict began when the curate, Luke McDonnell, a proselytizing member of the Reformation Society, broke established convention in the parish and insisted upon payment of tithe by the local Catholic priest, Fr. Martin Doyle, who was himself one of the new generation of militant priests emerging from the Bible war and Emancipation struggle. Doyle refused to pay, and McDonnell had the magistrates seize Doyle's cattle. With the support of his diocesan, Bishop Doyle of Kildare and Leighlin, Doyle organized an effective campaign of non-payment of tithe among the parishioners in Graigue—some of whom reportedly told a local magistrate that 'Daniel O'Connell will get the tithes taken off us, as he got us emancipation'. In March 1831 a force of some 350 police and 250 regular troops was brought in to collect the tithe and distrain the cattle of those in arrears. They were, however, not permitted by law to seize cattle that were under lock and key, or to distrain cattle between sunset and sunrise. By using an elaborate system of signals to warn of the approach of the police, the parishioners managed to get most of their cattle into pens before they could be legally seized. Further, when cattle were seized and offered for sale, communal pressure was applied to ensure that there would be no purchasers. After two months of hide-and-seek, the police and military had managed to recover only a third of the tithe arrears in Graigue.[173] From December 1830, meanwhile, the campaign of non-payment had spread to other parishes, especially in counties Kilkenny, Carlow, Wexford, and Tipperary—with hard-pressed

[172] P. O'Donoghue, 'Causes of the Opposition to Tithes, 1830–38', *Studia Hibernica*, 5 (1965), 7–28.

[173] P. O'Donoghue, 'Opposition to Tithe Payment in 1830–31', *Studia Hibernica*, 6 (1966), 69–72; A. MacIntyre, *The Liberator: Daniel O'Connell and the Irish Party 1830–1847* (New York, 1965), 176–7; O. Chadwick, *The Victorian Church, Part One, 1829–1859*, 3rd edn. (London, 1971), 49–50.

tenants, generally supported by local Catholic priests, employing similar methods to thwart the tithe collectors. On 21 February in the House of Lords, Lord Farnham described the campaign as 'a conspiracy against the Established Church'.[174] The efforts of the authorities to collect the tithe soon led to violent confrontations between police and rural communities. On 18 June 1831 at one of Lord Farnham's strongholds—Newtownbarry, county Wexford—a detachment of 250 yeoman, raised on Lord Farnham's estate, fired on a crowd of farmers protesting the distraining of their cattle, killing thirty-four, including three women.[175] The liberal *Dublin Evening Post* placed the blame for the tragedy largely on Lord Farnham, 'the Apostle of the Second Reformation'.[176] On 14 December 1831 local inhabitants ambushed a force of police sent to collect tithe in Carrickshock, near Knocktopher, county Kilkenny, killing thirteen.[177] In September 1832, police killed four men while collecting the tithe in Wallstown, county Cork, a parish with a population of 3,163 Catholics and one Protestant. As the loss of life mounted, with people being killed over the seizure of a cow or pig, the Irish liberal press pilloried the established clergy.[178] 'Must the Protestant Clergy', asked the *Dublin Evening Post* in June 1831, '. . . be under the necessity of killing and slaying the People, in order to exact the last penny of their dues?'[179]

Much as he deplored the violence and loss of life, Bishop Doyle, a long-time opponent of the system of tithes in Ireland, supported the anti-tithe campaign with his formidable pen. In a pamphlet on the Irish poor law published in March 1831, Doyle argued that the tithe had never been part of Irish ecclesiastical law, but was rather an alien tax imposed upon Ireland by the Norman conquerors against the will of the Irish people. Further, he maintained, the tithe in Ireland had never been rightly distributed even according to English law. According to both the ecclesiastical law and the common law of England, one-fourth of the tithe was to be devoted to the care of the poor. Because, he continued, the established clergy had not

[174] McGrath, *Politics, Interdenominational Relations and Education*, 148.

[175] Ibid. 149–50; *Dublin Evening Post*, 23, 25, 28, 30 June, 2, 5 July 1831, for full reports on the inquest into the Newtownbarry tragedy.

[176] *Dublin Evening Post*, 25 June 1831.

[177] *Dublin Evening Post*, 17 December 1831.

[178] O'Donoghue, 'Opposition to Tithe Payment in 1830–31', 77–81; Bowen, *The Protestant Crusade in Ireland*, 163–5; Chadwick, *The Victorian Church*, i. 50–1; Akenson, *The Church of Ireland*, 150–1.

[179] *Dublin Evening Post*, 25 June 1831.

provided, and did not provide, poor relief from the tithe, the tithe was therefore an illegal imposition.[180] The anti-tithe campaign continued to spread across much of Ireland through 1831 and 1832. Significantly, many of those parishes most affected by confrontations during the Bible war and New Reformation campaign now experienced the most concerted anti-tithe campaigns. In Graigue, it will be recalled, the curate whose actions sparked the tithe war was a zealous member of the Reformation Society. In towns such as Mountrath or Maryboro, the Scripture education and New Reformation movements had left a legacy of bitterness towards the established Church, which now found expression in resistance to the tithe. The Bible war and Emancipation campaign, moreover, had created political associations among Catholics in many parishes, and these associations were now revived to provide leadership in local anti-tithe struggles.[181] In evidence before the House of Commons Select Committee on Irish Tithes, Bishop Doyle argued that the New Reformation movement had 'tended very much to excite a bad feeling towards the clergy of the Established Church, which probably urged on this opposition to the tithe system'. The tithe war, in his view, was simply a continuation of the Bible war that had been initiated by the Reformation missionaries: 'the attack', he insisted, 'commenced and was carried on by the Protestants before the Catholics even resisted'.[182] By the end of 1832, only about half the tithe had been collected in much of the country outside Ulster. Many established clergymen received little or no income and were in considerable distress. Some were forced by threats, or poverty, to leave their parishes. In December 1831, both Houses of Parliament appointed select committees to enquire into the Irish tithe crisis. The Irish establishment seemed to be dying on the ground. Emancipation had not led to a revival of the Reformation movement. Rather, the Irish establishment was now gasping for breath. Its clergy were reduced either to calling upon military force to collect their tithes and acquiescing in the killing or maiming of their

[180] Fitzpatrick, *Life, Times and Correspondence of Dr. Doyle*, ii. 250–7; O'Donoghue, 'Opposition to Tithe Payment in 1830–31', 76–8; Akenson, *The Church of Ireland*, 149; Bowen, *The Protestant Crusade in Ireland*, 162.

[181] O'Donoghue, 'Causes of the Opposition to Tithes, 1830–38', 11–13, 19–21.

[182] 'Second Report from the Select Committee on Tithes in Ireland', *Parliamentary Papers*, 21 (508) (1831–2), 335–6; see also evidence from J. Dunn, ibid. 265, and T. Blakely, ibid. 353–4, 360–1.

parishioners, or else to facing personal destitution and the ruin of their Church. Many Protestants felt abandoned by the State. 'Our prospects in Ireland are very gloomy', Lord Farnham's moral agent, William Krause, lamented to his sister in April 1832. 'Popery, cherished and encouraged by the rulers of the land, seems to be holding its head high. The Protestants are emigrating in hundreds, feeling that they have no protection from the Government.'[183] This was far from Krause's mood five years earlier, when Farnham's Cavan estate had been viewed as the centre of the Reformation breakthrough.

Lord Grey's Whig Government approached Irish Church reform reluctantly. While some members of the Government, including Lords Grey and Holland, were not regular church attenders and were probably 'cultured despisers' of many Christian teachings, they did recognize the value of established Churches for inculcating social morals and respect for the social order. They had no wish to begin a process which might lead to the break-up of the Irish Church. Several younger Whig ministers, moreover, were committed Anglicans—either High Church Anglicans, as in the case of Edward Stanley and Sir James Graham, or liberal Anglicans, as with Lord John Russell, Lord Althorp, Lord Morpeth, and Thomas Spring Rice. These young Whigs had come under similar religious influences at Christ Church, Oxford, or Trinity College, Cambridge; in many cases they enjoyed a rich private devotional life. They also had no desire to damage the Irish establishment. None the less, the Whig ministers also acknowledged that the United Church of England and Ireland could not be made the Church of the Irish people.[184] The weakness of the Reformation movement, the passing of Emancipation and now the beginning of tithe war meant that Church reform in Ireland could not be evaded. Neither Reformation nor Emancipation had brought peace to Ireland. Parliament would have to accept the reality of a permanent Catholic majority in Ireland, and cease dreaming of a Union consolidated on the basis of conformity to the United Church.

In 1831, the Whig Government began the process of reform when it abandoned the long-standing policy of parliamentary grants in support of Scripture education and developed a new programme for

[183] Stanford, *Memoir of W. H. Krause*, 175.

[184] G. F. A. Best, 'The Whigs and the Church Establishment in the Age of Grey and Holland', *History*, 45 (1960), 103–18; R. Brent, *Liberal Anglican Politics: Whiggery, Religion, and Reform 1830–1841* (Oxford, 1987), 36–67.

popular education in Ireland. The new programme had first been recommended in 1828 by a select committee of the House of Commons. In its report, drafted as the New Reformation campaign was failing, the committee had called for a new system of state-subsidized popular education that would unite Catholic and Protestant children, and that would be under the direction of a board of education appointed by the Government without regard to religious affiliation. While the report had been well received by the Catholic hierarchy in Ireland, it had been bitterly opposed by both the Church of Ireland and the Kildare Place Society, and Wellington's Government had done nothing with it. Then in March 1831, amid the ferment of the tithe war, the lord-lieutenant, Lord Anglesey, pressed Grey's Government to consider again the report of 1828. Early in July 1831, Edward Stanley, the Irish Secretary—young, hard, aristocratic, talented, cool, and aloof—became converted to the recommendations of the report. With Lord Grey, Stanley developed during the summer a plan for a radical new departure in Irish education. The plan had three essential points. First, Parliament would cease making annual grants to the Protestant Kildare Place Society and Association for Discountenancing Vice, and would instead place those amounts, which totalled £30,000 per year, at the disposal of the lord-lieutenant for the support of a new national system of education. Second, to oversee the national system, Parliament would create a National Board of Education, made up of both Catholics and Protestants. The Board would be responsible for appointing and training teachers, determining the curricula, and selecting textbooks. Third, the majority of the school week in the national schools would consist of general instruction of a non-religious nature, with Catholic and Protestant children taught together. However, a portion of the week, either one day or an hour or so each day, was to be set aside for religious instruction. For this purpose, children would be separated, and instruction would be given by the clergy of the respective denominations, or their deputies.[185]

On 9 September 1831 Stanley introduced the new scheme for parliamentary grants to education in Ireland in the House of Commons.[186] While acknowledging the achievements of the Kildare Place Society and other Scripture education societies, he

[185] Akenson, *The Irish Education Experiment*, 102–13.

[186] *Hansard's Parl. Deb*, 3rd ser. vi (1831), cols. 1249–61.

also noted the obvious: most Catholics refused to send their children to these schools, and therefore the benefits of the parliamentary grants were restricted largely to Protestants. He did not dispute the value of a Scripture-based education, helping prepare children for salvation in the next world. However, another purpose of popular education was to teach children to live and work together in this world. One great aim of any scheme of education in Ireland, he argued, should be to bring Catholic and Protestant children together from an early age, so that friendships could 'be created and cemented at a period when human beings are the most soft and ductile, and under circumstances capable in some degree of resisting the separations and perhaps dissentions of after-life'.[187] This aim could not be achieved under the current system of Scripture education, and a Government with responsibility for a pluralist Ireland must therefore recommend a new system of 'mixed' schooling. Stanley's plan was opposed by a number of speakers, including James E. Gordon, a leading Protestant itinerant lay preacher during the New Reformation campaign and now Tory MP for Dundalk. Gordon defended the principle of Scripture education and vehemently rejected the notion that the State should cease supporting Protestant education because of opposition from the Catholic Church. Interestingly enough, Gordon was answered by Daniel O'Connell—the two men largely repeating the debate when they had confronted one another seven years before at the meeting of the Hibernian Bible Society in Cork, the debate that had marked the beginning of the Bible war in Ireland.[188] The passage of time had not diminished the rancour between the two. In the event, the House agreed to Stanley's proposals, and the Government moved to implement the scheme. By November 1831, the Government had appointed an Education Commission of seven members, including three from the established Church, two from the Catholic Church, and two from the Presbyterian Church. The duke of Leinster became president of the Commission, but from the beginning the dominant force was Richard Whately, the bearlike, bullying English Whig and former Oriel College Noetic, who in 1831 had succeeded the unfortunate Magee as archbishop of Dublin.[189]

[187] *Hansard's Parl. Deb*, 3rd ser. vi (1831), col. 1250.

[188] Ibid. cols. 1287–304; Wolffe, *The Protestant Crusade in Great Britain*, 70.

[189] D. H. Akenson, *A Protestant in Purgatory: Richard Whately, Archbishop of Dublin* (Hamden, Conn., 1981), 165–204.

Stanley had not described the Government's education scheme at length when he had requested general approval from the House of Commons. It was only in November 1831, when he issued instructions to the new Education Commission, that the details of the scheme became public. The result was a storm of Protestant protest. While Evangelicals took the lead in condemning the scheme, they were encouraged by Tory politicians anxious to embarrass the Government. On 10 January 1832 Irish opponents of the measure held a 'monster' meeting in the Rotunda of Dublin, with the Evangelical archbishop of Tuam in the chair, to petition Parliament against the education scheme. The meeting was followed by a bishops' protest against the scheme, signed by the seventeen Church of Ireland bishops, including the primate.[190] They were soon joined by Irish Presbyterian Evangelicals, under the leadership of the combative Henry Cooke of Belfast. The synod of Ulster held a special meeting in Cookstown on 11 January 1832, adopting a number of resolutions condemning the scheme. 'An attempt is making', warned the *Dublin Evening Mail* on 3 February, 'to strike at the very root of Protestantism, and indeed of religious education generally, and a moral and Christian people are called upon to resist such an attempt by every means within their power.'[191] In London, large public meetings were held by Evangelicals in Exeter Hall on 8 and 15 February to protest the plan. The London meetings were followed up by protest meetings in other English towns and cities.[192] Petitions against the scheme flowed into Parliament. In May 1832, with the warm support of the moderator Thomas Chalmers, the General Assembly of the Church of Scotland petitioned against portions of the scheme.[193] The House of Lords held a lengthy debate on 28 February 1832, when the earl of Roden and the archbishop of Armagh spoke at length against the plan.[194]

Those opposed to the Government's scheme for national education

190 *Dublin Evening Mail*, 11 January 1832; Sirr, *Memoir of Power le Poer Trench*, 691–6; N. D. Emerson, 'The Last Phase of the Establishment', in W. A. Phillips (ed.), *History of the Church of Ireland*, iii. 309–10.

191 *Dublin Evening Mail*, 3 February 1832.

192 *Dublin Evening Mail*, 13, 20 February 1832; Holmes, *Henry Cooke*, 94–104; Wolffe, *The Protestant Crusade in Great Britain*, 73–4; Hempton and Hill, *Evangelical Protestantism in Ulster Society*, 96–7.

193 Hanna, *Memoirs of Dr Chalmers*, iii. 321–38; *Scotsman* (Edinburgh), 4, 28 April, 26 May 1832; *Edinburgh Christian Instructor*, 31 (May 1832), 341–50.

194 *Hansard's Parl. Deb*, 3rd ser. x (1832), cols. 851–93.

in Ireland appealed to the familiar arguments for Scripture education—that children needed to be taught not only to read, but also to embrace the moral and spiritual truths found in the Bible. They claimed that the Scripture education schools of the Kildare Place Society and other societies had proved successful and popular among both Protestants and Catholics, and that the opposition to them came mainly from Catholic priests and political agitators. They insisted that the Government's scheme favoured the Catholic clergy, by permitting only extracts from the Bible acceptable to the priests to be read by children in the national schools, and they argued that such extracts distorted Scriptural meaning. They objected to religious instruction being separated from general instruction and relegated to a single day in the week, or to times before or after the normal teaching hours. They opposed the idea of the State assuming control of education and telling the Protestant clergy when they might provide religious instruction to children. Above all, opponents were outraged by the very idea that the State would allow Catholics a voicc in defining the national system of education in Ireland. Only two years after Emancipation, the State was rapidly moving beyond the mere toleration of Catholicism. 'You will observe', wrote one Church of Scotland clergyman, 'that this is not the mere case of Protestant and Catholic sitting in the same House of Commons and deliberating on civil affairs; but it is the case of Protestant and Roman Catholic, by *order of Government*, sitting at the same Board, and superintending, regulating, and providing instruction in the tenets of Romanism, for every town and village in Ireland.'[195] 'It is one thing to tolerate an error', complained the veteran New Reformation campaigner, James E. Gordon, 'it is another thing to teach it.' 'It is virtually conceded by a Protestant Government', he added, 'that the Roman Catholic religion, as it is administered in Ireland, is entitled to legislative sanction.'[196] Some Protestants feared that the Whig Government was not only removing educational authority from the established Church, but that it was also moving towards the establishment of Roman Catholicism in Ireland. The *Dublin Evening Mail* now called for the repeal of the Emancipation Act, which had clearly failed in its purpose of pacifying the Catholics

[195] Anon., *Irish Education: Letter on the Government Scheme of Education for Ireland . . . by a Clergyman of the Church of Scotland* (Glasgow, 1832), 16.

[196] J. E. Gordon, *Six Letters on the Subject of Irish Education, addressed to the Right Hon. E. G. Stanley* (London, 1832), 36, 41.

and securing the established Church; there was, it claimed, growing support for repeal.[197]

Despite the protests from many Protestants in Britain and Ireland, the Government persevered in its plans for the national system of education. As Stanley pointed out in a letter to Chalmers, 'we are [in Ireland] legislating . . . for a Catholic country [and] we are anxious to extend our instruction into that country as widely as possible'.[198] Stanley made some modifications in the Government's instructions to the Education Commission, which placated the more moderate opponents. The exaggerated claims by more extreme Evangelicals, moreover, weakened their case, while the presence of Richard Whately, the Protestant archbishop of Dublin, on the Education Board meant that the established Church in Ireland was not united against the scheme.[199] With the attention of the country focused on struggle over the parliamentary reform bill, it was difficult for opponents of the Irish education scheme to mobilize sustained Protestant resistance. By 1833, the national system was supporting 789 schools, with 107,042 children on the rolls, and by 1835, 1,106 schools, with 145,521 pupils.[200] The Education Board proceeded energetically in its work, erecting new school buildings, producing school textbooks, appointing inspectors of schools, and creating a model teacher training school for men and women in Dublin. By the mid-1830s, the national system of education was firmly in place in Ireland. The Catholic hierarchy gave it guarded support, at least during the early years, and gradually the National Board schools replaced the old hedge schools, which could not compete with the lower fees of the Board schools. Most of the established Church and the Presbyterian Synod of Ulster continued to oppose the scheme. Within the established Church, some now acted to create an alternative educational system. The Evangelical archbishop of Tuam founded a diocesan education society in 1833 and this example was followed in other dioceses, leading to the formation of the Church Education Society in 1839, with 825 schools and some 43,000 pupils.[201]

197 *Dublin Evening Mail*, 9 March 1832.

198 E. G. Stanley to T. Chalmers, 19 May 1832, in Hanna, *Memoirs of Dr Chalmers*, iii. 337.

199 *Dublin Evening Mail*, 8 February 1832.

200 Akenson, *The Irish Education Experiment*, 140.

201 Sirr, *Memoir of Power le Poer Trench*, 701–10; Emerson, 'The Last Phase of the Establishment', 311–12.

In April 1832, after months of political unrest, Parliament passed the parliamentary Reform Act, expanding the middle-class electorate, disenfranchising a number of small burghs, and increasing the representation of the counties and larger towns and cities. One effect of the Reform Act was to strengthen the political influence of middle-class urban Dissenters and shift the balance of power still further against the established Churches. Combined with the Repeal of the Test and Corporation Acts in 1828 and Catholic Emancipation in 1829, the Reform Act of 1832 represented a constitutional change of near revolutionary proportions. For the established Church in Ireland, the Reform Act rendered its position still more precarious. A more representative Parliament would be less patient with an establishment that could make no claim to be the national Church of the majority of the Irish people. Nor would the reformed Parliament be prepared to carry on the tithe war indefinitely. Time was running out for the Irish Church and its situation was desperate. The tithe in much of the country could not be collected, and many Irish clergymen were without any income. In June 1832, Parliament granted a modest sum of £60,000 to assist the Irish clergy, and empowered the Government now to collect the tithe arrears. In O'Connell's phrase, it transformed the viceroy into the 'Tithe Proctor-General for Ireland'. In August 1832, Parliament passed another Tithe Act, empowering the lord-lieutenant to impose a compulsory composition of tithe in those districts which had not already made voluntary compositions. The Act also set up procedures that aimed at making landlords rather than tenants responsible for the payment of tithe. These efforts, however, proved insufficient to resolve the crisis. In June 1832, the Government in Ireland launched a vigorous campaign to collect the tithe, which further alienated Irish communities from the State and also proved futile. During the next year, the authorities managed to collect little more than £12,000 in tithe, at a cost of some £26,000.[202]

By September 1832 Stanley was drafting a Government measure for a sweeping reform of the Irish establishment, intended to bring an end to the ten years' conflict over the Church of Ireland that had opened with Magee's controversial charge of October 1822. The lord-lieutenant, Anglesey, pressed the Government to move boldly.

[202] Akenson, *The Church of Ireland*, 152–7; MacIntyre, *The Liberator: Daniel O'Connell and the Irish Party*, 185–8; S. Walpole, *Life of Lord John Russell*, 2 vols. (London, 1889), i. 184–5.

'If you do not reform the Church to the full extent recommended', he warned Sir James Graham on 6 October, 'you will soon be without one.'[203] The Whigs were also prepared to treat the Irish Church separately from the English Church, ignoring the 1801 union of the Churches. 'The time has come', Lord Althorp wrote to Grey on 20 October 1832, 'when we must look at the two Churches as separate Churches as they are in fact and in reason.'[204] The Cabinet, however, was divided on the nature of the reform to be proposed. Lord John Russell, supported by Lords Althorp, Howick, and Durham, pressed for a drastic reduction of the Irish establishment, including the suppression of all parishes with few or no Protestants, and the appropriation of those parish revenues for the purposes of general education. Stanley and Grey, on the other hand, refused to accept Russell's sweeping proposals, which they believed would open the way for the complete disestablishment and disendowment of the Irish Church. The Cabinet supported Grey and Stanley, and Russell threatened to resign, arguing that both justice and humanity demanded an end to the collection of tithes and rents to 'be devoted exclusively to the use of one-tenth of the population'.[205] In the event, Russell did not resign. But the Cabinet was in some disarray when Althorp introduced the Irish Church bill to a stunned House of Commons on 12 February 1833.[206]

Although not as extensive as Russell had wanted, the Government bill was a radical measure, which signalled the effective end of the Church of Ireland as a national establishment.[207] Ten of the twenty-two bishoprics in the Irish Church were to be abolished. This would be achieved through the unions of specified dioceses, upon the deaths or resignations of the existing incumbents. With only about 850,000 members, there seemed no reason for the Irish established Church to have nearly the same number of bishops as that of England. The incomes of the two richest sees, Armagh and Derry, were to be significantly reduced. Cathedral dignitaries without specific ecclesiastical duties would be abolished. Parishes in which

[203] C. J. Parker, *Life and Letters of Sir James Graham*, 2 vols. (London, 1907), i. 174.

[204] Cited in I. Newbould, *Whiggery and Reform, 1830–41* (London, 1990), 138.

[205] M. D. Condon, 'The Irish Church and the Reform Ministries', *Journal of British Studies*, 3 (May 1964), 125–8; Walpole, *Life of Lord John Russell*, i. 188–93.

[206] *Hansard's Parl. Deb.*, xv (12 February 1833), cols. 561–77.

[207] For a thorough discussion of the content and passage of the bill, see O. J. Brose, 'The Irish Precedent for English Church Reform: The Church Temporalities Act of 1833', *Journal of Ecclesiastical History*, 7 (1956), 204–25.

no Protestant services had been held for three years or more were to be suspended as ecclesiastical units indefinitely. The bill called for the abolition of the church cess, a tax levied on property in parishes for the maintenance of church buildings and glebe-houses in the Establishment. In its place, there would be a graduated income tax on all Irish Church livings worth over £200 per annum, with the rate increasing from 5 per cent to 15 per cent (the base was later raised to £300). The ecclesiastical revenues released by the abolition of bishoprics, reduction of episcopal incomes and suspension of parishes, along with the proceeds of the new income tax on church livings, were to be vested in a new corporation, the Ecclesiastical Commission. This would be made up of the Church of Ireland primate and three other bishops, together with five lay members, three of whom would be salaried and appointed by the Government. The Commission would be responsible for employing the revenues for ecclesiastical purposes, including the repair of churches and glebe-houses, and the augmentation of small livings. Finally, and most controversially, the bill proposed to transform existing leases on bishop's lands into perpetual tenancies, which would provide tenants with greater security and encourage them to make improvements on their lands. Because the perpetual tenancy would be of greater value to the tenants, the rents would be increased, thus creating an additional income. And as this additional income would result exclusively through the action of the State, and therefore constitute an 'unearned increment', clause 147 of the bill proposed to appropriate the additional revenues for general purposes, such as education or hospitals.

The Irish Church temporalities bill was the subject of long and intense debate, in and out of Parliament, over the next several months. The Government had initially hoped for a rapid passage. However, they made an error regarding the parliamentary procedures for a money bill, which forced a postponement of debates in the Commons from mid-March to early May, and gave their opponents time to marshall their arguments. The bill was welcomed by O'Connell, who asserted that it gave him 'great satisfaction and delight'.[208] While some liberal MPs felt that it did not go far enough, they were prepared to support it as a first instalment of reform. Opposition to the bill focused on several main points. First, there was resistance to the abolition of the bishoprics. Opponents claimed

[208] *Hansard's Parl. Deb.*, xv (12 February 1833), col. 577.

that because of the geographic extent of many of its dioceses, and the unique problems facing the minority establishment in Ireland, the Irish Church needed its twenty-two bishops to provide leadership and discipline.[209] Sir Robert Inglis, Tory MP for Oxford and champion of the established Churches, also questioned whether Parliament had the authority to abolish bishoprics, which were spiritual offices, rooted in 'the sacred order of spiritual succession'. 'What right', he asked, 'had Parliament to interfere between one see and another, and what right had they to determine whether any see should exist or not?'[210] Secondly, opponents objected to the suppression of parishes in which there had been no worship for three years. This, they claimed, assured that the established Church could never gain an influence in those districts. It was a virtual admission that the Church of Ireland would never become the established Church of the whole of the country. As Wellington argued, it had been the policy of Parliament in recent years to support Church extension, that is, to help the Church build churches in parishes where there had hitherto been no Protestant worship. 'But now', he observed, 'if divine services have not been performed in any particular place for three years, Parliament, it seems, is to adopt, by way of remedy, the principle that divine service shall never be performed there again.'[211] For the *Dublin Evening Mail*, this clause would encourage Catholics to drive out parish incumbents: 'if the Roman Catholic Priests-Agitators and their agents, can only succeed in banishing the Protestant Clergy, as they already have banished the gentry, the work is complete, and Popery becomes *ipso facto* the Established Church of Ireland'.[212] Thirdly, opponents complained that the creation of an Ecclesiastical Commission introduced a new form of secular control over the Church. Authority was to be removed from the bishops, the spiritual leaders of the Church, and vested in a Board meeting in Dublin, which almost inevitably would be dominated by the full-time salaried lay members appointed by the Government, who alone would have the time to study at length the business of the Board.[213] Fourthly, opponents condemned the proposal in clause 147

[209] Ibid. xv (12 February 1833), col. 589; xvii (6 May 1833), cols. 977, 998; xvii (13 May 1833), cols. 1119–20; xix (19 July 1833), cols. 959, 969.

[210] Ibid. xvii (6 May 1833), cols. 987, 988–9.

[211] Ibid. xix (19 July 1833), cols. 959–60.

[212] *Dublin Evening Mail*, 20 February 1833.

[213] *Hansard's Parl. Deb.*, xvii (6 May 1833), col. 972; xix (19 July 1833), cols. 147–8.

to appropriate the increased rentals from the bishops' lands for non-ecclesiastical uses. Sir Robert Peel, for example, rejected the argument that as this was an unearned increment created as a result of State action, it could be legitimately appropriated by the State. All property, he maintained, increased in value through the actions of the State, which constructed roads, improved harbours, and provided security. If Parliament accepted the principle that the State could seize the increased Irish Church rentals, it would in logic have to allow the State to seize the increased rentals on all property.[214]

With its overwhelming majority in the Commons, the Whig Government was able to push the Irish Church temporalities bill through the Lower House. On 21 June, in order to facilitate the bill's passage through the House of Lords, the Government dropped the controversial clause 147 for the appropriation of increased bishops' rentals. This was largely the work of Stanley, who had always been uncomfortable with the idea of appropriation. But Radicals, Irish Catholics, Independents, and liberal Whigs were outraged by the dropping of clause 147. They had viewed the appropriation of bishops' rentals as opening the way for more extensive appropriations of Irish Church property in the future. O'Connell, who had supported the bill, now became a bitter opponent—repudiating it, he exclaimed grandly in the Commons, 'in the name of the people of Ireland'. Without appropriation, he argued, the chief merit of the bill was removed. The Tories, however, were prepared to accept the bill, with minor modifications, now that clause 147 had been dropped, and late in July the Lords passed the slightly amended bill. The Commons accepted the Lords' amendments and the Irish Church Temporalities Act became law on 14 August 1833.[215]

The Irish Church Temporalities Act meant the end of the Protestant establishment as a real force for the religious and moral instruction of the whole Irish people. While the appropriation of Church revenues had been defeated for the time being, the Act had nevertheless severely diminished the Irish Church and curtailed its future prospects. In reducing the number of bishoprics almost by half and suppressing parishes in which there had been no Protestant

[214] *Hansard's Parl. Deb.*, xvii (6 May 1833), cols. 1000–2.

[215] N. Gash, *Sir Robert Peel: The Life of Robert Peel after 1830*, 2nd edn. (London, 1986), 49–53; G. Kitson Clark, *Peel and the Conservative Party: A Study in Party Politics 1832–1841*, 2nd edn. (London, 1964), 115–37; Chadwick, *The Victorian Church*, i. 57–60; Akenson, *The Church of Ireland*, 174–7.

worship for three years, Parliament in effect decided that the Irish establishment was not the Church of the Irish people and would never become so. The State would never again endeavour to provide the Church with the resources it needed to extend its influence over the whole of Ireland. Unlike the State policy towards the Irish Church between 1801 and 1828, the Irish Church Temporalities Act of 1833 was intended neither to strengthen the Church's parish ministry nor to help it provide religious and moral instruction to the entire Irish people. Rather, the aim of the Act of 1833 was to reduce the expense of maintaining the Irish establishment and make it more tolerable to the Catholic majority—who were, of course, opposed in principle to its very existence. One of the most significant provisions of the Act was the abolition of the church cess, ending the power of parish vestries to tax the entire parish population for the maintenance of the established Church. The Church was now to maintain parish churches from its own resources; or in short, the Church was partly disestablished at the parish level.[216] These reforms had been carried by a Parliament which did not claim to be acting to uphold religious truth, but rather to be responding to popular opinion in Ireland. Indeed, the reforms reflected the new, more liberal political environment in which all institutions would now have to survive. In his pamphlet of 1831 on poor relief and tithe, Bishop Doyle had argued that the Irish establishment was in the process of being tried before 'a tribunal already established by public opinion in Ireland'. That tribunal, he added, would find it 'too revolting to allot the tenth of the lands and produce of the most fertile, but poorest nation in Europe, to a clergy whose followers do not amount to even a tithe of the people'.[217]

The position of the Irish Church was certainly unenviable. According to a census taken in 1834, there were 6,427,712 Catholics, comprising 80.9 per cent of the total population, and 852,064 members of the established Church, representing only 10.7 per cent of the population.[218] How much longer would such a minority establishment be tolerated in the post-Reform Act era, with government becoming more representative? The Irish Church remained a State Church, but not a national Church, especially as that nation was now being defined by the O'Connellites. The Irish Church would for now

[216] Akenson, *The Church of Ireland*, 177.
[217] Fitzpatrick, *Life, Times and Correspondence of Dr Doyle*, ii. 252–3.
[218] W. A. Phillips (ed.), *History of the Church of Ireland*, iii. 305–6.

receive some protection from the State, but only so long as it did not antagonize the surrounding Catholic and Presbyterian population by attempting to secure their conformity. It had been given a stay of execution, but it remained a prisoner before the tribunal of a hostile public opinion in Ireland. The State, complained the Evangelical *Christian Observer* in 1833, treated the Irish Establishment as 'an evil to be borne with and mitigated, rather than as a blessing of which we should wish the extension and perpetuity'.[219] This, then, was the result of the new mission of the established Church that had been launched by Archbishop Magee in October 1822, when he had sought to build upon the reform and extension movements of the first decades of the nineteenth century and achieve the conformity of the Irish Catholic population. This was the outcome of the Protestant project of the 1820s, which had aimed at consolidating the United Kingdom around a shared set of religious and moral values mediated through the national religious establishments, and especially the United Church of England and Ireland. That project, which had been supported by Parliament and promoted by the Scripture education societies, had been stopped in its tracks, mainly through the efforts of the Catholic Association. The assumption behind the Reformation campaign had been that the Irish Catholic population remained Catholic only because it was essentially ignorant, superstitious, and childlike. Ireland was in short a missionary field, in which the inhabitants had to be both Christianized and civilized by a religious establishment that had at last been awakened to its responsibilities. Through the New Reformation, the Irish establishment would transform semi-barbarous Irish Catholic peasants into loyal citizens of a Protestant United Kingdom. But the fatal weakness of the 'Second Reformationists', argued the O'Connellite *Dublin Evening Post* in August 1827, was that 'they despised their enemies too much'.[220] In the event, the Catholic Association had successfully resisted this campaign, in part by creating a new self-respect among Irish Catholics, and in the process it had asserted their civil rights in the United Kingdom. In a very real sense, the emergence of the 'tribunal' of Irish public opinion referred to by Doyle had been an unintended consequence of the New Reformation struggle of the 1820s. The United Kingdom State had failed to

[219] Cited in W. L. Mathieson, *English Church Reform, 1815–1840* (London, 1923), 78.
[220] *Dublin Evening Post*, 4 August 1827.

make the Irish Catholic population conform to the established Protestantism, and instead had been forced to reform itself in order to accommodate the Irish Catholic identity. This had led to the Repeal of the Test and Corporation Acts, Catholic Emancipation, and Parliamentary reform.

The Irish Church Temporalities Act of 1833 seriously threatened the Irish establishment as a Church. For many, Parliament's abolition of the ten bishoprics had been both an act of sacrilege and a blow to the spiritual independence of the Church. If Parliament were now prepared to suppress the spiritual office of bishop, ignoring the doctrine of apostolic succession, then what security did the Church of Ireland have against further encroachments? In Oxford, John Henry Newman conveyed to the archbishop of Dublin his horror at 'the extinction (without ecclesiastical sanction) of half her candlesticks, the witnesses and guarantees of the Truth and trustees of the Covenant'.[221] And if Parliament were willing thus to treat the Irish branch of the United Church of England and Ireland, what security did the English branch possess against a similar treatment? John Keble, the poet of *The Christian Year*, asserted in March 1833 that the Irish Church Temporalities Bill signalled that the '*persecution* of the church has begun'. The United Church, he added, would be well advised 'to throw from her those State privileges, which in such a case would prove only snares and manacles; and to excommunicate, as it were, the civil government'.[222] Thus ended the campaign to secure the conformity of the Irish Catholic population to the established Church.

[221] J. H. Newman to R. Whately, 28 October 1834, in E. J. Whately, *Life and Correspondence of Richard Whately*, 2 vols. (London, 1866), i. 235.

[222] [J. Keble], 'Church Reform, No. IV', *British Magazine*, 3 (March 1833), 366, 377.

3
'Tribunes of the People': The Struggle for the Established Churches in Britain, 1833–1841

Radicals and Voluntaries

The failure of the campaign to secure the conformity of the Irish Catholic majority to the established Church had effectively ended the project of consolidating the United Kingdom around a common set of religious and moral values mediated through the established Churches. The collapse of the New Reformation in Ireland had forced politicians to recognize that the confessional State would have to be sacrificed if the Union of 1801 with Ireland were to succeed. Dissenters and Catholics could not be kept outside the pale of the constitution. This recognition, in turn, had contributed to fundamental constitutional changes in the United Kingdom between 1828 and 1832—the Repeal of the Test and Corporation Acts, Catholic Emancipation, and the Reform Act. A more pluralistic, more democratic political order was being born, one in which conformity to one of the established Churches was no longer a requirement for full political participation in the State, and in which the old connection of the landed classes, mercantile élite, and established clergy no longer commanded the same authority. These changes had come so suddenly that the description of a 'constitutional revolution' is an appropriate one.[1] The confidence and sense of purpose that had characterized the established Churches in the 1820s evaporated; the balance of power in the parliamentary State seemed to be shifting away from supporters of the established Churches to religious Dissenters, whose numbers had so swelled since the 1790s. 'The revolution is made', wrote the Duke of Wellington to John

[1] G. Best, 'The Constitutional Revolution, 1828–32, and its Consequences for the Established Church', *Theology*, 52 (1959), 226–34.

Wilson Croker on 6 March 1833, 'that is to say, that power is transferred from one class of society, the gentlemen of England, professing the faith of the Church of England, to another class, the shopkeepers, being Dissenters from the Church, many of them Socinians, others atheists.'[2] The creation of the non-denominational system of national education in Ireland in 1831 suggested that Parliament might move towards a similar system in Britain. The reduction in 1833 of the established Church in Ireland, a branch of the United Church of England and Ireland, indicated that the established Churches throughout the United Kingdom were vulnerable. The confessional State had collapsed, and a new, more democratic political order was emerging. In a review of Southey's *Colloquies* in the *Edinburgh Review* in 1830, the young Whig historian Thomas Babington Macaulay (son of the Clapham Evangelical, Zachary Macaulay, but not sharing his father's piety) warned the United Church that its survival was contingent on its willingness to be tolerant and accept its diminished role in society. 'Mr Southey', Macaulay observed, 'thinks that the yoke of the Church is dropping off because it is loose. We feel convinced that it is borne only because it is easy, and that, in the instant in which an attempt is made to tighten it, it will be flung away.'[3] What was to be the role, if any, of the established Churches in the new order?

For one political group, the established Churches had no future role. They were destined to be flung away, as vestiges of the *ancien régime*, remnants of a corrupt social and political order that was now being reformed under rational influence. Radicalism, as the historian Jonathan Clark has argued, first emerged as a coherent ideology in England in the 1810s and 1820s, in opposition to the established order in Church and State.[4] Influenced by the thought of the Enlightenment and the explosive growth of Dissent, Radicals began directing attacks on the established Church of England from about 1815, portraying it as a prop of the old, irrational order. In 1818, the leading Radical author Jeremy Bentham published a sweeping attack on the establishment, *Church-of-Englandism and its Catechism Examined*, much of which focused on the Church's dominance over

[2] Cited in J. C. D. Clark, *English Society 1688–1832*, 413.

[3] T. B. Macaulay, 'Southey's Colloquies' (1830), in *Miscellaneous Works of Lord Macaulay*, ed. Lady Trevelyan, 5 vols. (New York, 1880), i. 421.

[4] J. C. D. Clark, 'Radicalism, Theology and Enlightenment', unpublished paper presented at the Tenth International Congress on the Enlightenment, Dublin, 1999.

popular education in England and its use of this dominance to indoctrinate the young.[5] For Bentham, whose position was essentially an atheist one, the whole system of the Church of England—its doctrine, discipline, and worship—was irrational and absurd. He focused attention on evidence of corruption in the Church—on widespread abuses of patronage, on non-residence, on sinecures, on the large incomes attached to many livings. At the same time, he argued, there was really no reason to reform the Church, as this would simply make it more efficient in disseminating untruths. Rather, he insisted, the whole 'Church of England system is ripe for dissolution', and he called for nothing less than the 'euthanasia of the Church'.[6] This would be accomplished by removing what he portrayed as the real essence of the Church, its wealth. 'The life', he asserted, 'of this Excellent person being in her gold,—[by] taking away her gold, you take away her life.' It would be an 'easy death', 'a death which no man will feel:—a death for which all men will be the better, and scarce a man the worse'. Its abolition would be 'death to so many of the sins of the *ruling* few [and] salvation to the *subject multitude*'. The money thus appropriated from the established Church could be used for pressing social needs.[7] Bentham would continue his attacks on the Church. For example, his *Constitutional Code*, published twelve years later in 1830, had a chapter entitled 'Established Religion—None'. His anti-Church attitudes were shared by his associates, among them Francis Place, a London tailor and journalist, and Richard Carlile, a journalist who was imprisoned from 1819 to 1825 for publishing Thomas Paine's theological works. Carlile, whose imprisonment raised serious questions about the extent of freedom of speech in England, was said to have entered prison a deist, and left it an atheist.[8]

In 1820, John Wade, a 'journeyman wool-stapler' before becoming a Radical journalist, published anonymously the *Black Book*, a jeremiad against the *ancien régime* in the three kingdoms, which directed some sixty pages to the abuses in the established Churches. It sold about 14,000 copies. Eleven years later, in 1831, Wade published an expanded version, the *Extraordinary Black Book; or Public*

[5] J. Bentham, *Church-of-Englandism and its Catechism Examined* . . . (London, 1818).

[6] Ibid. Appendix IV, 196–7, 198–9.

[7] Ibid. 396–9, 304.

[8] D. Baumbardt, *Bentham and the Ethics of Today* (Princeton, 1952), 478–88; E. Halévy, *The Growth of Philosophic Radicalism* (London, 1928), 295; D. Miles, *Francis Place 1771–1854* (Brighton, 1988), 102–3.

Abuses Unveiled, which sold 50,000 copies over the next four years. Described by the historian Norman Gash as the 'secular bible of radical reformers',[9] Wade's book devoted its first 117 pages to a sustained diatribe against the established Churches in England and Ireland. He greatly exaggerated the wealth of the establishments, putting the income of the Church of England at £7,600,000 a year (over double its actual income) and asserting that 'the clergymen of the Church of England and Ireland receive, in the year, more money than the rest of the Christian world put together'. 'In this respect', he added, 'they resemble the clergy of the Church of Rome before the Reformation.'[10] For all the exaggerations, there was enough truth in Wade's descriptions of gross inequalities in clerical incomes, pluralism and non-residence, sinecure livings, nepotism, and abuse of patronage, to make it an effective indictment.[11] There was also too much truth in Wade's portrayal of the established clergy as defenders of the existing political order:

> There is no question, however unpopular, which may not obtain countenance by the support of the clergy: being everywhere, and having much to lose, and a great deal to expect, they are always active and zealous in devotion to the interests of those on whom their promotion depends. . . . Whenever a loyal address is to be obtained, a popular petition opposed, or hard measure carried against the poor, it is almost certain some reverend rector, very reverend dean, or venerable archdeacon, will make himself conspicuous.[12]

In an article appearing in the *Jurist* for February 1833, the young Radical John Stuart Mill argued both for the end of the established Churches and the appropriation of their endowments to support a system of national education. Those endowments, Mill maintained, had originally been given by pious individuals for the spiritual cultivation of the nation. In the past, spiritual cultivation had been defined for the people by the established Church. But the enlightened society of the early nineteenth century had progressed to a more humanistic view of spiritual cultivation: it now meant the contributions of philosophers, educators, poets, historians, explorers, painters, sculptors, and architects. Thus, he argued, Parliament

[9] N. Gash, *Reaction and Reconstruction in English Politics 1832–1852* (Oxford, 1965), 62.

[10] [J. Wade], *The Extraordinary Black Book; or Public Abuses Unveiled* . . . (London, 1831), 41, 5, 6.

[11] Brose, *Church and Parliament*, 9.

[12] Ibid. 20–1.

should regard itself as permitted, even called upon, to transfer the endowments of the established Church to the support of educational institutions intended for the cultivation of modern men and women 'to the highest perfection of their mental and spiritual nature'.[13] For his father and fellow Radical James Mill, writing in the *London Review* of July 1835, the Church of England clergy had 'lost their influence among a people improving, now at last improving rapidly, in knowledge and intelligence'.[14]

By 1830, Protestant Dissenters in Britain were taking up the Radicals' call for the end of the established Churches. In May 1829, the Society for Promoting Ecclesiastical Knowledge was formed in London for the purpose of promoting the principles of Dissent and the separation of Church and State.[15] Early in April 1829, on the eve of the passing of Catholic Emancipation, a United Secession Church minister in Scotland, Andrew Marshall, argued in a published sermon that, in the interest of religious truth, Catholic Emancipation would have to be followed by the abolition of religious establishments.[16] The Roman Catholic majority in Ireland, Marshall maintained, would soon make use of their new political power to abolish the Irish Protestant establishment and establish and endow the Catholic Church in its place. It was difficult to see how this could be avoided. But to endow Roman Catholicism in Ireland, Marshall continued, would mean forcing the majority of Protestants in the United Kingdom as a whole to support the teaching of what they regarded as grievous error. This, he insisted, would be unacceptable. The only alternative, then, was for the State to abolish the religious establishments in the three kingdoms and make all religious denominations equal before the law. This was not only the one path to civil peace; more important, it would promote religious truth. It would liberate the gospel from any connection with the coercive power of the State. Ecclesiastical establishments, he maintained, were without warrant in the New Testament or the practice of the early Church; they were also unnecessary, inefficient, and divisive.

[13] J. S. Mill, 'The Right and Wrong of State Interference with Corporation and Church Property', in J. S. Mill, *Dissertations and Discussions: Political, Philosophical and Historical*, 2 vols. (London, 1859), i. 1–41, 38.

[14] [J. Mill], 'The Church, and its Reform', *London Review*, 1 (July 1835), 257–95, 271.

[15] H. S. Skeats and C. S. Miall, *History of the Free Churches of England 1688–1891* (London, 1891), 471–3.

[16] A. Marshall, *Ecclesiastical Establishments Considered: A Sermon, Preached on the Evening of Thursday, 9th April, 1829, in Greyfriar's Church, Glasgow* (Glasgow, 1829).

They tended only to 'secularise the church', turning it into a 'political institution'.[17]

R. M. Beverley, a Congregational layman and former Anglican, echoed much of the Radical critique when he called for an end of the established Church in his *Letter to the Archbishop of York on the Present Corrupt State of the Church of England*, a work which proceeded through fourteen editions and sold 30,000 copies in the four years after its publication in 1831.[18] For Beverley, the established Church had been fundamentally corrupted by the wealth, status, and privileges granted it by the State, and it no longer provided the people with either Christian discipline or sound Christian teaching. The problem was not with Anglicanism as a doctrinal system; rather, it was in the nature of establishment to corrupt any denomination that received its benefits. 'If the established Church', he asserted, 'were abolished to-morrow, and the sect of Ranters, or the disciples of Johanna [Southcott], or the followers of John Wesley, declared to be the dominant sect to whom tithes were due, then in ten years would the new Church be in every respect as corrupt as that under which the kingdom groans at present.' He attacked the church-building movement supported by the parliamentary grants of 1818 and 1824. 'The Churches', he maintained, 'are already far too numerous.' Further, the building of each new 'Parliament Church' was achieved through a 'long train of "jobbing"', in which clerics, builders, and property speculators conspired together to cheat the public, 'till at last, by dint of every sort of trickery, the matter is settled—a bad, ugly, pseudo-gothic lump of plastered brick is erected, and some favourite dandy Priest duly put in possession of the pulpit'. 'England', Beverley insisted, 'is thoroughly sick of the Church Establishment'; 'all Church property', he predicted, 'will, ere long, be confiscated'.[19]

There was indeed a widespread popular antagonism in Britain to the established Churches. In the countryside, many farmers and rural labourers objected to what they viewed as an exorbitant burden of tithe. The tensions between tithe-holders and tithe-payers had increased significantly during the 1820s. Rising agricultural prices during the Revolutionary and Napoleonic Wars had, as we

[17] Ibid. 20. [18] Mathieson, *English Church Reform*, 64–5.

[19] R. M. Beverley, *A Letter to his Grace the Archbishop of York, on the Present Corrupt State of the Church of England*, 5th edn. (Beverley, 1831), 36–7, 22–3, 4, 32; [I. Taylor], 'Church and State', *Eclectic Review*, 3rd series, 6 (July 1831), 16, 20.

have seen, meant halcyon days for the established clergy, providing many with substantial incomes, and enabling them to emulate the manners, tastes, and morals of the landed élite. This in turn aroused resentment among farmers and labourers, who often felt that the parish clergy were both excessively wealthy and too concerned to preserve the existing social hierarchy. Following the end of the Napoleonic Wars, falling agricultural prices placed severe pressures on small farmers, the spread of enclosures disrupted village communities, and the growth of textile factories brought ruin to handicraft weavers. For many country folk, the established clergy provided little support to suffering communities, but were quick to defend the rights of landowners. Popular hostility focused on the clerical magistrates—who enforced the strict laws against poaching, imprisoned persons for non-payment of tithe, supported enclosures, or kept poor-relief levels as low as possible.[20] During the 'Captain Swing' unrest that swept through the rural south-east of England in 1830, there were nearly one hundred physical attacks on Church of England clergymen, as small farmers and agricultural labourers demanded reductions in tithe demands.[21] Reports of the Irish tithe war encouraged resistance to the tithe in Britain. In December 1832, responding to rumours that the Whig Government planned to abolish the tithe in Ireland, the chairman at an anti-tithe meeting in Kent warned 'that a discontented ten millions in England might find themselves as able to accomplish this object as a discontented seven millions in Ireland'.[22] Some English landlords even seemed prepared to condone an Irish-style agitation against the tithe, as a means of diverting their tenants' attention away from high rents.[23]

Popular anti-establishment feeling was probably even stronger in the towns and cities. Dissent was particularly pronounced in the urban districts, where during the eighteenth century it had often found a space secure from the landlord–parson connection that dominated the countryside. There were also increasing numbers in

[20] E. Evans, 'Some Reasons for the Growth of English Rural Anti-clericalism, c.1750–c.1830', *Past and Present*, 66 (February 1975), 84–109; W. R. Ward, 'The Tithe Question in England in the Early Nineteenth Century', *Journal of Ecclesiastical History*, 16 (1965), 67–81; J. L. Hammond and B. Hammond, *The Village Labourer 1760–1832* (London, 1913), 216–24.

[21] E. Hobsbawm and G. Rudé, *Captain Swing: A Social History of the Great English Agricultural Uprising of 1830* (New York, 1975), 229–32.

[22] *The Times*, 4 January 1833.

[23] 'The Church and the Landlords', *Quarterly Review*, 49 (April 1833), 198–211.

the rapidly growing manufacturing and commercial districts who had no connections with any church. For many of these urban Dissenters and non-churchgoers, the established Church, with its legal church rates and claims of parochial authority, fulfilled no useful function and was simply one more burden upon the hard-pressed people. Many would have recalled, moreover, that two clerical magistrates, the Revds W. R. Hay and C. W. Etherston, had been involved in ordering the yeomanry to attack a peaceful demonstration at St Peter's Field, Manchester, in 1819, which had killed eleven and wounded 400. The efforts of the Church of England to recover its social influence through State-supported church extension efforts often served only to increase popular anticlericalism. The parliamentary church-building acts of 1818 and 1819 had empowered the Church Commissioners to create districts around each new church, and to levy church rates in the new districts for maintaining the new churches and repaying the Church Commission for the purchase of sites. Ratepayers in the new districts, however, also had to continue paying rates to the old parish church for a period of twenty years. This double liability could represent a heavy burden.[24] It was perhaps not surprising that in 1836, when a lay worker sought to collect money for church extension from the inhabitants of Bethnal Green, London, he was told that 'they would give him a shilling to hang the Bishop, but not sixpence [for church building]'.[25]

Popular hostility to the established Church flared into violence during the struggle for the passage of the parliamentary reform bill. When the House of Lords rejected the reform bill in October 1831 by a majority of 41 votes, reformers fastened blame on the United Church bishops, twenty-one of whom had voted against the bill while another six had abstained: had those twenty-one prelates not voted against it the bill would have passed. Amid the popular unrest of October and November 1831, clergy of the Church of England were singled out for threats and abuse. 'Judas Iscariot, Bishop of Worcester' was chalked on the walls of that cathedral city. A mob of 8,000 burnt the bishop of Carlisle in effigy; a crowd stoned the bishop of Bath and Wells while he travelled in his carriage; a mob accosted the archbishop of Canterbury, and the bishop of Durham feared

[24] J. P. Ellens, *Religious Routes to Gladstonian Liberalism: The Church Rate Conflict in England and Wales, 1832–1868* (University Park, Pa., 1994), 15; Watts, *The Dissenters*, ii. 477; *Hansard's Parl. Deb.*, xx (1834), col. 1019.

[25] Clarke, *Church Builders of the Nineteenth Century*, 26.

to show his face in his diocese. During the riots in Bristol on 29–31 October, a mob looted and burnt the bishop's palace, along with other public buildings on two sides of Queen's Square; for their participation in the riot, four men were hanged, before a silent crowd. The bishop of Exeter's palace had to be defended from a similar mob attack by the yeomanry. On Guy Fawkes Day in 1831, the figure of the local bishop replaced the pope on the bonfires.[26] In his Charge of 1831, Herbert Marsh, bishop of Peterborough, asserted that not since the Civil War of the 1640s had there been 'a time when the clergy were assailed with so much calumny and violence as they are at present'.[27] For John Wade, writing in a new edition of *The Extraordinary Black Book* published in 1832, the bishops' opposition to the reform bill signalled the end of the established Church:

> Your days are assuredly numbered; your lease is expired. The fatal vote given on the Reform-Bill has sealed your doom, and no depth of repentance can again establish you in the estimation of the people. Solemn pledges will be demanded from a reformed parliament that tithe shall be abolished, and that haughty prelates shall cease to haunt the chambers of legislation. A terrible storm is impending over the Church.[28]

The Irish Church struggles, it seemed, were now coming to Britain.

The first organized political campaign in Britain for the abolition of the established Churches began in Scotland, mainly in the industrializing central belt between Glasgow and Edinburgh.[29] The campaign opened amid the political unrest surrounding the reform bill. Early in 1832, the United Secession Church, the largest Dissenting denomination in Scotland, formed a committee to plan and co-ordinate a national movement for disestablishment in Scotland. They embraced the name of 'Voluntaries' to indicate that their aim was to base all religious organization on the voluntary decision of individuals for Christ. By the end of the year they had founded Voluntary Church Associations in both Edinburgh and Glasgow. Soon other local Voluntary societies mushroomed in towns across

[26] Chadwick, *The Victorian Church,* part 1, 24–30; J. Stevenson, *Popular Disturbances in England 1700–1870* (London, 1979), 220–3; M. Brock, *The Great Reform Act* (London, 1973), 248–53; J. R. M. Butler, *Passing of the Great Reform Act* (London, 1914), 296–310.

[27] Cited in Mathieson, *English Church Reform*, 45.

[28] [J. Wade], *The Extraordinary Black Book*, new edn. (London, 1832), 95.

[29] S. J. Brown, 'Religion and the Rise of Liberalism: The First Disestablishment Campaign in Scotland, 1829–1843', *Journal of Ecclesiastical History*, 48 (1997), 682–704; A. B. Montgomery, 'The Voluntary Controversy in the Church of Scotland, 1829–1843' (Univ. of Edinburgh Ph.D., 1953).

the central Lowlands, holding meetings and petitioning Parliament for the disestablishment of the Church of Scotland.[30] In March 1833, the Glasgow Voluntary Church Association founded the monthly *Voluntary Church Magazine*, which publicized the activities of the local Voluntary societies, and called upon Dissenters throughout the three kingdoms to follow the Scottish Voluntaries' lead. The campaign took the established Church in Scotland by surprise. Its clergy were paid modestly by English and Irish standards, and it had no bishops, cathedral establishments, and almost no non-residence or pluralities. In short, it had almost none of the abuses that so attracted the attention of English Radicals, and there seemed no reason for the Presbyterian establishment to be thus singled out. But the Scottish Voluntary agitation was not directed at abuses in the established Church, nor at specific grievances felt by Dissenters. Rather, the Scottish Voluntaries demanded the abolition of ecclesiastical establishments as a matter of principle.[31] Theirs was a thoroughgoing critique of the whole idea of a religious establishment. In this, they drew inspiration from the social ethics of the Scottish Enlightenment, with its emphasis on individual freedom, historical progress, and the self-regulating marketplace. Indeed, Voluntary inspiration came probably as much from Adam Smith and the political economists as from Scripture and the history of the Early Church. For perplexed supporters of the Scottish establishment, the Voluntaries were plunging Scotland into the evils of the Irish religious warfare. 'We shall soon be in a rather puzzling predicament in Scotland', wrote David Aitken, Church of Scotland minister of Minto, to his patron, the Whig earl of Minto, on 8 October 1832, 'in consequence of something like an Irish system of agitation, projected and begun by our Dissenters.'[32]

For the Scottish Voluntaries the times seemed propitious: the Irish tithe war, the Reform Act, the extension of popular education, and the growing political awareness among the common people—all seemed to point to a new relationship of Church and State. 'God has given us', enthused the *Voluntary Church Magazine* in September 1833, 'an excellent opportunity of acting efficiently in the purification

[30] *Voluntary Church Magazine*, 1 (September 1833), 320–4.

[31] *Eclectic Review*, 3rd ser., 10 (July 1833), 70–1; *Voluntary Church Magazine*, 1 (August 1833), 258–61; J. Sinclair to H. H. Norris, 20 June 1832, Bodl. MS Eng. Lett. c. 790, fos. 55–6.

[32] D. Aitken to Lord Minto, 8 Oct. 1832, National Library of Scotland, Minto Papers, MS 11801, fo. 120.

of his church. We have a liberal king—a liberal ministry—popular opinion is daily progressing in our favour; and high on the breast of the advancing tide of general education, there is held up to us the prospect of certain success.'[33] Voluntaries argued that individuals should make a positive decision to join a particular Church and that all Churches should be supported by the free-will offerings of their congregations. In advocating the voluntary system, they drew upon examples ranging from the practice of the Early Church to the vitality of the Churches in the United States. In political terms, they borrowed from the Radicals, portraying established Churches as tools of the dominant landed interest for the preservation of the existing hierarchical social order. They rejected the paternalism of the parish system, in which an alliance of patrons, property owners, parish clergymen, and parish schoolmasters claimed the authority to define the religious and moral values for the whole nation. They borrowed from the terminology of political economy, arguing that a free market in religion, with a healthy competition among different denominations, would draw forth the best efforts from clergy and congregations, and improve the effectiveness of home and foreign missions. They insisted that in their calls for disestablishment, their aim was not to destroy the established Churches, but rather to liberate and revive them. By placing all Churches on a voluntary basis, they would restore the purity and independence of the pre-Constantinian Faith and unleash those energies that had driven the expansion of Christianity during its first three centuries. 'I wish her delivered', proclaimed the Glasgow Congregational minister Ralph Wardlaw of the Church of Scotland in March 1834, 'from the thralldom and the indignity of being under state control.'[34] This aim—that is, the liberation of the established Churches from aristocratic patronage and state interference—won broad support, including that of many adherents of the established Church. When 550 persons in the Scottish Lowland town of Haddington signed a petition to Parliament for disestablishment in March 1833, no fewer than 347 claimed to be members of the established Church. Of 253 persons petitioning for disestablishment in the Scottish parish of Kilmaurs in March 1834, a majority were members of the established Church.[35]

[33] *Voluntary Church Magazine*, 1 (September 1833), 292–3.

[34] R. Wardlaw, *Speech . . . at the Public Meeting in Glasgow, for the Separation of Church and State, March 6, 1834* (Glasgow, 1834), 8.

[35] *Voluntary Church Magazine*, 1 (October 1833), 336–8; 2 (June 1834), 241.

In Scotland's capital of Edinburgh, the Voluntary campaign became associated with a popular agitation against the Annuity Tax.[36] This was an impost of 6 per cent on rentals of houses and shops in the city, which was used in part to pay the stipends of the Edinburgh parish clergy. The Annuity Tax had long been unpopular, with many Edinburgh citizens objecting to inequities in the imposition of the tax and claiming that the city was maintaining too many parish clergymen at too high a cost. Early in 1833, stimulated by the Voluntary movement, Edinburgh Dissenters began a campaign of non-payment of the Annuity Tax—a campaign resembling the tithe war raging across the Irish sea and indeed described as having an 'Irish flavour'.[37] Many adherents of the established Church joined with Dissenters in refusing to pay the tax. By April 1833, according to the Edinburgh lawyer Henry Cockburn, only £173 of the tax for the year had been collected, the arrears had grown to £11,000 ('a great part of which must inevitably be lost') and the city could not pay the stipends of the city clergy.[38] In the summer of 1833, the magistrates and town council began seizing and selling the household goods of non-payers. When this proved ineffective, they resorted to imprisoning non-payers until their arrears were paid. The Dissenters responded by turning the prosecuted non-payers into martyrs. In August 1833, for example, William Tait, proprietor of the liberal *Tait's Magazine*, was briefly imprisoned for non-payment. On his release on 13 August, he was conveyed home by a procession of 8,000, with banners and music, while thousands of cheering spectators lined the streets. A procession of 10,000 greeted the next man imprisoned for non-payment on his release on 26 August.[39] By the end of 1833, 846 Edinburgh citizens had been prosecuted for non-payment.[40]

During the summer of 1833, Parliament reformed burgh government in Scotland, broadening the franchise for the election of burgh councils. This in turn increased the influence of the ratepayers, who included many middle-class Dissenters. In January 1834, the first Edinburgh town council elected under the new franchise attempted

[36] D. McLaren, *History of the Resistance to the Annuity Tax* (Edinburgh, 1836); J. C. Williams, 'Edinburgh Politics, 1832–1852' (Univ. of Edinburgh Ph.D. thesis, 1972), 26–30.

[37] *Journal of Henry Cockburn*, 2 vols. (Edinburgh, 1874), i. 51.

[38] H. Cockburn to T. Chalmers, 22 Apr. 1833, New College Library, Edinburgh, Thomas Chalmers Papers, CHA 4.202.18.

[39] *Scotsman*, 22 June, 13, 17 July 1833; *Voluntary Church Magazine*, 1 (December 1833), 427–34.

[40] Machin, *Politics and the Churches*, 115.

to settle the city's Annuity Tax crisis. Their plan was ominous for the future of the established Church. For the Whig-controlled council proposed to reduce the budget by reducing the number of city clergy. It was all too reminiscent of the reduction of the Irish established Church several months earlier. In response to an organized campaign of non-payment of a Church rate, the town council would decrease the size of the Edinburgh establishment. The established presbytery of Edinburgh angrily rejected the proposals on 23 January. Led by Thomas Chalmers, Scotland's leading champion of the established Church, the presbytery maintained that Edinburgh needed not fewer but more clergy, to enable it to pursue an aggressive home mission among the unchurched urban poor. It would not quietly succumb to the Voluntary agitation.[41] Chalmers was in his element, giving one of the best speeches of his life. Immediately after the presbytery meeting, however, he suffered a stroke, which left him partially paralysed and seemed to mark the end of his career. The campaign against the Annuity Tax in Edinburgh continued, the Voluntary agitation in Scotland as a whole grew, and the Church of Scotland seemed set to share the fate of the Irish establishment.

From the middle of 1833, Scottish Voluntaries expanded their anti-establishment campaign into England, their efforts assisted by the family connections that linked many Scottish and English Dissenters.[42] By September 1833, a Voluntary Church Society had been established at Newcastle, and Voluntary agitations had commenced in Hexham, Blackburn, Bradford, and Leeds. The Scottish *Voluntary Church Magazine* for September heralded these developments and called upon Scottish Voluntaries to do all in their power to encourage the English movement.[43] Late in 1833, in an appendix to his published address given on laying the foundation stone for a new Weigh-house Congregational chapel in London, Thomas Binney, a 31-year-old Northumbrian Congregational minister of Scottish Presbyterian background, publicly announced his commitment to disestablishment. 'It is with me, I confess, a matter of deep, serious religious conviction, that the Established Church is a great national evil; that it is an obstacle to the progress of truth and godliness in the land; that it destroys more souls than it saves; and

[41] *Scotsman*, 25 Jan. 1834; Hanna, *Memoirs of Dr Chalmers*, iii. 429–33.

[42] For the influence of Scottish migrants on Voluntaryism in the North of England, see Ward, *Religion and Society in England*, 129–32.

[43] *Voluntary Church Magazine*, 1 (September 1833), 283–8.

that, therefore, its end is most devoutly to be wished by every lover of God and man.'[44] A growing number of English Dissenters were drawn to these views.[45] During early 1834 Voluntary Church Associations were formed in a growing number of English towns and cities, and leading Scottish Voluntaries travelled south to spread the Voluntary message: 'the whole machinery of popular agitation was put in motion . . . for the overthrow of the Church Establishment'.[46] Influenced by the Edinburgh Annuity Tax agitators, English Voluntaries directed their energies to opposing the Church rate that was levied in towns and cities to maintain established Church buildings and provide communion elements. In England, the vestry set the Church rate each year. Most English towns had open vestries, consisting of all ratepaying inhabitants. These open vestry meetings provided opportunities for public expressions of opposition to the Church rate, and, increasingly, to the continued existence of the established Church. There were angry exchanges over the Church rate at vestry meetings, with inhabitants loudly opposing the levying of any Church rate and meetings sometimes breaking up in confusion. The confrontations brought out local resentments over the increases in the Church rate resulting from recent church building; the new churches erected under the stimulus of parliamentary grants in 1818 and 1824 now required repairs and maintenance.[47] Many local Anglicans preferred to stay away from vestry meetings rather than participate in what they viewed as unseemly shouting matches. In early 1834, with Voluntaries taking the lead, the Church rate was defeated after bitter struggles in Manchester, Leeds, Rochdale, and Birmingham.[48] The Church establishment seemed to be dying in the towns and cities.

In the spring of 1834, the Whig Government sought to end the Church rate crisis by transferring part of the cost for the upkeep of the established Church in England to the land tax. Lord Althorp

[44] T. Binney, *An Address Delivered on Laying the First Stone of the New King's Weigh House*, 5th edn. (London, 1834), 34.

[45] Watt, *The Dissenters*, ii. 453–4.

[46] Skeats and Miall, *History of the Free Churches in England*, 477; W. H. Mackintosh, *Disestablishment and Liberation: The Movement for the Separation of the Anglican Church from State Control* (London, 1972), 5; R. Brent, 'The Whigs and Protestant Dissent in the Decade of Reform: The Case of Church Rates, 1833–1841', *English Historical Review*, 102 (1987), 897.

[47] Ellens, *Religious Routes to Gladstonian Liberalism*, 23–7; Chadwick, *The Victorian Church*, part 1, 85–7; Watt, *The Dissenters*, ii. 479–80.

[48] Ellens, *Religious Routes to Gladstonian Liberalism*, 41.

introduced the Government's plan in the Commons on 21 April.[49] It was, he insisted, a matter of saving the establishment: 'one of the consequences of having an Established Church was—that means should be provided by the Legislature for the support of the fabric of the Church'.[50] In the event, while Althorp's motion was approved by a substantial majority in the Commons, the Government chose not to pursue the bill in the face of widespread opposition from the larger Dissenting community, orchestrated by the United Committee of Dissenters, a new organization formed in March 1833. In May 1834, this United Committee held a General Convention in Nottingham, attended by some 400 delegates, to call for the total abolition of Church rates. The Convention also recommended the formation of local Voluntary Church Societies, and overwhelmingly approved a motion on disestablishment, with only 3 votes against.[51] English and Scottish Dissenters united to form the British Voluntary Society in London in May 1834, while petitions for disestablishment flowed to Parliament from local Voluntary Societies across Britain.[52]

As the Voluntary campaign in Britain gathered momentum, in Ireland the tithe war ground grimly on. The reduction of the established Church in Ireland in the summer of 1833 had not resolved the Irish tithe question, nor had it brought an end to pitched battles between Irish farmers and police.[53] Many Irish clergy had remained without incomes for nearly two years, and their situation was desperate. In 1833 Parliament approved a loan of £1,000,000 to the Irish clergy. But Parliament had no intention of paying the Irish clergy from the public purse in place of a tithe that could not be collected. A satisfactory measure had to be found to restore the regular payment of Irish tithe. For O'Connellites, Radicals, and many advanced Whigs, the solution was straightforward. The tithe war continued in Ireland, they argued, because the Irish Church Temporalities Act had not gone far enough. Parliament had not agreed in 1833 to appropriate the surplus revenues of the reduced Irish Church for the support of national education and other forms of general welfare in Ireland. Therefore, the Irish Catholic majority

[49] *Hansard's Parl. Deb.*, xxii (21 April 1834), cols. 1012–60.

[50] Ibid. 1014, 1022, 1030.

[51] Skeats and Miall, *History of the Free Churches in England*, 481–2; C. Binfield, *So Down to Prayers: Studies in English Nonconformity 1780–1920* (London, 1977), 72.

[52] H. M. MacGill, *The Life of Hugh Heugh* (Edinburgh, 1852), 255–8; Ellens, *Religious Routes to Gladstonian Liberalism*, 38.

[53] Akenson, *The Church of Ireland*, 180–1.

remained angry and alienated over the tithe. Until action was taken to appropriate the surplus revenues from the Irish Church, Irish Catholics would have no confidence in the good faith of Parliament and the tithe war would continue. While Radicals argued that Irish tithe revenues should go solely to secular purposes, some Whigs came to support sharing tithe revenues between the three main denominations in Ireland. During a tour of Ireland in September 1833, for example, Lord John Russell, paymaster-general in the Whig Cabinet, had become convinced that a just peace could only be achieved in Ireland if the surplus revenues of the Church of Ireland were appropriated, either for the concurrent endowment of the Catholic Church, Church of Ireland, and Presbyterian Churches, or for secular education.[54] More conservative Whigs, however, opposed any appropriation of Irish Church revenues, believing it would open the door for a general appropriation of revenues from all three established Churches.

In 1834 the Whig Government introduced a new Irish tithe bill, which proposed to resolve the issue by commuting the tithe into a land tax payable by the landlords. Russell had attempted in Cabinet to insert an appropriation clause in the bill, but failed to gain the support of the majority of his colleagues. Then on 6 May 1834, during a Commons debate on the bill, Russell broke from the Cabinet ranks and declared that once the Irish tithe bill had been passed, he would personally move for the appropriation of Irish Church revenues. His declaration was greeted with loud and general cheering from Radicals and liberal Whigs. The Radical Henry George Ward immediately introduced a motion for the appropriation of Irish Church revenues. While the Government managed to block Ward's motion, it now decided that it could not pursue its Irish tithe bill without widening its own divisions and those among its supporters in the Commons.[55] Russell had, by his Commons declaration, 'upset the coach' in a Government that was becoming increasingly divided over the future of the established Churches. By the end of May, four conservative Whig ministers,

[54] Walpole, *Life of Lord John Russell*, i. 197; Brent, *Liberal Anglican Politics*, 74–5; Machin, *Politics and the Churches in Great Britain*, 36.

[55] *Hansard's Parl. Deb.*, 3rd ser. xxiii (1834), cols. 664–6; Walpole, *Life of Lord John Russell*, i. 197–202; Brent, *Liberal Anglican Politics*, 76–8; Machin, *Politics and the Churches in Great Britain*, 36–8; R. W. Davis, 'The Whigs and Religious Issues, 1830–5', in R. W. Davis and R. J. Helmstadter (eds.), *Religion and Irreligion in Victorian Society* (London, 1992), 37–8; Halévy, *History of the English People 1830–1841*, 172–4.

including Edward Stanley and Sir James Graham—the ministers with the greatest commitment to the religious establishments—had resigned from the Government. 'Though anxious to reform the Church', wrote Graham to a friend and fellow Whig on 12 June, 'I could not consent to measures which appeared to me calculated to overthrow it.'[56] The continued Irish crisis also contributed, in early July 1834, to the resignation of Lord Grey. Viscount Melbourne became prime minister. Urbane, aristocratic, cool, and distant, with an intellectual interest in Christianity as a historical movement but with no strong commitment to the contemporary life and mission of the Church, Melbourne's leadership of the Government did not bode well for the established Churches. His Government, moreover, was increasingly dependent on the support of Radicals, Dissenters, and Irish Catholics—all committed to the reduction or abolition of the religious establishments. Many supporters of the Government continued to call for the appropriation of Irish Church revenues, and the issue promised to create a precedent for the established Churches in all three kingdoms.

Church Defence and Church Reform

The union of Church and State, which had appeared so strong in the mid-1820s, seemed to be breaking up throughout the three kingdoms by the early 1830s. Then there had been hopes that the established Churches would secure the conformity of nearly the whole population of the three kingdoms; now those Churches were struggling to survive. The failure of the Reformation in Ireland, the passing of Catholic Emancipation and the Reform Act of 1832 had resulted in a new political order. No longer could High Church defenders of the established Churches appeal, in Burke's language, to an 'indissoluble union' of Church and State. Old certainties and old securities were dissolving. During the reform bill crisis, the Whig prime minister, Lord Grey, had warned the bishops of the United Church of England and Ireland that they would have to set their house in order. The established Churches could no longer count on support from a friendly Parliament, but would now need to cultivate popular support. And if they hoped to win popular support, they would have to become more efficient and economical, and

[56] Parker, *Life and Letters of Sir James Graham*, i. 196.

demonstrate their usefulness to society. In short, they would have to accept reform. Charles James Blomfield, High Church bishop of London, was one who recognized that the Church could not avoid reform. 'How to secure the good and to exclude the evil', he admitted to William Howley, archbishop of Canterbury, on 11 December 1832, 'will be no easy problem.' 'Nevertheless', he added, 'we *must* attempt the solution of it; it is impossible that the Church (in so far as it is of human institution) can go on as it is.'[57]

'A fearful storm of pamphlets on Church Reform', lamented the High Church *British Magazine* in March 1833, 'has been spreading itself (and havoc with it) over the land.'[58] In England, the early 1830s witnessed the publication of an array of pamphlets, addresses, and articles, offering varied programmes for the reform of the established Church. As attacks on the Church mounted, numerous authors, clerical and lay, rushed into print with plans for reducing pluralities and non-residence, ending gross inequalities in clerical incomes, eliminating abuses of patronage, sinecures, and waste, improving clerical discipline, building new churches and schools, and promoting the Church's mission. Most of these works proved ephemeral, but a few authors did attract broad public interest. In three pamphlets published between 1831 and 1834, for example, Edward Burton, regius professor of Divinity at Oxford University, developed a scheme for increasing the incomes of small livings and thus improving the parish ministry.[59] This, he proposed, would best be achieved by introducing a graduated tax on church livings valued at over £200 a year, and abolishing a number of sinecure livings. The resulting fund would be managed by the Commissioners of Queen Anne's Bounty and be employed to raise small livings, thus gradually reducing any grounds for pluralism and non-residence.[60] More sweeping proposals were put forward by Lord Henley, the brother-in-law of Sir Robert Peel and a respected Evangelical lawyer.[61] Lord Henley's *Plan of Church Reform*, published in 1832, recommended

[57] C. J. Blomfield to W. Howley, 11 December 1832, in Blomfield, *Memoir of Charles James Blomfield*, 154–5.

[58] *British Magazine*, 3 (March 1833), 312.

[59] E. Burton, *Thoughts upon the Demand for Church Reform*, 2nd edn. (Oxford, 1831); E. Burton, *Sequel to Remarks upon Church Reform, with Observations upon the Plan Proposed by Lord Henley*, 2nd edn. (London, 1832); E. Burton, *Thoughts on the Separation of Church and State* (London, 1834).

[60] Burton, *Sequel to Remarks upon Church Reform*, 21–34, 54–5, 59, 70.

[61] [H. Brougham], 'Lord Henley on Church Reform', *Edinburgh Review*, 56 (October 1832), 203; Best, *Temporal Pillars*, 283–4.

the equalization of bishops' incomes (to discourage translations from poorer to wealthier sees), the creation of two new dioceses in populous districts and the equalization of the size of the dioceses, the removal of all bishops from the House of Lords, the creation of a representative Church Assembly, and the creation of a new ministry of Ecclesiastical Affairs to advise the Crown on the exercise of Church patronage. Perhaps most importantly, Henley called for the reduction of the size of cathedral chapters through the elimination of non-resident prebends. He estimated that a sum of £150,000 a year could thus be freed, which should be vested in a new body, an independent ecclesiastical Commission, which would use the fund to raise poor livings and create new parish churches where needed, and especially in the expanding cities.[62] Henley's pamphlet went through eight editions in the first year of its publication and was said to have gained the king's favour. Henley was also known to have Peel's confidence; indeed, much of his plan may have grown out of his conversations with the Conservative party leader.[63]

While Henley advocated the diversion of cathedral revenues to the parish ministry, another would-be Church reformer, Edward Pusey, an Oxford scholar of Hebrew, argued passionately that the cathedrals should not only be protected, but should be viewed as central to Church revival. In his *Remarks on the Prospective and Past Benefits of Cathedral Institutions*, published in 1833, Pusey argued that cathedral revenues should be used to endow a seminary for the training of priests at each cathedral.[64] England, he argued, was in need of additional provision for theological learning. While in Germany there were no fewer than twenty-three theological seminaries and at least 125 theological professors, England had only two universities with only seven theological professors.[65] Much of the new scholarship coming out of German universities, moreover, was suspect, bringing into question the biblical and historical foundations of Christian orthodoxy. It was therefore vital that England should become an international centre for sound Christian scholarship, by increasing the number of its teachers and seminaries. Cathedrals, Pusey argued, would make excellent seminaries. They

[62] Lord Henley, *A Plan of Church Reform, with a Letter to the King*, 5th edn. (London, 1832).

[63] Brose, *Church and Parliament*, 124; Best, *Temporal Pillars*, 288.

[64] E. B. Pusey, *Remarks on the Prospective and Past Benefits of Cathedral Institutions, in the Promotion of Sound Religious Knowledge and of Clerical Education*, 2nd edn. (London, 1833); R. Jupp, '"Nurseries of a Learned Clergy": Pusey and the Defence of Cathedrals', in P. Butler (ed.), *Pusey Rediscovered* (London, 1983), 139–55.

[65] Ibid. 63–4.

were spread evenly over the country, most of them had libraries, their canonical houses could provide residential and teaching facilities, and theological learning and scholarship could be conducted under the close supervison of the bishop. According to his plan, each candidate for orders might be required to pursue a further two years of theological study at a diocesan seminary after completion of the university course.[66] While recognizing the importance of the parish ministry, he insisted that an established Church had other functions to fulfil and that the Church of England must not sacrifice higher theological learning in its zeal to revive the parish system. Only a well-endowed religious establishment supporting a learned clergy and encouraging orthodox scholarship could in the long term preserve the foundations of Christian society in England against the spread of rationalism and irreligion. In presenting his case, he appealed to the writings of Thomas Chalmers, Presbyterian Scotland's 'brightest ornament', on the importance of the cathedral establishments as centres of learning. Chalmers, Pusey observed, lamented the appropriation of the Scottish cathedral revenues by the Crown and nobility at the Reformation.[67] Pusey was delighted when his work won Chalmers's praise, and he offered Chalmers his assistance in strengthening relations between the two 'national Churches' in their common struggle against infidelity and Dissent.[68]

Probably the most controversial of the various schemes of Church reform was that advanced by the liberal Anglican Thomas Arnold, disciple of Coleridge, former Oriel Noetic, and headmaster of Rugby, in his *Principles of Church Reform*, which appeared early in 1833.[69] Arnold recognized that a fundamental problem for Anglicans was how to justify maintaining an established Church in a society that now provided almost full civil rights to all Christian denominations. Arnold was convinced that the established Church was worth preserving. However, he insisted, it had to be transformed into a broad, inclusive national Church, one that could contribute to the religious life of an increasingly democratic and pluralistic society. It had to give less attention to theological and liturgical distinctions,

[66] Ibid. 74–80. [67] Ibid. 66–7, 94, 116, 119.

[68] H. P. Liddon, *Life of Edward Bouverie Pusey*, 4th edn., 4 vols. (London, 1894), i. 234–5; J. Lewis to T. Chalmers, 15 February 1833, New College Library, Edinburgh, Thomas Chalmers Papers, CHA 4.208.40; E. B. Pusey to T. Chalmers, 15 February [1833], ibid., CHA 7.1.33.

[69] T. Arnold, *Principles of Church Reform* (1833), ed. M. J. Jackson and J. Rogan (London, 1962); B. Willey, *Nineteenth Century Studies: Coleridge to Matthew Arnold* (London, 1949), 57–60.

which were of interest mainly to the professional clergy, and give more emphasis to social ethics. It had to become less dominated by the clergy and provide an enhanced role for the laity in ecclesiastical affairs. His specific proposals included creating new dioceses (thus reducing the size of each diocese), providing each bishop with an advisory council of lay and clerical members, establishing a representative ecclesiastical assembly in each diocese, broadening access to the ministry to include men who could not afford an Oxbridge education, allowing in many cases the parishioners to elect their own minister, and appointing lay church officers in every parish who would be responsible for regular house-to-house visiting. More controversial were his proposals to broaden the credal basis of the Church to make it inclusive of all trinitarian Protestant beliefs, and to permit different liturgies to be celebrated in the parish churches at different times. His aim with these proposals was to draw Protestant Dissenters back into a comprehensive national Church, reviving the ideal of a Christian society and ending the conflict of Church and Dissent. For Arnold, far more important than specific theological formulations or ecclesiastical structures was the need to restore Christian unity. Without some such comprehensive reorganization, he maintained, the established Church could not be saved. And disestablishment would be an evil of epic proportions, nothing less than 'the public renouncing of our allegiance to God; for without an Establishment . . . England will not be a Christian nation:—its government will be no Christian government:—we shall be wholly a kingdom of the world, and ruled according to none but worldly principles.'[70] 'I have been writing on Church Reform', Arnold wrote to a friend on 15 January 1833, 'and urging an union with the Dissenters as the only thing that can procure to us the blessing of an established Christianity; for the Dissenters are strong enough to turn the scale either for an establishment or against one; and at present they are leagued with the antichristian party against one, and will destroy it utterly if they are not taken into the camp in the defence of it'. 'And if we sacrifice', he added, 'that phantom Uniformity, which has been our curse ever since the Reformation, I am fully persuaded that an union might be effected without difficulty.'[71] Others, however, were not so prepared to sacrifice what they

[70] Arnold, *Principles of Church Reform*, 142.

[71] T. Arnold to W. K. Hamilton, 15 January 1833, in A. P. Stanley, *Life and Correspondence of Thomas Arnold*, 8th edn., 2 vols. (London, 1858), i. 282.

regarded, not as a 'phantom Uniformity' but as the essential doctrines and practices of the Church of England. Arnold's proposals were widely denounced; for one Oxford critic, Arnold sought to turn the Church into a 'withered spectre of religion', a 'cold incarnation of Deism, unanimated by the light and life of Scripture truth'.[72]

The variety of English Church reform proposals advanced between 1831 and 1834 indicated a Church that had no clear idea of how to proceed against the formidable forces suddenly calling for its overthrow. For one reformer, cathedral revenues should be diverted to the improvement of the parish ministry; for another, cathedral revenues must be preserved and cathedrals transformed into citadels of learning. For one reformer, the Church of England must break free of the bonds of strict orthodoxy and become inclusive of different shades of trinitarian belief; for another, it must become a bastion of strict Anglican orthodoxy. During these years Church supporters attempted little by way of Church reform in Parliament. The archbishop of Canterbury, William Howley, did propose three modest bills in the House of Lords in June 1831—one to facilitate the composition of tithes, one to restrict pluralities, and one to enable ecclesiastical persons or bodies, such as bishops or cathedral chapters, to divert some of their revenues to augment small livings. Parliament passed only the third bill and it had only a limited effect. In June 1832, the Whig Government appointed an Ecclesiastical Revenues Commission to investigate the state of the Church's finances.[73] But on the whole the Church of England lacked confidence in Parliament. Anglican clergy were understandably wary of reform at the hands of a Parliament that now included not only Catholics but also an increasing number of Radicals and Voluntaries.[74] Church leaders and Anglican politicians also feared that once Parliament began on the path of Church Reform, it would be rushed along by the momentum of events towards disestablishment. 'If we once begin to amend upon a system', the Tory journalist J. W. Croker observed to the High Church bishop of Exeter, Henry Phillpotts, on 21 October 1832, 'we shall, as in Parliamentary Reform, be carried away far beyond all improvement, and become implicated in and pledged to a series of plausible principles which can never be

[72] W. Palmer, *Remarks on the Rev. Dr. Arnold's Principles of Church Reform* (London, 1833), 29.
[73] Best, *Temporal Pillars*, 276–7.
[74] E. Burton, *Thoughts on the Separation of Church and State* (London, 1834), 63–71.

controul'd till they are satisfied, nor satisfied but by the annihilation of the Church.'[75]

It was not, in fact, the Church of England, but the much smaller Church of Scotland that took the lead in Church reform. This was largely because, unlike the Church of England which could only look to Parliament for reform, the Scottish establishment possessed its own legislative body, the General Assembly, that could enact ecclesiastical law independently of Parliament. In May 1834, moreover, the Evangelical party gained a working majority in the General Assembly, ending the dominance that the Moderate party, the traditional supporters of Crown and aristocratic patronage, had exercised in the Church since at least the 1750s. The Evangelicals had emerged as the party of reform in the 1820s, leading the efforts to eliminate remaining pluralities and improve the parish system. They had also worked to increase the popular voice in Church affairs, believing that the common people, with their roots in a traditional communal piety, often had a purer biblical faith than did the educated urban élite or the landed classes that controlled much of Scotland's ecclesiastical patronage. In 1825, largely through the efforts of Andrew Thomson, Edinburgh Evangelicals had founded a Society for the Improvement of Church Patronage, which by 1831 had thirty-seven branches outside Edinburgh. The Scottish Evangelicals thus had a clear view of how to reform the Church, and in 1834, with the Voluntary attacks on the Church increasing in intensity, the General Assembly gave its support to the Evangelical reform programme.[76]

The Evangelical-dominated General Assembly of 1834 embarked on two major initiatives that would fundamentally transform the established Church of Scotland. First, in an effort to increase popular support for the establishment, the Assembly passed the Veto Act, which restricted the operation of patronage and gave parishioners a greater voice in the selection of their ministers. The Veto Act gave a majority of male heads of family in communion with the Church the power to veto a patron's presentation to a parish living if they felt that the candidate would not be suitable as their minister. The heads

[75] J. W. Croker to H. Phillpotts, 21 October 1832, Exeter Cathedral Archives, Phillpotts Papers, ED 11/18/5.

[76] I. F. Maciver, 'The General Assembly of the Church, the State and Society in Scotland, 1815–1843' (Univ. of Edinburgh M.Litt., 1976), 34–6; N. L. Walker, *Robert Buchanan* (London, 1877), 118–19.

of family were not obliged to give reasons for their veto, though they were to affirm that they had not been influenced by any factious or malicious intent. If the patron's candidate was vetoed, the patron would be required either to present another candidate, or to allow the heads of family to select their own minister. The Veto Act would, it was hoped, strengthen the established Church at the parish level by ensuring that all appointments to the ministry were acceptable to parish communities. Moreover, by dealing at last with the contentious patronage issue and showing the established Church to be sensitive to popular opinion, the Veto Act might help attract moderate Dissenters back into the establishment.[77]

Secondly, the General Assembly of 1834 committed itself to a national campaign for church extension, aimed at expanding and strengthening the Church's parochial system. In order to encourage the building of new churches, the Assembly passed a Chapels Act, which enabled the Assembly to subdivide existing parishes for the purposes of pastoral care and ecclesiastical discipline. New churches would thus be given their own parochial jurisdictions, which were termed *quoad sacra* parishes, as opposed to the *quoad civilia* parishes that had been created by the civil authorities. The civil laws respecting the provision of poor relief and education did not apply to *quoad sacra* parishes, but the *quoad sacra* parishes would exercise authority over ecclesiastical discipline, catechizing, and house-to-house visiting. Each *quoad sacra* parish church would have a minister and kirk-session of elders, and would be represented in the ecclesiastical courts. The General Assembly hoped that the new *quoad sacra* jurisdictions would not only promote new church building, but also encourage many Dissenting Presbyterian congregations to apply to return to the established Church as *quoad sacra* parish churches (especially now that the abuses of patronage were being curbed by the Veto Act). Thirdly, the General Assembly reorganized and enlarged its standing Church Accommodation Committee, and charged this Committee to organize and lead a national campaign to build hundreds of new *quoad sacra* parish churches across Scotland. More specifically, the Committee was instructed to collect statistics

[77] A point made when the Veto was first introduced in the Assembly in the previous year: S. MacGregor (ed.), *Report of the Debate in the General Assembly of the Church of Scotland on the Overtures anent Calls, May 23, 1833* (Edinburgh, 1833), 50–1; see also R. M. W. Cowan, *The Newspaper in Scotland* (Glasgow, 1946), 227.

on Scotland's need for additional churches, to determine where new churches should be built and to collect money for church building.[78]

To head the enlarged Church Accommodation Committee and lead the national church extension campaign, the General Assembly of the Church of Scotland turned to Thomas Chalmers, Scotland's great advocate of the parochial establishment. Chalmers, it will be recalled, had suffered a stroke in January 1834, which had been expected to end his career. While he had made a partial recovery, his health remained delicate and he suffered from hazy vision and a hissing noise in his head. None the less he readily accepted the call, viewing it as the culmination of his life's work. He blamed the Voluntaries for his stroke and he believed that his life had been spared to enable him to take up the great work of saving and extending the established Church of Scotland against its Voluntary assailants. 'Nor can I regard it as otherwise than a gracious Providence', he stated in early June 1834 at the first meeting of the enlarged Church Accommodation Committee,

> that after having been unhinged, enfeebled, and well-nigh overborne in an arduous conflict with those who would despoil our beloved Church of her endowments, and abridge the number of her ministers, I should now be called upon, in the hour of my returning strength . . . to enlarge her means and multiply her labourers, instead of maintaining as heretofore, a weary struggle with the men whose unhallowed hands are lifted up against our Zion, to mutilate and destroy her.[79]

The General Assembly of 1834 proved of profound importance for the established Church of Scotland. That Church had ceased to look anxiously on while the Voluntary agitation gathered momentum, and now embraced a new militancy. Rather than wait upon its fate, the Church would advance to reclaim the ground lost to Dissent and irreligion and revive the parish system. It had moved from the defensive to the offensive. It had taken the initiative to reform patronage, facilitate the formation of new parish churches, and appeal to the Scottish people to support a national church-building movement. And Chalmers, the famed champion of the establishment principle, had come back from a near-fatal stroke to head the church extension campaign.

[78] T. Chalmers, *First Report of the Committee of the General Assembly on Church Extension* (Edinburgh, 1835), 20.

[79] Hanna, *Memoirs of Dr Chalmers*, iii. 450–1.

With unexpected energy, Chalmers proceeded immediately to organize the national campaign. His strategy was to encourage the formation of local societies, which would the mobilize local efforts to build churches to meet local needs. This, he believed, would inspire 'a far more intense local feeling and greatly more numerous contributions'.[80] A beginning in setting up local societies had already been made. A few months before, in January 1834, largely through the efforts of Chalmers's publisher, the Evangelical layman William Collins, a local church-building society had been formed in Glasgow. This society had announced a five-year plan to build and endow, through private contributions, twenty additional city churches, each with 1,000 sittings. Each new church was to be erected at a cost of £2,000 and to receive an additional £2,000 as an endowment. The endowment would pay part of the minister's stipend, with the rest of the stipend to be derived from modest seat rents, which would be set low enough to enable labouring families to attend church regularly.[81] The Glasgow church-building society, meanwhile, had inspired the formation of a similar church-building society in Aberdeen in February 1834.[82] Now, from June 1834, Chalmers's Church Accommodation Committee encouraged the multiplication of such local church-building societies across Scotland. It further instructed the local societies to adopt a penny-a-week scheme, in a move reminiscent of Daniel O'Connell's penny-a-week subscription scheme for the Catholic Association in the 1820s. While better-off families would subscribe larger amounts, labouring families would be encouraged to contribute small sums, as low as a penny each week, towards church building. The penny-a-week scheme, Chalmers argued, would lead to the accumulation of large sums through the combined efforts of tens of thousands of small contributors. It would also increase the attachment of the lower orders to the established Church, making even the poorest penny-a-week subscribers feel that they were stakeholders in the

[80] T. Chalmers to A. Gordon, 28 June 1834, New College Library, Edinburgh, Church Extension Letterbook, MS X13b, 6/3, 13–16.

[81] [W. Collins], *Proposal for Building Twenty New Parochial Churches in the City and Suburbs of Glasgow* [Glasgow, 1834], 1–15; W. Collins, *The Church of Scotland: The Poor Man's Church* [Glasgow, n.d.], 1–8; D. Keir, *The House of Collins* (London, 1952), 105–6.

[82] A. Thomson to A. Brunton, 19 February 1834, New College Library, Edinburgh, Alexander Thomson of Banchory Papers, THO 24; D. Chambers, 'The Church of Scotland's Parochial Extension Scheme and the Scottish Disruption', *Journal of Church and State*, 16 (1974), 271–2.

establishment. 'Every man whom you succeed in gaining as a penny-a-week contributor to our cause' Chalmers explained to a fellow minister on 9 July 1834, 'you will succeed in reforming as a friend to the Church of Scotland.'[83] His aim was to make church extension a genuinely popular movement. He would show that the established Church in Scotland was a people's Church, rooted in Scotland's history and popular culture, and not the creature of the Crown or Parliament.

As well as promoting the multiplication of local societies, Chalmers's Committee set up a general church extension fund, to be made up of contributions from wealthy members of the landed or mercantile élite. This general fund was used to cover administrative and printing costs for the campaign, and more importantly to supplement the collections by local church-building societies in poorer districts. In short, while the local penny-a-week schemes would encourage support from the poorer classes for local church building, the general fund would promote involvement by the upper classes in the campaign. The church extension campaign was thus to be a national movement, uniting rich and poor in support of a cause that would transcend selfish interests and class identities in industrial society. The campaign, Chalmers assured the duke of Buccleuch in a letter requesting his contributions on 9 July 1834, 'would serve more effectually than any other expedient, in these days of distemper and menace, to reunite the various orders of the state into a harmonious and pacific understanding with each other'.[84]

In August 1834, Chalmers established a model local church-building operation in the working-class Water of Leith district of Edinburgh. The aim was to show how church-building societies should proceed—first creating a Christian congregation in an area of low church attendance, and only then erecting church and school buildings. Chalmers began his operation by forming a local church-building society, which mapped out a manageable district and gathered statistics on church attendance. The society's enquiries revealed that out of a district population of 1,287, fewer than 150 individuals held seats in any church. Society members then began

[83] T. Chalmers to J. Cook, 9 July 1834, New College Library, Edinburgh, Church Extension Letterbook, MS X13b, 6/3, 33–6.

[84] T. Chalmers to the Duke of Buccleuch, 9 July 1834, New College Library, Edinburgh, Church Extension Letterbook, MS X13b, 6/3, 27–30.

conducting house-to-house visiting in the district, and holding week-night Bible and prayer meetings. They also employed an urban missionary to assist in the visiting and to conduct informal Sunday services in an abandoned malt granary. Chalmers himself would frequently conduct house-to-house visiting, assisted on occasions by a young Anglican friend, William Ewart Gladstone, whose father owned a house in Edinburgh and contributed financially to Chalmers's Water of Leith operation. Young Gladstone, recently elected to the Commons, became a convert to Chalmers's parish ideal.[85] By the end of 1834 nearly 400 Water of Leith inhabitants were regularly attending the Sunday services, despite the cold and damp of the unheated granary. Only at this point did the society begin building a new church, which was completed and constituted as a *quoad sacra* parish church in May 1836.[86] The Water of Leith operation signalled Chalmers's intentions for the church extension campaign. Local church-building operations were not simply to concentrate upon 'stone and lime', but were first to create the moral foundations of a Christian community. The local operations were not only to provide church accommodation for existing churchgoers, but were to endeavour through regular house-to-house visiting to reach the poor and marginalized in working-class districts, those who had lost all habits of church attendance. As the lower social orders embraced regular religious habits they would also embrace habits of thrift, hard work, self-sufficiency, and respectability. Such families would send their children to school, and seek to throw off all dependency on poor relief. The established Church, Chalmers argued, was the 'poor man's church'; one of its main purposes was to seek out the poor through aggressive visiting and prepare them for full citizenship in the Christian commonwealth. In this way an established Church differed from the Voluntary denominations, which in Chalmers's view were concerned primarily to attract congregations of better-off people who could afford to pay for the support of their

85 T. Chalmers to J. Gladstone, 14 March 1836, Glynne-Gladstone MSS, Flintshire Records Office, Harwarden, G.G. 98; *Gladstone Diaries*, 22, 24 Dec. 1835; *The Chalmers Centenary: Speeches delivered in the Free Assembly Hall, Edinburgh, on March 3, 1880* (Edinburgh, 1880), 15–16; J. Morley, *Life of William Ewart Gladstone*, 2nd edn., 2 vols. (London, 1905), i. 110.

86 *Parliamentary Papers*, First Report of the Commissioners on Religious Instruction in Scotland, 1837 (31), xxi. 19, 'Evidence of Thomas Chalmers, 13 Feb. 1836; Chalmers, *Collected Works*, xi. 347–53.

churches and clergy. 'It is on this', Chalmers maintained in a pamphlet published in February 1835, 'and this alone . . . that our plea for an Establishment, and a sufficiently extended one, is founded—on the moral and spiritual desolation of all remoter hamlets and villages in large country parishes, on the outcast thousands and tens of thousands in large towns—only to be assailed by the territorial methods of an Establishment, and by the aggressive forces which belong to it.'[87] Here, then, was a purpose for the established Church of Scotland, and indeed the established Churches of England and Ireland, in the era of reform following the end of the confessional State. They would become popular institutions, embracing a sense of responsibility for the poor and seeking to unite the social classes in a Christian commonwealth. They would look for worldly support, not primarily from Parliament, but from the people, and especially the labouring classes.

In order to reach the 'outcast' population, the Scottish church extensionists argued, the newly constructed churches had to be given endowments by the State. Only endowed parish churches, they maintained, would be able to carry on the home mission to the poor and marginalized in society, those who had little money to contribute to the support of their local church. Only endowed parish churches would be able to set their seat rents low enough to enable the labouring poor to attend church regularly in family units. Therefore, at the same time that the General Assembly began the church extension campaign, it also began negotiating with the Whig Government for a grant of public money sufficient to endow each new *quoad sacra* church with an income of £100 a year. This would not cover all the costs of the minister's stipend and the repair of the church, but it would pay a substantial part and allow the new churches to keep seat rents low. The Church felt its request was a reasonable one. It would form new *quoad sacra* parishes and build new churches. The State in return would provide a modest endowment for each new church, thus demonstrating its commitment to maintaining an established Church commensurate with Scotland's growing population. In July 1834, the General Assembly sent a deputation to London to put the Church's request to the Whig ministers. Melbourne's Government was encouraging. It was too

[87] T. Chalmers, *The Cause of Church Extension and the Question Shortly Stated, between Churchmen and Dissenters in Regard to It* (1835) in Chalmers, *Collected Works*, xviii. 136–7.

late in the parliamentary session to introduce a new bill, but the deputation was assured that the Government would introduce a motion during the next session. Chalmers confidently drafted a bill for the endowment grant, and circulated it among leading politicians.[88]

The situation for Melbourne's Government, however, was precarious. The momentum of reform had slowed and the ministry was increasingly torn in trying to meet the often conflicting demands of its Whig, Radical, Voluntary, and Irish Catholic supporters. Then in November 1834, before it could take any action on behalf of the Scottish Church, Melbourne's Government was suddenly dismissed by the king. The Conservative leader, Sir Robert Peel, who was on a visit to Rome, was summoned back to form a Government, and he dissolved Parliament on 28 December. In his manifesto to the electors in his constituency of Tamworth, Peel made it clear that he would work within the political system as defined in the Reform Act of 1832 and he acknowledged the value of many of the reforms initiated by the Whig Government. He also declared his commitment to the reform and extension of the established Churches. The Tories did well in the general election of January–February 1835, doubling their numbers in the Commons. Peel's Government held only a minority of seats in the new House of Commons, but it was a large minority and Peel was determined to persevere against a divided opposition. His return to power seemed a good sign for Scottish church extension. 'I do assure you', Peel informed Chalmers on 28 January 1835, 'that the Church of Scotland has few more attached friends among its own immediate members, than myself.' He added that he was 'favourably disposed' to Chalmers's proposals for the endowment bill, and would 'take them into very early consideration'.[89] Several weeks later, in his speech opening Parliament, the king announced that his Government would consider means to extend the Scottish Church establishment, and that it would also take up the much larger question of the reform and extension of the Church of England.

[88] T. Chalmers, 'Outline of the Scheme by which the Deficiencies of our Establishment Might be Repaired, September 1834', New College Library, Edinburgh, Church Extension Letterbook, MS X13b, 6/3, 82–3; T. Chalmers to W. E. Gladstone, 24 September 1834, BL Gladstone Papers, Add. MS 44354, fo. 58.

[89] Sir R. Peel to T. Chalmers, 24 January 1835, BL, Peel Papers, Add. MS 40411, fo. 200.

State Commissions, Church Extension, and Renewed Confidence

Peel's commitment to preserving and strengthening the established Churches was genuine. Although he bore the stigma of having 'betrayed' the Protestant establishment in 1829, Peel was in truth committed to the principle of a religious establishment. His own religion was essentially private and personal, a rational, broadly tolerant Protestantism, with emphasis on moral conduct and devotion to duty. He was not too concerned with differences in ecclesiastical structures, liturgies, and doctrine. He supported preserving the Episcopal Church of Ireland as a minority establishment in an overwhelmingly Catholic country, and he upheld the Episcopal Church of England as a distinctively English national Church. He supported the Presbyterian Church of Scotland as the Church commanding the religious loyalties of the majority of Scots, and could speak warmly of his experiences of Presbyterian worship while visiting Scotland. His primary concern was with the practical contributions of the established Churches at the parish level—with their role in elevating the morals of society and uniting individuals and social orders around shared values and beliefs.[90]

Peel recognized that there were real abuses needing reform within the established Churches.[91] In the tradition of Perceval and Liverpool, he had no patience with those who viewed the Church as a private corporation rather than a national institution. He refused to view the cathedral and college endowments as sacrosanct while the Church's parish ministry in many districts was starved of resources. For example, he was outraged to learn that King's College, Cambridge, took £2,000 a year from one parish, leaving the vicar of that parish only £24 a year. He rejected the argument that the Church needed to retain wealthy sinecures in order to attract well-connected and well-educated men into the clergy. 'Is the Church', he asked J. W. Croker on 2 February 1835, 'to be a provision for men of birth or learning? or is its main object the worship of God?'[92] Peel was under no illusions that his minority Government could survive for long. He did, however, believe that his unexpected call to power

[90] Gash, *Sir Robert Peel*, 184–7; Kitson Clark, *Peel and the Conservative Party*, 39–41.

[91] [T. H. Lister], 'Appropriation of Church Property', *Edinburgh Review*, 60 (January 1835), 485–6, 491.

[92] Parker, *Sir Robert Peel*, ii. 283–5.

was an opportunity for the established Churches. He hoped, as we have seen, to help the Church of Scotland gain the endowment grant. And he wanted to work with the Church of England in developing a programme of Church reform. It was, he wrote to Henry Phillpotts, bishop of Exeter, on 22 December 1834, 'possibly the last opportunity' for the Church of England to assist 'its true friends in the cause of judicious Reform' with hope of 'a satisfactory and final settlement'.[93] They could not let the opportunity pass. 'I am convinced of the absolute necessity', he wrote to Lord Harrowby, the veteran Church reformer, on 12 January 1835, 'of taking some effectual and practical step with a view not only to the satisfaction of the public mind, but to the higher object of promoting the spiritual efficiency of the Church, and the great moral and religious purposes for which the Church was founded.'[94]

For English Church reform, Peel proposed the appointment of a new commission, made up exclusively of clergymen and lay members of the Church of England, and charged to look into the organization and revenues of the Church and recommend a programme of reforms. The commission, Peel believed, could be constituted in such a manner that it would gain the confidence of the Church. It could, moreover, carry out its enquiries and deliberations at a distance from the House of Commons, where so many members were hostile or indifferent to the Church.[95] Only when it had backing for its reform proposals from Church leaders would the commission put its proposals to Parliament. The Church would thus be closely involved in the process from the beginning, and there would be no prospect of Parliament imposing reforms on the Church, with little consultation, as had been the case with the Irish Church Temporalities Act. After consultations at Lambeth in early January 1835, Peel gained the support of the two archbishops for the idea of the commission. In truth, Church leaders were in a corner, with little choice but to co-operate. There was a widespread public demand for Church reform, and resistance, according to one bishop, would have furnished 'proof, either that we were blind to the defects and abuses in the Church; or that, seeing them, we were, from interested

[93] Sir R. Peel to H. Phillpotts, 'Most Private', 22 December 1834, Exeter Cathedral Archives, Phillpotts Papers, ED 11/49/4; G. C. B. Davies, *Henry Phillpotts, Bishop of Exeter 1778–1869* (London, 1954), 323–4.

[94] Peel, *Memoirs*, ii. 72.

[95] Ibid. ii. 69–72; *Hansard's Parl.Deb.*, 3rd ser. xxxv (19 July 1836), cols. 356–7; G. I. T. Machin, *Politics and the Churches in Great Britain 1832–1868* (Oxford, 1977), 50–1.

motives, resolved not to correct them'.[96] The membership of the commission was agreed in mid-January, with the archbishop of Canterbury recruiting the clerical members (the archbishops of Canterbury and York and the bishops of Lincoln, Gloucester, and London) and Peel recruiting the lay members (Peel, Lord Lyndhurst, Henry Goulburn, Charles Wynn, and Sir Herbert Jenner).

Of the members of the new Ecclesiastical Commission, the energetic and commanding Charles James Blomfield, the bishop of London, was recognized as the dominant figure from the beginning—so much so that there was, Henry Goulburn, the home secretary, confided to Peel on 2 January 1835, 'great jealousy lest the Bishop of London should lead the Government [on the question of Church reform]'.[97] Born the son of a schoolmaster in 1786, Blomfield had attended Cambridge University, where he demonstrated from an early age an astounding capacity for work and won distinction as a classicist. Once ordained in 1810, he directed these energies to the parish ministry. Embracing moderate High Church and liberal Tory views, and associated with the influential Hackney Phalanx, he rose to prominence during the Church revival of the 1820s. In 1824, he became bishop of Chester, where he took a leading role in the emerging diocesan reform movement. Concerned over the poverty and growing class divisions in the industrializing society of his northern diocese, he was active in the distribution of charity. After 1826, under the influence of Thomas Chalmers and the Christian political economists, he became convinced that lasting social improvement would come only by building more parish churches and schools, and reviving a sense of Christian community among the labouring orders.[98] In 1828, Blomfield was translated to London. There he continued the work of improving the parish ministry through the reduction of pluralism and non-residency. 'The strongest argument for an established Church', he asserted in 1834, was that it was 'the most efficient instrument, of instructing the people in the doctrines of religion, and of habituating them to its decencies and restraints.'[99] By declining to issue licences for non-residence,

[96] J. Kaye, *A Letter to his Grace the Archbishop of Canterbury, on the Recommendations of the Ecclesiastical Commission* (London, 1838), 10.

[97] H. Goulburn to Sir R. Peel, 2 January 1835, BL Peel Papers, Add. MS 40333, fos. 211–12.

[98] Soloway, *Prelates and People*, 150–1.

[99] C. J. Blomfield, *The Uses of a Standing Ministry and an Established Church* (London, 1834), 35.

he managed between 1831 and 1835 to increase the number of resident incumbents in the diocese of London from 287 to 325. By 1834, there were only sixty-four parishes in the diocese of London without a resident clergyman.[100] He also became probably the most unpopular bishop in the Church; many felt, according to the historian Owen Chadwick, 'that he was high-handed, sarcastic, meddlesome, hasty, over-bearing, that even when he smiled he smiled episcopally, that he was always conscious of his dignity'.[101] He certainly supported the formation of the Ecclesiastical Commission; indeed, he had suggested the idea of just such a commission in a letter to the archbishop of Canterbury in December 1832.[102] In his Charge of July 1834, Blomfield expressed his belief that the Church should be prepared to redistribute its resources from the cathedral establishments to strengthen the parish ministry, the area of the Church's greatest social utility. The 'ornamental parts of the system', he insisted, while 'by no means unimportant . . . should not be suffered to stand in the way of improvements calculated to enhance and give lustre to the true beauty of the church—the beauty of its holy usefulness'.[103]

The Ecclesiastical Commission began its work in early February 1835. Peel made it clear from the beginning that for him, as for Blomfield, the Commission's main task should be to shift resources from the Church's 'ornamental parts' to its parish ministry: its priority should be raising poor livings to encourage residency and building new churches, especially in working-class districts in the growing towns and cities. 'I do earnestly ask', Peel wrote to William Van Mildert, the High Church bishop of Durham, on 23 February 1835, 'whether it be fit that the great manufacturing towns and districts of the country should be left, as to the means of spiritual instruction, in their present state?'[104] For Peel, the aims of English Church reform were essentially the same as those defined by the Church of Scotland six months previously—first, to diminish popular hostility to the established Church by reforming abuses, and second, to extend the parish system, especially in the new industrial

[100] Virgin, *The Church in an Age of Negligence*, 207–8; C. J. Blomfield, *A Charge delivered to the Clergy of the Diocese of London at the Visitation in July 1834*, 2nd edn. (London, 1834), 25.

[101] Chadwick, *Victorian Church*, i. 133; see also the caricature of 'Charles James Grantly' in Anthony Trollope's *The Warden* (London, 1855), ch. 8.

[102] C. J. Blomfield to W. Howley, 11 Dec. 1832, in Blomfield, *Memoir of Charles James Blomfield*, 153–5.

[103] Blomfield, *Charge . . . July 1834*, 16–17.

[104] Peel, *Memoirs*, ii. 81.

towns and cities. By 17 March 1835, the Commission had produced its first report, which focused on the administration of the dioceses. It included sweeping recommendations for the reorganization of diocesan boundaries, the redistribution of bishops' incomes, and the creation of two new dioceses.

Peel's Government, however, was now in serious difficulties. Once again the pressing problem was the established Church in Ireland, and the thorny question of the appropriation of its revenues. In Ireland the tithe war continued to spill blood; there was yet another pitched battle in county Cork shortly after Peel's appointment.[105] O'Connell had now declared that his party would not accept any measure of Irish tithe reform that did not include the appropriation of Irish Church revenues. On 30 March Lord John Russell gave notice of an appropriation resolution, and several days later, Peel's Government was defeated over Russell's resolution. Peel resigned on 8 April 1835, and Melbourne returned to office. There had been no time to introduce an endowment grant for the Church of Scotland, while the Ecclesiastical Commission for the Church of England had only begun its work. None the less, the Peel Government had done much to restore the confidence of the established Churches. In its brief 120 days in office, it had declared its firm support for church extension in Scotland, formed the Ecclesiastical Commission for the Church of England, and resisted appropriation from the established Church in Ireland. From 1835, the pressure for disestablishment eased, and the emphasis of public opinion shifted to the reform of the Churches. It was, moreover, reform aimed not at reducing the Churches, but at eliminating abuses and rationalizing administration, in order to make them more efficient in bringing religious and moral instruction to the growing industrial population.[106] Peel had made the reasoned defence of the religious establishments a main theme in the new Tory party that he was forging in the post-Reform Act era, and the Churches could now look forward to the day when the Tories would return to power.

The impact of Peel's brief Government could be seen in Parliament's changing attitude towards the Irish Church. A few

[105] Sir R. Peel to H. Goulburn, 27 December 1834, BL Peel Papers, Add. MS 40333, fos. 201–2.

[106] N. Gash, 'The Crisis of the Anglican Establishment in the Early Nineteenth Century', in A. M. Birke and K. Kluxen (eds.), *Church, State and Society in the 19th Century: An Anglo-German Comparison* (Munich, 1984), 35–7.

months after Peel's resignation, Melbourne's Government introduced another Irish tithe bill, this time with a provision for the appropriation of revenues from the Irish Church. With Government backing it seemed that appropriation would finally be implemented. But on 21 July 1835, Peel spoke powerfully in opposition to the bill, arguing that the work of the Irish Ecclesiastical Commission had revealed there were no surplus revenues in the Irish Church to be appropriated. Careful statistical research had demonstrated that the claims of excessive wealth in the Irish Church had been exaggerations. In fact, he argued, the Irish Church revenues were scarcely sufficient to provide decent support for its existing clergy. Parliament, Peel insisted, must now face up to the real implication of the Whig and Radical proposals to appropriate Irish Church revenues. The issue was the survival of the Irish Church establishment. Parliament should either bow to popular agitation and disestablish and disendow the Irish Church, or else recognize that the established Church was vital to real improvement in Ireland and preserve it. But it must cease pretending that there were vast Irish Church revenues surplus to the needs of that Church and ripe for appropriation. It would be best, Peel maintained, for Parliament to resist those whose real purpose was to undermine the Irish establishment and work for 'the slow extinction of Protestantism in Ireland'.[107] Peel gained the support of a substantial minority in the House, which was sufficient to convince the Government to drop its Irish tithe and appropriation bill. In his speech, which was subsequently published, Peel had shown the value of the Irish Ecclesiastical Commission in revealing the real financial circumstances of the Irish Church. The same service, he and his supporters believed, could be given to the English Church by the English Ecclesiastical Commission.

Melbourne's Cabinet had already decided that Peel's English Commission, reconstituted to reflect the change in Government, should continue its work. The Tory ministerial members of the Commission (Peel, Lyndhurst, Goulburn, and Wynn) resigned in April 1835 and were replaced by Whig ministers (Lords Melbourne, Lansdowne, and Cottenham, Lord John Russell, and Thomas Spring-Rice). Otherwise the membership, and the instructions to the Commission, remained the same, and Blomfield continued to

[107] Sir R. Peel, *Speech . . . in the House of Commons, on Tuesday, July 21, 1835, in support of his Amendment on the Irish Church Bill* (Edinburgh, 1835); Gash, *Sir Robert Peel*, 136–7.

dominate the proceedings. The second, third, and fourth reports of the Commission appeared in rapid succession in the spring and early summer of 1836. Taken together, the reports provided evidence of serious failings in the established Church in England and Wales. There were gross inequalities in the episcopal incomes, with the archbishop of Canterbury receiving £18,000 a year, the bishop of Durham £19,500 a year, and the bishop of London nearly £14,000 a year, while seven English and Welsh bishops received incomes of less than £3,000 a year.[108] The dioceses varied greatly in territory and population, with several far too large to be adequately supervised by the bishop. Among the parish clergy, there was widespread pluralism and non-residence, and considerable evidence of neglect of parish duties. Despite past parliamentary efforts to improve small livings, large numbers of clergy struggled on incomes insufficient to support a family. Perhaps most disturbing was the lack of church accommodation and the insufficient numbers of parish clergymen, especially in the rapidly expanding urban districts. In four London parishes, for example, with a total population of 166,000, the established churches offered seats for only 8,200. In the diocese of Chester, 38 parishes, representing a total population of 816,000, had room in the established churches for only 97,700.[109] It was therefore not surprising that Dissent had overtaken the Church in many urban districts. More disturbing for the Commissioners, a growing proportion of the population was now outside any form of organized religion.

To address this situation, the Commission drafted three parliamentary bills, which, taken together, offered a programme for the fundamental transformation of the established Church of England, rationalizing its administration and diverting resources from cathedral establishments to the parishes. The bills represented the principle that the Church of England must now do all it could from its own resources for church extension and improvement of small livings before it could expect any further help from the State. The Commissioners were under no illusions that their sweeping proposals would receive a warm welcome, especially from the Church. Their recommendations would have a negative impact on too many interests. And yet they believed that reform was imperative. They were haunted by the spectre of the unchurched masses, the hundreds

[108] *Hansard's Parl. Deb.*, 3rd ser. xxxv (1836), col. 18. [109] Ibid. 23.

of thousands of souls being lost to Christian influence by the Church's failure to fulfil its responsibilities of ministering to the labouring classes, especially in the expanding towns and cities. 'No man can be competent to deliver a fair judgment upon our recommendations', argued John Kaye, bishop of Lincoln and member of the Commission, 'who has not carefully perused and weighed that portion of the Report which particularly related to the deficiency of Church and Ministers in populous places.' 'When I regarded the frightful deficiency of spiritual instruction under which such numbers of my countrymen were suffering,' wrote another Commissioner, James Henry Monk, bishop of Gloucester, 'when it was clear that no earthly resource was available, except what might be spared from cathedral appointments, it became a question, not of predilection or of taste, but of duty to the sacred cause of Christ's church.'[110]

Melbourne's Government initially hoped to secure the passage of the three bills, one after another, through Parliament. In July and August 1836, Parliament considered the first of the three, the Established Churches bill. The bill made significant changes to the incomes of the archbishops and bishops, reducing the largest incomes and raising some of the others, with the aim of ensuring that all bishops received at least £4,500 a year. This, it was believed, would eliminate any need for bishops to hold parish livings *in commendam*. Further, it would reduce the temptation for ambitious prelates to seek translations to different sees in search of higher incomes. Secondly, the bill provided for the redrawing of diocesan boundaries to make the dioceses more equal in size and more rational and compact in territory. It also called for the creation of two new sees, Ripon and Manchester, in regions where there had been sizeable population growth. This would be matched by the suppression of two sees—to be accomplished by uniting the sees of Bristol and Gloucester and the sees of St Asaph and Bangor. The suppression of the sees was highly controversial, especially among High Churchmen who denied the authority of Parliament to suppress a bishopric. However, the Commission felt that the number of bishops could not be increased beyond twenty-six. Parliament would not approve the introduction of additional bishops in the House of Lords, and the Church would not wish to create two classes of

[110] Kaye, *Letter to the Archbishop of Canterbury*, 21; J. H. Monk, *A Charge delivered to the Clergy or the Diocese of Gloucester and Bristol, in August and September 1838* (London, 1838), 19.

bishop, a higher class with a seat in the Lords and a lower class without. Finally, the bill incorporated the Ecclesiastical Commission as a permanent governing body in the Church of England. The Commission was to consist of thirteen members, of whom only five were to be clergy (the two archbishops and three other bishops). The lay members were all to be members of the Church of England.

In introducing the bill in the Commons, Lord John Russell stated that the aim of the legislation was to strengthen the established Church. Despite pressure from the Radicals and Voluntaries, the Government had no intention of reducing the English Church or appropriating its revenues. The Commission's investigations, Russell observed, had demonstrated that there was a pressing need for the improvement of small livings and for church extension. Any revenues that could be freed up through internal reforms, therefore, were not to be viewed as surplus revenues; rather they must be invested in improving the Church's parochial system, especially in the crowded urban areas.[111] From the opposition benches, Peel spoke warmly in support of both the work of the Commission and the Government bill—hardly surprising, as it was largely his Commission and his programme. Opposition to the bill came from two directions. First, there were the Radicals and Voluntaries, who condemned the bill for not appropriating a large portion of the bishops' incomes for education or other national benefit.[112] Secondly, a number of High Churchmen, led by Sir Robert Inglis and the bishop of Exeter, claimed that if it enacted the bill Parliament would be interfering beyond its authority with the property and spiritual government of the Church.[113] In the event, Parliament passed the Established Church Act, though some felt the debates had been rushed and there had been insufficient consultation with the wider Church.

In response to these criticisms, the Government moved more slowly on the next two bills. It was not until 1838 that Parliament considered and passed the Commission's second bill, which dealt with pluralities and non-residence. The Pluralities Act of 1838 forbade any clergyman from holding more than one parish living except by special dispensation of the archbishop of Canterbury. Even

[111] *Hansard's Parl. Deb.*, 3rd ser. xxxv (1836), cols. 24–5.

[112] Best, *Temporal Pillars*, 312–13.

[113] *Hansard's Parl. Deb.*, 3rd ser. xxxv (1836), col. 347; Best, *Temporal Pillars*, 313–14; Mathieson, *English Church Reform*, 134–5.

with the archbishop's dispensation, no clergyman could hold more than two parish livings. The two parishes, moreover, could not be more than ten miles apart, neither could have a parish population of more than 3,000, and the combined annual income of the two benefices could not be more than £1,000. The Act placed restrictions on the amount of farming and trade in which the parish clergy could engage, it empowered bishops to require two full services, including a sermon or address, each Sunday, and it strengthened the bishop's power to enforce residence. There were additional clauses for the uniting and disuniting of parishes, for facilitating the building of parsonage houses, and for regulating the appointment and payment of curates. The Pluralities Act proved highly effective in achieving a resident parish clergy committed to forming parish communities by conducting regular worship services, house-to-house visiting, and charitable work. The Act did not affect existing interests, and as a result its full results were felt only gradually over the next generation. Yet it made an immediate impact on new appointments. In Lincolnshire before 1838, 25 per cent of incumbents instituted into parish livings were non-resident; after 1838 only 3 per cent of new incumbents were non-resident. In Nottinghamshire the figures were 20 per cent and 0 per cent respectively.[114] The Pluralities Act, the historian Frances Knight has argued, 'more than any other piece of legislation . . . set the tone for clerical life in the following decades'.[115] It conveyed the message that the parish ministry was a full-time responsibility and a high vocation, demanding the best efforts of incumbents.

The final of the Commission's three bills, that dealing with the diversion of resources from the cathedrals, would be the most contentious, and the Government allowed another delay before introducing it. In the mean time the Whigs were securing other reforms in the English ecclesiastical system. In 1836, with broad cross-party support, Parliament passed an act for the reform of the English tithe system, arranging for the commutation of tithe from payments in kind to a money payment based on the average price of grain over a period of seven years. The act proved effective, and most tithe was commuted over the next sixteen years, bringing an end to the cumbrous and unpopular methods of collecting the tithe in kind, and contributing to improved relations between the clergy and their

[114] Knight, *The Nineteenth-Century Church and English Society*, 121. [115] Ibid. 120.

parishioners. In the same session, Parliament passed the English Civil Marriage Act to legalize the celebration of marriages outside the parish church, either in Dissenting or Roman Catholic chapels, or before a civil registrar. In 1836, it also passed an act providing for the civil registration of births, marriages, and deaths in England, removing the responsibility for those records from the parish church to civil register offices and a new generation of civil servants.[116]

While Parliament from 1836 was gradually enacting the legislative programme outlined by the Ecclesiastical Commission, members of the Church of England were also active, forming and expanding diocesan church-building societies to promote local church extension efforts. The diocesan societies were intended to complement the church extension priorities of the Ecclesiastical Commission by raising voluntary contributions to build and enlarge local churches. These diocesan efforts were influenced by Thomas Chalmers and his Scottish church extension campaign. In 1834, for example, the Evangelical bishop of Chester, John Bird Sumner, took a leading role in forming a Chester Diocesan Church Building Society, for 'encouraging the erection of churches in the more populous parts of the diocese'. Sumner also advocated many of Chalmers's methods for the parish ministry, including the use of lay visitors to supplement the work of the parish clergyman. By 1838, the Chester Society had completed or begun more than fifty new churches in the diocese.[117] Sumner's brother, Charles Sumner, the Evangelical bishop of Winchester, helped to establish a diocesan church-building society at Winchester in 1837. By 1841, it had raised over £85,000 and provided 19,315 additional seats in new or rebuilt churches, with 11,350 seats free of pew rents.[118] Other church-building societies were formed in the dioceses of St Asaph (1834), Lichfield (1835), Worcester (1837), Bath and Wells (1836), Salisbury (1836), Norwich (1836), Exeter (1837), Chichester (1837), Bangor (1838), Peterborough (1838), Ripon (1838), and Hereford (1839).[119] The diocesan societies in turn encouraged the formation of numerous

[116] M. J. Cullen, 'The Making of the Civil Registration Act of 1836', *Journal of Ecclesiastical History*, 25 (1974), 39–59; a comparable act was not passed in Scotland until 1855.

[117] J. B. Sumner, *A Charge delivered to the Clergy of the Diocese of Chester . . . in 1838* (London, 1838), 21–2; Soloway, *Prelates and People*, 321; Smith, *Religion in Industrial Society*, 99–100; Scotland, *The Life and Work of John Bird Sumner*, 48–9, 54; R. B. Walker, 'Religious Changes in Cheshire, 1750–1850', *Journal of Ecclesiastical History*, 17 (1966), 87–8.

[118] C. R. Sumner, *A Charge delivered to the Clergy of Winchester . . . in 1841* (London, 1841), 11–12.

[119] Burns, *The Diocesan Revival in the Church of England*, 116.

local church-building societies and provided grants to aid these local church-building efforts. The result was the erection of hundreds of new churches within the establishment through purely voluntary means, which included the introduction of Chalmers's penny-a-week scheme for involving the labouring poor in the work of church extension.[120] By 1838, according to one Anglican observer, the Church of England was building more churches than all the other denominations combined.[121]

In 1836, a major church-building campaign was launched in London. The initiative came from Church Evangelicals, who called on the bishop of London to follow the example of the bishop of Chester's urban church-building efforts. In a published letter to the bishop of London, Baptist Noel, a veteran of the Irish Bible war during the 1820s and now the Evangelical pastor of St John's Chapel, Bedford Row, claimed that there were over 518,000 people in London without church accommodation, many of them living in conditions of appalling moral and physical deprivation. He called for the adoption in London of Chalmers's 'aggressive' system of urban ministry, and for the erection of new parish churches and schools, to be served by additional Anglican curates and teachers. Noel even advocated street preaching by lay preachers in order to reach the sunken population of London's slum districts.[122] Decisive measures would be needed if the established Church were not to lose the cities in Britain, as it had lost Ireland during the New Reformation campaign. The Evangelicals' London initiative gained other supporters, including the High Church Oxford professor of Hebrew, E. B. Pusey, who had been deeply impressed by the urban church extension plan begun by the Evangelicals of Glasgow in January 1834.[123] In November 1835 Pusey published a forceful article on 'Church-Building in Great Cities' in the High Church *British Magazine*, calling attention to the neglect of the religious and moral needs of the population of London and other large cities, and reminding merchants and manufacturers that they were members of a Christian commonwealth, with responsibilities to contribute to meeting the

[120] W. Dealtry, *Obligations of the National Church: A Charge delivered at the Visitation in Hampshire, September 1838* (London, 1838), 30–1.

[121] Ibid. 10–11.

[122] B. W. Noel, *The State of the Metropolis Considered* (London, 1835); G. Carter, 'Evangelical Seceders from the Church of England, *c.*1800–1850' (University of Oxford D.Phil., 1990), 398–400.

[123] E. B. Pusey to W. E. Gladstone, 2 February 1836, Pusey House, Oxford, Pusey Papers, 'Pusey and Gladstone', vol. I; Liddon, *Life of E. B. Pusey*, i. 327–30.

spiritual needs of the labouring poor. The Church of England must not simply wait upon the State to find the resources for urban church extension. It must remember that its existing churches, chapels, and cathedrals had been 'raised by the sacrifices, in some cases enormous sacrifices' of men and women in the past, and that the present generation must now do its part.[124]

In April 1836 the bishop of London, Blomfield, announced the formation of the Metropolis Churches Fund, with the goal of building and endowing at least fifty new churches in London. He acknowledged that there had been substantial church building in London since 1818, but noted that those efforts had been overwhelmed by the massive growth in the city's population. The need for churches was now greater than ever. In the east and north-east districts of London, for example, a population of 353,460 was served by only eighteen churches and chapels, and twenty-four clergymen of the established Church—or an average of one established church for every 19,000 people and one established clergyman for every 14,000. Blomfield insisted that the parish system could be restored in the urban environment, and that it must be the task of the established Church 'to divide the moral wilderness of this vast city into manageable districts, each with its place of worship, its schools, and its local institutions'.[125] The Church must seek to restore in the urban setting the traditional idea of Christian community, in which the rich would be reawakened to their responsibilities for the poor, and the poor learn again to respect the social order. Citing the example of church building in Glasgow, Blomfield called for voluntary contributions to build and endow the new churches. Endowments were particularly important as they would render the parish clergy 'independent of pew-rents' and thus strengthen the new churches' mission in poorer districts, where the inhabitants could not be expected to pay even modest seat rents. Blomfield hoped that the new district churches would restore traditional social harmonies and the old alliance of the clergy and upper social orders in the metropolis. Each district church would have a resident pastor, and affiliated schools and charities. Blomfield's scheme of urban church extension in London was very similar to that of Chalmers in Scotland, and

[124] [E. B. Pusey], 'Church Building in Great Cities', *British Magazine*, 8 (November 1835), 579–90, 582.

[125] C. J. Blomfield, *Proposals for the Creation of a Fund to be Applied to the Building and Endowment of Additional Churches in the Metropolis* (London, 1836), 8–9.

observers frequently linked the two.[126] In July Blomfield formed a committee, which included the High Churchmen Pusey and Gladstone and the Evangelical Lord Ashley.[127] William IV gave his patronage and special appeals were made to the wealthier classes of the city, especially the landlord class. Pusey contributed £5,000 to the Fund through considerable familial sacrifice, persuading his wife to sell her jewellery, while the family sold its carriage, adopted a stringent mode of living, and withdrew from society. By the end of 1836, Blomfield's Metropolis Churches Fund had raised over £106,000 for church-building in London.[128] William Cotton, a wealthy banker and cordage manufacturer, set a further example when in 1837–8 he personally financed the building of the campaign's first district church—St Peter's, Stepney. Within two years, St Peter's was a model district church, with a district visiting society, a hospice, two large schools, and a lending library with 570 volumes.[129] A similar urban church-building campaign was launched in 1836 in Manchester, and Glasgow, London, and Manchester now emerged as the main urban mission fields for the parochial establishments.[130]

With church extension came moves to improve pastoral provision in the Church of England. There was a recognition that more than 'stone and mortar' was required to revive the parish system in the towns and cities. In particular, more pastoral workers were needed. From 1832, J. B. Sumner, the bishop of Chester, advocated the appointment of lay visitors to assist parish incumbents in regular house-to-house visiting, on the model of the visiting elders and deacons in the Church of Scotland, as described in Chalmers's writings. In February 1836, Evangelicals in the Church of England formed the Church Pastoral-Aid Society, which endeavoured to increase the number of working clergy, in part by providing financial support for

[126] This included critics. John Henry Newman, for example, wrote of 'the miserable town Church extension system such as both Dr C. [Chalmers] and the Bishop of London advocate it'. Newman to Henry Wilberforce, 5 July 1838, in *Letters and Diaries of John Henry Newman*, vi. 261.

[127] P. J. Welch, 'Bishop Blomfield and Church Extension in London', *Journal of Ecclesiastical History*, 4 (1953), 204–6.

[128] D. Forrester, *Young Doctor Pusey: A Study in Development* (London, 1989), 66; Blomfield, *Memoir of Charles James Blomfield*, 177–9.

[129] A. Saint, 'Anglican Church-building in London, 1790–1890', in C. Brooks and A. Saint (eds.), *The Victorian Church: Architecture and Society* (Manchester, 1995), 35; Welch, 'Bishop Blomfield and Church Extension in London', 206.

[130] W. R. Ward, *Religion and Society in England*, 222–3.

the employment of assistant curates who would aid resident incumbents in the parishes. More controversially, the Society encouraged the appointment of lay assistants to the clergy in crowded urban parishes. The Evangelical Lord Ashley became the first president, and the Society was supported by the Evangelical bishops of Chester and Winchester. By 1838, it was supporting 137 curates and twenty-four lay assistants. In 1841, the society had over 1,700 members among the clergy. Its literature celebrated the ideal of the medieval parish, suggesting that similar close-knit parish communities could be restored in the new urban environment.[131] High Church members of the Society, meanwhile, opposed the employment of laymen for pastoral visiting and were unhappy with the Society's loose doctrinal positions. In the spring of 1837 a number of these High Church members, including the venerable Hackney Phalanx leader Joshua Watson and the young William Gladstone, broke away to found the Additional Curates Society. The new society restricted itself to supporting the employment only of ordained curates to assist the parish clergy, and it insisted on strict adherence to orthodox Anglican teachings.[132]

Some were developing new models for the urban ministry, as a means to maximize the church extension efforts. In 1838 the High Churchman Henry Wilberforce urged the creation of collegiate establishments for unmarried urban parish clergy, in which several incumbents of new urban churches would share a single residence, have common meals, pool their books into a common library, discuss together their experiences and pastoral methods, and provide one another with mutual support. These teams of urban clergy, he insisted, would prove far more effective than single parish incumbents in confronting the difficult challenges of community building in crime-ridden urban slum districts. The collegiate teams could work together to co-ordinate the work of lay visitors for district visiting and teaching in district Sunday schools and adult Bible classes. The collegiate residences could also serve as schools in practical theology for candidates for ordination who had recently completed

[131] F. W. Cornish, *The English Church in the Nineteenth Century*, 2 vols. (London, 1910), i. 84; Dealtry, *Obligations of the National Church*, 14; Chadwick, *The Victorian Church*, i. 446, 449–50; Knight, *The Nineteenth Century Church and English Society*, 62.

[132] Churton, *Memoir of Joshua Watson*, ii. 58; A. B. Webster, *Joshua Watson: The Story of a Layman*, 75; P. Butler, *Gladstone: Church, State and Tractarianism* (Oxford, 1982), 67–8; Dealtry, *Obligations of the National Church*, 14.

their university study, helping to provide ordinands with proper professional training.[133] The suggestion of residential collegiate establishments for the urban mission had first been made by the High Church fellow of Oriel College, Oxford, Richard Hurrell Froude, and with its monastic character, reminiscent of the early medieval monasteries that had helped to spread Christianity and Latin civilization across western Europe, the idea found particular favour among High Anglicans. During the summer of 1838, Pusey attempted to establish such collegiate establishments for urban mission in Manchester and London, and though the plan fell through in the short term, Pusey and his fellow High Anglicans remained committed to the project.[134]

There were also fresh efforts to strengthen the educational work of the established Church, especially through the revival of parish schools. In 1833 Parliament had agreed to make an annual grant of £20,000 per annum for building schools for the poor in Great Britain, with preference to be given to urban districts. The following year Parliament made an additional grant of £10,000 to Scotland, and agreed that the original annual grant of £20,000 would now be restricted to England and Wales. The Scottish grant of £10,000 was renewed in 1836, 1837, and 1838. In 1838, moreover, Parliament passed a Highlands Schools Act, which provided additional funds for building and endowing schools in the Highlands and Islands. In Scotland the grants went almost exclusively to schools in connection with the established Church of Scotland.[135] In England grants were awarded only on application from one of the two main educational societies—the National Society, which was the organ of the Church of England, or the British and Foreign Schools Society, supported primarily by the Dissenters. Grants were limited to the building of schools, and at least half the cost of the school had to be raised by private giving.[136] The result was a vigorous competition for the grants between the two educational societies, and this in turn mobilized considerable local effort. By the end of 1837 the total State

[133] H. W. Wilberforce, *The Parochial System: An Appeal to English Churchmen* (London, 1838), 34–40.

[134] P. Brendon, *Hurrell Froude and the Oxford Movement* (London, 1974), 134–5; Liddon, *Life of E. B. Pusey*, ii. 37–40.

[135] D. G. Paz, *The Politics of Working-Class Education in Britain, 1830–50* (Manchester, 1980), 14–15, 34; Anderson, *Education and the Scottish People 1750–1918*, 43, 45.

[136] F. Smith, *Life and Work of Sir James Kay-Shuttleworth* (London, 1923), 73–4; J. Hurt, *Education in Evolution: Church, State, Society and Popular Education* (London, 1971), 28–9.

grants of some £80,000 had encouraged private donations of over £165,000, and 153,600 pupils were being taught in the new schools.[137] In this competition, the established Church's National Society, with its superior resources, had won over 70 per cent of the state grants. The established Church was reasserting its authority over popular education in England.

Early in 1838 a circle of young Anglican London-based Tories, dubbed the 'Young Gentlemen' and including Lord Sandon, Thomas Acland, W. E. Gladstone, S. F. Wood, Philip Pusey, and W. M. Praed, developed a programme for the extension of the Church's educational provision, with the aim of achieving a national system of Church schools. The Young Gentlemen's scheme, which they pressed vigorously on the Church, comprised 'a regularly graduated scale of instruction from the Universities down to the Infant Schools, the whole essentially and intricately connected with the principles and Ministers of the Church'. Each diocese was to form a diocesan training college for teachers, and also a diocesan board of education, which would supervise a hierarchy of infant, parish, and middle schools, and would have power to inspect all diocesan schools.[138] The National Society, with the support of William Howley, archbishop of Canterbury, embraced much of the Young Gentlemen's programme, recommending the formation of diocesan boards of education and training schools for teachers in every diocese. In response, twenty-four diocesan and subdiocesan boards of education were established by 1839.[139] The first diocesan teacher training college opened at Chester in 1839, with twenty-one more such colleges formed by 1845.[140] The *Quarterly Review* observed in April 1838 that Church of England parish schools were multiplying rapidly in rural areas, with these schools becoming vital to the life of rural communities.[141] In July 1839 Howley asserted in the House of Lords that the parish clergy were awakening to their responsibilities and that

[137] *Hansard's Parl. Deb.*, 3rd ser. xlviii (14 June 1839), col. 245.

[138] R. J. W. Selleck, *James Kay-Shuttleworth* (Ilford, 1994), 144–5; Paz, *Politics of Working Class Education*, 62–5; Gash, *Reaction and Reconstruction in English Politics*, 78; E. S. Purcell, *Life of Cardinal Manning*, 2 vols. (London, 1895), 147–51.

[139] 'Diocesan Training Schools', *British Critic*, 27 (July 1840), 177–94; G. H. Sumner, *Life of Charles Richard Sumner, Bishop of Winchester* (London, 1876), 261; *Hansard's Parl. Deb.*, 3rd ser. xlviii (5 July 1839), col. 1239; G. F. A. Best, 'The Religious Difficulties of National Education in England, 1800–70', *Cambridge Historical Journal*, 12 (1956), 164; J. Morley, *Life of William Ewart Gladstone*, 2nd edn., 2 vols. (London, 1905), i. 148.

[140] Gash, *Reaction and Reconstruction in English Politics*, 78 n.

[141] [J. J. Blunt], 'Village Schools', *Quarterly Review*, 61 (April 1838), 451–3.

there would soon be a primary school in connection with the Church in every parish. For Blomfield, the Church was now recognizing that it was an educational as well as religious institution. 'A clergyman', he suggested to a public meeting in May 1839, 'was a clerical schoolmaster, and a schoolmaster was a lay parson.' 'A large and united movement', observed the High Church *British Critic* in July 1840, 'is now making by the Church of England to educate its people.'[142]

The new commitment to the established Church as a popular institution, a people's Church, was reflected in the first major work of Frederick Denison Maurice, the Anglican chaplain of Guy's Hospital, London, and a former Unitarian who had conformed to the established Church in adulthood. In *The Kingdom of Christ*, published in 1838, Maurice evoked Richard Hooker's view of the identity of Church and State—portraying the connection of the Church and State in England as an organic union, and further insisting that 'our nation of England acknowledged God for its King, just as much as the nation of the Jews did'.[143] In this godly commonwealth, this kingdom of Christ, the established Church was responsible before God for the religious instruction of the nation. The established Church, with its parish churches and schools, its parish ministers and schoolmasters, educated individuals to be free men and women, who willingly obeyed the civil laws because they understood that the social bonds were of divine ordinance.[144] The established Church embodied the vital principle of national unity, of shared religious and moral values, against the fragmentation of sects and proliferation of beliefs that characterized the Voluntary ideal. Maurice devoted particular attention to the parish system and the role of the parish clergy in shaping Christian communities at the grassroots level. The parish clergyman, he insisted, was both a servant of society and a servant of Christ:

> Not only at the baptism, and the sick-bed, and the grave is he claiming a dominion for his Master over all the incidents and transactions of life; but in watching over the interests of the poor, in administering charitable funds, and settling disputes, and presiding at vestries and explaining legislative measures, in the daily intercourse of life, at the house of the Squire or in the

[142] *Christian Guardian and Church of England Magazine* (July 1839), 278; *British Critic*, 27 (July 1840), 182.

[143] F. D. Maurice, *The Kingdom of Christ: or Hints on the Principles, Ordinances, and Constitution of the Catholic Church*, 3 vols. (London, 1838), iii. 41.

[144] Ibid. iii. 137–8.

cottage of the peasants, in directing the operations of the inferior schoolmaster, himself being the chief, he is still doing the Father's business.[145]

Maurice's vision of the Christian commonwealth of small, close-knit parish communities resembled that of Chalmers. While Maurice professed his preference for Anglicanism over Presbyterianism, he also acknowledged that Presbyterianism was the established Church in Scotland and therefore deserved Parliament's full support. He further suggested that the educated classes of Scotland were turning from the harsher aspects of Calvinism, and that Scottish Presbyterianism was moving towards closer congruence with Anglicanism in the essentials of Christianity.[146] The important point was that the established Churches throughout the three kingdoms expressed the ideas of the Christian society, and of a social gospel, and as such their revival was crucial for the future of the Kingdom of Christ in these islands.

After 1835, the threat of disestablishment was lifted from the established Churches, and the Churches of Scotland and England began to recover their confidence and sense of mission. There was no likelihood of a revival of the confessional State, or of the close relations of Church and State that had characterized the first quarter of the nineteenth century. But the Churches were now beginning to adapt to the new, more democratic political order that was emerging following the passing of the Reform Act. No longer able to look to the State for exclusive privileges, the established Churches began to redefine themselves as popular institutions, as 'poor men's churches', which provided religious instruction, pastoral care, and spiritual ordinances to the common people regardless of their ability to pay. They emphasized their social utility. 'An established Church', insisted one Anglican apologist in 1836, 'derives nothing from the State but its means of usefulness.'[147] In the social dislocations and suffering of early industrial society, the established Churches were finding a field for social service. They were working to revive Christian communities in the new urban environments through church extension and urban mission programmes. They were assuming responsibility for popular education among the labouring poor. Against the divisive forces of industrial capitalism, the established Churches were

[145] F. D. Maurice, *The Kingdom of Christ: or Hints on the Principles, Ordinances, and Constitution of the Catholic Church*, 3 vols. (London, 1838), iii. 227–8.

[146] Ibid. iii. 175–81.

[147] E. Osler, *The Church and Dissent, considered in their Practical Influence* (London, 1836), 13.

promoting a sense of social responsibility among the upper social orders, and of independence and self-help among the poor; they were seeking to ease class tensions through Christian social teachings. And as they regained popular support through their commitment to the parish ideal, as they did everything possible through the judicious management of their existing resources and the mobilization of voluntary giving, the Churches had reason to expect that the reformed Parliament would provide them with additional resources to carry on their work. The year 1838 marked a new high in this revived confidence and social mission of the established Churches in Scotland and England. It seemed that the established Churches in Britain were winning their version of the Irish New Reformation struggle, being fought now against Radicals and Voluntaries for the soul of an industrializing, urbanizing society. It was possible to envisage again the project of forging a Christian nation through the parochial institutions of the established Churches, if not in Ireland, at least in Britain. But this belief was soon to be tested, and the process began in Scotland.

The Crisis for Church Extension in Scotland

In Scotland, the church extension movement initiated by Thomas Chalmers and the Evangelical party had experienced considerable success during its first year. In May 1835 Chalmers had presented the first annual report of the Church Accommodation Committee to the General Assembly of the Church of Scotland. Subscriptions for church building, he observed, now totalled £65,626, while local societies in Scotland had built or were in the process of building sixty-four new *quoad sacra* parish churches. Contributions came from both the wealthy landed and commercial classes and from the labouring poor through the penny-a-week schemes. While the fall of the Peel Government in April 1835 had been a blow, Chalmers was confident that the broad popular support for church extension in Scotland would convince Melbourne's Whig Government to support the parliamentary grant that had been requested by the Church to provide partial endowments for the new churches.[148] In response to this glowing report, the General Assembly enlarged the standing Church Accommodation Committee to 130 members, increased its powers

[148] Chalmers, *First Report . . . on Church Extension*, 1–16.

and renamed it the Church Extension Committee. Chalmers was now convenor of the most powerful committee ever formed within the Church of Scotland, with authority over both the national church-building campaign and the negotiations with Parliament for the endowment grant. The name of the enlarged committee signalled that its purpose was not simply the 'stone and lime' of church building, but was rather to 'extend' the influence and authority of the established Church over the whole of Scotland through a reinvigorated parish system. Although Chalmers's health remained poor, he pressed himself to his limits in leading the campaign.

In July 1835 Chalmers led a deputation of the Church Extension Committee to London to lobby Melbourne's Whig Government for the parliamentary endowment grant. A year before, it will be recalled, Melbourne's Government had been encouraging. But now Chalmers and the church extensionists met with a lukewarm reception. The Government was uncertain about the religious situation in Scotland. It was also politically vulnerable, with a precarious majority in the Commons that depended on Radical, Voluntary, and Irish Catholic support. Government ministers acknowledged their responsibilities to the established Church in Scotland and promised that if there was genuine need for additional church accommodation it would be met. But the Government could not ignore a flood of petitions now pouring into Parliament. Organized by Scottish Voluntaries, these petitions insisted that there was already more than enough church accommodation in Scotland and that the Scottish people wanted no part of church extension.

Confronted by the conflicting claims of the Scottish church extensionists and Voluntaries, the Government announced in July 1835 that it would appoint a Royal Commission of Inquiry on Religious Instruction in Scotland. This Commission would investigate the total amount of church accommodation relative to the Scottish population and determine whether additional churches were actually needed. If it found a real need for new churches, the Commission would explore possible means of funding their construction and endowment. To a considerable extent, the Scottish Commission on Religious Instruction mirrored the English Ecclesiastical Commission, which had been formed six months previously. Both bodies were instructed to explore the extent of religious destitution, especially in the growing towns and cities, and both bodies were to investigate the resources available for church extension. But there was a critical difference. While the English Commission had included only members of the Church of England, the Scottish Commission of twelve members included a leading Scottish Voluntary, Andrew Dick, and several others who were openly sympathetic to the Voluntary cause. The convenor of the Commission, the Whig earl of Minto, was known to be personally hostile to Chalmers, the convenor of the Church Extension Committee. Moreover, in its investigation into religious accommodation in Scotland, the Commission was instructed to consider the accommodation offered by the Dissenters as well as by the established Church. The church extensionists were furious. The Government was, they believed, instructing the Commission to act as though the established Church and Dissent were equal in the eyes of the State.[149]

There was something still more ominous for the Church of Scotland in the Scottish Commission's instructions. The Government insisted that in considering possible sources of funding for church extension, the Commission should investigate the 'unappropriated teinds'. The teinds—that is, the Scottish version of tithe—had come under lay control after the Reformation. The bishops' teinds, which had originally supported the bishops and cathedral establishments, were now in the possession of the Crown and used to help fund the Civil List. The parish teinds were in the control of the heritors, or principal landowners. Only a portion of the parish teinds were used to pay the stipends of the parish clergy and provide for repair of the church and manse. The rest, the surplus or 'unappropriated teind', remained in the hands of the heritors and was treated as private income. No one knew in 1835 how much of the total teind in Scotland was unappropriated. The amount varied from parish to parish, depending on the value of the teind and the size of the minister's stipend. In some poorer parishes, the teinds were too small to pay the legal minimum stipend of the minister, and they had to be supplemented from State revenues. In such parishes, there was no unappropriated teind. In wealthier parishes, however, the heritors retained the bulk of the teinds for their personal use. In the parish of Blair Atholl, for example, the teinds were valued at £2,824 and the minister's stipend was about £300, leaving over £2,500 in the hands of the duke of Atholl, the single heritor.[150]

[149] Hanna, *Memoirs of Dr Chalmers*, iii. 470–87; S. J. Brown, *Thomas Chalmers*, 250–3.
[150] *Edinburgh Voluntary Churchman*, 5 (December 1835), 112–14.

No one knew how many Blair Atholls there were in the country. What was clear, however, was that Scottish landowners viewed any suggestion of using the unappropriated teinds for church extension as a threat to their property, and that if the Commission persisted in investigating the teinds it would set many landowners against church extension. One of the benefits of the church extension campaign, Chalmers argued, was that it united the different social orders behind the common cause of restoring traditional parish communities and elevating the condition of the poor through religious and moral instruction. The Commission's instructions regarding the unappropriated teinds now jeopardized this unity. Those instructions, complained the Scottish Tory Cuming Bruce in the House of Commons on 1 July 1835, were 'an attempt to throw a firebrand in between the landlords and the Church'.[151] For the Tory lawyer and church extensionist John Hope, 'the necessary and inevitable effect [of the Commission's instructions]'

> is to make the landowners feel their interests to be opposed to the Church—to create the feeling that the Church generally *wish* to appropriate the teinds now enjoyed by the landowners—to create heart-burning, distrust, and alienation in regard to the Church among the proprietors—to lead them to imagine that the *object of the Church* is to take possession of such Teinds to their spoliation and thus to set the proprietors generally against the Church.

'A more desireable result', he added, 'for the objects of the Voluntaries and the present Dissenters they could not desire.'[152] In the House of Lords, on 28 August, the Tory earl of Aberdeen vehemently opposed any suggestion of using the unappropriated teinds for church extension, insisting that those teinds were the property of the landowners. Melbourne, however, refused to accept this argument. The teinds, he maintained, had originally been intended to provide an endowment for the established Church, and so the Government must now regard them.[153] The Government held firm, and the Royal Commission on Religious Instruction in Scotland was instructed to investigate the teinds question. As suspected, the

[151] *Hansard's Parl. Deb.*, 3rd ser. xxix (1835), col. 139.

[152] J. Hope to Lord Aberdeen, 24 August 1835, BL Aberdeen Papers, Add. MS 43202, fo. 120; see also J. Hope to T. Chalmers, 25 August 1835, New College Library, Edinburgh, Thomas Chalmers Papers, CHA 4.237.75.

[153] *Hansard's Parl. Deb.*, 3rd ser. xxx (1835), cols. 1073–81.

support of the landed classes for church extension now began to fall away. The question of the unappropriated teinds, an Edinburgh Voluntary journal observed cattily in December 1835, was proving 'a test of the sincerity of many *warm and disinterested friends* of the Church'.[154]

The Scottish Voluntaries, meanwhile, were agitating furiously against any grant for church extension. Late in 1834, they had established a Scottish Central Board of Dissenters, which issued tracts, held public lectures, and organized petitions to Parliament. Voluntaries condemned church extension as a scheme for 'putting down the Dissenters'.[155] Public demonstrations against State support for church extension were held across Scotland. In July 1835, for example, a crowd of over 3,000 heard Dr John Ritchie, a leading Edinburgh Voluntary, with a coarse, biting sense of humour, inveigh against church extension for over four hours.[156] In September 1835, the Irish 'Liberator', Daniel O'Connell, made a triumphant tour of Scotland, calling for an alliance between Irish Catholics and Scottish Voluntaries, based on shared opposition to the established Churches. His meetings drew large and enthusiastic crowds.[157] 'There has not for a long time', observed David Aitken, minister of Minto, to Lord Minto, on 25 September 1835, 'been any question in Scotland which has called forth so much fervid zeal in a large class of the community.'[158]

In January 1836 the Commission travelled to Edinburgh, where it began taking evidence from both Dissenters and Church adherents on the amount of church accommodation and patterns of church attendance in the city. Only months later, in April 1836, did the Commission proceed to Glasgow for its second stage of enquiries. As it intended to visit a number of Scottish towns and cities, at this pace it would be years before it concluded its enquiries. The church extensionists suspected it was stalling. Its behaviour certainly contrasted with that of the English Commission, which had moved quickly to issue its first report. The controveries surrounding the

[154] *Edinburgh Voluntary Churchman*, 5 (December 1835), 114.

[155] *Scotsman*, 21 March 1835; *Hansard's Parl. Deb.*, 3rd ser. xxvii (3 April 1835), col. 783.

[156] *Edinburgh Voluntary Churchman*, 1 (August 1835), 18.

[157] *Tait's Edinburgh Magazine*, 2 (October 1835), 631–41; *Edinburgh Voluntary Churchman*, 3 (October 1835), 71; 4 (November 1835), 73–8.

[158] D. Aitken to Lord Minto, 25 September 1835, National Library of Scotland, Minto Papers, MS 11802, fo. 16.

Commission's enquiry, meanwhile, were placing a damper on the church extension movement. The second annual report of the Church Extension Committee, presented to the Church of Scotland in May 1836, showed a dramatic falling off of support. Total subscriptions had been halved—from £65,626 in 1834–5 to £32,359 in 1835–6—while only twenty-six new churches had been begun in 1835–6, as compared to sixty-four in 1834–5. The decline was most dramatic in the general fund, which had been set up specifically for contributions from wealthy landowners and merchants. Subscriptions to the general fund fell from £15,168 in 1834–5 to £1,547 in 1835–6, indicating a collapse in support from a propertied élite evidently concerned over their unappropriated teinds.[159] The Church responded to the waning support among the landed classes by strengthening the organization of the church extension campaign. Rather than rely on local initiative in forming church-building societies, the General Assembly now instructed every synod, presbytery, and kirk-session in the national Church to form church extension committees, and it instructed every parish church to hold at least one church extension collection each year. Further, the Church Extension Committee sent twenty agents on circuit around the country to hold public meetings and solicit subscriptions. Frustrated church extension leaders, meanwhile, especially Chalmers, publicly criticized both the Commission and the Whig Government.

Not everyone within the Church of Scotland was pleased with the more aggressive, new-style church extension agitation. Liberal Church members began questioning the wisdom of church extension. Was it right for the Church to intensify its agitation for multiplying churches when Dissenters viewed this as a threat to their religious liberty, landowners perceived it as a threat to their property, and the Whig Government regarded it as a threat to public order? Was not the church extension campaign, however laudable its goals, becoming dominated by clerics who were ambitious to revive not only the parochial establishment, but also the theocratic ideas of the seventeenth-century covenanters? 'For my own part', wrote David Aitken, minister of Minto, to Lord Minto, convenor of the Commission, in January 1836, 'I do not fear the Voluntaries, nor

[159] T. Chalmers, *Second Report of the Committee of the General Assembly on Church Extension* (Edinburgh, 1836), 3–25.

even your Lordship's very formidable commission, as some reckon it; the danger is in the unenlightened zeal of a large body of the clergy [of the established Church] who are bent on carrying into effect in the nineteenth century vigorous proceedings which men would not bear two hundred years ago.'[160] Late in 1836 the growing tensions within the Church surfaced in the moderatorship controversy. Chalmers and the church extensionists challenged the nomination of the respected Edinburgh Whig clergyman John Lee to be moderator of the General Assembly of 1837. Lee had been critical of church extension in his evidence before the Royal Commission; he had broken ranks, and as a result the church extensionists insisted that he could not be trusted with Church office. Liberal Church leaders supported Lee, who was defeated only after a bitter contest. The affair was a reflection of how desperate the church extensionists were to receive the endowment grant. Without endowments, they believed, the new churches would be unable to carry on their mission to the labouring poor; they would not be 'poor men's churches'. The endowment grant had also become a symbol of the idea of Church–State co-operation to create a great popular establishment in Scotland. In collecting pennies each week from labouring people for church extension, Church leaders had assured them that the State would be moved by their sacrifices and would do its part to make the Scottish parochial establishment commensurate with Scotland's growing population. Meanwhile, the aggressive new methods of popular agitation were beginning to achieve results for church extension, reversing the decline of the previous year. In 1836–7, subscriptions increased to £59,310 and sixty-seven new churches were begun.[161]

Events now hurried towards a culmination. Late in 1837 the Voluntaries increased their agitation against church extension, and threatened a campaign of passive resistance through the non-payment of teinds (in short, an Irish tithe war), should Parliament provide endowments to the new churches.[162] During December 1837 alone, Scottish Dissenters sent Parliament no fewer than 362 petitions, bearing some 148,000 signatures, against the endowment.[163] Early in 1838, the Royal Commission on Religious Instruction

[160] D. Aitken to Lord Minto, National Library of Scotland, Minto Papers, MS 11802, fo. 26.

[161] S. J. Brown, *Thomas Chalmers*, 256–66.

[162] *Voluntary Church Magazine*, 6 (January 1838), 23–34 (March 1838), 97–106.

[163] I. G. C. Hutchison, *A Political History of Scotland 1832–1924* (Edinburgh, 1986), 38.

published its first interim report. The report acknowledged that, even counting the Dissenting churches, there was a severe shortage of church accommodation in much of the country. In Glasgow, for example, the total church accommodation, both Church and Dissent, was sufficient for only 48.2 per cent of the population. Here, the church extensionists believed, was confirmation of their claims, even from the unfriendly Commission. With Tory support, they pressed the Government not to wait upon the full report of the Commission but to announce immediately how it intended to support Scottish church extension.

On 9 March 1838 Melbourne bowed to this pressure and outlined his Government's plan in a speech to the House of Lords.[164] The proposals were a devastating blow to Scottish church extension. First, the Government declined to support any endowment grants for new churches in the towns and cities, arguing that voluntary effort by the various denominations could meet the urban demand for church accommodation. Secondly, the Government agreed to support endowments for new established churches in the rural areas. However, its proposal for financing these endowments was precisely what friends of the established Church had feared in 1835: that is, the money would have to come from the unappropriated teinds, with the Church applying to the civil courts for their recovery. The Commission had by now discovered the amount of unappropriated teind. The bishops' teinds were modest, amounting to only about £10,200 a year. The unappropriated parish teinds, however, were much larger. Of the total parish teinds of £285,100 a year, about £138,200 a year, or almost half the total, was unappropriated and retained as private income by the landowners.[165] The Scottish landowners would hardly be expected to part willingly with this property, and in resisting the Church's claims they could expect sympathy from a Parliament dominated by the landed interest. For William Muir, a member of a deputation from the Church Extension Committee sent to London in early March, the Government's announcement was shattering. 'The measure', he informed his fiancée on 17 March, was 'evidently intended to set the landed proprietors against us by a threatened act of spoliation on

[164] *Hansard's Parl. Deb.*, 3rd ser. xli (1838), cols. 707–11.

[165] J. Skinner, *The Scottish Endowment Question, Ecclesiastical and Educational* (Glasgow, 1838), 30.

them.'[166] Melbourne was characteristically blunt in an interview with the Scottish Church Extension deputation on 24 March: 'Why, your Church mayn't be much better of our plan—but, hang it, you can't be worse.'[167] 'Gentlemen', a sympathetic duke of Wellington told the Church Extension deputation at that time, 'you will get nothing . . . . I am sorry for it; but so you will find it.' In Parliament, the Radicals and Dissenters would combine with the landed interest to ensure that the Church failed to receive even the unappropriated teinds. 'The real question which now divides this country', he continued,

> . . . is just this—Church or no Church. People talk of the war in Spain, and the Canada question; but all that is of little moment. The real question is Church or no Church; and the majority in the House of Commons—a small majority, it is true, but still a majority—are practically against it. It is a melancholy state of things, but such appears to me to be the critical position in which we now stand.[168]

On 30 March Lord Aberdeen challenged the Government's proposals in the Lords. The Scottish nation, he asserted, was thoroughly aroused: 'Never had any question of domestic policy so much agitated the people of Scotland since the union of the two kingdoms.' This should be the moment for Parliament to demonstrate its support for the principle of the established Church. But instead the Government offered a plan that was nothing more than an 'act of spoliation', that would throw an 'apple of discord between the proprietors and the clergy of Scotland', and that would fatally undermine all the efforts made for church extension.[169] Melbourne, however, refused to relent. It was, he observed, not simply a Scottish question. The need for additional church accommodation was greater in England than in Scotland, and if the State were to provide new grants of public money for church extension in Scotland, it would in fairness have to provide far larger grants for church extension in England. The demands of church extension for Britain's expanding population represented an open-ended commitment, which the State could not afford to undertake. 'The religious wants of Scotland', he maintained, 'should be provided for by Scotland

[166] W. Muir to A. Dixon, 17 March 1838, New College Library, Edinburgh, Muir Letterbook, Mul 2. I am grateful to Ms Christine Morrison for this reference.

[167] W. Muir to A. Dixon, 24 March 1838, ibid.

[168] Walker, *Robert Buchanan*, 76–7.

[169] *Hansard's Parl. Deb.*, 3rd ser. xlii (1838), cols. 110–24, 112, 120, 121.

itself.' 'It was better, much more wise, much more prudent, that this should be, than that they should rashly and imprudently plunge themselves into a course by which a great charge and burden should be imposed on the country for providing church accommodation.'[170]

In April 1838 an indignant Chalmers travelled to London to appeal for English support for the Scottish establishment with a series of 'Lectures on the Establishment and Extension of National Churches' under the auspices of the Church Influence Society.[171] The lectures were presented in rooms 'crowded to suffocation' with a fashionable audience, including several Church of England bishops and leading Tory and Whig politicians. Chalmers called upon supporters of the established Churches in both England and Scotland to stand together in calling for State grants for church extension. Despite the differences in doctrine and organization, the English and Scottish establishments shared a common purpose—the religious and moral elevation of society through the parish system. They had transformed themselves into great popular bodies, with a special commitment to the labouring poor of the industrial towns and cities. The established clergy had thrown off their former privileges, and now found their identity in service to the poor and outcast, those still outside the pale of the constitution. 'We appear', he exclaimed of the established clergy,

> for the families of our peasants and our artizans, and our men of handicraft and hard labour. We are the tribunes of the people, the representatives of that class to whom the law has given no other representatives of their own,—of the unfranchised multitude, who are without a vote, and without a voice in the House of Commons. Our sacred object is, the moral well-being of that mighty host who swarm and overspread the ground-floor of our commonwealth.[172]

It was rousing language, of a kind that might have been used by Bishop Doyle of Kildare and Leighlin in calling for Catholic Emancipation in the 1820s. But while Chalmers's lectures were warmly received, quickly published, and widely read, little came of their appeal for joint action by the English and Scottish establishments for church extension grants. Chalmers returned to Scotland to seek popular support against the Government proposals, embarking

[170] *Hansard's Parl. Deb.*, 3rd ser. xlii (1838), cols. 124–9, 129.

[171] T. Chalmers, *Lectures on the Establishment and Extension of National Churches* (1838) in *Collected Works of Thomas Chalmers*, xvii. 187–356.

[172] Ibid. 280.

in the late summer of 1838 on a six-week speaking tour of the south-west of Scotland, old covenanting country. One critic dubbed it a campaign of 'spiritual O'Connellism'. But his meetings were hounded by Radicals and Voluntaries, and he failed to raise a popular agitation.[173]

As it became clear that Parliament would provide no grants to endow the new Scottish churches, public donations for church extension rapidly dried up. Without endowments, the new churches had to require reasonably high seat rents, thus effectively excluding the poor. They became in effect no different from the churches of the Voluntary denominations. There now seemed little point in carrying on, and the campaign was wound up in 1841, when Chalmers resigned as Convenor of the Church Extension Committee. The achievements of the church extension campaign had been impressive. Between 1834 and 1841, the campaign had raised over £305,000 in voluntary subscriptions and erected 222 new churches, increasing the total number of churches in the Scottish establishment by over 20 per cent.[174] The church extensionists had inspired considerable effort, especially in the four years from 1834 to 1838. But the State's refusal to provide the endowment grant in 1838 had undermined public confidence in the campaign and created serious tensions between the established Church and landed classes in Scotland.

Conflict over the Cathedrals

While relations between the Scottish Church and Parliament were breaking down over the funding of church extension, a not wholly dissimilar controversy was by 1838 developing over the funding of church extension in England and Wales. Here the controversy focused not on the unappropriated teinds of Scottish landlords, but rather on the shady lawns, quiet closes, proud chapter houses, and majestic chancels of the English cathedrals, and the lives, learning, and usefulness of their prebendaries and dignitaries. In 1836, in the third of its proposed bills for the reform of the Church of England, the Ecclesiastical Commission had recommended sweeping reforms of the cathedral establishments, aimed at reducing the numbers of

173 S. J. Brown, *Thomas Chalmers*, 273–5.
174 Hanna, *Memoirs of Dr. Chalmers*, iv. 87.

prebendaries and diverting the money saved to church extension and the improvement of small livings. In particular, the Commission's proposed bill had called for the suppression of all non-resident prebends, the limitation of the number of prebends in each cathedral chapter to four, and the removal of certain lands held by deans and prebends. Through these reforms, the Commission had maintained that £130,000 a year would be generated from the Church's existing resources for the improvement of the parish ministry.[175]

The proposals for the reduction of the cathedrals had been the most controversial of the Ecclesiastical Commission's recommendations, and they had aroused intense opposition from some quarters within the Church.[176] The cathedral chapters, under the leadership of the chapter at Canterbury, had united against the proposals, and had received support from High Church leaders, including Pusey and Henry Phillpotts, bishop of Exeter.[177] In 1836, a committee of chapters was established to co-ordinate the defence of the cathedrals, and pamphlets appeared denouncing the Commission's proposals. These opponents of the Commission's proposed cathedral bill insisted on the vital importance of cathedrals for the life and work of the national Church. In proposing the reduction of the cathedrals, the Ecclesiastical Commissioners were laying their hands on a fundamental part of Anglicanism. While much of Protestant Europe had dismantled its cathedrals, the Church of England had preserved and venerated them as parts of 'a system which took root in the first days of Christianity, and has grown up for 1800 years'. England's cathedrals were 'the oldest incorporations in the kingdom, coeval with the conversion of the country to Christianity'.[178] They expressed the English Church's continuity with the primitive Church. For Henry Manning, High Church rector of Lavington, the cathedral establishments represented the best hope for restoring a pure apostolic government within the Church of England.[179] Their buildings provided for worship on a grand scale; they were

[175] Best, *Temporal Pillars*, 303–4.

[176] For an overview of the debate, see P. J. Welch, 'Contemporary Views on the Proposals for the Alienation of Capitular Property in England (1832–1840)', *Journal of Ecclesiastical History*, 5 (1954), 184–95; Best, *Temporal Pillars*, 331–45.

[177] Liddon, *Life of E. B. Pusey*, i. 396–9.

[178] [W. Sewell], 'The Cathedral Establishments', *Quarterly Review*, 58 (February 1837), 200, 205.

[179] H. E. Manning, *The Principle of the Ecclesiastical Commission Examined, in a Letter to the Right Rev. The Lord Bishop of Chichester* (London, 1838), 30.

inspiring monuments to the faith of past generations. Cathedrals formed central points of communication. For Phillpotts, their endowments supported men of talent and learning, trained to defend the faith through their preaching and publications, to nurture Church music and liturgical practice, and to advise the bishop on the affairs of the diocese.[180] They were lamps set upon hills, guiding and inspiring the parish clergy as they struggled amid the harsh realities of the world. They were guardians of orthodoxy. Without the cathedrals, the High Church Tory MP, William Ewart Gladstone, was convinced 'of the inadequacy of a purely parochial ministry in the long-run to maintain the truth of religion unimpaired'.[181] The cathedral endowments had been provided by the faith and charity of previous generations and were held in trust by the Church for the purpose of maintaining their buildings and chapters. Parliament could not divert cathedral revenues to other purposes without infringing on the rights of property and the law respecting trusts.[182] Nor was it clear that the diversion of the cathedral revenues would have much real impact on the parish ministry. The sum of money expected to be realized by the suppression of non-resident canons—an estimated £130,000 per annum—was modest in comparison to the need.[183]

Some advanced less elevated arguments for not reducing the cathedrals. Even if many of the cathedral prebendaries were sinecure positions, that did not mean they were not useful to the institutional Church. Sydney Smith, the witty Whig dean of St Paul's, and a man of the old order, argued that canonries represented prizes by which the Church was enabled to reward some of its clergy. The Church, he observed, was a human as well as a divine institution, and its all too human clergy needed to be motivated by hope of reward. Cathedral establishments offered positions of wealth and leisure to which parish clergymen might aspire. Because the nation would not provide a substantial income to all the incumbents, the only way the Church could attract educated 'gentlemen' into its ministry was by offering the hope of prizes. 'What then remains', he asked, 'if you

[180] H. Phillpotts, Bishop of Exeter, *Charge delivered to the Clergy of the Diocese of Exeter* (London, 1836), 29–30.

[181] W. E. Gladstone to H. E. Manning, 27 September 1837, in D. C. Lathbury (ed.), *Correspondence on Church and Religion of William Ewart Gladstone*, 2 vols. (London, 1910), i. 40.

[182] *Quarterly Review*, 58 (February 1837), 201; Welch, 'Contemporary Views on the Proposals for the Alienation of Capitular Property', 185.

[183] C. Thorp, *A Charge to the Clergy of the Archdeaconry of Durham* (Durham, 1838), 7.

will have a Clergy and not pay them equitably and separately, than to pay them unequally and by lottery?'[184] Others feared that the proposed reduction of cathedral establishments would be but the first step towards their complete abolition. William Selwyn, a canon of Ely cathedral, suspected that the Commission's proposed bill would reduce the cathedral establishments to 'such a wretched state of inefficiency' that it would provide 'a fair pretext to the next Church Reformers, to suppress the remaining canonries'.[185] Pusey asserted that the Ecclesiastical Commission's only concern had been to find money, and that it had given little attention to the activities of the cathedrals before calling for their reduction. 'The cathedrals', he observed in the *British Critic* of April 1838, 'are sentenced first, tried afterwards; the thing to be done is decided upon unhesitatingly and without knowledge of the case.'[186]

Underlying the opposition to the Commission's proposed reduction of the cathedrals was a widespread fear of the Ecclesiastical Commission itself—a fear that it was emerging as a permanent governing body over the Church of England, answerable only to Parliament. It was replacing the Church's government by bishops, who were the successors of the apostles, with administrators and civil servants. 'We cannot', William Selwyn observed to Gladstone on 20 April 1838, 'help looking upon this [cathedral plan] as one more step towards riveting the Commission on the Church, and erecting it as a new and perpetual authority in Ecclesiastical Affairs.'[187] The Commission represented, according to Phillpotts of Exeter, 'the vice of modern legislation', that is, the love of administrative 'centralization', which was destined to destroy local differences and initiatives.[188] 'Under an idea of centralisation and efficiency', asked Manning in January 1838, 'is the whole genius of apostolic government to be superseded by an external parliamentary board?' For Manning, the weakening of the cathedral chapters was part of a larger plan for strengthening parliamentary control over the Church. 'The next patriarch of the English Church', he warned, 'will be

[184] S. Smith, *A Letter to Archdeacon Singleton, on the Ecclesiastical Commission*, 2nd edn. (London, 1837), 10.

[185] W. Selwyn to W. E. Gladstone, 31 January 1837, BL, Gladstone Papers, Add. MS 44355, fos. 178–83.

[186] [E. B. Pusey], 'The Royal and Parliamentary Ecclesiastical Commissions', *British Critic*, 28 (April 1838), 488.

[187] W. Selwyn to W. E. Gladstone, 20 April 1838, BL, Gladstone Papers, Add. MS 44356, fos. 55–8.

[188] Phillpotts, *Charge* (1836), 33.

Parliament, and on its votes will hang our orders, mission, discipline and faith.'[189] For Pusey, writing in the *British Critic*, the Commission was helping Parliament to 'render the clergy mere stipendiaries of the state'. 'In a short time', he insisted, 'if things go on thus . . . we shall live under the supremacy of the Commission; it will be our legislature, executive, the ultimate appeal of our bishops; it will absorb our Episcopate; the prime minister will be our Protestant pope.' He maintained that the Church of England was now being shackled in the same way that the established Church of Ireland had been 'laid in iron' by Parliament: 'we are fettered now, that we may be plundered hereafter'.[190] Within the cathedral chapters, there was anger that the bishops were not giving them more support in what they perceived as a struggle for the spiritual independence of the Church. In response, some prebendaries began calling for the revival of Convocation, arguing that only a representative Church assembly could now preserve the integrity of the English Church. The cathedrals question, observed Charles Thorp, archdeacon of Durham, was calling the clergy's attention 'to the loss we have sustained by the suspension of our constitutional assemblies, our Synods, and our Convocations'.[191] As far back as 1836, Henry Goulburn had warned Peel that the proposals for the cathedral chapters were likely 'to raise in the Church a republican spirit adverse to the Bishops'.[192]

On the other hand, there were many in the Church who accepted, however reluctantly, the proposals of the Ecclesiastical Commission. They respected the history and contributions of the cathedral establishments. However, they also pointed to a far more pressing need for improving small livings to promote clerical residency, and for church extension, especially in the urban districts. Money was needed if the Church's parish system were to be revived. 'We were not insensible to the benefits which Cathedral institutions were capable of conferring, and have conferred on the country,' wrote John Kaye, bishop of Lincoln and a member of the Ecclesiastical Commission, in 1838. 'But . . . we knew that in many districts of the kingdom the Established Church was not answering

[189] Manning, *The Principle of the Ecclesiastical Commission Examined*, 30, 38.

[190] [Pusey], 'The Royal and Parliamentary Ecclesiastical Commissions', 514, 526, 521.

[191] Thorp, *Charge to the Clergy of the Archdeaconry of Durham*, 14; see also [Pusey], 'The Royal and Parliamentary Ecclesiastical Commissions', 525.

[192] H. Goulburn to Sir R. Peel, 2 September 1836, BL, Peel Papers, Add. MS 40333, fos. 360–1.

the end of its institution, was not providing for the Cure of Souls.' The alternative before them was either to take the money from the cathedrals or 'to allow whole districts to remain destitute of the Bread of Life'.[193]

By 1839 the Church of England was increasingly divided over the respective claims of the cathedrals and the parishes, and perhaps more important, over the Ecclesiastical Commission and its meaning for the spiritual independence of the Church. The Tory MP and confidant of Peel, Sir James Graham, feared that the growing crisis in the Church of England was threatening to bring home to England the same religious disorder that was so prevalent on the peripheries of the United Kingdom, in Ireland and Scotland. 'In this sad state of affairs', he wrote to Gladstone on 15 December 1839,

> what a blessing it would be, if there were peace within the walls of the Church of England: but alas! here also a tendency to schism prevails. Bishop is arrayed again Bishop: Chapters against their Visitors: Canons lampoon their Metropolitans, and the Head of the Church is confederated with her enemies. I know not what concession will avail any thing. I know not what resistance can be made against dangerous innovations, amidst discord and divisions such as these.[194]

In forming the Ecclesiastical Commission, Graham insisted, Peel had been motivated by a sincere desire to save the established Church of England and make it more efficient in providing moral and religious instruction to the 'growing multitudes'. There had been no secret agenda for weakening the cathedrals, diminishing the power of the bishops, or imposing parliamentary control.

In 1840 the Melbourne Government finally brought the bill for the diversion of cathedral revenues, the ecclesiastical duties and revenues bill, before Parliament. By now, nearly all the cathedral chapters, both Oxford and Cambridge Universities, and some 3,000 clergymen had petitioned against the bill.[195] In the Commons, opposition to the bill was led by Sir Robert Inglis, Tory MP for Oxford. However, the Tory leader Sir Robert Peel supported the bill, ensuring that it received cross-party support. For Peel, the over-

[193] Kaye, *Letter to the Archbishop of Canterbury*, 34. Similar views were expressed by Kaye's fellow Commission member, John Monk, bishop of Gloucester and Bristol: Monk, *Charge delivered to the Clergy of the Diocese of Gloucester and Bristol . . . in 1838*, 19.

[194] Sir J. Graham to W. E. Gladstone, 15 December 1839, BL, Gladstone Papers, Add. MS 44163, fos. 1–5.

[195] *Hansard's Parl. Deb.*, 3rd ser. liii (1840), cols. 590–619; lv (1840), cols. 1115–55.

riding concern was the crying need for church extension in the expanding cities. He acknowledged that the revenues to be generated by cathedral reform would be insufficient on their own for that purpose. However, if the Church were seen to be doing all it could with its existing revenues, he was confident that Parliament would provide additional funds for church extension. 'The Church setting an example of making a sacrifice', he insisted, 'would be the most likely way to induce the Legislature to assist the Church.'[196] He warned friends of the Church not to reject cathedral reform in the belief that the Church no longer had to fear an onslaught of the kind that had nearly overwhelmed it in the early 1830s.[197] That onslaught might have abated, but the cry for disestablishment would be revived if Parliament were now to reject a key part of the reform programme developed by the Ecclesiastical Commission. With Peel's support, the bill had a relatively easy passage through the Commons.

In the Lords, there was more formidable opposition to the bill, led by Henry Phillpotts of Exeter, who combined a vigorous defence of the cathedral establishments with an assault on the Ecclesiastical Commission and all its works. The assault brought forth an eloquent reply on 30 July 1840 from Blomfield, who deprecated what he viewed as gross misrepresentations of the Commission. For Blomfield, the Commissioners had no dark ulterior motives, no plan of setting themselves up as the governors of the Church, no desire to demolish time-honoured institutions or impose a centralized administration. Rather, they had been motivated solely by the desire to extend the influence of the Church to the growing population. The aim was to save not only the Church, but the Christian commonwealth, amid the profound social dislocations associated with urbanization and industrialization. But above all, they sought to reach out to the vast numbers in the city slums who had no church connection, who were without pastoral care or religious instruction. As bishop of London, Blomfield was acutely aware of the unchurched urban masses. 'I am continually brought into contact', he observed,

> in the discharge of my official duties, with vast masses of my fellow-creatures, living without God in the world. I traverse the streets of this crowded city with deep and solemn thoughts of the spiritual condition of

[196] Ibid. 3rd ser. liii, col. 602.
[197] Ibid. 603.

its inhabitants. I pass the magnificent church which crowns the metropolis, and is consecrated to the noblest of objects, the glory of God, and I ask of myself in what degree it answers that object. I see there a dean, and three residentiaries, with incomes amounting in the aggregate to between £10,000 and £12,000 a-year. I see, too, connected with the cathedral twenty-nine clergymen, whose offices are all but sinecures, with an annual income of about £12,000 at the present moment, and likely to be very much larger after the lapse of a few years, I proceed a mile or two to the east and north-east and find myself in the midst of an immense population in the most wretched state of destitution and neglect, artizans, mechanics, labourers, beggars, thieves, to the number of at least 300,000. I find there, upon an average, about one church, and one clergyman, for every 8,000 or 10,000 souls; in some districts a much smaller amount of spiritual provision; in one parish, for instance, only one church, and one clergyman for 40,000 people. I naturally look back to the vast endowments of St. Paul's, a part of them drawn from these very districts, and consider whether some portion of them may not be applied to remedy, or alleviate, those enormous evils. No, I am told, you may not touch St. Paul's. It is an ancient corporation which must be maintained in its integrity. Not a stall can be spared.[198]

It was a heart-felt plea; however valuable the cathedral establishments, the needs of church extension were far more pressing. In the final analysis, he insisted, the strength of the established Church lay not in its cathedrals, but in its 'division of the country into parishes and districts of manageable size, each with its church, its pastor, its schools, its local charities'.[199] Only the revival of the parish system could preserve the Christian commonwealth. And unless the Church were seen to be doing all it could with its own resources, it could look for no new resources from Parliament for church extension.

Despite opposition from twelve bishops, the House of Lords passed the bill on 6 August 1840, and it received the royal assent on 11 August 1840. The Ecclesiastical Duties and Revenues Act gradually suppressed, at the deaths of the present incumbents, 317 non-resident cathedral canonries and sixty-eight sinecure rectories (though it preserved the non-resident canonries as purely honorific titles of distinction). The Act also provided for the gradual restriction in the number of resident canons to four per cathedral in most cases, with Canterbury, Oxford, Durham, Ely, and Westminster

[198] *Hansard's Parl. Deb.*, 3rd ser. lv (30 July 1840), cols. 1137–8.
[199] Ibid. 1142.

allowed six, and Winchester and Exeter allowed five. This meant that of 205 residential canonries, seventy-two were to be gradually suppressed. With a few exceptions, the incomes of the suppressed cathedral livings were vested in the Ecclesiastical Commission. Further, while the corporate estates attached to cathedral chapters were not touched, the separate estates attached to individual deanships and canonries were vested in the Ecclesiastical Commission on the deaths of the present incumbents. The ecclesiastical patronage in the hands of individual deans and canons was transferred to the bishops. Finally, the Act enlarged the Ecclesiastical Commission, adding all the bishops of England and Wales, the deans of Canterbury, St Paul's, and Westminster, the lord chief justice and five other judges, and several other lay members—increasing the size of the Commission from thirteen members to forty-nine, with about three-fifths of the members clerical and two-fifths lay.[200] For many, the Act was a devastating defeat not only for the ancient cathedrals, but for theological learning, property rights, and ecclesiastical diversity within the Church of England. James Stephen, writing to Samuel Wilberforce on 27 August 1840, insisted that the Act 'should be printed with a black margin, as a perpetual record of the snatching, hasty, impatient, short-sightedness of our age'.[201] Nor did the Church see much immediate financial benefit from the sacrifice of the cathedrals, largely because of the Act's respect for the life interests of incumbents of cathedral livings.[202]

In any event, the Church had now submitted to the reform programme as outlined by the Ecclesiastical Commission in 1835–6, and many now looked for what had been presented as the primary aim of reform—the extension of the Church's parochial structures. The Church, supporters of the Ecclesiastical Commission had argued, had to be seen to be doing all that it could with its own resources before it could look to Parliament for additional public money for church extension. There had been an assumption that once the Church had done its part, parliamentary assistance for church extension would follow. In the early months of 1840, then, as the Government introduced the cathedral chapters bill, Church leaders opened a campaign for a new parliamentary grant for building and

[200] Chadwick, *The Victorian Church*, i. 137–9; Mathieson, *English Church Reform*, 152–4; Brose, *Church and Parliament*, 136–56.

[201] J. Stephen to S. Wilberforce, 27 August 1840, Bodl. Wilberforce MSS d. 46, fos. 45–6.

[202] Best, *Temporal Pillars*, 348–97.

endowing churches, especially in the expanding urban districts. A London Committee sent circulars to every parish in the country, encouraging petitions to Parliament for the church extension grant. In 1840, Hugh McNeile, the fiery Evangelical preacher and perpetual curate of St Jude's, Liverpool, delivered a series of lectures on Church establishments in London under the auspices of the Church Interests Committee. They were intended to build upon Chalmers's celebrated lectures on establishments in 1838 and mobilize public support for church extension in England.[203] Sir Robert Inglis announced that he would bring forward a church extension motion in Parliament before the end of the session. In a pamphlet addressed to the prime minister, the Evangelical Baptist Noel claimed that an additional 2,000 new churches were required in order to bring religious instruction to the unchurched masses.[204] By June 1840, Parliament had received 2,546 petitions, bearing 213,580 signatures, pressing for the new church extension grant.[205] The church extensionists made much of the dangers of Radicalism and Socialism, insisting that only the sound religious instruction of the labouring orders could preserve the social order.[206] The Dissenters, in turn, responded with their own petitioning campaign against any parliamentary grant, recreating some of the controversy that had rocked Scotland two years before.

On 30 June 1840 Inglis introduced his church extension motion in the Commons with a 3-hour speech.[207] He opened by noting the explosive growth of population in recent decades, and the failure of either the established Church or the Dissenters to provide sufficient church accommodation for the expanding numbers. As a result, an increasing proportion of the population, especially in the expanding cities, were deprived of opportunities for public worship and were without religious and moral instruction. Private donations, while they had accomplished much for church building, were still woefully inadequate to meet the need. Only the State could provide the money needed to build the required new churches. And only the

203 Carter, 'Evangelical Seceders from the Church of England, c. 1800–1850', 49–51; *Christian Observer*, 40 (April 1840), 253–4; (May 1840), 319–20.

204 *Hansard's Parl. Deb.*, 3rd ser. lv (30 June 1840), 347.

205 Ibid. 273–4.

206 *The Times* (9 June 1840), 3; (30 June 1840), 6; *Christian Observer*, 40 (May 1840), 319–20.

207 *Hansard's Parl. Deb.*, 3rd ser. lv (30 June 1840), cols. 272–326; the speech was subsequently published: R. H. Inglis, *Church Extension: Substance of a Speech delivered in the House of Commons, on . . . the 30th June, 1840* (London, 1840).

State could provide the endowments that would enable the new churches to offer free sittings for the poor and pursue a vigorous home mission. It was, he maintained, the duty of the nation to ensure that its established Church had the resources to provide religious instruction and ordinances to the whole population, the poor as well as the rich. The Church had done all that it could with its existing resources. Now, the moment had arrived for Parliament to play its part. Inglis denied that church extension represented a threat to Dissent; rather, its aim was to evangelize among the unchurched population that both the established Church and the Dissenting denominations had hitherto failed to reach. Echoing the teachings of Chalmers and Blomfield, he insisted that Parliament must provide an adequate parish system to combat crime, improve the condition of the poor, and above all preserve the Christian identity of the nation. 'The duty of the nation, having an Established National Church', he continued,

> is to make provision out of the national resources for the increase of that National Church, in proportion to the increase of the people forming that nation . . . you mock the people, if you say, that you establish a Church to teach them, and then repel and exclude three-fourths of them, without any fault of their own, from the sound of that teaching.[208]

He then moved that, as the former parliamentary grants of 1818 and 1824, supplemented by 'private and local liberality', had proved inadequate for the nation's need, Parliament must provide additional public money for church extension.

There was some confusion at the close of Inglis's speech, as no member of the Whig Government rose to reply. After a pause, Inglis was eventually answered by the Radical H. G. Ward, by the Whig Dissenter Edward Baines, MP for Leeds and proprietor of the *Leeds Mercury*, and by Daniel O'Connell. Ward focused on the vagueness of Inglis's motion, which had not specified an amount for the proposed church extension grant. If it approved such a motion, he warned, Parliament would be taking on an open-ended commitment. Further, he questioned the morality of requiring the nation as a whole to support the extension of what he described as a minority sect—'but one sect out of the many sects'. 'Would he tax', Ward asked Inglis, 'the Catholics of Ireland, and Presbyterians of Scotland, for that portion of the people of England which belonged to the

[208] Inglis, *Church Extension*, 65.

Established Church of England?'[209] Baines questioned Inglis's claims on the extent of the problem of insufficient church accommodation, arguing that if the Nonconformist churches and chapels were taken into account, there was more than enough church room. For O'Connell, the Church of England was not only a minority denomination in the United Kingdom, but it was also 'the richest Church in the world', well able to build and endow its churches without putting 'its hands into the pockets of those who did not believe in its doctrines'.[210] Finally, Lord John Russell rose to speak on behalf of the Government. The debate, he argued, had illustrated the extent to which the nation was divided over the issue of church extension. Any new grant would only increase these divisions and inflame popular opinion against the clergy. Despite this opposition from the Government, Inglis's motion was only narrowly defeated by a vote of 166 to 149, or a majority of 17.

'Though defeated', the Evangelical Lord Ashley noted in his diary the following day, '. . . we gained a victory; the question will, under God, be carried another year.'[211] Inglis pledged to reintroduce his motion in the next parliamentary session and the petitioning campaign was revived in the early months of 1841, with the London Committee again circulating forms to every parish in the country. None the less, the defeat of June 1840 had been a serious blow to the cause of church extension in England. It had been widely assumed that once Parliament had enacted the reform programme outlined by the Ecclesiastical Commission, and the Church was seen to be doing all that it could for church extension, Parliament would feel obligated to provide additional funds. The Church of England, it must be noted, was making impressive efforts through its diocesan societies in stimulating private giving for church extension. Between 1831 and 1841, according to the report on the religious census of 1851, the Church of England had built, almost entirely through its own efforts, 667 new churches—a significant increase over the 276 churches built in the previous decade under the stimulus of the parliamentary grants of 1818 and 1824.[212] But while the Church had done so much, Parliament had declined in June 1840 to

[209] *Hansard's Parl. Deb.*, 3rd ser. lv (30 June 1840), col. 336.

[210] Ibid. 352–3.

[211] E. Hodder, *Life and Work of the Seventh Earl of Shaftesbury*, 2nd edn. (London, 1887), 158.

[212] H. Mann, 'Report of the Census, 1851—Religious Worship', *Parliamentary Papers*, 89, Sess. 1852–53, p. xl.

provide further public funds and make church extension a truly national effort. It seemed that Parliament's refusal to provide additional public money to the Church of Scotland in 1838 was forming a precedent for the English Church. The petitioning campaign of early 1841 did not inspire much confidence. J. C. Hare, liberal Anglican archdeacon of Lewes, confided to his friend Henry Manning on 6 March 1841 that many clergymen in his archdeaconry were 'very loth to undertake the trouble of [parish petitions], unless some object is to be gained'.[213] The Church of England, it seemed, was in 1840 learning the same lesson that had been driven home to the Church of Scotland in 1838: Parliament was growing hesitant to take on what would amount to an open-ended commitment to church building, in order to restore the parish system in the developing urban-industrial society. Meanwhile, every month that passed brought further population increase, further urbanization. The difficulty of reviving the parish system increased, while the likelihood of new State investment in the parochial establishment receded.

In the field of education, meanwhile, the impressive efforts of the established Churches were also being frustrated. In 1833, it will be recalled, Parliament had approved a recurring grant of £20,000 a year for building schools for the poor. In England, the grants were awarded to local school-building projects on application from one of the two major educational societies—the Anglican National Society and the Dissenting British and Foreign Society—on the condition that the society raise at least half the cost of building the school. This had promoted a vigorous competition between the two societies, with the wealthier Anglican National Society taking a clear lead, winning over 70 per cent of the total educational grant each year. By the beginning of 1839, some 1,118,000 children were being educated in Anglican schools, as compared with about 597,000 children in Dissenting schools.[214] An increasingly confident Church of England was looking to the day when it would educate nearly the whole of the youth of England and Wales. The Scottish establishment

[213] J. C. Hare to H. Manning, 6 March 1841, Bodl. MS. Eng. Lett. c. 653/1, fos. 90–3; see also H. Manning to J. C. Hare, 16 February 1841, 26 February 1841, fos. 74–8, 82–5, and W. Gresley, *Remarks on the Necessity of Attempting a Restoration of the National Church* (London, 1841).

[214] Figures cited by W. F. Hook, vicar of Leeds, in a speech in March 1839; W. R. W. Stephens, *Life and Letters of Walter Farquahar Hook*, 2 vols. (London, 1878), i. 452.

was also drawing upon Parliament's education grant, and in 1838, Parliament had agreed to build and endow an additional forty-one established parish schools in the Highlands of Scotland.[215] Dissenters sought to halt this flow of State funds into the schools of the establishments. In 1836, they formed the Manchester Society for Promoting National Education, to agitate for the restriction of State funds to non-denominational popular education. That same year, liberal advocates of non-denominational education in London, including Lord Brougham, Lord John Russell, and Thomas Spring Rice, formed the Central Society of Education. Thomas Wyse, Irish Catholic MP for Waterford and veteran of the struggle against the New Reformation in the 1820s, became its first chairman. The Central Society agitated for a national system of non-denominational schools, with democratic control and a system of state inspection. In 1838, Wyse introduced a motion in the Commons for a national system of education in England, which gained a significant number of votes, and encouraged Russell, long an advocate of non-denominational national education, to bring forward a Government proposal.[216]

On 12 February 1839 Russell proposed in the Commons a new system for the support of popular education in Britain. First, the Government proposed a modest increase in the annual educational grant to England, from £20,000 to £30,000 a year (with the separate Scottish grant continuing). Secondly, grants would no longer be restricted to one of the two main educational societies in England or to the established Church of Scotland, but would be open to other reputable schools. Thirdly, the State would insist upon the right to inspect all schools that received a grant, to ensure that taxpayers received value for their money. Fourthly, the Government proposed to establish a normal school for the training of teachers, in which there would be general religious education, but in which specific religious instruction would be left to visiting clergymen from the different denominations. Finally, the Government would establish a new committee of the Privy Council to act as a Board of Education to oversee the new national system. The education committee would include no bishops or other official representatives of the

[215] *Hansard's Parl. Deb.*, 3rd ser., xl (1838), 820–3; xlii (1838), cols. 1166–9; xliv (1838), 548–9.

[216] Paz, *Politics of Working-Class Education*, 69–72; R. G. Cowherd, *Politics of English Dissent* (New York, 1956), 119–20.

established Churches of England and of Scotland.[217] Russell's proposals were intended to move the country towards a national, non-denominational system of popular primary education.[218] 'It could no longer be said', Russell asserted when introducing his programme in the Commons, 'with respect either to education or to the general distribution of political power in the country, that the principle of exclusion (the Church of England being alone favoured) was any longer the principle of the State. On the contrary, the principle was, that there should be general admission of all persons, without distinction of religion, to an equal participation of civil rights.'[219]

The Church of England rallied against the Whig plan, viewed as yet another blow struck at the revival of the established Churches. (The established Church of Scotland, by now expecting little from the State, was not active in this agitation.) Protest meetings were held across England, and over 3,000 petitions against Russell's proposals were presented to Parliament. Some English Dissenters, especially Wesleyans, also opposed the plan, which they suspected would lead to a secularized national education system.[220] There was strong opposition in Parliament, and the Government was forced to relinquish part of its plan—that of the normal school to provide a non-denominational teacher training. The Education Committee, however, was set up in June 1839, and after over a year of controversy a system of State inspection of schools was established in July 1840, after the Government agreed to a compromise with leaders of the Church of England over inspection procedures. By this 'concordat', the archbishops of the Church of England received the right to veto the appointment of individual inspectors, the power to end inspector's appointments, and the right to review instructions to inspectors.[221] It was further agreed that the Education Committee would consult the Education Committee of the General Assembly of the Church of Scotland on the appointment of inspectors in

[217] *Hansard's Parl. Deb.*, 3rd ser. xlv (1839), cols. 273–84; Chadwick, *Victorian Church*, i. 338–9; Paz, *Politics of Working-Class Education*, 83–4.

[218] [T. Spring Rice], 'Ministerial Plan of Education', *Edinburgh Review*, 70 (October 1839), 149–80; Smith, *Life of Kay-Shuttleworth*, 79–94.

[219] *Hansard's Parl. Deb.*, 3rd ser. xlv (1839), col. 278.

[220] *Christian Observer*, 39 (July 1839), 447–8; *Christian Guardian* (July 1839), 274–9; D. Hempton, *Methodism and Politics in British Society 1750–1850* (London, 1984), 160–3; Hodder, *Life of Shaftesbury*, 132–5; Stephens, *Life of W. F. Hook*, i. 444–5.

[221] Hurt, *Education in Evolution*, 35–6; Paz, *Politics of Working-Class Education*, 98–103.

Scotland.[222] None the less, the changes of 1839–40 marked a significant movement forward towards a State-supported system of non-denominational national education. For despite the concordat, the Church had made a critical concession, accepting the appointment of inspectors who were responsible to the Education Committee, and not to the Churches.[223] It was further demonstration that by 1840 the revival of the established Churches was reaching its limit.

The established Churches of England and Scotland had, in many respects, been remarkably successful in accommodating to the new, more democratic political order that had emerged with the constitutional revolution of 1828–32. The failure of the New Reformation campaign in Ireland and the reduction of the Irish establishment had effectively ended the project of consolidating the United Kingdom into a single nation-state under the guidance of the established Churches. But the leaders of the established Churches had defended their property and status against the onslaught by political Radicals between 1831 and 1833, and against the more serious challenge from political Dissent and Voluntaryism after 1832. Amid the fires of religious conflict, they had embarked upon significant programmes of reform, redefining themselves as popular institutions that provided useful social functions: in Blomfield's memorable phrase, the established Church was to be valued for 'the beauty of its holy usefulness'. The church extension campaign in Scotland and the Church reform programme in England had provided a new rationale for the religious establishments. They would promote social harmony, provide religious and moral education to the masses, improve conditions for the poor, and help to build viable communities. They would become 'poor men's churches', providing pastoral care, religious observances, and educational opportunities to those who were unable to contribute to the support of voluntary churches and schools. Their clergy, as Chalmers had proclaimed in his London lectures of 1838 would be 'tribunes of the people', discovering the needs of the people through their house-to-house visiting, and providing a voice to those without a vote in parliamentary and municipal elections. By the later 1830s, the danger that the two established Churches in Britain would be disestablished and disendowed had receded. It became clear that

[222] *Presbyterian Review*, 13 (July 1840), 116–21.
[223] Selleck, *James Kay-Shuttleworth*, 173.

the established Churches in Britain would not follow the minority established Church in Ireland and be reduced in size and harried with threats of appropriation. The established Churches of England and of Scotland emerged from their ordeal in the early 1830s as much strengthened institutions, with enhanced perceptions of their social mission. By 1838, these Churches were making significant advances in strengthening their parochial ministry, developing national systems of education, and expanding their social influence through ambitious programmes of church extension. Their leaders were beginning to revive the project of the 1820s, albeit without the Irish part. They were again envisaging a British nation-state consolidated around the parochial and educational institutions of the national establishments, a unified Christian commonwealth of close-knit parish communities with values defined by popular national Churches.

However, the refusal of Parliament in 1838 and 1840 to provide additional funds for church extension dealt serious blows to these aspirations. Without additional resources from the State, the established Churches would be unable to build and endow a sufficient number of new churches to provide pastoral care and religious instruction to the whole of Britain's expanding population; they would not be able to unite the social classes into a Christian commonwealth. Despite the impressive efforts by the Churches on their own to build new churches and schools during the 1830s, those efforts were not keeping pace with the growth of population.[224] In declining to support the extension of the established Churches to a level commensurate with the growth of population, Parliament was saying in effect that a steadily smaller proportion of Britain's growing population would be accommodated within the established Churches. As the population continued to grow, the influence of the established Churches would correspondingly decline. The church extensionists in England and Scotland had logic and fairness on their side in their request for additional resources from the State. So long as the Churches of England and of Scotland remained national establishments, it was the responsibility of the State to provide additional resources to enable them to expand the number of their parish churches and schools, their pastors and schoolmasters, at a rate commensurate with the increasing population.

[224] Mann, 'Report of the Census, 1851—Religious Worship', p. xxxix.

This was, however, a responsibility that probably no Government could have met in the new political order that had emerged after the Reform Act. However 'glorious' the prospect of a nation united under the influence of reformed, popular established Churches, the reality was that the British peoples were divided in their Church affiliations. They were far too divided for the more representative Parliament after 1832 to have approved major grants of public money for extending the established Churches. Further, the needs of church extension were open-ended. As Melbourne had pointed out in the debate over Scottish church extension in March 1838, if Parliament had accepted the argument that the establishments must be made commensurate with the growing population, it would have needed to build an indefinite number of new parish churches and schools, and to commit the nation to meeting an indefinite cost. Probably no Government could have secured parliamentary approval in the later 1830s for such an open-ended financial commitment, and certainly not the embattled Whig Government, dependent as it was on the support of Radicals, Voluntaries, and Irish Catholics.

But was it true that the nation was deeply divided religiously, or that it could not have afforded the costs of church extension? The church extensionists could reasonably claim that the religious divisions in Britain at least were not very deep. After all, most British Dissenters were Protestants, with theological views not so distant from those in the established Churches. Further, the large-scale growth of religious Dissent in Britain was a recent development, something that had occurred only amid the extraordinary conditions prevailing between 1790 and 1815, when the attention of the nation was focused on the struggle with revolutionary and Napoleonic France. Many had been drawn into Dissent during these years because Evangelical Dissenters had been passionate home missionaries, while there had been insufficient pastoral zeal or church accommodation in the established Churches. But if the nation was now prepared to support its established Churches, the growth of Dissent might be reversed, and British society return to the situation that had prevailed before 1790, when Dissenters had been a tolerated minority, representing about 10 per cent of the population. And as Britain returned to prosperity in the 1830s, as it emerged as the wealthiest nation in the world, with an expanding global influence, surely the nation could afford to build and endow a sufficient number of established parish churches and schools for its population.

This brings us to the real point at issue. The nation *could* have afforded church extension. But many did not want parliamentary support for church extension—because they sensed that it represented a danger to civil liberty. However attractive the idea of the closely knit parish community, centred upon the parish church and united by shared religious and moral values, it was also an idea that was likely to prove authoritarian. Moreover, the idea of a popular established Church, a people's Church, shaping social ethics for parish communities, as emphasized by such champions of church extension as Chalmers and Inglis, might prove especially dangerous for civil liberties, with the potential to create a tyranny of the majority in the different parishes of the land. The church extensionists might loudly, and sincerely, proclaim their support for the full toleration of religious Dissent. But in their godly commonwealth of close-knit parish communities under the direction of the established Churches, Dissenters would have necessarily been marginalized. The revived and more numerous parish churches, with their zealous resident clergymen and armies of parish visitors, would have sought to reassert their control over education, poor relief, moral discipline, and philanthropy within their parish bounds. They would have revived control over the rites of passage—baptism, confirmation, marriage, and burial. Theirs would be a communitarian, but also an authoritarian social order, with community opinion articulated and directed by parish clergy, parish schoolmasters, parish visitors, parish philanthropists. Dissenters would again feel themselves to be outsiders, their congregations would again become, as in the early eighteenth century, 'little gardens walled around'. The Edinburgh Dissenter and publisher Adam Black acknowledged in 1835 that Chalmers's ideal parish system offered, at first view, a 'gorgeous' prospect, but Black went on to argue that it also promised to impose a regimented social regime. 'If it were possible', he asked of the proposals to revive the system in Edinburgh, 'would it be desirable that the Presbytery or Town-Council should have the power of causing the inhabitants to form themselves into parishes, as the King of Prussia orders his troops to form themselves into squares?'[225] For the English Congregational minister Thomas Binney, writing in opposition to the church extension campaign of 1840, the ideal

[225] A. Black, *The Church its own Enemy, being an Answer to the Pamphlets of the Rev. Dr. Chalmers*, 3rd edn. (Edinburgh, 1835), 21, 22.

parish system was 'confessedly beautiful'. However, such a degree of social order could only be achieved at the cost of religious liberty and of the evangelical dynamism that accompanied religious liberty and free competition among the sects. 'The Parliamentary extension of the Establishment', he maintained, 'fully and fairly carried out, would come ultimately to this—the ecclesiastical ascendancy of *one* church secured by the forcible treatment of every other . . . as if [their] very existence . . . were an impertinence'.[226] At issue between the church extensionists and their opponents were the conflicting claims of unity and freedom, of the ideal of close-knit Christian communities representing common values and beliefs, and the ideal of an open society, representing a diversity of beliefs and opinions. This tension is an enduring one for any society. 'That we have not freedom and unity together', observed the Whig historian Thomas Babington Macaulay in April 1839, 'is a very sad thing.' But it was also sad, he added, 'that we have not wings', and we are 'just as likely to see the one defect removed as the other'.[227]

Unlimited State support for church extension would have threatened the open society and civic liberties that were becoming increasingly attractive to inhabitants of Britain. It might also have threatened the freedom of the established Churches. That is, it might well have transformed them into little more than departments of a paternalistic State, bodies with broad concerns for social welfare, but ultimately responsible to their parliamentary paymaster. Could the Churches have long maintained their spiritual independence had they come to rely on regular grants from the State? The Irish dramatist Oscar Wilde once remarked that 'when the gods wish to punish us they answer our prayers'. Had the established Churches received all they had wanted in 1838–41, had their prayers been answered, had massive State support for church and school extension been placed at their disposal, it might well have come at a price—their subordination to the State and the sacrifice of their spiritual independence.

[226] T. Binney, *Righteousness Exalteth a Nation: A Lecture on Church Extension* (London, 1840), 23, 29.

[227] T. B. Macaulay, 'Gladstone on Church and State' (April 1839), in Lady Trevelyan (ed.), *Miscellaneous Works of Lord Macaulay*, 5 vols. (New York, 1880), ii. 589.

4
'Troublers of Israel': Prophetic Protests within the Established Churches, 1833–1841

Spiritual Independence

The movements for Church defence, Church reform, and church extension had constituted one line of response to the crisis confronting the established Churches following the failure of the New Reformation in Ireland, the constitutional changes of 1828–32, and the Voluntary onslaught. Ecclesiastical leaders had immersed themselves in the political struggle for established religion. They had made vigorous efforts to defend the established Churches in the new political environment, to reform abuses in their organization and then to extend their influence to a rapidly growing population. These efforts had increasingly politicized the Churches, bringing them into active political involvement with parliamentary parties, royal commissions, voluntary societies for church and school building, public meetings, petitioning campaigns, and popular journalism. Church leaders had sought, in the event without success, to revive that close, co-operative alliance of Church and State that had characterized the early decades of the century.

For some within the established Churches, however, the challenges confronting Christian society in the United Kingdom were more profound than the external threats posed by Irish Catholics, Radicals, and Voluntaries. For them, the real crisis for established religion had resulted from the loss of prophetic fervour, dogmatic certainty, and ecclesiastical authority within the established Churches themselves. The Churches were losing their influence and authority in society because, in emphasizing their alliance with the State, they had not given sufficient emphasis to their identity as Churches of Christ—as branches of the universal Church, guided by the Holy

Spirit, embodying the teachings, liturgy, and discipline of the Early Church, and recognizing only the headship of Christ. In their former years of plenty between 1808 and 1828, the established Churches had devoted too much attention to cultivating their relations with the State, to emphasizing their role as upholders of the social order, and to lobbying for State grants. In looking so much to the State for support, they had lost sight of the power and the glory that were theirs by divine right. They had, to a large degree, subordinated themselves to the State. After 1828, however, the support of the State proved a broken reed. In response, some began arguing that there would be no security for the established Churches until they recognized that they must be grounded in something other than State support, and must embrace a higher purpose than the preservation of the social order.

During the late 1820s and 1830s three movements emerged that aimed at reviving a high view of the established Churches as independent from the State in spiritual matters and transcending temporal political and social arrangements. The first of these was the prophetic movement inspired by Edward Irving, Henry Drummond, and the Albury Circle. For those involved in this movement, the established Churches had to recover their faith in the Holy Spirit and their role as witnesses of the Spirit. They had to proclaim the special providence that had been bestowed upon Britain, and the responsibilities that being an elect nation entailed. They had to regain their belief that the arrangements of this world were transitory and that Christ would return in glory and usher in the millennium. The prophetical movement found expression in the preaching and publications of Irving, in the Albury meetings, and in the quarterly journal the *Morning Watch*. It also influenced the work of John Nelson Darby and the beginnings of the Brethren. The second movement emerged at Oxford University in the late 1820s and early 1830s, inspired by a group of younger divines including John Henry Newman, John Keble, Richard Hurrell Froude, and Edward Pusey. The Oxford divines endeavoured to revive a conception of the Church of England as a branch of the ancient catholic and apostolic Church. They venerated episcopal government, the ordained priesthood, the sacraments as vehicles of divine grace, strict spiritual discipline, dogmatic teaching, and the traditions of the Church. Their movement was promoted through their sermons and treatises, through the quarterly *British Critic*, through the development of a party organization, and especially through the series of

Tracts for the Times. Thirdly, there was the Non-Intrusionist movement that developed within the established Church of Scotland in the mid-1830s under the leadership of a number of younger high Presbyterian Evangelicals including Robert Smith Candlish, William Cunningham, and James Begg, and gradually drawing in the veteran ecclesiastic Thomas Chalmers. The Non-Intrusionists defended the Church of Scotland as a true branch of the universal Church, embodying the discipline and organization of the primitive Church, and preserving its spiritual independence under the sole headship of Christ.

All three movements shared a vision of the established Churches as reflections of Christ's continuing sovereignty over the world. They held a common view of the established Churches as foundations of Christian society, but also as independent in their spiritual functions from the State. They found support from many of those Church adherents who were distressed over the recent actions of the State—who had opposed repealing the Test and Corporation Acts, granting Catholic Emancipation, reducing the established Church of Ireland, creating the Ecclesiastical Commission, weakening the cathedral establishments, or refusing new grants for church extension. Their struggle for the prophetic witness of the Churches was pursued alongside the movements of the 1830s for Church defence, Church reform, and church extension. But in their uncompromising zeal for the spiritual authority of the Church the three movements also diverged from the political Church reform movements, embraced a profound distrust of the State, and contributed to widening divisions within the Churches.

Prophetical Movements: The Church in the Last Days

The prophetical movement within the established Churches was closely connected with the career of the Scottish Presbyterian divine Edward Irving. In the later 1820s, Irving and his church at Regent Square in London became the storm centre of a movement to revive prophecy in the established Churches and proclaim the imminent second coming of Christ. Irving's career formed one of the most extraordinary stories in the history of nineteenth-century Christianity.[1]

[1] Irving's life continues to fascinate. Significant biographical studies include M. Oliphant, *The Life of Edward Irving*, 2 vols. (London, 1862); A. L. Drummond, *Edward Irving and his Circle*

He was born in 1792, the son of a tanner in Annan, Dumfriesshire. This was Covenanter country, and as a boy Irving visited all the graves of the martyred Covenanters in the district, embracing the ideal of their heroic piety. He was educated at the University of Edinburgh, where he prepared for the ministry in the Church of Scotland. Failing to gain presentation by a patron to a parish living, he supported himself as a schoolmaster in the Fife town of Kirkcaldy, and gained a reputation for being unduly severe in disciplining his pupils. In 1818, he resigned his teaching post, moved to Edinburgh, had an unsuccessful love affair with the lively and talented Jane Welsh (who later married Irving's close friend, the Scottish historian and critic Thomas Carlyle), and contemplated becoming an overseas missionary. Instead, in 1819 he became the assistant minister in Glasgow to Thomas Chalmers, who was then beginning his celebrated St John's experiment in the urban ministry. It was a curious partnership. Chalmers was primarily concerned with his schemes for improving social cohesion and popular education in the crowded urban parish, and especially for reducing the levels of legal poor relief. Irving, on the other hand, never entered fully into the ethos of Chalmers's St John's experiment, with its emphasis on political economy. Rather, he embraced a high view of his ministry, adopting a priestly character in his pastoral visiting, pronouncing solemn blessings upon the humble dwellings of the Glasgow poor. With his great height, powerful build, striking features, dark eyes, and long, flowing black hair, Irving seemed to many St John's parishioners to have the appearance of a brigand chief rather than a Presbyterian divine. There was also adverse comment on the length and demanding nature of his sermons. Chalmers, however, defended his assistant, noting on one occasion that 'whatever they say, they never think him like anything but a leader of men'.[2]

In 1822, feeling undervalued in his native Scotland, Irving accepted an invitation to become minister to the Caledonian Chapel in Hatton Garden, London. This was a small, struggling congregation that was in communion with the Church of Scotland. Soon after arriving in London, he experienced a sensational rise to fame as a

(London, 1937); C. G. Strachan, *The Pentecostal Theology of Edward Irving* (London, 1973); A. Dallimore, *Forerunner of the Charismatic Movement: The Life of Edward Irving* (Chicago, 1983); S. Gilley, 'Edward Irving: Prophet of the Millennium', in J. Garnett and C. Matthew (eds.), *Revival and Religion since 1700* (London, 1993), 95–110.

[2] Drummond, *Edward Irving and his Circle*, 33.

preacher. Reports circulated of a fiery new preacher with an arresting appearance, a protégé of the great Chalmers. Early in 1823 the foreign secretary, George Canning, a man renowned for his eloquence, praised Irving's preaching during a debate in the House of Commons. There followed a great crush for seats at Sunday worship in the Caledonian Chapel, with cabinet ministers and peers struggling for room. Irving was invited into wealthy and cultivated social circles. He became a regular visitor to Samuel Taylor Coleridge's Highgate home, where he absorbed the transcendental thought of Lake poets and German Romantics. In 1824, his growing, prosperous congregation contracted for the building of a magnificent twin-towered, neo-Gothic building in Regent Square, which was completed in 1827. But Irving's fame as a preacher proved fleeting. His novelty value began to fade, his fashionable hearers grew impatient with his lengthy sermons and prayers, the rows of coroneted carriages outside his church disappeared, and from 1825 his congregations no longer boasted the élite of London society. Moreover, he became immersed in controversy. An uncompromising defender of the principle of established religion, he warmly supported the New Reformation movement in Ireland and denounced any concessions to Dissenters or Catholics. He was critical of missionary societies, delivering in 1825 a sermon before the London Missionary Society in which he contrasted the heroic, martyr missionaries of the Early Church with the financial pragmatism and businesslike organization of the modern missionary enterprise.[3] And after 1825, Irving was increasingly drawn to writings on prophecy.

A strain of prophetical writing had appeared in Britain and Ireland in the early years of the nineteenth century, stimulated by the upheavals of the French Revolution and Napoleonic Wars, and fed by the social unrest that had followed the end of the wars in 1815.[4] The outbreak of the French Revolution had seemed to initiate a series of events of transcendent import, including the de-Christianization campaign of the Jacobin republic, the occupation of Rome by French armies, and the seizure of the pope, which for many portended the end of the papacy. The career of Napoleon, his obscure origins, his spectacular victories and conquests, the making

[3] E. Irving, *For Missionaries after the Apostolic School* (London, 1825); Oliphant, *Life of Edward Irving*, i. 195–207.

[4] D. N. Hempton, 'Evangelicalism and Eschatology', *Journal of Ecclesiastical History*, 31 (1980), 182–4.

of his empire, the high tragedy of the invasion of Russia and the destruction of the grand army, the battle of nations at Leipzig, Napoleon's fall, exile, return, and final defeat at Waterloo, his imprisonment, like a modern Prometheus, on the rocky island in the South Atlantic—these events seemed larger than life, with a meaning that transcended mundane human history. Many in Britain turned to Scripture, and especially the books of Daniel and Revelation, for an explanation. Millennial speculations ceased to be confined to the apocalyptic subculture of Richard Brothers and Joanna Southcott and the Southcottians, and now became the subject of learned treatises and part of élite culture.[5] Spencer Perceval, the Evangelical prime minister, was drawn to biblical prophecy to explain the events in the great struggle with Napoleonic France. Prophetic speculation was rife at Trinity College, Dublin, from the 1790s and the Trinity College author William Hales published a 3-volume *New Analysis of Chronology* between 1808 and 1811, employing prophecy to understand the revolutionary events of his times.[6] In 1812, the former Chilean Jesuit Manuel Lacunza Y Diaz published a treatise on the Second Coming of Christ under the pseudonym Ben Ezra. A string of prophetical works by English and Scottish authors followed, including William Cuninghame of Lainshaw's *Dissertation on the Seals and Trumpets* (1813), James Hatley Frere's *Combined View of the Christian Prophecies* (1814), Bayford's *Messiah's Kingdom* (1816), Peter Roberts's *Manual of Prophecy* (1818), Lewis Way's letters of 'Basilicus' in the *Jewish Expositor* (1820–2), and James Cooper's *The Crisis; or, an Attempt to Shew from Prophecy . . . the Prospects and Duties of the Church* (1825).[7] During the 1820s the painter John Martin drew inspiration from the prophetical movement, exhibiting in London lurid depictions of *Belshazzar's Feast* and *The Fall of Babylon*.[8] The London Society for Promoting Christianity among the Jews, founded in 1809, emerged as a major force after 1815 under the direction of

[5] Carter, 'Evangelical Seceders from the Church of England', 221–2.

[6] Liechty, 'Irish Evangelicalism, Trinity College Dublin, and the Mission of the Church of Ireland', 275–86.

[7] E. R. Sandeen, *The Roots of Fundamentalism 1800–1830* (Chicago, 1970), 5–14; S. Gilley, 'Newman and Prophecy, Evangelical and Catholic', *Journal of the United Reformed Church History Society*, 3 (1985), 160–9; Hempton, 'Evangelicalism and Eschatology', 184–5; E. Miller, *The History and Doctrines of Irvingism*, 2 vols. (London, 1878), i. 10–11; Martin, *Evangelicals United*, 174–91.

[8] Gilley, 'Edward Irving: Prophet of the Millennium', 97.

Lewis Way—reflecting the growing belief that the conversion of the Jews and the Second Coming of Christ were near.[9]

It was into this world of prophecy and millenarian expectations that Irving was drawn. In 1825, he delivered a sermon before the Continental Society, an organization formed in 1819 for the evangelization of the European Continent. He published the sermon in 1826, now expanded into a lengthy treatise entitled *Babylon and Infidelity Foredoomed of God: A Discourse on the Prophecies of Daniel and the Apocalypse.* Reviewing history in the light of scriptural symbolism, he gave his support to the argument, already advanced by Cuninghame of Lainshaw and other recent writers, that the French Revolution had marked the end of the 1260 years of the Christian dispensation (corresponding to the 1260 'days' in Revelations 12:6), which had begun with the code of Justinian in 533 and ended with the de-Christianization campaign of the Jacobin republic in 1793. Our world, Irving taught, was now in its last days, and would soon see the return of Christ in glory and the thousand-year reign of the saints on earth. Napoleon was the 'great Infidel', who 'began his career with the spoliation of Rome, the sacred city of the Latin, and . . . ended it with the spoliation of Moscow, the sacred city of the Greek Church'.[10] Britain, Irving continued, had triumphed over the Napoleonic Antichrist, because Britain was the 'sealed' or elect nation, a covenanted people, the only one of the 'ten horns', or ten former provinces of the Roman Empire, that had both cast off the papal supremacy and restored the true Christian faith.[11] This covenanted status brought great gifts but also heavy responsibilities. As long as Britain remained steadfast in the faith, 'the Lord will preserve his glory in the midst of us', even through the cataclysms of the last days. However, he added (with reference to contemporary politics), should Britain cease its opposition to the papal 'Antichrist' and grant Catholic Emancipation, should it commit this act of national apostasy, this sin against the covenant, then it would share in the divine vengeance that was destined soon to fall on the rest of corrupt Christendom.[12] More particularly, should Parliament enact Catholic Emancipation, 'our national character is forfeited in heaven, and we are sealed no longer'.[13] In 1828 Irving appealed to biblical prophecy

[9] Sandeen, *Roots of Fundamentalism*, 9–13.

[10] E. Irving, *Babylon and Infidelity Foredoomed of God: A Discourse on the Prophecies of Daniel and the Apocalypse*, 2nd edn. (Glasgow, 1828), 528.

[11] Ibid. 534–5.

[12] Ibid. 533.

[13] Ibid. 546.

in vigorously opposing the repeal of the Test and Corporation Acts.[14] He supported the New Reformation campaign, and called for religious war in Ireland. In 1829, as Catholic Emancipation was passed, he published *The Church and State Responsible to Christ, and to one Another*, in which he employed the symbolism of Daniel's vision of the four beasts to denounce liberalism, Dissent, and especially Roman Catholicism. God, he argued, intended that Church and State, though distinct bodies, must be united. Irving compared the unity of Church and State to the unity of the human and divine natures in Christ.[15] For Irving, the repeal of the Test and Corporation Acts and the passing of Catholic Emancipation were acts of national apostasy, sins against the divinely ordained unity of Church and State. Catholic Emancipation, which had 'given the Pope the full swing of his fearful influence over seven or eight millions of his majesty's lieges' was a cause of 'nation guilt', 'a great evil in the sight of God', which if not speedily repented would bring the nation to ruin.[16] 'The crisis of this nation is come,' he proclaimed, 'and upon the [Catholic] question now at issue in the kingdom—for the whole kingdom is now roused to consider it—depends the salvation or perdition of this island for ever.'[17] Irving's prophetical writings portrayed history as grand spectacle, as epic poetry, a Miltonic struggle between cosmic evil, represented by the great Infidel and the Antichrist, Napoleon and the pope, and cosmic good, represented by the sealed nation of Britain and its established Churches.

After 1826 Irving became a leading figure in a circle for the study of prophecy that was formed by Henry Drummond, a wealthy ultra-Tory banker and nephew of the Scottish Lord Melville (Pitt's close friend and confidant). Educated at Harrow and Oxford, Drummond had been elected to Parliament for Plympton Earl in 1810, at the age of 24 (he resigned his seat in 1813). With a growing fortune earned through banking, he founded a professorship of political economy at Oxford in 1825. He was a rich, well-connected, devout Anglican, firmly committed to the union of Church and

[14] E. Irving, *A Letter to the King, on the Repeal of the Test and Corporation Laws* (London, 1828).

[15] E. Irving, *The Church and State Responsible to Christ, and to One Another: A Series of Discourses on Daniel's Vision of the Four Beasts* (London, 1829), 554–63.

[16] Ibid. 300–1.

[17] Ibid. 16; the theme of national apostasy was further explored in E. Irving, 'On the Doctrine and Manifestation and Character of the Apostasy in the Christian Church', *Morning Watch*, 1 (March 1829), 100–15.

State, and drawn to prophetical explanations.[18] Between 1826 and 1830, Drummond hosted five annual conferences, or retreats, at his country estate at Albury Park, Surrey, for the purpose of exploring 'unfulfilled prophecy'. There were about forty clergymen and lay people involved in the conferences, including Lewis Way, Cuninghame of Lainshaw, and Spencer Perceval, the son of the murdered prime minister. Nearly all of them were adherents of the Church of England or Church of Scotland.[19] Each conference lasted for about a week, and involved extensive searching of the Scriptures and interpretations of prophetic symbolism and imagery. The mood of the conferences was pessimistic, predicting that division and devastation would result from the growth of liberalism, the toleration of Dissent, and the emancipation of Catholics.[20] They embraced a gloomy premillenarianism, with the belief that the world had entered the time of evil and confusion that would culminate in the collapse of civilization, the restoration of the Jews to Palestine, the return of Christ in glory, and the establishment of the thousand-year rule of the saints on earth—followed by the last judgement and the end of the world. There was no real hope for progress or improvement in a world that had entered its last days. Some expected the Second Coming to occur between 1843 and 1847. 'I see', observed Henry Drummond, in his published account of the deliberations of the Albury conference,

> the councils of the kingdom ignorant of the first principles of a Christian state. I see the nation falling into factions. I see the people despising their superiors and their rulers. I see the church ignorant of its foundations, indifferent to its dignity, and ready to sacrifice all upon the altar of liberality. I see one half of the nation arrayed under the banner of dissent, and united into one band, to say and to swear that an established church is an offence to God, and to man, and must be pulled down. I see education without principle; and literature without seriousness. In one word, I see a glorious nation crumbling into dissolution.[21]

Other circles for the study of prophecy emerged around Britain, with Irving's London household hosting one of them. In 1826, a Society for the Investigation of Prophecy was founded in London.

[18] Henry Drummond has found no biographer, but see R. A. Davenport, *Albury Apostles: The Story of the Body Known as the Catholic Apostolic Church*, 2nd edn. (London, 1973), 15–20; E. Miller, *History and Doctrines of Irvingism*, i. 30–5.

[19] Sandeen, *Roots of Fundamentalism*, 20.

[20] Henry Drummond published anonymously a 3-vol. account, based largely on notes taken during the conferences: [H. Drummond], *Dialogues on Prophecy*, 3 vols. (London, 1828?).

[21] Ibid. iii. 434–5.

In the spring of 1828, Irving visited his native Scotland, presenting a series of twelve early morning lectures on the Apocalypse to packed halls in Edinburgh during the meeting of the General Assembly.[22] Although Chalmers found the lectures to be 'quite woful', others in Scotland were drawn into the movement, and a study circle emerged in Edinburgh.[23] In 1829, the movement founded a quarterly journal, the *Morning Watch*, which was financially supported by Drummond and edited by the Welsh Anglican John Tudor.[24] The journal became the main forum for the movement, taking the place of the Albury conferences which came to an end in 1830.

In Ireland, a prophetical circle of Church of Ireland Evangelicals took shape on the county Wicklow estate of Theodosia, Lady Powerscourt, an attractive young widow, and a wealthy and influential patron of Evangelicalism. She worshipped at Irving's church when she was in London and evidently attended the first Albury conference in 1826, becoming a zealous proponent of the prophetical and premillenarist movement. In the autumn of 1827, as the hopes of the New Reformation campaign were fading, she began hosting annual conferences on unfulfilled prophecy at Powerscourt—modelled on Drummond's Albury conferences. Irving travelled to Ireland in September 1830, preaching to large crowds in the Dublin area and visiting Powerscourt. In 1830, the monthly *Christian Herald* magazine was founded in Dublin by 'a Clergyman of the Established Church' (E. N. Hoare), to provide a forum for the discussion of unfulfilled prophecy. The Powerscourt conferences became more formal in October 1831, when the event attracted some seventy participants and was presided over by the Church of Ireland incumbent of Powerscourt and veteran New Reformationist, Robert Daly—a formidable, energetic figure compared by his prophetical admirers to Martin Luther and dismissed by the liberal *Dublin Evening Post* as 'mad, beyond a doubt'.[25] The annual conferences on prophecy were held at Powerscourt House until 1833.[26] They attracted Evangelicals who were probing for answers after the failure of the New

[22] Oliphant, *Life of Irving*, ii. 17–23.

[23] Hanna, *Memoirs of Dr Chalmers*, iii. 220; *Scotsman*, 7 June 1828.

[24] E. Miller, *History and Doctrines of Irvingism*, i. 46–7.

[25] *Dublin Evening Post*, 12 Jan., 23 Feb. 1832; Mrs Hamilton Madden, *Memoir of Robert Daly* (London, 1875), 149–53; Stunt, *From Awakening to Secession*, 165.

[26] H. H. Rowdon, *The Origins of the Brethren, 1825–1850* (London, 1967), 50, 86–99; Carter, 'Evangelical Seceders from the Church of England', 273–8; F. R. Coad, *A History of the Brethren Movement* (Exeter, 1968), 109–10.

Reformation movement. One of these was William Krause, Lord Farnham's moral agent, who from about 1830 embraced premillenarian views, informing his sister in November 1831 that 'I firmly believe that the day of the Lord's coming is not far off'.[27] The Powerscourt conferences were increasingly dominated by the powerful personality of John Nelson Darby (1800–82), the Church of Ireland curate of the parish of Calary, which adjoined Lady Powerscourt's estate. Darby, the youngest son of a well-off Anglo-Irish landowner and the godson of the great Admiral Nelson, had been ordained in 1825 by Archbishop Magee and had been active in the New Reformation movement.[28] He was described at this time by his friend Francis Newman, the brother of John Henry Newman, as an otherworldly figure with 'a fallen cheek, a bloodshot eye . . . a seldom shaven beard, a shabby suit of clothes and a generally neglected person' who might have 'vied in emaciation with a monk of La Trappe'.[29] Darby had been disillusioned by the failure of the New Reformation campaign in Ireland, which he attributed in part to the Erastian attitudes of the Anglican hierarchy, especially Archbishop Magee. It had been, he believed, too political in orientation. He also came to believe that the New Reformation mission had failed because the Irish Church was too bound to its parish structures and its ordained clergy, and feared to make use of itinerant evangelists and lay preachers. By 1828, Darby had resigned his curacy in the Church of Ireland. He grew convinced that the visible Church everywhere was in ruins, that the world had entered its last days, and that true Christians should withdraw from a fallen world and testify against its errors in preparation for the Second Coming. Although he remained within the established Church, he began 'breaking bread', or sharing communion, with a circle of like-minded Christians in Dublin. He also began questioning the scriptural warrant for an ordained clergy and seeking to restore the purity of the primitive Church.[30]

[27] Stanford, *Memoir of W. H. Krause*, 169–71.

[28] W. G. Turner, *John Nelson Darby: A Biography* (London, 1926), 14–17.

[29] W. B. Neatby, *A History of the Plymouth Brethren* (London, 1901), 46.

[30] J. N. Darby, 'Considerations addressed to the Archbishop of Dublin and the Clergy who Signed the Petition to the House of Commons for Protection' (1827), in *The Collected Writings of J. N. Darby*, ed. W. Kelly, 34 vols. (London, 1984), i. 1–19; J. N. Darby, 'Thoughts on the Present Position of the Home Mission' (1833) in *Collected Writings*, i. 52–67; Carter, 'Evangelical Seceders from the Church of England', 284–6; Stunt, *From Awakening to Secession*, 168–75.

In Scotland, the arrival of the prophetical movement coincided with a questioning of the doctrines of the Westminster Confession of Faith, the Church of Scotland's standard of faith. Under early nineteenth-century humanitarian and Evangelical influences, some Scots had grown to doubt the harsher teachings of the Westminster Confession, especially the doctrines of the total depravity of humankind and of double predestination, with some souls predestined from before all time to eternal bliss and others to eternal torment. During the 1820s Thomas Erskine of Linlathen (1788–1870), a Scottish Episcopalian and a landed gentleman residing in the neighbourhood of Dundee, published a series of theological treatises that called for a more heartfelt, personal, experiential faith, with emphasis on the paternal love of God for all his children. He rejected the Calvinist doctrine of predestination. God, according to Erskine, willed the salvation of all humankind, and not simply the elect; God's love was filial, the Church was the family of God, and it was God's aim to overcome all alienation and draw all humankind into his family. Christ, Erskine maintained, had died for every person, in order to sanctify all life.[31] Although an Episcopalian, Erskine's writings had a profound impact on many Scottish Presbyterians. One of these was John Macleod Campbell, the young Church of Scotland minister of the western Highland parish of Row, a beautiful spot on the shores of the Gareloch, some 30 miles north-west of Glasgow. From his arrival in the parish in 1825, Campbell had been disturbed by the morose religion that he encountered among his parishioners, a religion shaped more by fear of God's wrath than by joy over the gospel message. He became convinced that this religion of fear resulted largely from the doctrine of predestination, and its consignment of much of the human race to eternal fires. In about 1827, Campbell began to preach that Christ had died to atone for the sins of all humankind, and not simply for the sins of the elect, and that assurance of God's love and of salvation through Christ's atonement was essential to the Christian faith.[32] It was a bright, bold message of

[31] J. Tulloch, *Movements of Religious Thought in Britain during the Nineteenth Century* (London, 1885), 129–45; Drummond and Bulloch, *The Scottish Church 1688–1843*, 194–200; D. Finlayson, 'Aspects of the Life and Influence of Thomas Erskine of Linlathen, 1788–1870', *Records of the Scottish Church History Society*, 20 (1978), 31–45.

[32] R. H. Story, *Memoir of the Life of the Rev. Robert Story* (Cambridge, 1862), 143–51; Tulloch, *Movements of Religious Thought*, 145–50; B. A. Gerrish, *Tradition and the Modern World: Reformed Theology in the Nineteenth Century* (Chicago, 1978), 71–98.

individual hope, which broke like sunlight through the grey clouds covering the Row community. Edward Irving met Campbell in Edinburgh during his visit in May 1828. Impressed by Campbell's views on universal atonement, he travelled to Row the following month. There Irving preached to the Row community that our world had entered its last days, and could expect to witness 'signs and wonders', including the miraculous gifts of the Holy Spirit. His proclamation of the imminent return of Christ in glory evidently had a profound impact on the rural parishioners, whose beliefs had already been unsettled by the new teachings of their young minister. The devout at Row began looking in expectation for the promised signs and wonders.

They did not have long to wait. In March 1830, Campbell's parish of Row experienced an outbreak of the Spirit gifts, including healing, prophecy, and extra-sensory communications. The gifted ones also began speaking and singing in tongues (utterances purporting to be in unknown languages) and speaking with the power (unnaturally loud and forceful exclamations, which were believed to result from the Holy Spirit speaking directly through the gifted person). Among those affected were Mary Campbell of Fernicarry, a young consumptive local woman, whose saintly sister, Isabella, had died of tuberculosis amid ecstatic visions in 1827, and two unmarried brothers, George and James Macdonald, who were shipbuilders. But others in the district also claimed the gifts. Soon large numbers of the devout and curious flocked to Row to witness the gifts, many of them remaining.[33] Thomas Erskine visited Row and became convinced that the Spirit gifts were genuine. The manifestations, he observed in a pamphlet in 1830, were meant to call people away from a merely nominal acceptance of God's existence, to a knowledge of 'the *living God*, and the life-giving God'. They were also harbingers of things to come. 'My dear reader', he pleaded, 'these things which are now taking place, are just signs of the times—Listen to the voice of the sign. It tells of the near coming of Christ.'[34] Several hundred miles away in London, Irving was initially sceptical when he read the reports from Row, but discussions with his assistant minister and fellow Scot, Alexander J. Scott, convinced him that the gifts of the Spirit, given to the Church at Pentecost, had never been taken from

[33] Drummond, *Edward Irving and his Circle*, 136–51; E. Miller, *History and Doctrines of Irvingism*, i. 51–61; Strachan, *Pentecostal Theology of Edward Irving*, 61–9.

[34] [T. Erskine], *On the Gifts of the Spirit* (Greenock, 1830), 20–1, 23.

the Church, but had only lapsed through the faithlessness of Christians. There was no reason why the Spirit gifts should not return to a community of the faithful.[35] In the autumn of 1830, the Albury circle sent a deputation, including the lawyer and member of Irving's London congregation John B. Cardale, north to Row to observe the phenomena. They returned convinced that the gifts were genu-ine.[36] Irving's London congregation began praying that the Spirit gifts would appear among them as well.

But while Irving's congregation prayed, in Scotland the Rowite movement was coming under attack. The forces of Calvinist orthodoxy in the Church of Scotland moved quickly to suppress the movement in its midst. With the established Church feeling threatened by the recent passage of Catholic Emancipation and now by the Reform Bill agitation, its leaders were not prepared to allow the Church's unity to be undermined by new doctrines and prophetic enthusiasm. Established clergymen were sent to Row to gather evidence. Late in 1830, the Church courts commenced formal proceedings for heresy against ministers prominent in the Rowite movement. These proceedings claimed their first victims in May 1831, when the General Assembly deposed John Macleod Campbell and Hugh Baillie McLean from the ministry of the Church of Scotland, and deposed Irving's assistant minister, Alexander Scott, from the position of probationer minister. The same General Assembly denounced Irving for heretical views concerning the human nature of Christ, and instructed the Presbytery of Annan, which had ordained him, to initiate proceedings for his heresy trial.[37] Five more ministers were deposed for heretical views over the next few years.

In April 1831, meanwhile, the first manifestations of the Spirit gifts had appeared among members of Irving's London congregation. At first, the manifestations—speaking and singing in tongues or speaking with power—were confined to private homes. The spread of the manifestations was assisted by Mary Campbell of Row, who had married a law clerk, William Caird, and who in March 1831 had moved to the London area, staying with Lady Olivia Sparrow, a leading figure in the Irvingite circle. On 16 October 1831, amid the excitement of the reform bill crisis and widespread terror

[35] Strachan, *The Pentecostal Theology of Edward Irving*, 61–2, 70–84.

[36] *Morning Watch*, 2/4 (December 1830), 869–73.

[37] Drummond and Bulloch, *The Scottish Church 1688–1843*, 202–5.

over the approach of cholera, a Miss Hall broke out loudly in tongues during a regular Sunday service in Irving's church. She was soon joined by others. Irving endeavoured for some weeks to silence the outbursts, but he gradually became convinced that the manifestations were the very baptism of the Spirit for which his congregation had been praying. Late in November, he began allowing gifted persons to speak in tongues or with power during regular services.[38]

The result, for many, was pandemonium. Gifted persons interrupted services with their prophetic messages, and curious or mocking onlookers intruded themselves into the services. Some found the utterances—delivered in loud, unnatural voices, often from darkened corners of the church—deeply disturbing, and more conventional Church members began leaving the congregation. The trustees of the recently completed Regent Square church, which was burdened with a heavy debt, grew concerned that the 'tongues' were not only bringing the church into disrepute, but also threatening it with financial ruin. In March 1832, the trustees appealed against Irving's innovations in worship to the Presbytery of London, a court of the established Church of Scotland. At the trial, Irving denied that he had done anything contrary to 'the word of God . . . the people or the customs of our fathers'. In determining how the gifted should be permitted to prophesy in services, he had acted 'according to the best records of ecclesiastical antiquity' and 'was at great pains to consult the best records'.[39] In the event, the Presbytery decided in favour of the trustees, and on 2 May 1832 Irving and his supporters—including the large majority of his congregation, some 800 communicants—were locked out of the Regent Square church. They worshipped for several months in rooms in Gray's Inn Road, previously home to a group of Owenite socialists. Irving, together with several evangelists from his congregation, also began preaching in the open air around London. In the autumn of 1832, the congregation moved into a large house with attached picture gallery in Newman Street, which had once been occupied by the painter Benjamin West.

There, in October 1832, John B. Cardale, a solicitor and one of the gifted persons, announced that he had been called by the Spirit to become an 'apostle', with a divine commission to rule and ordain.

[38] Stunt, *From Awakening to Secession*, 261–5.

[39] Oliphant, *Life of Irving*, ii. 277, 279.

Irving and most of the congregation accepted Cardale's claim. By now, however, some former supporters of the prophetical movement were beginning to fall away. Richard Baxter, one of the foremost gifted persons in Irving's congregation, became convinced that he had been deluded by a 'lying spirit', and published in 1833 a lengthy retraction, 'for the sake of those whom I may have hardened or betrayed into a false faith'.[40] In Scotland, Macleod Campbell dissociated himself from the gifted persons at Row.[41] However, others remained committed to the prophetical movement, including Henry Drummond and a group residing in the neighbourhood of his Albury estate. In December 1832 the 'apostle', Cardale, ordained Drummond as 'angel', or chief pastor, of the church in Albury.

In March 1833, Irving returned to Scotland to face trial for heresy before the Presbytery of Annan. There was no obvious reason why he should have returned, as he was now practically separated from the established Church of Scotland and there could be no doubt about the trial's outcome. Irving insisted, however, upon defending his views in the town of his birth, in the church where he had been baptized and ordained, before the presbytery that had ordained him. On 13 March 1833, following a day-long trial, the Presbytery formally deposed Irving from the ministry of the Church of Scotland for holding heretical views on the human nature of Christ. Night had fallen when the sentence was solemnly pronounced in the darkened parish church of Annan, crowded with some 2,000 spectators and lit by a single candle. David Dow, a fellow Church of Scotland minister who had also been drawn into the prophetical movement, broke out in tongues and then spoke with the power, pronouncing the Spirit's condemnation of the proceeding and commanding all present to flee from the church. There was considerable confusion, and the meeting broke up amid screams in the dark and a scramble for the doors. The following day, Irving preached to thousands in the open air.[42] Returning to London, he was ordained by Cardale on 5 April 1833 to the office of 'angel' of the Newman Street church. Soon other congregations emerged—at Bishopsgate Street, London (May 1833), at Brighton (December 1833), at Chatham, Chelsea,

[40] R. Baxter, *Narrative of Facts characterising the Supernatural Manifestations in Members of Mr Irving's Congregation, and other Individuals in England and Scotland*, 2nd edn. (London, 1833), 3; Davenport, *Albury Apostles*, 54–61.

[41] Drummond and Bulloch, *The Scottish Church 1688–1843*, 205.

[42] Oliphant, *Life of Irving*, ii. 338–54; Drummond, *Edward Irving and his Circle*, 217–21.

and Southwark in London, and at Edinburgh (January 1834).[43] In September 1833, Henry Drummond felt called by the Spirit to join Cardale as a second 'apostle', and by the end of 1833, two more 'apostles' were called, making a total of four. In June 1833, the *Morning Watch*, the journal of the prophetical movement, was brought to an end. It had been directed primarily to members of the established Churches, with the aim of reviving the national Churches through a restoration of their prophetic witness. But now the followers of the prophetical movement were leaving the established Churches to form a new communion.[44]

Irving, meanwhile, the prince of the prophetical movement within the established Churches, was dying of consumption. He grew frail, ceased his open-air evangelizing in London by the end of 1832, and restricted his ministry to the Newman Street congregation, largely withdrawing from the world. Seeing him after a lapse of two years in the summer of 1834, his old friend Thomas Carlyle was shocked by Irving's grey hair, pale, hollow, deeply lined face, and slow, unsteady walk.[45] In September 1834, Irving returned to his native Scotland. He died, aged 42, on 7 December 1834 in Glasgow, where he had begun his Church of Scotland ministry, and he was buried in a tomb donated by a stranger in the crypt of Glasgow cathedral.[46] As the mourners departed, there remained a number of young women dressed in white, confident that he would rise again from the grave. So ended the career of one of the most extraordinary Churchmen of the nineteenth century—a champion of established religion, who sought with prophetic fervour to revive the apostolic authority of the national Churches of Scotland and England in preparation for the moment of Christ's return—but who in the end was driven out of the established Church of Scotland.

The movement that Irving had inspired survived him in the form of the Catholic Apostolic Church, which from the mid-1830s took form as a new denomination, made up mainly of seceders from the established Churches. By the end of 1836, there were some thirty-six Catholic Apostolic churches in England, Scotland, and Ireland.[47]

[43] E. Miller, *History and Doctrines of Irvingism*, i. 134–41, 176; Stunt, *From Awakening to Secession*, 265–7.

[44] Ibid. i. 131–3.

[45] T. Carlyle, *Reminiscences*, ed. J. A. Froude, 2 vols. (London, 1881), ii. 328–9.

[46] Drummond, *Edward Irving and his Circle*, 227–8.

[47] E. Miller, *History and Doctrines of Irvingism*, i. 176.

The Catholic Apostolic Church claimed to restore the primitive offices of the early Church—the fourfold ministry of apostles, prophets, evangelists, and pastors—in preparation for Christ's return.[48] At the head of the Church was the restored apostolate. A total of twelve apostles had been called by June 1835. They were a varied group of landed aristocrats, middle-class professional men, and former clergymen in the established Churches. Most were in their thirties, energetic men with practical experience of the world. Their call was viewed as inaugurating a new epoch in the world. Just as Jesus had appointed the twelve apostles to the Jews at the beginning of the Christian era, so now, they believed, at the end of the Christian era, the Holy Spirit had appointed twelve apostles to the Gentiles. The task of the twelve was to gather a divided Christendom together and present it, restored to its wholeness, to Christ when he returned to open the millennium. In addition to the apostles, there were the prophets, whose office it was to interpret Scripture and communicate the messages of the Spirit, the evangelists, who were to preach the gospel to all people, and the pastors, who were to provide care to the individual local churches. The chief pastor, or 'angel', of each local church was assisted by a number of elders. Of particular importance were the seven churches of London, portrayed as the new Zion of the universal Church, with the Council of the Seven Churches, or, as it was called, the Council of Zion, exercising special leadership. Their elaborate liturgy, as defined in the service book of 1842, was decidedly high, containing a mixture of Roman Catholic, Greek Orthodox, and Anglican influences. As a denomination, the 'Irvingites' became known largely for the rich symbolism and colour of their church decor and liturgy.

In Ireland, meanwhile, the prophetical movement associated with Dublin and Powerscourt was contributing to another secession from the established Church. John Nelson Darby, it will be recalled, had resigned his curacy in the Church of Ireland in 1828, and established about the same time a circle in Dublin for regular prayer, the study of unfulfilled prophecy, and the breaking of bread or celebration of holy communion. The group included Anthony Norris Groves, an Englishman who had recently withdrawn from Trinity College,

[48] For the early development of the Catholic Apostolic Church, see especially E. Miller, *History and Doctrines of Irvingism*, i. 107–241; Davenport, *Albury Apostles*, 67–136.

Dublin, where he had been preparing for the Anglican priesthood, and John Gifford Bellett, a barrister and established Churchman. In 1832, Darby publicly denounced the Whig archbishop of Dublin, Richard Whately, for supporting the Government's abandonment of the Scripture education societies and creation of the National System of Education in Ireland. The resulting controversy brought Darby, after much struggle, finally to break his connection with the established Church. In 1833, he convinced Lady Powerscourt to follow him out of the established Church. She died three years later, at the age of only 36. Darby's Dublin circle, meanwhile, had taken the name of 'Brethren', and combined their studies of prophecy with a puritanical style of life and worship, aimed at restoring the purity of the Early Church. A second circle of Brethren was formed in Plymouth in 1830, where the movement took on a strong Calvinist doctrine. From Plymouth the Brethren movement spread in the early 1830s to Bristol, Barnstaple, London, Torquay, and Bath, clearly emerging as a loose grouping of independent assemblies by the mid-1830s. A Brethren periodical, the *Christian Witness*, began in January 1834. There was a small Brethren assembly established in Edinburgh by 1838. The Plymouth Brethren, as the new communion became known, rejected apostolic succession, the historic creeds of the Church, infant baptism, and the idea of an ordained, salaried ministry. They viewed themselves as an assembly of the faithful, called out of a ruined Church to restore the primitive purity of the first Christians and to await the Second Coming. They rejected the Irvingite claims to a revival of the Spirit gifts, while their puritanical worship and predestinarian beliefs contrasted sharply with the liturgy and teachings of the Catholic Apostolic Church. None the less, both groups shared a belief that the world was in its last days, and that the return of Christ was imminent.[49]

The prophetical movements of Irving and Darby—of the Albury apostles, the Rowite manifestations, and Powerscourt circle—developed from efforts to renew the embattled established Churches of England, Ireland, and Scotland in the late 1820s and early 1830s. These movements represented efforts to find meaning in the changing relations of Church and State and to recover the independent

[49] Rowdon, *Origins of the Brethren*; Coad, *History of the Brethren Movement*, 25–90; Neatby, *History of the Plymouth Brethren*, 1–65; Carter, 'Evangelical Seceders from the Church of England', 272–321.

spiritual authority of the established Churches. They stood against the spirit of the times, opposed Catholic Emancipation, and rejected the liberal creed of progress and toleration. The world, the Irvingites and Brethren believed, was in its last days. For Irving, writing in early 1830, the three evil 'spirits' of the times were the Evangelical, the Liberal, and the papal—the Evangelical, because it elevated individual piety and voluntary religious societies over 'the church and its ordinances'; the Liberal, because it elevated private reason over religious authority; and the papal, because it threatened the spiritual independence and doctrinal purity of Britain's national Churches.[50] For Darby, the visible Church was in ruins and society had fallen into evil and corruption. The propheticals' obsession with unfulfilled prophecy reflected their belief that God was directing history and that the revolutionary upheavals and warfare in Europe since 1789 had a higher meaning. They viewed the Church, not as an establishment supporting the existing social order, but as a mystical body, separate from the world, but also holding the key to the coming kingdom. They sought to revive the spiritual power of the early Church.[51] For Irving, as his lifelong friend Thomas Carlyle later reminisced, 'Christian religion was to be a truth again, not a paltry form, and to rule the world.'[52] In the event, the propheticals failed to infuse the established Churches with their vision, and they seceded, forming two very different bodies, the Catholic Apostolic Church and the Plymouth Brethren, differing in much, but united by their shared belief that the Second Advent was near. The prophetical movement continued to exercise influence in the established Churches, affecting many who remained within the established Church with a premillenarian vision of a world in its last days. These included Edward Bickersteth, secretary of the Church Missionary Society from 1824 and rector of Watton from 1830, who embraced a premillenarianism in 1832, and Lord Ashley, the future seventh earl of Shaftesbury, who in the mid-1830s was brought to embrace a prophetical and premillenarian vision through the influence of the Irish Anglican and missionary to the Jews, Alexander McCaul.[53]

[50] E. Irving, 'Signs of the Times and the Characteristics of the Church', *Morning Watch*, 2 (March 1830), 152–4.

[51] E. Irving, 'The Church, with her Endowment of Holiness and Power', in *The Collected Writings of Edward Irving*, ed. G. Carlyle, 5 vols. (London, 1865), v. 449–506.

[52] Carlyle, *Reminiscences*, ii. 236.

[53] Bebbington, *Evangelicalism in Modern Britain*, 75–94; M. Hennell, *Sons of the Prophets: Evangelical Leaders of the Victorian Church* (London, 1979), 43–4, 54.

The prophetical movement also touched John Henry Newman, the Oxford scholar, whose younger brother, Francis, had been strongly influenced by Darby.[54] The Irvingite movement would exercise an influence on the High Church movement for revitalizing the established Church of England that emerged in Oxford in the early 1830s.[55]

The Tractarian Movement in the Church of England: The Apostolic Succession

The Oxford Movement is generally regarded as beginning in the spring and summer of 1833. Its founders were a group of romantic High Church Anglicans, who were alarmed over challenges to the authority of the established Church. Like Irving, Drummond, and the propheticals, the Oxford divines feared that their society was throwing off its belief in a providence that guided the destiny of nations. Their apprehensions were deepened by the changing relations between the State and established Church. In the 1820s, the Church–State alliance had seemed strong and vibrant, and the Church seemed destined to reassert its influence and authority. By the early 1830s, however, those halcyon days were over. The New Reformation movement in Ireland had failed. Dissenters had been given a new confidence by the Repeal of the Test and Corporation Acts and Roman Catholics by Emancipation. Parliament had been reformed amid violent attacks on the Anglican clergy. In Ireland the established Church seemed to be disintegrating amid the violence of the tithe war. The Revolution of 1830 in France portended a return of political unrest in Europe, with renewed danger to Christian society. 'At the beginning of the summer of 1833', the High Church William Palmer later recalled, 'the Church of England and Ireland seemed destined to immediate desolation and ruin'.[56] The transformation in the relations of Church and State had come so suddenly, so violently, that it seemed to defy rational explanation. Portentous forces were at work, and the Church of England would need to marshall all its spiritual resources for the coming struggle.

[54] Gilley, *Newman and his Age*, 47–8, 76–7.

[55] Brilioth, *The Anglican Revival*, 306–7.

[56] W. Palmer, *A Narrative of Events connected with the Publication of the Tracts for the Times* (London, 1883), 96.

The leaders of the Oxford Movement had come to maturity in the 1820s, the years of Anglican promise; they were products of the revival in the established Church. Oxford in the 1820s, as we have seen, had been a centre of the Anglican revival. Early nineteenth-century administrative and educational reforms had transformed the University from a quiet haven of privileged leisure into a place of lively debate and serious study, a seminary for training the clergy of a resurgent Anglican establishment. There were, to be sure, criticisms of the devotional life in the University—including allegations of spiritual lethargy, high and dry preaching, unseemly student conduct at chapel, and lack of moral earnestness. Yet within its colleges, many were being stirred by the brightened prospects for established Protestantism and stimulated by the theological and historical learning of such figures as Charles Lloyd (Regius professor of Divinity 1822–9) and Edward Burton (Regius professor of Divinity 1829–36). Lloyd, for example, gave a course of private lectures in the 1820s on the history of liturgy, which awakened considerable interest in the worship and devotional practices of the early and medieval Church.[57] The early nineteenth century had brought a revival of interest in the 'Hutchinsonians', followers of the eccentric eighteenth-century Hebraist and mystic John Hutchinson, who had embraced a high view of the sacraments, an interest in patristics, the practice of asceticism, fervent devotion, and strong sense of a pervasive providence in the world. High Church scholars such as William Palmer and Martin Joseph Routh inspired renewed veneration for the seventeenth-century Caroline divines.[58] They preserved the view of the Church of England as a branch of the universal Church, its bishops the successors to the apostles, its doctrine and liturgy rooted in antiquity. In the 1820s the writings of the Irish High Churchmen John Jebb, bishop of Limerick, and Alexander Knox not only celebrated the ideal of the historic apostolic Church, but also directed Oxford interest to the efforts being made to revive the established Church in Ireland.

If there was a strong commitment in Oxford to reviving the established Church, there was also an awareness that the Church of England was more than an establishment, however much it might value its connection with the State. The Church was a spiritual body,

[57] W. J. Baker, 'Hurrell Froude and the Reformers', *Journal of Ecclesiastical History*, 21 (July 1970), 247; [F. Oakeley], 'The Church Service', *British Critic*, 27 (April 1840), 251.

[58] F. L. Cross, *The Oxford Movement and the Seventeenth Century* (London, 1933), 7–40.

instituted by Christ, its doctrines and liturgy rooted in Scripture and tradition, and with a duty to elevate the whole of society. At Oriel College, the Noetics called on the Church to exercise its powers of independent judgement, untrammelled by patronage and party politics, and to secure its independence from the State in matters of ecclesiastical discipline. It was the Noetic and future archbishop of Dublin, Richard Whately, who penned the anonymous *Letters on the Church, by an Episcopalian*, published in 1826, which called for a full separation of the Church from the State.[59] Separation, he argued, would free the Church from its governmental responsibilities and allow it to concentrate on developing its character as a spiritual institution. 'The Church', he argued, 'as a *Church*, i.e., as a spiritual community, has no concern with secular government.'[60] Such a separation, he further maintained, would not require the Church to give up its tithes and endowments, for these were the Church's own corporate property, given to the Church by pious individuals in previous generations, and not by the State. Whately's work touched nerves in an Oxford community awakening to the Church's inherent power. John Henry Newman recalled that one friend, 'after reading it . . . could not keep still, but went on walking up and down his room'.[61] John Keble, the author of *The Christian Year*, was initially critical of Whately's arguments; however, by 1827 he was sharing Whately's doubts about the benefits of the State alliance for the Church.[62] Another fellow of Oriel College, Richard Hurrell Froude, was drawn to the writings of Felicité de Lamennais, the French ultramontane Roman Catholic priest, who from 1829 called on the French clergy to assert the Church's independence from State interference, even if this meant giving up their State stipends.[63]

The occasion for the beginning of the Oxford Movement was the

[59] [R. Whately], *Letters on the Church. By an Episcopalian* (London, 1826).

[60] Ibid. 133–41, 178. [61] J. H. Newman, *Apologia Pro Vita Sua* (New York, 1950), 43.

[62] Nockles, *Oxford Movement in Context*, 82–3; J. R. Griffin, 'John Keble: Radical', *Anglican Theological Review*, 53/3 (July 1971), 167–73.

[63] W. G. Roe, *Lamennais and England: The Reception of Lamennais's Religious Ideas in England in the Nineteenth Century* (Oxford, 1966), 93–9; C. Dawson, *The Spirit of the Oxford Movement* (London, 1933), 68; J. R. Griffin, 'The Radical Phase of the Oxford Movement', *Journal of Ecclesiastical History*, 27 (1976), 50. Peter Nockles warns against over-emphasizing Lamennais's influence on the Oxford Movement, but does acknowledge Lamennais's influence on Froude: P. Nockles, '"Church and King": Tractarian Politics Reappraised', in P. Vaiss (ed.), *From Oxford to the People: Reconsidering Newman and the Oxford Movement* (Leominster, 1996), 93–4.

Government's plan, announced early in 1833, to reform the established Church of Ireland. The Irish Church temporalities bill, it will be recalled, provided for the gradual abolition of ten dioceses, the suppression of a number of parishes, the introduction of a graduated tax on clerical incomes, and the establishment of an ecclesiastical commission. There was widespread, and not unreasonable, fear that the Irish bill would form a precedent for the similar reduction of the Church of England, which had, of course, been united to the Church of Ireland in 1801, and which was itself being assailed by Radicals and Voluntaries. The High Church party in England had strongly supported the Irish New Reformation movement in the 1820s, and they now felt incensed over Parliament's treatment of the Irish Church. In an article in the High Church *British Magazine* of March 1833, Keble denounced the Whig plans for the Irish Church as a 'persecution of the church'. The State, he insisted, had no authority to abolish bishoprics, which were spiritual offices instituted by Christ. If the Government persevered with its plans, it would force the Church 'to throw from her those state privileges . . . and excommunicate, as it were, the civil government'. The choice was becoming one 'between separation and virtual apostasy'.[64] In the following month, Keble predicted in the same journal that Irish precedents would soon be applied to the Church of England, and that English bishoprics and cathedral establishments would 'be sacrificed to the Moloch of Radicalism, whenever it is found necessary to propitiate that greedy and bloody deity'.[65] On 14 July 1833, Keble delivered his famous Assize Day sermon in the University Pulpit of Oxford. There he maintained that the 'Apostolical Church' faced being 'forsaken, degraded, nay trampled on and despoiled by the State and people of England' in an act of 'national apostasy'. The nation, in short, was proclaiming, 'We will be as the heathen . . . aliens to the Church of our Redeemer'.[66] Keble's language was reminiscent of Irving's 'prophetic' warning four years earlier that Catholic Emancipation was an act of national apostasy by which Britain would forfeit its status as a 'sealed nation'. A few weeks after Keble's sermon, in early August 1833, the Irish Church Temporalities Act received the royal assent. In response, Keble

[64] [J. Keble], 'Church Reform, no. iv', *British Magazine*, 3 (March 1833), 360–78, 377; Rowlands, *Church, State and Society*, 87.

[65] [J. Keble], 'Church Reform, no. v', *British Magazine*, 3 (April 1833), 484–91, 490.

[66] J. Keble, *National Apostasy*, ed. A. Stephenson (Abingdon, 1983), 22, 16.

told the High Churchman John Henry Newman on 8 August that the established Church must prepare to relinquish its tithes and endowments, even if this meant leaving the State under 'the curse of Sacrilege'.[67]

Others shared Keble's alarm. Late in July 1833 the High Church editor of the *British Magazine*, Hugh James Rose, organized a three-day meeting, or retreat, at his rural rectory at Hadleigh, Suffolk, to consider responses to Whig threats to the spiritual independence and integrity of the established Church.[68] The meeting was attended by Richard Hurrell Froude, William Palmer, R. C. Trench, and Arthur Perceval. Perhaps significantly, of the four, two had connections with the Irvingites. Trench, who was Rose's curate, was a young Anglican of Irish background. He had regularly attended Irving's services in 1832–3, both before and after the congregation had been expelled from the Regent Square church by the Presbytery of London, and as late as March 1833 he was struggling to believe 'in the powers manifested in the midst of Mr. Irving's Church'.[69] Arthur Perceval was the cousin of Spencer Perceval, who was the son of the assassinated Evangelical prime minister and a leading figure, soon to become an 'apostle', in the emerging Catholic Apostolic Church.[70] The discussions conducted among the five meeting at Hadleigh reflected the larger divisions that were developing between the old High Church group (represented at Hadleigh by Rose and Palmer), whose main concern was to preserve the union of Church and State, and an emerging 'Apostolical' group (represented at Hadleigh by Froude and to a lesser extent Perceval), who believed with Keble that the Church of England had to be prepared to give up the privileges of establishment in order to maintain its character as a Christian Church. Rose and Palmer urged caution and advocated the formation of a committee to plan a long-term strategy for Church defence. They were both prudent men, with responsible positions within the established Church. Froude, on the other hand, opposed action by committee, which he suspected would be ineffectual, and called for an immediate appeal for direct popular support.[71]

67 Keble to Newman, 8 August 1833, in *Letters and Diaries of John Henry Newman*, iv. 23; Griffin, 'John Keble: Radical', 172–3.

68 Machin, *Politics and the Churches in Great Britain 1832 to 1868*, 79.

69 R. C. Trench, *Letters and Memorials*, 2 vols. (London, 1888), i. 113–42, 135.

70 Gilley, *Newman and his Age*, 113.

71 Brendon, *Hurrell Froude and the Oxford Movement*, 129–30; R. H. Froude to J. Keble, 18 August 1833, Keble College, Oxford, Keble Papers, MS 62a.

The discussions continued in Oxford through the summer, with a growing divergence between the old High Church group and the less moderate 'Apostolicals'. Palmer and Rose assumed the leadership of the old High Church group and employed committee methods in seeking to generate broad support for the defence of the established Church. In August 1833, they formed an Association of Friends of the Church, and urged the formation of branch societies throughout the country. The Association drafted a petition to the archbishop of Canterbury, expressing support for the existing doctrine, liturgy, and polity of the Church of England, and affirming that any reforms in the Church must have the approval of the bishops. The cautious petition was signed by some 7,000 clergy of the established Church and submitted to the archbishop in February 1834. It was followed by a similarly worded address by the laity, signed by some 230,000 heads of family, and submitted to the king in May 1834. Both the clerical petition and lay address conveyed little more than platitudes, and their chief merit lay in demonstrating support in the country for the established Church.

Froude and John Henry Newman, meanwhile, assumed the leadership of the Apostolicals. They pursued a more vigorous programme aimed at reviving the spiritual independence of the Church of England. The two men had recently returned from a tour of Italy. Newman had nearly died of a fever in Sicily and he now believed that his life had been spared for a purpose—to preserve and restore the English national Church. While Froude and Newman gave their general support to the Association's petition and address, they did not place much confidence in such methods: Newman described the address as 'milk and water', and saw it as only a hesitant beginning towards the real goal of preparing the clergy for independent action and redefining 'the Church as a body and power distinct from the State'.[72] The Apostolicals did not share the hope, prevalent among the old High Church group, that the former alliance of Church and State could be restored. The confident days of the 1820s, they believed, were gone forever. Froude, suffering from the consumption that would soon claim his life, was the dominant voice among the Apostolicals. As his own hold on the world loosened, he called for bold action to free the Church from what he

[72] Newman to H. J. Rose, 23 November 1833, *Letters and Diaries of John Henry Newman*, iv. 121.

viewed as its worldly chains. 'With Froude', Newman later recalled, 'Erastianism,—that is, the union (so he viewed it) of Church and State,—was the parent, or if not the parent, the serviceable and sufficient tool, of liberalism. Till that union was snapped, Christian doctrine never could be safe.'[73] In the *British Magazine* of July 1833, Froude argued that it was 'impossible for the Church of England to recover her lost ascendancy in the councils of this nation'. The old order in Church and State had changed utterly. But neither could the Church sit still and hope to be left alone in these troubled times. 'Open your eyes', Froude proclaimed to the Church, 'to the fearful change which has been so noiselessly affected; and acknowledge that BY STANDING STILL YOU BECOME A PARTY TO REVOLUTION'.[74] The Church found itself in a changed world; old certainties and landmarks were gone. Perhaps, as leaders of the prophetical movement were then proclaiming, the world had entered the chaos and evil of its last days. The Church would have to look to its own resources. By August Newman was contemplating a disruption of the Church of England, and envisaging the day when the clergy would call on 'the people' to follow them out of a corrupt establishment.[75] If the State continued to interfere in the spiritual authority of bishops, and if bishops such as Blomfield of London continued to co-operate with this 'Tyranny', Newman observed to a friend on 7 August, it 'will cause a schism in the Church, such as it has never known'.[76] 'We have stood by Monarchy and Aristocracy', Newman wrote to another correspondent on 8 September, 'till they have refused to stand by themselves. Surely it is time to "flee to the mountains".'[77] In the *British Magazine* of October 1833, he suggested that the 'time-honoured instrument' of the established Church, based upon 'the regal and aristocratic power', was broken. Stripped of the protection of State power, the apostolic Church must now '*look to the people*'.[78]

In August 1833, the Apostolicals began issuing the 'Tracts for the

[73] Newman, *Apologia*, 66.

[74] [R. H. Froude], 'Conservative Principles', *British Magazine* (July 1833); repr. in *Remains of Richard Hurrell Froude*, ed. J. Keble and J. H. Newman, 2 vols. (Derby, 1839), i. 189–96.

[75] Newman to Keble, 5 August 1833, *Letters and Diaries of John Henry Newman*, iv. 20–2; J. R. Griffin, 'The Anglican Politics of Cardinal Newman', *Anglican Theological Review*, 55 (1973), 434–43.

[76] Newman to H. A. Woodgate, 7 August 1833, *Letters and Diaries of John Henry Newman*, iv. 27.

[77] Newman to R. F. Wilson, 8 September 1833, ibid. iv. 44.

[78] [J. H. Newman], 'Letters on the Church of the Fathers', *British Magazine*, 4 (October 1833), 422; Ker, *John Henry Newman*, 82–3.

Times' that gave a name to their movement. The Tracts were largely Newman's idea. They were intended as brief, provocative expressions of individual opinion on fundamental Church principles that would excite imaginations, stir debate, and incite action. Newman would allow no editorial committee, which he felt would impose a stultifying conformity, and he wrote many of the early Tracts himself. 'They were not', he explained to Rose, 'intended as symbols *è cathedrâ*, but as the expression of individual minds . . . No great work was ever done by a system; whereas systems rise out of individual exertions.'[79] The Tracts would in a sense provide the forum for open discussion and debate that the Church had lost with the suppression of Convocation. The early Tracts, then, were short, bold, categorical, argumentative. Their essential message was that the Church of England was not simply an establishment, nor was it a creation of the State. It did not exist to further the purposes of the parliamentary State; it was not defined by its relationship to the State. Rather, it was nothing less than a true branch of the holy, catholic, and apostolic Church, which had been instituted by Christ, guided by the Holy Spirit, served by the apostles and their episcopal successors, preserved against doctrinal error by the Fathers and doctors, renewed by the blood of the martyrs, venerated by generations of the faithful, and destined to abide until the return of Christ in glory. It was the dwelling-place of the Spirit and the divinely ordained instrument for communicating grace to the world. A key theme in the early Tracts was that of the apostolic succession as a defining mark of the Church. The clergy of the Church of England were part of a mystical chain, unbroken through the centuries, linking them to the apostles and to Christ; they had the authority to preach Christ's gospel and administer Christ's sacraments and discipline, not because they held appointments in a State establishment, but because they were commissioned to do so by the successors of the apostles. 'The Lord JESUS CHRIST', wrote Newman of the clergy in the first Tract, 'gave His Spirit to His Apostles; they in turn laid their hands on those who should succeed them; and these again on others; and so the sacred gift has been handed down to our present Bishops, who have appointed us as their assistants, and in some sense representatives.'[80] The clergy of the Church of England were not civil servants. 'Are we content', asked Newman in the second Tract,

79 Newman, *Apologia*, 69.

80 [J. H. Newman], *Thoughts on the Ministerial Commission*, Tract 1 (London, 1833), 2.

to be accounted the mere creation of the State, as schoolmasters and teachers may be, or soldiers, or magistrates, or other public officers? Did the State make us? can it unmake us? can it send out missionaries? can it arrange dioceses? Surely all these are spiritual functions; and Laymen may as well set about preaching, and consecrating the Bread and Wine, as assume these.[81]

The Church must resist State encroachments on its spiritual autonomy, even if this meant persecution and the loss of its property. It must not allow Radical or Voluntary threats to intimidate it into accepting State-imposed reforms that would further limit its spiritual influence and muzzle its prophetic voice. Stripping the Church of its property and its clergy of their social status might well be the means intended by providence to restore the Church to a proper understanding of itself. Newman called on the bishops to lead the Church's protest, even if it meant 'the spoiling of their goods, and martyrdom'. He envisaged a clergy denuded of wealth, status, privilege, forced to share the poverty of the common people, but shining forth all the brighter as Christ's ambassadors. He told the common people to be ready for that day of apostolic poverty: 'Then you will look at us, not as gentlemen, as now; not as your superiors in worldly station, but still, nay, more strikingly so than now, still as messengers from Him, who seeth and worketh in secret, and who judgeth not by outward appearance.'[82] At the same time, he held that the apostolical Church should not initiate the break with the State; rather, the Church should abide in patience and maintain its witness until forced to give up its established status by the action of the State.[83]

In the fourth Tract, John Keble echoed Newman's claim that the established clergy had lost sight of their true commission, and that the Church might be more effective if liberated from the State connection. 'For many years', he observed, 'we have been much in the habit of resting our claim on the general duties of submission to authority, of decency, and order, of respecting precedents long established; instead of appealing to that warrant, which marks us, *exclusively*, for GOD'S AMBASSADORS'. The Church needed to recover the purity of the 'Primitive Church', when the clergy had elevated

[81] [J. H. Newman], *The Catholic Church*, Tract 2 (London, 1833), 2.

[82] [J. H. Newman], *Heads of a Week-Day Lecture, delivered to a Country Congregation*, Tract 10 (London, 1833), 4.

[83] Griffin, 'The Radical Phase of the Oxford Movement', 49, 53–5.

'canonical obedience' over State service.[84] This theme of returning to the purity of the ancient, or pre-Constantinian, Church, ran through several early Tracts. It was in the Church of the apostles, and not the political theory of establishment, that the Church should seek its identity, the model for its offices, and its path of duty. The early Tracts, Newman later recalled, were urgent summons not for mere Church reform, but for a 'second Reformation'; they were aimed at restoring the 'primitive Christianity that had been delivered for all time by the early teachers of the Church'.[85] Newman concluded his first book, *The Arians of the Fourth Century*, published in 1833, with a call to the Church of his own day to look to its 'Spiritual Rulers' in resisting 'the presence in the Church, of an Heretical Power enthralling it . . . and interfering with the management of her internal affairs'.[86]

These calls for spiritual independence initially found broad support in the Church of England. Twenty Tracts had appeared by the end of 1833. They were discussed in the streets and the common-rooms of Oxford. Newman and his friends carried the Tracts around the country on horseback, and posted bundles to sympathetic clerics or lay people for local distribution. Though it is unclear how widely the early Tracts circulated outside Oxford, the movement did begin to be known nationally.[87] Froude, now dying of consumption, left England for the Barbados in November 1833, but Newman found new allies and authors. The Tracts' uncompromising language, vigorous argumentation, and call for a people's Church appealed to Church adherents, and especially younger clerics, who felt threatened on all sides by Dissenters, Radicals, and Catholics, and largely abandoned by the Church's traditional supporters, the Crown, Parliament, and aristocracy. In late 1833 and early 1834 the threat of disestablishment and disendowment was a very real one throughout the three kingdoms. The Irish Church Temporalities Act had gravely weakened the Church of Ireland and undermined its capacity to carry on a mission to the whole Irish population. The Whigs had seemed to say to the Irish Church that it could retain its

[84] [J. Keble], *Adherence to the Apostolical Succession the Safest Course*, Tract 4 (London, 1833), 1–2.

[85] J. H. Newman, *Apologia*, 70–1.

[86] J. H. Newman, *The Arians of the Fourth Century* (London, 1833), 422.

[87] Ker, *John Henry Newman*, 85; T. Mozley, *Reminiscences chiefly of Oriel College and the Oxford Movement*, 2 vols. (London, 1882), i. 329–30; F. Knight, 'The Influence of the Oxford Movement in the Parishes 1833–1860: A Reassessment', in Vaiss (ed.), *From Oxford to the People*, 128–30.

tithes and endowments, provided that it did not try to act as a branch of the true Church in Ireland. The early Tractarians were prepared to resist such a fate for the Church of England, even at the cost of a disruption of the established Church; they professed themselves ready to 'flee to the mountains' rather than submit to a State control that would compromise the Church's apostolic commission to minister to all people. The Oxford Movement shared much in common with the prophetical movement of Drummond and Irving, which had broken from the established Church in the months before the launching of the Tracts.[88] Supporters of both the Irvingite and Tractarian movements felt alienated from the State by the constitutional revolution of 1828–32; they felt that the United Kingdom was in a condition of national apostasy for having abandoned the Church's mission in Ireland. Both movements perceived a distinction between a true Church and a religious establishment. Both looked for a revival of the purity of the primitive apostolic Church—the Irvingites through a second coming of the apostolate and the renewed exercise of the Spirit gifts; the Tractarians through a restoration of the spiritual authority of the bishops as the successors of the apostles, and a revived understanding of the Church as the vehicle of living grace. There were, to be sure, differences. Most importantly, the Tractarians did not believe in the return of the Spirit gifts. In the fifth Tract, for example, J. W. Bowden asserted that the miraculous gifts of the Spirit had been withdrawn from the Church, once they had 'answered their purpose in giving it its first footing in the world', while in the thirty-sixth Tract, Arthur Perceval (whose cousin was now an apostle in the Catholic Apostolic Church) compared the Irvingites to Roman Catholics, and claimed that their 'pretended gifts' were a 'mixture of delusion and imposture'.[89]

As the year 1834 progressed, the danger that the reformed Parliament would disestablish or disendow the Church of England receded, and leaders of the established Church began to recover their confidence. The Tracts continued to appear, but they grew less alarmist and more academic in tone. The jeremiads of late 1833 against an apostate Whig State mellowed into scholarly elaborations of Church principles. In addition to the Tracts, Newman and his

[88] Gilley, 'Newman and Prophecy', 170–1.

[89] [J. W. Bowden], *A Short Address to his Brethren on the Nature and Constitution of the Church of Christ*, Tract 5 (London, 1833), 7; [A. P. Perceval], *Account of Religious Sects at present Existing in England*, Tract 36 (London, 1834), 5.

supporters now issued a series of 'Records of the Church', with stories of the apostles, aimed at educating people about the apostolic Church.[90] The Tractarians also began acting as an ecclesiastical party, employing political tactics to defend the Church's privileges and powers. In 1834, for example, they organized resistance to the liberal campaign to remove religious tests at the English universities.[91] Both universities required subscription to the Thirty-Nine Articles. At Oxford, subscription to the Articles was required for matriculation in the university; at Cambridge, subscription was required before the award of a degree. Radicals, Dissenters, and liberal reformers sought to end subscription, arguing that the universities were national institutions, and that a significant portion of the nation should not be excluded because of their denominational affiliation. A bill for the abolition of subscription was introduced by the Unitarian MP George Wood, in April 1834, and passed its third reading in the Commons in July 1834, only to be thrown out by the Lords in August. In the autumn of 1834, the former Oriel Noetic R. D. Hampden issued a pamphlet in support of admitting Dissenters to the university—arguing that the real unity of the Church was 'an invisible one' and that real religion was 'distinct from Theological Opinion'. He called upon Oxford University itself to remove the tests, rather than wait for Parliament to do so.[92] The Tractarians, in response, rallied opinion within the University against any dilution of the subscription requirement. For the Tractarians, the colleges of Oxford and Cambridge were independent corporations, offering a religious education; the removal of religious tests would undermine their educational mission. The relationship between tutor and student, Newman argued in March 1834, was a pastoral one and would be disrupted if they could not freely discuss religious truths. Ending subscription would mean that attendance at chapel could no longer be required, for how could the colleges allow 'our places of worship to be profaned by the presence of those who scorn them'?[93] In the spring of

[90] Ker, *John Henry Newman*, 87.

[91] P. B. Nockles, '"Lost Causes and . . . Impossible Loyalties": The Oxford Movement and the University', *The History of the University of Oxford*, vi. *Nineteenth-Century Oxford, Part 1*, ed. M. G. Brock and M. C. Curthoys (Oxford, 1997), 212–22; W. R. Ward, *Victorian Oxford*, 87–98; Chadwick, *The Victorian Church*, Part 1, 89–95.

[92] R. D. Hampden, *Observations on Religious Dissent, with particular reference to the Use of Religious Tests in the University*, 2nd edn. (Oxford, 1834), 28, 40–1.

[93] Newman to Hugh James Rose, 17 March 1834, Newman to the editor of the *Standard* [26 April, 1 May 1834], *Letters and Diaries of John Henry Newman*, iv. 208–12, 241–4, 245–7.

1835 the Tractarians thwarted a move to have Oxford University act unilaterally to ease the terms of the religious test, while in July 1835 a second bill to abolish subscription was rejected by the House of Lords. In the subscription campaign, the Tractarians had entered the political arena, organizing petitions and addresses, writing to the newspapers, and co-operating with other parties in Church and State.

From 1834, Tractarians developed further their defence of the established Church as a spiritual institution with a divine claim to the allegiance of the people. In doing so, they turned to the seventeenth-century Caroline divines and their conception of the Anglican communion as representing a *via media* between the extremes of Roman Catholicism and Puritanism. In the summer of 1834 Newman developed this theme in Tracts 38 and 41. Sixteenth-century Anglicans, he argued, in reforming the liturgy, practices, and discipline of their branch of the catholic and apostolic Church, had resisted 'foreign interference' from both Rome and Geneva. Instead, the English Church followed a path '*between* the (so called) Reformers and the Romanists', avoiding the errors of both.[94] The Church of England was not in its essentials a Protestant Church, but neither was it Roman. It had not broken from the apostolic tradition, even amidst the upheavals of the sixteenth and seventeenth centuries. The Anglican liturgy was rooted in the practice of the primitive Church. Anglican doctrine was firmly rooted in antiquity. The Thirty-Nine Articles, though drafted in the sixteenth century, were not a new body of doctrine, 'but in a great measure only protests against certain errors of a certain period of the Church'.[95] The idea of Anglicanism as a *via media* conformed to the national pride of an England emerging as the workshop of the world, with a great commercial empire. Here was an England central to the religious as well as political world—religiously a *via media* between Catholic authoritarianism and Protestant individualism, politically a *via media* between European despotism and American democracy.

In early 1837 Newman published his *Lectures on the Prophetical Office of the Church, viewed relatively to Romanism and Popular Protestantism*, which provided his fullest exposition of the doctrine of the *via media*. The work grew out of his prolonged controversy in the Paris religious press with the French Roman Catholic priest

[94] [J. H. Newman], *Via Media, No. I*, Tract 38 (London, 1834), 6.

[95] Ibid. 9–10; [J. H. Newman], *Via Media, No. II*, Tract 41 (London, 1834), 3.

Abbé Jean-Nicholas Jager.[96] In the lectures, Newman began by observing that the old idea of establishment, which had defined the Church of England since the Revolution of 1688, had been abandoned by the State with the constitutional revolution of 1828–32. 'We accepted', he maintained, 'the principles of 1688 as the Church's basis, while they remained, because we had received them: they have been surrendered.'[97] The Church of England, he argued, must now ground itself solely in the Anglo-Catholic faith rooted in antiquity and preserved within Church tradition. This ancient Anglo-Catholic faith stood opposed both to the popular Protestantism of the Dissenters and to the authoritarian system of the Roman Catholics. Popular Protestantism, in its emphasis on private judgement and private Bible study, tended to view the Church's discipline, doctrine, and tradition as merely 'human systems'.[98] In truth, Newman argued, popular Protestantism was itself a 'human system', 'in which only so much of the high doctrines of the Gospel is admitted, as is seen and felt to tend to our moral improvement'.[99] Popular Protestantism was concerned primarily with legitimizing our own ideas of social harmony and moral improvement. Because human nature was essentially self-interested, private judgement all too often meant extracting from Scripture materials with which to construct a comfortable personal religion. Private judgement, moreover, like human nature, was inherently 'rebellious' towards external authority and led invariably to schism.[100] Roman Catholics, on the other hand, placed their emphasis on the infallibility of the Church, but in so doing they too constructed an essentially 'human system'. The contemporary Roman Catholic Church, he maintained, was at variance with the Church of antiquity. To the testimony of the early Church, the Roman Church had added new doctrines and teachings, including the doctrine of purgatory, prayers for the dead, and the supreme authority of the Roman Pontiff.[101]

Against the errors of both popular Protestantism and Romanism, the Church of England stood firm, preserved by the guidance of tradition, which he defined as 'uniform custom'.[102] For Newman,

[96] J. H. Newman, *Apologia*, 89; Gilley, *Newman and his Age*, 132–9; Ker, *John Henry Newman*, 110–11; H. Tristam, 'In the Lists with the Abbé Jager', in H. Tristam *et al.*, *John Henry Newman: Centenary Essays* (London, 1945), 201–22.

[97] J. H. Newman, *Lectures on the Prophetical Office of the Church, viewed relatively to Romanism and Popular Protestantism*, 2nd edn. (London, 1838), 12–13.

[98] Ibid. 194. [99] Ibid. 120. [100] Ibid. 173.

[101] Ibid. 205–30. [102] Ibid. 39.

Anglican tradition took two forms. First, there was what he now termed the 'Episcopal Tradition', represented by the historic creeds and liturgical practices of the Church, which were delivered from hand to hand through the apostolic succession. Second, and more problematical, there was what he termed the 'Prophetical Tradition'. This consisted in the whole body of teachings in the Church, including the vast writings of the Fathers, and the inspired writings, sermons, stories, and customs that have been passed from generation to generation among the faithful. The Prophetical Tradition, for Newman, was made up of that

> body of Truth, pervading the Church like an atmosphere, irregular in its shape from its very profusion and exuberance; at times separable only in idea from Episcopal Tradition, yet at times melting away into legend and fable; partly written, partly unwritten, partly the interpretation, partly the supplement of Scripture, partly preserved in intellectual expressions, partly latent in the spirit and temper of Christians; poured to and fro in closets and upon the housetops, in liturgies, in controversial works, in obscure fragments, in sermons, in popular prejudices, in local customs.[103]

Newman acknowledged that the Prophetical Tradition contained both essentials and non-essentials of the faith, and that there was a difficulty in distinguishing the one from the other. In a profound sense, however, this diversity was also the strength of the Church. The Prophetical Tradition offered teachings suited to the needs of each individual, intended to nurture personal growth within the larger body of the faithful. The Church offered its teachings in a spirit of love, and asked 'for a dutiful and simple-hearted acceptance of her message growing into faith, and that variously, according to the circumstances of individuals'.[104] For Newman, the Church of England was suffused with prophetic power; the gifts of the Spirit were found in its preaching, its liturgy, its discipline, its theological scholarship, its popular stories, its church architecture, and its artistic representations. It did not need to fear, like the Church reformers, the threats posed by Radicals and Voluntaries; it did not need to look, like the Irvingites, for extraordinary signs of the last days. Rather, the Church was always under threat, always in its last days, always expecting the imminent return of Christ in glory:

> The Church is ever ailing, and lingers on in weakness . . . Religion seems ever expiring, schisms dominant, the light of Truth dim, its adherents

[103] Ibid. 305–6. [104] Ibid. 315.

scattered. The cause of Christ is ever in its last agony, as though it were but a question of time whether it fails finally this day or another. The Saints are ever all but failing from the earth, and Christ all but coming; and thus the Day of judgment is literally ever at hand.[105]

In Newman's Anglo-Catholic vision, the apostles were ever alive in the persons of the bishops, the visible Church was ever in the end time, and the Second Coming was always near.

After 1835, the Tractarians took an increasing interest in the diverse traditions of the Church, including the sacraments, ancient liturgies, the teachings of the Fathers, ancient and medieval forms of devotion, and church architecture. Tradition was elevated almost to the level of Scripture. Had not the Church Fathers, asked Keble in a sermon in 1836, employed 'Church tradition as parallel to Scripture, not as derived from it?'[106] The Tracts grew from racy leaflets into longer, more scholarly dissertations on aspects of the Anglo-Catholic tradition. This change resulted in part from the influence of Edward Bouverie Pusey, Regius professor of Hebrew and canon of Christ Church. A former liberal Anglican of aristocratic background, and a former admirer of the Evangelical Presbyterian Thomas Chalmers, Pusey had undergone a profound change in the mid-1830s. Deeply disturbed over the spread of 'infidel' ideas from Germany, Pusey had thrown aside his liberal and tolerant views, and embraced a stern, dogmatic Anglicanism. He took on a grave and grim religiosity, making it a rule never to smile and subjecting his wife and children to a harsh discipline. He fully associated himself with the Tractarians in 1835. In the summer and autumn of 1835, he contributed his *Scriptural Views of Holy Baptism*, a lengthy work of scholarly erudition which comprised Tracts 67–9. Drawing upon the teaching of the Greek as well as the Latin Fathers, he developed a closely reasoned argument for baptismal regeneration, or the traditional Catholic teaching that at baptism the individual is sanctified by the Holy Spirit, accorded remission of sins, and received into the Church. The work inspired new interest in the Church as vehicle of sacramental grace; it also, as his biographer later observed, 'at once . . . placed Pusey before the world as a leader of the Oxford

[105] J. H. Newman, *Lectures on the Prophetical Office of the Church, viewed relatively to Romanism and Popular Protestantism*, 429.

[106] J. Keble, *Primitive Tradition Recognised in Holy Scripture: A Sermon preached in the Cathedral Church of Winchester . . . September 27, 1836* (London, 1839), 23.

Movement'.[107] Pusey brought to the movement a distinguished academic reputation, political connections, a gravity of demeanour, an intense devotional life, and a rigorous self-discipline. There were also gloomy apocalyptic beliefs; like the Irvingites and Brethren, Pusey perceived signs of the approaching end of the world.[108] Were we entering, he asked in a sermon in November 1837, the last days? 'We have signs', he observed, 'that God is more than heretofore visiting the earth, and that Satan more than heretofore is let loose upon it.'[109] In the autumn of 1835 Pusey, together with Newman, Keble, and Frederick Oakeley, formed a Theological Society, to promote the view of the Church of England as both Catholic and Reformed. The following year, Pusey and Newman began The Library of the Fathers, a series of scholarly editions intended to bring the Fathers more prominently before the mind of the English Church. The first two volumes appeared in 1838.[110]

Along with their interest in antiquity, the Tractarians were also increasingly drawn to the medieval Church.[111] From the 1820s there had been in England a revival of interest in the Middle Ages, a revival associated with the historical novels and poetry of Sir Walter Scott, and the celebration of chivalry in Kenelm Digby's *The Broad Stone of Honour*, first published in 1822 and expanded to four volumes in 1828–9.[112] There was, moreover, a renewed interest in Gothic church architecture from at least the last quarter of the eighteenth century. This interest was promoted in the mid- and late 1830s through the work of the eccentric but brilliant Catholic convert Augustus Welby Pugin, with the support of his aristocratic patron, the Catholic earl of Shrewsbury. As a boy, Pugin had been taken regularly by his mother to Edward Irving's church in London, and Irving's prophetic visions may well have affected Pugin's romantic ecclesiology.[113] Converting to Roman Catholicism in 1835, at the

[107] Liddon, *Life of E. B. Pusey*, i. 346–50; Rowell, *The Vision Glorious*, 74–7; Forrester, *Young Doctor Pusey*, 65, 73–4.

[108] H. C. G. Matthew, 'Edward Bouverie Pusey: From Scholar to Tractarian', *Journal of Theological Studies*, NS 32 (1981), 101–24.

[109] E. B. Pusey, *Patience and Confidence the Strength of the Church* (Oxford, 1837), 53.

[110] Liddon, *Life of E. B. Pusey*, i. 332–42, 409–44.

[111] R. Chapman, 'Last Enchantments: Medievalism and the Early Anglo-Catholic Movement', in L. J. Workman (ed.), *Medievalism in England*, Studies in Medievalism, 4 (Cambridge, 1962), 170–86.

[112] M. Girouard, *The Return to Camelot: Chivalry and the English Gentleman* (New Haven, Connecticut, 1981), 30–66.

[113] Clarke, *Church Builders of the Nineteenth Century*, 47.

age of 23, Pugin advocated a revival of medieval Christian architecture as a stage towards the revival of a Christian society. In his *Contrasts*, published in 1836, he provided a series of twinned illustrations of medieval and modern architecture, aimed at demonstrating the superiority of the medieval vision. These illustrations included a subtle social commentary. He contrasted, for example, an illustration of a medieval monastery and a modern workhouse, to demonstrate what he believed were more humane attitudes to the poor in the Middle Ages.[114] Pugin's buildings, and even more his published writings and drawings, were soon inspiring efforts to restore existing medieval cathedrals and churches.[115]

This movement was encouraged by the Oxford Society for Promoting the Study of Gothic Architecture, formed in 1838, and still more by the Cambridge Camden Society, formed in 1839 to promote 'ecclesiology', or 'the principles which . . . guided medieval builders'. The Cambridge Camden Society was largely the brainchild of the Cambridge undergraduate John Mason Neale, a supporter of the Tractarian movement who viewed the revival of early English ecclesiastical architecture as a corollary to Tractarian efforts to revive catholic liturgical practices. Gothic architecture was, in the words of the historian Geoffrey Rowell, 'the outworking of liturgical and theological principle, an architectural medium which proclaimed a theological message'.[116] When Newman had a chapel-of-ease erected at Littlemore in 1835, it had pointed arches and a stone altar, with a cross over the altar and a side table for storing the elements.[117] In early 1839 the Tractarian *British Critic* called for the restoration of medieval interior decoration in churches, especially that of the fifteenth century, 'the gorgeous era of church architecture', which had been characterized by pointed arches, crosses over the altars, gilded rood-lofts and screens, fresco paintings, stone altars adorned with rich hangings, shrines and statues, stained glass—a richness of light and colour, all in 'perfect harmony'.[118] By the early 1840s new churches were being constructed and existing

[114] N. Yates, 'Pugin and the Medieval Dream', in G. Marsden (ed.), *Victorian Values: Personalities and Perspectives in Nineteenth-Century Society* (London, 1990), 59–70.

[115] D. Gwynn, *Lord Shrewsbury, Pugin and the Catholic Revival* (London, 1946).

[116] J. F. White, *The Cambridge Movement* (Cambridge, 1962), 24–47; M. Chandler, *The Life and Work of John Mason Neale* (Leominster, 1995), 30–44; Rowell, *The Vision Glorious*, 101.

[117] *Christian Observer*, 37 (August 1837), 502–4.

[118] 'Interior Decorations of English Churches', *British Critic*, 25 (April 1839), 368–95, 377, 381–2.

churches restored according to medieval patterns, while high-backed Georgian box pews were being removed.[119] The Tractarian Frederick Oakeley argued in the *British Critic* that the restoration of medieval church interiors should be accompanied by a revival of ancient and medieval liturgical practices and signs of devotion—the people making signs of obeisance on entering church, priests consecrating the communion elements while facing the altar, alms being offered at the altar in the kneeling position, weekly communion, turning to the east in prayer, the marking of feast days and saint's days.[120]

Tractarian writers were drawn to the history of the medieval Church. Before his premature death in 1836 Richard Hurrell Froude had written a lengthy treatise on the conflict between Thomas Becket and Henry II as an episode in the Church's continuing struggle to preserve its spiritual independence. He had portrayed Becket as a heroic figure guided by Providence.[121] The first two volumes of Froude's *Remains*, edited by Newman and Keble, were published in March 1838, with the second two volumes, including the treatise on Becket, following in 1839. The *Remains* abounded in denunciations of the Reformation and veneration for medieval piety and devotion. 'The *Remains*', Peter Nockles has observed, 'were in perfect tune with the romantic medievalism which the Movement consciously fostered and identified with historic Oxford.'[122] In 1840 the Tractarian J. W. Bowden published his *Life and Pontificate of Gregory the Seventh*, chronicling the eleventh-century conflict between the reforming pontiff and the Holy Roman Emperor, a conflict in which, like Froude's Becket, Gregory struggled to vindicate the Church's spiritual independence against the encroachments of the State. Through Gregory's efforts, Bowden maintained, the Church had 'permanently escaped . . . secularization, or amalgamating incorporation into the state'. 'To the papacy', he added, '. . . the Church of after-times unquestionably owes, on this account, a debt

[119] N. Yates, *Anglican Ritualism in Victorian Britain* (Oxford, 1999), 48–63; N. Yates, *Kent and the Oxford Movement* (Gloucester, 1983), 6–14; O. Chadwick, *The Spirit of the Oxford Movement: Tractarian Essays* (Cambridge, 1990), 46–7.

[120] [F. Oakeley], 'The Church Service', *British Critic*, 27 (April 1840), 249–76.

[121] R. H. Froude, *Remains of Richard Hurrell Froude*, Second Part, ed. J. Keble and J. H. Newman (London, 1838), ii. 1–558; Baker, 'Hurrell Froude and the Reformers', 249; Chapman, 'Last Enchantments', 171; Rowlands, *Church, State and Society*, 113–16; Newman, *Apologia*, 53.

[122] Nockles, 'The Oxford Movement and the University', 235.

of gratitude.'[123] In his highly favourable review of Bowden's book, Newman observed that Gregory had forced the world to confront the question of 'whether the Church was or was not a creature of the State'. The Church at this time had 'needed a champion, such as, through God's providence, she found'.[124] The Tractarians promoted a view of the Middle Ages, not as a time of superstition and corruption for the Church, a dark night before the dawn of the Reformation, but as an age of faith, when imposing cathedrals sent their Gothic spires to the heavens, church interiors reflected the symbolism and mystery of the faith, humble parish priests provided selfless pastoral care, and heroic popes and bishops defended the Church from the power of kings and emperors. In reclaiming the Middle Ages, Tractarians sought to recapture the fullness of the Prophetical Tradition.[125]

But if God had not forsaken the medieval Roman Church in the time of Becket and Gregory, why were Anglicans to believe so confidently that God had abandoned the modern Roman Church? Did not the Roman Catholic Church share in Newman's Prophetical Tradition? Had not the medieval popes defended the Church's spiritual independence? The Tractarians' growing awareness of the rich history of the Church soon drew them to more positive attitudes towards the Roman Catholic Church. After 1838, there was a new mood within the Tractarian movement, associated with the younger Oxford men who felt a romantic attraction to the medieval Church. This group included Frederick Oakeley, fellow of Balliol until 1839, when he took charge of Margaret Chapel, London, Frederick William Faber, fellow of University College, William George Ward, fellow of Balliol, John D. Dalgairns, John Brande Morris, and Charles Seager. They became warmly attracted to the devotional practices not only of the medieval Church, but also of the contemporary Roman Catholic Church, including fasting, private confession, and the keeping of saint's days. Weary of the political struggles over Voluntarism and establishment, Church reform and church extension, they sought a new ideal in catholic tradition and began to question traditional views of Roman 'popery' and superstition. 'The new party', wrote Newman's early biographer, 'was characterised by

[123] J. W. Bowden, *The Life and Pontificate of Gregory the Seventh*, 2 vols. (London, 1840), ii. 375, 376.

[124] J. H. Newman, *Essays Critical and Historical*, 2 vols. (London, 1887), ii. 306.

[125] Chapman, 'Last Enchantments', 177.

great enthusiasm, a disposition to startle the older and more moderate spirits, a recklessness of consequences, a certain love of paradox.'[126] They looked to Newman, with his Prophetical Tradition, as their guide and inspiration. These were the young men for whom, as one of their number, James Anthony Froude, later recalled, '*Credo in Newmannum* was the genuine symbol of faith'. The disciples now pressed their mentor relentlessly to follow the logic of his own writings on Church tradition. These would liberate the English Church from the stale debates over establishment, and lead the Church of England to look on the Roman Church, not as the arch-foe of the gospel, but as a guide to the Prophetical Tradition.[127] They themselves sat lightly on Anglicanism, and wished to see closer relations between the Anglican and Roman communions, perhaps even a corporate union. In this they received encouragement from members of the Roman Catholic communion in England, and especially the young, well-connected English Catholic converts, George Spencer (the youngest son of Earl Spencer) and Phillipps de Lisle—who in 1839–40 inaugurated a Crusade of Prayer in Catholic Europe for the return of England to the Roman communion.[128] During the summer of 1839, Newman grew alarmed over the possibility that his young protégés might begin moving as individuals into the Roman Catholic Church. 'I am conscious', he wrote to Henry Manning on 1 September 1839, 'that we are raising longings and tastes which we are not allowed to supply—and till our Bishops and others give scope to the development of Catholicism externally and visibly, we *do* tend to make impatient minds seek it where it has ever been, *in* Rome.' 'It is comparatively easy to get up a Catholic movement', he confided to H. A. Woodgate on 20 October 1839, 'it is not easy to see what barriers are to be found to its onward progress.'[129] Newman was particularly distressed over the prospect of conversions, as he was himself growing less certain that the Church of England's claims were superior to those of Rome. It was during the summer of 1839, as he later recalled in his *Apologia*, that his historical researches into the fifth-century Monophysite controversy provided him with the

[126] W. Ward, *The Life of John Henry Cardinal Newman*, 2 vols. (London, 1912), i. 67.

[127] W. Ward, *William George Ward and the Oxford Movement* (London, 1889), 136–49; Froude, *Short Studies on Great Subjects*, iv. 272–93.

[128] E. S. Purcell, *Life and Letters of Ambrose Phillipps de Lisle*, 2 vols. (London, 1900), i. 172–80.

[129] J. H. Newman to H. Manning, 1 September 1839; J. H. Newman to H. A. Woodgate, 20 October 1839, *Letters and Diaries of John Henry Newman*, vii. 133–4, 169.

unsettling vision that the Church of England might be, like the fifth-century Monophysites, a schismatic movement, and that the present-day Roman Catholic Church might be the one true Church. 'It was like a spirit rising from the troubled waters of the old world', he remembered,

> with the shape and lineaments of the new. The Church then, as now, might be called peremptory and stern, resolute, overbearing, and relentless; and heretics were shifting, changeable, reserved, and deceitful, ever courting civil power, and never agreeing together, except by its aid; and the civil power was ever aiming at comprehensions, trying to put the invisible out of view, and substituting expediency for faith.

Was not the Church of England in 1839, he implied, simply another heretical sect, competing with the Dissenters for the favour of the civil power, while the Roman Catholic Church remained stern, resolute, spiritually independent? He tried to put the thought away, but it was, he later recalled, like the vision of a ghost, and 'he who has seen a ghost, cannot be as if he has never seen it'.[130]

There was by now a renewed sense of urgency among the Tractarians. In part, this reflected a sense that the Church was again in danger. The Government and Ecclesiastical Commission proposed the reduction of the cathedrals, while Voluntaries and Radicals revived their call for disestablishment. Confidence in the *via media* was breaking down, and younger Tractarians moved in a Romeward direction. There was also growing criticism of the Oxford Movement. The first major attack had come in April 1836 when the liberal Anglican Thomas Arnold published an article on the Tractarians in the *Edinburgh Review* under the title of 'the Oxford Malignants'. He denounced 'the Oxford conspirators' as 'formalist Judaizing fanatics', seeking to impose on the Church of England the 'mere foolery' of rituals and clerical dress. Oxford, he insisted, needed to be rescued from the 'sectarian' spirit of 'High Church fanaticism'.[131] Unease over Tractarian teachings, especially their 'Popery', grew steadily among liberal Anglicans, Evangelicals, and High Anglicans. In January 1837, the Islington Clerical Association, a leading forum for Church Evangelicals, condemned the Tracts.[132]

[130] J. H. Newman, *Apologia*, 133, 135.

[131] [T. Arnold], 'The Oxford Malignants and Dr Hampden', *Edinburgh Review*, 63 (April 1836), 225–39, 234, 235, 238; T. W. Bamford, *Thomas Arnold* (London, 1960), 91–106.

[132] Hylson-Smith, *Evangelicals in the Church of England*, 115.

From mid-1837 the Evangelical *Christian Observer* regularly attacked the Tractarians for their 'Popish' innovations in liturgy and clerical dress.[133] The High Church bishop of Down and Connor, Richard Mant, published a pamphlet in 1837 in response to Tractarian Romanizers, in which he defended the Anglican Thirty-Nine Articles against the decrees and canons of the Council of Trent.[134] The publication in March 1838 of the first two volumes of Froude's *Remains*, with their expressions of hatred for the Reformers, further aroused distrust of the Tractarians and their real aims. Those who had once sympathized with Tractarian efforts to assert the spiritual independence of the Church now drew back. In May 1838, Godfrey Faussett, Margaret professor of Divinity at Oxford, preached a sermon on the 'Revival of Popery', which drew examples from Froude's *Remains* and the Tracts.[135] In his Charge of 1838, Richard Bagot, bishop of Oxford, reflected the growing sense of alarm at the Romeward direction of the movement, especially among the younger adherents. 'I would implore them', he stated with reference to the Tractarian leaders, 'to take heed . . . lest in their exertions to re-establish unity, they unhappily create fresh schism; lest in their admiration of antiquity, they revert to practices which heretofore have ended in superstition.'[136] What had begun as a movement to defend the independence and revive the authority of the national Church was, by 1838, threatening a disruption of that Church. In 1837, Newman had had reason to believe that his movement would renew the Church from within, and enable it to present a united front to Parliament. But by late 1838, he was anxious over the divisive effects of his movement and was preparing to give up the Tracts.[137] The movement was facing defeat.

In February 1841, Newman responded to the crisis in the movement with Tract 90, 'Remarks on Certain Passages in the Thirty-Nine Articles'. His aim was to halt secessions to Rome from among advanced Tractarians; it was, he later recalled, 'a matter of life and

[133] e.g. *Christian Observer*, 37 (August 1837), 502–11; 38 (February 1838), 109–14; 38 (March 1838), 164–87.

[134] R. Mant, *The Churches of Rome and England Compared in their Declared Doctrines and Practices* (London, 1837).

[135] G. Faussett, *Revival of Popery; a Sermon preached before the University of Oxford, at St. Mary's, on Sunday, May 20, 1838* (Oxford, 1838).

[136] R. Bagot, *A Charge delivered to the Clergy of the Diocese of Oxford* (Oxford, 1838), 21.

[137] D. Newsome, *The Convert Cardinals: John Henry Newman and Henry Edward Manning* (London, 1993), 128.

death'.[138] The Tract opened in a curious manner by arguing that the Thirty-Nine Articles were deeply flawed as a statement of the Church's faith. They were not only vague and uncertain. They were also Erastian in origin, adopted by the State and then imposed on the national Church. None the less, until such time as the Church reasserted its spiritual independence in doctrinal matters, it would have to be content with its defective creed. 'Till her members are stirred to this religious course', he stated, 'let the Church sit still; let her be content to be in bondage; let her work in chains; let her submit to her imperfections as a punishment.'[139] Having denigrated the Articles, Newman then proceeded to argue that for all their flaws, they did point towards Catholic truth. Reviewing the language of fourteen of the Thirty-Nine Articles, he maintained that they could be interpreted in a Catholic sense. The Articles, he observed, had been drafted in the late sixteenth century, when perhaps half the population of England and Wales remained Catholic, and the Articles had been intended to define a body of doctrine that would be as comprehensive as possible, enabling both Catholics and Protestants to subscribe. Providence had thus used the flawed Articles to frustrate the designs of Protestant extremists, and to ensure that the Church of England, as a national Church, was both Catholic and Protestant. This meant there was no need for those attracted by Catholic practices to secede from the Church in which Providence had placed them. Rather, it was the 'duty' of Anglo-Catholics 'to take our reformed confessions in the most Catholic sense they will admit' in the interest of Christian unity. 'The Protestant Confession', he insisted, 'was drawn up with the purpose of including Catholics; and Catholics now will not be excluded. What was an economy in the reformers, is a protection to us.'[140] Tract 90 was a defensive document, a plea to preserve the unity of the national Church by retaining the Anglo-Catholics within its communion.

For the growing number of opponents of the Tractarians, however, Tract 90 was not a defensive statement but a subtle form of Romish aggression, an attempt to subvert the Church of England from within by undermining confidence in its Protestantism, and

[138] J. H. Newman, *Apologia*, 147.

[139] J. H. Newman, *Remarks on Certain Passages in the Thirty-Nine Articles*, Tract 90 (London, 1841), 5.

[140] Ibid. 98, 101–2.

indeed its doctrinal foundations. The doubts about the Romanizing tendencies of the movement seemed confirmed. The Tract, which sold some 12,500 copies within the year, was widely denounced in the press. Opponents objected to what they viewed as dishonesty on Newman's part, a willingness to strain the meaning of the Articles in order to achieve a Catholic interpretation. There was outrage over Newman's descriptions of the Church of England as 'in bondage' and 'in chains', and as teaching only a vague body of doctrine. In suggesting that the Church could not be trusted in doctrinal matters, was he not undermining the very confidence in the Church that his movement allegedly sought to revive? Did not the Tractarian leader now reveal unmistakably that it was his intention to 'unprotestantize' the Church of England, to corrupt it from within? If so, was he not a more dangerous enemy of the established Church than all the Radicals and Voluntaries combined? At Oxford, all but four of the heads of houses censured the Tract, while the vice-chancellor and hebdomadal board published a statement disclaiming any university sanction for its ideas. In April 1841, at the insistence of the archbishop of Canterbury and the bishop of Oxford, a chastened Newman agreed to end the Tracts. Over the coming months, thirteen bishops, ranging from the High Church Phillpotts of Exeter to the Evangelical Sumner of Winchester, criticized Tractarian teachings in their charges. At the same time, Tractarians, including Keble, Pusey, Arthur Perceval, and W. G. Ward, came to the defence of Newman and Tract 90. Party divisions deepened. 'We can no longer blind ourselves', proclaimed W. F. Hook in 1841, 'to the fact that the Church of England is now a divided body.'[141] 'What just hope', asked John Kaye, bishop of Lincoln, of the Tract 90 conflict, 'can we entertain of the permanence of the National Church, if these divisions are to continue?'[142]

The Oxford Movement was now in crisis. What had begun as an effort to revive the influence and authority of the Church of England against the threats from Whig and Radical reformers, had become a divisive force, threatening the unity of that Church. From a movement for the assertion of the spiritual independence of the

[141] W. F. Hook, *Letter to the Bishop of Ripon, on the State of Parties in the Church of England*, 3rd edn. (London, 1841), 4; see also, F. D. Maurice, *Reasons for Not Joining a Party in the Church* (London, 1841); G. A. Poole, *On the Present State of Parties in the Church of England* (London, 1841).

[142] J. Kaye, *A Charge to the Clergy of the Diocese of Lincoln* (London, 1843), 57.

Church, it had developed into a movement for the revival of Church principles and eventually for the revival of ancient and medieval Catholic devotion and liturgy. Like the Irvingites, the Oxford Tractarians had endeavoured to revive the prophetic voice of the established Church through a recovery of its apostolic character. While the Irvingites had sought that character through a restored apostolate of the Spirit, a revival of the Spirit gifts of healing and tongues, and the development of a new liturgy, the Tractarians looked to the apostolic succession, the prophetical tradition of Church teachings, and the revival of ancient and medieval liturgies and devotional practices. What the Irvingites sought in futurist prophecy, the Tractarians sought in the prophetical traditions of the Church. Both groups had a sense of the world in its last days, under the shadow of divine judgement. Both groups sought to realize the full powers of the Church, its mystery, and the beauty of its holiness. For both, the Church was more than a creation of the State, it was a body of believers, founded by Christ and guided by the Spirit, and conveying divine grace through the sacraments. Both spoke of 'priests' and 'the holy catholic church'. Both were anxious to make the Christian religion again a truth 'to rule the world'. In the event, however, as both movements failed to transform the national Church, they became divisive forces. Denounced as enthusiasts and fanatics, the Irvingites left the established Church by 1833. Several years later, a far larger secession appeared to be looming. Denounced as Romanizers, papists, and conspirators, it seemed that the Tractarians were also to be forced out of the established Church.

The Non-Intrusionist Movement in the Church of Scotland: The Covenanted Nation

While the Anglican establishment was being both aroused and divided by the Tractarian movement, within the established Church of Scotland a party emerged that had a similar impact on the national Church. This party, the Non-Intrusionist party, shared the Tractarian commitment to restoring the prophetic voice and spiritual independence of the Church against encroachments (intrusions) from the parliamentary State. As the Tractarian party had emerged from the larger High Church party in the Church of England, so the Non-Intrusionist party developed from the larger Evangelical party in the Church of Scotland. And like the Tractarians, the Scottish Non-Intrusionists would soon become 'troublers of Israel', challenging complacency and ease within the national Church, calling for resolution and sacrifice, but also bringing bitter divisions to the Church they sought to restore.

The Non-Intrusionist movement developed out of the controversy over the role of patronage in the appointment of ministers in the established Church. A few words of explanation are in order here. Ecclesiastical patronage in Scotland, it will be recalled, was a property right, recognized and protected by the Patronage Act passed by Parliament in 1712. The person or body possessing the patronage of a parish was entitled to present a candidate to become minister of that parish. Nearly every parish in Scotland had a legal patron, with about two-thirds of the patronages owned by members of the landed gentry and aristocracy, almost one-third by the Crown, and about 5 per cent by colleges or burghs. Patrons could present only candidates who had been duly licensed by a presbytery of the Church of Scotland, and each presentation had to be accompanied by a 'call', signed by the male heads of family in the parish, signifying their willingness to have the patron's candidate as their minister. In the Church of Scotland, candidates for the ministry were ordained on being presented to their first charge. A minister was ordained only once, and previously ordained ministers who were presented to another parish were simply admitted to the living. But most presentations meant settling the candidates in their first charges. This meant that once the patron had presented a candidate to a parish living, the candidate was taken on 'trials' by the local presbytery. Only after being satisfied with the candidate's learning, doctrine, and morals, would the presbytery proceed to ordain him, with ordination carried out in the presence of the congregation.

During the eighteenth century, the parishioners' 'call' became viewed as a mere formality by the civil and ecclesiastical courts, and the courts would not allow the lack of a 'call' to interfere with the settlement of a patron's presentee. This was deeply resented by many Church members, who felt that the needs and concerns of parishioners were being ignored, while the Church deferred to the wishes of the patrons. But protests against the patronage law had proved unavailing, and during the long dominance of the Moderate party in the Church, between 1766 and 1833, Church leaders came to accept patronage. Some Moderate clergymen, such as Principal William

Robertson of Edinburgh University, leader of the Moderate party from 1766 to 1780, and a man suspicious of popular opinion, viewed patronage as a means to place 'moderate and literary' men in the pulpits, men who would contribute to intellectual improvement, social harmony, and political stability. The patron class, moreover, saw patronage as a means to fill local church pulpits with men of conservative social and political views who would teach the common people to accept their place. They also looked for men who could provide congenial company over dinner or cards at the patron's house. If these traits could be combined with effectiveness in communicating the gospel to the parishioners, so much the better, but for probably most patrons correct political views and good manners were the main criteria.

In 1834, as we have seen, the Evangelical party in the Church broke the dominance of the Moderates in the General Assembly and used its new majority to reform procedures for the settlement of ministers. The Veto Act, passed by the General Assembly of 1834, was in fact a compromise measure, intended to steer a middle course between those who wanted the complete abolition of patronage and those who wished to preserve the institution of patronage as both a property right and a link between the landed classes and the established Church. The aim of the Veto Act was to strengthen the role of parish opinion in the appointment of ministers, while at the same time respecting the rights of patrons. By the terms of the Act, a majority of the male heads of family in a parish who were in communion with the Church received the right to veto a patron's candidate, provided they sincerely believed the candidate would not be effective as their minister. In exercising their power of veto, the heads of family were not obligated to articulate the reasons for their dissatisfaction with the candidate, although they were to affirm that they had not been influenced by any factious or malicious motivations. If a presentee was vetoed, the patron had six months in which to make another presentation; if he failed to do so, the heads of family would be allowed to select their own minister. Although the House of Commons had appointed a select committee in February 1834 to look into the question of Church of Scotland patronage, the majority in the General Assembly saw no need to wait on the results of this enquiry.[143] Rather, Evangelical leaders sought legal advice from

[143] Machin, *Politics and the Churches in Great Britain*, 121.

leading Whig lawyers, including Lords Jeffrey and Moncrieff, who assured them that the Church's Veto Act was legal and would be the best way to reform patronage.[144] Indeed, Jeffrey had informed Henry Cockburn in May 1833 that he had 'lately had many conversations with Lord Melbourne, and others in high station in his Majesty's Councils, on the subject of the excitement which prevails in Scotland as to Church Patronage'. 'Their opinion', he reported, 'is, that no presentee should be forced upon a parish against the serious and earnest reclamation of a decided majority of the people; and that when this is evinced, the settlement ought not to be proceeded with, but the patron set to present anew.'[145] With such advice coming from the Government, Evangelical leaders had not believed it necessary to ask Parliament to legalize the Church's Veto Act. For them, the Veto Act was simply a means to restore the popular 'call' to its lawful place in the settlement of ministers.[146]

During the next four years, the Church of Scotland, now with a more democratic character, exhibited a new dynamism. Under Chalmers's energetic leadership, as we have seen, the church extension movement raised voluntary contributions to build about 180 new churches between 1834 and 1838. There was an extension of pastoral care, with increased house-to-house visiting by parish ministers, elders, and deacons. Parish churches appointed more elders and deacons, and exercised greater care over poor relief and moral discipline.[147] From 1835, there was a revival of the system of presbyterial visitations, with presbyteries making regular visits to each parish within their jurisdiction to examine its religious and moral condition.[148] The General Assembly began exercising a more activist leadership in the Church. In the mid-1830s, the General Assembly created a new system of standing committees to oversee what became known as the four great schemes of the Church: Church Extension, Education, Foreign Missions, and Colonial Churches.

[144] Hanna, *Memoirs of Dr Chalmers*, iii. 351–4; A. Turner, *The Scottish Secession of 1843* (Edinburgh, 1859), 169–72; J. Moncrieff to H. Brougham, 3 March and 22 May 1833, Brougham Papers, University College, London, fos. 33,269, 33,653.

[145] F. Jeffrey to H. Cockburn, 7 May 1833, Cockburn Papers, National Library of Scotland, Adv. MSS 9.1.9./Letter 218, fos. 163–5.

[146] R. Buchanan, *The Ten Years' Conflict*, 2 vols. (Glasgow, 1852), i. 258–61.

[147] G. Lewis, *The Eldership in the Church of Scotland* (Glasgow, 1834); 'The Eldership in the Church of Scotland', *Presbyterian Review*, 6 (November 1834), 28–44; R. Buchanan, *The Ten Years' Conflict*, i. 333–9.

[148] *Scottish Guardian* (Glasgow), 26 January 1836; 'Presbyterian Visitations', *Presbyterian Review*, 11 (July 1838), 77–86.

The Church Extension Committee encouraged the erection of new churches. The Education Committee raised funds for the building of new parish schools and worked to revive the system of parish education throughout Scotland. The Foreign Missions and Colonial Churches Committees oversaw the Church of Scotland's overseas mission, which had grown steadily since its beginning in 1824. Regular collections were held for these schemes, annual reports were presented and discussed in the Assembly, public meetings were conducted, and tracts and pamphlets circulated. During the five-year period from 1834 to 1838, voluntary contributions for the support of the missionary and philanthropic work of the Church of Scotland increased fourteenfold.[149]

Within the Church, there was an increased interest in Scotland's Presbyterian heritage. The writings of the Presbyterian historian Thomas McCrie—the *Life of John Knox* (1811) and *Life of Andrew Melville* (1819)—had fired the popular imagination with depictions of the Reformers as romantic heroes, standing fearlessly for the spiritual independence of the Church and the rights of a Christian people. Sir Walter Scott's *Old Mortality* (1816) had offered an engaging, but largely negative portrayal of the seventeenth-century Presbyterian Covenanters as courageous but misguided zealots. This had led to a heated exchange between Thomas McCrie and Scott in the pages of the *Edinburgh Christian Instructor* and the *Quarterly Review.* Public interest in the Covenanting experience was aroused, and Scott's novel was followed by more sympathetic fictional accounts of the Covenanters, including James Hogg's *The Brownie of Bodsbeck* (1818) and John Galt's *Ringan Gilhaize* (1823).[150] These writings contributed to a renewed veneration of the Covenanting martyrs. They were portrayed as heroes who rose from the ranks of the common people, and died for their faith on the lonely hills and moors. The new appreciation of Presbyterianism was furthered in the pages of the *Presbyterian Review*, a quarterly journal founded in 1831, and the *Scottish Guardian* newspaper, established in Glasgow in 1832.

On 20 December 1838, public meetings were held in towns across Scotland to mark the 200th anniversary of the Glasgow Assembly,

149 R. Buchanan, *The Ten Years' Conflict*, i. 330.

150 D. Mack, '"The Rage of Fanaticism in Former Days": James Hogg's *Confessions of a Justified Sinner* and the Controversy over *Old Mortality*', in *Nineteenth-Century Scottish Fiction*, ed. I. Campbell (Manchester, 1979), 37–50; D. M. Murray, 'Martyrs or Madmen? The Covenanters, Sir Walter Scott and Dr Thomas McCrie', *Innes Review*, 43 (1992), 166–75.

which had endorsed the National Covenant of 1638, abolished episcopacy, and restored Presbyterianism in the Scottish national Church.[151] At the public meeting in Edinburgh, Sir George Sinclair MP took the chair, while the packed hall responded with loud enthusiasm as speaker after speaker, mainly younger Evangelical clergymen, lauded Scotland's Presbyterian inheritance, won through the sacrifices of the Covenanters. For Charles James Brown and Robert S. Candlish, Presbyterianism rather than episcopacy was the pattern of the Church governance enjoined by Scripture and practised by the primitive Church.[152] For Thomas McCrie, the son of the celebrated historian, Presbyterianism best expressed the spirit of the Scottish nation. 'Scotsmen', he asserted, 'have never been fond of bishops from the commencement [of the Christian era].' The ancient Scottish Church, he maintained, had been Presbyterian, 'governed *communi consilio Presbyterorum*, by a common council of Presbyters'. Bishops had arrived late, in the medieval Scottish Church, 'intruded upon Scotland . . . without the consent of the Church, by one Palladius, who was sent from Rome for that purpose'.[153] The great strength of Presbyterianism, for William Cunningham, was its insistence on the strict separation of Church and State, and on the spiritual independence of the Church. In this, the Scottish Presbyterian Church provided a model for Christendom. 'I should like to know', he asked, 'what portion of the Christian Church has more interest in this truth, or a better right to proclaim it? and I should like to know what Church has done so much, or half as much, to assert and maintain it, as the Established Church of Scotland?'[154] For these Evangelicals, the Presbyterian Church of Scotland was a branch of the true Church, rooted in the practices of the primitive Church, teaching a pure Scriptural doctrine, preserved through the blood of the martyrs, and maintaining its spiritual independence and prophetic witness into the present day. The Presbyterian revival found further expression in 1839, when the 'Old Light Burgher Secession Church', which had its roots in the Presbyterian secession in 1733 and maintained a particular

[151] 'Commemoration of the Assembly 1638', *Presbyterian Review*, 11/44 (April 1839), 628–49.

[152] *Report of the Great Public Meeting in the Assembly Rooms, Edinburgh, on Thursday evening, December 20, 1838, to Commemorate the Restoration of Civil and Religious Liberty, and of Presbyterian Church Government, as Secured by the Glasgow Assembly of 1638* (Edinburgh, 1838), 22–3, 36–7.

[153] Ibid. 29–30. [154] Ibid. 53.

attachment to the Covenants, reunited with the Church of Scotland. It was, Candlish assured the Assembly of 1839 in moving the Act of Union, 'the beginning of that ingathering by which the church of Scotland might yet be the church of all the people of the land'. The Evangelical-led Church of Scotland was also beginning to perceive itself as the centre of a world Presbyterianism, with universal claims that rivalled the Anglican *via media* and an ultramontane Roman Catholicism. The Presbyterian Churches in England, in Ireland, and in Canada had all sent deputations to the Church of Scotland General Assembly of 1839.[155]

In the later 1830s, amid this revival of popular Presbyterianism, a conflict broke out between the civil and ecclesiastical courts in Scotland over the Church's Veto Act of 1834. During its first few years of operation, the Veto Act had worked reasonably well to ensure a greater popular voice in the appointment of parish ministers. The Whig Government respected the terms of the Veto Act in administering the Crown's church patronage. Private patrons endeavoured to canvass parish opinion before making presentations, and the heads of families in the parishes exercised restraint in using their veto power. Of 150 settlements of ministers between 1834 and 1839, only ten presentations were vetoed—five of them during the first year of the act's operation, when, according to Chalmers, people had been 'set agog' by their new power.[156] A crisis developed, however, when one of these vetoed presentations was challenged in the civil courts.

In October 1834, the earl of Kinnoull, patron of the Perthshire parish of Auchterarder, presented Robert Young, a probationer minister, to be ordained as the parish minister. After hearing Young preach, however, the male heads of family in Auchterarder voted overwhelmingly, 286 votes to 2, to veto Young's presentation. Young appealed against the veto in the ecclesiastical courts, but on 30 May 1835, the General Assembly, the highest ecclesiastical court, decided to uphold the veto. At this point, Young was approached by John Hope, the dean of faculty and son of the lord president of the Court of Session, the supreme civil court in Scotland. Hope was an ardent opponent of the Veto Act. An elder in the Church, he had been a member of the General Assembly of 1834, and had formally

[155] R. Buchanan, *The Ten Years' Conflict*, i. 472.

[156] Hanna, *Memoirs of Dr Chalmers*, iv. 116; T. Chalmers, *Remarks on the Present Position of the Church of Scotland* (Edinburgh, 1839), 17.

registered his dissent after the passing of the Veto Act. He now decided to test its legality in civil law. On Hope's advice, Young took his case from the ecclesiastical to the civil courts, where Hope, acting as his counsel, argued that the Church's Veto Act was an illegal encroachment on the civil rights of both patrons and presentees. The lawyers acting for the Church responded that the settlement of ministers was an internal Church matter, and that the civil courts could not interfere without intruding on the Church's spiritual independence. The Court of Session agreed to hear the case, and on 8 March 1838, it found in Young's favour by a vote of eight judges to five. According to the majority of judges, the right of patronage was a civil right, protected by civil law, over which the Church had no authority. Patronage was enshrined in the parliamentary act of 1712, and the established Church of Scotland was bound to enforce the law. In delivering his judgement, the lord president, Charles Hope, dealt summarily with the Presbyterian Church's claims to spiritual independence under the sole headship of Christ. 'That our Saviour', he maintained, 'is the Head of the Kirk of Scotland in any *temporal*, or *legislative*, or *judicial* sense, is a position which I can dignify by no other name than absurdity. THE PARLIAMENT is the temporal head of the Church, from whose acts, and from whose acts alone, it exists as the *National* Church, and from which alone it derives all its powers.'[157] Following the decision, Young raised an action in the civil courts to force the local presbytery to take him on his trials, and, if it found him sound in learning, doctrine, and morals, to ordain him minister of Auchterarder. Further, he submitted a notarial protest, holding the individual members of the presbytery liable to him for damages.

Most Church leaders were outraged by the Court's decision, and especially the language used in the judgement. They bristled over the lord president's dictum that Parliament was the 'temporal head of the Church'. In truth, the Church of Scotland had never recognized the Crown, or the Crown-in-Parliament, as its temporal head. The lord president seemed to be promulgating a new doctrine, aimed at the heart of the resurgent Presbyterianism. The General Assembly of the Church of Scotland considered the Court of Session's Auchterarder decision at its annual meeting in May 1838. It took two major actions. First, following an impassioned speech by a young

[157] R. Buchanan, *The Ten Years' Conflict*, i. 393.

Glasgow minister, Robert Buchanan, the Assembly passed, by a vote of 183 to 142, a strongly worded resolution affirming its spiritual independence. Christ, according to the resolution, was the head of the Church of Scotland, and 'therein appointed a government in the hands of Church officers distinct from the civil magistrates'. The Presbyterian courts of the Church of Scotland possessed 'an exclusive jurisdiction founded on the word of God' and this 'power Ecclesiastical . . . flows from God and the Mediator, Jesus Christ, and is spiritual, not having a temporal head on earth'. The Church's strength was in 'that great God who, in the days of old, enabled their fathers, amidst manifold persecution, to maintain a testimony, even to the death, for Christ's kingdom and crown'.[158] Secondly, the Assembly agreed to appeal against the Court of Session's Auchterarder decision to the House of Lords, the highest civil court in the United Kingdom. But the General Assembly was not united on this matter. Both these actions were opposed by a significant minority of Moderates, led by George Cook, professor of Ecclesiastical History at St Andrews University. For Cook and the Moderate party, the Church must accept the judgement of the Court of Session and rescind the Veto Act.

The House of Lords agreed to hear the Auchterarder appeal and gave its decision on 4 May 1839. It found in favour of the patron and the presentee, and declared the Church's Veto Act to be illegal. In delivering his judgement, the mercurial Whig law lord Lord Brougham (who in July 1834 had congratulated the General Assembly in the House of Lords for having passed the Veto Act) insisted that the Church had no case whatsoever. It was perfectly clear, he argued, that the law recognized only the patron's presentation as binding and that the parishioners' 'call' had always been a mere formality—of no more importance, he quipped, than the presence of the 'champion's horse' at the coronation ceremony. The desires of the parishioners, whether expressed through a 'call' or a veto, could have no bearing on the Church's legal obligation to enforce the patron's right of presentation. Brougham also dismissed the Church's claim to spiritual independence, insisting that it was 'indecent' even to suggest that the civil courts could not instruct the Church in the appointment and ordination of its ministers.[159] Needless to say, the majority in the Scottish Church was outraged by

[158] R. Buchanan, *The Ten Years' Conflict*, i. 402–9. [159] Ibid. 421–33.

the Lords' decision against the Veto, and even more by the flippant manner in which the Lords had dismissed the Church's historic claims to spiritual independence. As Lord Cockburn noted in his diary on 6 May 1839: 'The ignorance and contemptuous slightness of the judgement did great mischief. It irritated and justified the people of Scotland in believing that their Church was sacrificed to English prejudices.'[160]

There was good reason for anger and defiance in the Scottish Church. The civil courts had contemptuously dismissed two principles that most Scottish Presbyterians regarded as fundamental to the mission and identity of their Church. The first was the principle of non-intrusion, which held that the civil power must not intrude any person into the ministry of a parish against the conscientious objections of the parishioners. Such intrusions were offences against the rights of a Christian people. They would serve to alienate communities from the established Church and swell the ranks of Dissent. How, Evangelicals asked, could a minister intruded into a parish against the will of its people ever hope to gain their trust and develop a pastoral connection with them? The second, and more fundamental principle was that of the spiritual independence of the Church. The appointment of parish ministers, Evangelical leaders observed, was a spiritual act, which very often involved ordination. It was thus an internal Church matter. The Church could not grant the civil courts authority over the appointment and ordination of its ministers without reducing itself to a department of State, and turning its ministers from Christ's ambassadors into State officials.

Thomas Chalmers, the stalwart champion of the established Church idea, had initially kept a distance from the developing patronage controversy. He was not opposed in principle to patronage, provided that the wishes of the parishioners were recognized in some way. And he did not view the Veto Act as the only, or even necessarily the best, way to give expression to the popular voice. However, he was outraged by the House of Lords' Auchterarder judgement, and he took the leadership of what was now being called the Non-Intrusionist party. He blazed into action at the General Assembly of May 1839. In a stirring speech, he introduced a three-part motion in response to the Lords' Auchterarder judgement. First, the Church should refuse to ordain Robert Young as minister

[160] H. Cockburn, *Journal 1831–1854*, 2 vols. (Edinburgh, 1874), i. 225–6.

of the parish church of Auchterarder. If the State wished, it could seize the teinds, manse, church building, and parish school building at Auchterarder. But the Church would never ordain Young at the bidding of the civil courts. Secondly, the Church should reaffirm its commitment to the principle of non-intrusion, as fundamental to its identity as a Christian Church. Thirdly, the General Assembly should appoint a special committee to confer with the Government about how to end the conflict between the civil and ecclesiastical courts in Scotland, perhaps through the drafting of parliamentary legislation to legalize the Church's Veto Act. In presenting his three motions, Chalmers observed that the Church of England would never submit to the 'degradation' that the Lords proposed for the Scottish Church. 'Ask any English ecclesiastic', he stated, 'whether the Bishop would receive an order from any civil court whatever on the matter of ordination; and the instant, the universal reply is, that he would not.' Chalmers appealed to the memory of the seventeenth-century Covenanters, and insisted that their spirit still lived in the Scottish Church. 'Should the emancipation of our Church require it', he insisted, 'there are materials here . . . for upholding the contest between principle and power; and enough of the blood and spirit of the olden time for sustaining that holy warfare.'[161] He also raised the possibility of a disruption of the Church of Scotland, with the Non-Intrusionists leaving the Church, rather than submitting to control by the civil courts in spiritual matters. The General Assembly approved all three of Chalmers's motions by overwhelming majorities, and the 'holy warfare' began. A few days after the close of the Assembly, Chalmers assured the English Tory MP Sir James Graham that he was in earnest when he spoke of a possible disruption. 'Rather than be placed at the feet of an absolute and uncontrolled patronage,' he assured Graham, 'there are . . . very many of our Clergy, and these the most devoted and influential in Scotland, who are resolved to quit the Establishment.'[162]

Following the Assembly of 1839, the Non-Intrusionists began appealing for popular support through a series of *Tracts on the Intrusion of Ministers*, modelled on the Oxford Tracts and written by prominent Non-Intrusionist leaders, including Chalmers, Cunningham, Candlish, Alexander Dunlop, and Thomas Guthrie.

161 Hanna, *Memoirs of Dr Chalmers*, iv. 110, 112.
162 Machin, *Politics and the Churches in Great Britain*, 123.

It was reminiscent of the early Tractarian days in Oxford, when Newman had spoken of the Church 'looking to the people' and 'fleeing to the mountains'. The Scottish Tractarians stressed the spiritual independence of the Church, the importance of the pastoral connection between minister and parishioners, and the imperative, in a Reformed Church, of gaining the consent of the people before settling a minister among them. As Cunningham asserted: 'The power of forcing a minister upon a congregation who openly declare their decided refusal to enter into the pastoral relation with him, has no foundation in Scripture, reason, or expediency.'[163] To those who accused the Non-Intrusionists of rebellion against the State, these Presbyterian Tractarians responded that theirs was an episode in the timeless struggle between Church and State, the kingdom of Christ and the kingdom of the world. 'The world', Robert Candlish maintained,

> never sets itself against the kingdom of Christ simply as such. But it charges as rebels those who recognise another king besides Caesar, and pretends to punish them accordingly. In the days of Charles II, it was largely argued that the Covenanters were hunted and slaughtered, not at all for their religion, but for their disobedience to lawful authority.[164]

By now other vetoed candidates were taking their case to the civil courts, and the civil courts were ordering presbyteries to ordain them. In June 1839 the Court of Session threatened to imprison the entire presbytery of Dunkeld when it refused to obey the Court's instructions to proceed to the ordination of a vetoed patron's candidate. The Court also warned that the next presbytery that refused its instructions to ordain would most assuredly be imprisoned.

With tensions growing in Scotland, attention now shifted to Westminster, and the prospect of parliamentary action to bring a halt to the conflict. In May 1833, it will be recalled, leading Whigs, including Melbourne, had encouraged the General Assembly to adopt something like the Veto. Non-Intrusionist leaders, therefore, had reason to expect that Melbourne's Government would introduce legislation to legalize the Church's Veto Act. A deputation from the General Assembly's Non-Intrusion Committee visited London in July 1839, and were assured that the Government would introduce legislation in the parliamentary session of 1840. The

[163] *Tracts on the Intrusion of Ministers* [W. Cunningham], Tract 10 (Edinburgh, 1839), 6.

[164] *Tracts on the Intrusion of Ministers* [R. S. Candlish], Tract 3 (Edinburgh, 1839), 4.

Melbourne Government, however, was only limping along, and was dependent on Radical, Voluntary, and O'Connellite supporters who had no wish to rescue the established Church of Scotland from disruption. Then, in late December 1839, the earl of Aberdeen, a member of the Church of Scotland, prominent Tory politician, and close friend of the Tory party leader, Sir Robert Peel, informed Chalmers that he would be willing to introduce a bill. Chalmers, who distrusted the Whigs, jumped at Aberdeen's proposal, and in January 1840 a deputation of the Non-Intrusion Committee met with Aberdeen. Melbourne's Government was only too happy now to back away and leave the question to the Tories, and Aberdeen set about drafting a bill. Aberdeen intended legislation that would legalize some form of a congregational veto, but he also felt that the Veto Act in its present form was flawed, as it enabled the male heads of family to veto presentees without giving reasons. This, he believed, could lead to injustices. Male heads of family might veto a candidate for frivolous reasons or simply out of prejudice—because, for example, they disliked the colour of his hair—and such a rejection, with no reasons assigned, would cast a shadow over the candidate's future prospects in the Church. Aberdeen's bill, therefore, required the heads of family to state their reasons for vetoing a presentee, with presbyteries to review these reasons and decide whether or not they were valid. This would have been acceptable to most of the Non-Intrusionists. But Aberdeen's bill went farther, and allowed the civil courts to review and overturn the decisions of the presbyteries. Thus his bill continued to give the civil courts final authority over the ecclesiastical courts in matters of ordination, and failed to address the Church's main concern. This the majority of Non-Intrusionists could not accept, and in May 1840, by a vote of 221 to 134, the General Assembly decided to oppose Aberdeen's bill. Aberdeen was forced to abandon his bill, in July 1840, after its second reading in the House of Lords. Angered by what he perceived as the Non-Intrusionists' ingratitude, Aberdeen now became their implacable enemy.

Amid these growing tensions, a number of Church of Scotland Evangelicals turned to prophecy, and sought consolation in a special providence. Some looked with hopeful expectation to the launch of a Church of Scotland mission to the Jews.[165] This movement

[165] D. Chambers, 'Prelude to the Last Things: The Church of Scotland's Mission to the Jews', *Records of the Scottish Church History Society*, 19 (1977), 43–58.

had begun in the spring of 1838, when several presbyteries sent overtures to the General Assembly, requesting the formation of a Jewish mission. The initiative was inspired in part by the writings of such early nineteenth-century millenarians as Lewis Way, for whom the conversion of the Jews would be a sign of the Second Coming. It also reflected the revived interest in the seventeenth-century Covenanters, and the sense of the Scottish people as a covenanted nation, with a special connection to the people of God's first covenant. Further, the movement expressed the sense of impending crisis within the Church of Scotland and the feeling that the Church needed to recover its identity as an agent of Providence. As the historian Don Chambers observed of the origins of the Church of Scotland's Jewish mission: 'Amid the gathering storm-clouds of church-state warfare, missionary activity was insurance against disaster, because Jehovah would not desert those who held to the covenants.'[166] The General Assembly of 1838 appointed a special committee to consider the overtures, and this committee sent, in 1839, a deputation to the Middle East to explore the ground for a Church of Scotland mission to the Jews. The deputation included Alexander Keith, Scotland's foremost author on unfulfilled prophecy, and Robert Murray McCheyne, a popular, sensitive, saintly young Evangelical minister who shared the fascination with prophecy.[167] In response to their report, the General Assembly of 1840 created a standing committee on the Mission to the Jews. This became the fifth of the great 'schemes' of the Church, with a special attraction for the Non-Intrusionists. While the Oxford Tractarians embraced the language of the apostolic succession and sought inspiration in the early and medieval Church, Scottish Non-Intrusionists embraced the language of the Covenants and sought a connection with the Jewish people, the first covenanted nation.

Others in the Scottish Church looked for special Providence through religious revival. Preparations had been made by the *Presbyterian Review*, which in October 1838 called for the Church courts to be transformed into forums of prayer for a downpouring of

[166] Ibid. 51.

[167] A. Bonar, *Narrative of a Mission of Enquiry to the Jews from the Church of Scotland in 1839* (Edinburgh, 1843); A. Bonar, *Memoir and Remains of the Rev. Robert Murray McCheyne* (Edinburgh, 1844), 91–121.

the Holy Spirit upon the troubled Church of Scotland.[168] Then in the summer of 1839, a religious revival began near Glasgow in Kilsyth, a parish which had been one of the centres of the great revival of 1741–2. In July, large numbers began flooding into the parish to hear the preaching of its Evangelical Non-Intrusionist minister, William H. Burns. There were open-air meetings, conducted amid groans, wailing, prostrations, and shouts of joy. Tents were set up to accommodate the crowds, which grew to an estimated 12,000–15,000 for the celebration of communion in September. The Kilsyth community organized numerous nightly prayer and fellowship meetings, publicly burned 'infidel' books, and imposed a rigid moral discipline. Ministers travelled from as far as Aberdeen to assist at the Kilsyth services, and carried the revival back with them to their own parishes. The revival movement spread to Dundee in August 1839. There Robert Murray McCheyne provided revival leadership when he returned from the Holy Land in November 1839. During 1840 there were clusters of revivals throughout much of Lowland Scotland, and the movement spread north to Ross-shire and Skye by 1842.[169] In 1840 leading Evangelical Non-Intrusionists delivered a series of fourteen addresses in Glasgow to promote the revival. In these addresses, the conflict of Church and State formed a dark background to the revivalist zeal. For example, the Non-Intrusionist Glasgow minister John G. Lorimer insisted that 'the very warfare in which the Church has been and is at present engaged' bore 'witness to her decided growth as a spiritual church of Christ'. John Macnaughtan, minister of Paisley, observed that the struggle of 'these troublous times' had 'thrown the Church on her spiritual resources'.[170] 'As the result of this', he added, 'her strength is consolidating, even while her difficulties increase.' The revival served to heighten the sense of anticipation. 'It seems', the *Presbyterian Review* observed in January 1840, 'as if some universal convulsion were on the point of bursting forth, to wrench and shake asunder the entire fabric of society.'[171]

[168] 'Finney's Lectures on the Revival of Religion', *Presbyterian Review*, 11/42 (October 1838), 264–91.

[169] 'Revival at Kilsyth', *Presbyterian Review*, 12/46 (October 1839), 36–75; Bonar, *Robert Murray McCheyne*, 108–33; T. Brown, *Annals of the Disruption*, 2nd edn. (Edinburgh, 1893), 7–19; I. Burns, *The Pastor of Kilsyth; or Memorials of the Life and Times of W. H. Burns* (London, 1860); I. Burns, *Memoir of Wm. C. Burns* (London, 1870), 83–216; W. J. Couper, *Scottish Revivals* (Dundee, 1918), 118–29.

[170] *The Revival of Religion* (Glasgow, 1840), 234, 402.

[171] 'Doctrine of Revivals', *Presbyterian Review*, 12/47 (January 1840), 470.

It was amid these revivalist enthusiasms and apocalyptic visions that the Evangelical Non-Intrusionists confronted another major patronage dispute, that involving the Aberdeenshire parish of Marnoch. In 1837, there was a vacancy in the living at Marnoch, and a firm of lawyers representing the earl of Fife, patron of the parish, presented John Edwards. It was a curious presentation. Edwards, who had been a schoolmaster in the district for twenty years, had briefly served the assistant minister at Marnoch and had proved so unpopular that in late 1835 he had been dismissed at the parishioners' request.[172] His presentation two years later was, not surprisingly, vetoed by an overwhelming vote of 261 to 1. The patron then made a second presentation, of David Henry, who was acceptable to the parishioners. Edwards, however, appealed to the Court of Session, which in June 1839 issued an interdict forbidding the local presbytery of Strathbogie from proceeding with Henry's ordination as minister of Marnoch. The Commission of the General Assembly instructed the presbytery of Strathbogie to obey the interdict and suspend all ordination proceedings. There would, the General Assembly hoped, be a general suspension of the patronage conflict while the Non-Intrusion Committee carried on its discussions at Westminster for a legislative solution. But the Court of Session was determined to impose its authority over the Church and would recognize no truce. In July 1839, it instructed the presbytery of Strathbogie to ignore the patron's second presentation to Henry and proceed immediately to the trials and ordination of Edwards to the Marnoch ministry. It would force Edwards on the parish of Marnoch. The presbytery of Strathbogie had a narrow majority of Moderate ministers, seven men who were prepared to obey the command of the civil Court. The General Assembly instructed them to take no action. But the seven Moderate ministers of Strathbogie presbytery decided to ignore the Assembly's instruction and proceed to Edwards's trials and ordination. They would obey what they viewed as the superior authority of the Court of Session.

Rather than allow the seven Strathbogie ministers to ordain Edwards, the Commission of the General Assembly, at its meeting in December 1839, suspended the seven from their ministerial functions. The General Assembly further agreed to send other Church of Scotland ministers to the Strathbogie district to conduct religious

[172] H. Duncan, 'Mr Edwards and the Parish of Marnoch', *Witness*, 29 February 1840.

services in the churches of the suspended ministers. The seven Strathbogie ministers in turn appealed for protection to the Court of Session. On 26 December 1839, the Court of Session issued an interdict forbidding any minister from entering the churches or churchyards of any one of the seven suspended ministers without that minister's express permission. The ministers sent by the General Assembly respected the letter of the interdict and did not enter the church buildings or churchyards. Instead, they conducted religious services in the open air, in tents or in barns. The Court of Session responded on 14 February 1840 with the notorious 'extended interdict'. This forbade any Church of Scotland minister from setting foot anywhere in the parishes of the suspended Strathbogie ministers without their permission, to preach, or administer the sacraments. Non-Intrusionists responded angrily to what they portrayed as an effort by the civil authorities to forbid Church of Scotland services in part of the country. The Strathbogie ministers had been suspended from their offices by the ecclesiastical courts, and the Church felt obligated to send ministers to provide religious services to the people of those parishes. Were they returning to the days when the troopers of Charles II had hunted down Covenanting preachers and forced Presbyterians to worship in secret on the hillsides and moors? At a public meeting in Edinburgh on 24 February, Chalmers was defiant. 'Be it known, then, unto all men', he asserted, 'that we shall not retreat one footstep,—we shall make no submission to the Court of Session . . . They may force the ejection of us from our places: they shall never, never force us to the surrender of our principles.'[173] On 4 March the Commission of the General Assembly pledged to resist what it viewed as an unlawful interdict. It sent ministers into the parishes of the suspended Strathbogie seven, and, although served with interdicts and threatened with imprisonment, the ministers conducted worship.[174] 'When these Lords of Session', the Non-Intrusionist minister Thomas Guthrie later recalled, 'forbade me to preach my Master's blessed Gospel, and offer salvation to sinners anywhere in that district under the arch of heaven, I put the interdict under my feet and preached the Gospel.'[175] In the event, the Court of Session did not attempt to imprison the Non-Intrusionist

[173] Hanna, *Memoirs of Dr Chalmers*, iv. 145–6.

[174] Ibid. iv. 149–50; *Witness*, 7 March 1840; T. Brown, *Annals of the Disruption*, 33–42.

[175] T. Guthrie, *Autobiography of Thomas Guthrie and Memoir*, ed. D. K. Guthrie and C. J. Guthrie, 2 vols. (London, 1875), ii. 18.

ministers for breach of interdict. It would have been difficult, for the Non-Intrusionists were receiving considerable popular support. In August 1840, at a public meeting in Edinburgh, the Non-Intrusionists called upon the people of Scotland to sign the 'Engagement in Defence of the Liberties of the Church and People of Scotland', a document portrayed as a new national covenant, expressing commitment to the principles of non-intrusion and spiritual independence in the Church of Scotland.[176] During 1840, petitions bearing over 265,000 signatures were laid before Parliament in support of non-intrusion and spiritual independence.[177]

But the Church of Scotland was not united. The Moderate minority in the Church warmly supported the seven suspended ministers of Strathbogie, applauding their obedience to the civil law and ignoring their suspension by the General Assembly. In January 1841, on the instructions from the Court of Session, the seven suspended ministers ordained John Edwards as minister of Marnoch. The ordination took place in the face of a hostile crowd, and also a number of newspaper reporters, who fed the growing national interest in the affair. Members of the congregation had taken their places in the church at the beginning of the service. Then, as the ordination ceremony began, they all filed out in silent protest, holding worship outside in the snow. The ordination ceremony was then conducted in the presence of jeering onlookers—'outsiders', insisted the parishioners—who occupied the galleries of the church and tossed down snowballs.[178] The ordination, at the orders of the Court of Session and against the express will of the parishioners, the General Assembly, and even the patron, was, for the Non-Intrusionists, an outrage and a sacrilege. 'Can the civil court', asked the Non-Intrusionist *Witness* newspaper on 27 January, 'stretch out its arm . . . and be as God between this man and the people?'[179] Meetings of protest over the 'Marnoch intrusion' were held across Scotland and within weeks £8,000 had been raised to build a new church for the Marnoch parishioners.[180] The General Assembly, meanwhile, felt it

[176] 'Engagement in Defence of the Liberties of the Church and People of Scotland', *Presbyterian Review*, 13 (January 1841), 295–310; *Witness*, 12 August 1840; R. Buchanan, *The Ten Years' Conflict*, ii. 161–71.

[177] Ibid. ii. 121.

[178] *Witness*, 27 January 1841; *Scottish Guardian*, 26 January 1841.

[179] [H. Miller], 'The Outrage at Marnoch', *Witness*, 27 January 1841.

[180] *Scottish Guardian*, 29 January, 2 February 1841.

had to respond to the insubordination of the Strathbogie ministers. The seven suspended ministers had openly defied the sentence of the supreme ecclesiastical court in the Church of Scotland, treating its decisions as not binding when overridden by the civil courts. In an effort to end the confrontation, the Commission of the General Assembly arranged a 'brotherly' conference which the seven suspended ministers agreed to attend. But when the representatives of the Assembly arrived in Aberdeen for the meeting, they were met only by the lawyers for the seven, and informed that the suspended ministers refused to recognize the authority of the General Assembly to take any disciplinary action for their actions at Marnoch.

The General Assembly considered the defiance of the Strathbogie seven at its meeting in May 1841. The Court of Session imposed an interdict forbidding the Assembly from taking any disciplinary action, and leading politicians warned that any punishment of the seven would prove fatal to the Scottish Church. None the less, by a vote of 222 to 125, the General Assembly deposed the seven from the ministry of the Church of Scotland for their defiance of Church discipline.[181] The Church, Chalmers insisted, could not shrink from the exercise of ecclesiastical discipline out of fear of civil authority. 'If the vindication of her outraged authority', he exclaimed, 'is to be indeed the precursor of her dissolution as a national Church . . . if this is to be the last knell of the Presbyterian Establishment in Scotland, only let the Legislature say so.'[182]

With this act, a disruption of the established Church of Scotland became almost inevitable. Leading Whig and Tory politicians denounced the General Assembly for its 'ecclesiastical tyranny'. 'The presumption manifested by the general assembly in their proceedings', asserted Lord Aberdeen in presenting a petition from the Strathbogie seven in the House of Lords on 15 June 1841', 'was never equalled by the church of Rome'.[183] The Moderate minority in the Church refused to recognize the Assembly's authority to depose the seven, and rallied behind the deposed ministers, who continued to conduct worship, meet as a presbytery, occupy their churches and manses, and draw their stipends. Moderate ministers travelled to Strathbogie to assist the seven in worship and the celebration of communion. When the Commission of the General Assembly

181 *Presbyterian Review*, 14 (July 1841), 338–58.

182 Ibid. 343.

183 R. Buchanan, *The Ten Years' Conflict*, ii. 286.

warned the Moderates to cease such open flouting of its authority, the Moderate leader, George Cook, threatened to go to the civil courts and ask them to decide whether the Moderates or the Non-Intrusionists constituted the established Church of Scotland.[184]

The Non-Intrusionist movement in the Church of Scotland, like the Tractarian movement in the Church of England, had reached a crisis in early 1841. By coincidence, the publication of Tract 90 in England and the ordination of Edwards at Marnoch in Scotland occurred within two weeks of each other. For their opponents, both the Tractarians and the Non-Intrusionists were intent on emulating the absolutist model of the Roman Catholic Church. Tract 90 was denounced as an attempt to revive a Roman doctrine and liturgy within the Church of England. The General Assembly's act deposing of the Strathbogie ministers was portrayed as an attempt to impose a 'Roman' ecclesiastical tyranny in Scotland. The events of 1841 were indeed devastating blows to the Church revival movements that had promised so much only a few years before. Both the Tractarian and the Non-Intrusionist movements had emerged as efforts to revive the threatened religious establishments of England and Scotland as Churches—to convince their adherents that the established Churches were not departments of State, to be reformed and reduced by Parliament or to have ministers imposed on their congregations by the civil courts. Both movements had insisted that the national establishments were also Churches of Christ, grounded not in acts of Parliament but in the history of the Church universal, defined not by civil law but possessing spiritual independence from the State and bearing a prophetic witness to their nations. As leaders of the respective Church renewal movements, Newman and Chalmers were arguably the greatest Churchmen of their day, appealing with great eloquence for a vision of the Churches as popular, independent, spiritual institutions. An established Church, these leaders insisted, was not a creation of the State, but was an *imperium in imperio*—within the State but transcending the State with prophetic power. The task of the Church was not to serve the interests of the State by preserving social harmony through the moral instruction of the people; rather it was to transform society

[184] R. W. Vaudry, 'The Constitutional Party in the Church of Scotland 1834–1843', *Scottish Historical Review*, 62 (1983), 36–7; *Scottish Guardian*, 4, 11 June 1841; Hanna, *Memoirs of Dr Chalmers*, iv. 232–3.

and redeem humanity. In the event, however, the uncompromising zeal of the Tractarians and Non-Intrusionists had come to divide the Churches they had sought to revive. Their opponents came to feel threatened and decided to resist Tractarian 'Romanizing' and Non-Intrusionist 'tyranny'. By early 1841, with the collisions over Tract 90 and Marnoch, it became increasingly clear that Newman and Chalmers, with their respective supporters, were to be forced from the Churches they had sought so desperately to preserve and renew.

Tractarians and Non-Intrusionists: A Shared Struggle for Spiritual Independence?

The conflicts surrounding the Tractarian and Non-Intrusionist movements within England and Scotland were complicated by the antipathy that developed between supporters of the two movements. Despite their common emphasis on the spiritual independence and prophetic witness of the Church, there was no co-operation between Anglican Tractarians and Presbyterian Non-Intrusionists, and all too little Christian charity. On the contrary, the exclusive claims of the two Church movements had come to revive deep-seated, historical animosities between the Anglican and Reformed communions. During the eighteenth and early nineteenth centuries, the Church of England and Church of Scotland, linked through their common connection with the State, had, for probably the large majority of their adherents, been 'sister establishments'. There was, to be sure, a legacy of distrust. High Anglicans sometimes blamed Presbyterians for the revolutionary upheavals of the 1640s; High Presbyterians sometimes blamed Anglicans for the hunting down of Covenanters between 1660 and 1688. But the overriding emphasis in both establishments had been on what they shared in common: the Church–State connection, the parish system, and the Churches' role as guardians of the faith, inculcating loyalty to the Protestant State, preserving the social hierarchy, and promoting social harmony. This was especially true of the years of plenty for the establishments between 1808 and 1828. Most supporters of the establishments had played down the differences in ecclesiastical government, doctrine, and liturgy between the English and Scottish establishments.

In the 1830s, however, as the established Churches came under threat, as the Churches lost confidence in the State and as Tractarians and Non-Intrusionists sought to define the foundations of ecclesiastical authority, both groups came to view the differences between Anglicanism and Presbyterianism as fundamental. For the Tractarians, as we have seen, apostolic succession through bishops was an essential mark of the Church. The authority of the Church was conveyed only through this mystical and unbroken chain, stretching back through the centuries, from bishop to bishop, to Christ's laying his hands on the Apostles. Only a bishop, a successor to the Apostles, could communicate the divine commission that gave men the authority to preach, teach, and celebrate the sacraments in Christ's name. This led the Tractarians to reject openly the idea that the Scottish establishment could be a Church. In the seventh Tract of the series, for example, Newman had maintained that the clergy of the Church of Scotland were not properly ordained and therefore had no spiritual authority. 'The Presbyterian Ministers', he insisted, 'have assumed a power, which was never entrusted to them. They have presumed to exercise the power of ordination, and to perpetuate a succession of ministers, without having a commission to do so.'[185] John Keble, in the fourth Tract, insisted that 'we in England cannot communicate with Presbyterians' and compared virtuous Presbyterians to 'virtuous Heathens, Jews, or Mahometans'.[186] In Tract 20, on *The Visible Church*, Newman called on Christians to support the exclusive authority of the 'Apostolic Church' against 'all self-originated forms of Christianity'.[187]

This Tractarian critique of Presbyterianism spread within the Church of England. In April 1835, for example, the High Anglican Samuel Wilberforce informed a friend that he had become convinced that Presbyterianism was unscriptural and 'that the Episcopal form of Government is the appointment of God through his inspired apostles'.[188] In his influential sermon, 'Hear the Church', preached before the Queen in June 1838 (the published version went through 28 editions and sold over 100,000 copies), the High Church vicar of Leeds, W. F. Hook, insisted that episcopal government was necessary to a Church, and compared 'Presbyterians in Scotland' to 'Papists in France and Italy' and 'worshippers of the Mosque and votaries of Brahma'. 'The consistent English Churchmen', he insisted, would

185 [J. H. Newman], *The Episcopal Church Apostolical*, Tract 7 (London, 1833), 2.
186 [Keble], *Adherence to the Apostolic Succession the Safest Course*, Tract 4, 5–6.
187 [J. H. Newman], *The Visible Church*, Tract 20 (London, 1833), 4.
188 Newsome, *The Parting of Friends*, 173.

not worship in an established church when visiting Scotland.[189] In August 1837, Pusey assured the High Church Scottish Episcopalian lawyer James Hope that the establishment of Presbyterianism in Scotland had grievously injured, and continued to injure, the influence of the Church within the United Kingdom. He could not accept the argument that it had been right for the State to establish Presbyterianism in Scotland on the grounds that it was acceptable to most Scottish people. 'On the same grounds', he insisted, 'that Presbyterianism is established in Scotland, Romanism ought to be in Ireland, and I see no ground for thinking Romanism the worst of the two. . . . A member of the Church who upholds Presbyterianism in Scotland is, pro tanto, keeping down his own Church.' 'Our English politicians', he added, 'have much embarrassed themselves (e.g., Sir R. Peel) with the Scotch kirk . . . The identification of the interests of the two establishments I think, works serious mischief; making people think our church only an establishment, and their's altogether a sound church, because established.' The recovery of a sound understanding of Church principles, he trusted, would bring Parliament to recognize that Anglican and Presbyterian establishments were incompatible in the same Christian State.[190] In 1839–40, as the Scottish Non-Intrusionists struggled against civil interference in matters of ordination, the High Anglican *British Magazine* published a prolonged correspondence on the question of whether any minister in the Church of Scotland could be regarded as ordained. Virtually every Anglican contributor agreed that the Scottish establishment did not have an ordained clergy, because it did not maintain the apostolic succession through bishops.[191] For one correspondent, the Presbyterian clergy were 'mockers before God' in 'assuming a power which they do not possess'. In 'presuming to impart blessings to others which they have not the power to bestow', they made 'shipwreck of the souls of men'.[192] Another contributor could see no difference between the English Dissenters and the Scottish establishment; both were schismatics, in rebellion against proper episcopal

[189] W. F. Hook, *Hear the Church: A Sermon preached at the Chapel Royal, in St James Palace, on . . . June 17, 1838*, 2nd edn. (London, 1838), 6; Stephens, *Life of W. F. Hook*, i. 425–31.

[190] E. B. Pusey to J. Hope, '*Very Private*', 4 August 1837, National Library of Scotland, Hope-Scott Papers, MS 3675, fos. 192–3.

[191] *British Magazine*, 15 (January–June 1839), 37–43, 178–80, 181–4, 277–83; 16 (July–December 1839), 300–1, 532–4, 629–33, 635–8; 17 (January–June 1840), 35–8, 51–4, 198–201, 274–5, 301–7, 415–17, 656; 18 (July–December 1840), 54–5, 241–8, 372–9, 617–24.

[192] *British Magazine*, 15 (June 1839), 184.

government.[193] Still another insisted 'that nothing sacramental could be received from Scottish Kirk "presbyters" because they have nothing to give, having received nothing, neither the power of giving orders, nor of absolution, nor of retaining sins, nor of celebrating the holy communion, or any other divine office'.[194]

In July 1840, the Tractarian *British Critic*, under Newman's editorship, published a lengthy article on 'The Courts and the Kirk'.[195] The article opened by expressing admiration for the stand taken by the Scottish Non-Intrusionists in defence of the principle of spiritual independence. It agreed with the Non-Intrusionists that an established Church must have freedom from the civil power in matters of ordination and internal discipline, and it applauded their apparent willingness to suffer for their principles. But the article then went on to maintain that, having rejected apostolic government through bishops, the Scottish establishment, or Kirk, had no claim to be a Church. On the contrary, it was a schismatic body, 'founded on rebellion against the most sacred ordinances of God'; its whole history, 'down to its triumph in 1689, is stained with blood shed in rebellion'. 'It is unquestionable', the author asserted, 'that the founders of the Kirk had never received from the Church the power of ordaining . . . It is quite certain that the kirk is no Church.'[196] While the insubordinate ministers of the presbytery of Strathbogie might well deserve to be disciplined by the rules of the Presbyterian system, the Kirk had no more authority to suspend them from Christ's ministry than it had had to ordain them in the first place. The leaders of the Kirk were bound to fail in their quest for spiritual independence, because they had laid claim to a spiritual authority they did not possess.

For their part, Presbyterian Non-Intrusionists, with a revived sense of their Covenanting heritage, were equally strident against what they termed 'Oxford Popery'. There appears to have been little awareness of the Oxford Movement in Scotland before 1836 and the publication of Thomas Arnold's attack on the 'Oxford Malignants' in the *Edinburgh Review*. But after that, Scottish Presbyterians laid into the Tractarians. Beginning in January 1837, the *Presbyterian Review* published a series of articles on the Tractarians, in which it rejected their claims that episcopacy and

[193] Ibid. 16 (December 1839), 629–33. [194] Ibid. 17 (January 1840), 38.

[195] 'The Courts and the Kirk', *British Critic*, 28 (July 1840), 1–92.

[196] Ibid. 24, 86, 35.

tradition were defining marks of the Church.[197] Scripture, the *Presbyterian Review* insisted, must be the sole authority in Christianity, and Scripture, it maintained, sanctioned neither an episcopal form of Church government nor a doctrine of apostolic succession. The *Presbyterian Review* rejected the Tractarian emphasis on the Fathers and Church tradition, arguing that neither was authoritative in matters of the Faith; on the contrary, both often led people into error. There was, it insisted, 'an immeasurable distance, an impassable gulf' between the inspired canon of Scripture, and the human testimony of the Fathers and Church tradition.[198] Further, it rejected the Tractarian argument that apostolic succession was essential to a Church, arguing instead that the Church derived its authority solely from Scripture. The Tractarian claims for the exclusive authority of their Church were all too reminiscent of those earlier claims of Archbishop Laud, Charles I, and Charles II, whose efforts to suppress Presbyterianism and impose an episcopal Church upon Scotland had brought persecution and civil strife. 'Instead of glorying over us', the *Presbyterian Review* observed of the Tractarians, 'and imputing such matchless and unsullied perfection to their church, their more becoming posture would be one of solemn penitence for the wrongs [their Church] has wrought us, for the blood of the saints she has shed upon our mountains, as well as for her own grievous shortcomings in practice and flagrant errors in doctrine.'[199] In truth, it added, the Church of England was 'under a cloud' for the sin of having ejected at the Restoration of 1660 the largely Presbyterian Puritan clergy, 'two thousand of her godliest ministers', from their pastoral charges.[200]

Non-Intrusionists condemned Tractarian efforts to play down the Reformation and revive the liturgy, architecture, and practices of the Middle Ages, which Scottish Presbyterians viewed as a time of darkness and corruption. For the Evangelical *Edinburgh Christian Instructor*, the Tractarian writings revealed the Church of England to be a 'half-reformed Church', whose Reformation had been circumscribed by the Tudor monarchs. Under Tractarian influence, it was

[197] 'Oxford Popery, No. I', *Presbyterian Review*, 9/34 (January 1837), 185–210; 'Oxford Popery, No. II', *Presbyterian Review*, 9/35 (May 1837), 289–328; 'Hear the Church!', *Presbyterian Review*, 11/43 (January 1839), 559–69; 'Tracts for the Times', *Presbyterian Review*, 14/55 (January 1842), 615–52.

[198] *Presbyterian Review*, 9/35 (May 1837), 299.

[199] Ibid. 327.

[200] Ibid. 9/34 (January 1837), 204.

being corrupted by those remnants of 'Popery' which the Reformation had failed to root out of its liturgy and doctrine. The Tractarians had not invented these 'Popish' elements, but they were bringing them again to the surface.[201] There was, then, no possibility that Non-Intrusionists could make common cause with Tractarians in the struggle for the spiritual independence of the established Churches against the expanding power of the parliamentary State. In 1840, for example, while the Non-Intrusionists were decrying State interference in ministerial appointments in their Church, the Non-Intrusionist *Witness* newspaper warmly endorsed Parliament's decision to reduce the cathedral chapters, which the Tractarians viewed as an unpardonable act of State interference. The *Witness* found the High Anglican defence of the 'richly endowed Cathedrals' ridiculous and it applauded Parliament for at last doing 'a little of what the Reformation ought to have done' to the English establishment.[202]

The growing distance between the two established Churches was reflected in the changing relations between two leading defenders of the established Churches, Thomas Chalmers and the rising young Tory and High Anglican politician William Ewart Gladstone.[203] In the mid-1830s, Chalmers and Gladstone had been allies in the cause of preserving and extending the established Churches of both Scotland and England. Chalmers had been a friend of Gladstone's parents (who were both Scots) and he had cultivated a connection with their brilliant son, who had been elected to Parliament in 1832 and was committed to advancing the interests of established Christianity. The two men became friends, despite the nearly 30-year difference in their ages. During Peel's short-lived Government in 1834–5, Gladstone, who held minor office in the Government, acted as an adviser to Chalmers's campaign to secure a parliamentary grant for Scottish church extension, and as a channel of communication between Chalmers and Peel.[204] During his visits to the family home

[201] 'The Church of England a Half-Reformed Church', *Edinburgh Christian Instructor*, NS 2 (February 1839), 54–66.

[202] *Witness*, 11 April 1840.

[203] S. J. Brown, 'Gladstone, Chalmers and the Disruption of the Church of Scotland', in D. Bebbington and R. Swift (eds.), *Gladstone Centenary Essays* (Liverpool, 2000), 10–28.

[204] W. E. Gladstone to T. Chalmers, 30 December 1834; 9, 16, 26 January 2, 13, 15, 18 February, 12, 28 March 1835, New College Library, Edinburgh, Thomas Chalmers Papers, CHA 4.223.31, CHA 4.223.37, CHA 4.236.60–70, CHA 4.336.4–6; T. Chalmers to W. E. Gladstone, 13, 27 December 1834; 28 January, 10, 14, 16, 21 February, 7, 19 March 1835, BL Gladstone Papers, Add. MSS 44354, fos. 108, 134, 153, 172, 176, 177, 182, 186.

in Edinburgh in 1835, Gladstone accompanied Chalmers in pastoral visiting in destitute areas of the city, and listened sympathetically while Chalmers described his dream of transforming Scotland into a godly commonwealth through the parish structures of the established Church.[205]

After 1835, however, Gladstone came under Tractarian influence, in part through new friendships with the High Church rector of Lavington, Henry Manning, and the Anglican lawyer of Scottish background, James Hope.[206] Manning and Hope pressed Gladstone to cease his support for the Scottish Presbyterian establishment. By August 1837, Pusey was able to report to Hope that Gladstone had come around to the Tractarian position that the establishment of Presbyterianism in Scotland had been 'very injurious' to the interests of the apostolic Church.[207] In the spring of 1838 Chalmers discovered the extent of the change in Gladstone's views. The Whig Government, it will be recalled, announced in March that it would not support a parliamentary grant for Scottish church extension, and the following month Chalmers travelled to London to deliver his lectures on the establishment and extension of national Churches, in an attempt to gain Anglican support for the Scottish Church. In his lectures, Chalmers argued that it was a matter of relative indifference which denomination the State chose to establish, provided that the denomination was Protestant with a commitment to mission. Anglicans, he insisted, should support efforts to reform and extend the Presbyterian Church of Scotland, and they should in turn expect the same support from the Church of Scotland for Anglican Church reform and extension. Chalmers expected help from Gladstone, who had done so much for Scottish church extension in 1834–5 and who attended the lectures regularly. During Chalmers's series of lectures, a deputation from the Church of Scotland visited Gladstone to ask his help. They received a cold reception. Gladstone explained that he could no longer assist Scottish church extension on 'conscientious grounds', because the Church of Scotland lacked apostolic

[205] W. E. Gladstone to H. Wellwood Moncreiff, March 1880, cited in *The Chalmers Centenary: Speeches delivered in the Free Assembly Hall, Edinburgh, on March 3, 1880* (Edinburgh, 1880), 15–16; Morley, *Life of Gladstone*, i. 110; Lord Rosebery, *Miscellanies, Literary and Historical*, 2 vols. (London, 1921), i. 249–50.

[206] P. Butler, *Gladstone: Church, State and Tractarianism: A Study of his Religious Ideas and Attitudes, 1809–1859* (Oxford, 1982), 70–3.

[207] E. B. Pusey to J. R. Hope, *Very Private*, 4 August 1837, National Library of Scotland, Hope-Scott Papers, MS 3675, fos. 192–3.

succession.[208] On 14 May 1838 Gladstone conveyed to Manning his disappointment with Chalmers's lectures: 'Such a jumble of church, unchurch, and anti-church principles as that excellent and eloquent man Dr Chalmers has given us in his recent lectures, no human being ever heard.' 'He flogged', Gladstone added, 'the apostolic succession grievously.'[209]

Stung into action by Chalmers's lectures, Gladstone began writing his own book on the relations of Church and State, a subject that had been ripening in his mind for some months. He completed the first draft by late July 1838, and published the book, *The State in its Relations with the Church*, by the end of the year. In this work, Gladstone maintained that Chalmers was wrong to claim that it did not much matter which Protestant Church a State chose to establish. On the contrary, argued Gladstone, the State, in its corporate character, had the capacity to recognize religious truth and it was morally bound to enter into a connection only with a branch of the true Church. And this, he now believed, meant a Church that preserved the apostolic succession through government by bishops. Chalmers, he asserted, had 'surrendered the condition without which all others fail, in omitting from his calculation the divine constitution of the visible Church'. Gladstone could not recognize the Presbyterian establishment, whatever its virtues, as a branch of the catholic and apostolic Church. 'The Scottish establishment', he insisted, 'has deprived herself of the episcopal succession, and therein, we cannot but believe, of her strongest argument as an establishment against the competing claims of any other religious body.'[210]

Gladstone's book marked a break in his personal friendship with Chalmers, who could view the book only as a cruel blow, a further High Anglican attempt to 'unchurch' the Scottish establishment. There was no communication between the men for over a year. During that period, Scottish church extension ground to a halt, and the patronage controversy threatened the unity of the Presbyterian establishment. Then, in January 1840, Chalmers broke the silence and wrote to Gladstone, appealing for his help in finding a legislative solution to the Scottish Church crisis. Gladstone was friendly but evasive in his reply, expressing regret that their differences over Church principles had brought a breach in their former friendship,

[208] J. F. Leishman, *Matthew Leishman of Govan and the Middle Party of 1843* (Paisley, 1921), 93–6 .

[209] Morley, *Life of Gladstone*, i. 171.

[210] W. E. Gladstone, *The State in its Relations with the Church* (London, 1838), 21, 105.

and conveying a vague hope that Chalmers's attempts to secure a legislative settlement would be successful. Chalmers, increasingly desperate to find a friend at Westminster, begged Gladstone for his help. 'Let me implore', he wrote on 17 February 1840, 'your best services on behalf of our Religious Establishment in Scotland, if not as a True Church, at least as an efficient practical organ for the distribution of Christian truth and principle among the families of our land.'[211] Gladstone did not respond.

There was, in truth, little chance of gaining Gladstone's 'best services' on behalf of the Presbyterian establishment in Scotland. Since 1839, Gladstone's Scottish interests had focused, not on the difficulties of the Presbyterian Church of Scotland, but on his work, in conjunction with his High Church friend James Hope, for the restoration of the Scottish Episcopal Church to its rightful place as the true Church in Scotland. There is evidence that he perceived the impending break-up of the Church of Scotland as promising a new dawn for the Scottish Episcopal Church. In October 1839, he assured Hope that the prospects were good for the Episcopal revival, as the coming months were likely to be 'critical to the Kirk, both as an Establishment, I fear—and as Presbyterianism'. 'Do look well', he advised, 'at the Patronage question.'[212] By the summer of 1840 Gladstone and Hope had embraced the plan of establishing a college at Glenalmond, in Perthshire, that would aim both to train ordinands for the Scottish Episcopal Church and to educate Episcopalian lay leaders, who would help to guide the Scottish people back into the apostolic Church.[213] Gladstone and Hope invested considerable time and effort in raising subscriptions for the project. 'Perhaps it is perverseness', Gladstone admitted to Hope on 25 August 1840, but he had to believe that the increasing extremism of the 'Vetoists' in the Church of Scotland indicated 'that now is the time' to press forward vigorously with the college project.[214] The bishops of the Scottish Episcopal Church approved the college project in 1841,

[211] W. E. Gladstone to T. Chalmers, 7 February 1840, New College Library, Edinburgh, Thomas Chalmers Papers, CHA 4.291.30; T. Chalmers to W. E. Gladstone, 17 February 1840, BL Gladstone Papers, Add. MSS 44357, fos. 72–4.

[212] W. E. Gladstone to J. R. Hope, 24 October 1839, National Library of Scotland, Hope-Scott Papers, MS 3672, fos. 44–5.

[213] R. Ornsby, *Memoirs of James Robert Hope-Scott of Abbotsford*, 2 vols. (London, 1884), i. 206–12, 242–5.

[214] W. E. Gladstone to J. R. Hope, 25 August 1840, National Library of Scotland, Hope-Scott Papers, MS 3672, fo. 73.

buildings were erected in Glenalmond and The College of the Holy and Undivided Trinity opened in 1847. Nor were Gladstone and Hope alone in suspecting that the patronage crisis in the Presbyterian establishment was opening the way for Episcopal revival. There was, from the later 1830s, a growing interest among English Tractarians in the Scottish Episcopal Church, as a Church that had preserved its apostolic ministry amid persecution.[215] In September 1841 the *British Magazine* acknowledged that High Anglicans were attracted to the Scottish Episcopal Church in part 'because of the internal dissensions by which her ancient rival, the Kirk, has been made to totter to its base'.[216] It was perhaps not surprising that some Non-Intrusionists came to believe there was a Tractarian conspiracy behind the threatened disruption of the Church of Scotland.[217]

By 1841, then, the Tractarian and Non-Intrusionist movements were not only threatening to lead to secessions from the established Churches of England and Scotland, but they were also contributing to antagonism between the Anglican and Presbyterian establishments. Tractarians and Non-Intrusionists shared much in common—in their efforts to ground the authority of the Church in something other than Parliament, in their striving to recover the prophetic voice of the Church, in their struggle for the spiritual independence of their respective Churches. But their very different views of religious authority had also revived old enmities, which the more latitudinarian leaders of the eighteenth-century established Churches had sought to lay to rest. For the Tractarians, episcopal government and the apostolic succession were essential marks of the Church; without these, there was no Church. They also believed that authority rested in the traditions of the Church, and they were increasingly drawn to the Gothic architecture and devotional practices of the medieval Church. For them, Presbyterianism

[215] P. Nockles, '"Our Brethren of the North": The Scottish Episcopal Church and the Oxford Movement', *Journal of Ecclesiastical History*, 47 (1996), 655–82; W. Perry, *The Oxford Movement in Scotland* (Cambridge, 1933).

[216] *British Magazine*, 20 (September 1841), 241.

[217] In her novel of the Disruption, Lydia Miller, wife of the prominent Non-Intrusionist journalist Hugh Miller, suggested that Tractarianism represented a Jesuit conspiracy, committed to undermining the established Protestant Churches of both Scotland and England. [L. Miller], *Passages in the Life of an English Heiress or Recollections of Disruption Times in Scotland* (London, 1847); A. Calder, 'The Disruption in Fiction', in Brown and Fry (eds.), *Scotland in the Age of the Disruption*, 116–25.

represented the spirit of rebellion that had overthrown for a time the true apostolic Church in Britain in the mid-seventeenth century. The Presbyterian 'kirk' in Scotland, they believed, was not a true Church, but a schismatic movement born of human pride; its ministers were not properly ordained, and had no authority to preach or administer the sacraments.

For the Non-Intrusionists, on the other hand, Presbyterianism best conformed to the practice of the Church of the New Testament. Authority was derived from Scripture alone, and there was a fundamental divide between Scripture and the traditions of the Church. For Non-Intrusionists, apostolic succession was a human invention without divine warrant. Episcopal government placed too much power in the hands of fallible human beings, it surrounded the clergy with an air of superstitious mummery, and it introduced privilege into the Church. Further, episcopacy recalled for Scottish Presbyterians the civil warfare of the seventeenth century, when Covenanters had died on the hillsides in resisting the Stewart monarchs' imposition of episcopacy. Non-Intrusionists regarded the Reformation as a profound discontinuity in Christian history, a return to the true Church. They did not view the Church Fathers as authoritative and they dismissed the medieval period as a time of superstition, ignorance, and corruption. For them, the Anglican establishment was not a true Church, but a 'half-reformed Church', corrupted by elements of 'Popery'. Providence, they believed, had restored Presbyterianism to Scotland in 1690 not because Presbyterianism was agreeable to the Scottish people, but because it was the true form of Christ's Church. When they looked to more distant history, it was particularly the people of the Old Testament, the people of the Covenant, with whom they perceived a special connection.

Both movements had sought to revive the prophetic voice of the Church in modern Britain, to make the Church an independent force for the redemption of Britain's industrializing, urbanizing, class-divided society. It might well be said of both Tractarians and Non-Intrusionists, as Thomas Carlyle had said of Edward Irving, that for them 'Christian religion was to be a truth again, not a paltry form, and to rule the world'. To a very considerable extent, the two movements breathed new life into the religious establishments. Their leaders were people of ability and zeal. The movements gained broad support among the clergy of the two establishments. On the eve of the crisis over Tract 90, in January 1841, an anonymous writer in the Evangelical *Christian Observer* claimed that 'a majority of the clergy [in the Church of England] are what is nick-named "Puseyites", and we have also the testimony of their opponents that they are fast increasing in numbers and influence'.[218] This was probably an exaggeration, but not a wildly inaccurate one, if all those influenced by the Tractarian vision of the Church are described as 'Puseyites'. Within the Church of Scotland, the majority of the clergy were Non-Intrusionists in early 1841, as reflected in the strong Non-Intrusionist majorities in the General Assembly and other Church courts—majorities that held up despite the threats of punitive action from the Court of Session. The English Tractarians and Scottish Non-Intrusionists represented prophetic movements of considerable power and vision. They had grasped a vital truth in their insistence that the established Churches had to recover a sense of themselves as mystical bodies of believers, with spiritual independence from the State. But Edward Irving and John Nelson Darby had also grasped this truth, and it had taken them and their supporters out of the established Church. Prophetic movements can also be unpredictable and uncontrollable—they can pull down as well as build, divide as well as unite—and the Tractarian and Non-Intrusionist movements were by 1841 threatening to break up the established Churches that they had sought to renew.

[218] *Christian Observer*, 41 (January 1841), 20.

5

Hopes Frustrated: The Peel Government and the Established Churches, 1841–1846

Peel Returns to Power

At the beginning of June 1841, Melbourne's Whig Government, weary, distracted, and ineffectual, was brought down on a no-confidence vote. At the general election that followed, the Tories gained a majority of almost 80 in the Commons, and on 30 August 1841, Peel was called to form a Government. For the first time since the 'constitutional revolution' of 1828–32, the United Kingdom had a Tory Government with a parliamentary majority. The Tory party, after its acrimonious divisions over Catholic Emancipation, had been reconstructed during the 1830s. Under Peel's leadership, it had come to accept much of the new post-1832 political and religious order. By 1841, there was no likelihood that a Tory Government would seek to reverse the Repeal of the Test and Corporation Acts or revoke Catholic Emancipation. However, the party leader was committed to the project of building national unity around the influence and authority of the established Churches in England, Scotland, and Ireland. 'I mean to support', Peel had affirmed, amid great cheering, at a Glasgow meeting on 13 January 1837, 'the National Establishment which connects Protestantism with the State in the three countries.'[1]

Four years on from that Glasgow speech, however, the prospects of restoring the 'National Establishment' in all three countries had faded. On the 'Celtic fringe' of the United Kingdom, in Ireland and Scotland, the established Churches now seemed past hope of being made builders of national unity. However, with the formation of the Peel Government, many Anglicans did at least look for a new

[1] Kitson Clark, *Peel and the Conservative Party*, 328.

beginning for the union of Church and State in England. There a restoration of the established Church still seemed possible. A principal aim of the English Church reform movement that had been initiated by Peel's short-lived minority Government of 1834–5 had been to make the most efficient use of the Church's existing resources, so that it could extend its parish system, and in Peel's words, 'advance its banners into the desolate and unclaimed wastes of religious indifference or profligacy'.[2] Many had assumed that once the Church of England had acquiesced in the reform programme developed by the Ecclesiastical Commission, Parliament would provide new grants for church extension. The House of Commons, it will be recalled, had only narrowly defeated Sir Robert Inglis's motion for a church extension grant in June 1840. Now, with Peel in power, surely this decision would be reversed. Peel had voted for Inglis's motion in June 1840. Since 1835, moreover, he had maintained a close, co-operative relationship with Charles James Blomfield, the leading force on the Ecclesiastical Commission and the chief promoter of church extension in London.[3] In October 1841, *Fraser's Magazine* proclaimed that it had 'not the slightest possible doubt' that Peel's Government would sponsor a major church extension programme.[4] That same month the *Church of England Quarterly Review* called on Peel's Government to declare 'at once that they have accepted office with the view of . . . restoring to *Protestantism* that influence in the government of the land which for centuries belonged to it'.[5] The Church of England had, through its own efforts and with its own resources, accomplished much under the difficult conditions of the 1830s—in church extension, popular education, ecclesiastical discipline. Now, with a sympathetic Government at Westminster, the hour had surely arrived for a combined Church–State campaign aimed at restoring the influence and authority of the English Church. In October 1841, *Fraser's Magazine* claimed that more than 16,000 of the Church of England's approximately 18,000 clergymen were confident that Peel would do just that.[6]

[2] *Scottish Guardian*, 17 January 1837.

[3] P. J. Welch, 'Blomfield and Peel: A Study in Co-operation between Church and State, 1841–1846', *Journal of Ecclesiastical History*, 12 (1961), 72–3.

[4] 'Sir Robert Peel's Claim to the Confidence of the Clergy', *Fraser's Magazine*, 24 (October 1841), 387.

[5] 'Church Extension, in Relation to the Present National Crisis', *Church of England Quarterly Review*, 10 (October 1841), 367–8.

[6] 'Sir Robert Peel's Claim to the Confidence of the Clergy', 385.

At the same time, many Anglicans had doubts about Peel's religious policies. There was still considerable distrust of Peel for his 'great betrayal' of the Protestant constitution in 1829.[7] Most Tractarians, moreover, even if they acknowledged that Peel would seek to revive the influence of the established Church, questioned Peel's motives and the nature of his religious beliefs. For them, Peel was a pragmatist, with unsound religious views. As evidence for this they fastened on his address at the opening of the new Tamworth Library and Reading Room in January 1841. On this occasion, Peel (who had, it will be recalled, achieved a brilliant double First at Oxford in 1808) had praised the new spirit of intellectual improvement permeating all levels of society, and had argued that the expansion of practical knowledge in the arts and sciences would also contribute to the moral progress of humankind. Society, he maintained was entering a new era, in which technological innovation would bring an improved quality of life for all. The future was bright: there would be increased food production, increased manufactures, increased employment, and more leisure. It was time for society to put behind it the narrow religious divisions of the past, and to find unity in a broad, inclusive religious faith, with emphasis on the harmonies of the universe, the benevolence of the Creator, and the progress of humanity. Popular education, as represented by such institutions as the Tamworth Reading Room, should shun 'Controversial Divinity' and promote instead the benefits of 'mental improvement and increasing knowledge' and 'the most comprehensive view of the order of the Universe'.[8] Many applauded Peel's address, with its expression of a new national creed of work and progress.

John Henry Newman, however, was appalled. He could not abide in silence what he viewed as Peel's glib vision of moral progress through the 'march of mind'. Such ideas were especially dangerous in a man of Peel's ability, power, and influence. Writing under the name Catholicus, he laid into Peel's Tamworth Reading Room address with a series of letters in *The Times*, which were republished early in 1841 as *The Tamworth Reading Room*.[9] For Newman, Peel's

[7] 'Sir Robert Peel's Claim to the Confidence of the Clergy', 384.

[8] Sir Robert Peel, *An Inaugural Address delivered by the Right Hon. Sir Robert Peel, President of the Tamworth Library and Reading Room, on Tuesday, 19th January 1841* (London, 1841), 11, 31, 29–30.

[9] J. H. Newman, 'The Tamworth Reading Room', reprinted in *Discussions and Arguments on Various Subjects* (London, 1872), 254–305.

creed failed to take account of the stubborn reality of human sin. Mental improvement, Newman contended, would not in itself elevate morals, technological improvement would not bring happiness. This was because human nature was inherently sinful, and fallen humanity needed salvation not enlightenment. No one, Newman argued, would be saved from sin through contemplation of the natural world or through a more comfortable material standard of living. The nation was in need of redemption, insisted Newman, and Peel offered only a vague natural religion, shorn of doctrinal belief and conviction, in which reliance on Christ's atonement gave way to the cultivation of the intellect.[10] If this was the 'national religion' that Peel planned to extend into the country's 'desolate and unclaimed wastes' through a revived established Church, it would, Newman maintained, be worse than useless. The Tractarian *British Critic*, in its review of Peel's address, shared Newman's hostility and went on to denigrate Peel's reputation as a friend and defender of the Church:

> If Sir Robert Peel had even for one hour—for one half sentence—made a stand for a single sacred verity or principle, one might be encouraged to assign a milder interpretation to this loose, doubtful, tottering style of talk; but unhappily the whole career of this statesman has been one continual defalcation. From the first moment that our too-confiding Church began to lean upon this staff of a broken reed, it has never ceased to pierce her.[11]

While harsh, there were grounds for such criticism. Peel's commitment to maintaining the established Churches may have been sincere; yet there was also an element of political expediency.[12] A cultivated man, a patron of the arts and sciences, Peel seemed to value the established Churches primarily as civilizing agencies, providing religious and moral instruction to the population, promoting benevolence and virtue, preserving social harmony in the parishes, elevating tastes through the beauty of public worship, and knitting together the diverse peoples of the United Kingdom with shared values. His idea of the established Church was largely that of the 1820s. He had no appreciation for the Tractarians' prophetic fervour, uncompromising beliefs, and exclusive claims. Among the 'Puseyites', he observed to Lord Ashley in August 1841, 'Christian

[10] Ker, *John Henry Newman*, 207–12; Gilley, *Newman and his Age*, 195–8.

[11] 'The Tamworth Reading Room', *British Critic*, 30 (July 1841), 46–99, 64; see also 'The Age of Unbelief', *British Critic*, 31 (January 1842), 91–123.

[12] Machin, *Politics and the Churches in Great Britain*, 148–9.

charity is consumed in their burning zeal for their own opinions'.[13] Peel's essentially eighteenth-century religion was cool, balanced, rational, rooted in natural theology, and distrustful of dogmatic claims. In advising the Crown on Church patronage, he preferred pragmatic men like himself, committed to duty and avoiding extremes.[14]

Peel's Government, as it came to power in 1841, represented probably the last hope of restoring the old alliance of Church and State in England, the last opportunity to build a Christian nation-state around the parochial structures and educational provision of the established Church of England. The coming years would determine whether unity could be restored within the established Church in England, the church extension movement be revived and a Church-directed system of popular education be expanded. The prospects for the established Churches in Ireland and Scotland seemed doubtful. But if the old alliance of Church and State could be revived in the predominant kingdom, there might be a possibility of its revival on the Celtic periphery. Otherwise, society would continue to move in the direction of religious pluralism, of voluntaryism in Church adherence, and of more tenuous links of Church and State.

Corn, Chartism, and Young England

The formation of Peel's Government coincided with a severe downturn in the economy. Beginning in 1837, a succession of four poor harvests forced bread prices up to near famine levels, while business failures threw tens of thousands out of work. By March 1842, the home secretary, Sir James Graham, reported that over a million people in England and Wales, out of a total population of about sixteen million, were receiving poor relief.[15] The optimism of Peel's Tamworth Reading Room address now seemed misplaced. The year 1842 witnessed the worst distress experienced by Britain in the nineteenth century. 'The picture which the manufacturing districts now present', lamented the *Manchester Times* on 9 July 1842, 'is absolutely frightful. Hungry and half-clothed men and women are

[13] Parker, *Sir Robert Peel*, ii. 475. [14] Chadwick, *The Victorian Church*, i. 226–30.

[15] *Hansard's Parl. Deb.*, 3rd ser. lxiii (1841), col. 437, cited in G. Kitson Clark, 'Hunger and Politics in 1842', *Journal of Modern History*, 25 (1953), 356.

stalking through the streets begging for bread.'[16] In the Scottish town of Paisley, the collapse of the cotton shawl industry resulted in the bankruptcy of 67 out of 112 businesses between 1841 and 1843. More than a quarter of the town's population was on relief by January 1842, overwhelming the existing poor-relief system. Only urgent appeals for subscriptions throughout Britain averted widespread starvation.[17] Paisley may have been an extreme case, but the social misery was widespread, bringing a new urgency to the 'condition of England' question. Denunciations were hurled at the Government for failing to manage the economy. Peel and Graham were 'haunted men', feeling the country's suffering acutely.[18] Of England's working people, observed Thomas Carlyle in *Past and Present*, published early in 1843, 'some two millions, it is now counted, sit in Workhouses, Poor-law Prisons; or have "out-door relief" flung over the wall to them,—the workhouse Bastille being filled to bursting, and the strong Poor-law broken asunder by a stronger. They sit there, these many months now; their hope of deliverance as yet small.'[19]

The economic distress of the later 1830s and early 1840s served to direct public attention to what was becoming known as the 'condition of England' question, and the reason why Britain's world economic dominance was not assuring steadily improving living conditions for the mass of its population. The 'condition of England' question received a number of different answers. But for many, the chief cause of the distress was the corn law, with its artificial restriction on the importation of foreign grain. The corn law had been enacted in 1815 by a Parliament dominated by the landed interest. Its purpose had been to protect British agriculture from the effects of imports of cheap imported grain from the war-ravaged Continent. Initially, the law prohibited the importation of foreign grain when the market price fell below 80*s*. a quarter, which was a virtual famine price. The result was excessively high bread prices, which contributed to the acute suffering of the post-war years. The law proved increasingly difficult to defend, even in a political order

[16] Cited in D. Read, 'Chartism in Manchester', in A. Briggs (ed.), *Chartist Studies* (London, 1959), 53.

[17] T. C. Smout, 'The Strange Intervention of Edward Twistleton: Paisley in Depression 1841–3', in T. C. Smout (ed.), *The Search for Wealth and Stability* (London, 1979).

[18] Kitson Clark, 'Hunger and Politics in 1842', 357.

[19] T. Carlyle, *Past and Present* (1843) in *The Works of Thomas Carlyle*, 30 vols. (London, n.d.), x. 1–2.

dominated by the landed interest, and in 1828 a new corn law was enacted, which provided a sliding scale, with the duty on imported grain increasing as the market price fell below 73*s*. a quarter. But the revised corn law remained unpopular. For its opponents, the corn law was a form of 'class legislation', protecting the opulence of the gentry and aristocracy by keeping the price of bread for the masses artificially high. This in turn stifled the growth of manufactures and trade by thwarting the profitable exchange of British manufactured goods for foreign foodstuffs and by forcing employers to pay unnaturally high wages to their workers. Labouring families, moreover, were kept in poverty by the need to devote a considerable portion of their wages, half or more, to paying for food.

In March 1839 a group of liberal urban middle-class manufacturers, merchants, and journalists based in Manchester founded the Anti-Corn Law League, to press for the total repeal of the corn law. Influenced by the methods of mass agitation developed by the Voluntary and Church defence campaigns of the 1830s, the League issued tracts, founded journals, sent paid lecturers on circuits, formed local societies, collected subscriptions, and petitioned Parliament. The campaign was infused with missionary fervour; it was a struggle for good against evil. League agitators maintained that abolishing the corn laws would reduce class divisions and restore social harmony at home through a more equitable distribution of wealth. Abroad, it would promote universal peace among the nations through increased international commerce and global interdependence. Dissenters were particularly active in the League, perceiving a connection between landlord privilege and the privileges of the established clergy.[20] Nor was such a perception without foundation. In England and Wales, the Tithe Commutation Act of 1836 had linked the incomes of the established clergy to the price of corn, with the result that the clergy benefited from the high corn duties. 'The Church clergy', Richard Cobden, one of the founders of the League, wrote to the Quaker John Bright on 12 May 1842, 'are almost to a man guilty of causing the present distress by upholding the Corn Law—*they having themselves an interest* in the high price of bread.'[21] Dissenting ministers portrayed the corn laws as contrary to both natural justice

[20] R. F. Spall, 'The Anti-Corn-Law League's Opposition to English Church Establishment', *Journal of Church and State*, 32 (Winter, 1990), 97–123; K. R. M. Short, 'English Baptists and the Corn Laws', *Baptist Quarterly*, 21 (July 1966), 309–20.

[21] Ibid. 26.

and the word of God, and summoned their congregations to support the League as a religious duty. League journals, such as the *Anti-Corn-Law Circular*, denounced the 'Bread-Taxing Bishops'. 'The value of the tithes and teinds on which [the established clergy] fatten', observed the *Scottish Patriot* on 31 July 1841, 'is vastly enhanced, they know, by the aristocratic restrictions on the food of the community.'[22] On 17 August 1841 the League organized a conference of clergymen in Manchester, which brought together 645 ministers to denounce the corn laws as 'opposed to the law of God . . . anti-scriptural and anti-religious'. It was a Dissenting event, with only two ministers of the established Church of England and two ministers of the established Church of Scotland attending. A similar conference of Welsh clergymen, again almost exclusively Dissenters, was held in December 1841 in Caernarfon. In January 1842 Scottish Dissenters, led by the Voluntary agitator Duncan MacLaren, organized a three-day conference for clergymen in Edinburgh, which attracted 580 ministers, once again virtually all of them Dissenters.[23]

In their combined attacks on the established clergy and the corn laws, League propaganda challenged the ideal of the stable, harmonious parish community, presided over by the paternalistic alliance of squire and parson, to which defenders of the established Churches had so often appealed. In July 1843 the League propagandist Alexander Somerville, a largely self-taught former Scottish labourer who wrote under the pseudonym 'The Whistler at the Plow', published in the *Morning Chronicle* an account of a visit to an English rural parish, in which poor parishioners denounced their parson, who hunted, dined, and drank with the landed élite, while wages in the parish fell and the poor went hungry. When Somerville asked these labouring people why they continued to attend the parish church, they replied it was either from fear of dismissal or hope of charity. 'The condition of these people', Somerville asserted, 'their poverty, their hatred of the churches, their outward compliance with, but inward bitterness towards, its dignitaries, is the rule throughout rural England.'[24]

Some adherents of the established Churches, including the

[22] Cited in N. McCord, *Anti-Corn Law League 1838–1846* (London, 1958), 26–7.

[23] Ibid. 103–7; R. G. Cowherd, *The Politics of English Dissent* (New York, 1956), 134–6; Watts, *The Dissenters*, ii. 525–7; Ward, *Religion and Society in England*, 199–201.

[24] *Morning Chronicle*, 6 July 1843, cited in F. Engels, *The Condition of the Working Class in England* (1844), trans. W. O. Henderson and W. H. Chaloner (London, 1958), 303–4.

Evangelicals Thomas Chalmers and Baptist Noel, supported the repeal of the corn laws. But many others were strident in defence of those laws, portraying the corn laws and established Churches as inextricably linked, joint guardians of a paternalistic social order. In July 1841, the *Blackburn Standard* denounced the Manchester meeting of clergy against the corn laws as 'a conspiracy for the overthrow of Mother Church'.[25] The *Church of England Quarterly Review* of October 1841 argued that Christianity and the corn laws together formed the divinely ordained foundation of the social order. 'The two great elements of national peace and welfare', it averred, 'set before us in the word of God, are the culture of the social and the culture of the human heart.' Therefore, 'the two great remedies that can alone avail for our safety, are a diligent national pursuit of Christian faith, truth and righteousness, and a sedulous repression and counteraction of the artificial, mercenary, and feverish spirit of trade'.[26] By January 1843, the same journal was calling for the forcible suppression of the Anti-Corn Law League, which it denounced as an unholy alliance of 'Dissenters, Papists and Infidels', fomenting rebellion and seeking to make the State '*practically Atheist*'.[27]

The economic distress from the later 1830s also contributed significantly to the national working-class agitation for fundamental political reform, associated with the People's Charter. This movement had emerged in 1837, when members of the London Workingmen's Association had drafted the People's Charter, which contained a series of demands aimed at achieving a more representative House of Commons. A largely working-class agitation for the Charter spread across Britain in 1838–9, with mass meetings and demonstrations. In this agitation, some Chartists had directed attacks at the established Churches, embracing the Radical and Voluntary critique of the establishments as props of a corrupt and oppressive social order. In the summer of 1839, Chartists had disrupted Sunday worship in established churches in Sheffield and other Midlands towns.[28] The Chartist movement had been largely

[25] Cited in Spall, 'The Anti-Corn-Law League's Opposition to English Church Establishment', 103.

[26] 'Christianity and the Corn Laws', *Church of England Quarterly Review*, 10 (October 1841), 431–47, 432, 444.

[27] 'National Retrospects and Prospects', *Church of England Quarterly Review*, 13 (January 1843), 178–9, 196.

[28] E. Yeo, 'Christianity in Chartist Struggle 1838–1842', *Past and Present*, 91 (May 1981), 109–39; H. U. Faulkner, *Chartism and the Churches* (New York, 1916), 35–9; Soloway, *Prelates*

suppressed during the winter of 1839–40, which had been a time of violent confrontations and mass arrests. In the early 1840s, however, its leaders had revived the movement and adopted new methods, creating a National Charter Association, with local branches and regular penny-a-week subscriptions, designed to mobilize mass support. In May 1842 the Chartists presented a petition to Parliament bearing, they claimed, over 3,300,000 signatures—which the Commons then voted overwhelmingly not to receive. Frustrated over the failure of constitutional tactics, and suffering from falling wages and rising unemployment, working people in the Midlands turned to direct industrial action in July and August 1842, forcing stoppages of work, often by pulling the plugs from factory boilers. Once the stoppages began, working-class leaders attempted to organize a general strike. The movement spread widely, reaching as far as Glasgow and South Wales before being suppressed by military action.

The established clergy were deeply alarmed by the Chartist violence, viewing it as a further rejection of the paternalistic Christian social order and a revival of the working-class violence that in 1831 had led to the torching of the episcopal palace at Bristol, the torching of effigies of Anglican bishops and threats on the lives of clerics. The High Church author of Tract 83, published in 1840, portrayed Chartism as satanic, another fiery sign of these 'Times of Antichrist'.[29] For the Church of England Evangelical Edward Bickersteth, the Chartist unrest represented the 'Unclean Spirit out of the Mouth of the Beast', the 'spirit of lawlessness, self-will, and anarchy'—a sign that the Second Coming was nigh.[30] Others viewed Chartism in less cosmic terms, portraying it as a damning indictment of the existing social order, which was failing to provide a decent life for a large portion of the labouring population. Many supporters of the established Churches were profoundly influenced by Thomas Carlyle's influential pamphlet on *Chartism*, published in 1839, in which he had maintained that the sunken condition of the working classes demonstrated the fallacy of the dominant creed of political

and People, 222–4; Ward, *Religion and Society in England*, 201–2; E. R. Wickham, *Church and People in an Industrial City* (London, 1957), 99–102.

[29] Cited in Faulkner, *Chartism and the Churches*, 71.

[30] E. Bickersteth, *The Divine Warning to the Church, at this Time, of our Present Enemies, Dangers, and Duties, and as to our Future Prospects: A Sermon Preached . . . November 5, 1842* (London, 1842), 10.

economy, with its doctrine of *laissez-faire*. The country, he insisted, needed not less government, but more. Chartism was in truth a cry of a confused and abandoned people for a revival of the paternalist Christian order, in which the aristocracy would once again lead and the clergy would once again teach.[31] In *Past and* Present, published in 1843, Carlyle continued his attack on *laissez-faire*. In this work, he compared the anarchic conditions of contemporary society, driven by the impersonal forces of the market-place, with the order and spiritual values that had prevailed in medieval England. The hero of the work was the medieval monk Abbot Samson, who had not been afraid to bear a paternalist rule over his community.[32] Carlyle's comparisons of the medieval and modern resembled Pugin's book of illustrations praising medieval and denigrating modern architecture, *Contrasts* (1836), which had been reissued in 1841. Calls for a return to a paternalistic social order were in the air. In 1841, the Tory Anglican factory reformer Richard Oastler called in his *Fleet Papers* for an alliance of 'the Altar, the Cottage, and the Throne', and looked to a purified national Church to restore a paternalist England.[33] In 1840–1, in the midst of the Church–State conflict that was tearing his beloved Church of Scotland apart, Carlyle's fellow Scot Thomas Chalmers had taken time to write a new book on the care of the poor, in which he called again for a revival of the parish community ideal. Denouncing the English Poor Law Act of 1834 as a 'moral gangrene' and workhouses as 'pauper bastilles', he insisted that Scotland and indeed the whole United Kingdom needed a revival of close-knit Christian parish communities, in which better-off inhabitants would willingly assist their poorer brethren out of a spirit of Christian benevolence, directed by visiting pastors and church officers. Chartism, he maintained, was 'a vehement, but most natural outcry' against the breakdown of traditional communal sentiment and the growth of secular, legal systems of poor relief. Only a revival of communal sentiment, nurtured by national Churches, could overcome the growing class divisions in industrial society.[34]

[31] T. Carlyle, *Chartism* (London, 1839).

[32] T. Carlyle, *Past and Present* (London, 1843).

[33] C. Driver, *Tory Radical: The Life of Richard Oastler* (New York, 1946), 416, 424–34, 508–12.

[34] T. Chalmers, *The Sufficiency of a Parochial System, without a Poor Rate, for the Right Management of the Poor* (Glasgow, 1841), in *Collected Works*, xxi. 140, 162, 152; Brown, *Thomas Chalmers*, 288–96.

Within the Church of England, a group of young laymen responded to the renewed social unrest by calling for a Christian communal paternalism, infused with a romantic medievalism. This group included the young aristocrats Lord John Manners and George Smythe, who in the summer of 1838, while undergraduates at Cambridge University, had been drawn into the Tractarian movement during a visit to the Lake district. Here they had encountered the Tractarian incumbent of Ambleside, Frederick Faber, with whom they developed a close friendship. Manners and Smythe were attracted by Faber's fervent spirituality and Christian communitarianism.[35] Together with a third friend, Alexander Baillie-Cochrane, Manners and Smythe were returned to the House of Commons at the general election of 1841. In the Commons they formed a friendship with the extravagant Tory society novelist and politician Benjamin Disraeli, with his black ringlets of hair, perfumed handkerchiefs, and female conquests. By 1843 the four had formed themselves into a Tory pressure group under the name of Young England. They were influenced by the chivalric ideas of Kenelm Digby's *Broad Stone of Honour* and they venerated the romantic Anglican poet Robert Southey, viewing him as the real founder of their movement. They advocated paternalistic government, a hierarchical social order, the maintenance of the corn laws, and aristocratic responsibility for the poor. In a volume of poetry published in 1841 under the title *England's Trust*, Manners expressed his ideal of medieval Christian society, in which

> Each knew his place—king, peasant or priest,
> The greatest owed connexion with the least.
> From rank to rank the generous feeling ran,
> And linked society as man to man.

Above all, the Young Englanders looked to the Anglo-Catholic Church—redolent with medieval traditions, with rituals, prayer book, saints' days, cathedrals, quiet country churches and churchyards—as the means to reunite the diverse social orders through a shared national faith.[36] Early in 1843 Manners published *A Plea for*

[35] C. Whibley, *Lord John Manners and his Friends*, 2 vols. (Edinburgh, 1925), i. 63–74, 110; R. Faber, *Young England* (London, 1987), 9–44.

[36] Whibley, *Lord John Manners*, 96–156; Faber, *Young England*, 45–99; R. Blake, *Disraeli* (London, 1966), 168–75; D. Roberts, *Paternalism in Early Victorian England* (London, 1979), 212–15; Girouard, *The Return to Camelot*, 82–4; 'Young England', *Edinburgh Review*, 80 (October 1844), 517–25.

National Holy-Days, calling for a revived celebration of the traditional Christian holidays, both to restore the social influence of the national Church and to provide the labouring orders with the opportunity for healthy outdoor sports and recreation.[37] The following year Manners called for the formation of an Anglican sisterhood of mercy (unmarried women, living in community and dedicated to caring for others) in memory of Southey. For Manners, according to his biographer, the Church of England 'was a Church of the whole people, the centre of a revived religious life, a general and diffused worship, in which rich and poor, high and low, should join devoutly. Thus from a beneficent aristocracy and a reawakened Church a continual stream of blessings should flow. England, once more merry, should rejoice in a happy and prosperous peasantry.'[38] The Young Englanders soon attracted a wide circle of supporters, including Henry Baillie, Stafford O'Brien, Peter Borthwick, Monckton Milnes, and Henry Hope. They also received positive attention from the press, most notably *The Times*, the *Morning Post*, and the *Spectator*, which gave them an influence far greater than might have been expected from their numbers.[39]

During the session of 1843, the Young England group in the Commons evinced a special concern for the working classes. They supported legislation to limit the hours of factory labour. They advocated conciliation for Ireland and the provision of land allotments for the Irish poor. Although ostensibly supporting Peel, they grew critical of the Tory leader's pragmatism. The Tory party, they insisted, needed more attention to ideals, more commitment to reviving the influence of the Church. In May 1844 Disraeli published *Coningsby; or the New Generation*. The novel served as a manifesto for Young England. In it, he portrayed the established Church as a people's Church and a pillar of a new Tory democracy. 'The estate of the Church', insisted Millbank, the novel's voice of Anglo-Catholicism, 'is the estate of the people, so long as the Church is governed by its real principles. The Church is the medium by which the despised and degraded classes assert the native equality of man, and vindicate the rights and power of intellect.' 'It is . . . by the Church alone', he added, 'that I see any chance of regenerating the national character. The parochial system, though shaken by the fatal

[37] Lord J. Manners, *A Plea for National Holy-Days* (London, 1843).

[38] Whibley, *Lord John Manners*, i. 153–4.

[39] Gash, *Sir Robert Peel*, 386–7; Roberts, *Paternalism in Early Victorian England*, 194, 204–5, 212.

poor law, is still the most ancient, the most comprehensive, and the most popular institution of the country.'[40] In *Sybil, or the Two Nations*, published in the following year, Disraeli focused on the growing social divide. Perhaps the most memorable scene was that in which the hero first met the heroine and her father in a summer evening amid the ruins of a medieval monastery. Here Sybil's father spoke with passion of the communal ideal of the medieval Church, in which monasteries had acted as paternalistic landlords and had promoted hospitality, learning, and the arts. He contrasted this with the coldness of the present, with England divided into the 'two nations' of rich and poor. In the end, the novel suggested that the paternalist ideal might live again, if the national Church and aristocracy would again teach and lead the people.[41] More controversial was Disraeli's suggestion, running throughout the novel, that to fulfil its task the national Church must recover its spiritual independence by breaking free from its connection with the State.[42]

The beginning of the 1840s witnessed severe economic distress and a real fear of social revolution. It was also a time of crusades and high ideals—of the Anti-Corn Law League, Chartism, Young England—of visions of fundamental social reform, and a recognition that the common people were finding a voice. It was an era of ideals. 'Black, Atheistic, unsympathizing Radicalism is ended', wrote Thomas Carlyle in October 1841, 'a new nobler sort seems to me on all hands to be struggling to begin.'[43] Surely this was a time for bold action to revive the influence and authority of the Church of England.

The Limits of Establishment in England

During the parliamentary session of 1842 Peel's Government came under growing pressure to increase the provision for religious and moral instruction in England and Wales. There was a widespread feeling that the extension of the Church of England should be a priority. While the Church was doing much through its own

[40] B. Disraeli, *Coningsby; or the New Generation* (London, 1844), bk. vii. ch. 2.

[41] B. Disraeli, *Sybil; or the Two Nations* (London, 1845), bk ii. ch. 5.

[42] 'Modern Theories and Politics', *Church of England Quarterly Review*, 19 (Jan. 1846), 190–1.

[43] T. Carlyle to J. G. Marshall, 27 October 1841, *Collected Letters of Thomas and Jane Welsh Carlyle*, ed. C. L. Ryals and K. J. Fielding (Durham, North Carolina, 1987), xiii. 288–9.

resources to increase its church accommodation, Church leaders continued to urge Parliament to provide a grant for church extension. The High Church William Palmer argued in 1841 that an additional 6,000 clergymen were needed for the Church to revive its traditional pastoral care for England's greatly enlarged population. For the liberal Anglican J. C. Hare, speaking in 1842, it was 'right and fitting that the State should publicly acknowledge its obligation of providing for the spiritual wants of its people, and should not excommunicate itself from the duties of Christian love'.[44] On 7 February 1842 Sir Robert Inglis promised the Commons that he would introduce a church extension motion during that session, a pledge that he renewed on several occasions in subsequent weeks.[45] Then on 18 July 1842, near the end of the session, Peel announced that his Government would come forward with definite church extension proposals for England and Wales in 1843. The disturbances during the summer of 1842 gave church extension an added urgency, with some arguing that if there had been adequate pastoral supervision of the industrial population there would have been no Chartist agitation.[46] It was to church extension, insisted Blomfield in his Charge of October 1842, 'that the country must look, under God, for the cure of its most dangerous diseases'.[47] Throughout the autumn and winter, Government ministers deliberated on how best to support church building.[48] Outside the Cabinet there were calls for an enormous parliamentary grant. Inglis, for example, pressed for between £2,000,000 and £3,000,000, while the *Church of England Quarterly Review* argued that a large portion of the reparations required from China after the Opium War of 1839–42 should go to fund church extension (a curious proposal that would, had it been acted on, no doubt have appealed to the young Karl Marx).[49]

[44] H. E. Manning to J. C. Hare, 16, 26 February 1841, Bodl. Library, Oxford, MS. Eng. Lett., c.653/1, fos. 74–8, 82–5; W. Palmer, *An Enquiry into the Possibility of Obtaining Means for Church Extension without Parliamentary Grants* (London, 1841), 8–13; J. C. Hare, *Privileges Imply Duties: A Charge to the Clergy of the Archdeaconry of Lewes* (London, 1842), 38–9.

[45] *Hansard's Parl. Deb.*, 3rd ser. lx (1842), cols. 104, 1270; lxi (1842), col. 1115; lxii (1842), col. 1382; lxiii (1842), cols. 1611–12.

[46] S. Wilberforce, *A Charge, delivered at the Ordinary Visitation of the Archdeaconry of Surrey, November 1842*, 2nd edn. (London, 1842), 29–31; *The Times*, 26 May 1843.

[47] C. J. Blomfield, *A Charge, delivered to the Clergy of the Diocese of London at the Visitation in October 1842*, 2nd edn. (London, 1842), 63–4.

[48] Best, *Temporal Pillars*, 356–7; Gash, *Sir Robert Peel*, 382–3.

[49] 'National Retrospects and Prospects', *Church of England Quarterly Review*, 13 (January 1843), 200.

Peel, however, had pragmatically come to a very different conclusion: Parliament's decision against new State grants for church extension in June 1840, he decided, could not be reversed. A Parliament of the three kingdoms, even this Parliament with its firm Tory majority, could not be brought to provide new grants of public money for the extension of the Church of England, and any attempt to do so would raise powerful forces against both the Church and Government. 'I dread', he confided to Graham on 22 December 1842, 'for the sake of the Church and its best interests, stirring up that storm, which large demands on the public purse would inevitably excite. Ireland, Scotland, Dissent, and religious indifference, might be brought by skilful management to combine against a vote for Church Extension in England.' However compelling the arguments for new church extension grants, the Church of England would have to face political reality. Its position was vulnerable in the increasingly pluralistic society of the 1840s. 'It is very well', he continued to Graham,

> for clergymen, and for Sir Robert Inglis, to argue that it is the duty of the State to provide religious edifices wherever they are wanted, and that Dissenters are bound to build and repair and endow their own churches and those of the Establishment also, and this by new taxation wherever requisite. But you and I know that the Church and religion would suffer, and peace and charity would be sacrificed, were we in practice to push these arguments to their just logical conclusions.[50]

Any money for church extension, he concluded, would have to be found from the Church's existing resources or from private donations.

Peel introduced his Government's long-awaited church extension bill for England and Wales in the Commons on 5 May 1843. He began by acknowledging the pressing need for additional parish churches. In the diocese of Chester, he noted, there were eight districts comprising a total population of 816,000, but with church accommodation for only 97,700; in the diocese of York there were twenty districts with a total population of 402,000 but with church accommodation for only 48,000. Something clearly needed to be done. And yet, he continued, the time when Parliament could have provided major sums of public money to extend the parochial establishment had passed. It was unfortunate, but with the growth of

[50] Sir R. Peel to Sir J. Graham, 22 December 1842, *Peel Papers*, BL Add. MSS 40448, fos. 116–19.

Dissent, that was their situation. He then proceeded to describe what his Government would do. Their bill would enable the Church to borrow up to £600,000 from Queen Anne's Bounty (the fund created out of the first fruits and tenths that had been diverted from Rome to the Crown in 1533, and which in 1703 Queen Anne had directed to be used to augment the livings of the poorer clergy). This £600,000 loan would be paid to the Church of England in annual instalments of £30,000 over a period of about seventeen years. This money would be used to provide endowments to pay the stipends of new clergymen, who would be appointed to minister in heavily populated areas. Each of these newly endowed clergymen would be assigned a district, over which he would have full pastoral responsibility, free from the interference of any existing parish incumbents. That clergyman would then be encouraged to gather a congregation and to seek private donations to build and maintain a district church. It was a reversal of the previous church extension acts of 1818 and 1824, which had begun with the building of the church, and then relied on private giving and seat rents to support the minister. Peel's district churches bill began by providing a clergyman, who would be obliged to exert himself and compete in the religious market-place. Through his pastoral visiting and preaching, especially among the unchurched urban poor, he would be expected to form a parish community, and so inspire it with religious feeling and industrious habits that it would help raise the money for the stone and mortar, assisted by one of the many diocesan church-building societies. The Church of England, meanwhile, would repay the loan from Queen Anne's Bounty for the new clergymen from the savings that were gradually being accumulated through the Ecclesiastical Duties and Revenues Act of 1840. Peel acknowledged that many would be disappointed that his bill provided no new public money, but he insisted that the country would not support any such grant.[51]

The bill encountered virtually no resistance and became law in July 1843. It interfered with no interests and provided no public revenues to the Church. Even the leader of the Opposition, Lord John Russell, observed dryly that the bill 'did not appear to be of vast extent or high principle, or to be likely to produce any extraordinary results'.[52] And that was the problem. For those who had from at least

[51] *Hansard's Parl. Deb.*, 3rd ser. lxviii (1843), cols. 1277–92.

[52] Ibid. cols. 1292–95, 1297; Best, *Temporal Pillars*, 356–8.

1835 expected a significant measure of church extension from a Peel Government, the bill was profoundly disappointing. Peel's caution did not result from personal coolness towards the cause of church extension; he personally subscribed £4,000 for church building in London and the industrial districts of Staffordshire, Warwickshire, and Lancashire (while modestly forbidding any public notice of his donation).[53] Rather, the feebleness of the Act reflected his Government's conviction that there was no longer any consensus for increased State financial support for the established Church. As one German commentator observed, the power of Dissent was now such that a Government would risk its survival were it to ask for State grants for church extension.[54] Charles-Thomas Longley, bishop of Ripon, shared this conclusion, observing in his Charge of September 1844 that 'however much *we* may be inclined to rely on parliamentary precedents of former years, they will, I fear, weigh but little with that branch of the Legislature, whose constitution has been so materially altered since the last national grants were made'.[55] Whatever the pragmatic politics behind Peel's decision, however, many within the Church felt betrayed by the Government's refusal even to attempt to persuade Parliament of its obligation to provide the established Church with the resources needed to extend religious instruction and pastoral care to a rapidly growing population. The Government had surrendered without a fight a fundamental principle of a religious establishment—that it be commensurate with the size of the population. 'The Government', insisted the *Church of England Quarterly Review* in July 1843, 'has no right to assume, and has no grounds for assuming, that the Parliament would refuse to make such grants as it would propose.'[56]

Anglicans were further disappointed by the Peel Government's efforts to expand popular education. During the late 1830s, it will be recalled, the Church of England had made major strides in educating the poor. In the competition with the Dissenter-dominated British and Foreign Society for State grants in aid of school building,

[53] Gash, *Sir Robert Peel*, 383.

[54] F. Uhden, *The Anglican Church in the Nineteenth Century*, trans. W. C. C. Humphreys (London, 1844), 157–8.

[55] Charles-Thomas Longley, Bishop of Ripon, *A Charge addressed to the Clergy of the Diocese of Ripon . . . in September 1844* (London, 1844), 17.

[56] 'Church Extension, by Clerical Endowment', *Church of England Quarterly Review*, 14 (July 1843), 121.

the Church's National Society won the lion's share. The Church established diocesan education societies and diocesan teacher training schools across the country. As the Tories came to power in 1841, many expected that the Government would provide large-scale support to the Church's efforts to educate the children of the poor. In late 1842 the home secretary, Sir James Graham, drafted a bill for the improvement of the Factory Act of 1833, which included a provision for the education of child-workers in the factories. It was a sweeping measure, and a response in part to the working-class unrest. 'The education of the rising youth', he had insisted to James Kay of Manchester on 31 August 1842, 'should be the peculiar care of the Government: its neglect is one of the principal causes of the Evil spirit, which now actuates large masses of the community.'[57] Graham's bill proposed to reduce the working day for children between the ages of 8 and 13 to six-and-a-half hours, and then require factory children to attend school for at least three hours daily, five days a week. The schools for factory children were to be supported from local rates on property and from small deductions from the children's incomes. Each school would be managed by a board of seven trustees, of which the chairman would be either the parish clergyman or (if the school district included more than one parish) a local established clergyman named by the bishop of the diocese. The rest of the board would be made up of two churchwardens, two members named by the factory masters, and two representatives of the ratepayers, selected annually by the magistrates. The schools were to provide religious instruction, which would include teaching from the Church of England catechism and prayer book for up to an hour daily. The schoolmaster was also to lead the children in daily prayer and ensure their attendance at a Church of England Sunday school. Dissenting parents were allowed to remove their children during the daily hour of Anglican instruction, and if the parents requested it, licensed Dissenting clergymen could provide religious instruction to Dissenting children for up to one hour a week. While the bill would initially have affected only about 30,000 children, Graham viewed it as the beginning of a national system of rate-aided schools, governed by local boards and under central State supervision. It was also to be an Anglican system.[58] 'By the education

[57] Selleck, *James Kay Shuttleworth*, 201.

[58] Ibid. 202–4; Paz, *Politics of Working-Class Education*, 114–18, 124.

clauses, as they now stand', he privately assured the High Anglican Gladstone, 'the Church has ample security that every master in the new schools will be a Churchman, and that the teaching of the Holy Scriptures, as far as the limited exposition may be carried, will necessarily be in conformity with his creed.'[59] For supporters of the bill, it seemed obvious that State-supported popular education must be directed by the established Church.[60]

For opponents of the bill, this appeared far less obvious. Graham introduced his bill on 28 February 1843, and immediately Dissenters mounted a ferocious and brilliantly organized opposition. Under the editorship of Edward Miall, the *Nonconformist* newspaper, founded in April 1841 to oppose the principle of established religion, took a leading role in rousing Dissenting feeling against Graham's bill and orchestrating a national campaign.[61] For Dissenters, the bill was both an assault on the liberties of Dissenters and an attempt to regain the conformity of the whole nation to the established Church by winning over the next generation. 'It is', insisted the *Eclectic Review* of Graham's plan in May 1843, 'a church-extension scheme which the government has propounded.'[62] Dissenters were united as never before since the agitation for the Repeal of the Test and Corporation Acts, while their organization reflected the methods developed by the Voluntary campaign and the Anti-Corn Law League. By the end of April opponents of the bill had sent in 13,369 petitions bearing over 2,068,000 signatures. These petitions, Graham admitted to the Commons on 1 May, were 'numerous almost without a parallel'.[63] He attempted to soften opposition by amending the bill, but the Dissenting campaign continued unabated, with eventually some 24,000 petitions bearing over 4,000,000 signatures being presented. It was unprecedented. 'The old spirit of the puritans', enthused the *Eclectic Review* of June 1843, 'has returned to their children.' One MP

[59] Parker, *Life and Letters of Sir James Graham*, i. 344.

[60] *The Times*, 26 May 1843; 'The Factory Education Bill and the Dissenters', *Church of England Quarterly Review*, 14 (July 1843), 161–84.

[61] For the controversy over Graham's bill of 1843, see J. T. Ward and J. H. Treble, 'Religion and Education in 1843: Reaction to the "Factory Education Bill"', *Journal of Ecclesiastical History*, 20 (1969), 79–110; Paz, *Politics of Working-Class Education*, 114–25; D. Hempton, *Methodism and Politics in British Society 1750–1850* (London, 1984), 164–71; Machin, *Politics and the Churches in Great Britain, 1832 to 1868*, 151–60; Soloway, *Prelates and People*, 411–18.

[62] 'Factories Education Bill', *Eclectic Review*, NS 13 (May 1843), 594; A. Miall, *Life of Edward Miall* (London, 1884), 90.

[63] *Hansard's Parl. Deb.*, 3rd ser. lxviii (1843), col. 1104.

presented over 500 petitions on a single night, requiring the assistance of four fellow MPs to carry them to the table.[64] Finally, on 15 June 1843, Graham announced that due to the 'insuperable objections' from a large portion of the Dissenting community, the Government would withdraw the education clauses from the bill, and reintroduce a truncated factory bill in the next session. 'It is', Peel confided to the Evangelical Anglican Lord Ashley, on 16 June 1843, 'but a sorry and lamentable triumph that Dissent has achieved.'[65]

The defeat was a devastating blow to the idea of a Church-directed national system of education in England and Wales. The Peel Government now concluded that it could never raise again the proposal for a national system of education. In the view of many Church supporters, the Government's withdrawal of the bill had been another miserable climbdown, reflecting lack of commitment to the established Church. For Samuel Wilberforce, writing to J. W. Croker on 19 April 1843, Peel was facing 'the very crisis of the moral power of his government'. The established Church, Wilberforce insisted, was recovering its former influence, and now had the support of some twelve million of England's sixteen million people. 'A marvellous change', he insisted, 'has come over the mind of England.' It made no sense to sacrifice the religious and moral instruction of the factory children in an effort to conciliate four million Dissenters who would, in any event, be satisfied with nothing less than the end of the established Church.[66] The failure of Graham's bill raised further questions about the future of the establishment. Church reformers during the past decade had emphasized the social duties of the established Church. But now that the Church was embracing its responsibilities, the State was unable to give it support, because of what Church supporters viewed as the selfishness of a Dissenting minority. If even a Tory Government dared not provide the established Church of England with the resources it needed to extend pastoral care and popular education, would not the Church be better off without the trappings of establishment? Had not the time arrived for the Church to throw off its reliance on the State and look to the voluntary support of the people?

64 'The Government Education Bill', *Eclectic Review*, NS 13 (June 1843), 698; Miall, *Life of Edward Miall*, 91.

65 Parker, *Sir Robert Peel*, ii. 560–2.

66 *The Times*, 26 May 1843; S. Wilberforce to J. W. Croker, 19 April 1843, Bodl. MS Eng. Lett., d. 367, fos. 69–72.

Walter Hook, High Church vicar of Leeds, was one of those incensed by the withdrawal of Graham's bill. Hook was a magnanimous figure, with real empathy for working-class suffering. He had been striving in his urban pastorate to convince the labouring population that the established Church was indeed the Church of the whole people, committed to serving the needs of all social orders. He attended Chartist meetings and engaged in dialogue with them, winning their respect with his insistence that his was a Church of the common people.[67] Graham's bill had symbolized Hook's vision of a Church–State alliance working for the elevation of the working classes, and its withdrawal was a bitter blow. He now argued that the Church must go forward on its own, making a dramatic gesture that would capture the imagination of the nation and convince the working classes of its sincerity. The Church, he insisted to Samuel Wilberforce in July 1843, should sacrifice its property in order to establish and endow a national Christian system of popular education. It should give up most of its episcopal incomes, sell off the episcopal palaces, and call on the wealthier clergy to offer up as much of their incomes as possible. By thus impoverishing itself to bring education to the people, the Church would recover its independence, its sense of mission, its popular support, and its self-respect. 'The Church must try', he continued, 'for God's sake to win the people by making a great sacrifice. We want not the State to take our funds and expend them, but the Church to use its own funds and to say, "We will educate the people in our own way out of our own funds".'[68] Henry Manning, High Church archdeacon of Chichester, also believed that the Church must now proceed on its own and provide a national system of education from its own resources. This, he believed, might well be the plan of providence.[69] These calls to sell off the ecclesiastical silver found little support within the Church. However, in the late summer of 1843 a special meeting of the governing committee of the Anglican National Society, with the archbishop of Canterbury in the chair, did respond to the failure of Graham's bill by appealing for private donations for 'extending and improving elementary education in the manufacturing and mining

[67] E. Rose, 'W. F. Hook and the Dark Satanic Mills', in P. T. Phillips (ed.), *The View from the Pulpit: Victorian Ministers and Society* (Toronto, 1978), 117–41.

[68] A. R. Ashwell, *Life of Samuel Wilberforce*, 3 vols. (London, 1880), i. 225–7.

[69] H. E. Manning, *A Charge delivered at the Ordinary Visitation of the Archdeaconry of Chichester, in July 1843* (London, 1843), 26–7.

districts'. By September, some £43,730 had been subscribed, including a donation of £1,000 from the prime minister; by November, the figure had reached £115,000. The Church, Samuel Wilberforce asserted in November 1843, 'has declared that the children of our factories should have a Christian education; [and] that if the state cannot train them, she will undertake the charge'.[70] J. C. Hare even argued that, having assumed the financial burden, the Church should now refuse to allow any State inspection of its schools—thus effectively disestablishing its educational wing.[71]

With Graham's factory education bill, then, as with Peel's District Churches Act, Parliament declined to provide additional public money to assist the established Church of England in extending its pastoral and educational work among the urban working classes. The Church Reform Acts of 1836, 1838, and 1840 had raised the expectation that, if the Church accepted the reform programme and made efficient use of its existing resources, the State would be forthcoming with additional money to support the Church's mission. But the Peel Government failed to meet this expectation, backing down before Dissenting pressure and placing pragmatic political considerations over what Church leaders viewed as the highest possible aim—the Christian education of the nation. The events of 1843 seemed to confirm the Tractarian position—that the established Church of England must cease leaning on the 'broken reed' of the State connection, and look to its inner resources as a Church. It was perhaps not surprising that 1843 witnessed a renewed movement within the Church for the revival of Convocation, to provide the Church once again with an independent form of synodical government, nor that there should be calls for the revival of ecclesiastical discipline within the Church of England, through ecclesiastical courts that would be entirely independent of the civil power.[72]

[70] *Christian Observer*, 43 (September 1843), 573–4; S. Wilberforce, *A Charge delivered at the Ordinary Visitation of the Archdeaconry of Surrey, November 1843* (London, 1843), 26.

[71] J. C. Hare to H. Manning, 17 September 1844, Bodl., MS. Eng. Lett., c. 653/1, fos. 300–6.

[72] R. I. Wilberforce, *A Charge, delivered at the Ordinary Visitation [of the Archdeaconry] of the East Riding* (York, 1843), 6–12; R. I. Wilberforce, *Church Courts and Church Discipline* (London, 1843); 'Revival of Convocation', *Christian Remembrancer*, 7 (April 1844), 466–81; 'Convocation, or a Synod', *English Review*, 2 (October 1844), 36–54; R. Whately, *Thoughts on Church-Government* (London, 1844); F. Knight, 'Ministering to the Ministers: The Discipline of Recalcitrant Clergy in the Diocese of Lincoln, 1830–1845', in W. J. Sheils and D. Wood (eds.), *The Ministry: Clerical and Lay*, Studies in Church History, 26 (Oxford, 1989), 357–66.

By 1843, moreover, there was a growing movement in the Church to resist the union of the Welsh bishoprics of St Asaph and Bangor, which had been one of the provisions of the Established Churches Act of 1836. The union was to take place following the death of one of the bishops, and was meant to enable the State to create a new bishopric of Manchester without increasing the number of bishops. But Anglicans now argued that the Church needed more bishops to provide proper discipline and pastoral leadership, and they were less concerned about the arguments that the number of bishops must be defined according to the traditional number who sat in the House of Lords. Bishops, they argued, were first and foremost pastors and their functions as figures of State were secondary; the Church must be free to increase the number of bishops as it saw fit, without reference to considerations of State.[73] After the disappointing events of 1843 many believed that the old alliance of Church and State in England was finally drawing to a close. 'Every year shows me more and more', Gladstone observed in his diary in December 1843, 'that the idea of Christian politics can not be realised in the State according to its present conditions of existence.'[74] Some High Anglicans welcomed the waning of the alliance, believing it was forcing the Church of England to stand on its own and thus to recover its spiritual independence. 'The more Government withdraws its support from the Church', Hook observed to the veteran High Churchman H. H. Norris, on 17 March 1843, 'in my opinion the better: we shall thus gradually cease to be worldly Establishmentarians and become self-denying Churchmen.'[75] 'We shall be wise', observed Henry Manning in July 1843, 'if we give over looking to the civil power for measures conceived in the spirit.'[76] 'The great want of the Church of England in the present day', maintained the High Church *Christian Remembrancer* of April 1844, 'is obviously independence'—for only by restoring its spiritual independence would the Church revive its discipline, its mission, and its national influence.[77] The traditional Church–State connection in England had been dealt fatal blows in 1843 and the Church of England was finding itself but the leading

[73] 'Dioceses of St. Asaph and Bangor—Additional Bishoprics', *English Review*, 1 (April 1844), 44–105.

[74] P. Butler, *Gladstone: Church, State and Tractarianism*, 109.

[75] W. F. Hook to H. H. Norris, 17 March 1843, Bodl. MS Eng. Lett., c. 790, fos. 112–15.

[76] Manning, *Charge delivered . . . in July, 1843*, 18.

[77] 'Revival of Convocation', *Christian Remembrancer*, 7 (April 1844), 474.

denomination competing with other denominations for members in a religious market-place. 'The theory of the alliance between Church and State', maintained the *English Review* in April 1844, 'on which the Reformation proceeded, is already, for the most part, abandoned by statesmen and politicians: the identity of the Church and State, on which Hooker argued, does not exist; *practically* the Church stands related to the State, as the chief, the oldest, the most *formally* recognized, of many religious bodies.'[78]

The Disruption of the Church of Scotland

In Scotland, the Church–State conflict was drawing to a climax when Peel entered office in September 1841. The Court of Session had in 1838 declared the Church's Veto Act to be an illegal infringement on the civil rights of patrons and presentees; the House of Lords had confirmed the decision in 1839. The civil courts had begun instructing presbyteries to ordain patron's candidates to parish livings, regardless of the conscientious objections of the congregations. The General Assembly of the Church in turn had instructed presbyteries to resist such 'intrusions'. Lord Aberdeen had failed to gain the Church's support for his bill to legalize a modified form of the Church's Veto Act, while the 'intrusion' at Marnoch and the deposing of the seven Moderate ministers at Strathbogie in the winter and spring of 1841 left little room for compromise between the civil and ecclesiastical courts.

Peel had no love for the Scottish Non-Intrusionists. He viewed what he termed 'the Popish Presbyterian party' as little different from Chartists and Anti-Corn Law League agitators. 'I suppose', he wrote to Aberdeen on 16 December 1840, 'that many of them, when they find their own schemes impracticable, will try to shelter their retreat under a popular cry, and be content to transfer to democracy the influence which they wished to secure for the priesthood.'[79] For Peel, the General Assembly's act deposing the Strathbogie ministers was an act of rebellion against the State, and this rebellion would have to be broken before Parliament could offer any conciliation. He had made his position clear a few months before forming his Government. On 6 May 1841 the Tory duke of Argyll had

[78] *English Review*, 1 (April 1844), 84.

[79] F. Balfour, *The Life of George, Fourth Earl of Aberdeen*, 2 vols. (London, 1922), ii. 84.

introduced in the House of Lords a bill which would have legalized the veto, provided it could be demonstrated that the congregation had not acted from malice or prejudice. Argyll's bill was endorsed by the General Assembly of the Church of Scotland on 20 May. However, in early June, when Argyll approached Peel for his support, Peel responded that he would not support Argyll's bill, or any bill to end the crisis, until the General Assembly first reinstated the Strathbogie ministers and admitted it had been wrong to discipline them for obeying the civil courts. The parliamentary session ended before Argyll's bill could be read a second time.[80]

In the autumn of 1841 a Scottish Tory landowner and MP, Sir George Sinclair, attempted to mediate a settlement among the different parties. Sinclair seemed uniquely qualified for the job. He was an Evangelical and had at one time been president of the Anti-Patronage Society in Scotland; he was close to Chalmers, Candlish, and other leaders of the Non-Intrusionist party. He was also a long-time personal friend of Peel, with whom he had attended school at Harrow. Sinclair hoped to revive Aberdeen's bill, though with modifications that would give presbyteries full discretionary power to reject a patron's candidate as unsuitable if the congregation sincerely objected to the candidate for whatever reason. With a tenacious optimism, Sinclair corresponded with politicians, lawyers, and leaders of both the Non-Intrusionist and the pro-patronage Moderate parties in the Church of Scotland.[81] The Non-Intrusionist leaders were prepared to accept Sinclair's proposed bill. The Moderate party in the Church, on the other hand, confident that they had the support of the civil courts and fearful of their future in a popular, Evangelical Church, opposed Sinclair's bill. George Cook, leader of the Moderate party, assured Sinclair on 15 September 1841 that the Church courts could not be entrusted with independent authority, as they would only abuse power, 'as in ages past'. To allow presbyteries full discretion to reject unpopular patron's candidates, Cook added, 'would be equivalent to the extermination of all who hold the opinions which I, and they with whom I act, entertain'.[82] After reviewing Sinclair's correspondence with the Church leaders, Peel

[80] R. Buchanan, *Ten Years' Conflict*, ii. 287–93; Duke of Argyll to Sir R. Peel, 24 June 1841; Peel to Argyll, 25 June 1841, *Peel Papers*, BL Add. MSS 40429, fos. 383–7.

[81] G. Sinclair (ed.), *Selection from the Correspondence carried on during Certain Recent Negociations for the Adjustment of the Scottish Church Question* (Edinburgh, 1842).

[82] Ibid. 31.

decided that his Government should do nothing. Writing to Sinclair on 27 November, he insisted that there could be no settlement so long as the Non-Intrusionist party retained its leadership in the Church. Any action by his Government, he believed, would only 'arm the violent party with weapons to be directed against those who are in favour of a peaceful and practicable settlement'. He therefore proposed to leave the Church to suffer the consequences of its illegal actions, until the majority rejected the Non-Intrusion leaders and made a 'public avowal' of their submission to the patronage law.[83]

In November 1841 the 'intrusion' of a patron's candidate into a parish church, this time in the Aberdeenshire parish of Culsamond, culminated in a riot. The patron's candidate, William Middleton, a man of about 60 who had served as interim minister in the parish for some years, had been vetoed by eighty-nine of the 139 male heads of family, in accordance with the Church's Veto Act. In this case, the heads of family were forthright about their reasons for vetoing the candidate, citing his 'cold, unscriptural preaching' and 'secular pursuits' on the Sabbath. The Moderate members of the presbytery of Garioch, on instructions from the civil courts, ignored the veto and proceeded to ordain Middleton. The parishioners physically resisted the ordination on 11 November 1841, and the candidate had to be ordained in the manse, behind closed doors, while police battled with rioters outside.[84] The Commission of the General Assembly, on 17 November, summoned all the parties involved in the Culsamond affair to appear before the next General Assembly meeting in May and explain their behaviour, and in the mean time it prohibited Middleton from officiating in the parish church until the Assembly had reviewed the case. On 10 March 1842, however, the Court of Session placed an interdict on any review of the Culsamond affair by the Church courts. First, the Court of Session noted that it had already ruled that Middleton was to be minister of Culsamond and the Church could have no further say in the matter. But secondly, the Court stated that if the General Assembly were to consider the parishioners' objections to Middleton, it would damage his reputation and thus infringe on his civil rights. With this

[83] R. Peel to G. Sinclair, 'Private', 27 November 1841, *Peel Papers*, BL Add. MSS 40496, fos. 30–1.

[84] For a vivid description of the Culsamond riot, see W. Alexander's novel, *Johnny Gibb of Gushetneuk* (Aberdeen, 1871), ch. 18.

ruling the Court of Session effectively claimed complete authority over the Church courts in all matters of ecclesiastical discipline—for any disciplinary action by the Church courts would touch on the reputations of the persons involved.[85] In the wake of the Culsamond decision, some Church of Scotland ministers began appealing to the civil courts to block any disciplinary actions by the ecclesiastical courts, including discipline in cases involving theft and sexual misconduct. Pressure on the Non-Intrusionists seemed to increase by the day. In March, the Government moved troops into Aberdeenshire to crush any further popular resistance to patronage. 'Chartism was put down by the military', observed the Non-Intrusionist *Witness* bitterly on 19 March, 'and why not put down non-intrusion by the military too?'[86]

The growing pressure on the Church seemed to have desired results for the Government when in March 1842 approximately forty ministers and elders from the Synod of Glasgow and Ayr, who until now had adhered to the Non-Intrusionist party, signed a declaration expressing their distress over the increasing 'difficulties and dangers with which the Church of Scotland is now surrounded' and their willingness to accept a Government bill to regulate the settlement of ministers based on Sir George Sinclair's amended version of Aberdeen's bill of 1840. In the coming weeks, the 'forty' formed themselves into a 'Middle party' under the leadership of William Muir of Edinburgh and Matthew Leishman of Glasgow. They formally broke with the Non-Intrusionist leadership, condemned the deposing of the Strathbogie ministers, and called for obedience to the civil courts.[87] To Peel and his Government, it seemed that moderate Non-Intrusionists were at last coming to their senses, and that the forty represented the beginning of the break-up of the Non-Intrusion party.

The Non-Intrusionist solidarity, however, did not break up. Early in 1842, Non-Intrusionists began forming local Church Defence Associations throughout the country, to defend the spiritual independence of the Church and the religious rights of the Scottish

[85] Hanna, *Memoirs of Dr. Chalmers*, iv. 275–9; H. Watt, *Thomas Chalmers and the Disruption* (Edinburgh, 1943), 235–9; F. Lyall, *Of Presbyters and Kings: Church and State in the Law of Scotland* (Aberdeen, 1980), 41–2.

[86] *Witness*, 19 March 1842.

[87] Leishman, *Matthew Leishman of Govan*, 121–47; Turner, *The Scottish Secession of 1843*, 266–84; W. Muir to R. Peel, 2 March 1842, *Peel Papers*, BL. Add. MSS 40503, fos. 281–90.

people and also (in language reminiscent of the Irish Catholic Association in the mid-1820s) to protect non-intrusionist tenants from victimization by pro-patronage landlords.[88] The aim, according to one observer, was 'to enlist the masses'.[89] 'We are, in truth', Chalmers observed to Lord Lorne on 19 February 1842, 'fighting not only our own battles, but the battles of the people; and why should not the people be made aware of it?'[90] The Church Defence Associations appealed to Scotland's popular, Presbyterian, Covenanting heritage. For Hugh Miller, editor of the Edinburgh *Witness*, the Non-Intrusionists were struggling not only against the civil courts and landlords in Scotland, but also against English Tories and High Anglicans, who were in turn infused with 'Puseyism' and committed to destroying the Scottish Presbyterian establishment. The present confrontation was but a new version of the old seventeenth-century struggle between the Covenanters and Laudian Anglicans. The open hostility of such High Church Anglicans as Blomfield to the Non-Intrusionist cause gave credence to this interpretation.[91] 'The English hierarchy', warned the *Witness* on 1 January 1842, 'seem to anticipate the possibility of rearing a prelatic Church on the ruins of ours.'[92]

The General Assembly took decisive action in support of non-intrusion at its meeting in May 1842. First, it reasserted its independent jurisdiction. At the opening of its proceedings, the Assembly was confronted with two rival sets of commissioners from the presbytery of Strathbogie, one made up of ministers and elders who recognized the General Assembly's authority, and the other made up of the seven deposed ministers who maintained, with the support of their Moderate allies, that they were the true commissioners of the presbytery, because they were so defined by the Court of Session. The Assembly brushed aside the claim of the deposed ministers and refused to admit them. When the Court of Session responded by interdicting the General Assembly's meeting, the Assembly ignored

[88] *Witness*, 8, 12 January 1842.

[89] D. Aitken to Lord Minto, 12 February 1842, *Minto Papers*, National Library of Scotland, MS 11802, fos. 184–6.

[90] *A Selection from the Correspondence of the Late Thomas Chalmers*, ed. W. Hanna (Edinburgh, 1853), 390.

[91] G. Sinclair (ed.), *Selection from the Correspondence carried on during Certain Recent Negociations*, 50.

[92] *Witness*, 1 January 1842; also 19, 23 February, 2, 26 March 1842; see also J. Buchanan, *On the 'Tracts for the Times'* (Edinburgh, 1843).

it. Secondly, the Assembly proceeded to adopt a motion calling for the complete abolition of patronage in the Church of Scotland. The Church's efforts to find a compromise between the rights of patrons and the rights of parishioners had clearly failed. Now, with their backs against the wall, the Non-Intrusionists decided to strike at the root of the crisis, and petition Parliament for an end to patronage.

Thirdly, and most importantly, the General Assembly adopted the 'Claim of Right', an assertion of the Church's spiritual independence, drafted by the Non-Intrusionist lawyer Alexander Dunlop. The Claim of Right represented both the Church's final appeal to the State and also a summons to the people of Scotland in language that was reminiscent of the National Covenant of 1638. The document began by reviewing a series of legal acts passed since the sixteenth century that supported the principles of both non-intrusion and spiritual independence. It gave particular attention to the Union of 1707 and the pledges then made to preserve Scotland's Presbyterian establishment. While recognizing the power of the State to deprive the Church of its property, it denied the authority of the civil courts over ordination and ecclesiastical discipline. The Church could not relinquish its spiritual independence to the civil courts without also relinquishing its identity as a Christian Church. It was for its steadfastness to 'the great doctrine of the sole Headship of the Lord Jesus over his Church' that Scotland's Church was now 'subjected to hardship'. In introducing the Claim of Right in the Assembly, Chalmers proclaimed with Covenanting fervour that we 'shall know how to suffer, even as the fathers of our martyred Church have done before us'.[93]

For Peel, the proceedings of the General Assembly of May 1842 sealed the fate of the Scottish establishment. The hopes raised by the emergence of the Middle party in April 1842 had been dashed; the Church had not overthrown Chalmers and the other Non-Intrusionist leaders. Now the Church would have to pay. In mid-June 1842 Peel announced in the House of Commons that his Government 'had abandoned all hope of settling the [Scottish Church] question in a satisfactory manner, or of effecting any good by introducing a measure relative to it'.[94] Some weeks later the House of Lords struck yet another blow at the Scottish establishment,

[93] *The Church of Scotland's Claim of Right, to which are Prefixed the Speeches of Dr Chalmers, Dr Gordon and Mr Dunlop in the General Assembly, in Support of the Same* (Edinburgh, 1842), p. v.

[94] Hanna, *Memoirs of Dr. Chalmers*, iv. 302.

when it delivered its judgement in the second Auchterarder case. Robert Young, it will be recalled, had been vetoed by the male heads of family in the parish of Auchterarder, and together with the patron, the earl of Kinnoull, had challenged the legality of the veto in the civil courts. In 1838 the Court of Session had found in Young's favour, and awarded him the stipend, manse, and church building. The Church had duly relinquished these 'temporalities' to Young, but on instructions from the General Assembly the presbytery had refused to ordain him as minister of the parish. Young and Kinnoull had then raised a civil action against the presbytery for refusing to ordain. The Court of Session found in their favour and awarded them a massive £10,000 in damages, with the clerical members of the presbytery individually responsible for payment. If unable to pay, they would be imprisoned. The Church appealed, but on 9 August 1842 the House of Lords upheld the Court of Session's decision. There were now thirty-nine patronage cases in the civil courts, and the large award to Young and Kinnoull would encourage still more. It was clear that while the Government looked on, the Court of Session would force the Non-Intrusionists out of the Church through a series of crippling legal judgements. Some now argued that the Non-Intrusionists should adopt a policy of passive disobedience—refusing to ordain patron's candidates as commanded by the civil courts, and allowing the Court of Session to fill the prisons with conscientious clergymen, until an aroused public opinion forced Parliament to intervene.[95] The Non-Intrusionist leaders, more prosaically, resolved that should the Queen-in-Parliament reject their final petition, their Claim of Right, they would peacefully leave the establishment.

At the same time, there was considerable uncertainty among the rank-and-file Non-Intrusionist clergy and laity about secession. It was not clear how many clergymen would actually go out, or how those who did would be supported. Many were still unconvinced that secession was necessary. There were lengthy, often acrimonious discussions in presbyteries across the country.[96] In an effort to strengthen resolve and instil confidence, the Non-Intrusion leaders

[95] *An Address to the People of Scotland, issued by Appointment of the Convocation of Ministers, held at Edinburgh, November 1842* (Edinburgh, n.d.), 10; G. F. C. Duncan, *Memoir of the Rev. Henry Duncan* (Edinburgh, 1848), 290; [J. F. Ferrier], *Observations on Church and State* (Edinburgh, 1848), 24.

[96] G. D. Henderson, *Heritage: A Study of the Disruption* (Edinburgh, 1943), 98.

organized a special Convocation in Edinburgh over a seven-day period between 17 and 24 November 1842. Only Non-Intrusionist clergymen were invited, and 465 ministers attended. At the meeting, leading Non-Intrusionists reviewed the issues at stake and the reasons why they must prepare to leave the State connection. There was much prayer and personal testimony; the proceedings, one commentator observed, had a 'Millennial character'.[97] Chalmers introduced a plan for the financial maintenance of the proposed Free Church. Money would be collected by local congregations, with penny-a-week subscriptions from the poor and larger donations from wealthier persons. The money would be redistributed, according to need, by a central committee—which would ensure that every minister, no matter how poor the local community, would receive a decent stipend. No outgoing minister need fear poverty. Despite these assurances, many continued to hold back. Of the 465 ministers present, only 354 signed the pledge to resign their livings if the State rejected their Claim of Right.[98]

Peel was not impressed by the Convocation. 'I believe', he wrote to Sir George Sinclair on 2 December 1842, 'the main cause of the present embarrassment is the subjection of very many Ministers of the Church of Scotland, through fear and against their own conscientious convictions, to the violence and menaces of their leaders.'[99] On 4 January 1843 home secretary Graham informed the General Assembly that the Government refused to consider the Church's Claim of Right. 'Pretensions such as these', Graham observed, 'have heretofore been successfully resisted by the Sovereign and the people of this realm; nor could they be conceded without the surrender of civil liberty, and without the sacrifice of personal rights.'[100] Two weeks later, on 20 January, the Court of Session struck again at the Church, when it declared the Church's Chapels Act of 1834 to be illegal and ruled that ministers and elders of *quoad sacra* churches, which included all the new churches erected by the church extensionists since 1834, should

[97] Duncan, *Memoir of Henry Duncan*, 291.

[98] W. Wilson and R. Rainy, *Memorials of Robert Smith Candlish* (Edinburgh, 1880), 219–59; D. Aitken to Lord Minto, 13 December 1842, *Minto Papers*, National Library of Scotland, MS 11802, fos. 201–4.

[99] R. Peel to G. Sinclair, 'Confidential', 7 December 1842, *Peel Papers*, BL Add. MSS 40520, fos. 29–30.

[100] *Letter from Sir James Graham, Principal Secretary for the Home Department, to the Moderator of the General Assembly, with the Reply, being the Minute of the General Assembly's Special Commission* (Edinburgh, 1843), 3.

never have been allowed to sit on the ecclesiastical courts. As virtually all ministers and elders of the *quoad sacra* churches were Non-Intrusionists, denying them membership in the Church courts ensured that the Non-Intrusionists would not have a majority in the next General Assembly. The decision also brought into question the legality of any act by any Church court since 1834, thus threatening the breakdown of all ecclesiastical order. On 7–8 March 1843 the House of Commons held a two-day debate on the Scottish Church crisis. Both Peel and Graham now acknowledged that there would be a serious disruption of the Scottish establishment, with many of the most able and committed ministers departing. None the less, they argued, the Government could not concede the Non-Intrusionists' claims. An established Church was in their view a branch of the State. Its ecclesiastical jurisdiction was limited by civil law, and in particular the ecclesiastical courts could not have exclusive authority over questions relating to patronage and ecclesiastical discipline, as those questions invariably involved civil rights. The ecclesiastical courts had to be subject to review by the civil courts, with any fundamental disagreements between the civil and ecclesiastical courts to be decided by the House of Lords (in which, unlike the Church of England, the Church of Scotland had no representation). Those in the Scottish Church who were unable to accept these terms of establishment as defined by the State would have to go. The overwhelming majority in the Commons agreed with the Tory leaders, and the Commons declined to intervene to avert the break-up of the Scottish establishment.[101]

Following the Convocation of November 1842, meanwhile, the Non-Intrusionists had thrown themselves into the work of mobilizing popular support. The Convocation had revealed continued uncertainties among the Non-Intrusionist clergy; the leadership therefore now made a concerted effort to present their case to the Scottish people. They began by issuing *An Address to the People of Scotland*. 'One only alternative remains to us', it proclaimed, 'and that is to forfeit the benefits of an establishment, that we may preserve to ourselves and our children the inalienable privileges of a church of Christ.'[102] A standing Convocation Committee was created, with an office in Edinburgh. From early January 1843, it sent

[101] *Hansard's Parl Deb.*, 3rd ser. lxvii (1843), cols. 354–422, 442–512. Graham's speech appears in cols. 378–94; Peel's speech in cols. 491–506.

[102] *An Address to the People of Scotland, issued by Appointment of the Convocation of Ministers, held at Edinburgh, November 1842* (Edinburgh, n.d.), 6.

Non-Intrusionist ministers, usually in pairs, on circuits around the country, to conduct public meetings and enlist support. This speaking campaign built upon the excitement aroused by the religious revival which had begun in 1839, and the meetings often had an apocalyptic tone. Despite his poor health, the revivalist preacher Robert Murray McCheyne of Dundee travelled extensively through rural Aberdeenshire on behalf of the Convocation Committee in late February; the exertion may have contributed to his premature death, at the age of 29, on 25 March 1843. John McDonald and Henry Allan toured Sutherlandshire in January, gathering crowds of 2,000–3,000 for open-air meetings in the snow. For the Evangelical preacher and hymn-writer Andrew Bonar, the movement was God's call to his people to withdraw from a worldly establishment: 'Come, my people, enter into thy chambers.'[103] The public meetings were followed by the formation of local associations, with collectors responsible for gathering subscriptions for the new Church. By mid-April 1843, 405 local associations had been formed. For Chalmers, speaking at a public meeting on 16 February in Edinburgh, the people were rallying to Scotland's national Church now that they saw it under attack by the State. It was showing itself to be a popular Church. 'For Church Extension', he observed, 'I knocked at the door of a Whig ministry, and they refused to endow. I then knocked at the door of a Tory ministry, but they offered to enslave. I now therefore turn aside from both, and knock at the door of the general population.'[104] There was also a Scottish nationalist dimension to the agitation. At a public meeting in early 1843 in rural Dumfriesshire, a Non-Intrusionist minister asserted that Parliament's treatment of the established Church of Scotland was 'enough to justify Scotland in demanding the repeal of the Union'. 'With that', the minister later recalled, '. . . the meeting rose as one man, waving hats and handkerchiefs, and cheering again and again.'[105]

On 18 May 1843 the opening day of the General Assembly, the Non-Intrusionists left the Church of Scotland. As the Assembly

[103] Bonar, *Memoir of R. M. McCheyne*, 163–7; J. Kennedy, *The 'Apostle of the North': The Life and Labours of the Rev. Dr. McDonald* (London, 1866), 301–9; A. Beith, *Memories of Disruption Times* (London, 1877), 35–141; T. Brown, *Annals of the Disruption*, 58–74; A. Bonar, *Diary and Life*, ed. M. Bonar (Edinburgh, 1893), 110.

[104] Hanna, *Memoirs of Dr. Chalmers*, iv. 332–3; Duncan, *Memoir of Henry Duncan*, 297–8; *Witness*, 1 March 1843.

[105] T. Brown, *Annals of the Disruption*, 69.

opened in St Andrew's church in Edinburgh's New Town, the retiring Moderator David Welsh read a lengthy protest, laid it on the table, and walked out of the church, followed by Chalmers and the other leaders. Then, row by row, the Non-Intrusionist commissioners solemnly departed the church, and moved out into the street, where a huge crowd had gathered to witness the event. The outgoing commissioners, joined by other outgoing ministers, walked in procession through the pressing crowd to a large hall, fitted out in a disused tannery. There they signed a deed of demission, relinquishing their charges, stipends, glebes, manses, and status as ministers of the established Church of Scotland. They constituted themselves the Free Protesting Church of Scotland and threw themselves on an uncertain future. Some 454 out of 1,195 ministers in the Church of Scotland, or over a third of the total, entered the Free Church. They were joined by between a third and half of the lay membership. The new body claimed to be Scotland's true national Church—the historic Church of the Scottish people, the Church of the Reformation and of the martyrs of the Covenant—which had severed its connection with an Erastian State and looked to the Scottish people. The new Free Church had its main strength in the Lowland urban centres and in the Highlands, but congregations were formed throughout the country. And those who left included the most energetic and most committed of the ministers.

'The people must stand firm', insisted the *Witness* on 3 June 1843, at the close of the first Free Church General Assembly. 'Their ministers have stood the trial nobly; it is *they* [the people] who are on trial now.'[106] The next few years were a time of trial for the whole Free Church. The Disruption came at a time of acute economic distress and widespread unemployment, and communities were often hard-pressed to support the outgoing ministers while at the same time paying their teinds to the 'residuary' establishment. The landowners were almost uniformly hostile to this movement of popular Presbyterianism. In 1843, according to one estimate, 86 per cent of the high nobility and some two-thirds of the landed classes were Episcopalian; thus, the religious differences between landlords and tenants were almost as great in rural Scotland as in rural Ireland.[107] Many landowners viewed Free Church membership as an attack on their authority and a rebellion against the civil law: it was their duty

[106] *Witness*, 3 June 1843.

[107] C. G. Brown, *Religion and Society in Scotland since 1707* (Edinburgh, 1997), 34.

to crush the movement. On some estates, Free Church tenants were evicted and Free Church labourers dismissed. For example, Lord MacDonald evicted some forty-five Free Church tenants from his estate on Skye and another nine from his lands on North Uist. Lord Ross of Cromarty dismissed twenty-two Free Church labourers from his Ross-shire estate.[108] In many rural districts, the landowners refused to sell or lease sites to the Free Church for its churches or manses. This could cause particular hardship in areas where a single landlord owned virtually all the land—as in the southern uplands, where the largest landowner, the Episcopalian duke of Buccleuch, was an implacable foe of the Free Church, or in Sutherland, where the duke of Sutherland, notorious for his role in the Highland Clearances, the clearing of tenant farmers to make way for sheep runs, also sought to suppress the Free Church. Congregations were forced to worship in the open air along the sea shores, on public highways, or on remote hillsides. In the mining village of Wanlockhead, on land belonging to the duke of Buccleuch, the Free Church congregation was forced to worship unsheltered in a ravine through six winters. In Canonbie, also on Buccleuch land, the congregation was forced to worship through one winter on the public highway. Some landowners refused to allow Free Church ministers to reside on their estates, and threatened tenants with eviction if they provided Free Church ministers with hospitality.[109] The refusals of sites and victimization of Free Church adherents grew so blatant that in March 1847, the House of Commons appointed a Select Committee to investigate.

Despite the intimidation and economic distress, the Free Church managed through voluntary contributions to create a national Church. By 1847 they had erected over 730 buildings for worship, most of them unpretentious wooden structures that were later replaced by more substantial stone and mortar structures. The new Church also developed a system, devised by Chalmers, by which wealthier congregations in the urban centres contributed to the support of poorer churches—providing all clergy with a minimum stipend of over £120 a year during the first years, which was only slightly lower than the minimum stipend in the established

[108] *Third Report of the Select Committee of the House of Commons on Sites*, Parliamentary Papers, 1847 (237), xiii, p. 24, questions 4438–59; p. 36, questions 4724–49.

[109] S. J. Brown, 'Martyrdom in Early Victorian Scotland: Disruption Fathers and the Making of the Free Church', in D. Wood (ed.), *Martyrs and Martyrologies*, Studies in Church History, 30 (Oxford, 1993), 326–31.

Church. By 1848, moreover, the Free Church had erected over 400 new manses, or residences, for its ministers. They also created a national system of popular education, and by 1847 they were maintaining 513 teachers and teaching some 44,000 children—nearly equal to the number being taught in the endowed schools of the established Church. From 1844, the Free Church initiated a movement for urban mission through aggressive house-to-house visiting combined with church-directed educational and social services. Further, as all but one of the pre-Disruption Church of Scotland overseas missionaries joined the Free Church, the new Church assumed the costs of their support and also had to provide the missionaries with new churches, schools, and residences, as existing mission structures—such as the school and library at Calcutta—were seized by agents of the established Church. Free Church contributions to overseas missions averaged nearly £40,500 a year between 1843 and 1848, as compared to an average of £16,400 in the established Church between 1838 and 1843. Finally, the new Church established a college in Edinburgh for the training of its ministers. Initially envisaged as a great free university, the New College in Edinburgh, begun in 1846 and completed in 1850, instead became one of the world's leading Reformed theological seminaries, drawing students from throughout the world to its majestic building on the Mound overlooking the city's new town. By 1846 there were nearly 200 students of divinity enrolled at New College. By 1848, moreover, the Free Church General Assembly had established additional theological colleges at Glasgow and Aberdeen.[110]

This rapid creation of a national Church through voluntary means alone was unprecedented. Hundreds of new churches and schools were added for the religious instruction and pastoral care of Scotland's rapidly growing population. The Free Church emerged as arguably the most dynamic denomination in Scotland, a great popular Church. In Glasgow there was evidence of a strong working-class Free Church membership, with many of its elders and managers coming from the skilled working classes.[111] In 1846 the Free Church General Assembly agreed that local presbyteries should be permitted to allow women

[110] S. J. Brown, 'The Disruption and the Dream: the Making of New College 1843–1861' in D. F. Wright and G. D. Badcock (eds.), *Disruption to Diversity: Edinburgh Divinity 1846–1996* (Edinburgh, 1996), 29–50.

[111] P. Hillis, 'Presbyterianism and Social Class in Mid-Nineteenth Century Glasgow: A Study of Nine Parishes', *Journal of Ecclesiastical History*, 32 (1981), 47–64.

communicants to vote in the election of ministers, and the practice became widespread.[112] And yet at the same time the Disruption of 1843 was also a tragedy, breaking up the established Church of Scotland. The established Church survived, but now as a minority Church, which had, following the Disruption, rescinded the Veto Act and Chapels Act and accepted the authority of the civil courts. It was no longer able to fulfil its responsibilities in the distribution of poor relief, and in 1845 Parliament passed a New Poor Law for Scotland, which had the effect of transferring authority over poor relief from the kirk-sessions of the established Church to elected poor-law boards. By 1851 the established Church represented less than a third of Scotland's churchgoing population. The Disruption had been accompanied by angry confrontations between supporters of the Free and established Churches, which embittered religious life in Scotland for generations. Chalmers termed the remnant establishment in Scotland a 'moral nuisance', and Free Church publicists compared the persecution of Free Church members, especially in the Highlands, to that of the martyrs of the Covenants. The Scottish Disruption also sent shock waves through the establishments of the three kingdoms, further weakening the foundations of established religion, while it gave impetus to the disestablishment movement. In England, Dissenters collected contributions to assist the Scottish Free Church.[113] The Presbyterian Church of Ireland, including its leader, the staunchly Tory Henry Cooke, gave its full support to the Free Church of Scotland, recognizing it as the true 'sister Church' of Irish Presbyterianism and raising money for its support.[114] William Gibson, Presbyterian minister in Belfast and a future Moderator of the Irish Presbyterian General Assembly, predicted that the break-up of the Scottish Presbyterian establishment would be followed by the end of the Episcopal establishments in England and Ireland. 'Now that the breakwater is removed', he asked, 'what is to hinder the swelling tide to sweep away more ambitious structures, and overwhelm them in one common ruin?'[115]

[112] L. Orr MacDonald, 'Women and Presbyterianism in Scotland, c. 1830 to c. 1930' (University of Edinburgh Ph.D., 1995), 263–71.

[113] Miall, *Life of Edward Miall*, 89–90.

[114] J. L. Porter, *Life and Times of Henry Cooke* (London, 1871), 417–33; Holmes, *Henry Cooke*, 151–6; Wilson and Rainy, *Memorials of Robert Smith Candlish*, 181–4; *Minutes of the General Assembly of the Presbyterian Church in Ireland* (Belfast, 1843), 190–1, 220–1; T. Brown, *Annals of the Disruption*, 544–5.

[115] Porter, *Life of Henry Cooke*, 431–3; W. Gibson, *The Flock in the Wilderness; or, the Secession of 1843* (Belfast, 1843), 28.

In the 1820s the Church of Scotland had been, in the view of English as well as Scottish defenders of the alliance of Church and State, a model establishment, popular, efficient, and economical. Now in Scotland, as in Ireland, the established Church was a minority Church, its existence resented by the majority of the population. For this, much of the responsibility lay with Peel. His Government could have brought forward legislation to increase the popular voice in the selection of ministers—a version of Sinclair's bill or the duke of Argyll's bill—that would have satisfied the Non-Intrusionist party and preserved the unity of the Scottish establishment. That his Government declined to do so indicates in part an underestimate of the religious commitment of the Non-Intrusionists, an unwillingness on the part of pragmatic English politicians to believe that so many Scottish Non-Intrusionists would actually sacrifice their worldly interests for their principles. It also suggests a lack of sympathy for the Scottish establishment among the overwhelmingly Anglican governing classes in the United Kingdom. While there is no evidence that High Anglicans genuinely planned to erect an episcopal establishment on the ruins of the Presbyterian one, neither did many Anglicans, including Evangelicals, express concern over the break-up of the Church of Scotland.[116]

National but not Established: The Roman Catholic Church in Ireland

Early in 1843, Daniel O'Connell, the Irish Catholic 'Liberator', began a national campaign to repeal the Act of Union of Great Britain and Ireland and restore an independent Irish Parliament in Dublin. Proclaiming that '1843 is and shall be the great Repeal year',[117] he revived the methods of agitation that had proved so effective in the campaign for Catholic Emancipation. These included appeals to Irish national pride through the popular press, the collection of a 'Repeal Rent' and the conduct of 'monster meetings'

[116] B. W. Noel, *Free Church of Scotland. The Substance of a Speech delivered at a Public Meeting held at Exeter Hall, on . . . 11th October 1844* (London, 1844), 4; For Gladstone, the Disruption was further demonstration that Presbyterianism was fundamentally flawed: W. E. Gladstone, 'The Theses of Erastus and the Scottish Church Establishment' (1844), in *Gleanings of Past Years*, 7 vols. (London, 1879), iii. 1–40.

[117] MacDonagh, *O'Connell*, 502.

throughout the country. By the summer of 1843, Ireland was ablaze with Repeal agitation and many feared that civil war was imminent.

Before the formation of the Peel Government in 1841, there had been signs of success for the Union. From the mid-1830s, O'Connell and his Irish parliamentary party had maintained an uneasy alliance with the Whigs, wishing to see whether Catholic Emancipation would lead to improved civil government in Ireland and more impartial treatment of Catholics.[118] Would there, in short, be a more open, liberal society, of the sort envisaged in the 1820s by the Catholic Bishop Doyle? Under the Whigs, there certainly was progress towards that ideal in the 1830s. There were improvements in the administration of local justice, with an increased reliance on professional, stipendiary magistrates and a professional police force, rather than on magistrates drawn from the ranks of the almost exclusively Protestant landed classes.[119] A new Board of Works, formed in 1831, promoted the construction of roads and bridges, which provided employment and developed an infrastructure for economic development. In 1838, Parliament enacted an Irish poor law, with a Central Board in Dublin and local poor-law unions administered by elected poor-law boards and empowered to levy rates and erect workhouses. While the act was in some respects flawed, it did at least attempt to introduce an impartial, non-sectarian system for the care of the poor, based on principles of local democracy, and Catholics were well represented on the local poor-law boards.[120] In 1840, Parliament enacted a measure of municipal reform in Ireland, based on the Scottish act of 1833 and the English act of 1835. The Board of Education formed by the Whigs in 1831 steadily expanded its provision of a non-denominational popular education. There were 789 schools with some 107,000 pupils in 1833. By 1841 that had increased to 2,337 schools and over 281,000 pupils.[121]

The question of tithes proved a far more thorny issue. The Irish Church Temporalities Act of 1833 had reduced the size of the established Church in Ireland. It had not, however, dealt with the vexed

[118] Macintyre, *The Liberator: Daniel O'Connell and the Irish Party*.

[119] M. A. G. O'Tuathaigh, *Thomas Drummond and the Government of Ireland 1835–41* (Dublin, 1978), 8–22.

[120] G. O'Brien, 'The Establishment of Poor-law Unions in Ireland, 1838–43', *Irish Historical Studies*, 23 (1982), 97–120; Macintyre, *The Liberator*, 211–26; G. O'Tuathaigh, *Ireland before the Famine 1798–1848* (Dublin, 1972), 108–14.

[121] Akenson, *The Irish Education Experiment*, 140.

issue of tithes, and the tithe war had continued. It was largely the appropriation issue that stifled Whig attempts to get a tithe reform bill through Parliament. In Ireland, Catholic leaders, including James Doyle, bishop of Kildare and Leighlin (until his death in 1834), and John MacHale, archbishop of Tuam from 1834, had pressed strenuously for the appropriation of tithe revenues from the Church of Ireland, insisting that the money should be devoted to the Irish poor. Advanced Whigs, especially Lord John Russell, had taken up the appropriation cause, viewing it as a matter of natural justice to the hard-pressed Irish peasantry. However, the Tories, with their firm majority in the House of Lords, made it clear by 1835 that they would not approve any tithe bill involving appropriation. A stalemate continued for the next two years. Finally, after the election of 1837, even the advanced Whigs conceded that appropriation would have to be dropped if any tithe reform measure were to be enacted. O'Connell and his Irish party agreed to give up appropriation, recognizing that any tithe revenues surplus to the needs of the Church of Ireland would be very small, and that in any event the Church of Ireland was no longer a major force in Irish national life.[122] In 1838 an Irish tithe act, without appropriation, was passed. The act abolished the tithe in Ireland, replacing it with a rent charge equal to 75 per cent of the value of the tithe and payable by the landlords. It also erased all arrears in tithe, and brought to an end the seven years of tithe war.

Despite these gains, by 1838 O'Connell had become disenchanted with Westminster politics. The Whig alliance was bringing diminishing returns, while the weakness of the Whig Government was all too apparent. He was alarmed over the prospect of his old enemy, Peel, coming to power, believing as he did that a Peel Government would work to revive the power of the Protestant landlords and established Church. He began tentatively exploring possible support in Ireland for a movement aimed at repealing the Union. In August 1838, he formed a Precursor Society, with branches set up around the country. This was transformed into a Repeal Association in 1840. In November 1841, O'Connell was elected for a year's term as lord mayor of Dublin, and devoted himself to this office, in part to demonstrate that Catholics were capable of governing Ireland. In October 1842, as O'Connell's year in office drew to a close, he again

[122] Akenson, *The Irish Education Experiment*, 180–94; Brent, *Liberal Anglican Politics*, 76–103; Macintyre, *The Liberator*, 188–200.

turned his attention to repeal. At the same time, the repeal movement received important support from a new journal, *The Nation*, founded by a circle of young Protestant and Catholic journalists and lawyers, including Thomas Davis, John Blake Dillon, and Charles Gavan Duffy. Embracing a romantic nationalism that looked to France and the Continent rather than England for its political ideas, the writers of *The Nation* called for Irish national self-determination. Only thus would Ireland achieve its cultural potential. By 1843 *The Nation* had a circulation of over 10,000 and an estimated readership of 250,000. Its group of authors and promoters were dubbed 'Young Ireland' by an English journalist, with comparisons made to the Young England movement of Disraeli and Manners.[123]

In the spring of 1843 the repeal campaign took off, spreading through Ireland with all the fervour of a religious revival. Tens of thousands enrolled in the Repeal Association, either as volunteers, subscribing £10 a year, as members, subscribing £1 a year, or as associates, paying a penny a month. Branches multiplied, many providing reading rooms with repeal newspapers and pamphlets. The Repeal Rent, used to finance the campaign, rose from about £100 a week in January to around £1,900 a week by July. Although now nearly 70, O'Connell pushed himself to the limit, travelling over 5,000 miles to speak at public meetings. Approximately forty great public gatherings, dubbed 'monster meetings' by the English press, were held around Ireland during the spring and summer, some attracting crowds of 100,000 or more, with the vast numbers marshalled by repeal wardens, or 'O'Connell's police'. The meeting on the historic hill of Tara, in mid-August, attracted numbers estimated between 500,000 and 1,000,000. These monster meetings had a flavour of early Wesleyan gatherings or American revivalist camp meetings, generating intense excitement with reminders of the sins and humiliations of Ireland's past, and promising a new birth through repeal.

The Catholic clergy took a highly visible role in the agitation.[124] Priests enrolled their parishioners in the Repeal Association,

[123] R. Davis, *The Young Ireland Movement* (Dublin, 1987); D. Gwynn, *Young Ireland and 1848* (Cork, 1949), 1–10; T. W. Moody, *Thomas Davis 1814–45* (Dublin, 1945); S. Cronin, *Irish Nationalism: A History of its Roots and Ideology* (Dublin, 1980), 65–72; D. G. Boyce, *Nationalism in Ireland* (London, 1982), 158–64.

[124] D. A. Kerr, *Peel, Priests and Politics: Sir Robert Peel's Administration and the Roman Catholic Church in Ireland, 1841–1846* (Oxford, 1982), 75–92; K. B. Nowlan, 'The Catholic Clergy and Irish Politics in the Eighteen Thirties and Forties', *Irish Historical Studies*, 9 (1974), 119–35;

collected the Repeal Rent, and led processions of parishioners to the great outdoor gatherings. 'The Catholic clergy', observed the historian Donal Kerr, 'were prominent on the Repeal platforms and no Repeal banquet was complete without a rousing speech from a priest or bishop.'[125] For these clerics, repeal would be the culmination of Catholic Emancipation, the real liberation of the Catholic people of Ireland. Fr. Tom Maguire, for example, who had achieved fame as a Catholic debater during the Bible war of the 1820s, now directed his formidable oratory to the repeal movement—insisting that repeal 'was the consideration next in importance to eternity itself, for the Irish people'. The great repeal gathering at Tara was held on the feast of the Assumption, a temporary altar was erected on the hill, and four masses were offered during the morning. Local priests reportedly led thirty-one processions from their various parishes to the monster meeting at Lismore in September.[126] Speaking on 14 May 1843 at a repeal banquet in Mullingar, William Higgins, bishop of Ardagh, proclaimed that 'every Catholic bishop in Ireland, without an exception, is an ardent Repealer'. This was an exaggeration. However, the majority of Irish bishops—fifteen out of the twenty-seven—did support the movement. They were led by Archbishop MacHale, the staunch foe of the New Reformation movement of the 1820s, who joined the Repeal Association in August 1840 and encouraged the clergy of his diocese to do the same. For MacHale, the repeal movement was a means to strengthen the discipline and cohesion of the Catholic community.[127] Catholic Ireland, he believed, must cease looking to party politics at Westminster. Rather, he assured O'Connell on 11 April 1840, it must be 'fully impressed with the conviction, *that it is not on Whig or Tory or Radical it is to rely*,—for they are all hostile to our holy religion,—*but on our own concentrated efforts*'.[128] Although O'Connell attempted to gain support for repeal among Irish Protestants, his failure to do so, combined with MacHale's militant Catholicism, gave the repeal agitation a sectarian character. By June there were fears of

O. MacDonagh, 'The Politicisation of the Irish Catholic Bishops', 1800–1850, *Historical Journal*, 18 (1975), 37–53; J. F. Broderick, *The Holy See and the Irish Movement for the Repeal of the Union with England 1829–1847* (Rome, 1951), 109–62.

[125] Kerr, *Peel, Priests and Politics*, 80.

[126] Broderick, *The Holy See and the Irish Movement for Repeal*, 144–5, 152–3.

[127] E. Larkin, *The Historical Dimensions of Irish Catholicism* (Washington, DC, 1984), 97.

[128] B. O'Reilly, *John MacHale, Archbishop of Tuam: His Life, Times and Correspondence*, 2 vols. (New York, 1890), i. 500.

sectarian warfare.[129] The Protestant *Tipperary Constitution*, for example, claimed on 9 June that the monster meetings were inciting hatred towards Protestants: 'this fearful tide of agitation which overflows the country now threatens to deluge her in one sea of blood'.[130] 'It is', the home secretary, Sir James Graham, wrote of repeal to Lord Stanley on 16 July, 'a religious struggle, directed by the R. Catholic Hierarchy and Priesthood.'[131]

In a search for allies outside Ireland, the Repealers sought to establish links with the Presbyterian Non-Instrusionists in Scotland, suggesting analogies between the struggles in Ireland and Scotland and calling for an alliance. The Westminster State, Irish Repealers argued, treated the Presbyterians of Scotland with no less contempt than it did the Catholics of Ireland. The aim of both Scots Non-Intrusionists and Irish Repealers was the same—to restore the dignity and respect due the Churches of the large majority of their respective populations. *The Nation* began reporting on the non-intrusionist controversy in Scotland in November 1842.[132] The non-intrusionist story was taken up by other repeal newspapers, which printed flattering descriptions of the Scottish Presbyterian establishment and defended its claims to spiritual independence. 'The government of the Church of Scotland', insisted the Catholic *Freeman's Journal* on 11 March, should be left solely to 'its general assembly of experienced, able, and pious ministers.' 'What the Scotch had better do', asserted the O'Connellite *Pilot* on 13 March, 'is, to join us in repealing both Unions. Then a Presbyterian people would be capable of regulating a Presbyterian Church, and not be the slaves of the interpretations of English judges or tribunals.' 'Hereafter', announced the *Dublin Evening Post* on 27 May, several days after the Disruption, 'the Seceding [Free] Church must be—like the Catholic Priesthood of Ireland—democratic,' while the remnant Scottish establishment 'will become like the Irish Establishment, a sinecure'.[133] In the event, the Presbyterian Non-Intrusionist leaders, who had no real interest in ending the Union, declined to respond to these repeal overtures.

[129] J. Graham to R. Peel, 'Private', 4, 18 June 1843, Peel Papers, BL Add. MSS 40448, fos. 305–6, 325–6.

[130] *Tipperary Constitution*, 9 June 1843.

[131] MacDonagh, *O'Connell*, 517.

[132] *The Nation*, 26 November, 3 December 1842, 28 January, 11, 18 March 1843.

[133] *Freeman's Journal*, 11 March 1843; *Pilot* (Dublin), 13 March 1843; *Dublin Evening Post*, 27 May 1843.

Early in July the House of Commons devoted five evenings to the repeal crisis in Ireland. The debate began with a motion from the liberal Protestant landowner William Smith O'Brien, asking that the Commons form itself into a Committee to consider the grievances that lay behind the repeal movement. In the course of the debate it became apparent that, for many speakers, the chief Irish grievance was the established Church of Ireland, which was portrayed as a constant, galling reminder of Protestant ascendancy and Catholic subordination. A considerable portion of the country's agricultural wealth continued to go to support the established Church. O'Brien compared the large endowments to the Protestant Church with the 'miserable grant' that Parliament renewed each year to the Catholic College at Maynooth, a grant which could not 'pass through this House, without furnishing topics of invective and insult against the Roman Catholic clergy'. 'Is it surprising then', he asked, 'that they [the Irish Catholic clergy] should, almost without exception, strenuously advocate the repeal of the Union?'[134] The Irish Catholic MP Thomas Wyse conveyed the humiliation and distress experienced by many poor Catholics at weekly worship:

> congregations of four or five thousand persons were to be seen kneeling in the rain round some miserable hovel, (there was no cover for them within), under the name of a parish chapel, probably built on the site, and often from the ruins of one of their own ancient churches, while not far distant they might perceive the handsome, English-built, new raised, well lit, well ventilated, well warmed Protestant Church, with a lady-and-gentleman congregation of four persons.[135]

(A similar description might have been made of Scottish Highland Free Church congregations at this moment, worshipping on a windswept shoreline or a bleak hillside, while the patron and his family sat in the comfortable established church.) The Radical MP H. G. Ward insisted 'that the establishment, as now constituted, must be given up, if the Union was to be preserved'; in support of this assertion he quoted O'Connell's statement in *Ireland, Irish and Saxon*, that 'the Union is a living lie, until Ireland is placed on equal terms as regards its Church establishment with England and Scotland'.[136] For Villiers Stuart, 'until they removed the crying injustice of the state of the church in Ireland, they never could do anything permanently to

[134] *Hansard's Parl. Deb.*, 3rd ser. lxx (4 July 1843), col. 654.

[135] Ibid. (4 July 1843), col. 691.

[136] Ibid. (7 July 1843), col. 765.

establish tranquillity'.[137] Other speakers shrank from calling for disestablishment, but did demand a further reduction in the size of the Protestant establishment, combined with some form of concurrent endowment of the Irish Catholic Church.[138] In the end, Smith O'Brien's motion to go into Committee was defeated. But the debate had advanced the idea that the established Church was a root cause of the repeal agitation, and might have to be sacrificed to save the Union.

Early in October 1843, Peel's Government moved to suppress the repeal agitation. It prohibited the monster meeting that was to be held at Clontarf, outside Dublin, on 8 October, and threatened to break up the meeting by force should it be held. Although informed of the prohibition only hours before the meeting was due, O'Connell immediately called it off and turned the crowds away rather than risk a bloodbath. A few days later the civil authorities arrested O'Connell and a number of his supporters, charging them with seditious conspiracy. In February 1844 O'Connell and the others were found guilty by a packed Protestant jury. O'Connell was fined £2,000 and sentenced to a year's imprisonment, while his associates received lesser sentences. The Government, meanwhile, also exerted diplomatic pressure on Rome to halt the involvement of the Catholic bishops and priests in the repeal movement.[139] The Government's repressive policies were not very successful. O'Connell was viewed as a martyr in Ireland, and both the repeal Rent and membership in the repeal Association increased. The convictions of the 'repeal Martyrs' were overturned on appeal to the House of Lords, and in September 1844 a triumphant O'Connell was set free, his liberation celebrated with a Te Deum in the Dublin pro-cathedral. For many devout Catholics his release was a miracle from heaven. None the less, the promised 'year of repeal' had now passed, and there was no effort to revive the monster meetings. While the repeal campaign continued in a more subdued manner, O'Connell, who had aged considerably under the strain of his trial and imprisonment, now looked for more limited gains—what he

[137] Ibid. (10 July 1843), col. 865.

[138] e.g. More O'Ferrall, ibid. (7 July 1843), col. 787; T. B. Macaulay, ibid. (7 July 1843), cols. 807–8; Viscount Howick, ibid. (10 July 1843), cols. 886–9; M. Milnes, ibid. (11 July 1843), cols. 956–8; Lord J. Russell, ibid. (11 July 1843), cols. 1006–8.

[139] Kerr, *Peel, Priests and Politics*, 100–9; Broderick, *The Holy See and the Irish Movement for Repeal*, 171–82.

termed 'instalments' towards the ultimate goal of repeal. These he had sketched out in a letter to the English radical Charles Buller, in January 1844. At the top of the list was the disestablishment of the Church of Ireland, which he described as 'the monster grievance which festers in the mind of the Catholic clergy'.[140] There was a growing perception that the disestablishment of the Irish Protestant Church, and perhaps the endowment of the Catholic Church in Ireland, might be enough to end the repeal agitation. 'So long', maintained the Catholic *Dublin Review* in August 1843, 'as the people are of one religion and the national Church-Establishment—for *Church* it is not—of another, so long will there be disunion, dissention, discontent and loud complaint.'[141]

Peel's Government had certainly not shown itself to be a particular friend of the established Church in Ireland, despite all Peel's professions of support for the Irish establishment during the 1830s. When Peel had come to office in 1841, many Irish Protestants had looked for a new beginning for the Protestant establishment. In particular, they had expected that the Tories would replace the Whig national system of education, introduced in 1831, with a return to the old system of State grants in support of Protestant Scripture education schools. In 1839 the Church of Ireland had formed the Church Education Society to co-ordinate the work of diocesan educational societies being formed throughout the country. Its presidents included twelve prelates of the Irish Church, while there was a managing committee of prominent lay and clerical members in Dublin. By 1842, the Church Education Society was maintaining through voluntary donations 1,372 schools with 86,102 pupils—nearly a quarter of the total number of pupils in the State-supported national system—offering a Scripture-based education. The primate of the Irish Church, Lord John George Beresford, archbishop of Armagh and a president of the Church Education Society, pressed the lord lieutenant, who in turn pressed Peel, to give up the national system and return to the system of State grants for Scripture education. By November 1842, however, Peel had decided in favour of maintaining the national system, believing that the key to Ireland's future welfare lay in the mixed Protestant and Catholic education offered by the national schools. In August 1844 he instructed the

[140] MacDonagh, *O'Connell*, 540.

[141] 'Ireland and her Grievances', *Dublin Review*, 15 (August 1843), 165.

lord lieutenant to use the Crown's ecclesiastical patronage to reward those who supported the national schools.[142] The Church of Ireland continued the pressure. Support for the national system of education, insisted the *Dublin University Magazine* in May 1844, was 'utterly impossible for a conscientious minister of the Established Church, without forgetting his ordination vows'.[143] In May 1845 Beresford presented Peel with a petition for a parliamentary grant to the Church Education Society signed by 1,700 clergymen of the Church of Ireland, 1,600 members of the Irish gentry and aristocracy, and over 60,000 lay people. Peel, however, rejected the petition flatly, in what some Protestants viewed as an insulting dismissal.[144] He was, concluded the veteran Bible warrior and New Reformationist Robert J. McGhee, even worse than the Whigs. 'All the "heavy blows and great discouragements" to the Protestant Church which Lord Melbourne had the temerity to threaten, Sir Robert Peel had the treachery to inflict.'[145]

At the same time that it was disappointing the Irish establishment, Peel's Government was also deciding that it would make efforts to conciliate the Irish Catholics in the hope of weakening Catholic support for repeal. On 18 June 1843 Graham had assured Peel that 'we cannot abandon the Protestant Church in Ireland' and 'we cannot give to the Roman Catholics an Establishment'. But otherwise, he added, 'no opportunity should be omitted of winning [the Catholics] to the State; of softening their resentments; of improving their education; of reconciling their clergy'.[146] During the early months of 1844, the Government worked on measures to conciliate the Irish Catholics, without either disestablishing the Protestant Church or establishing Catholicism. The Government's programme included two main provisions. First, they would sponsor legislation aimed at promoting private donations to Catholic churches, schools, hospitals, and other institutions by reforming the law governing charitable bequests in Ireland. This, they believed, would increase the endowments of the Catholic Church without introducing any

[142] Sir R. Peel to Lord Heytesbury, 8 August 1844, Peel Papers, BL Add. MSS 40479, fos. 23–30.

[143] 'The Church Education Society', *Dublin University Magazine*, 23 (May 1844), 628.

[144] Akenson, *The Irish Educational Experiment*, 197–200.

[145] R. J. McGhee, *Reflections on the Endowment of the College of Maynooth* (London, 1845), 34–5.

[146] J. Graham to R. Peel, 'Private', 18 June 1843, Peel Papers, BL Add. MSS 40448, fos. 328–9.

State-funded scheme of endowment or any suggestion of a Catholic establishment. Secondly, the Government would introduce measures for improving and expanding higher education in Ireland, aimed at increasing the numbers of middle-class professionals, breaking down sectarian barriers, and creating a better-educated and more independent Catholic priesthood. The measures included the creation of three new colleges, to be located in the provinces of Ulster, Connaught and Munster. More controversially, there was also a plan to improve the amenities and finances of the Catholic College at Maynooth. Peel was cautious in outlining the programme in a Cabinet memorandum on 11 February 1844. 'Many we shall never reclaim or conciliate', he observed of the Irish Catholics, 'but it is of immense importance to detach, if we can, from the ranks of those who cannot be reclaimed or conciliated, all those who are not yet committed to violent counsels, and are friendly to the connection between the two countries.'[147]

The Government introduced the charitable bequests bill in the Commons in June 1844.[148] It was a modest bill that proposed reforms in the mechanisms for resolving disputes that often arose over private bequests made to corporate bodies. Previously there had been a large board for arbitrating such disputes. It had included some fifty members, nearly all Protestants, and had shown a persistent bias against bequests made to Catholic churches, schools, hospitals, or other bodies. This large board was now to be replaced with a leaner board of thirteen members, at least five of whom had to be Catholics, including three Catholic bishops. This smaller, more representative body, it was believed, would effectively end the bias against Catholic bequests. The bill clarified and simplified procedures for making Catholic bequests, though it also imposed restrictions on some types of Catholic bequests, forbidding both bequests to religious orders and deathbed bequests. The bill encountered virtually no opposition in Parliament and became law in August 1844. In Ireland, however, the majority of Catholics, led by MacHale and O'Connell, vehemently opposed the act. They denounced its clause invalidating deathbed bequests, with its offensive suggestion that Catholic priests would abuse their spiritual office in order to secure such bequests. They were outraged by the prohibition of bequests to

[147] Parker, *Sir Robert Peel*, iii. 101–3.

[148] Kerr, *Peel, Priests and Politics*, 122–223; Macaulay, *William Crolly*, 305–26.

schools or hospitals run by religious orders. Above all, they were angry that the Government had not consulted with the Catholic Church before drafting a bill so vital to its future. In a public letter to Peel in July 1844, MacHale attacked the measure as 'surpassing, in its odious provisions, the worse enactments of penal times'.[149] A minority of Catholic bishops, however—'fawning prelates' in the view of the MacHaleites—were prepared to accept the act, for all its faults, as at least an improvement over previous practice. By the end of 1844 three bishops, among them the Catholic primate William Crolly, archbishop of Armagh, and Daniel Murray, archbishop of Dublin, had agreed to serve on the new Charitable Bequests Board, thus ensuring that the act could be made to work. The Government was not unhappy over the result. Although the act had not won Catholic public favour, it had at least gained a degree of public support from moderate prelates. Further, as Graham observed to the lord lieutenant, Lord Heytesbury, in November, it did no harm to the State 'when the heads of the Church, whose boasted strength is unity . . . break out into unseemly conflict'.[150] Castle officials now entered into regular contact with Murray, Crolly, and other moderate bishops, inviting them to meetings, addressing them by their titles, and recognizing their diocesan authority. There were even rumours that a concordat for Ireland was being negotiated between London and Rome.

Encouraged by these results, the Government now proceeded to the most controversial aspect of its conciliation policy—assistance to the college at Maynooth. The College of Saint Patrick in Maynooth, some 15 miles west of Dublin, had been established by the Irish Parliament in 1795 with an annual grant of £8,000, to provide training for Catholic priests in Ireland. The aim had been to ensure that priests were educated in Ireland, where the State could watch over their training, rather than on the Continent, where young priests might have been infected by the ideas of the French Revolution. After the Union of 1801 the Westminster Parliament continued to grant the annual subsidy to Maynooth, with the amounts remaining at about £9,000 up to the mid-1840s. The numbers of students at Maynooth, meanwhile, steadily increased, from 40 in 1795 to 250 in 1809 and 437 by 1843. The modest size of the State subsidy, combined with the growing student numbers and

[149] Kerr, *Peel, Priests and Politics*, 130. [150] Ibid. 177.

the poverty of the Irish Catholic Church, meant that the college was in chronic financial crisis, burdened with a mounting debt, while its 'mean, rough-cast and white-washed range of buildings' were overcrowded and dilapidated. The condition of the college was said to put off young men from the middle and upper classes from attending, so that Maynooth students—numbering 437 in 1840—came mainly from the ranks of the small tenant farmers. The priests educated at Maynooth, the Irish novelist Maria Edgeworth had quipped in 1831, were 'so vulgar that no gentleman can, let him wish it ever so much, keep company with them'.[151] In 1841 and 1842, the bishops had appealed for increased aid from the Government, but Peel had at that time seen no reason to oblige.[152]

On 4 February 1845 Peel announced in the Commons his Government's intention to increase the grant to Maynooth.[153] Two months later, on 3 April, he introduced the Maynooth bill. The proposals were threefold. First, the bill would nearly triple the money provided, raising it from £9,000 to £26,360 a year. Second, the payment would be transformed from an annual grant, which had to be approved each year, into a permanent charge on the consolidated fund. This meant the State would now endow Maynooth, something the policy of annual grants had been intended to avoid. Finally, the bill provided a non-recurrent grant of £30,000 to cover the cost of badly needed repairs on the college buildings. The proposals received a warm reception from the Catholic Church in Ireland, with even the MacHaleites admitting that they were a positive step. O'Connell expressed himself satisfied, saying of his old foe, Peel, in a speech before the Repeal Association in April that 'nothing was ever more fair, manly and excellent in all its details, than his plan respecting Maynooth'.[154] In Ireland, on the whole, Protestant opposition was muted.[155]

[151] M. Edgeworth to H. Edgeworth, 12 August 1831, cited Kerr, *Peel, Priests and Politics*, 240.

[152] Ibid. 249–51.

[153] Detailed accounts of the Maynooth affair include Kerr, *Peel, Priests and Politics*, 224–89; G. I. T. Machin, 'The Maynooth Grant, the Dissenters and Disestablishment, 1845–1847', *English Historical Review*, 82 (1967), 61–85; Wolffe, *Protestant Crusade in Great Britain*, 198–210; E. R. Norman, *Anti-Catholicism in Victorian England* (London, 1968), 23–51; G. A. Cahill, 'The Protestant Association and the Anti-Maynooth Agitation of 1845', *Catholic Historical Review*, 43 (1957), 273–308.

[154] Kerr, *Peel, Priests and Politics*, 287.

[155] Lord Heytesbury to Sir R. Peel, 24 April, 24 May 1845, Peel Papers, BL Add. MSS 40479, fos. 333–4, 364–5.

In Britain, however, the response was one of outrage. Since the mid-1830s there had been a mounting opposition to the Maynooth grant, driven by Evangelical zeal and growing distrust of the Tractarian Romanizers. Now the simmering resentments came to a boil, and a loose alliance of Voluntary Dissenters, Anglican Evangelicals, Wesleyan Methodists, Free Church Scots, and High Anglicans came together, committed to inflaming Protestant opinion and forcing the withdrawal of the Maynooth proposals, as Protestant Dissenters had forced the withdrawal of Graham's factory education bill two years before. Opponents of the proposals claimed that they were a step towards the general endowment of the Catholic Church in Ireland, that they would complete the destruction of the established Church of Ireland, that they would lead to the establishment of the Catholic Church, and that they would bring down the wrath of God on an apostate nation. The Protestant Society, which had been formed in 1827 to lead the New Reformation campaign in Ireland, took the first steps to awaken the British people to the danger. By late February activists had formed a Central Anti-Maynooth Committee, based at Exeter Hall in London and chaired by the English landowner Sir Culling Eardley Smith.[156] The Committee orchestrated a national campaign of public meetings and petitions. Soon the country was on fire. On 18 March the Anti-Maynooth Committee organized a large public meeting in London. There the Anglican Evangelical Baptist Noel, who had played such a prominent role in the Irish Bible war twenty years before, asserted grimly that 'the present measure was only the commencement of a system of legislation which would inevitably terminate in the endowment of the Romish Church'.[157] Their struggle, Culling Smith assured Thomas Chalmers on 18 April, was that 'between Christ and anti-Christ'.[158] Dissenters were prominent in the agitation—their campaign publicized by Miall's *Nonconformist* newspaper and co-ordinated by the pro-disestablishment Anti-State Church Society, an organization formed in 1844 in the aftermath of the successful campaign against Graham's factory education bill. In Scotland, the Free Church dominated the anti-Maynooth

[156] A. S. Thelwall (ed.), *Proceedings of the Anti-Maynooth Conference of 1845* (London, 1845), p. vii.

[157] Norman, *Anti-Catholicism in Victorian England*, 36.

[158] C. E. Smith to T. Chalmers, 18 April 1845, Thomas Chalmers Papers, New College Library, Edinburgh, CHA 4.320.24.

campaign. The same Government, Free Church leaders noted, that had presided over the break-up of the Protestant establishment in Scotland now proposed to endow the Catholic Church in Ireland. The Government, they further observed, was prepared to endow Maynooth with no attempt to impose State control, while in Scotland they had insisted that the civil courts must exercise control over a State-endowed Church.[159] For the old High Church party, struggling to preserve the Church–State alliance against Tractarian Romanizers, the Maynooth grant came as a slap in the face. Christopher Wordsworth, canon at Westminster Abbey, and William Palmer of Worcester College, Oxford, headed the High Church opposition to what they viewed as an assault on the established Church, reminiscent of the suppression of the Church of Ireland bishoprics in 1833.[160] Between February and May 1845, 10,204 petitions, bearing 1,284,296 signatures, were presented to the House of Commons against the bill, as opposed to only 90 petitions, with 17,482 signatures, presented in its support.[161]

In the Commons, the veteran Churchman Robert Harry Inglis, still smarting from the Government's refusal to provide grants for Anglican church extension, led the anti-Maynooth forces. The second reading of the bill brought six furious nights of debate. The Tory party split on the issue, with over half the Tory MPs opposing the Government, and the bill was carried through its second reading only with Whig support. Peel, it seemed, was being deserted by supporters of the established Protestantism that was to have been one of the foundations of his new Tory party. On 14 April the Whig historian and MP for Edinburgh, Thomas Babington Macaulay, delivered a telling blow, when he portrayed Peel as a sorcerer's apprentice, being overwhelmed by those forces of bigoted Protestantism that he had summoned up for political purposes during his years in opposition. During the 1830s, Macaulay claimed, Peel had encouraged attacks on the Whig Government for attempting to do justice to the Irish Catholics. Now he was reaping the whirlwind.

All those fierce spirits, whom you hallooed on to harass us, now turn round and begin to worry you. The Orangeman raises his war-whoop: Exeter hall

[159] G. F. Millar, 'Maynooth and Scottish Politics: the Role of the Maynooth Grant Issue, 1845–1857', *Records of the Scottish Church History Society*, 27 (1997), 223–5.

[160] Nockles, *Oxford Movement in Context*, 90–3; Wolffe, *Protestant Crusade in Great Britain*, 206; 'Policy of England toward Ireland', *English Review*, 3 (June 1845), 417.

[161] Machin, 'The Maynooth Grant, the Dissenters and Disestablishment', 64.

sets up its bray . . . and the Protestant operatives of Dublin call for impeachments in exceedingly bad English. But what did you expect? Did you think, when, to serve your own turn, you called the devil up, that it was as easy to lay him as to raise him? Did you think, when you went on, session after session, thwarting and reviling those whom you knew to be in the right, and flattering all the worst passions of those whom you knew to be in the wrong, that the day of reckoning would never come? It has come.[162]

While Parliament deliberated, the anti-Maynooth agitation grew, culminating between 30 April and 3 May with a London conference that drew over 1,000 delegates from Protestant Churches throughout the three kingdoms. The agitation failed to halt the Maynooth bill. It did, however, divide and weaken Peel's Tory party. Gladstone had resigned from the Government on the issue. Peel staked the survival of his Government on the Maynooth bill; none the less, in the third reading of the bill in the Commons, Tory MPs voted against it by 149 to 148.[163] Peel's Government held firmly to its Maynooth policy, and with Whig support the bill passed through both Houses of Parliament and became law on 30 June 1845. 'The bill will pass but our party is destroyed', wrote Graham to Heytesbury on 12 April.[164] For many Tory supporters of established religion, Maynooth was Peel's second great betrayal of the established Churches, comparable to Catholic Emancipation in 1829. Peel, who had refused to recommend additional State money for the Protestant establishments in England and Scotland, who refused to provide a grant to the Irish establishment's successful Church Education Society, now provided endowments to the Catholic Church in Ireland.[165] Was this not further evidence of his lack of religious conviction? If he were prepared to endow Maynooth, and perhaps the whole Irish Catholic Church, in an attempt to silence the repeal agitation, was he not using religion as a form of social control? If so, was not the Government confirming the Voluntary claim that an established Church was essentially a tool of State? The Maynooth affair contributed to growing doubts about any State involvement in religion. 'We are scarcely warranted', maintained the *Church of England Quarterly Review* of July 1845, 'in saying that the destruction of the English Church, as a national Church, is the end which our legislators propose.' But, it added, 'it is very clear that it is the end which their measures will

[162] Macaulay, *Miscellaneous Works*, v. 365.
[163] Gash, *Reaction and Reconstruction in English Politics*, 151.
[164] Ibid. 152.
[165] Chadwick, *The Victorian Church*, i. 223.

effect'.[166] 'What think you of Maynooth?', the High Anglican Samuel Wilberforce asked his brother Robert on 29 April. 'It seems to me quite unavoidable,—but another step towards the ultimate dissolution of all established religion.'[167] Church and State, he now believed, 'are rather at the fag end of an old alliance'.[168]

Many of those who agitated against the Maynooth grant were also committed to disestablishment.[169] The *Quarterly Review* claimed that three-quarters of the petitioners against Maynooth were Dissenters.[170] Miall announced that he opposed the grant not from dislike of Roman Catholicism, but from dislike of all establishments, and support for his Anti-State Church Association swelled as a result of the agitation.[171] In August 1845, moreover, a group of Scottish Dissenting and Free Church leaders, including Chalmers, called for the formation of an 'Evangelical Alliance' to carry on the struggle against 'the encroachments of Popery and Puseyism, and to promote the interests of scriptural Christianity'.[172] This call reflected the belief, widespread in the Free Church, that there had been a conspiracy of Roman Catholics and Tractarians behind the Disruption, and that this same conspiracy was behind the Maynooth grant. In a pamphlet defining the aims of the Evangelical Alliance, Chalmers observed that 'whether the Anti-Christ that is now appearing be in the ancient and unmitigated form of Popery, or in the no less dangerous though milder form of Puseyism,—surely there is the most urgent call for vigilance and alarm.'[173] Until now, the Free Church had steadfastly insisted that it held to the principle of an established Church, even if it had been forced to break its alliance with an 'Erastian' State. However, this attitude began to change in the aftermath of Maynooth. In August 1845, the Free Church leader Robert Candlish asserted in a speech before a special meeting of the General Assembly that the choice now before them was 'between the abolition of all establishments and the establishment and endowment of Popery'. Establishments, he warned, were becoming the instruments

[166] 'The Prospects of the English Church', *Church of England Quarterly Review*, 18 (July 1845), 109.

[167] Ashwell, *Life of Samuel Wilberforce*, i. 266.

[168] Ibid. i. 265.

[169] Cowherd, *Politics of English Dissent*, 159–60.

[170] *Quarterly Review*, 76 (June 1845), 257.

[171] Watts, *The Dissenters*, ii. 549.

[172] J. Wolffe, 'The Evangelical Alliance in the 1840s: An Attempt to Institutionalise Christian Unity', *Voluntary Religion*, Studies in Church History, 23 (Oxford, 1986), 333–46.

[173] T. Chalmers, *On the Evangelical Alliance* (Edinburgh, 1846), 28–9.

through which the 'Man of Sin' would accomplish his ends.[174] The Evangelical Alliance, inaugurated in the autumn of 1845, was dominated by Dissenters.

Among supporters of the Maynooth grant, meanwhile, many were indeed coming to the view that there should be a general State endowment of the Catholic Church in Ireland. Most advocated concurrent endowment, that is the endowment of both the Catholic and Protestant Churches. Ideas of concurrent endowment of the two Churches had been around since at least the beginning of the century, and these had been revived after 1843 in response to the involvement of the Catholic clergy in the repeal agitation. In January 1844, the Whig Nassau Senior recommended in the *Edinburgh Review* that the State should provide an endowment of £320,000 per annum to the Catholic Church in Ireland. He even suggested that, were it politically possible, the best course would be to give the whole endowment of the existing Protestant establishment in Ireland, including the rent charge on land, to the Catholic Church, and then to provide a new State grant to support the smaller Church of Ireland.[175] During the Maynooth agitation liberal newspapers, including the *Manchester Guardian*, joined in the call for concurrent endowment in Ireland.[176] By June 1845, even the Tory J. W. Croker, writing in the conservative *Quarterly Review*, was advocating concurrent endowment.[177] There could, Croker argued, be no peace in Ireland until the Catholic Church there was established and endowed by the State, and thus given a stake in the United Kingdom. Against the argument that a Protestant State could never endow Roman Catholicism, he emphasized political reality. 'We are *not* a Protestant people', he asserted. 'We are an Anglican and Presbyterian and Roman Catholic people, and we all contribute in various ways, direct as well as indirect, in the maintenance of each other's worship.'[178] If the same State could establish both Anglicanism and Presbyterianism in Britain, why could it not establish both Catholicism and Anglicanism in Ireland?

Others, however, were convinced that the solution was not to

[174] Wilson and Rainy, *Memorials of Robert Smith Candlish*, 366.

[175] [N. W. Senior], 'Ireland', *Edinburgh Review*, 79 (January 1844), 223, 228; T. B. Macaulay to Charles Napier, 25 November 1843, in G. O. Trevelyan, *Life and Letters of Lord Macaulay*, 2nd edn., 2 vols. (London, 1883), ii. 149–52.

[176] D. Read, *Peel and the Victorians* (Oxford, 1987), 144.

[177] [J. W. Croker], 'Ireland', *Quarterly Review*, 76 (June 1845), 247–98.

[178] Ibid. 268.

create two rival established Churches in Ireland, but to disestablish the Church of Ireland. On 23 April 1845 Macaulay made a forthright appeal for Irish disestablishment in the House of Commons. 'Of all the institutions existing in the civilized world', he insisted, 'the Established Church of Ireland seems to me the most absurd.' That Church, he continued, had received a trial of nearly 300 years, and it had failed. It had failed to provide religious and moral instruction to the Irish people, it had failed to achieve any significant number of conversions from Catholicism to Protestantism, and it had failed to promote social harmony and civil peace. 'In the name of common-sense, then', Macaulay asked, 'tell us what good end this Church has attained.' Irish disestablishment was 'a concession, which ought in justice to have been made long ago, and which may be made with grace and dignity even now'.[179] Significantly, the Evangelical Anglican Baptist Noel had come to a similar view, which he expressed in a pamphlet in 1845.[180] Noel, it will be recalled, had been a champion of established Protestantism in Ireland during the Bible war and New Reformation campaign; indeed, his confrontation with O'Connell and Sheil in September 1824 in Cork had marked the first clash of that war. But now even Noel called for an end to the Irish establishment. The State, he maintained, was confronted in Ireland with the stark alternative of 'religious equality or repeal', that is, either to grant full equality under the law to both Catholics and Protestants, or to risk the repeal of the Union. The Maynooth endowment, he argued, indicated that the Government had decided on a policy of concurrent endowment. Yet it would be absurd for the State to maintain two rival establishments in the same country, 'each bent on the rout and ruin of the other'.[181] The only real solution, Noel concluded, was to disestablish and disendow the Church of Ireland, and leave all the Churches in Ireland equal before the law as Voluntary Churches. (By 1848, Baptist Noel had left the Church of England to become, yes, a Baptist.) In November 1845 the Scottish Free Church leader R. S. Candlish, writing in the *North British Review*, a Free Church organ, supported Noel's view.[182] 'Few

[179] Macaulay, *Miscellaneous Works*, v. 367–87, 368, 380, 387.

[180] B. W. Noel, *The Catholic Claims: A Letter to the Lord Bishop of Cashel*, 3rd edn. (London, 1845).

[181] Ibid. 25.

[182] [R. S. Candlish], 'Church and State—Ireland', *North British Review*, 4 (November 1845), 255–80.

probably among the friends of Establishment', that same journal observed in November 1846, 'would hesitate, between the two alternatives, to prefer the system of Voluntary Churches to [one] of universal endowment.' They would, it added, 'think it far better that the State should *negatively* decline to acknowledge Christianity, than *positively* represent it as giving an uncertain, varying, if not unmeaning, sound'.[183]

In the event, the calls for concurrent endowment made little headway. The British public would not have accepted the scheme. Further, there was no enthusiasm among Irish Catholics for State endowment and establishment. The Catholic Church had, during the previous twenty years, grown to pride itself on its independence from the State and its reliance on the free-will offerings of its congregations. Whatever might be the situation for the Catholic Church elsewhere in Europe, in Ireland it was a Voluntary Church, rooted in the communities that supported it. It was free from State control and identified with the suffering masses; its clerical leaders were not prepared to relinquish its spiritual independence. 'The people', an Irish Catholic priest in the diocese of Tuam had informed the French historian Alexis de Tocqueville in July 1835, 'gives the fruit of its labours liberally to me, and I give them my time, my care and my entire soul.' But, he added, 'the day I received government money, the people would no longer regard me as their own'.[184] One line of Catholic polemic against Anglicanism was that the Church of England, unlike the Catholic Church, was 'the slave of the state'.[185] The *Dublin Review* of March 1844 insisted that the Catholic Church in Ireland had from its beginning been a voluntary Church and it had no desire 'now, in the nineteenth century, to exchange the voluntary system for a government pension'. Through voluntary means alone, it noted, the Catholic Church ministered to seven million Catholics, supported twenty-six archbishops and bishops, some 2,500 priests, over 2,000 churches, and numerous schools. 'Behold the fruits of the voluntary principle', it concluded. 'Then look to its past history in Ireland, and say whether any people

[183] [G. Moncrieff], 'Religion in its Relation to Politics', *North British Review*, 6 (November 1846), 264.

[184] A. de Tocqueville, *Journeys to England and Ireland*, trans. G. Lawrence and K. P. Mayer, ed. J. P. Mayer (London, 1958), 172.

[185] [N. Wiseman], 'Church and State', *Dublin Review*, 17 (September 1844), 236–41.

should readily abandon a principle so old and so good.'[186] It might have added that established religion was no longer so secure in the United Kingdom; this mess of pottage was hardly worth a birthright. In 1801 or 1825, the Catholic Church in Ireland might have accepted State payment of its clergy as part of an emancipation package. But the offer, had it been made, would not have been so attractive in 1844–5—not from a State that had declined to provide additional funds to the Church of England for church extension or popular education and that had insisted on civil control over clerical appointments in the Church of Scotland.

Early in May 1845, with the Maynooth grant safely through the Commons, the Government introduced the third of its conciliatory measures for Ireland—the academic colleges bill. This bill provided for the establishment of three new colleges, at Belfast, Galway, and Cork. These colleges were to have no religious lectures or religious tests. While the plan did not forbid the creation of theological chairs, such chairs would have to be endowed from private sources and not by the State. The aim of the colleges scheme was to provide a non-denominational higher education, along the lines of the national system of education set up in 1831. The plan was reminiscent of Peel's Tamworth Reading Room address of January 1841, with its assumption that social harmony would be achieved through the spread of 'useful knowledge' and avoidance of 'Controversial Divinity'. The plan found little favour. On its introduction, it was denounced by that intrepid Protestant champion Robert Harry Inglis as 'a gigantic scheme of Godless education'. O'Connell took up Inglis's phrase, denouncing the 'godless colleges', and in this he was joined by the majority of Irish Catholic bishops. Parliament passed the bill in the autumn of 1845, and the Crown issued charters for the new colleges by the end of 1845. Irish Catholic opposition to the scheme, however, intensified. Amid claims that the new colleges would be proselytizing agencies, the Vatican issued a papal rescript in 1846 condemning the scheme and the Irish hierarchy forbade Catholics to attend the colleges. The Government's programme of conciliating the Catholic Church now drew to a close.[187] The policy had failed in its aim of winning widespread Catholic support for

[186] [P. Leahy], 'State Provision for the Irish Clergy', *Dublin Review*, 16 (March 1844), 186–220, 217, 219.

[187] Kerr, *Peel, Priests and Politics*, 290–351; Gwynn, *Young Ireland and 1848*, 40–8.

the Union, while it had further weakened the principle of established religion in the three kingdoms. In the autumn of 1845, meanwhile, the potato crop in Ireland failed. Soon famine—a 'judgement of God', in the view of Sir James Graham[188]—overshadowed the Government's conciliatory policies in Ireland.

Siren Songs: Catholic Revival and Oxford Secessions

Within the Church of England, support for the Tractarians had waned steadily following the storm over Tract 90 in 1841, and the Tractarians in turn had grown increasingly defensive, narrowly focused, and doctrinaire.[189] Adherents of the movement found their prospects for preferment and influence in the national Church diminishing.[190] For many, Tractarianism was a reactionary movement, lost in medieval mummery, with no place in the modern world of industry and progress. 'To Puseyism', wrote Thomas Carlyle in October 1841, 'one has to say with emphasis: "Foolish ghost, be silent! LABORARE *est orare* [to work is to pray]".'[191] In the parishes Tractarian clergymen encountered growing opposition when they attempted to introduce changes in liturgy and church decoration. 'The puseyites', complained Robert Slaney, a Shropshire country gentleman and MP for Shrewsbury, in his diary for August 1843, 'cause great alarm at Oxford and elsewhere—wishing to introduce the authority of the Fathers, and other usages of the Roman Catholic Church, and to limit the right of private judgement as to the Scriptures, and requiring generally prostration of the understanding before Authority.'[192]

Undaunted by such hostility, advanced Tractarians, including W. G. Ward, Frederick Oakeley, J. D. Dalgairns, and Frederick Faber, grew outspoken about their intention to move the Church of England, or at least their section of it, towards corporate union with the Roman Catholic Church. Apart from their disillusionment with

[188] Hilton, *The Age of Atonement*, 249.

[189] Nockles, 'The Oxford Movement and the University', 244.

[190] Knight, 'The Influence of the Oxford Movement in the Parishes', 133; W. Ward, *W. G. Ward and the Oxford Movement*, 185–6.

[191] T. Carlyle to J. G. Marshall, 27 October 1841, *Collected Letters of Thomas and Jane Welsh Carlyle*, xiii. 289.

[192] Cited in D. G. Paz, *Popular Anti-Catholicism in Mid-Victorian England* (Stanford, Calif., 1992), 133.

the Protestant establishment, there was reason for these Tractarian Romanizers to look hopefully to the Catholic Church in England. That Church had grown increasingly confident and expansive in the decade following Emancipation. 'Catholicity in England', the convert Ambrose Phillipps de Lisle enthused in 1840, 'is proceeding at a railroad pace.'[193] There was substantial growth in Catholic numbers in England and Wales. In 1780, there had been an estimated 54,000 Catholics out of a population of 7,500,000. By 1840, according to reports of the Catholic vicars-apostolic, there were over 450,000 Catholics out of a population of some 16,000,000. Even allowing for exaggeration, there had been significant growth. Most of this increase was due to migration from Ireland; in 1840, there were in England some 420,000 Irish-born residents, perhaps two-thirds of whom were Catholics; the failure of the New Reformation in Ireland was now being brought home to Britain by this influx of Irish Catholics. In order better to serve the growing numbers, Propaganda in Rome had reorganized the ecclesiastical structures of the Catholic Mission in England in 1840, doubling the number of vicariates, from four to eight. Many English Catholics were now pressing for their Church to restore bishoprics with territorial dioceses.[194] There was an enhanced mission to the urban poor, with a multiplication of Catholic philanthropic societies, led by the Associated Catholic Charities, founded in 1811, and the Catholic Institute, established in the 1820s and reorganized in 1838. Catholic charities revived the medieval ideal of holy poverty, with the poor blessed because they were poor, and to be helped without distinguishing between the 'worthy' and the 'unworthy' poor.[195] The number of Catholic places of worship had increased from about 350 churches and chapels in the mid-1820s to some 450 churches and chapels in 1840.[196] Augustus Pugin, now professor of Ecclesiastical

[193] E. R. Norman, *The English Catholic Church in the Nineteenth Century* (Oxford, 1984), 201.

[194] J. Connell, *The Roman Catholic Church in England 1780–1850: A Study in Internal Politics* (Philadelphia, 1984), 152–85.

[195] Paz, *Popular Anti-Catholicism*, 81–100; R. K. Donovan, 'The Denominational Character of English Catholic Charitable Effort, 1800–1865', *Catholic Historical Review*, 62 (1976), 200–23; S. Gilley, 'Heretic London, Holy Poverty and the Irish Poor, 1830–70', *Downside Review*, 89 (1971), 64–89; J. L. Altholz, 'Social Catholicism in England in the Age of the Devotional Revolution', in S. J. Brown and D. W. Miller (eds.), *Piety and Power in Ireland 1760–1960* (Belfast, 2000), 209–19.

[196] J. D. Holmes, *More Roman than Rome: English Catholicism in the Nineteenth Century* (London, 1978), 101.

Antiquities at Oscott, continued to promote the Gothic revival in Catholic church architecture; in 1840, he was at work building seventeen new Catholic churches.[197] The wealthy convert Phillipps de Lisle made his country house named Grace-Dieu, near Loughborough, a centre for mission. He founded a monastery, erected schools and churches, and dreamed of the conversion of England. In 1840, the Italian Rosminian Fr. Luigi Gentili (1801–48) arrived at Grace-Dieu to conduct missions in the neighbouring villages. He broke with Phillipps in 1842, but carried on his mission in the Midlands through a village preaching that was reminiscent of the Evangelical Dissenters fifty years before. Encountering considerable verbal and physical abuse in the early years of his mission, he persevered and is said to have made nearly 3,000 converts before his death in 1848.[198]

From 1840, the leading force in the Catholic Church in England was Bishop Nicholas Wiseman (1802–65), former rector of the English College in Rome, and, from 1840, coadjutor to the vicar-apostolic of the Central District and president of St Mary's College, Oscott, near Birmingham. Born in Spain to an Irish family, Wiseman had spent some twenty-two years on the Continent before coming to England. An able linguist and scholar, an imposing speaker and writer, imperious and magnanimous, sleek, charming, and urbane, Wiseman brought an aura of intellectual respectability to the Catholic Church. Unlike many Catholics in England, he was sympathetic to the Oxford Movement, viewing it in 1840 as a step towards the re-Catholicizing of England.[199] In 1836 he had founded the *Dublin Review*, a quarterly Catholic journal of literature and politics; later he noted that its original purpose had been 'to watch . . . and to correct, where necessary, the Religious Movement . . . then becoming prominent in the English Church'.[200] Wiseman meant to transform the college at Oscott into a magnet, or beacon, to attract the Anglo-Catholics into the Roman Church.[201] By the beginning of 1843, he was sounding a triumphalist note. 'During the past

[197] Norman, *The English Catholic Church*, 201.

[198] C. R. Leetham, *Luigi Gentili: A Sower for the Second Spring* (London, 1965).

[199] W. Ward, *Life and Times of Cardinal Wiseman*, 2nd edn., 2 vols. (London, 1897), i. 381–2; Norman, *The English Catholic Church*, 209; B. Fothergill, *Nicholas Wiseman* (London, 1963), 62–3.

[200] [N. Wiseman], 'The Religious Movement', *Dublin Review*, 19 (December 1845), 538–9.

[201] Holmes, *More Roman than Rome*, 64.

twelve months', he informed Cardinal Acton on 1 January 1843, 'there have been more converts than for ten years previously.' He spoke of regularly receiving converts in groups of twenty to forty around his vicariate.[202] Such language was reminiscent of the New Reformation rhetoric two decades before in Ireland; only now it was Catholics praying—and praying with confidence—for the conformity of Protestant England.

Within the Oxford Movement, probably the most enthusiastic advocate of union with Rome was W. G. Ward (1812–82), the jovial, expansive, opera-loving fellow of Balliol College, Oxford, and a University lecturer in mathematics and logic. While a student, Ward had embraced the Christian social idealism of the liberal Anglican Thomas Arnold. Later he had flirted briefly with Radicalism, but then had been drawn into the Tractarian movement. Early in 1841, he published two pamphlets in response to Newman's Tract 90, in which he pushed Newman's line of argument further in a Romeward direction. For Ward, Newman's argument that the Thirty-Nine Articles could be interpreted in a Catholic sense had been inconsistent and unconvincing. If anything, Ward maintained, Tract 90 had demonstrated that the Anglican Articles were a failed compromise between Catholicism and Protestantism. No one, Anglican or Catholic, could subscribe to all the articles without prevarication; the Church of England was fundamentally flawed and could provide no certain spiritual home. It was his task, he avowed, to set before these foundering Christians 'that one image of the Catholic Church, which, would they but see it, is the real satisfaction for their restless cravings'.[203] Ward's critique of Anglicanism aroused intense opposition within the established Church, and he was forced to resign his University lectureships.[204]

He now became a still more outspoken advocate of a corporate union of the Anglican and Catholic Churches—a mouthpiece for those younger Romanizers who were less concerned with the apostolic purity of the ancient Church (so important to the early Tractarians), and more concerned with the living, catholic, and universal Church. In July 1841, and again in October 1841, Ward visited the college at Oscott, where he had discussions with Wiseman

202 Cardinal Gasquet, 'Letters of Cardinal Wiseman', *Dublin Review*, 164 (1919), 5–6.

203 [W. G. Ward], *A Few Words in Support of No. 90 of the Tracts for the Times* (Oxford, 1841), 44.

204 W. Ward, *William George Ward and the Oxford Movement*, 185–210.

and Phillipps de Lisle about prospects for reunion. It was Ward's belief that the Romanizers should remain in the Church of England, the Church in which providence had placed them, and work from within for union. He counselled patience on the part of Roman Catholics. 'You cannot be more anxious than I am', he assured Phillipps on 28 October 1841, 'for the return of the greatest possible number of Englishmen *in the most Catholic and Christian temper possible* to visible unity.' 'You must believe', he added, 'that the spirit working at present within the English Church is certain in God's good time to bring His elect to you.'[205] Phillipps de Lisle hastened to spread Ward's assurances. 'The leading Men in the Anglican Church', Phillipps informed the Catholic earl of Shrewsbury in 1841, 'are determined to reunite their Church to the Holy See.' 'You may rest assured', he continued to Shrewsbury, 'that the reunion of the Churches is certain. Mr Newman has lately received the adhesion of *several hundreds* of the Clergy: this is publickly known, and therefore I may state it.'[206] When in July 1841 Newman resigned as editor of the *British Critic*, the editorship passed to his brother-in-law, the compliant Thomas Mozley. During Mozley's editorship, Ward and Oakeley contributed a series of articles, highly critical of the Reformers and favourable to Roman Catholicism. The State connection, they maintained, had proved a broken reed for the Anglican Church, and the much vaunted apostolic succession had not ensured the Church strong leadership under the bishops. Older Tractarian leaders, especially Pusey, were uneasy with the Romanizers. Yet Pusey also acknowledged the attractions that the Roman Catholic Church, with its unity, discipline, independence, and certainty, could have for members of the distracted Church of England.[207]

The Church of England grew still more distracted over the Jerusalem bishopric affair.[208] During the summer of 1841, the British and Prussian Governments took up a proposal by the Prussian diplomat and devout Protestant Chevelier Bunsen to create a joint Anglo-Prussian bishopric in Jerusalem, which would provide

[205] W. Ward, *William George Ward and the Oxford Movement*, 195, 198.

[206] Purcell, *Life of Ambrose Phillipps de Lisle*, i. 216–17.

[207] E. B. Pusey, *A Letter to his Grace the Archbishop of Canterbury, on some Circumstances in connection with the Present Crisis in the English Church* (Oxford, 1842), 8–13.

[208] There is an extensive literature on the Jerusalem bishopric affair. See especially R. W. Greaves, 'The Jerusalem Bishopric, 1841', *English Historical Review*, 64 (1949), 328–52; P. J. Welch, 'Anglican Churchmen and the Establishment of the Jerusalem Bishopric', *Journal of Ecclesiastical History*, 8 (1957), 193–204; Nockles, *Oxford Movement in Context*, 156–64.

support to Protestants residing in the Middle East. There were, in fact, virtually no Protestants in the region, and for the politicians the project was primarily a means to enhance British and Prussian influence in the Levant. It was also influenced by a renewed interest in the Jewish mission, and Church Evangelicals embraced the project with enthusiasm.[209] The Prussian king, Frederick William IV, agreed to endow the Jerusalem bishopric, while nomination of the bishop would alternate between the British and Prussian Crowns. Queen Victoria and Prince Albert warmly supported the scheme, the bill passed through both Houses of Parliament without a division and received the royal assent in October 1841. The first bishop, the Anglican Michael Soloman Alexander, was consecrated in November 1841.

Although the scheme received broad support within the Church of England, the Tractarians denounced it as unashamedly Erastian, an agreement by two States to use their established Churches for political ends. The politicians had taken the lead; the Churches had obediently followed. Tractarians warned that the Anglo-Prussian bishopric would be viewed as an unwelcome intrusion by the Orthodox Church. Above all, they objected to such a union between their own Anglo-Catholic Church and an overtly Protestant Church, rooted in both the Lutheran and Calvinist Reformations. The scheme, insisted the Young Englander Lord John Manners, was 'a flag of alliance held out to Zurich and Geneva from Lambeth'.[210] The joint bishopric, according to Pusey, aimed 'to bring together persons, one knows not whom, sound or unsound, pious or worldly, bound together by no associations, accustomed to no obedience'.[211] For Newman, the affair confirmed his growing fears about the established Church. 'It seems', Newman confided to his fellow Tractarian J. W. Bowden on 10 October 1841, 'we are *in the way* to fraternise with Protestants of all sorts—Monophysites, half-converted Jews and even Druses. If any such event should take place, I shall not be able to keep a single man from Rome. They will be all trooping off sooner or later.'[212] 'Such acts as were in progress', Newman later recalled, 'led me to the gravest suspicion, not that [the Anglican Church] would soon cease to be a Church, but that it had never been a Church all along.'[213]

[209] Hylson-Smith, *Evangelicals in the Church of England*, 120.
[210] Welch, 'Anglican Churchmen and the Establishment of the Jerusalem Bishopric', 198.
[211] Pusey, *Letter to the Archbishop of Canterbury*, 114.
[212] A. Mozley (ed.), *Letters and Correspondence of J. H. Newman*, i. 352–3.
[213] J. H. Newman, *Apologia*, 159.

In February 1842, Newman—on his 'death-bed, as regards my membership with the Anglican Church'—moved to Littlemore, just outside Oxford. Here he had leased a row of several two-roomed cottages, and gathered around himself a small community of Anglo-Catholic scholars, creating what he described as a 'half College half monastery'.[214] One of the aims of his community was to keep the younger Romanizers within the established Church by providing them with the regular discipline and devotion they craved. The young men, whom he referred to as 'monks', assisted Newman in the preparation of a work of piety, *The Lives of the Saints of the English Church*. Questions, meanwhile, were raised about Newman's honesty in remaining within the Church of England, and about the influence he exercised over the young men at Littlemore. Was he not 'rearing at Littlemore a nest of Papists', training them for the delicate work of subverting the Protestant Church of England from within? It was a charge that hurt him deeply. He continued to hold his position as vicar of St Mary's in Oxford—a sign, he insisted, of his allegiance to the Church of England.[215] However, he also confessed privately to Pusey in October 1842 that his 'sympathies' were with the Romanizers.[216] Other Tractarians set up religious houses with a monastic character, including F. W. Faber, who established a house at Elton in 1843, and Robert Aitken, who formed one at St James, Leeds, in the same year.[217]

Opposition to the Tractarians intensified. Pusey had been in virtual retirement from public life following the devastating blow of his wife's death in 1839. In May 1843 he was dealt another blow, when he was charged with heretical teaching for a sermon preached at Christ Church on the eucharist as a comfort to the penitent sinner—a work which reflected his own personal experience with anguish and consolation. A court of six doctors decided that Pusey's views on the real presence of Christ in the eucharist contravened the Anglican Articles, approaching too close to the Roman doctrine of transubstantiation, and the Oxford authorities suspended him from preaching within the University for two years. The proceedings against Pusey seemed to many not only insensitive and unjust but also calculated, part of a move to silence or force the more extreme

[214] Ker, *Newman*, 241, 245–50.

[215] W. Walsh, *The Secret History of the Oxford Movement*, 6th edn. (London, 1899), 16–28; Liddon, *Life of Pusey*, ii. 293.

[216] Ker, *Newman*, 253.

[217] Yates, *Anglican Ritualism in Victorian Britain*, 78.

Tractarians from the Church. There were rumours that the Peel Government was behind Pusey's suspension.[218] Certainly Peel despised the Tractarians, while Queen Victoria, with her moderate Evangelical leanings, described the Puseyites as 'snakes in the grass'.[219] The Cambridge-educated moderate Evangelical William Goode was insisting by 1842 that it was time the Tractarians left the Church.[220] The following year, William Lockhart, an undergraduate and member of Newman's Littlemore community, joined the Catholic Church against the wishes of his family. Here was evidence of the corrupting influence of the Romanizers. In 1843, the Evangelical Lord Ashley presided at a meeting to petition the authorities at Oxford University to suppress the Tractarians. High Churchmen were also openly denouncing the Tractarian Romanizers. In 1842 W. F. Hook published a sermon warning Anglicans against the growth of Romanism and the 'peril of idolatry.' In 1843, William Palmer of Worcester College, who had contributed some of the early Tracts, published his *Narrative of Events Connected with the Publication of the 'Tracts for the Times'*, accusing the Romanizers of corrupting the Tractarian movement. Henry Manning preached a fiercely anti-Catholic sermon on 5 November 1843 in Oxford's St Mary's church.[221] Under mounting pressure, the *British Critic*, the chief organ of the Romanizers, was discontinued in October 1843. For some, the growing rage against the Tractarians was going too far, and threatened to become a witch-hunt. In 1843, the liberal Anglican F. D. Maurice blamed the press for stirring up popular hostility to the Tractarians: 'a religious school for scandal is opened in every town and village; men employ themselves in the house of God in observing the tones and gestures of their pastors, that they may report something evil of them in next week's newspapers'.[222] The year 1843—the year of the defeat of Graham's scheme for an Anglican national system of education, of the Disruption of

[218] Liddon, *Life of Pusey*, ii. 328–63; Nockles, 'The Oxford Movement and the University', 249–50; Ker, *Newman*, 276–7.

[219] W. Arnstein, 'Queen Victoria and Religion', in Malmgreen (ed.), *Religion in the Lives of English Women*, 99.

[220] W. Goode, *The Case as it is; or, A Reply to the Letter of Dr. Pusey to his Grace the Archbishop of Canterbury* (London, 1842), 42–3.

[221] W. F. Hook, *Peril of Idolatry: A Sermon* (London, 1842); Purcell, *Life of Cardinal Manning*, i. 244–53.

[222] F. D. Maurice, *On the Right and Wrong Methods of Supporting Protestantism* (London, 1843), 3, 13.

the Church of Scotland, of the repeal movement in Ireland—was also witnessing the crisis of the Oxford Movement.

On 18 September 1843 Newman resigned as vicar of St Mary's, preaching his final sermon, 'The Parting of Friends', on 25 September. 'I do so despair of the Church of England', he confided to his sister, Harriet, on 29 September, 'and am so evidently cast off by her, and, on the other hand, I am so drawn to the Church of Rome, that I think it *safer*, as a matter of honesty, *not* to keep my living.'[223] Newman's resignation, though not unexpected, gave a certain finality to the break-up of the Tractarian movement. 'How vividly', the Scottish Episcopalian John Campbell Shairp, then a student at Balliol, later recalled, 'comes back the remembrance of the aching blank, the awful pause, which fell on Oxford when that voice had ceased, and we knew that we should hear it no more. It was as when, to one kneeling by night, in the silence of some vast cathedral, the great bell tolling solemnly overhead has suddenly gone still.'[224] Four months earlier Thomas Chalmers, who had led the campaign from 1833 to revive the influence and authority of the established Church of Scotland, had resigned his professorship of divinity. He had grown to view the established Church that he had championed as fundamentally flawed. Now Newman, who had led an influential campaign from 1833 to revive the established Church of England as a force for national redemption, also felt obliged to resign his office in that Church. The two men held radically different views of the nature of the Church; they were fundamentally opposed in their views on apostolic succession, the place of tradition, the nature of the sacraments. Yet during the 1830s they had been arguably the most influential Churchmen in the United Kingdom. And on one fundamental point they were agreed: a Church, even an established Church, must be independent of the State in its spiritual functions; it must exercise an independent spiritual discipline, and it must speak with a prophetic voice. Now, in the long summer of 1843, both demitted their offices in their respective established Churches, and sought elsewhere for the true Church.[225] Chalmers had departed amid a fanfare of popular adulation and had been followed out of the established Church by

[223] A. Mozley (ed.), *Letters and Correspondence of J. H. Newman*, i. 425.

[224] W. Ward, *Life of John Henry Cardinal Newman*, 2nd edn., 2 vols. (London, 1913), i. 77.

[225] For a comparison of Newman and Chalmers, see H. J. Laski, *Studies in the Problem of Sovereignty* (London, 1917), 114.

thousands; he became the venerated leader of the Free Church. Newman's resignation was a lonely affair, as he wept for the friends he left behind and they wept to watch him depart. Nor had he yet made his way to that other Church.

The summer of 1843 also saw the beginnings of open warfare over ritual, as the controversies surrounding the Oxford Movement erupted in violent confrontations in the parishes. The tensions had been building for years, with deep-seated popular anti-Catholicism fed by denunciations of the Tractarian Romanizers in the press and in pulpits. There was, *Fraser's Magazine* noted in December 1842, growing hostility over Tractarian innovations in worship, including:

> their endeavour to introduce the keeping of the saints' days, their practice of praying with faces turned towards the East, their decorating the communion-tables with candlesticks and tapers, and, in some instances, even with flowers, their opening their Churches daily for the celebration of divine worship, their rigid observance of the Church's fasts . . . their dislike to the black gown, and preference of the white surplice . . . their chanting of the liturgy, or reading it in a monotonous tone, their bowing towards the altar as often as they passed it.[226]

The ritualist war began with moves in late 1842 by the High Church bishops Blomfield of London and Phillpotts of Exeter to require the clergy of their dioceses to observe the Church's rubrics governing public worship, including the requirement that preachers wear the surplice at morning worship.[227] These calls encountered an angry popular response. In the diocese of London, Blomfield's instructions were ignored in many parishes; in churches where the clergy did seek to obey their diocesan, worshippers walked out or loudly protested. In Exeter, opposition to the rubrics, and especially the surplice, led to riots in late 1844 and early 1845. Broadsheets summoned people to 'save your church from the horrors of Popery', congregations walked out of services or disrupted services at which the surplice was worn, and angry mobs roughed up and chased the offending clergymen through the streets.[228] English Protestants were

[226] 'Movements in the Church', *Fraser's Magazine*, 26 (Dec. 1842), 717.

[227] C. J. Blomfield, *Charge delivered to the Clergy of the Diocese of London . . . in October 1842*, 2nd edn. (London, 1842), 36–54; H. Phillpotts, *Charge delivered to the Clergy of the Diocese of Exeter* (London, 1842); [J. W. Croker], 'Rubrics and Ritual of the Church of England', *Quarterly Review*, 72 (May 1843), 232–90.

[228] Chadwick, *The Victorian Church*, i. 212–21; Blomfield, *Memoir of Charles James Blomfield*, 247–62; Davies, *Henry Phillpotts*, 180–9; Yates, *Anglican Ritualism in Victorian Britain*, 182–3.

emulating the methods of the Irish Catholics during the Bible war of the 1820s—only now it was threatened Protestants disrupting High Church services which they feared were bringing England's national Church into conformity with Rome. For their part, High Anglicans were outraged at what they portrayed as Evangelical-incited mobs seeking to intimidate conscientious clergymen from observing the rubrics of their Church. The situation, the High Church *Christian Remembrancer* averred, was threatening the disruption of the Church of England; the Evangelicals, it predicted, would find 'that they have called up a devil which is not to be laid by their puny Establishmentism'.[229]

Amid the gathering ritualist storm, in June 1844 W. G. Ward published *The Ideal of a Christian Church*, partly in response to William Palmer's attack on the Tractarian Romanizers in his *Narrative* of the previous year.[230] It was a rambling, ponderous, contentious, impolitic, but also intensely honest work. For Ward, the ideal Christian Church was an independent spiritual entity, outside the control both of the civil State and of the rich and powerful in society, and exercising an elevating influence on the population through the example of its sanctity, moral discipline, and dogma. Ward placed considerable emphasis on the social ethics of the Church, and especially its commitment to the poor. In language reminiscent of the church extensionists of the 1830s, he maintained that the ideal Church was a 'poor man's Church'; its 'high and peculiar prerogative' was 'to alleviate the misery of the humble and oppressed'.[231] It was to carry out an aggressive mission 'among our crowded manufacturing towns', gaining the trust of the poor, teaching social responsibility to the upper and middle classes, rejecting political economy with its 'deliberate calculations of methodical and cool-headed science', and enhancing social harmony.[232] It should assist men and women to grow in sanctity and compassion. To achieve these purposes, the ideal Church had to be independent of all outside authority in its spiritual life, for 'it is impossible for Christians to ripen into saints, if ordinary men are allowed to sit in judgement on their conduct and expressions'.[233] The Anglican establishment, Ward continued, had, in the three hundred years since the Reformation,

[229] 'The Rubical Question', *Christian Remembrancer*, 9 (April 1845), 488, 499, 501.

[230] W. G. Ward, *The Ideal of a Christian Church considered in Comparison with Existing Practice*, 2nd edn. (London, 1844).

[231] Ibid. 420. [232] Ibid. 414, 373–4, 415. [233] Ibid. 418.

failed to achieve this ideal. It had identified itself too closely with the civil State and the social élite. It lacked proper discipline. With a few honourable exceptions, its clergy and laity had neglected their duties to the poor. It had 'been swayed by a spirit of arrogance, self-contentment, and self-complacency'.[234] This in turn reflected its over-reliance on private judgement and on mirroring the prevailing values of society. It desired too much to be a respected part of the social and constitutional order, to be the national religion, rather than to be the often unwelcome witness to the universal truths of the catholic and apostolic Church. The remedy, for Ward, was for the Church of England to look to the example of the Roman Catholic Church. Here it would find the model of an authoritative, spiritually independent, socially committed, missionary Church.

Ward's book stung the defenders of the established Church to action. This critique of Anglicanism and advocacy of Roman Catholicism could not be ignored—not with a confident Catholic Church calling openly for the re-conversion of England, not with many prominent journalists and politicians recommending the endowment of the Catholic Church in Ireland, not with ritualists alienating parishioners with 'popish' innovations in worship. Late in 1844 the Oxford authorities brought formal charges against both Ward and his book—charges which they widened to include a censure of Newman's Tract 90. The convocation of Oxford University considered these charges on 13 February 1845, several days after the Maynooth bill had been introduced in Parliament and while anti-Catholic feeling was intense. The Sheldonian Theatre was packed; over 1,000 attended, with political and religious leaders coming to Oxford for what was viewed as a crucial decision on the Tractarian movement. Ward spoke ably in his own defence, but convocation decided by an overwhelming majority to condemn the book and then by a smaller majority to deprive Ward of his University degrees. The motion to censure Newman was blocked before it could come to a vote, although Newman suspected that it was only a matter of time before his opponents would revive the proceedings against him. Ward's 'degradation' sent a clear message to the Romanizers. The majority in the Church of England would no longer tolerate calls for union with the Roman Catholic Church. Shortly after Ward's degradation, Bishop Blomfield of London instituted proceedings

[234] W. G. Ward, *The Ideal of a Christian Church considered in Comparison with Existing Practice*, 55.

in the Court of Arches against Frederick Oakeley, the Romanizing incumbent of the Margaret Chapel. The Court proceeded to suspend Oakeley from the living in July 1845, despite the fact that he had already resigned.[235] The Church, it seemed, was forcing the Romanizers out of its communion. 'I would', Blomfield asserted in his Charge of 1846, 'rather see a member of our communion pass over at once to the adversary's camp, and from thence hurl defiance and reproach against those whom he has deserted, than that he should continue amongst us only for the dishonest purpose . . . of trying how much of the Romish system can be engrafted upon our own.'[236]

In the summer of 1845, the advanced Tractarians began going over to the Roman Church. The prospect of a corporate union of the Anglican and Roman Churches had ended, and the proceedings against Ward, Newman, and Oakeley showed that the Romanizers now had the choice of keeping silent or leaving the Anglican Church. They followed their individual consciences. There was no grand procession out of the Church of England, as had been the case with the exodus from the Church of Scotland two years before. Rather, Tractarian seceders went over one by one, in individual acts of conformity to Rome—W. G. Ward, Frederick Oakeley, J. D. Dalgairns, Frederick Faber, Ambrose St John, and a number of others. 'It was not till the summer', the Anglo-Catholic R. W. Church later recalled, 'that the first drops of the storm began to fall. Then through the autumn and the next year, friends, whose names and forms were familiar to Oxford, one by one disappeared and were lost to it. Fellowships, curacies, intended careers, were given up.'[237] Newman was received into the Roman Catholic Church on 8 October 1845, and the community at Littlemore was, in the words of one of their number, 'scattered like chaff'.[238] The secessions to Rome did not bring the end of the Oxford Movement. The Tractarians within the Church of England regrouped after 1845 under the leadership of Pusey and Keble, and they continued to exercise influence—pressing for greater reverence for the sacraments

[235] F. Oakeley, *Historical Notes on the Tractarian Movement* (London, 1865), 95–7; Blomfield, *Memoir of Charles James Blomfield*, 268; W. Ward, *William George Ward and the Oxford Movement*, 352–6.

[236] Blomfield, *Memoir of Charles James Blomfield*, 270.

[237] Church, *The Oxford Movement*, 394.

[238] M. Pattison, *Memoirs of an Oxford Don* (1885), ed. V. H. H. Green (London, 1988), 113.

as vehicles for divine grace, greater commitment to the pastoral ministry, greater appreciation for the beauty of holiness, and a heightened sense of the universal Church. The commitment of these Anglo-Catholics, illustrated especially in the careers of selfless parish priests in the urban slums, won widespread respect. In 1847, the Tractarians gained their first bishop, when the Oxford-educated Tractarian Alexander Forbes was consecrated to the see of Brechin in the Scottish Episcopal Church, setting an example of service in the slums of Dundee.[239] Yet the secessions of 1845, and especially the departure of Newman, were an end to the first phase of the Oxford Movement. Those going out testified that in their view the established Church of England was not a branch of the true Church. They rejected what Oakeley termed 'the exclusiveness and mere nationality of the Anglican Church'.[240] They contributed significantly to the Roman Catholic revival in Victorian England, weakening the image of the Protestant nation.

Other advanced Tractarians could not follow Newman into the authoritative Catholic Church, but instead moved in a liberal direction. Mark Pattison, who had been a young member of Newman's Littlemore community, fell into a prolonged depression in 1846–7. Oxford, after the secessions to Rome, seemed to him to lose all direction. 'The sensation to us', he later recalled, 'was as of a sudden end of all things, and without a new beginning.' As he recovered his bearings, he came to view the Tractarian years in Oxford as a 'nightmare', and gradually moved from Christianity to embrace a vague, personal belief in an 'Unseen Power'.[241] In his autobiographical novel, *The Nemesis of Faith*, James Anthony Froude, the younger brother of Richard Hurrell Froude and an ardent Newmanite, wrote of his personal crisis in 1845. He felt himself torn between the influence of the era's two men of genius—Newman, with his calls for the 'surrender of reason' and renunciation of the world; and Thomas Carlyle, with his affirmations of human capacity and worldly progress; in the event, Froude could not follow Newman into the Catholic Church and instead embraced Carlyle, humanism, and the gospel of progress.[242]

[239] R. Strong, *Alexander Forbes of Brechin: The First Tractarian Bishop* (Oxford, 1995), 47–100.

[240] F. Oakeley, *A Letter on Submitting to the Catholic Church, addressed to a Friend* (London, 1845), 26.

[241] Pattison, *Memoirs of an Oxford Don*, 113, 120, 122–3, 164.

[242] J. A. Froude, *The Nemesis of Faith* (London, 1849), 150–78.

Peel's Fall and the Gospel of Free Trade

Gods! were there ever two such bores?
  Nothing else talked of, night or morn—
Nothing *in* doors, or *out* of doors,
  But endless Catholics and Corn!

Thomas Moore

Several months after Newman's departure, in June 1846, Peel resigned as prime minister, bringing his Government to an end. The Government's fall resulted not from its handling of the mounting crises in the established Churches, though these crises had certainly weakened confidence. Rather the fall resulted from the prime minister's conversion to free trade. Peel had come to power in 1841 pledged to support the corn laws. The landed classes had given him their confidence, believing that he would preserve their interests against those of middle-class merchants and manufacturers. However, prompted by economic distress, especially in the manufacturing districts, Peel's Government had soon begun moving away from its protectionist commitments. The Government reintroduced the income tax in 1842 and in successive budgets removed over 400 items from the customs duty. Then in the autumn of 1845, the potato crop in Ireland was destroyed by fungus. Much of the Irish population, especially the rural inhabitants of Munster and Connaught, were dependent on the potato. With Ireland facing mass famine, the Government brought forward legislation in January 1846 to repeal the corn laws. The end of these laws, Peel and his ministers believed, would promote imports of grain, bring down food prices, and thus alleviate the famine in Ireland. Repeal of the corn laws would also improve conditions for the labouring orders in Britain, by lowering the cost of food and stimulating manufactures. It was a conversion as dramatic as that of the outgoing Scottish Non-Intrusionists or English Tractarians. The Dissenter-dominated Anti-Corn Law League was triumphant. For most of the Conservative party, however, Peel had betrayed his promises and principles. In the Commons, two-thirds of the Tory party now turned against Peel's Government, and the repeal of the corn laws could be carried through the Commons only with Liberal support. The House of Lords, threatened with an influx of new peers, reluctantly passed repeal on 25 June. A few hours later, Peel's Government was defeated on an Irish crimes bill and resigned. Peel made it clear that he would not continue to lead the Tory party and he and his supporters separated from the main body of protectionist Tories. For the second time in his career, Peel had reversed his position on a fundamental issue, and in so doing split the Tory party. In 1829 the issue had been Catholic Emancipation; in 1846 it was the corn laws. In 1829, it was believed, he had undermined the Protestant constitution; in 1846, it was feared, he overthrew the social order. Many conservatives predicted that the end of the corn laws would mean the ruin of the landed classes and the triumph of the shopkeepers and manufacturers; it was social revolution.

The final stages in the passing of repeal had brought out tensions between the Anglican clergy and the landed classes. Protectionist landowners had expected the clergy of the established Church to support them in defending the corn laws. The Church, they believed, would surely recognize that the corn laws provided protection for the ideal rural parish community, with its hierarchical social order and squire–parson connection. The corn laws, like the rural parish system, represented traditional social relationships, continuity, and stability. The repeal of the corn laws, on the other hand, meant free trade, individualism, social mobility, and social change; it meant promoting the pluralist city with its cacophony of religious voices; it meant marginalizing the traditional Anglican society. The Anti-Corn Law League was dominated by urban Dissenters, who combined their calls for economic freedom with demands for a free market in religion.

And yet, in 1846 the Anglican clergy did not take their stand with the corn laws, landed classes, and Old England. They did not as a body petition Parliament, or otherwise signal their support for the corn laws. In the second reading of the repeal bill in the House of Lords, two-thirds of the bishops supported repeal. Some protectionist peers openly branded this as a betrayal, not only of the traditional social order, but of the Church's economic interests. The duke of Buckingham observed in the House of Lords that the commutation of the tithes for the English clergy in 1836 had linked the clerical incomes to the price of corn. The repeal of the corn laws, by reducing corn prices, would, he insisted, force down clerical incomes by 25 per cent.[243] How could any conscientious clergyman allow such

[243] *Hansard's Parl. Deb.*, 3rd ser. lxxxvii (11 June 1846), col. 269; Norman, *Church and Society in England*, 137–8; Soloway, *Prelates and People*, 219–22.

damage to the clerical order? The earl of Malmesbury reminded the bishops that they were 'guardians of the interests of the parochial clergy'.[244]

In response, Connop Thirlwall, bishop of St David's, and Samuel Wilberforce, bishop of Oxford, angrily denied that there was a separate clerical interest, and insisted that in opposing protection they acted for the 'vast mass of the community'. Thirlwall praised his fellow Anglican clergymen for not having petitioned to preserve the corn laws; for this, they 'had earned the approbation and respect of all classes'.[245] The clergy, insisted Wilberforce, believed that without the corn laws 'they will minister to a happier, a more contented, a better provided for, and a greatly elevated peasantry'.[246] The old alliance of the established Church of England and landed interest, of parson and squire, was strained. A large and increasing proportion of the Church of England clergy now ministered to urban parishes, and their links with the old paternalist ideal were tenuous. But did this not remove one more support from the established Church? The conservative *English Review* certainly feared for the Church's future, warning that the repeal of the corn laws would encourage Dissenters and might well be followed by a renewed Radical and Voluntary onslaught on the Church, comparable to the storm that had followed the Reform Act of 1832.[247] The Church was again in danger, only now it might find that its traditional allies had joined its foes. 'Hitherto', it observed, 'the Church has been identified with the agricultural interest.' Now there was danger that the landed interest would respond to their loss of incomes by 'concurring in measures for the alienation of Church property'.[248] But the majority of the established clergy seemed prepared to accept the risk, and remained silent as the corn laws were abolished.

With Peel's resignation in late June, public opinion swung to his favour. Probably the majority in the country welcomed his conversion to free trade, or if not, at least respected his willingness to sacrifice his career for his conscience. From being denounced as a cold, unfeeling, unprincipled pragmatist, Peel now became a martyr—a martyr to the new gospel of free trade, cheap bread, increased manufactures, and international brotherhood. His resignation speech,

[244] *Hansard's Parl. Deb.*, 3rd ser., lxxxvi (26 May 1846), col. 1264.

[245] Ibid. 3rd ser., lxxxvii (12 June 1846), col. 307.

[246] Ibid. 3rd ser., lxxxvii (12 June 1846), col. 329.

[247] 'Church and State', *English Review*, 5 (June 1846), 449.

[248] Ibid. 450, 451.

expressing hope that his name might be remembered with good will 'in the abodes of those whose lot it is to labour, and to earn their daily bread by the sweat of their brow', left a memorable impression. For the liberal Anglican A. P. Stanley, Peel retired from the political stage with great dignity, giving the country 'free trade with one hand and universal peace with the other, and casting under foot the miserable factions which had dethroned him'.[249] For Thomas Carlyle, Peel was a heroic figure, a missionary of the progressive order.[250] His Government of 1841–6 would be remembered chiefly for repealing the corn laws.

It would not, however, be remembered for securing the restoration of the established Churches. He had come to power in 1841 pledging 'to support the National Establishment which connects Protestantism with the State in the three countries'.[251] Many had looked to Peel's Government not only to support, but to revive the established Church of England, to make it once again a guardian of the faith in the predominant partner of the United Kingdom. With a renewed alliance of Church and State in England, pushing forward programmes of church extension and Church-directed national education, it might have been possible to move again towards strengthening the established Churches on the Celtic periphery. It might have been possible to revive the project of the early decades of the century, with Church and State co-operating to achieve a paternalist Christian social order throughout the three kingdoms. After five years of Tory Government, however, these hopes had ended, and the established Churches had been considerably weakened. The Government had ended with Peel joining the forces of an emerging liberalism. 'Sir Robert Peel', observed the *Church of England Quarterly Review* of April 1846, 'now stands at the head of the democratic and liberal party, where, as is now apparent, he ought to have stood ever since the year 1829, when he abandoned all his former statements.'[252] In a sense, Peel had, by his resignation in 1846, followed Chalmers and Newman out of the old corporate order of Church and State, and into a more liberal, pluralistic, individualistic, and fluid society.

Between 1841 and 1846, Peel's Government had failed to provide

[249] Read, *Peel and the Victorians*, 240.

[250] J. Seigel, 'Carlyle and Peel: The Prophet's Search for a Heroic Politician and an Unpublished Fragment', *Victorian Studies*, 26 (1983), 181–95.

[251] Kitson Clark, *Peel and the Conservative Party*, 328.

[252] 'The Peel Crisis', *Church of England Quarterly Review*, 19 (April 1846), 466.

additional State funds for church extension in England, or to enable the Church of England to begin developing a national system of State-supported popular education. It had failed to avert the Disruption of the established Church of Scotland, which had reduced that Church to the position of a minority establishment. It had given no real support to the minority established Church of Ireland, and it had failed to draw the majority Roman Catholic Church in Ireland into alliance with the State. The Church of England had become increasingly divided into conflicting parties. The Church had begun to be distracted by the ritualist war between Evangelicals and Anglo-Catholics, and many of the most zealous Tractarians had entered the resurgent Roman Catholic Church. Tory efforts to revive the traditional authority of established religion had been thwarted by a combination of religious dissent, democratic sentiment, free trade, Irish nationalism, and economic distress. Peel's Government had been the last opportunity to re-knit the old alliance of Church and State. It had failed. 'As far as we can see', the *Church of England Quarterly Review* observed of the Anglican establishment in July 1845, 'there is no reasonable prospect that she will ever recover the position from which she has been thrust by a succession of legislative measures.'[253] Established religion could no longer be seen as binding the three kingdoms together. The United Kingdom was becoming increasingly pluralistic in its religious faith: it had become a multi-faith State of Anglicans and Presbyterians and Roman Catholics and Dissenters. Reviewing the position of the Churches in the three kingdoms in April 1845, the liberal *Edinburgh Review* insisted that this movement towards religious pluralism was a healthy one. 'A fact which the best men of the Middle Ages, and even of the Reformation, would have deemed incredible, has been verified by succeeding generations. Commonwealths, composed of men of different beliefs, are now prosperous and happy; and have not only more peace, but more religion.'[254] Many people, including the Peelite William Gladstone, were coming to believe that the ethical Christian commonwealth would be achieved through the moral gospel of free trade rather than a revival of established religion.[255]

[253] 'The Prospects of the English Church', *Church of England Quarterly Review*, 18 (July 1845), 112.

[254] [W. Emerson], 'The Churches of the Three Kingdoms', *Edinburgh Review*, 81 (April 1845), 529.

[255] H. C. G. Matthew, *Gladstone: 1809–1874* (Oxford, 1986), 76.

The United Kingdom was also a State in which it was becoming increasingly acceptable to hold no Christian faith. In the second half of the nineteenth century, hope for social harmony and progress came to focus increasingly on the city hall, the philanthropic businessman, and Thomas Carlyle's gospel of work, rather than on the parish church, the resident pastor, and the Sunday sermon.

Conclusion

In the first quarter of the nineteenth century, many had looked to the established national Churches—the United Church of England and Ireland, the Church of Scotland—to play a vital role in the process of uniting the diverse peoples of the three historic kingdoms of England, Ireland, and Scotland into a single Protestant nation. Through the influence of the established Churches, the inhabitants of the United Kingdom would receive a shared set of values and beliefs, a common identity, and a sense of national mission. The established Churches would be the guardians of the nation's faith. In thousands of parishes across the three kingdoms, from Lincolnshire to Galway, from Sutherland to Devon, established clergymen would provide pastoral care and weekly sermons, while parish churches would support schools, distribute charity, and promote a communal morality. The parish church would form the physical centre of the community, the most important public building, the place where the records of births, marriages, and deaths were kept, where the community found its identity. In the churchyard, where the ancestors were buried, parish inhabitants would meet to exchange news before and after worship. The Anglican Prayer Book or the Church of Scotland Shorter Catechism would shape minds and provide continuity between the generations. Church services would mark national anniversaries; church bells would ring out the news of national victories. Through their parochial structures, the established Churches would help form the diverse peoples of England, Ireland, and Scotland into Britons, loyal subjects of the Protestant State. Church and State would co-operate to build a Christian commonwealth that would be stable, hierarchical, traditional, paternalist, communal, and homogenous. This conservative Protestant nation-state would be in contrast to the nationalism that had emerged with the French Revolution and inspired Napoleonic expansion. It would also confront the spirit of religious Dissent that had grown so significantly in Britain during the years of warfare with revolutionary and Napoleonic France.

In the quarter century after 1801, leaders in Church and State made significant efforts to advance this project of Protestant nation-building. The Act of Union of 1801 had created a single United Church of England and Ireland, intended to breathe new life into the Irish Protestant establishment. Parliament commissioned enquiries, enacted legislation, and invested unprecedented amounts of public money in the established Churches. There were improvements in clerical residency and discipline, a reduction in pluralism, and the construction of new churches and schools. There were diocesan reform movements in England and Ireland, and reform movements in the presbyterian courts of Scotland. A vibrant Christian idealism began to permeate the universities in the three kingdoms. Young graduates, inspired by the writings of Robert Southey, Samuel Taylor Coleridge, William Wordsworth, and Thomas Chalmers, joined the ranks of the established clergy with a new sense of vocation.

Then came the deluge. It began with the failure of the New Reformation campaign in Ireland in 1827–8, and the end of the hopes of securing the conformity of the majority of the Irish people to the established order in Church and State. The project of forming a Protestant United Kingdom around the established Churches now began to unravel. The Repeal of the Test and Corporation Acts in 1828, the passing of Catholic Emancipation in 1829, and the Parliamentary Reform Act of 1832 changed the political environment. By 1833, Ireland was torn by the Tithe War, while in Britain, Voluntaries and Radicals had launched a large-scale disestablishment campaign. Against the onslaught, Church leaders struggled to defend, and revive, the influence and authority of the parochial establishments, and such leaders as Blomfield, Chalmers, the Sumner brothers, Phillpotts, and Kaye acted with extraordinary energy and commitment. But they found the more representative Parliament less and less supportive. In the 1830s, the future of the established Churches formed arguably the most important question in the politics of the United Kingdom. 'The real question which now divides this country', the Duke of Wellington had insisted in 1838, 'is . . . Church or no Church'.[1] The struggle of the 1830s had been one to decide the nature of the United Kingdom. Was it to be an essentially unitary Protestant State, characterized by a close connection of Church and State, with a common set of religious beliefs

[1] Walker, *Robert Buchanan*, 77.

and moral values mediated to the people through the parochial institutions of the established Churches? Or was it to be a more pluralist, multi-faith State, in which there would be a number of denominations enjoying equality under the law, in which church affiliation would be a matter of individual choice, and religious beliefs and moral values would be matters of private conscience? The ideals of the paternalist Protestant State and close-knit parish community offered much that was attractive, including the inculcation of a communal identity and responsibility, a shared sense of national mission, and a common social ethic. But the paternalist Protestant State also had an authoritarian aspect, and would have left Dissenters and unbelievers marginalized, and denied the benefits of the projected Church-controlled systems of national education.

In the event, the parliamentary State declined to invest the additional public money in the established Churches that would have enabled them to extend their pastoral and educational provision to the rapidly expanding population. The Churches were not disestablished in the 1830s, but they were told that if they wished to extend their influence to the expanding population, they would have to rely on their own efforts, which meant they would increasingly resemble voluntary associations. By the later 1830s, meanwhile, many adherents of the established Churches had come to question the value of the State connection. At a time of heightening Church–State tensions, some Church members had turned to prophetical movements. They sought a grounding for Church authority outside the State connection; they sought to recover the sense of the Church as a spiritual body; they insisted upon the spiritual independence of the Church. If the State were to withdraw its support from the ideal of building the Protestant commonwealth, if it were to commit this act of apostasy, could the established Churches continue their connection with the State? For many, the answer was no. The national Churches, they believed, would have to cease being establishments, and become Churches of Christ alone. They would have to throw off the State connection, in obedience to the sole headship of Christ. These attitudes (though precious little besides) were shared by leaders of both the Oxford Movement in the Church of England and the Non-Intrusionist movement in the Church of Scotland. By 1841, the prospects of building a Christian paternalist nation-state in the United Kingdom around the parochial structures of the established Churches had effectively ended. The end became clear during the

Peel Government of 1841–6, which saw the significant secessions of Scottish Non-Intrusionists and English Tractarians from the established Church, the revival of Roman Catholicism in Britain, and the controversial, largely unsuccessful efforts by the State to develop connections with the Catholic Church in Ireland. The old ideal of the parish community receded to the margins of British and Irish life, the Protestant State faded, and the nation looked to other ideals, among them free trade and global commerce, to shape its future.

By the later 1840s the situation of the national Churches of the three kingdoms was certainly not what had been envisaged by the reformers and theorists of the 1810s and 1820s. In Ireland, despite the massive State investment of the first quarter of the century, the established Church remained a minority Church, with the adherence of less than 10 per cent of the population. Protestant missionaries continued to seek converts among the Catholic population, but they now felt a need to organize their converts into colonies under the protection of Protestant landlords—such as the colonies at Dingle, in county Kerry, or on Achill Island. The famine that devastated Irish society between 1845 and 1849 brought a revival of Protestant mission activity, with the formation of the Society for Irish Church Missions to Roman Catholics giving the Protestant mission a new importance. By 1851 there were claims that over 35,000 Catholics had converted to Protestantism.[2] But the famine also brought renewed hostility to the established Church in Ireland, as stories of 'souperism', or claims that Protestants used food to try to 'buy' the conversions of starving Catholics (similar to the claims made against the New Reformationists in 1826–7), became part of the famine mythology. The conversions ceased, and in 1870 Gladstone's Liberal Government disestablished the Church of Ireland. Between the late 1840s and early 1870s, meanwhile, the Catholic Church strengthened its religious authority over Ireland's famine-devastated population, in what the historian Emmet Larkin has termed a 'devotional revolution'.[3] It established its position as the Irish national Church, while it remained independent from the State.

In Scotland, the Disruption of 1843 had reduced the established Church of Scotland to a minority establishment. According to the

[2] D. A. Kerr, *'A Nation of Beggars?': Priests, People and Politics in Famine Ireland 1846–1852* (Oxford, 1994), 210–14.

[3] E. Larkin, 'The Devotional Revolution in Ireland', *American Historical Review*, 77 (June 1972), 625–52.

State religious census of 1851, only some 32 per cent of church attendees on census Sunday in Scotland attended the established Church. In sections of the country, such as the Highland county of Ross-shire, virtually the whole population had deserted the established Church in 1843, leaving the congregation of many a parish church to consist solely of the patron's family and servants. The post-Disruption establishment was derided in the children's rhyme as 'the auld kirk, the cauld kirk, the kirk without the people'. The Scottish poor law, passed in 1845, transferred authority over poor relief from the kirk-sessions and heritors to elected poor-law boards. The Free Church national educational system rivalled the parish schools of the establishment, until the Educational Act for Scotland in 1872 formed a national system of education which absorbed most of the denominational schools. Between 1872 and 1906, Scottish politics was dominated by a prolonged national campaign to disestablish the Church of Scotland. Although unsuccessful, the campaign convinced leaders of the Church of Scotland that if their Church hoped to exercise a greater national influence, it would need to distance itself from the Westminster State and demonstrate a greater degree of spiritual independence. In 1922 Parliament agreed to a new constitution for the Church of Scotland, the Articles Declaratory, which effectively redefined the Church of Scotland from an established Church to a free national Church, possessing spiritual independence from the State. This opened the way for a Presbyterian Church reunion in 1929, when the United Free Church, made up of most of those congregations that had left at the Disruption of 1843, united with the Church of Scotland.

The Church of England weathered the struggles of the 1830s and 1840s better than the establishments in Ireland and Scotland. While the State after 1832 declined to provide funding for church extension or an Anglican system of national education, the Church of England managed to mobilize considerable private giving for these goals and to hold considerable popular support. 'If there is much that is unsatisfactory in its external relations with the State', observed Bishop Kaye of Lincoln of the Church in his Charge of 1846, 'there is much to cheer and encourage us in its internal condition. Never, I believe, did it possess a stronger hold upon the affections of its Lay Members, especially of the poorer classes.'[4] In his Charge of 1845, Charles

[4] J. Kaye, *A Charge to the Clergy of the Diocese of Lincoln* (London, 1846), 37.

Sumner pointed to the increased provision of churches and schools in his diocese of Winchester since 1829, an increase achieved through voluntary effort alone: in 1829, there were 491 churches; in 1845, there were 599 churches; in 1829, there had been 88 parish churches with no school; in 1845, there were only 19 such parish churches; in 1829, 30,461 children attended a school in connection with the Church of England; in 1845, 60,936 children were attending a Church of England school.[5] For Henry Manning, in his Charge to the archdeaconry of Chichester, the fifteen years from 1830 to 1845 had been difficult ones for the Church of England, with the State refusing additional financial support to the Church, and Dissenters and Roman Catholics calling boldly for disestablishment. 'And yet', Manning continued, 'despite of all this, there has arisen within the Church, our enemies themselves being judges, an energy and power of expansion never seen before.' Taken on the whole, the years of trial had left the Church more confident, more self-reliant.

> What have been the fruits of these years of adverse events? A thousand Churches; a work of almost universal restoration, never to be estimated; an increase of clergy, probably far exceeding the increase of Churches; a number of congregations newly formed, exceeding the number of individual minds which have been drawn from us; more than half-a-million of money in the last five years offered to the work of national education; a whole system of institutions for training school teachers; the reorganisation of almost every diocese on the principle of its spiritual unity and government.

'If such', he added, 'be the [results] of external conflict, may the shadows of worldly adversity for ever hang upon the Church of England!'[6] The 1830s and 1840s were indeed decades of unprecedented Anglican church building. Manning's estimate of 1,000 new churches was far too low. According to Horace Mann's report on the Religious Census of 1851, 2,029 churches in connection with the Church of England had been built between 1831 and 1851.[7]

Yet for all this, the established Church of England in 1850 was not what had been envisaged by the Church reformers and Anglican authors of the first quarter of the century. Manning himself soon grew disillusioned, and in 1851 he left the established Church of

[5] C. R. Sumner, *A Charge delivered to the Clergy of the Diocese of Winchester* (London, 1845), 10–22.

[6] H. E. Manning, *A Charge delivered at the Ordinary Visitation of the Archdeaconry of Chichester in July 1845* (London, 1845), 50–3.

[7] Mann, 'Report of the Census, 1851—Religious Worship', p. xli.

England for the Roman Catholic Church, where he provided leadership to the continued Catholic revival in Victorian England. The Church of England had not reasserted its influence and authority over the rapidly expanding population of England and Wales. For all the church building in his diocese of Winchester, Sumner also had to admit that church extension had barely kept up with the increase of population, and that the ratio of church sittings to population was no different in 1845 than it had been in 1829.[8] According to the religious census of 1851, the proportion of Anglican churches to population in England and Wales as a whole was worse in 1851 than 1831—with one established church for every 1,175 people in 1831 and one established church for every 1,296 inhabitants in 1851.[9] The census also revealed that less than half of the eligible population of England and Wales attended any church service on census Sunday, while of those who did attend worship, only about 51 per cent attended the Church of England.[10] There is evidence that the revival of the Church of England had reached its limit by 1850, while by 1870, in the words of Frances Knight, 'the Church of England could no longer claim to be the Church of the English nation'.[11] Despite the impressive efforts in Anglican church extension from the 1820s, the Church remained relatively thin in the large industrial towns and cities. Its strength was concentrated south of the Trent, and especially in the rural south-east, while it was far weaker in the north and west. In Wales, the established Church in 1851 accounted for only about a quarter of all worshippers.

But if the struggles of the 1830s and early 1840s had not brought a revival of the establishment ideal, it was probably true that the national Churches of England, Ireland, and Scotland emerged from those struggles strengthened as Christian Churches. They were after 1850 characterized less by their connection with the State, and more by a sense of responsibility for the religious and moral well-being of individuals. They were less concerned about exercising authority over their populations (because they had less power to do so), and they grew more concerned to provide religious instruction, sacraments, and the religious rites of passage to those who needed

[8] Sumner, *Charge . . . Winchester*, 10–11.

[9] Mann, 'Report of the Census, 1851—Religious Worship', p. xxxix.

[10] Chadwick, *The Victorian Church, Part one*, 363–9.

[11] J. Cox, *The English Churches in a Secular Society: Lambeth, 1870–1930* (Oxford, 1982), 7; Knight, *The Nineteenth-Century Church and English Society*, 201.

them. They learned to function in an increasingly pluralistic, democratic, and secular society, not as guardians of the national faith, but as societies of believers. As the prospects for revived alliance of Church and State faded, religion for probably the majority of the British and Irish people became increasingly a matter of personal choice, of individual quest and discovery. From a Protestant State, the United Kingdom had become a Liberal State, and the national Churches had embraced the ideal of a free Church in a free State. Religion became viewed less as a body of teachings to be accepted on authority from a religious establishment as an expression of loyalty to the State, and more as a faith, a hope, and a charity, internal to the individual believer.

Select Bibliography

A comprehensive bibliography would add considerably to the length of the book. The bibliography is therefore restricted to the more important published books, pamphlets, theses, and post-1900 journal articles. For manuscripts, nineteenth-century periodicals, parliamentary reports, and other primary sources, the reader should refer to the full references cited in the footnotes.

BOOKS AND PAMPHLETS PUBLISHED BEFORE 1900

An Address to the People of Scotland, issued by Appointment of the Convocation of Ministers, held at Edinburgh, November 1842 (Edinburgh, n.d.).

Alexander, W., *Johnny Gibb of Gushetneuk* (Aberdeen, 1871).

Arnold, T., *The Christian Duty of Granting the Claims of the Roman Catholics* (Oxford, 1829).

Ashwell, A. R., *Life of Samuel Wilberforce*, 3 vols. (London, 1880).

Authenticated Report of the Discussion which took place between the Rev Richard T. P. Pope and the Rev Thomas Maguire (Dublin, 1827).

Bagot, R., *A Charge delivered to the Clergy of the Diocese of Oxford* (Oxford, 1838).

Baxter, R., *Narrative of Facts characterising the Supernatural Manifestations in Members of Mr Irving's Congregation, and other Individuals in England and Scotland*, 2nd edn. (London, 1833).

Beith, A., *Memories of Disruption Times* (London, 1877).

Bentham, J., *Church-of-Englandism and its Catechism Examined . . .* (London, 1818).

Beverley, R. M., *A Letter to his Grace the Archbishop of York, on the Present Corrupt State of the Church of England*, 5th edn. (Beverley, 1831).

—— *A Letter to Lord Henley, on the Deficiencies of his Plan of Church Reform* (Beverley, 1833).

Bickersteth, E., *The Divine Warning to the Church, at this Time, of our Present Enemies, Dangers, and Duties, and as to our Future Prospects: A Sermon Preached . . . November 5, 1842* (London, 1842).

Binney, T., *An Address Delivered on Laying the First Stone of the New King's Weigh House*, 5th edn. (London, 1834).

BINNEY, T., *The Ultimate Object of the Evangelical Dissenters Avowed and Advocated* (London, 1834).

—— *Righteousness Exalteth a Nation: A Lecture on Church Extension* (London, 1840).

BLACK, A., *The Church its own Enemy, being an Answer to the Pamphlets of the Rev. Dr. Chalmers*, 3rd edn. (Edinburgh, 1835).

BLOMFIELD, A., *Memoir of Charles James Blomfield* (London, 1864).

BLOMFIELD, C. J., *A Charge delivered to the Clergy of the Diocese of London at the Visitation in July 1834*, 2nd edn. (London, 1834).

—— *The Uses of a Standing Ministry and an Established Church* (London, 1834).

—— *Proposals for the Creation of a Fund to be Applied to the Building and Endowment of Additional Churches in the Metropolis* (London, 1836).

—— *Three Sermons on the Church* (London, 1842).

—— *A Charge, delivered to the Clergy of the Diocese of London at the Visitation in October 1842*, 2nd edn. (London, 1842).

BONAR, A., *Narrative of a Mission of Enquiry to the Jews from the Church of Scotland in 1839* (Edinburgh, 1843).

—— *Memoir and Remains of the Rev. Robert Murray McCheyne* (Edinburgh, 1844).

—— *Diary and Life*, ed. M. Bonar (Edinburgh, 1893).

[BOWDEN, J. W.], *A Short Address to his Brethren on the Nature and Constitution of the Church of Christ*, Tract 5 (London, 1833).

—— *The Life and Pontificate of Gregory the Seventh*, 2 vols. (London, 1840).

BROOKE, R. S., *Recollections of the Irish Church* (London, 1877).

BROWN, T., *Annals of the Disruption*, 2nd edn. (Edinburgh, 1893).

BUCHANAN, J., *On the 'Tracts for the Times'* (Edinburgh, 1843).

BUCHANAN, R., *The Ten Years' Conflict*, 2 vols. (Glasgow, 1852).

BURGON, J. W., *Lives of Twelve Good Men* (London, 1891).

BURKE, E., *Speeches of the Right Honourable Edmund Burke in the House of Commons*, 4 vols. (London, 1816).

BURNS, I., *The Pastor of Kilsyth; or Memorials of the Life and Times of W. H. Burns* (London, 1860).

—— *Memoir of William C. Burns* (London, 1870).

BURNS, R., *Plurality of Offices in the Church of Scotland Examined* (Glasgow, 1824).

BURTON, E., *Thoughts upon the Demand for Church Reform*, 2nd edn. (Oxford, 1831).

—— *Sequel to Remarks upon Church Reform, with Observations upon the Plan Proposed by Lord Henley*, 2nd edn. (London, 1832).

—— *Thoughts on the Separation of Church and State* (London, 1834).

CARLETON, W., *The Works of William Carleton*, 2 vols. (New York, 1881).

CARLYLE, T., *Chartism* (London, 1839).

—— *Past and Present* (1843), in *The Works of Thomas Carlyle*, 30 vols. (London, n.d.), x.

—— *Reminiscences*, ed. J. A. Froude, 2 vols. (London, 1881).

The Chalmers Centenary: Speeches delivered in the Free Assembly Hall, Edinburgh, on March 3, 1880 (Edinburgh, 1880).

CHALMERS, T., *Church Establishments Defended* (London, 1833).

—— *The Collected Works of Thomas Chalmers*, 25 vols. (Glasgow, 1835–42).

—— *First Report of the Committee of the General Assembly on Church Extension* (Edinburgh, 1835).

—— *Second Report of the Committee of the General Assembly on Church Extension* (Edinburgh, 1836).

—— *Remarks on the Present Position of the Church of Scotland* (Edinburgh, 1839).

—— *On the Evangelical Alliance* (Edinburgh, 1846).

—— *A Selection from the Correspondence of the Late Thomas Chalmers*, ed. W. Hanna (Edinburgh, 1853).

The Church of Scotland's Claim of Right, to which are Prefixed the Speeches of Dr Chalmers, Dr Gordon and Mr Dunlop in the General Assembly, in Support of the Same (Edinburgh, 1842).

CHURTON, E., *Memoir of Joshua Watson*, 2 vols. (London, 1861).

COCKBURN, H., *Journal 1831–1854*, 2 vols. (Edinburgh, 1874).

[COLLINS, W.], *Proposal for Building Twenty New Parochial Churches in the City and Suburbs of Glasgow* (Glasgow, 1834).

—— *The Church of Scotland: the Poor Man's Church* (Glasgow, n.d.).

COOK, G., *Substance of a Speech delivered in the General Assembly, 22 May 1816, containing an Inquiry into the Law and Constitution of the Church of Scotland respecting Residence and Pluralities* (Edinburgh, 1816).

COPLESTON, E., *Charge delivered to the Clergy of the Diocese of Llandaff* (London, 1833).

CUNNINGHAM, J., *The Church History of Scotland*, 2 vols. (Edinburgh, 1859).

CUNNINGHAM, J. W., *The State of the Country: A Sermon* (London, 1819).

DAUBENY, C., *A Guide to the Church* (1798), 3rd edn., 2 vols. (London and Bath, 1830).

—— *On the Nature, Progress and Consequences of Schism; with Immediate Reference to the Present State of Religion in this Country* (London, 1818).

DAUNT, W. J. O'NEILL, *Eighty-five Years of Irish History 1800–1885*, 2 vols. (London, 1886).

DEALTRY, W., *Religious Establishments Tried by the Word of God* (London, 1833).

—— *Obligations of the National Church: A Charge delivered at the Visitation in Hampshire, September 1838* (London, 1838).

DISRAELI, B., *Coningsby; or the New Generation* (London, 1844).

DISRAELI, B., *Sybil; or the Two Nations* (London, 1845).

[DOYLE, J.], *A Vindication of the Religious and Civil Principles of the Irish Catholics*, 3rd edn. (Dublin, 1823).

[——], *Letters on the State of Education in Ireland; and on Bible Societies* (Dublin, 1824).

[——], *A Reply by J.K.L. to the late Charge of the Most Rev Doctor Magee, Protestant Archbishop of Dublin* (Dublin, 1827).

[DRUMMOND, H.], *Dialogues on Prophecy*, 3 vols. (London, 1828?).

DUNCAN, G. F. C., *Memoir of the Rev. Henry Duncan* (Edinburgh, 1848).

[ERSKINE, T.], *On the Gifts of the Spirit* (Greenock, 1830).

FAUSSETT, G., *The Claims of the Established Church to Exclusive Attachment and Support* (Oxford, 1820).

—— *Revival of Popery; a Sermon preached before the University of Oxford, at St. Mary's, on Sunday, May 20, 1838* (Oxford, 1838).

[FERRIER, J. F.], *Observations on Church and State* (Edinburgh, 1848).

FITZPATRICK, W. J., *The Life, Times, and Correspondence of the Right Rev. Dr. Doyle, Bishop of Kildare and Leighlin*, 2 vols. [1st edn, Dublin, 1861] (Boston, 1869).

FORSTER, C. (ed.), *Thirty Years' Correspondence between John Jebb, Bishop of Limerick, and Alexander Knox*, 2 vols. (London, 1834).

—— *The Life of John Jebb*, 2 vols. (London, 1836).

FROUDE, J. A., *The Nemesis of Faith* (London, 1849).

—— 'The Oxford Counter-Reformation', in J. A. Froude, *Short Studies on Great Subjects*, 4 vols. (London, 1890), iv. 231–360.

FROUDE, R. H., *Remains of the Late Richard Hurrell Froude*, ed. J. Keble and J. H. Newman, 4 vols. (i–ii, London, 1838; iii–iv, Derby, 1839).

GIBSON, W., *The Flock in the Wilderness; or, the Secession of 1843* (Belfast, 1843).

GLADSTONE, W. E., *The State in its Relations with the Church* (London, 1838).

—— 'The Theses of Erastus and the Scottish Church Establishment' (1844), in *Gleanings of Past Years*, 7 vols. (London, 1879), iii. 1–40.

GLASSFORD, J., *Letter to the Right Honourable the Earl of Roden, on the Present State of Popular Education in Ireland* (Ireland, 1829).

GOODE, W., *The Case as it is; or, A Reply to the Letter of Dr. Pusey to his Grace the Archbishop of Canterbury* (London, 1842).

GORDON, J. E., *Six Letters on the Subject of Irish Education, addressed to the Right Hon. E. G. Stanley* (London, 1832).

GRESLEY, W., *Remarks on the Necessity of Attempting a Restoration of the National Church* (London, 1841).

GREVILLE, C., *The Greville Memoirs*, ed. H. Reeve, 3 vols. (London, 1874).

GUTHRIE, T., *Autobiography of Thomas Guthrie and Memoir*, ed. D. K. Guthrie and C. J. Guthrie, 2 vols. (London, 1875).

HALDANE, A., *The Lives of Robert Haldane of Airthey and of his Brother, James Alexander Haldane*, 4th edn. (Edinburgh, 1855).

HAMPDEN, R. D., *Observations on Religious Dissent, with particular reference to the Use of Religious Tests in the University*, 2nd edn. (Oxford, 1834).

HANNA, W., *Memoirs of Dr Chalmers*, 4 vols. (Edinburgh, 1849–52).

HARE, J. C., *Privileges Imply Duties: A Charge to the Clergy of the Archdeaconry of Lewes* (London, 1842).

HARFORD, J. S., *Life of Thomas Burgess* (London, 1840).

HARROWBY, LORD, *Substance of the Speech of the Earl of Harrowby, on Moving for the Recommitment of a Bill for the Better Support and Maintenance of Stipendiary Curates, on Thursday, the 18th of June, 1812* (London, 1812).

HENLEY, LORD, *A Plan of Church Reform, with a Letter to the King*, 5th edn. (London, 1832).

HILL, G., *View of the Constitution of the Church of Scotland* (1803), 3rd edn. (Edinburgh, 1835).

HODDER, E., *Life and Work of the Seventh Earl of Shaftesbury*, 2nd edn. (London, 1887).

HOOK, W. F., *Hear the Church: a Sermon preached at the Chapel Royal, in St James Palace, on . . . June 17, 1838*, 2nd edn. (London, 1838).

—— *Letter to the Bishop of Ripon, on the State of Parties in the Church of England*, 3rd edn. (London, 1841).

—— *Peril of Idolatry: A Sermon* (London, 1842).

HORSLEY, S., *Sermons by Samuel Horsley*, 2 vols. (London, 1824).

INGLIS, J., *The Importance of Ecclesiastical Establishments; a Sermon, preached . . . before the Society . . . for the Benefit of the Sons of the Clergy of the Church of Scotland* (Edinburgh, 1821).

INGLIS, R. H., *Church Extension: Substance of a Speech delivered in the House of Commons, on . . . the 30th June, 1840* (London, 1840).

Irish Education: Letter on the Government Scheme of Education for Ireland . . . by a Clergyman of the Church of Scotland (Glasgow, 1832).

IRVING, E., *For Missionaries after the Apostolic School* (London, 1825).

—— *Babylon and Infidelity Foredoomed of God: A Discourse on the Prophecies of Daniel and the Apocalypse*, 2nd edn. (Glasgow, 1828).

—— *A Letter to the King, on the Repeal of the Test and Corporation Laws* (London, 1828).

—— *The Church and State Responsible to Christ and to One Another: A Series of Discourses on Daniel's Vision of the Four Beasts* (London, 1829).

—— *The Collected Writings of Edward Irving*, ed. G. Carlyle, 5 vols. (London, 1865).

JEBB, J., *A Charge, delivered to the Clergy of the Diocese of Limerick . . . on Thursday, the 19th of June 1823* (Dublin, 1823).

JEBB, J., *A Speech delivered in the House of Peers, Thursday, June 10, 1824, on Occasion of the Third Reading of the Irish Tithe Composition Amendment Bill* (London, 1824).

JOHNES, A. J., *An Essay on the Causes which have Produced Dissent from the Established Church, in the Principality of Wales*, 3rd edn. (London, 1835).

KAYE, J., *A Letter to his Grace the Archbishop of Canterbury, on the Recommendations of the Ecclesiastical Commission* (London, 1838).

—— *A Charge to the Clergy of the Diocese of Lincoln* (London, 1843).

—— *A Charge to the Clergy of the Diocese of Lincoln* (London, 1846).

[KEBLE, J.], *Adherence to the Apostolical Succession the Safest Course*, Tract 4 (London, 1833).

—— *Primitive Tradition Recognised in Holy Scripture: A Sermon preached in the Cathedral Church of Winchester . . . September 27, 1836* (London, 1839).

—— *Sermons, Academical and Occasional* (Oxford, 1847).

KENNEDY, J., *The 'Apostle of the North': The Life and Labours of the Rev. Dr. McDonald* (London, 1866).

KENNEY, A. H., *Principles and Practices of Pretended Reformers in Church and State* (London, 1819).

—— 'Memoir of William Magee', in *Works of William Magee*, 2 vols. (London, 1842), i. pp. ix–lxxx.

KILLEN, W. D., *The Ecclesiastical History of Ireland*, 2 vols. (London, 1875).

KNOX, A., *Remains of Alexander Knox*, 2nd edn., 4 vols. (London, 1836).

LAPSLIE, J., *A Foederal Union amongst the Different Sects of Christians, and particularly of this Kingdom, Proposed and Recommended. A discourse, delivered before the Synod of Glasgow and Air, at Glasgow, April 1791* (Glasgow, 1795).

Letter from Sir James Graham, Principal Secretary for the Home Department, to the Moderator of the General Assembly, with the Reply, being the Minute of the General Assembly's Special Commission (Edinburgh, 1843).

LEWIS, G., *The Eldership in the Church of Scotland* (Glasgow, 1834).

LIDDON, H. P., *Life of Edward Bouverie Pusey*, 4th edn., 4 vols. (London, 1894).

LONGLEY, C.-T., *A Charge addressed to the Clergy of the Diocese of Ripon . . . in September 1844* (London, 1844).

MACAULAY, T. B., *History of England*, 5 vols. (New York, 1862).

—— *Miscellaneous Works of Lord Macaulay*, ed. Lady Trevelyan, 5 vols. (New York, 1880).

MCGHEE, R. J., *Reflections on the Endowment of the College of Maynooth* (London, 1845).

MACGILL, H. M., *The Life of Hugh Heugh* (Edinburgh, 1852).

MACGREGOR, S. (ed.), *Report of the Debate in the General Assembly of the Church of Scotland on the Overtures anent Calls, May 23, 1833* (Edinburgh, 1833).

MacHale, J., *Letters of John MacHale, Archbishop of Tuam* (Dublin, 1893).
McKerrow, J., *History of the Secession Church*, 2nd edn. (Edinburgh, 1854).
McLaren, D., *History of the Resistance to the Annuity Tax* (Edinburgh, 1836).
McNeile, H., *Letters to a Friend, Who Has Felt it his Duty to Secede from the Church of England* (London, 1834).
Madden, Mrs. H., *Memoir of Robert Daly, Lord Bishop of Cashel* (London, 1875).
Madden, S., *Memoir of the Life of the Late Rev Peter Roe, Rector of Odagh and Minister of St. Mary's, Kilkenny* (Dublin, 1842).
Magee, W., *A Charge delivered at his Primary Visitation, in St Patrick's Cathedral, Dublin, on Thursday, the 27th of October, 1822* (London, 1822).
—— *The Evidence of his Grace, the Archbishop of Dublin, before the Select Committee of the House of Lords on the State of Ireland* (Dublin, 1825).
—— *The Works of William Magee, Archbishop of Dublin*, 2 vols. (London, 1842).
Manners, Lord J., *A Plea for National Holy-Days* (London, 1843).
Manning, H. E., *The English Church: Its Succession, and Witness for Christ* (London, 1835).
—— *The Principle of the Ecclesiastical Commission Examined, in a Letter to the Right Rev. The Lord Bishop of Chichester* (London, 1838).
—— *A Charge delivered at the Ordinary Visitation of the Archdeaconry of Chichester, in July 1843* (London, 1843).
—— *A Charge delivered at the Ordinary Visitation of the Archdeaconry of Chichester in July 1845* (London, 1845).
Mant, R., *The Churches of Rome and England Compared in their Declared Doctrines and Practices* (London, 1837).
Mant, W. B., *Memoirs of the Right Reverend Richard Mant, Lord Bishop of Down and Connor and of Dromore* (Dublin, 1857).
Marsh, H., *The National Religion the Foundation of National Education*, 2nd edn. (London, 1811).
—— *An Enquiry into the Consequences of Neglecting to give the Prayer Book with the Bible* (Cambridge, 1812).
—— *An Appendix to the 'Comparative View of the Churches of England and Rome'* (Cambridge, 1816).
Marshall, A., *Ecclesiastical Establishments Considered: A Sermon, Preached on the Evening of Thursday, 9th April, 1829, in Greyfriar's Church, Glasgow* (Glasgow, 1829).
Massy, D., *Footprints of a Faithful Shepherd: A Memoir of the Rev Godfrey Massy, Vicar of Bruff* (London, 1855).
Maurice, F. D., *The Kingdom of Christ: or Hints on the Principles, Ordinances, and Constitution of the Catholic Church*, 3 vols. (London, 1838).

Maurice, F. D., *Reasons for Not Joining a Party in the Church* (London, 1841).

—— *On the Right and Wrong Methods of Supporting Protestantism* (London, 1843).

Miall, A., *Life of Edward Miall* (London, 1884).

Mill, J. S., 'The Right and Wrong of State Interference with Corporation and Church Property', in J. S. Mill, *Dissertations and Discussions: Political, Philosophical and Historical*, 2 vols. (London, 1859), i. 1–41.

Miller, E., *The History and Doctrines of Irvingism*, 2 vols. (London, 1878).

[Miller, L.], *Passages in the Life of an English Heiress or Recollections of Disruption Times in Scotland* (London, 1847).

Monk, J. H., *A Charge delivered to the Clergy or the Diocese of Gloucester and Bristol, in August and September 1838* (London, 1838).

Mozley, A. (ed.), *Letters and Correspondence of John Henry Newman*, 2 vols. (London, 1891).

Mozley, T., *Reminiscences chiefly of Oriel College and the Oxford Movement*, 2 vols. (London, 1882).

Murray, J. W., *Sketches of the Lives and Times of Eminent Irish Churchmen from the Reformation Downwards* (Dublin, 1874).

Newland, H., *An Apology for the Established Church in Ireland* (Dublin, 1829).

Newman, J. H., *The Arians of the Fourth Century* (London, 1833).

[——], *Thoughts on the Ministerial Commission,* Tract 1 (London, 1833).

[——], *The Catholic Church,* Tract 2 (London, 1833).

[——], *The Episcopal Church Apostolical,* Tract 7 (London, 1833).

[——], *Heads of a Week-Day Lecture, delivered to a Country Congregation*, Tract 10 (London, 1833).

[——], *The Visible Church*, Tract 20 (London, 1833).

[——], *Via Media, No. I*, Tract 38 (London, 1834).

[——], *Via Media, No. II*, Tract 41 (London, 1834).

—— *Lectures on the Prophetical Office of the Church, viewed relatively to Romanism and Popular Protestantism*, 2nd edn. (London, 1838).

—— *Remarks on Certain Passages in the Thirty-Nine Articles*, Tract 90 (London, 1841).

—— 'The Tamworth Reading Room' (1841), *Discussions and Arguments on Various Subjects* (London, 1872), 254–305.

—— *Essays Critical and Historical*, 2 vols. (London, 1887).

Noel, B. W., *The State of the Metropolis Considered* (London, 1835).

—— *A Plea for the Poor* (London, 1841).

—— *Free Church of Scotland. The Substance of a Speech delivered at a Public Meeting held at Exeter Hall, on . . . 11th October 1844* (London, 1844).

—— *The Catholic Claims: A Letter to the Lord Bishop of Cashel*, 3rd edn. (London, 1845).

Norris, H. H., *A Practical Exposition of the Tendency and Proceedings of the British and Foreign Bible Society*, 2nd edn. (London, 1814).

Oakeley, F., *A Letter on Submitting to the Catholic Church, addressed to a Friend* (London, 1845).

—— *Historical Notes on the Tractarian Movement* (London, 1865).

O'Donoghue, D. J., *The Life of William Carleton*, 2 vols. (London, 1896).

Oliphant, M., *The Life of Edward Irving*, 2 vols. (London, 1862).

Ornsby, R., *Memoirs of James Robert Hope-Scott of Abbotsford*, 2 vols. (London, 1884).

O'Reilly, B., *John MacHale, Archbishop of Tuam: His Life, Times and Correspondence*, 2 vols. (New York, 1890).

Orme, W., *Memoirs of John Urquhart* (Philadelphia, 1855).

Osler, E., *The Church and Dissent, considered in their Practical Influence* (London, 1836).

Otway, C., *Letter to J. K. L., on the Subject of his Reply to Lord Farnham* (Dublin, 1827).

Paley, W., *The Principles of Moral and Political Philosophy*, 21st edn., 2 vols. (Edinburgh, 1814).

Palmer, W., *Remarks on the Rev. Dr. Arnold's Principles of Church Reform* (London, 1833).

—— *An Enquiry into the Possibility of Obtaining Means for Church Extension without Parliamentary Grants* (London, 1841).

—— *A Narrative of Events connected with the Publication of the Tracts for the Times* (London, 1883).

Parker, C. S., *Sir Robert Peel*, 3 vols. (London, 1891).

Peel, R., *Speech . . . in the House of Commons, on Tuesday, July 21, 1835, in support of his Amendment on the Irish Church Bill* (Edinburgh, 1835).

—— *An Inaugural Address delivered by the Right Hon. Sir Robert Peel, President of the Tamworth Library and Reading Room, on Tuesday, 19th January 1841* (London, 1841).

—— *Memoirs, by the Right Honourable Sir Robert Peel*, 2 vols. (London, 1856).

[Perceval, A. P.], *Account of Religious Sects at present Existing in England*, Tract 36 (London, 1834).

Phelan, W., *The Bible, not the Bible Society, being an Attempt to Point Out that Mode of Disseminating the Scriptures, which would most Effectually Conduce to the Security of the Established Church, and the Peace of the United Kingdom* (Dublin, 1817).

[——], *The Case of the Church of Ireland Stated, in a Letter Respectfully Addressed to His Excellency the Marquis Wellesley . . . by Declan* (Dublin, 1823).

Phillimore, R., *The Ecclesiastical Law of the Church of England*, 2 vols. (London, 1873).

PHILLPOTTS, H., *Charge delivered to the Clergy of the Diocese of Exeter* (London, 1833).
—— *Charge delivered to the Clergy of the Diocese of Exeter* (London, 1836).
—— *Charge delivered to the Clergy of the Diocese of Exeter* (London, 1842).
POOLE, G. A., *On the Present State of Parties in the Church of England* (London, 1841).
PORTER, J. L., *Life and Times of Henry Cooke* (London, 1871).
Practical Observations upon the Views and Tendencies of the First Report of the Commissioners of Irish Education Inquiry (London, 1826).
PURCELL, E. S., *Life of Cardinal Manning*, 2 vols. (London, 1895).
PUSEY, E. B., *Remarks on the Prospective and Past Benefits of Cathedral Institutions, in the Promotion of Sound Religious Knowledge and of Clerical Education*, 2nd edn. (London, 1833).
—— *Patience and Confidence the Strength of the Church* (Oxford, 1837).
—— *A Letter to his Grace the Archbishop of Canterbury, on some Circumstances in connection with the Present Crisis in the English Church* (Oxford, 1842).
PUGIN, A. W., *Contrasts: or, A Parallel between the Noble Edifices of the Middle Ages and Corresponding Buildings of the Present Day* [1st edn. 1836], 2nd edn. (London, 1841).
RANKEN, A., *The Importance of Religious Establishments* (Glasgow, 1799).
Report of the Debate of the General Assembly of the Church of Scotland on the Overtures anent the Union of Offices (Edinburgh, 1825).
Report of the Great Public Meeting in the Assembly Rooms, Edinburgh, on Thursday evening, December 20, 1838, to Commemorate the Restoration of Civil and Religious Liberty, and of Presbyterian Church Government, as Secured by the Glasgow Assembly of 1638 (Edinburgh, 1838).
The Revival of Religion (Glasgow, 1840).
ROSE, H. J., *The State of the Protestant Religion in Germany* (London, 1826).
—— *The Commission and Consequent Duties of the Clergy*, 4th edn. (London, 1847).
RYDER, H., *Charge delivered to the Clergy of the Diocese of Lichfield and Coventry* (Stafford, 1824).
[SEELING, R. B.], *Essays on the Church* (London, 1833).
SINCLAIR, G. (ed.), *Selection from the Correspondence carried on during Certain Recent Negociations for the Adjustment of the Scottish Church Question* (Edinburgh, 1842).
SINCLAIR, J., *Analysis of the Statistical Account of Scotland* (London, 1826).
SIRR, J. D., *A Memoir of the Hon. and Most Revd. Power le Poer Trench, Last Archbishop of Tuam* (Dublin, 1845).
SKEATS, H. S., and MIALL, C. S., *History of the Free Churches of England 1688–1891* (London, 1891).
SKINNER, J., *The Scottish Endowment Question, Ecclesiastical and Educational* (Glasgow, 1838).

SMITH, S., *A Letter to Archdeacon Singleton, on the Ecclesiastical Commission*, 2nd edn. (London, 1837).
—— *Second Letter to Archdeacon Singleton* (London, 1838).
SOUTHEY, C. C., *The Life and Correspondence of Robert Southey*, 6 vols. (London, 1850).
SOUTHEY, R., *The Book of the Church*, 2 vols. (London, 1824).
STANFORD, C. S., *Memoir of the Late Rev. W. H. Krause* (Dublin, 1854).
STANLEY, A. P., *Life and Correspondence of Thomas Arnold* (1844), 8th edn., 2 vols. (London, 1858).
STEPHEN, L., 'The Clapham Sect', in *Essays in Ecclesiastical Biography*, 2 vols. (London, 1849), i. 287–383.
STEPHENS, W. R. W., *Life and Letters of Walter Farquahar Hook*, 2 vols. (London, 1878).
STEVEN, R., *Remarks on the Present State of Ireland* (London, 1822).
STORY, R. H., *Memoir of the Life of the Rev. Robert Story* (Cambridge, 1862).
STRUTHERS, G., *The History of the Rise, Progress and Principles of the Relief Church* (Glasgow, 1843).
SUMNER, C. R., *A Charge delivered to the Clergy of Winchester . . . in 1841* (London, 1841).
—— *A Charge delivered to the Clergy of the Diocese of Winchester* (London, 1845).
SUMNER, G. H., *Life of Charles Richard Sumner, Bishop of Winchester* (London, 1876).
SUMNER, J. B., *Charge addressed to the Clergy of the Diocese of Chester at the Primary Visitation in August and September 1829* (London, 1929).
—— *A Letter to the Clergy of the Diocese of Chester, occasioned by the Act of the Legislature granting Relief to his Majesty's Roman Catholic Subjects* (London, 1829).
—— *A Charge delivered to the Clergy of the Diocese of Chester . . . in 1838* (London, 1838).
THELWALL, A. S. (ed.), *Proceedings of the Anti-Maynooth Conference of 1845* (London, 1845).
THORP, C., *A Charge to the Clergy of the Archdeaconry of Durham* (Durham, 1838).
TISDALL, W., *A Seasonable Enquiry into that Most Dangerous Political Principle of the Kirk in Power* (Dublin, 1713).
[——], *The Case of the Sacramental Test, Stated and Argued* (Dublin, 1715).
Tracts on the Intrusion of Ministers on Reclaiming Congregations, 11 tracts (Edinburgh, 1839).
TRENCH, R. C., *Letters and Memorials*, 2 vols. (London, 1888).
TREVELYAN, G. O., *Life and Letters of Lord Macaulay*, 2nd edn., 2 vols. (London, 1883).

Trollope, A., *The Warden* (London, 1855).
—— *Clergymen of the Church of England* (London, 1866).
Tulloch, J., *Movements of Religious Thought in Britain during the Nineteenth Century* (London, 1885).
Turner, A., *The Scottish Secession of 1843* (Edinburgh, 1859).
Twiss, H., *The Public and Private Life of Lord Chancellor Eldon,* 2 vols. (London, 1846).
Uhden, F., *The Anglican Church in the Nineteenth Century*, trans. W. C. C. Humphreys (London, 1844).
[Wade, J.], *The Extraordinary Black Book; or Public Abuses Unveiled . . .* (London, 1831).
Walker, N. L., *Robert Buchanan* (London, 1877).
Walpole, S., *Life of Spencer Perceval,* 2 vols. (London, 1874).
—— *Life of Lord John Russell*, 2 vols. (London, 1889).
Walsh, W., *The Secret History of the Oxford Movement*, 6th edn. (London, 1899).
Warburton, W., *The Alliance between Church and State, or, the Necessity and Equity of an Established Religion and a Test-Law Demonstrated* (London, 1736).
Ward, W., *William George Ward and the Oxford Movement* (London, 1889).
—— *Life and Times of Cardinal Wiseman*, 2nd edn., 2 vols. (London, 1897).
[Ward, W. G.], *Few Words in Support of No. 90 of the Tracts for the Times* (Oxford, 1841).
—— *The Ideal of a Christian Church considered in Comparison with Existing Practice*, 2nd edn. (London, 1844).
Wardlaw, R., *Speech . . . at the Public Meeting in Glasgow, for the Separation of Church and State, March 6, 1834* (Glasgow, 1834).
Wellwood, H. Moncrieff, *Account of the Life and Writings of John Erskine* (Edinburgh, 1818).
Whately, E. J., *Life and Correspondence of Richard Whately*, 2 vols. (London, 1866).
Whately, R., *The Use and Abuse of Party-Feeling in Matters of Religion considered in Eight Sermons preached before the University of Oxford* (Oxford, 1822).
[——], *Letters on the Church. By an Episcopalian* (London, 1826).
—— *Thoughts on Church-Government* (London, 1844).
Wilberforce, H. W., *The Parochial System: An Appeal to English Churchmen* (London, 1838).
Wilberforce, R. I., *A Charge, delivered at the Ordinary Visitation [of the Archdeaconry] of the East Riding* (York, 1843).
—— *Church Courts and Church Discipline* (London, 1843).

WILBERFORCE, S., *A Charge, delivered at the Ordinary Visitation of the Archdeaconry of Surrey, November 1842*, 2nd edn. (London, 1842).

—— *A Charge delivered at the Ordinary Visitation of the Archdeaconry of Surrey, November 1843* (London, 1843).

WILSON, W. and RAINY, R., *Memorials of Robert Smith Candlish* (Edinburgh, 1880).

WYSE, T., *Historical Sketch of the Late Catholic Association of Ireland*, 2 vols. (London, 1829).

YATES, R., *The Church in Danger . . . in a Letter to the Right Hon. Earl of Liverpool* (London, 1815).

—— *The Basis of National Welfare* (London, 1817).

—— *Patronage of the Church of England: Concisely Considered in Reference to National Reformation and Improvement* (London, 1823).

BOOKS AND ARTICLES PUBLISHED SINCE 1900

ACHESON, A. R., *'A True and Lively Faith': Evangelical Revival in the Church of Ireland* (Belfast, 1992).

ADDISON, W. G., *Religious Equality in Modern England, 1714–1914* (London, 1944).

AKENSON, D. H., *The Irish Education Experiment: The National System of Education in the Nineteenth Century* (London, 1970).

—— *The Church of Ireland: Ecclesiastical Reform and Revolution, 1800–1885* (New Haven, 1971).

—— *A Protestant in Purgatory: Richard Whately, Archbishop of Dublin* (Hamden, Conn., 1981).

ALLEN, P., 'S. T. Coleridge's *Church and State* and the Idea of an Intellectual Establishment', *Journal of the History of Ideas*, 46 (1985), 89–106.

ANDERSON, R. D., *Education and the Scottish People 1750–1918* (Oxford, 1995).

ANGLESEY, MARQUESS OF, *One-Leg: The Life and Letters of Henry William Paget, First Marquess of Anglesey* (London, 1961).

ANSDELL, D., *The People of the Great Faith: The Highland Church, 1690–1900* (Stornoway, 1998).

ARNOLD, T., *Principles of Church Reform* (1833), ed. M. J. Jackson and J. Rogan (London, 1962).

BAKER, W. J., 'Hurrell Froude and the Reformers', *Journal of Ecclesiastical History*, 21 (1970), 243–59.

BALFOUR, F., *The Life of George, Fourth Earl of Aberdeen*, 2 vols. (London, 1922).

BALLEINE, G. R., *A History of the Evangelical Party in the Church of England* (London, 1933).

BAMFORD, T. W., *Thomas Arnold* (London, 1960).

BARKLEY, J. M., 'The Presbyterian Minister in Eighteenth Century Ireland', in J. L. M. Haire *et al.*, *Challenge and Conflict: Essays in Irish Presbyterian History and Doctrine* (Antrim, 1981), 46–60.

BARRETT, P., *Barchester: English Cathedral Life in the Nineteenth Century* (London, 1993).

BARTLETT, T., *The Fall and Rise of the Irish Nation: The Catholic Question 1690–1830* (Dublin, 1992).

BAUMBARDT, D., *Bentham and the Ethics of Today* (Princeton, 1952).

BEBBINGTON, D. W., 'The Life of Baptist Noel: Its Setting and Significance', *Baptist Quarterly*, 24 (1972), 389–411.

—— *Evangelicalism in Modern Britain* (London, 1989).

BEST, G. F. A., 'The Religious Difficulties of National Education in England, 1800–70', *Cambridge Historical Journal*, 12 (1956), 155–73.

—— 'The Protestant Constitution and its Supporters, 1800–1829', *Transactions of the Royal Historical Society*, 5th ser., 8 (1958), 105–27.

—— 'The Constitutional Revolution, 1828–32, and its Consequences for the Established Church', *Theology*, 52 (1959), 226–34.

—— 'The Evangelicals and the Established Church in the Early Nineteenth Century', *Journal of Theological Studies*, NS 10 (1959), 63–78.

—— 'The Whigs and the Church Establishment in the Age of Grey and Holland', *History*, 45 (1960), 103–18.

—— *Temporal Pillars: Queen Anne's Bounty, the Ecclesiastical Commissioners and the Church of England* (Cambridge, 1964).

BINFIELD, C., *So Down to Prayers: Studies in English Nonconformity 1780–1920* (London, 1977).

BLAKE, R., *Disraeli* (London, 1966).

BOLTON, F. R., *The Caroline Tradition of the Church of Ireland* (London, 1958).

BOTTIGHEIMER, K., 'The Failure of the Reformation in Ireland: *Une Question Bien Posée*', *Journal of Ecclesiastical History*, 36 (1985), 196–207.

BOWEN, D., *Souperism: Myth or Reality? A Study of Catholics and Protestants during the Great Famine* (Dublin, 1970).

—— *The Protestant Crusade in Ireland 1800–70: A Study of Protestant–Catholic Relations between the Act of Union and Disestablishment* (Dublin, 1978).

BOYCE, D. G., *Nationalism in Ireland* (London, 1982).

—— *Nineteenth-Century Ireland: The Search for Stability* (Dublin, 1990).

BRADLEY, J. E., *Religion, Revolution, and English Radicalism* (Cambridge, 1990).

BRADSHAW, B., 'Sword, Word and Strategy in the Reformation in Ireland', *Historical Journal*, 21 (1978), 475–502.

BRENDON, P., *Hurrell Froude and the Oxford Movement* (London, 1974).

BRENT, R., *Liberal Anglican Politics: Whiggery, Religion, and Reform 1830–1841* (Oxford, 1987).

—— 'The Whigs and Protestant Dissent in the Decade of Reform: The Case of Church Rates, 1833–1841', *English Historical Review*, 102 (1987), 887–910.

BRIGGS, A. (ed.), *Chartist Studies* (London, 1959).

BRILIOTH, Y., *The Anglican Revival: Studies in the Oxford Movement* (London, 1925).

BROCK, M., *The Great Reform Act* (London, 1973).

BROCK, W. R., *Lord Liverpool and Liberal Toryism 1820 to 1827*, 2nd edn. (London, 1967).

BRODERICK, J. F., *The Holy See and the Irish Movement for the Repeal of the Union with England 1829–1847* (Rome, 1951).

BROOKE, P., *Ulster Presbyterianism: The Historical Perspective 1610–1970*, 2nd edn. (Belfast, 1994).

BROOKS, C. and SAINT, A. (eds.), *The Victorian Church: Architecture and Society* (Manchester, 1995).

BROSE, O. J., 'The Irish Precedent for English Church Reform: The Church Temporalities Act of 1833', *Journal of Ecclesiastical History*, 7 (1956), 204–25.

—— *Church and Parliament: The Reshaping of the Church of England 1828–1860* (Oxford, 1959).

BROWN, C. G., *Religion and Society in Scotland since 1707* (Edinburgh, 1997).

BROWN, F. K., *Fathers of the Victorians* (Cambridge, 1961).

BROWN, S. J., *Thomas Chalmers and the Godly Commonwealth in Scotland* (Oxford, 1982).

—— 'Martyrdom in Early Victorian Scotland: Disruption Fathers and the Making of the Free Church', in D. Wood (ed.), *Martyrs and Martyrologies*, Studies in Church History, 30 (Oxford, 1993), 319–32.

—— 'The Disruption and the Dream: The Making of New College 1843–1861', in D. F. Wright and G. D. Badcock (eds.), *Disruption to Diversity: Edinburgh Divinity 1846–1996* (Edinburgh, 1996), 29–50.

—— 'Religion and the Rise of Liberalism: The First Disestablishment Campaign in Scotland, 1829–1843', *Journal of Ecclesiastical History*, 48 (1997), 682–704.

—— 'Gladstone, Chalmers and the Disruption of the Church of Scotland', in D. Bebbington and R. Swift (eds.), *Gladstone Centenary Essays* (Liverpool, 2000), 10–28.

—— and FRY, M. (eds.), *Scotland in the Age of the Disruption* (Edinburgh, 1993).

—— and MILLER, D.W. (eds.), *Piety and Power in Ireland 1760–1960* (Belfast, 2000).

BRYNN, E., 'Some Repercussions of the Act of Union on the Church of Ireland, 1801–1820', *Church History*, 40 (1971), 284–96.

BRYNN, E., *The Church of Ireland in the Age of Catholic Emancipation* (New York, 1982).

BURLEIGH, J. H. S., *A Church History of Scotland* (Oxford, 1960).

BURNET, G. B., *The Holy Communion in the Reformed Church of Scotland 1560–1960* (Edinburgh, 1960).

BURNS, A., *The Diocesan Revival in the Church of England, c.1800–1870* (Oxford, 1999).

BUTLER, J. R. M., *The Passing of the Great Reform Bill* (London, 1914).

BUTLER, P., *Gladstone: Church, State and Tractarianism: A Study of his Religious Ideas and Attitudes, 1809–1859* (Oxford, 1982).

—— (ed.), *Pusey Rediscovered* (London, 1983).

BUTLER, M., *Romantics, Rebels and Reactionaries* (Oxford, 1981).

CAGE, A., and CHECKLAND, E. O. A., 'Thomas Chalmers and Urban Poverty: The St. John's Parish Experiment in Glasgow, 1819–1837', *Philosophical Journal* (Glasgow), 13 (1976), 37–56.

CAHILL, G. A., 'The Protestant Association and the Anti-Maynooth Agitation of 1845', *Catholic Historical Review*, 43 (1957), 273–308.

CANNY, N., 'Why the Reformation Failed in Ireland: *Une Question Mal Posée*', *Journal of Ecclesiastical History*, 30 (1979), 423–50.

—— 'The Formation of the Irish Mind: Religion, Politics and Gaelic Irish Literature', *Past and Present*, 95 (1982), 91–116.

CARLESS-DAVIS, H. W., *The Age of Grey and Peel* (Oxford, 1929).

CARLETON, W., *Traits and Stories of the Irish Peasantry* (1842–4), 2 vols. (Gerrard's Cross, 1990).

CARLYLE, T., *Collected Letters of Thomas and Jane Welsh Carlyle*, ed. C. R. Sanders, C. L. Ryals, K. J. Fielding, I. Campbell, *et al.* 27 vols., ongoing (Durham, NC, 1970–).

CARWARDINE, R., *Trans-atlantic Revivalism: Popular Evangelicalism in Britain and America 1790–1865* (Westport, Conn., 1978).

CHADWICK, O., *The Victorian Church, Part One, 1829–1859*, 3rd edn. (London, 1971).

—— *The Spirit of the Oxford Movement: Tractarian Essays* (Cambridge, 1990).

CHAMBERS, D., 'The Church of Scotland's Parochial Extension Scheme and the Scottish Disruption', *Journal of Church and State*, 16 (1974), 263–86.

—— 'The Church of Scotland's Highlands and Islands Education Scheme, 1824–1843', *Journal of Educational Administration and History*, 7 (1975), 8–17.

—— 'Prelude to the Last Things: The Church of Scotland's Mission to the Jews', *Records of the Scottish Church History Society*, 19 (1977), 43–58.

CHANDLER, M., *The Life and Work of John Mason Neale* (Leominster, 1995).

CHAPMAN, R., 'Last Enchantments: Medievalism and the Early Anglo-

Catholic Movement', in L. J. Workman (ed.), *Medievalism in England*, Studies in Medievalism, IV (Cambridge, 1962), 170–86.

Clark, I. D. L., 'From Protest to Reaction: The Moderate Regime in the Church of Scotland, 1752–1805', in N. T. Phillipson and R. Mitchison (eds.), *Scotland in the Age of Improvement* (Edinburgh, 1970), 200–24.

Clark, I. M., *A History of Church Discipline in Scotland* (Aberdeen, 1929).

Clark, J. C. D., *English Society 1688–1832* (Cambridge, 1985).

—— 'England's *Ancien Regime* as a Confessional State', *Albion*, 21 (1989), 450–74.

—— 'Radicalism, Theology and Enlightenment', unpublished paper presented at the Tenth International Congress on the Enlightenment, Dublin, 1999.

—— 'Protestantism, Nationalism, and National Identity, 1660–1832', *Historical Journal*, 43 (2000), 249–76.

Clarke, B. F. L., *Church Builders of the Nineteenth Century* (London, 1938).

Coad, F. R., *A History of the Brethren Movement* (Exeter, 1968).

Coleridge, S. T., *On the Constitution of the Church and State* (1829), ed. J. Colmer (London, 1976).

Colley, L., *Britons: Forging the Nation 1707–1837* (New Haven, 1992).

Collinson, P., Ramsay, N., and Sparks, M. (eds.), *A History of Canterbury Cathedral* (Oxford, 1995).

Condon, M. D., 'The Irish Church and the Reform Ministries', *Journal of British Studies*, 3 (1964), 121–62.

Connell, J., *The Roman Catholic Church in England 1780–1850: A Study in Internal Politics* (Philadelphia, 1984).

Connolly, S. J., *Priests and People in Pre-Famine Ireland 1780–1845* (Dublin, 1982).

—— *Religion, Law and Power: The Making of Protestant Ireland 1660–1760* (Oxford, 1992).

Cooper, A., 'Ireland and the Oxford Movement', *Journal of Religious History*, 19 (1995), 62–74.

Corish, P. J. (ed.), *A History of Irish Catholicism* (Dublin, 1970–1), v. pts. 6–10.

—— *The Catholic Community in the Seventeenth and Eighteen Centuries* (Dublin, 1981).

Cornish, F. W., *The English Church in the Nineteenth Century*, 2 vols. (London, 1910).

Couper, W. J., *Scottish Revivals* (Dundee, 1918).

Cowan, R. M. W., *The Newspaper in Scotland* (Glasgow, 1946).

Cowherd, R. G., *The Politics of English Dissent* (New York, 1956).

Cox, J., *The English Churches in a Secular Society: Lambeth, 1870–1930* (Oxford, 1982).

CRONIN, S., *Irish Nationalism: A History of its Roots and Ideology* (Dublin, 1980).

CROSS, F. L., *The Oxford Movement and the Seventeenth Century* (London, 1933).

CULLEN, M. J., 'The Making of the Civil Registration Act of 1836', *Journal of Ecclesiastical* History, 25 (1974), 39–59.

DALLIMORE, A., *Forerunner of the Charismatic Movement: The Life of Edward Irving* (Chicago, 1983).

D'ALTON, I., *Protestant Society and Politics in Cork 1812–1844* (Cork, 1980).

DARBY, J. N., *The Collected Writings of J. N. Darby*, ed. W. Kelly, 34 vols. (London, 1984).

DAVENPORT, R. A., *Albury Apostles: The Story of the Body Known as the Catholic Apostolic Church*, 2nd edn. (London, 1973).

DAVIES, G. C. B., *Henry Phillpotts, Bishop of Exeter 1778–1869* (London, 1954).

—— *The First Evangelical Bishop: Some Aspects of the Life of Henry Ryder* (London, 1958).

DAVIS, R., *The Young Ireland Movement* (Dublin, 1987).

DAVIS, R. W., 'The Strategy of "Dissent" in the Repeal Campaign, 1820–28', *Journal of Modern History*, 38 (1966), 374–93.

—— *Dissent in Politics 1780–1830: The Political Life of William Smith, MP* (London, 1971).

—— 'The Tories, the Whigs and Catholic Emancipation, 1827–1829', *English Historical Review*, 97 (1982), 89–98.

—— 'The Whigs and Religious Issues, 1830–5', in R. W. Davis and R. J. Helmstadter (eds.), *Religion and Irreligion in Victorian Society* (London, 1992), 29–50.

DAWSON, C., *The Spirit of the Oxford Movement* (London, 1933).

DEWEY, C., *The Passing of Barchester: A Real Life Version of Trollope* (London, 1991).

DICKINSON, H. T., *Liberty and Property: Political Ideology in Eighteenth-Century Britain* (London, 1977).

DITCHFIELD, G. M., 'Ecclesiastical Legislation during the Ministry of the Younger Pitt, 1782–1801', in J. P. Parry and S. Taylor (eds.), *Parliament and the Church, 1529–1960* (Edinburgh, 2000), 64–80.

DONNELLY, J. S., JR., 'Pastorini and Captain Rock: Millenarianism and Sectarianism in the Rockite Movement of 1821–4', in S. Clark and J. S. Donnelly, Jr. (eds.), *Irish Peasants: Violence and Political Unrest* (Dublin, 1988), 102–39.

DONOVAN, R. K., 'The Denominational Character of English Catholic Charitable Effort, 1800–1865', *Catholic Historical Review*, 62 (1976), 200–23.

DOWLING, P. J., *The Hedge Schools of Ireland* (Dublin, 1968).

DRIVER, C., *Tory Radical: The Life of Richard Oastler* (New York, 1946).
DRUMMOND, A. L., *Edward Irving and his Circle* (London, 1937).
—— and BULLOCH, J., *The Scottish Church 1688–1843: The Age of the Moderates* (Edinburgh, 1973).
ECCLESHALL, R., 'Anglican Political Thought in the Century after the Revolution of 1688', in D. G. Boyce, R. Eccleshall, and V. Geoghegan (eds.), *Political Thought in Ireland since the Seventeenth Century* (London, 1993), 36–72.
EDGAR, A., 'The Discipline of the Church of Scotland', in R. H. Story (ed.), *The Church of Scotland*, 5 vols. (Edinburgh, n.d.), v. 427–556.
ELLENS, J. P., *Religious Routes to Gladstonian Liberalism: The Church Rate Conflict in England and Wales, 1832–1868* (University Park, Pa., 1994).
ELLIS, S. G., 'Economic Problems of the Church: Why the Reformation Failed in Ireland', *Journal of Ecclesiastical History*, 41 (1990), 239–65.
ENGELS, F., *The Condition of the Working Class in England* (1844), trans. W. O. Henderson and W. H. Chaloner (London, 1958).
ESCOTT, H., *A History of Scottish Congregationalism* (Glasgow, 1960).
EVANS, E., 'Some Reasons for the Growth of English Rural Anti-clericalism, c.1750–c.1830', *Past and Present*, 66 (1975), 84–109.
FABER, R., *Young England* (London, 1987).
FALVEY, J., 'The Church of Ireland Episcopate in the Eighteenth Century: An Overview', *Eighteenth-Century Ireland*, 8 (1993), 103–14.
FAULKNER, H. U., *Chartism and the Churches* (New York, 1916).
FIGGIS, J. N., 'William Warburton, Bishop of Gloucester, 1698–1779', in W. E. Collins (ed.), *Typical English Churchmen: From Parker to Maurice* (London, 1902), 215–53.
—— *Churches in the Modern State*, 2nd edn. (London, 1914).
FINLAYSON, D., 'Aspects of the Life and Influence of Thomas Erskine of Linlathen, 1788–1870', *Records of the Scottish Church History Society*, 20 (1978), 31–45.
FORRESTER, D., *Young Doctor Pusey: A Study in Development* (London, 1989).
FOSTER, R. F., *Modern Ireland 1600–1972* (London, 1988).
FOTHERGILL, B., *Nicholas Wiseman* (London, 1963).
FRUCHTMAN, J., JR., 'The Apocalyptic Politics and Richard Price and Joseph Priestley: A Study in Late Eighteenth-Century English Republican Millenialism', *Transactions of the American Philosophical Society*, 73/4 (1983).
FRY, M., *The Dundas Despotism* (Edinburgh, 1992).
GALLOGLY, D., *The Diocese of Kilmore 1800–1950* (Cavan, 1999).
GASH, N., *Mr Secretary Peel: The Life of Sir Robert Peel to 1830* (London, 1961).
—— *Reaction and Reconstruction in English Politics 1832–1852* (Oxford, 1965).

GASH, N. 'The Crisis of the Anglican Establishment in the Early Nineteenth Century', in A. M. Birke and K. Kluxen (eds.), *Church, State and Society in the 19th Century: An Anglo-German Comparison* (Munich, 1984), 31–43.

—— *Sir Robert Peel: The Life of Robert Peel after 1830*, 2nd edn. (London, 1986).

GERRISH, B. A., *Tradition and the Modern World: Reformed Theology in the Nineteenth Century* (Chicago, 1978).

GIBSON, W., 'The Tories and Church Patronage: 1812–30', *Journal of Ecclesiastical History*, 41 (1990), 266–74.

—— *Church, State and Society, 1760–1850* (London, 1994).

GILBERT, A. D., *Religion and Society in Industrial England* (London, 1978).

GILL, S., *William Wordsworth: A Life* (Oxford, 1989).

GILLEY, S., 'Heretic London, Holy Poverty and the Irish Poor, 1830–70', *Downside Review*, 89 (1971), 64–89.

—— 'Nationality and Liberty, Protestant and Catholic: Robert Southey's Book of the Church', in S. Mews (ed.), *Religion and National Identity*, Studies in Church History, 18 (Oxford, 1982), 409–32.

—— 'John Keble and the Victorian Churching of Romanticism', in J. R. Watson (ed.), *An Infinite Complexity: Essays in Romanticism* (Edinburgh, 1983), 226–39.

—— 'Newman and Prophecy, Evangelical and Catholic', *Journal of the United Reformed Church History Society*, 3 (1985), 160–83.

—— *Newman and his Age* (London, 1990).

—— 'Edward Irving: Prophet of the Millennium', in J. Garnett and C. Matthew (eds.), *Revival and Religion since 1700* (London, 1993), 95–110.

GIROUARD, M., *The Return to Camelot: Chivalry and the English Gentleman* (New Haven, 1981).

GRAY, D., *Spencer Perceval: The Evangelical Prime Minister 1762–1812* (Manchester, 1963).

GREAVES, R. W., 'The Jerusalem Bishopric, 1841', *English Historical Review*, 64 (1949), 328–52.

—— 'The Working of the Alliance: A Comment on Warburton', in G. V. Bennett and J. D. Walsh (eds.), *Essays in Modern English Church History: In Memory of Norman Sykes* (London, 1966), 163–80.

GREGORY, J. (ed.), *The Speculum of Archbishop Thomas Secker*, Church of England Record Society, 2 (Woodbridge, 1995).

GRIFFIN, J. R., 'John Keble: Radical', *Anglican Theological Review*, 53 (1971), 167–73.

—— 'The Anglican Politics of Cardinal Newman', *Anglican Theological Review*, 55 (1973), 434–43.

—— 'The Radical Phase of the Oxford Movement', *Journal of Ecclesiastical History*, 27 (1976), 47–56.

GUNSTONE, J. T. A., 'Alexander Knox, 1757–1831', *Church Quarterly Review*, 157 (1956), 463–75.

GWYNN, D., *Lord Shrewsbury, Pugin and the Catholic Revival* (London, 1946).

—— *Young Ireland and 1848* (Cork, 1949).

HAMMOND, J. L., and HAMMOND, B., *The Village Labourer 1760–1832* (London, 1913).

HALÉVY, E., *The Growth of Philosophic Radicalism*, trans. M. Morris (London, 1928).

—— *A History of the English People in the Nineteenth Century*, trans. E. I. Watkin, 6 vols., 2nd edn. (London, 1949).

HARRISON, J. F. C., *Quest for the New Moral World: Robert Owen and the Owenites in Britain and America* (New York, 1969).

—— *The Second Coming: Popular Millenarianism 1780–1850* (London, 1979).

HART, A. TINDAL, *The Curate's Lot: The Story of the Unbeneficed English Clergy* (London, 1970).

HEMPTON, D. M., 'Evangelicalism and Eschatology', *Journal of Ecclesiastical History*, 31 (1980),179–94.

—— 'The Methodist Crusade in Ireland, 1795–1845', *Irish Historical Studies*, 22 (1980), 33–48.

—— *Methodism and Politics in British Society 1750–1850* (London, 1984).

—— *Religion and Political Culture in Britain* (Cambridge, 1996).

—— and HILL, M., *Evangelical Protestantism in Ulster Society 1740–1890* (London, 1992).

HENDERSON, G. D., *The Scottish Ruling Elder* (Aberdeen, 1935).

—— *Heritage: A Study of the Disruption* (Edinburgh, 1943).

HENNELL, M., *John Venn and the Clapham Sect* (London, 1958).

—— *Sons of the Prophets: Evangelical Leaders of the Victorian Church* (London, 1979).

HENRIQUES, U., *Religious Toleration in England 1787–1833* (London, 1961).

HILL, J. R., 'National Festivals, the State and "Protestant Ascendancy" in Ireland, 1790–1829', *Irish Historical Studies*, 24 (1984), 30–51.

—— 'The Meaning and Significance of "Protestant Ascendancy", 1781–1840', in *Ireland after the Union*, Proceedings of the Second Joint Meeting of the Royal Irish Academy and the British Academy (Oxford, 1989), 1–22.

—— *From Patriots to Unionists: Dublin Civic Politics and Irish Protestant Patriotism, 1660–1840* (Oxford, 1997).

HILLIS, P., 'Presbyterianism and Social Class in Mid-Nineteenth Century Glasgow: A Study of Nine Parishes', *Journal of Ecclesiastical History*, 32 (1981), 47–64.

HILTON, B., *The Age of Atonement: The Influence of Evangelicalism on Social and Economic Thought 1785–1865* (Oxford, 1988).

HINDE, W., *Catholic Emancipation: A Shake to Men's Minds* (Oxford, 1992).

HOBSBAWM, E., and RUDÉ, G., *Captain Swing: A Social History of the Great English Agricultural Uprising of 1830* (New York, 1975).

HOLE, R., *Pulpits, Politics and Public Order in England 1760–1832* (Cambridge, 1989).

HOLMES, J. D., *More Roman than Rome: English Catholicism in the Nineteenth Century* (London, 1978).

HOLMES, R. F., *Henry Cooke* (Belfast, 1981).

HOOKER, R., *Of the Laws of Ecclesiastical Polity* (1593–1662), Folger edn., ed. G. Edelen, W. Speed Hill, P. G. Stanwood, 3 vols. (Cambridge, Mass., 1977, 1981).

HORSLEY, S., 'Thoughts on Civil Government', ed. A. Robinson, in S. Taylor (ed.), *From Cranmer to Davidson: A Church of England Miscellany* (Woodbridge, 1999), 203–12.

HOWSE, E. M., *Saints in Politics: The Clapham Sect and the Growth of Freedom* (London, 1953).

HUGHES, E., 'The Bishops and Reform, 1831–3: Some Fresh Correspondence', *English Historical Review*, 56 (1941), 459–90.

HURT, J., *Education in Evolution: Church, State, Society and Popular Education* (London, 1971).

HUTCHISON, I. G. C., *A Political History of Scotland 1832–1924* (Edinburgh, 1986).

HYLSON-SMITH, K., *Evangelicals in the Church of England 1734–1984* (Edinburgh, 1988).

—— *High Churchmanship in the Church of England* (Edinburgh, 1993).

JENKINS, B., *Era of Emancipation: British Government of Ireland 1812–1830* (Kingston and Montreal, 1988).

KEBLE, J., *National Apostasy* [1833], ed. A. Stephenson (Abingdon, 1983).

KEIR, D., *The House of Collins* (London, 1952).

KELLY, J., 'The Genesis of "Protestant Ascendancy"', in G. O'Brien (ed.), *Parliament, Politics and People: Essays in Eighteenth-Century Irish History* (Dublin, 1989), 93–127.

KER, I., *John Henry Newman: A Biography* (Oxford, 1988).

KERR, D. A., *Peel, Priests and Politics: Sir Robert Peel's Administration and the Roman Catholic Church in Ireland, 1841–1846* (Oxford, 1982).

—— *'A Nation of Beggars?': Priests, People and Politics in Famine Ireland 1846–1852* (Oxford, 1994).

KIDD, C., 'The Kirk, the French Revolution, and the Burden of Scottish Whiggery', in N. Aston (ed.), *Religious Change in Europe 1650–1914* (Oxford, 1997), 213–34.

Kiely, B., *Poor Scholar: A Study of William Carleton* (1948), 2nd edn. (Dublin, 1997).

Kitson Clark, G., 'Hunger and Politics in 1842', *Journal of Modern History*, 25 (1953), 355–74.

—— *Peel and the Conservative Party: A Study in Party Politics 1832–1841*, 2nd edn. (London, 1964).

—— *Churchmen and the Condition of England 1832–1885* (London, 1973).

Knight, F., 'Ministering to the Ministers: The Discipline of Recalcitrant Clergy in the Diocese of Lincoln, 1830–1845', in W. J. Sheils and D. Wood (eds.), *The Ministry: Clerical and Lay*, Studies in Church History, 26 (Oxford, 1989), 357–66.

—— *The Nineteenth-Century Church and English Society* (Cambridge, 1995).

Langford, P., *Public Life and the Propertied Englishman 1689–1798* (Oxford, 1991).

Laqueur, T. W., *Religion and Respectability: Sunday Schools and Working Class Culture 1780–1850* (New Haven, 1976).

Larkin, E., 'The Devotional Revolution in Ireland, 1850–75', *American Historical Review*, 77 (June 1972), 625–52.

—— *The Historical Dimensions of Irish Catholicism* (Washington, DC, 1984).

—— 'The Rise and Fall of Stations in Ireland, 1750–1850', unpublished paper (1997).

Laski, H. J., *Studies in the Problem of Sovereignty* (London, 1917).

Lathbury, D. C. (ed.), *Correspondence on Church and Religion of William Ewart Gladstone*, 2 vols. (London, 1910).

Leetham, C. R., *Luigi Gentili: A Sower for the Second Spring* (London, 1965).

Leishman, J. F., *Matthew Leishman of Govan and the Middle Party of 1843* (Paisley, 1921).

Leneman, L. and Mitchison, R., 'Acquiescence in and Defiance of Church Discipline in Early Modern Scotland', *Records of the Scottish Church History Society*, 25 (1995), 19–39.

Lewis, C. J., 'The Disintegration of the Tory-Anglican Alliance in the Struggle for Catholic Emancipation', *Church History*, 29 (1960), 25–43.

Lovegrove, D. W., *Established Church, Sectarian People: Itinerancy and the Transformation of English Dissent, 1780–1830* (Cambridge, 1988).

Lyall, F., *Of Presbyters and Kings: Church and State in the Law of Scotland* (Aberdeen, 1980).

Macaulay, A., *William Crolly: Archbishop of Armagh, 1835–49* (Dublin, 1994).

McBride, I., *Scripture Politics: Ulster Presbyterians and Irish Radicalism in the Late Eighteenth Century* (Oxford, 1998).

McClatchey, D., *Oxfordshire Clergy 1777–1869* (Oxford, 1960).

McCord, N., *The Anti-Corn Law League 1838–1846* (London, 1958).

MacDonagh, O., 'The Politicisation of the Irish Catholic Bishops', 1800–1850, *Historical Journal*, 18 (1975), 37–53.

—— *The Life of Daniel O'Connell 1775–1847*, 2nd edn. (London, 1991).

McDowell, R. B., *Public Opinion and Government Policy in Ireland 1801–1846* (London, 1952).

McFarland, E. W., *Ireland and Scotland in the Age of Revolution* (Edinburgh, 1994).

McGrath, T., *Politics, Interdenominational Relations and Education in the Public Ministry of Bishop James Doyle of Kildare and Leighlin, 1786–1834* (Dublin, 1999).

—— *Religious Renewal and Reform in the Pastoral Ministry of Bishop James Doyle of Kildare and Leighlin, 1786–1834* (Dublin, 1999).

Machin, G. I. T., *The Catholic Question in English Politics 1820–1830* (Oxford, 1964).

—— 'The Maynooth Grant, the Dissenters and Disestablishment, 1845–1847', *English Historical Review*, 82 (1967), 61–85.

—— *Politics and the Churches in Great Britain, 1832–1868* (Oxford, 1977).

—— 'Resistance to Repeal of the Test and Corporation Acts', *Historical Journal*, 22 (1979), 115–39.

—— 'Canning, Wellington, and the Catholic Question', *English Historical Review*, 99 (1984), 94–100.

MacInnes, A., 'Evangelical Protestantism in the Nineteenth-Century Highlands', in G. Walker and T. Gallagher (eds.), *Sermons and Battle Hymns: Protestant Popular Culture in Modern Scotland* (Edinburgh, 1990), 43–68.

MacInnes, J., *The Evangelical Movement in the Highlands of Scotland 1688 to 1800* (Aberdeen, 1951).

McIntosh, J., *Church and Theology in Enlightenment Scotland: The Popular Party, 1740–1800* (Edinburgh, 1998).

MacIntyre, A., *The Liberator: Daniel O'Connell and the Irish Party 1830–1847* (New York, 1965).

Maciver, I. F., 'Unfinished Business? The Highland Churches Scheme and the Government of Scotland, 1818–1835', *Records of the Scottish Church History Society*, 25 (1995), 376–99.

Mack, D., '"The Rage of Fanaticism in Former Days": James Hogg's *Confessions of a Justified Sinner* and the Controversy over *Old Mortality*', in I. Campbell (ed.), *Nineteenth-Century Scottish Fiction* (Manchester, 1979), 37–50.

Mackintosh, W. H., *Disestablishment and Liberation: The Movement for the Separation of the Anglican Church from State Control* (London, 1972).

Maclean, A., *Telford's Highland Churches* (Inverness, 1989).

Malmgreen, G. (ed.), *Religion in the Lives of English Women, 1760–1930* (London, 1986).

MARTIN, R. H., *Evangelicals United: Ecumenical Stirrings in Victorian Britain, 1795–1830* (Metuchen, NJ, 1983).

MATHER, F. C., 'Georgian Churchmanship Reconsidered: Some Variations in Anglican Public Worship 1714–1830', *Journal of Ecclesiastical History*, 36 (1985), 255–83.

—— *High Church Prophet: Bishop Samuel Horsley (1733–1806) and the Caroline Tradition in the Later Georgian Church* (Oxford, 1992).

MATHIESON, W. L., *English Church Reform 1815–1840* (London, 1923).

MATTHEW, H. C. G., 'Edward Bouverie Pusey: From Scholar to Tractarian', *Journal of Theological Studies*, NS 32 (April 1981), 101–24.

—— *Gladstone: 1809–1874* (Oxford, 1986).

MECHIE, S., *The Church and Scottish Social Development 1780–1870* (Oxford, 1960).

MEEK, D. E., 'Evangelical Missionaries in the Early Nineteenth-Century Highlands', *Scottish Studies*, 28 (1987), 1–34.

MILES, D., *Francis Place 1771–1854* (Brighton, 1988).

MILLAR, G. F., 'Maynooth and Scottish Politics: The Role of the Maynooth Grant Issue, 1845–1857', *Records of the Scottish Church History Society*, 27 (1997), 220–79.

MILLER, D. W., *Queen's Rebels: Ulster Loyalism in Historical Perspective* (Dublin, 1978).

MITCHISON, R., 'The Making of the Old Scottish Poor Law', *Past and Present*, 63 (May 1974).

—— and LENEMAN, L., *Sexuality and Social Control: Scotland 1660–1780* (Oxford, 1989).

MOODY, T. W., *Thomas Davis 1814–45* (Dublin, 1945).

MORLEY, J., *Life of William Ewart Gladstone*, 2nd edn., 2 vols. (London, 1905).

MORROW, J., 'The National Church in Coleridge's *Church and State*: A Response to Allen', *Journal of the History of Ideas*, 47 (1986), 646–52.

MURRAY, D. M., 'Martyrs or Madmen? The Covenanters, Sir Walter Scott and Dr Thomas McCrie', *Innes Review*, 43/2 (Autumn 1992), 166–75.

NEATBY, W. B., *A History of the Plymouth Brethren* (London, 1901).

NEWBOULD, I., *Whiggery and Reform, 1830–41* (London, 1990).

NEWMAN, J. H. *Apologia Pro Vita Sua* (1864), Modern Library Edition (New York, 1950).

NEWMAN, J. H., *Letters and Diaries of John Henry Newman*, ed. C. S. Dessain, E. E. Kelly, T. Gornall, I. Ker, G. Tracey, 31 vols. (London, 1961–72; Oxford, 1973–).

NEWSOME, D., *Godliness and Good Learning: Four Studies on a Victorian Idea* (London, 1961).

—— *The Parting of Friends: A Study of the Wilberforces and Henry Manning* (London, 1966).

NEWSOME, D., *The Convert Cardinals: John Henry Newman and Henry Edward Manning* (London, 1993).

NOCKLES, P. B., *The Oxford Movement in Context: Anglicanism High Churchmanship 1760–1857* (Cambridge, 1994).

—— '"Our Brethren of the North": The Scottish Episcopal Church and the Oxford Movement', *Journal of Ecclesiastical History*, 47/4 (October 1996), 655–82.

—— '"Lost Causes and . . . Impossible Loyalties": The Oxford Movement and the University', in M. G. Brock and M. C. Curthoys (eds.), *The History of the University of Oxford*, vi. *Nineteenth-Century Oxford, Part 1* (Oxford, 1997), 195–267.

—— 'Church or Protestant Sect? The Church of Ireland, High Churchmanship and the Oxford Movement, 1822–1869', *Historical Journal*, 41 (1998), 457–93.

NORMAN, E. R., *Anti-Catholicism in Victorian England* (London, 1968).

—— *Church and Society in England 1770–1970* (Oxford, 1976).

—— *The English Catholic Church in the Nineteenth Century* (Oxford, 1984).

NOWLAN, K. B., 'The Catholic Clergy and Irish Politics in the Eighteen Thirties and Forties', *Irish Historical Studies*, 9 (1974), 119–35.

O'BRIEN, G., 'The Establishment of Poor-law Unions in Ireland, 1838–43', *Irish Historical Studies*, 23 (November 1982), 97–120.

O'CONNELL, D., *The Correspondence of Daniel O'Connell*, ed. M. R. O'Connell, 8 vols. (Dublin, 1972–9).

O'DONOGHUE, P., 'Causes of the Opposition to Tithes, 1830–38', *Studia Hibernica*, 5 (1965), 7–28.

—— 'Opposition to Tithe Payment in 1830–31', *Studia Hibernica*, 6 (1966), 69–98.

O'FERRALL, F., *Catholic Emancipation: Daniel O'Connell and the Birth of Irish Democracy 1820–30* (Dublin, 1985).

OLIVER, W. H., 'Owen in 1817: The Millennialist Moment', in S. Pollard and J. Salt (eds.), *Robert Owen: Prophet of the Poor* (London, 1971), 166–87.

O'TUATHAIGH, G., *Ireland before the Famine 1798–1848* (Dublin, 1972).

—— 'Gaelic Ireland, Popular Politics and Daniel O'Connell', *Journal of the Galway Archaeological and Historical Society*, 34 (1974–5), 21–34.

—— *Thomas Drummond and the Government of Ireland 1835–41* (Dublin, 1978).

PALLISER, D. M., 'Introduction: The Parish in Perspective', in S. J. Wright (ed.), *Parish, Church and People: Local Studies in Lay Religion 1350–1750* (London, 1988), 5–28.

PARKER, C. J., *Life and Letters of Sir James Graham*, 2 vols. (London, 1907).

PATTISON, M., *Memoirs of an Oxford Don* (1885), ed. V. H. H. Green (London, 1988).

PAZ, D. G., *The Politics of Working-Class Education in Britain, 1830–50* (Manchester, 1980).
—— *Popular Anti-Catholicism in Mid-Victorian England* (Stanford, Calif., 1992).
PERRY, W., *The Oxford Movement in Scotland* (Cambridge, 1933).
PHILLIPS, P. T. (ed.), *The View from the Pulpit: Victorian Ministers and Society* (Toronto, 1978).
PHILLIPS, W. A. (ed.), *History of the Church of Ireland*, 3 vols. (Oxford, 1933).
PORT, W. H., *Six Hundred New Churches: A Study of the Church Building Commission, 1815–1856* (London, 1961).
POWER, T. P., and WHELAN, K. (eds.), *Endurance and Emergence: Catholics in Ireland in the Eighteenth Century* (Dublin, 1990).
PRICKETT, S., *Romanticism and Religion: The Tradition of Coleridge and Wordsworth in the Victorian Church* (Cambridge, 1976).
PURCELL, E. S., *Life and Letters of Ambrose Phillipps de Lisle*, 2 vols. (London, 1900).
PYM, D., 'The Idea of Church and State in the Thought of Three Principal Lake Poets: Coleridge, Southey and Wordsworth', *Durham University Journal*, 83 (1991), 19–26.
RACK, H. D., 'Domestic Visitation: A Chapter in Early Nineteenth Century Evangelism', *Journal of Ecclesiastical History*, 24 (1973), 357–76.
READ, D., *Peel and the Victorians* (Oxford, 1987).
ROBERTS, D., *Paternalism in Early Victorian England* (London, 1979).
ROBERTS, M. J. D., 'Private Patronage and the Church of England, 1800–1900', *Journal of Ecclesiastical History*, 32 (1981), 199–223.
ROE, W. G., *Lamennais and England: The Reception of Lamennais's Religious Ideas in England in the Nineteenth Century* (Oxford, 1966).
ROSEBERY, LORD, *Miscellanies, Literary and Historical*, 2 vols. (London, 1921).
ROWDON, H. H., *The Origins of the Brethren, 1825–1850* (London, 1967).
ROWELL, G., *The Vision Glorious: Themes and Personalities of the Catholic Revival in Anglicanism* (Oxford, 1983).
—— (ed.), *Tradition Renewed: The Oxford Movement Conference Papers* (London, 1986).
ROWLANDS, J. H. L., *Church, State and Society: The Attitudes of John Keble, Richard Hurrell Froude and John Henry Newman, 1827–1845* (Worthing, 1989).
SACHS, W. L., *The Transformation of Anglicanism* (Cambridge, 1993).
SACK, J. J., *From Jacobite to Conservative* (Cambridge, 1993).
SANDEEN, E. R., *The Roots of Fundamentalism 1800–1830* (Chicago, 1970).
SCHMIDT, L. E., *Holy Fairs: Scottish Communions and American Revivals in the Early Modern Period* (Princeton, 1989).

SCOTLAND, N., *John Bird Sumner, Evangelical Archbishop* (Leominster, 1995).

SEIGEL, J., 'Carlyle and Peel: The Prophet's Search for a Heroic Politician and an Unpublished Fragment', *Victorian Studies*, 26 (1983), 181–95.

SELLECK, R. J. W., *James Kay-Shuttleworth* (Ilford, 1994).

SHER, R. B., *Church and University in the Scottish Enlightenment: The Moderate Literati of Edinburgh* (Princeton, 1985).

—— and MURDOCH, A., 'Patronage and Party in the Church of Scotland, 1750–1800', in N. McDougall (ed.), *Church, Politics and Society: Scotland 1408–1929* (Edinburgh, 1983), 197–220.

SHORT, K. R. M., 'English Baptists and the Corn Laws', *Baptist Quarterly*, 21 (1966), 309–20.

—— 'The English Indemnity Acts 1726–1867', *Church History*, 42 (1973), 366–76.

SMITH, F., *Life and Work of Sir James Kay-Shuttleworth* (London, 1923).

SMITH, M., *Religion in Industrial Society: Oldham and Saddleworth 1740–1865* (Oxford, 1994).

SMOUT, T. C., 'The Strange Intervention of Edward Twistleton: Paisley in Depression 1841–3', in T. C. Smout (ed.), *The Search for Wealth and Stability* (London, 1979).

SMYTH, C., *Simeon and Church Order: A Study of the Origins of the Evangelical Revival in Cambridge in the Eighteenth Century* (Cambridge, 1940).

SOLOWAY, R. A., *Prelates and People: Ecclesiastical Social Thought in England 1783–1852* (London, 1969).

SPALL, R. F., 'The Anti-Corn-Law League's Opposition to English Church Establishment', *Journal of Church and State*, 32 (1990), 97–123.

STEVENSON, J., *Popular Disturbances in England 1700–1870* (London, 1979).

STRACHAN, C. G., *The Pentecostal Theology of Edward Irving* (London, 1973).

STRONG, R., *Alexander Forbes of Brechin: The First Tractarian Bishop* (Oxford, 1995).

STUNT, T. C. F., 'Evangelical Cross-Currents in the Church of Ireland, 1820–1833', in W. J. Sheils and D. Wood (eds.), *The Churches, Ireland and the Irish*, Studies in Church History, 25 (Oxford, 1989).

—— *From Awakening to Secession: Radical Evangelicals in Switzerland and Britain 1815–35* (Edinburgh, 2000).

SWORDS, L., *A Hidden Church: The Diocese of Achonry 1689–1818* (Blackrock, co. Dublin, 1997).

SYKES, N., *Church and State in England in the XVIIIth Century* (Cambridge, 1934).

TAYLOR, S., 'William Warburton and the Alliance of Church and State', *Journal of Ecclesiastical History*, 43 (1992), 271–86.

THOMPSON, E. P., *Witness against the Beast: William Blake and the Moral Law* (Cambridge, 1993).

TOCQUEVILLE, A. DE, *Journeys to England and Ireland*, trans. G. Lawrence and K. P. Mayer, ed. J. P. Mayer (London, 1958).

TRISTAM, H., 'In the Lists with the Abbé Jager', in H. Tristam *et al.*, *John Henry Newman: Centenary Essays* (London, 1945), 201–22.

TURNER, W. G., *John Nelson Darby: A Biography* (London, 1926).

VAISS, P. (ed.), *From Oxford to the People: Reconsidering Newman and the Oxford Movement* (Leominster, 1996).

VALENZE, D. M., *Prophetic Sons and Daughters: Female Preaching and Popular Religion in Industrial England* (Princeton, 1985).

VARLEY, E. A., *The Last of the Prince Bishops: William Van Mildert and the High Church Movement of the Early Nineteenth Century* (Cambridge, 1992).

VAUDRY, R. W., 'The Constitutional Party in the Church of Scotland 1834–1843', *Scottish Historical Review*, 62 (1983), 35–46.

VINCENT, E., 'The Responses of Scottish Churchmen to the French Revolution, 1789–1802', *Scottish Historical Review*, 73 (1994), 191–215.

VIRGIN, P., *The Church in an Age of Negligence* (Cambridge, 1989).

WALKER, R. B., 'Religious Changes in Cheshire, 1750–1850', *Journal of Ecclesiastical History*, 17 (1966), 77–94.

WALSH, J., HAYDON, C., and TAYLOR, S. (eds.), *The Church of England, c.1689–c.1833: From Toleration to Tractarianism* (Cambridge, 1993).

WARD, J. T., and TREBLE, J. H., 'Religion and Education in 1843: Reaction to the "Factory Education Bill"', *Journal of Ecclesiastical History*, 20 (1969), 79–110.

WARD, W., *The Life of John Henry Cardinal Newman*, 2 vols. (London, 1912).

WARD, W. R., 'The Tithe Question in England in the Early Nineteenth Century', *Journal of Ecclesiastical History*, 16 (1965), 67–81.

—— *Victorian Oxford* (London, 1965).

—— *Religion and Society in England 1790–1850* (London, 1972).

—— *The Protestant Evangelical Awakening* (Cambridge, 1992).

—— (ed.), *Parson and Parish in Eighteenth-Century Surrey: Replies to Bishops' Visitations* (Guildford, 1994).

—— (ed.), *Parson and Parish in Eighteenth-Century Hampshire: Replies to Bishops' Visitations* (Winchester, 1995).

WARNE, A., *Church and Society in Eighteenth-Century Devon* (Newton Abbot, 1969).

WATERMAN, A. M. C., *Revolution, Economics and Religion: Christian Political Economy 1798–1833* (Cambridge, 1991).

—— '"The Grand Scheme of Subordination": The Intellectual Foundations of Tory Doctrine', *Australian Journal of Politics and History*, 40, Special Issue (1994), 121–33.

WATERMAN, A. M. C., 'The Nexus between Theology and Political Doctrine in Church and Dissent', in K. Haakonssen (ed.), *Enlightenment and Religion: Rational Dissent in Eighteenth-Century Britain* (Cambridge, 1996), 193–218.

WATT, H., *Thomas Chalmers and the Disruption* (Edinburgh, 1943).

WATTS, M. R., *The Dissenters*, 2 vols. (Oxford, 1978, 1995).

WEBSTER, A. B., *Joshua Watson: The Story of a Layman, 1771–1855* (London, 1954).

WEBSTER, M., 'Simeon's Doctrine of the Church', in A. Pollard and M. Hennell (eds.), *Charles Simeon (1759–1836): Essays Written in Commemoration of his Bi-Centenary* (London, 1959), 123–35.

WELCH, P. J. 'Bishop Blomfield and Church Extension in London', *Journal of Ecclesiastical History*, 4 (1953), 203–15.

—— 'Contemporary Views on the Proposals for the Alienation of Capitular Property in England (1832–1840)', *Journal of Ecclesiastical History*, 5 (1954), 184–95.

—— 'Anglican Churchmen and the Establishment of the Jerusalem Bishopric', *Journal of Ecclesiastical History*, 8 (1957), 193–204.

—— 'Blomfield and Peel: A Study in Co-operation between Church and State, 1841–1846', *Journal of Ecclesiastical History*, 12 (1961), 71–84.

WESTERKAMP, M. J., *Triumph of the Laity: Scots-Irish Piety and the Great Awakening 1625–1760* (Oxford, 1988).

WHELAN, K., *The Tree of Liberty: Radicalism, Catholicism and the Construction of Irish Identity 1760–1830* (Cork, 1996).

WHIBLEY, C., *Lord John Manners and his Friends*, 2 vols. (Edinburgh, 1925).

WHITE, J. F., *The Cambridge Movement* (Cambridge, 1962).

WILLEY, B., *Nineteenth Century Studies: Coleridge to Matthew Arnold* (London, 1949).

WHETSTONE, A. E., *Scottish County Government in the Eighteenth and Nineteenth Centuries* (Edinburgh, 1981).

WICKHAM, E. R., *Church and People in an Industrial City* (London, 1957).

WITHRINGTON, D., 'Non-Church-Going, c.1750–c.1850', *Records of the Scottish Church History Society*, 17 (1972), 99–113.

WOLFFE, J., 'The Evangelical Alliance in the 1840s: An Attempt to Institutionalise Christian Unity', *Voluntary Religion*, Studies in Church History, 23 (Oxford, 1986), 333–46.

—— *The Protestant Crusade in Great Britain 1829–1860* (Oxford, 1992).

YATES, N., *Kent and the Oxford Movement* (Gloucester, 1983).

—— 'Pugin and the Medieval Dream', in G. Marsden (ed.), *Victorian Values: Personalities and Perspectives in Nineteenth-Century Society* (London, 1990), 59–70.

—— *Anglican Ritualism in Victorian Britain* (Oxford, 1999).

YEO, E., 'Christianity in Chartist Struggle 1838–1842', *Past and Present*, 91 (1981), 109–39.

THESES

BRADLEY, I., 'The Politics of Godliness: Evangelicals in Parliament, 1784–1832' (Univ. of Oxford D.Phil., 1974).

CARTER, G., 'Evangelical Seceders from the Church of England, c. 1800–1850' (Univ. of Oxford D.Phil., 1990).

CLAYTON, H. R., 'Societies Formed to Educate the Poor in Ireland in the late 18th and early 19th Centuries' (Trinity College, Dublin, M.Litt., 1981).

EVERSHED, W. A., 'Party and Patronage in the Church of England 1800–1945 (Univ. of Oxford D.Phil., 1985).

GARRARD, J. R., 'William Howley (1766–1848), Bishop of London, 1813–28, Archbishop of Canterbury, 1828–48' (Univ. of Oxford D.Phil., 1992).

HEHIR, I., [now I. Whelan] 'Evangelical Religion and the Polarization of Protestant–Catholic Relations in Ireland, 1780–1840' (Univ. of Wisconsin, Madison, Ph.D., 1994).

LIECHTY, J., 'Irish Evangelicalism, Trinity College Dublin, and the Mission of the Church of Ireland at the End of the Eighteenth Century' (St Patrick's College, Maynooth, Ph.D., 1987).

MACDONALD, L. ORR, 'Women and Presbyterianism in Scotland, c.1830 to c.1930' (Univ. of Edinburgh Ph.D., 1995).

MACIVER, I. F., 'The General Assembly of the Church, the State and Society in Scotland, 1815–1843' (Univ. of Edinburgh M.Litt., 1976).

MONTGOMERY, A. B., 'The Voluntary Controversy in the Church of Scotland, 1829–1843' (Univ. of Edinburgh Ph.D., 1953).

MURRAY, N. U., 'The Influence of the French Revolution on the Church of England and its Rivals' (Univ. of Oxford D.Phil., 1975).

NOCKLES, P. B., 'Continuity and Change in Anglican High Churchmanship in Britain, 1792–1850' (Univ. of Oxford D.Phil., 1982).

WHITLEY, L., 'The Operation of Lay Patronage in the Church of Scotland from the Act of 1712 until 1746' (Univ. of St Andrews Ph.D., 1993).

WILLIAMS, J. C., 'Edinburgh Politics, 1832–1852' (Univ. of Edinburgh Ph.D., 1972).

Index